The Fight for the Right to Food

International Relations and Development Series

As tomorrow's challenges become increasingly global and the North–South divide narrows, the **International Relations and Development series** edited by the Graduate Institute in Geneva relies on an approach to global problems that integrates international relations and development studies. It aims to promote research concentrating on global and multi-level governance, involving the United Nations and other international organisations as well as key regions and regional organisations. The distinctiveness of this series lies in the combination of a wide disciplinary range, including political science, international economics, international law, anthropology and history from an interdisciplinary perspective.

International Relations and Development Series
Series Standing Order ISBN 978–0–230–27988–9 (hardback) 978–0–230–27989–6 (paperback)
(*outside North America only*)

You can receive future titles in this series as they are published by placing a standing order. Please contact your bookseller or, in case of difficulty, write to us at the address below with your name and address, the title of the series and one of the ISBNs quoted above.

Customer Services Department, Macmillan Distribution Ltd, Houndmills, Basingstoke, Hampshire RG21 6XS, England

363.8
Z6f
2011

The Fight for the Right to Food

Lessons Learned

Jean Ziegler
Christophe Golay
Claire Mahon
Sally-Anne Way

LASELL COLLEGE LIBRARY
80A Maple St.
Auburndale, MA 02466

THE GRADUATE INSTITUTE | GENEVA
INSTITUT DE HAUTES ÉTUDES
INTERNATIONALES ET DU DÉVELOPPEMENT
GRADUATE INSTITUTE OF INTERNATIONAL
AND DEVELOPMENT STUDIES

© Jean Ziegler, Christophe Golay, Claire Mahon and Sally-Anne Way 2011

All rights reserved. No reproduction, copy or transmission of this publication may be made without written permission.

No portion of this publication may be reproduced, copied or transmitted save with written permission or in accordance with the provisions of the Copyright, Designs and Patents Act 1988, or under the terms of any licence permitting limited copying issued by the Copyright Licensing Agency, Saffron House, 6-10 Kirby Street, London EC1N 8TS.

Any person who does any unauthorized act in relation to this publication may be liable to criminal prosecution and civil claims for damages.

The authors have asserted their rights to be identified as the authors of this work in accordance with the Copyright, Designs and Patents Act 1988.

First published 2011 by
PALGRAVE MACMILLAN

Palgrave Macmillan in the UK is an imprint of Macmillan Publishers Limited, registered in England, company number 785998, of Houndmills, Basingstoke, Hampshire RG21 6XS.

Palgrave Macmillan in the US is a division of St Martin's Press LLC, 175 Fifth Avenue, New York, NY 10010.

Palgrave Macmillan is the global academic imprint of the above companies and has companies and representatives throughout the world.

Palgrave® and Macmillan® are registered trademarks in the United States, the United Kingdom, Europe and other countries.

ISBN: 978–0–230–28464–7 hardback

This book is printed on paper suitable for recycling and made from fully managed and sustained forest sources. Logging, pulping and manufacturing processes are expected to conform to the environmental regulations of the country of origin.

A catalogue record for this book is available from the British Library.

A catalog record for this book is available from the Library of Congress.

10 9 8 7 6 5 4 3 2 1
20 19 18 17 16 15 14 13 12 11

Transferred to Digital Printing in 2012

Contents

Preface xiii

List of Acronyms and Abbreviations xvi

1 Introduction: Hunger and the Right to Food 1
   1.1 The state of hunger in the world today 1
   1.2 The development of the right to food 4
      1.2.1 World Food Summit 1996 4
      1.2.2 World Food Summit: five years later 6
      1.2.3 Voluntary Guidelines on the Right to Food 7
      1.2.4 The United Nations human rights system and the right to food 10

Part I The Right to Food in International Law 13

2 The Definition of the Right to Food in International Law 15
   2.1 The definition of the right to food 15
   2.2 Correlative States' obligations 18
      2.2.1 The obligation to respect the right to food 19
      2.2.2 The obligation to protect the right to food 19
      2.2.3 The obligation to fulfil the right to food 19
      2.2.4 The concept of progressive realization of the right to food 20
      2.2.5 The obligation to provide a basic minimum subsistence 21
      2.2.6 The obligation of non-retrogression 21
      2.2.7 The obligation of non-discrimination 21

3 The Right to Food of the Most Vulnerable People 23
   3.1 Women 23
      3.1.1 Gender dimensions of the right to food 24
      3.1.2 International instruments protecting women's right to food 27
   3.2 Children 28
      3.2.1 The extreme vulnerability of children to hunger and malnutrition 29
      3.2.2 Children's right to food under international law 29
      3.2.3 Child combatants in armed conflicts and the right to food 31

	3.3	Farmers and peasants	34
		3.3.1 Rural poverty and access to land	34
		3.3.2 Agrarian reform	35
	3.4	Fisherpeople	41
		3.4.1 Linkages between fisheries and the right to food	42
		3.4.2 Challenges to the right to food for fishing and fish-farming communities	42
		3.4.3 A right-to-food approach to fisheries	49
	3.5	Indigenous people	50
		3.5.1 Key issues facing the right to food of indigenous peoples	53
		3.5.2 Legal framework governing the right to food of indigenous peoples	55
		3.5.3 Government obligations vis-à-vis the right to food of indigenous peoples	57
	3.6	Refugees from hunger	58
		3.6.1 Fleeing from hunger	61
		3.6.2 The need to recognize refugees from hunger	63
4	The Right to Food in an Era of Globalization		68
	4.1	International trade and the right to food	68
		4.1.1 Trade and food security	68
		4.1.2 Trade liberalization and the right to food	72
		4.1.3 Progress in international trade negotiations and the right to food	74
	4.2	Extraterritorial obligations of states to the right to food	78
		4.2.1 Legal framework for extraterritorial obligations	79
	4.3	The responsibilities of international organizations concerning the right to food	84
		4.3.1 Key impacts of international organizations on the right to food	84
		4.3.2 The legal framework: international organizations and the right to food	86
	4.4	The responsibilities of private actors regarding the right to food: transnational corporations	91
		4.4.1 The impact of transnational corporations on the right to food	91
		4.4.2 Holding corporations accountable for human rights violations	94
5	The Right to Food in Situations of Armed Conflict		101
	5.1	The protection of the right to food under international humanitarian law	101
		5.1.1 Prohibition of starvation of civilians as a method of warfare	102

		5.1.2 Forced displacement	103
		5.1.3 Rules for specific categories of person	103
	5.2	Principles and rules for humanitarian assistance	104
		5.2.1 Principles of humanitarian assistance	104
		5.2.2 Rules of humanitarian assistance	105
	5.3	Enforcement mechanisms for international humanitarian law	107

Part II The Right to Food in Practice: Country Missions in Africa, Asia and Latin America   109

6	Niger		111
	6.1	First mission to Niger	111
	6.2	Food insecurity and the right to food in Niger	112
		6.2.1 Threats of famine	112
		6.2.2 Overview of food insecurity situation	113
	6.3	Legal framework for the right to food in Niger	116
		6.3.1 International obligations	116
		6.3.2 National obligations	117
		6.3.3 Access to justice and human rights institutions	118
	6.4	Policy framework for addressing food insecurity	119
		6.4.1 Government policies and institutions	119
		6.4.2 Non-governmental organizations and associations	122
	6.5	Main findings and concerns regarding the realization of the right to food	123
		6.5.1 Progressive realization	123
		6.5.2 Violations of the right to food	124
		6.5.3 Obstacles to the realization of the right to food	126
	6.6	Conclusions and recommendations	131
	6.7	Emergency follow-up	132

7	Brazil		135
	7.1	Introduction	135
	7.2	Overview of hunger and poverty in Brazil	136
	7.3	Legal framework for the right to food in Brazil	139
		7.3.1 International obligations	139
		7.3.2 National constitutional norms	139
		7.3.3 Access to justice and human rights institutions	140
	7.4	Policy framework to address food insecurity and the right to food	141
		7.4.1 Government policies for food security and the right to food	141
		7.4.2 Activities of non-governmental organizations and social movements	145

viii Contents

7.5	Main findings and concerns regarding the realization of the right to food	147
	7.5.1 Progressive realization	147
	7.5.2 Violations of the right to food	148
	7.5.3 Obstacles to the realization of the right to food	150
7.6	Conclusions and recommendations	151

8 Bangladesh 155
- 8.1 Introduction 155
- 8.2 Hunger and poverty in Bangladesh 156
  - 8.2.1 Overview of food insecurity in Bangladesh 156
  - 8.2.2 Progress 157
- 8.3 Legal framework for the right to food in Bangladesh 159
  - 8.3.1 International obligations 159
  - 8.3.2 National obligations 160
  - 8.3.3 Access to Justice and human rights institutions 161
- 8.4 Policy framework for the right to food 163
  - 8.4.1 Government policies and institutions 163
  - 8.4.2 Non-governmental organizations and associations 166
- 8.5 Main findings and concerns regarding the realization of the right to food 166
  - 8.5.1 Progressive realization 166
  - 8.5.2 Violations of the right to food 168
  - 8.5.3 Obstacles to the realization of the right to food 169
- 8.6 Conclusions and recommendations 172

9 The Occupied Palestinian Territories 175
- 9.1 Introduction 175
- 9.2 Malnutrition and food insecurity in the Occupied Palestinian Territories 177
  - 9.2.1 On the verge of humanitarian catastrophe 177
  - 9.2.2 Causes of the food crisis 178
- 9.3 Legal framework governing the right to food in the Occupied Palestinian Territories 181
  - 9.3.1 International law status of the Occupied Palestinian Territories in 2003 181
  - 9.3.2 Obligations of the Government of Israel 182
  - 9.3.3 Obligations of the Palestinian Authority 183
  - 9.3.4 Other key laws and institutions 184
- 9.4 Main findings and concerns 185
  - 9.4.1 The humanitarian crisis 185
  - 9.4.2 Violations of the right to food 185
- 9.5 Conclusions and recommendations 190

10 Ethiopia 194
- 10.1 Introduction 194

10.2	Famine and food insecurity in Ethiopia		195
	10.2.1	Famine in Ethiopia in 2003	195
	10.2.2	Overview of hunger and food insecurity in Ethiopia	197
10.3	Legal framework for the right to food		199
	10.3.1	International obligations	199
	10.3.2	National constitutional norms	199
	10.3.3	Access to justice and human rights institutions	201
10.4	Policy framework for the right to food		202
	10.4.1	Government policies and programmes	202
	10.4.2	Policies and programmes of the United Nations system in Ethiopia	205
10.5	Main findings and concerns		207
	10.5.1	Progressive realization	207
	10.5.2	Violations of the right to food	208
	10.5.3	Obstacles to the realization of the right to food	209
10.6	Conclusions and recommendations		211

11	Mongolia			214
	11.1	Introduction		214
	11.2	Hunger and food insecurity in Mongolia		215
		11.2.1	The harsh winters and dzuds	215
		11.2.2	Overview of hunger and food insecurity in Mongolia	217
	11.3	Legal framework for the right to food in Mongolia		221
		11.3.1	International obligations	221
		11.3.2	Domestic constitutional and legislative framework	221
		11.3.3	Access to justice and human rights institutions	224
	11.4	Policy framework for the right to food		224
		11.4.1	Government policies and institutions	224
		11.4.2	International agencies and donors	227
		11.4.3	Non-governmental organizations	228
	11.5	Main findings and concerns		228
		11.5.1	Progressive realization of the right to food	228
		11.5.2	Violations of the right to food	229
		11.5.3	Obstacles to the realization of the right to food	230
	11.6	Conclusions and recommendations		233

12	Guatemala			236
	12.1	Introduction		236
	12.2	Hunger and food insecurity in Guatemala		237
		12.2.1	Hunger and food insecurity	237
		12.2.2	A history of social conflict	241
		12.2.3	The 1996 Peace Accords: framework for a more equitable future	242

	12.3	Legal framework for the right to food in Guatemala	243
		12.3.1 International obligations	243
		12.3.2 Domestic constitutional and legislative framework	243
		12.3.3 Access to justice and human rights institutions	245
	12.4	Policy framework for the right to food	246
		12.4.1 Government policies and institutions	246
		12.4.2 United Nations specialized agencies	249
		12.4.3 Non-governmental organizations and associations	249
	12.5	Main findings and concerns	250
		12.5.1 Progressive realization of the right to food	250
		12.5.2 Violations of the right to food	250
		12.5.3 Obstacles to the realization of the right to food	252
	12.6	Conclusions and recommendations	253
13	India		257
	13.1	Introduction	257
	13.2	Hunger and food insecurity in India	258
		13.2.1 Hunger and food insecurity	258
		13.2.2 Recent developments	262
	13.3	Legal framework for the right to food in India	263
		13.3.1 International obligations	263
		13.3.2 Domestic constitutional and legislative framework	263
		13.3.3 Access to justice and human rights institutions	265
	13.4	Policy framework for the right to food	266
		13.4.1 Government policies and institutions	266
		13.4.2 Non-governmental organizations and associations	270
	13.5	Main findings and concerns	271
		13.5.1 Progressive realization of the right to food	271
		13.5.2 Violations of the right to food	271
	13.6	Conclusions and recommendations	274
14	Lebanon		277
	14.1	Introduction	277
	14.2	General context	278
	14.3	Legal framework related to the right to food in Lebanon	278
	14.4	Main findings and concerns related to the right to food and water	280
		14.4.1 During the war	280
		14.4.2 After the war	282
	14.5	Conclusions and recommendations	287

15	Bolivia		290
	15.1 Introduction		290
	15.2 Malnutrition and food insecurity in Bolivia		291
		15.2.1 The current situation of malnutrition and food insecurity in Bolivia	291
		15.2.2 Social crisis and recent developments in Bolivia	295
	15.3 Legal framework for the right to food in Bolivia		298
		15.3.1 International obligations	298
		15.3.2 Domestic constitutional and legislative framework	299
		15.3.3 Access to justice and human rights institutions	300
	15.4 Policy framework for the right to food		301
		15.4.1 Government policies and institutions	301
		15.4.2 United Nations specialized agencies and bilateral assistance	303
		15.4.3 Social movements and non-governmental organizations	303
	15.5 Main findings and concerns		304
		15.5.1 Progressive realization of the right to food	304
		15.5.2 Violations of the right to food	305
		15.5.3 Obstacles to the realization of the right to food	307
	15.6 Conclusions and recommendations		308
16	Cuba		310
	16.1 Introduction		310
	16.2 Malnutrition and food insecurity in Cuba		311
		16.2.1 The current situation of malnutrition and food insecurity	311
		16.2.2 The dissolution of COMECON	313
		16.2.3 The reinforcement of the United States embargo	315
		16.2.4 Increases in world food prices	316
	16.3 Legal framework for the right to food in Cuba		316
		16.3.1 International obligations	316
		16.3.2 Domestic constitutional and legislative framework	317
		16.3.3 Access to justice and human rights institutions	318
	16.4 Policy framework for the right to food		320
		16.4.1 Government policies and institutions	320
		16.4.2 United Nations specialized agencies	324
		16.4.3 Civil society	325
	16.5 Main findings and concerns		326
		16.5.1 Progressive realization of the right to food	326
		16.5.2 Main concerns	326
		16.5.3 Obstacles to the realization of the right to food	328

	16.6	Conclusions and recommendations	329
17	Conclusion		332
	17.1	Where are the structural problems?	333
		17.1.1 Schizophrenia in the UN system and in States' policies	333
		17.1.2 Exclusion and discrimination	335
		17.1.3 Powerful non-state actors: transnational corporations	337
	17.2	What are the new threats?	338
		17.2.1 Desertification	338
		17.2.2 Biofuels	343
	17.3	Where is hope?	350
		17.3.1 The Right to Food Guidelines	350
		17.3.2 The adoption of the Optional Protocol to the ICESCR and progress in the justiciability of the right to food	351
		17.3.3 The strategy of food sovereignty	352

Annexures 357

1. The work of the Special Rapporteur on the right to food and his team 357
2. The right to food: Commission on Human Rights Resolution 2000/10 361
3. The right to food: Commission on Human Rights Resolution 2001/25 364
4. The right to food: Human Rights Council Resolution 7/14 367
5. List of the Special Rapporteur's reports to the United Nations 374
6. Main recommendations of the Special Rapporteur on the right to food to the Members States of the United Nations and international organizations 375

Notes 385

Index 431

Preface

Every five seconds a child below ten dies from hunger. Twenty-five thousand persons die from hunger or immediately-related causes every day. Every four minutes, somebody loses his or her eye-sight from lack of Vitamin A. Over one billion people are gravely, permanently undernourished. According to the 2008 report on world food insecurity by the Food and Agriculture Organization of the United Nations (FAO), world agriculture, in its present state, could nourish 12 billion people (at 2700 kilocalories per adult per day) – double the current world population.

Therefore there is no reason that world hunger should continue.

At the beginning of my mandate as UN Special Rapporteur on the Right to Food, I identified seven major problems which directly affect or prevent the realization of the right to food:

(a) problems linked to developments in world trade;
(b) external debt servicing and its impact on food security;
(c) developments in biotechnology and their impact on access to food;
(d) wars and their destructive impact on food security;
(e) corruption;
(f) access to land and credit;
(g) discrimination against women and its impact on food security.

Today, I am convinced that one of the key obstacles to the realization of the right to food is the schizophrenia in the United Nations system and in States' policies, which, on the one hand support the promotion of the right to food, yet at the same time act to undermine it.

The first aspect of this 'schizophrenia' is the existence of profound internal contradictions within the international community. On the one hand, United Nations agencies such as the FAO, the World Food Programme, the United Nations Development Programme and the United Nations Children's Fund emphasize social justice and human rights and do excellent work in promoting the right to food, as evidenced for example by the FAO's Right to Food Guidelines. On the other hand, the Bretton Woods institutions, along with the Government of the United States of America and the World Trade Organization, refuse to recognize the mere existence of a human right to food and impose on the most vulnerable States the 'Washington Consensus' emphasizing liberalization, deregulation, privatization and the compression of State domestic budgets, a model which in many cases produces greater inequalities.

Let's take an example. My two missions to Niger showed how the market-based paradigm of development, largely imposed by the International Monetary Fund and the World Bank, has destroyed food security for the most vulnerable. Cost-recovery policies in health centres mean that many poor children are not being treated for malnutrition. The privatization of government support services, including the logistics and food distribution system and the National Veterinary Office, has exacerbated food insecurity among small-scale farmers and pastoralists. Niger possesses wealth in the form of 20 million head of cattle, sheep and camels, which are historically prized and exported widely. The animals constitute essential revenue for millions of nomads and peasants. But the privatization of the national veterinary office led to disaster; many pastoralists can no longer afford the prices of vaccinations, medicines and vitamins charged by commercial traders. They lose their cattle, their livelihood and migrate to the urban slums where many of them perish.

The second aspect of this 'schizophrenia' is that many States are not at all coherent as far as their own practices are concerned. Far too often, one part of a government undertakes to protect and promote the right to food, while another part of the government takes decisions or implements policies that directly undermine this right. The great majority of States have recognized the right to food in the World Food Summit Declarations and the Right to Food Guidelines. One hundred and sixty States are parties to the International Covenant on Economic, Social and Cultural Rights, and more than 190 to the Convention on the Rights of the Child. They have to respect, protect and fulfil the right to food in all their policies and decisions. Unfortunately today there is an increasing lack of coherence in policies implemented by Governments. For example, while they remain committed to a rights-based approach to development, they might also adopt trade policies that have negative effects on human rights in other countries. They vote for the right to food in the UN Human Rights Council and they vote against it in the World Trade Organization.

Wide disparities in economic power between States mean that powerful States negotiate trade rules that are neither free nor fair. Such rules severely affect small farmers and threaten food security, especially in developing countries that have been required to liberalize agriculture to a much greater extent than developed countries. The heavy production and export subsidies that OECD countries grant their farmers – more than US$ 349 billion in 2008 or almost US$ 1 billion per day – mean that subsidized European fruit and vegetables can be found in a market stall in Dakar, Senegal, at lower prices than local produce. Although developed countries, including European Union member States, made promises at the World Trade Organization Hong Kong Ministerial Conference in December 2005 to eliminate export subsidies that result in dumping, there has been little concrete progress so far. In Mexico, it is estimated that up to 15 million Mexican farmers and their families (many from indigenous communities) may be displaced from their livelihoods as a result of the North American Free Trade Agreement and competition with subsidized United States maize.

Some governments and important intergovernmental organizations support the neo-liberal theory. This theory does not recognize the existence of economic, social and cultural human rights and claims that only political and civil rights are human rights. According to this totally irrational theory, only a totally liberalized and privatized, unified world market can gradually eliminate hunger and malnutrition in the world. The evidence shows the contrary – liberalization and privatization have progressed rapidly in most countries during the last 10 years. At the same time, more people than ever before suffer from grave, permanent undernourishment. Only the normative approach can gradually eliminate hunger and permanent malnutrition in the world. The human right to food has to be implemented by all States, by all intergovernmental organizations and by all non-state actors including multinational corporations. As Jean Jacques Rousseau wrote almost 250 years ago in *The Social Contract*:

> Between the rich and the poor, it is freedom which oppresses and it is law which liberates.

Let's hope that the right to food will become a useful weapon to halt the daily massacre of hunger.

My deep gratitude goes to the Swiss Development Cooperation (SDC). Without its generous help, this book could not have been published. The SDC also very efficiently supported my mandate as Special Rapporteur, including the essential work of Sally-Anne Way, Claire Mahon and Christophe Golay.

JEAN ZIEGLER
Vice President of the UN Human Rights
Council Advisory Committee
Former UN Special Rapporteur on the Right to Food

Acronyms and Abbreviations

AAY	Antyodaya Anna Yojana (India)
ACC/SCN	Administrative Committee Coordination/Subcommittee on Nutrition
ADLI	Agricultural Development-Led Industrialization Strategy (Ethiopia)
AEUO	All-Ethiopia Unity Organization
AFP	Agence France Presse
AIPE	Asociación de Instituciones de Promoción y Educación (Bolivia)
ALBA	Bolivarian Alternative for the Americas
ANAP	National Association of Small Farmers (Cuba)
ANAPQUI	Bolivia's National Association of Quinoa Producers (Asociación Nacional de Productores de Quinoa)
ANDDH	Niger Association for the Defence of Human Rights
APDHB	Asamblea Permanente de Derechos Humanos de Bolivia
AREN	Association pour la redynamisation de l'elevage (Niger)
ASAP	Action Professionals' Association for the People (Ethiopia)
ASAP	Disaster Prevention and Preparedness Commission (Ethiopia)
BINP	Bangladesh Integrated Nutrition Project
BLAST	Bangladesh Legal Aid and Services Trust
BRAC	Bangladesh Rural Advancement Committee
CAFTA	Central American Free Trade Agreement
CCA	United Nations Common Country Assessment
CCSs	Credit and Service Cooperatives (Cuba)
CESCR	Committee on Economic, Social and Cultural Rights
CESE	Ecumenical Coordination of Service (Brazil)
CIPCA	Centro de Investigación y Promoción del Campesinado (Bolivia)
CMEA	Council for Mutual Economic Assistance
CNSA	Committee on National Food Security (Niger)
COMECON	Council for Mutual Economic Support
CONAN	National Council for Food and Nutrition (Bolivia)
CONASAN	National Council on Food and Nutrition Security (Guatemala)
COPREDEH	Presidential Commission for the Coordination of Human Rights Policies (Guatemala)
COS	Colectivo de Organizaciones Sociales (Guatemala)
CPT	Comissão Pastoral da Terra (Brazil)

CPT	Pastoral Land Commission (Brazil)
CRC	Convention on the Rights of the Child
CSOs	civil society organizations
DCH	Dhaka Community Hospital (Bangladesh)
DSB	Dispute Settlement Body
EHRCO	Ethiopian Human Rights Council
EIU	Economist Intelligence Unit
EPRDF	Ethiopian Peoples Revolutionary Democratic Front
ESAF	Enhanced Structural Adjustment Facility
ETC	Erosion, Technology and Concentration
EU	European Union
EWLA	Ethiopian Women Lawyers Association
FAO	Food and Agriculture Organization of the United Nations
FASE	Federation of Organizations for Social and Educational Assistance (Brazil)
FIAN	Foodfirst Information and Action Network
GAJOP	Center for Judicial Counsel for Grassroots Organizations (Brazil)
GDP	Gross Domestic Product
GMOs	genetically modified organisms
GNI	Gross National Income
GNP	Gross National Product
HEPG	Humanitarian and Emergency Policy Group (OPT)
HIPC	Heavily Indebted Poor Countries
HNP	Health, Nutrition, Population
HREV	Human Rights Everywhere
IACHR	Inter-American Commission on Human Rights
IBASE	Brazilian Institute for Social and Economic Analysis
ICCPR	International Covenant on Civil and Political Rights
ICDS	Integrated Child Development Scheme (India)
ICDS	Integrated Child Development Services Programmes (India)
ICESCR	International Covenant on Economic, Social and Cultural Rights
ICRC	International Committee of the Red Cross
IDPs	internally displaced persons
IFAD	International Fund for Agricultural Development
IFHR	International Federation for Human Rights
IFPRI	International Food Policy Research Institute
IGWG	Inter-Governmental Working Group on the Elaboration of Voluntary Guidelines to Support Member States' Efforts to Achieve the Progressive Realization of the Right to Adequate Food in the Context of National Food Security
IHEID	Graduate Institute of International and Development Studies
ILO	International Labour Organization
ILRI	International Livestock Research Institute

IMF	International Monetary Fund
INESC	Instituto de Estudos Socioeconomicos (Brazil)
INFOE	Institute for Ecology and Action Anthropology
INRH	National Institute of Hydraulic Resources (Cuba)
IPEA	Institute for Applied Economic Research
IPRFD	International Project on the Right to Food in Development
ITQ	Individual Transferable Quotas
IUED	Graduate Institute of Development Studies
IUHEI	Graduate Institute of International Studies
IUU fishing	illegal, unreported and unregulated fishing
LACC	Local Aid Coordination Committee (OPT)
LRA	Lord's Resistance Army (Uganda)
MDGs	Millennium Development Goals
MDMS	Mid-Day Meals Scheme (India)
MLAA	Madaripur Legal Aid Association (Bangladesh)
MNDH	Brazilian Forum on Food and Nutritional Security (Movimento Nacional para Direitos Humanos)
MSF	Médecins Sans Frontières
MST	Movimento dos Trabaladores Rurais Sim Terra (Landless Workers Movement)
NAFTA	North American Free Trade Agreement
NGO	non-governmental organization
NHRC	National Human Rights Commission (India)
NNP	National Nutrition Programme (Bangladesh)
NTCs	non-trade concerns
OAS	Organization of American States
OCHA	Office for the Coordination of Humanitarian Affairs
OECD	Organization for Economic Cooperation and Development
OHCHR	Office of the United Nations High Commissioner for Human Rights
ONPVN	Office des Produits Vivriers du Niger (The National Office for Basic Foodstuffs of Niger)
OPT	Occupied Palestinian Territories
PAHO	Pan American Health Organization
PDS	Public Food Distribution System (India)
PFDS	Public Food Distribution System (Bangladesh)
PIDhDD	Plataforma Interamericana de Derechos Humanos, Democracia y Desarollo
PNIC	Palestinian National Information Center
PRSP	Poverty Reduction Strategy Paper
PUCL	People's Union for Civil Liberties (India)
RAIPON	Russian Association of Indigenous Peoples of the North
REST	Relief Association of Tigray (Ethiopia)
SDC	Swiss Agency for Development and Cooperation

SDPRP	Sustainable Development Poverty Reduction Programme (Ethiopia)
SESAN	Secretariat for Food and Nutrition Security (Guatemala)
SGRY	Sampoorna Grameen Rozgar Yojana (India)
SINASAN	National System for Food and Nutrition Security (Guatemala)
SNE	Société nigérienne des eaux
SNNPR	Southern Nations, Nationalities and Peoples Region (Ethiopia)
TCO	Tierra Comunitaria de Orígen (Bolivia)
TNCs	transnational corporations
TPDS	Targeted Public Distribution Scheme
TRIPS	Trade-Related Aspects of Intellectual Property Rights
UBPC	Unidad Básica de Produción Cooperativa (Cuba)
UDAPE	Unidad de Análisis de Políticas Sociales y Económicas
UK	United Kingdom (of Great Britain and Northern Ireland)
UN	United Nations
UNAIDS	United Nations World Conference on Environment and Development
UNCHS	United Nations Centre for Human Settlements
UNCTAD	United Nations Conference on Trade and Development
UNDAF	United Nations Development Assistance Framework
UNDP	United Nations Development Programme
UNEP	United Nations Environment Programme
UNESCO	United Nations Educational, Scientific and Cultural Organization
UNFPA	United Nations Fund for Population Activities
UNHCR	United Nations High Commissioner for Refugees
UNICEF	United Nations Children's Fund
UNIDO	United Nations Industrial Development Organization
UNIFIL	United Nations Interim Force in Lebanon
UNMAC	United Nations Mine-Action Centre
UNRWA	United Nations Relief and Works Agency for Palestine Refugees in the Near East
UNSCO	Office of the United Nations Special Coordinator in the Occupied Territories
UNSECOORD	United Nations Security Coordinator
US	United States
USA	United States of America
USAID	United States Agency for International Development
UXO	unexploded ordnance
WANAHR	World Alliance on Nutrition and Human Rights
WFP	World Food Programme
WFS:fyl	World Food Summit: five years later

WHA	World Health Assembly
WHO	World Health Organization
WIDER	World Institute for Development Economics Research
WMO	World Meteorological Organization
WSSCC	Water Supply and Sanitation Collaborative Council
WTO	World Trade Organization
WWF	World Wildlife Fund

1
Introduction: Hunger and the Right to Food

1.1 The state of hunger in the world today

It is an affront to human dignity to see how many people starve to death or live a life not worthy of the name, in conditions of squalor and unable to escape, with minds and bodies that are not whole. In the period 1997–1999, there were 815 million undernourished people in the world – mainly in the 122 third world countries.[1] The shocking news is that in the last decade global hunger has continued to increase. The Food and Agriculture Organization's (FAO) 2008 report, *The State of Food Insecurity in the World*, showed that hunger had increased to 923 million gravely undernourished children, women and men, compared to 848 million in 2007, despite already warning in 2003 of a 'setback in the war against hunger'. In 2009, FAO announced that for the first time, more than one billion people were undernourished in the world, primarily in developing countries. Before the world food crisis of 2007–2008, important progress in reducing hunger had been made in a few countries. But hunger is now on the rise everywhere. The overall trend is one of regression, rather than the progressive realization of the right to food.

Every five seconds a child under the age of 10 dies, directly or indirectly, of hunger somewhere in the world.[2] Over 2.2 million people, mostly babies and children, die from diarrhoea every year as a result of unclean drinking water.

Sixteen million of the undernourished people in the world live in the economically developed countries of the North.[3] The countries worst affected by extreme hunger are mostly in sub-Saharan Africa (18 countries), the Caribbean (Haiti) and Asia (Afghanistan, Bangladesh, the Democratic People's Republic of Korea and Mongolia). Most of the victims live in Asia – 583 million. However, if we look at the number of victims relative to the size of the population, sub-Saharan Africa is the worst affected: there, 236 million women, men and children, or 30 per cent of the region's population, are permanently and seriously undernourished.[4] More than 33 per cent of Africa's youngest children suffer from the effects of permanent, severe, chronic undernourishment in the form of stunted physical growth, but 70 per cent of the world's stunted children live in Asia.

A distinction should be drawn between two concepts – hunger or undernourishment on the one hand, and malnutrition on the other. Hunger or undernourishment refers to an insufficient supply or, at worst, a complete lack of calories. Malnutrition, however, is characterized by the lack or shortage of food which otherwise provides sufficient calories, of micronutrients – chiefly vitamins (organic molecules) and minerals (inorganic molecules). These micronutrients are vital for the functioning of cells and especially of the nervous system. Many of the women, men and children suffering from chronic undernourishment suffer from what the FAO calls 'extreme hunger'. This means that their daily ration of calories is well below the minimum necessary for survival. Many people die on a daily basis from starvation.

Malnutrition handicaps people for life. It can retard mental and physical development. Malnourishment also heightens vulnerability to other illnesses and almost always has serious physical and mental effects. Brain cells do not develop, bodies are stunted, blindness and diseases become rife, limiting potential and condemning the hungry to a marginal existence. Children are stunted and do not grow properly if they do not receive adequate food, in terms of both quantity and quality. A child may be receiving sufficient calories, but if he lacks micronutrients, he will suffer from stunted growth, infections and other disabilities, including impaired mental development.[5] What the United Nations Children's Fund (UNICEF) calls 'hidden hunger' is undernourishment and/or malnutrition between birth and the age of five, and it has disastrous effects: A child suffering from undernourishment and/or malnutrition in the first years of life will never recover. He cannot catch up later and will be disabled for life.[6]

Permanent, serious undernourishment and malnutrition prevent men and women from developing their full potential and becoming economically active, condemning them to a marginal social existence. They are decisive factors in the underdevelopment of many third world economies. Hunger costs developing countries up to US$ 500 billion in lost productivity given that hungry men, women and children are mentally and physically incapacitated by hunger and malnutrition, despite the fact that it would cost only US$ 25 million per year to halve undernourishment in 15 of the world's poorest countries.[7]

So the impacts of hunger and malnutrition are extreme: underdevelopment of brain cells, heightened vulnerability to disease, including HIV/AIDS, physical deformities and blindness are only some of these terrible effects.[8] These can also be passed on from generation to generation over the life cycle, as malnourished mothers give birth to babies who are themselves physically and mentally underdeveloped, and then pass these problems onto their own children.[9] Every year, tens of millions of seriously undernourished mothers give birth to tens of millions of seriously affected babies – Régis Debray has called these babies 'crucified at birth'.[10] This leads to a vicious cycle of poverty and underdevelopment. The impacts of hunger and malnutrition therefore affect the very possibility of a country to develop. Children cannot concentrate at school without food in their stomachs. No one can do a productive day's work, physically or mentally, if they are hungry. This means that poor countries can be trapped in a cycle of underdevelopment.

As George McGovern wrote in his book, *The Third Freedom: Ending Hunger in Our Time*:

> Of the world's hungry people, 300 million are school-age children. Not only do they bear the pangs of hunger but also their malnutrition leads to loss of energy, listlessness, and vulnerability to diseases of all kinds. Hungry children cannot function well in school – if, indeed, they are able to attend school at all. Hunger and malnutrition in childhood years can stunt the body and mind for a lifetime. No one can even guess at the vastly larger number of older children and adults who lead damaged lives because of malnutrition in their foetal or infant days.[11]

Action contre la Faim (Action Against Hunger), a French non-governmental organization (NGO), writes: 'Many poor people around the world do not get enough to eat because food production is geared to cash payment.' In many cases, the equation is simple: those who have money eat and those without suffer from hunger and the ensuing disabilities and often die.

This silent tragedy occurs daily in a world overflowing with riches. A world which already produces enough food to feed the global population of 6.2 billion people. According to the FAO, we produce more than enough food to feed the whole world population; enough food to give each person every day the equivalent of 2700 calories. And yet there are currently more than one billion gravely undernourished children, women and men living on the planet.

Hunger, like poverty, is still a predominantly rural problem. Of the 1.4 billion people who suffer from extreme poverty in the world, 75 per cent live and work in rural areas.[12] The rural poor suffer from hunger because they lack access to resources such as land, do not hold secure tenure, are bound by unjust sharecropping contracts or have properties that are so small that they cannot grow enough food to feed themselves. It is clear that reducing hunger does not mean increasing the production of food in rich countries, but rather in finding ways of increasing access to resources for the poor in the poorest countries.

Famine and food crises are not inevitable. In Africa, a study by the well-respected International Food Policy Research Institute (IFPRI) has shown that chronic food insecurity in Africa has been increasing since 1970, with the number of malnourished people in sub-Saharan Africa soaring from 88 million to 200 million in 1999–2001,[13] and to 236 million in 2008.[14] Chronic food insecurity means that as soon as drought strikes, it can quickly turn into catastrophic famine. Yet the IFPRI study shows that hunger could be reduced by investing in development and reducing dependence on rain-fed agriculture. Investments in simple water-harvesting technologies, agricultural extension, education and HIV/AIDS prevention and treatment would dramatically reduce the percentage of malnourished children in Africa.[15] This would put African countries on course to meeting the Millennium Development Goals and help prevent recurrent famine.

Persistent hunger is neither inevitable, nor acceptable. Hunger is not a question of fate; it is manmade. It is the result either of inaction, or of negative actions that violate the right to food. It is therefore time to take action. It is time to recognize the right to food as a human right and to realize the right to food across the world.

It is clear that if people come to believe that hunger is intolerable, that starving to death is an affront to human dignity, then the human right to food will become a necessity and a reality. As Georges Abi-Saab, eminent Professor of International Law, says:[16]

> [I]nternational law, like all law, does not arise from a vacuum or a social void, and does not always emerge in the legal universe in some 'big bang'. In most cases, it is the result of progressive and imperceptible growth, through the process of development of the values of a society; new ideas appear and take root; they strengthen into values which become more and more imperative in the social consciousness, to the point where they give rise to the irresistible conviction that they must be formally approved and protected. That is the point which marks the threshold of law.

If people believe that we should not let people die from starvation, that we should not let people be mentally and physically underdeveloped by constant malnourishment, then they will believe in the right to food. The right to food is inherent in everyone as a human being. There are always actions that can be taken to prevent hunger, prevent famine and prevent people dying from starvation. One step that can be taken is to make the right to food a reality. This would make a difference.

1.2 The development of the right to food

1.2.1 World Food Summit 1996

In the history of ideas, two things are vital: the truth of a concept and its timing. How can the truth of a concept be defined? A concept is the intelligible unity of a perceptible plurality. The truth of a concept may therefore be measured by its greatest and best possible appropriateness to its subject. The problem of the 'right time', on the other hand, is more complicated.

Kairos is a keyword in classical Greek philosophy. It means the 'right time', the propitious moment when an idea – a proposition – is liable to be accepted by the collective consciousness. There is an unexplained mystery in the history of ideas: an idea may be right and true for generations, sometimes centuries, without impinging on public debate or taking shape in a social movement, in other words in the collective consciousness. The idea remains unacceptable until that mysterious moment the Greeks call *kairos*.[17]

As far as the right to food is concerned, the 'right time' came in November 1996 in Rome, at the World Food Summit organized by FAO. However, the right to food has been considered a human right since 1948, when it appeared in paragraph 1 of Article 25 of the Universal Declaration of Human Rights in these terms:

> Everyone has the right to a standard of living adequate for the health and well-being of himself and of his family, including food, clothing, housing and medical care and necessary social services, and the right to security in the event of unemployment, sickness, disability, widowhood, old age or other lack of livelihood in circumstances beyond his control.

The Universal Declaration dates from 1948 and the World Food Summit took place in 1996. So it took almost half a century to produce the first coherent plan of action intended to make the right to food a reality.[18] A similar case is that of the United Nations Convention on the Prevention and Punishment of the Crime of Genocide, which dates from 1948, while the Rome Statute of the International Criminal Court responsible for enforcing it was adopted only in 1998.

In 1996, 180 nations met at the World Food Summit in Rome, at the FAO headquarters. Here they pledged to eradicate hunger and committed themselves to a basic target: reducing the number of undernourished people by half by 2015. On 13 November 1996, the World Food Summit adopted the Rome Declaration on World Food Security, in which those attending the Summit undertook to implement, monitor and follow up the Summit Plan of Action at all levels, in cooperation with the international community (commitment seven). In the Rome Declaration, governments reaffirmed the right of everyone to have access to safe and nutritious food, consistent with the right to adequate food and the fundamental right of everyone to be free from hunger. It also gave a specific mandate to the High Commissioner for Human Rights to better define the rights related to food and propose ways to implement and realize them.

The Rome Declaration set out seven commitments that form the basis for achieving sustainable food security for all. The Plan of Action spells out the objectives and actions relevant for practical implementation of these seven commitments. The following five objectives were defined in the Plan of Action:

> Objective 7.1: To adopt actions within each country's national framework to enhance food security and enable the implementation of the commitments of the World Food Summit Plan of Action.
>
> Objective 7.2: To improve subregional, regional and international cooperation and to mobilize, and optimize the use of, available resources to support national efforts for the earliest possible achievement of sustainable world food security.
>
> Objective 7.3: To monitor actively the implementation of the World Food Summit Plan of Action.
>
> Objective 7.4: To clarify the content of the right to adequate food and the fundamental right of everyone to be free from hunger, as stated in the International Covenant on Economic, Social and Cultural Rights and other relevant international and regional instruments, and to give particular attention to implementation and full and progressive realization of this right as a means of achieving food security for all.
>
> Objective 7.5: To share responsibilities in achieving food security for all so that implementation of the World Food Summit Plan of Action takes place at the lowest possible level at which its purpose could be best achieved.

1.2.2 World Food Summit: five years later

It soon became clear that little action was being taken with respect to the 1996 commitments. To check on progress being made, another meeting was convened in 2002 – the World Food Summit: five years later (WFS:fyl). The Declaration of that Summit called for the creation of an International Alliance Against Hunger to join forces in efforts to eradicate hunger. Another glimmer of hope appeared: Governments promised to draw up voluntary guidelines for the implementation of the right to food.

The WFS:fyl was held in Rome in June 2002 to review progress on the commitments made at the 1996 World Food Summit. The key commitment made by governments in 1996 was to halve the number of victims of hunger by 2015. However, the clearest, and shocking, conclusion of the 2002 Summit was that little progress had been made in meeting this goal. Five years later there were still 815 million hungry people, according to the FAO.[19] At the slow rate of progress witnessed at the time, it would take until at least 2030 to meet the goal of halving hunger.[20] Yet the situation was even worse than the aggregate statistics suggest. If the impressive progress of China was taken out of the figures, world hunger had increased since 1996. According to the IFPRI, the number of food-insecure or chronically malnourished people increased by 40 million in the 1990s, without counting China. Countries where the number of malnourished people increased included Afghanistan,

Bangladesh, the Democratic Republic of the Congo, India, Iraq, Kenya, the Democratic People's Republic of Korea, the United Republic of Tanzania and Uganda. In Africa, the situation in most countries was worse than it was ten years previously. On average, a third of all people in the countries of sub-Saharan Africa suffered from chronic severe hunger and malnourishment. FAO reported that, of the 91 countries that reported on their implementation of the 1996 commitments, 'few, if any' could claim substantive progress.[21]

Despite the fundamental importance of eradicating hunger, only two member countries of the Organization for Economic Cooperation and Development (OECD) were represented at the Summit by Prime Ministers, although many developing countries were represented by Heads of State. The final Declaration of the Summit, adopted after three days of intense negotiations, was disappointing in terms of the solutions proposed for world hunger, and it recognized that the goal of halving hunger by 2015 was unlikely to be attained. Few concrete solutions to speed up action were proposed, except for stimulating free trade and biotechnological progress. However, these elements proved to be highly controversial in the negotiations between representatives of various Governments, because of their different assessments of their potential impacts on hunger. The concept of the right to food was also hotly debated in the negotiations on the final Declaration. There was pressure from some Governments to replace the concept of the right to food with the concept of food security. However, the concept of the right to food is much stronger than the concept of food security. The right to food includes all the elements of food security – including availability, accessibility and utilization of food – but it also goes beyond the concept of food security because it emphasizes accountability. A rights-based approach focuses attention on the fact that making progress to reduce hunger is a legal obligation, not just a preference or choice.

Eventually, after intense negotiation, the right to food was reaffirmed in the final Declaration, and Governments agreed to draw up a set of voluntary guidelines on the right to food. The final Declaration reaffirms in its third preambular paragraph 'the right of everyone to have access to safe and nutritious food', and in paragraph 10 calls for the establishment of an intergovernmental working group to elaborate over the next two years a set of 'voluntary guidelines ... to achieve the progressive realization of the right to adequate food'. These important developments represent small seeds of hope in the fight against hunger. This success was thanks to the efforts of a number of countries and groups, particularly the Group of 77, Norway, Switzerland, Germany, France, Cuba and Venezuela, in fighting for the inclusion of the right to food and voluntary guidelines on the right to food.

1.2.3 Voluntary Guidelines on the Right to Food

In November 2002 the FAO Council established the first Intergovernmental Working Group to elaborate Voluntary Guidelines on the Progressive

Realization of the Right to Adequate Food, as requested in paragraph 10 of the Declaration of the WFS:fyl. In November 2004, the 'Voluntary Guidelines' were adopted by the FAO Council and approved by all Governments.[22] This was an important step, because in adopting the Voluntary Guidelines, Governments reaffirmed a solid commitment to the right to adequate food and agreed on an internationally accepted understanding of the right to food. This marked important progress. Indeed, the FAO hailed this effort as a 'landmark commitment to human rights' as it signified universal acceptance of what the right to food means and provides a practical tool that will 'empower the poor and hungry to claim their rights'.[23]

Although the Voluntary Guidelines are not the code of conduct that many States and non-governmental organizations had been fighting for, they were still an important step forward. The process of drawing up the guidelines helped strengthen governments' understanding of the right to food. The elaboration of the Guidelines provided an important space for reaffirming the importance of human rights in the fight against hunger and malnutrition and for developing a better understanding of international obligations with respect to the right to food. The process also provided an important forum for discussion and sharing of experiences to fight hunger and to clarify the right to food, as promised in objective 7.4 of the 1996 Plan of Action.

The Voluntary Guidelines were, and still are, ground-breaking in the sense that they provide an internationally accepted definition of the right to food. The definition adopted by governments closely follows the definition adopted by the Committee on Economic, Social and Cultural Rights (CESCR). It also follows the interpretation offered by the Committee that States are obliged to *respect, protect* and *fulfil* the right to adequate food, which has important implications for the acceptance of this framework across all economic, social and cultural rights.[24] Paragraph 17 of the Voluntary Guidelines states that:

> …States Parties to the International Covenant on Economic, Social and Cultural Rights (ICESCR) have the obligation to respect, promote and protect and to take appropriate steps to achieve progressively the full realization of the right to adequate food. States Parties should respect existing access to adequate food by not taking any measures that result in preventing such access, and should protect the right of everyone to adequate food by taking steps so that enterprises and individuals do not deprive individuals of their access to adequate food. States Parties should promote policies intended to contribute to the progressive realization of people's right to adequate food by proactively engaging in activities intended to strengthen people's access to and utilization of resources and means to ensure their livelihood, including food security. States Parties should, to the extent that resources permit, establish and maintain safety

nets or other assistance to protect those who are unable to provide for themselves.

The Guidelines are also ground-breaking in recognizing the international dimension related to the right to food, addressing questions of international trade, food aid and embargoes, for example. This is important because it extends understanding of the right to food beyond the traditional relation between a State and its citizens towards a greater recognition of 'extraterritorial' responsibilities. This set of guidelines also addresses questions of non-State actors, encouraging direct responsibility for the right to food and improved regulation of markets to ensure food security.

The Voluntary Guidelines also show how the right to food can be incorporated into government strategies and institutions. They show how the key human rights principles – non-discrimination, participation, transparency, accountability and access to justice – can be incorporated into a rights-based approach to food security. They also call on States to promote 'broad-based economic development that is supportive of their food security policies' (guideline 2.1), to 'pursue inclusive, non-discriminatory and sound economic, agriculture, fisheries, forestry, land use, and, as appropriate, land reform policies' (guideline 2.5) and to incorporate the right to food into poverty reduction strategies. They urge States to 'take account of shortcomings of market mechanisms in protecting the environment and public goods' (guideline 4.10) and that, particularly for women (guideline 8.3) and vulnerable groups:

> ...States should respect and protect the rights of individuals with respect to resources such as land, water, forests, fisheries, and livestock without any discrimination. Where necessary and appropriate, States should carry out land reforms and other policy reforms consistent with their human rights obligations and in accordance with the rule of law in order to secure efficient and equitable access to land and to strengthen pro-poor growth. Special attention may be given to groups such as pastoralists and indigenous people and their relation to natural resources. (guideline 8.1)

The Voluntary Guidelines also call on States to set up mechanisms to inform people of their rights and improve access to justice for the right to food (guideline 7). Greater recognition of the right to adequate food at the national level and assuring access to justice for all, with priority for the poorest and most vulnerable, will significantly improve the realization of the right to food. The Voluntary Guidelines therefore have the potential to have a very positive impact in the struggle for the right to food. It is essential that they are adopted as a practical instrument to guide government policies and programmes in order to have a real impact on hunger and food insecurity in the world.

1.2.4 The United Nations human rights system and the right to food

In other parts of the UN system the human rights bodies had also been addressing the right to food. In 1999, the CESCR discussed the right to food, as contained in Article 11 of the International Covenant on Economic, Social and Cultural Rights. The CESCR adopted a General Comment on the right to adequate food at its twelfth session, on 11 May 1999.[25] This General Comment sought to elaborate the CESCR's interpretation of Article 11 and the content of the right to food, including the corresponding State obligations. In General Comment No. 12 the Committee affirmed, *inter alia*, that the right to adequate food is indivisibly linked to the inherent dignity of the human person and is indispensable for the fulfilment of other human rights enshrined in the International Bill of Human Rights[26] and is also inseparable from social justice, requiring the adoption of appropriate economic, environmental and social policies, at both the national and international levels, oriented to the eradication of poverty and the fulfilment of all human rights for all.

Other human rights bodies had been addressing the right to food well before this time. As early as 1983, the United Nations Sub-Commission on Prevention of Discrimination and Protection of Minorities had appointed a Special Rapporteur on the Right to Food. After many years of work, the Sub-Commission on the Promotion and Protection of Human Rights adopted an updated final study on the right to food, submitted by Mr Asbjørn Eide, in August 1999.[27]

The Office of the High Commissioner had also been facilitating discussions on the right to food, organizing expert consultations, and submitting a report on the topic to the Commission on Human Rights.[28]

Finally, in July 2000 the Commission on Human Rights passed Resolution 2000/10 to create the post of Special Rapporteur on the Right to Food. On 4 September 2000, the Chairperson of the Commission appointed Mr Jean Ziegler, from Switzerland, as Special Rapporteur. Jean Ziegler's mandate finished at the end of April 2008 after the appointment of Professor Olivier de Schutter, from Belgium, as the new Special Rapporteur on the Right to Food.[29]

The role of the Special Rapporteur on the Right to Food is to ensure that governments are meeting their obligations to respect, protect and fulfil the right to food of all people. The Commission on Human Rights created the role of Special Rapporteur on the Right to Food 'in order to respond fully to the necessity for an integrated and coordinated approach in the promotion and protection of the right to food'.[30] Resolution 2000/10 outlined the mandate of the Special Rapporteur, requesting the Special Rapporteur to accomplish the following main activities:

(a) To seek, receive and respond to information on all aspects of the realization of the right to food, including the urgent necessity of eradicating hunger;

(b) To establish cooperation with Governments, intergovernmental organizations, in particular the Food and Agriculture Organization of the United Nations, and non-governmental organizations, on the promotion and effective implementation of the right to food, and to make appropriate recommendations on the realization thereof, taking into consideration the work already done in this field throughout the United Nations system;
(c) To identify emerging issues related to the right to food worldwide.

In 2001, the Research Unit on the Right to Food was created as an independent academic research project – at the Graduate Institute of Development Studies in Geneva[31] – to provide research support to the UN Special Rapporteur on the Right to Food, in collaboration with the United Nations Office of the High Commissioner for Human Rights. The staff of the Research Unit on the Right to Food were Christophe Golay (2001–2008), Sally-Anne Way (2001–2007) and Claire Mahon (2007–2008) – all co-authors of this book with Jean Ziegler.

Together, we promoted the right to food in many ways during these seven years (see Annex 1). We elaborated 15 thematic reports for the United Nations General Assembly, the Commission on Human Rights and the Human Rights Council. We also undertook country missions to assess the implementation of the right to food in different countries in the various regions of the world, including in Brazil, Guatemala, Bolivia, Cuba, Niger, Ethiopia, Niger, India, Bangladesh, Mongolia, Lebanon and the Occupied Palestinian Territories (see Part II). In hundreds of cases of alleged violations of the right to food, we sent communications to Member States as well as to international and regional financial institutions, national development agencies and transnational corporations.

The objective of this book is to publish the research we have undertaken during the mandate of the first UN Special Rapporteur on the Right to Food, in a format that can be accessible to the widest possible audience. To reach that objective, we have chosen to divide the book in two parts. The first part is devoted to the theoretical development of the right to food in international law, while the second part is devoted to analyzing the right to food in practice, by presenting the results of our 11 country missions in Africa, Asia and Latin America.

Part I
The Right to Food in International Law

The development of the right to food in international law has been very important in the last 10 years, in particular since the adoption of the General Comment on the right to adequate food by the CESCR in 1999, and the adoption of the voluntary guidelines on the right to food by all Members States of the FAO in 2004.

In this first part, devoted to the analysis of this development, we will present the definition of the right to food in international law in Chapter 2, the right to food of the most vulnerable people, including women, children, farmers and peasants, fisherpeople indigenous people and refugees from hunger in Chapter 3, the protection of the right to food in an era of globalization in Chapter 4 and its protection in situations of armed conflict in Chapter 5.

2
The Definition of the Right to Food in International Law

2.1 The definition of the right to food[1]

All human beings have a right to live in dignity, free from hunger. The right to food is a human right. It is a right protected under international human rights and international humanitarian law.

We have adopted the following definition in all our work:

> The right to food is the right to have regular, permanent and unrestricted access, either directly or by means of financial purchases, to quantitatively and qualitatively adequate and sufficient food corresponding to the cultural traditions of the people to which the consumer belongs, and which ensures a physical and mental, individual and collective, fulfilling and dignified life free of fear.

The right to food includes both the right to solid food and to liquid food (safe water).[2] In general, the right to food embodies the practical idea that all people should have a decent standard of living, especially enough to eat and drink, both in peacetime and in war. Like all the other economic and social rights, the right to food is about the concern for human dignity that underlies the Universal Declaration on Human Rights. It is also about the fight for President Roosevelt's 'Third Freedom' – the freedom from want and freedom from hunger.[3]

The right to food means that Governments must not take actions that result in increasing levels of hunger, food insecurity and malnutrition. It also means that Governments must protect people from the actions of others that might violate the right to food. Governments must also, to the maximum of available resources, invest in eradicating hunger. The right to food is not about charity, but about ensuring that all people have the capacity to feed themselves in dignity.

The right to food is a binding obligation well established under international law, recognized in the Universal Declaration on Human Rights and the International Covenant on Economic, Social and Cultural Rights, as well as other instruments.[4] The right to food has also been recognized in numerous national constitutions.

The right to food, and the measures that must be taken, are laid out precisely in Article 11 of the International Covenant on Economic, Social and Cultural Rights. Article 11, paragraph 1, states that States parties recognize 'the right of everyone to an adequate standard of living for himself and his family, including adequate food, clothing and housing, and to the continuous improvement of living conditions'. In paragraph 2 of the same article, they recognize that measures may be needed to guarantee 'the fundamental right of everyone to be free from hunger'. Paragraph 2 provides that States parties shall take, individually and through international cooperation, the measures, including specific programmes, which are needed:

(a) To improve methods of production, conservation and distribution of food by making full use of technical and scientific knowledge, by disseminating knowledge of the principles of nutrition and by developing or reforming agrarian systems in such a way as to achieve the most efficient development and utilization of natural resources;
(b) Taking into account the problems of both food-importing and food-exporting countries, to ensure an equitable distribution of world food supplies in relation to need.

As pointed out by the CESCR, the body responsible for monitoring implementation of the Covenant, in its General Comment No. 12: 'The human right to adequate food is of crucial importance for the enjoyment of all rights. It applies to everyone ...'.[5] So the words 'for himself and his family' in Article 11, paragraph 1, do not imply limitations on the applicability of this right in the case of individuals or in the case of households headed by a woman.

Article 1 of the International Covenant on Economic, Social and Cultural Rights sets forth the right of peoples to self-determination, by virtue of which they freely determine their political status and pursue their economic, social and cultural development. For this purpose, 'All peoples may ... freely dispose of their natural wealth and resources' and, consequently, 'In no case may a people be deprived of its own means of subsistence (para. 2).'[6]

The concept of the right to food comprises different components. The first of these is the notion of adequate food, as set forth in Article 11, paragraphs 1 and 2, of the Covenant. In its General Comment No. 12, the CESCR gives the following definition:

> The right to adequate food is realized when every man, woman and child, alone or in community with others, has physical and economic access at all times to adequate food or means for its procurement. The right to

adequate food shall therefore not be interpreted in a narrow or restrictive sense which equates it with a minimum package of calories, proteins and other specific nutrients. The right to adequate food will have to be realized progressively. However, States have a core obligation to take the necessary action to mitigate and alleviate hunger... even in times of natural or other disasters.[7]

Two other components of the concept of the right to food are the notions of adequacy and sustainability:

> The concept of *adequacy*... serves to underline a number of factors which must be taken into account in determining whether particular foods or diets that are accessible can be considered the most appropriate under given circumstances... The notion of *sustainability* is intrinsically linked to the notion of adequate food or food *security*, implying food being accessible for both present and future generations. The precise meaning of 'adequacy' is to a large extent determined by prevailing social, economic, cultural, climatic, ecological and other conditions, while 'sustainability' incorporates the notion of long-term availability and accessibility.[8]

A further component is the notion of a diet:

> *Dietary needs* implies that the diet as a whole contains a mix of nutrients for physical and mental growth, development and maintenance, and physical activity that are in compliance with human physiological needs at all stages throughout the life cycle and according to gender and occupation.[9]

According to the definition of the right to food, everyone has the right to food corresponding to their own particular culture:

> *Cultural or consumer acceptability* implies the need also to take into account... perceived non-nutrient-based values attached to food and food consumption and informed consumer concerns regarding the nature of accessible food supplies.[10]

Lastly, there is the component of accessibility:

> Economic accessibility implies that personal or household financial costs associated with the acquisition of food for an adequate diet should be at a level such that the attainment and satisfaction of other basic needs are not threatened or compromised. Economic accessibility applies to any acquisition pattern or entitlement through which people procure their food and is a measure of the extent to which it is satisfactory for the enjoyment of the right to food.[11]

Our definition of the right to food,

> the right to have regular, permanent and unrestricted access, either directly or by means of financial purchases, to quantitatively and qualitatively adequate and sufficient food corresponding to the cultural traditions of the people to which the consumer belongs, and which ensures a physical and mental, individual and collective, fulfilling and dignified life free of fear

tries to capture the dimension of human suffering that is missing from many formal descriptions of food insecurity: the unbearable nagging dread that tortures starving persons from the moment they wake up. How, during the day that lies ahead, will they be able to feed their family, provide nourishment for their children and feed themselves? This dread may be even more terrible than the physical suffering and the many aches and diseases that strike an undernourished body.

This definition is very close to the definition of food security, indeed the corollary of the right to food is food security. The definition of food security is given in the first paragraph of the World Food Summit Plan of Action: 'Food security exists when all people, at all times, have physical and economic access to sufficient, safe and nutritious food to meet their dietary needs and food preferences for an active and healthy life.' The parameters for food security vary with age: at birth, babies need 300 calories a day; between the ages of 1 and 2, 1000 calories a day; by the age of 5, children need 1600 calories a day. To maintain their strength every day, adults need between 2000 and 2700 calories, depending on where they live and what kind of work they do.[12] Understanding food security is therefore vital to understanding the right to food, as it gives us an understanding of the minimum standards that are considered necessary.

The rights-based approach to food security adds a new and vital element: accountability. Commitment to the right to food and food security entails obligations of Governments to ensure freedom from hunger for all people at all times. States parties to the International Covenant on Economic, Social and Cultural Rights are legally bound to respect, protect and fulfil the right to food. By committing themselves to advancing the right to food through ratification of international conventions, Governments are bound to respect, protect and fulfil the right to food, which also means that they should be accountable to their populations if they violate those obligations. However, this will only happen if the justiciability of the right to food is established.[13]

2.2 Correlative States' obligations[14]

The existence of the right to food gives rise to obligations for States. Asbjørn Eide, in his outstanding report on the right to adequate food,[15] sets out three main obligations that can be paraphrased as follows: to respect, protect and fulfil the right to food. These three levels of obligations have been further defined by the CESCR in its General Comment No. 12 on the right to adequate food, before being accepted by the States in the Voluntary Guidelines on the Right to Food.

2.2.1 The obligation to respect the right to food

The obligation to respect means that the Government should not arbitrarily take away people's right to food or make it difficult for them to gain access to food. The obligation to respect the right to food is effectively a negative obligation, as it entails limits on the exercise of State power that might threaten people's existing access to food. Violations of the obligation to respect would occur, for example, if the Government arbitrarily evicted or displaced people from their land, especially if the land was their primary means of feeding themselves, if the Government took away social security provisions without making sure that vulnerable people had alternative ways to feed themselves, or if the Government knowingly introduced toxic substances into the food chain, as the right to food entails access to food that is 'free from adverse substances'. In situations of armed conflict, it would mean that the Government troops must not destroy productive resources and must not block, delay or divert relief food supplies to civilian populations.

2.2.2 The obligation to protect the right to food

The obligation to protect means that the Government must pass and enforce laws to prevent powerful people or organizations from violating the right to food. The obligation to protect requires States to regulate non-State actors, including corporations or individuals who may threaten other people's right to food. The Government must also establish bodies to investigate and provide effective remedies, including access to justice, if that right is violated. For example, if the Government does not intervene when a powerful individual evicts people from their land, then the Government violates the obligation to protect the right to food. The Government would also fail to protect the right to food if it took no action if a company polluted a community's water supply. To protect the right to food, the Government might also have to take action if people were denied access to food on the basis of gender, race or other forms of discrimination. It might also, for example, have to introduce laws to protect consumers against harmful food products or against unsustainable means of production or to combat corruption. That could include the introduction of labelling on foods or legislation on the use of pesticides or genetically engineered food.

2.2.3 The obligation to fulfil the right to food

The obligation to fulfil (facilitate and provide) means that the Government must take positive actions to identify vulnerable groups and to implement policies to ensure their access to adequate food by facilitating their ability to feed themselves. General Comment No. 12 summarizes this obligation as follows:

> ...whenever an individual or group is unable, for reasons beyond their control, to enjoy the right to adequate food by the means at their disposal, States have the obligation to *fulfil (provide)* [the right to food] directly.[16]

The obligation to fulfil is a positive obligation, as this means that the Government must actively seek to identify vulnerable groups and implement policies to improve those people's access to adequate food and their ability to feed themselves. That could mean improving employment prospects by introducing an agrarian reform programme for landless groups or promoting alternative employment opportunities. It could also include, for example, free milk programmes in schools in order to improve child nutrition. The further obligation to provide goes beyond the obligation to facilitate, but only comes into effect when people's food security is threatened for reasons beyond their control. As a last resort, direct assistance may have to be provided by means of safety nets, such as food voucher schemes or social security provisions to ensure freedom from hunger. In most cases, access to food is a question of affordability, and therefore income. This obligation to fulfil the right to food imposes duties on the State such as the duty to promote redistributive taxation and social security.

This support should be provided as a matter of right, rather than charity, in order to ensure human dignity. As FAO has outlined, 'a rights-based approach to food security emphasizes the satisfaction of people's basic needs as a matter of right, rather than of benevolence'.[17]

The Government would violate its obligations if it let people starve when they were in desperate need and had no way of helping themselves. An appeal by a State for international humanitarian aid, when it is itself unable to guarantee the population's right to food, also comes under this third obligation. States that, through neglect or misplaced national pride, make no such appeal or deliberately delay such appeals are violating their obligation (as in the case of Ethiopia under the dictatorship of Haile Mengistu in the early 1980s).

2.2.4 The concept of progressive realization of the right to food

The fulfilment of the right to food, like other economic, social and cultural rights, is qualified to the extent that it must be achieved progressively and to the maximum of available resources. Under, Article 2 paragraph 1, of the International Covenant on Economic, Social and Cultural Rights (emphasis added): '

Each State Party...undertakes to take steps...to the *maximum of its available resources*...[with a view to achieving] *progressively* the full realization of the rights recognized in the present Covenant by all appropriate means'.

That means that a poor country is not expected immediately to ensure the same level of economic, social and cultural benefits that a rich country can afford. However, even the poorest country is bound to ensure the highest level its resources will permit and, at the very least, a basic minimum level of economic, social and cultural rights.[18] The concept of 'progressive realization' cannot be used to justify persistent injustice and inequality. It requires Governments to take immediate steps to continuously improve people's ability to feed themselves and to eliminate hunger.

There are certain limits on the application of the concept of progressive realization of the right to food. In accordance with General Comment No. 12, '... States have a core obligation to take the necessary action to mitigate and alleviate hunger...even in times of natural or other disasters'.[19]

In addition, General Comment No. 3 provides examples of minimum State obligations of immediate nature and puts some limits on the concept of progressive realization.[20]

2.2.5 The obligation to provide a basic minimum subsistence

There is a clear minimum core obligation on all States to provide, at the very least, a minimum essential level of economic, social and cultural rights, including the right to food, regardless of the limitation of progressive realization. The minimum core obligation is an immediate obligation, although it is still subject to available resources. As the CESCR has clarified:

> In order for a State party to be able to attribute its failure to meet at least its minimum core obligations to a lack of available resources it must demonstrate that every effort has been made to use all resources that are at its disposition in an effort to satisfy, as a matter of priority, those minimum obligations.[21]

2.2.6 The obligation of non-retrogression

The concept of progressive realization of the right to food also implies the 'principle of non-regression', which means that Governments must not adopt regressive policies that lead to deterioration in access to food. What Governments must do, therefore, is adopt an action plan with concrete goals and fixed time frames and monitor progress over time to measure progressive realization. Current national efforts to monitor the Millennium Development Goal on hunger provide an important step in this direction. However, Governments must also be called upon to explain and account for any regression in the realization of the right to food.

2.2.7 The obligation of non-discrimination

Under international law, the prohibition of discrimination is not subject to the limitation of progressive realization. The obligation not to discriminate is an immediate duty, and discrimination in access to food on the basis of race, colour, sex, language, religion, political or other opinion, national or social origin, property, birth or other status, as stated in Article 2, paragraph 2, of the International Covenant, cannot be justified under any circumstances, including low levels of resources. This means that it should be ensured, whatever the level of resources, that resources are shared fairly and that specific groups are not discriminated against in the distribution of resources by the State. We believe very strongly that non-discrimination policies must be implemented immediately, and not subjected to progressive realization.

3
The Right to Food of the Most Vulnerable People

3.1 Women[1]

Women are disproportionately affected by hunger, food insecurity and poverty, largely as a result of gender inequality and their lack of social, economic and political power. In many countries, girls are twice as likely to die from malnutrition and preventable childhood diseases than boys, and it is estimated that almost twice as many women suffer from malnutrition than men. Unfortunately, however, there are still no global statistics on malnutrition or undernourishment rates disaggregated for men and women.

Yet women are key to food security. Women play vital roles in the production and preparation of food, in agriculture and in earning incomes to feed their families, and as mediators of nutrition education within the family, if they themselves are educated. It is now widely agreed that women produce 60–80 per cent of food crops in developing countries and play a crucial part in ensuring the food security of households. And it is increasingly recognized that the health of women is crucial to the health of entire societies, because malnourished women are more likely to give birth to malnourished and underdeveloped babies. In countries where there are high rates of children dying before the age of five, this is being increasingly linked to maternal malnutrition. New scientific evidence in nutrition calls for a 'lifecycle' approach to nutrition which recognizes the intergenerational links in nutritional status.[2] Underweight and malnourished mothers are more likely to give birth to underweight babies, whose mental and physical capacities may be severely stunted. These children may never recover and in turn have malnourished babies, passing hunger on through the generations.

Despite their key role in ensuring food security, 70 per cent of the world's hungry are women or girls. Women often face discrimination in gaining secure access to and control over other productive resources, such as land, water and credit, as they are often not recognized as producers or juridical equals. According to FAO, while the proportion of women heads of rural households continues to grow, exceeding 30 per cent in some developing countries, women own less than 2 per cent of all land.[3] Despite legal and often constitutional rights in many countries, women still face considerable obstacles to inheritance, purchase and control of land. In many countries, despite formal protection against discrimination, women lack any real access to land, a problem which is exacerbated by a lack of inheritance rights.[4]

3.1.1 Gender dimensions of the right to food

Although significant advances have been made in developing legal protections for women, including protection of the right to food, there remains a gap between principle and practice in many contexts around the world. Even where legislation exists, women do not always have access to justice or the laws may not be enforced, and legal equality does not always amount to substantive equality. While advances have been made in women's formal rights, this has not been accompanied by adequate attention focused on making these rights meaningful and substantive, so the real impact of international instruments on women's lives remains limited. Women continue to suffer de facto discrimination in access to and control over food, land and incomes and other resources.

Intra-household discrimination in the distribution of food and income can severely affect women's right to food. As Amartya Sen so graphically illustrated in his article 'More than 100 Million Women are Missing', discrimination against girl children can result in high child malnutrition and high female mortality, with young girls dying from malnutrition and neglect.[5] During our mission to Bangladesh,[6] we found a marked gender disparity in malnutrition levels, with far more girl children underweight and stunted than boy children. In Bangladesh, social and cultural customs demand in many regions that women eat last, after the male members of the family, which also means that women often eat least, contributing to high rates of female mortality. In Bangladesh discrimination and devaluation of women are sometimes expressed in other very violent ways, including acid-throwing, where a woman is intentionally disfigured as an act of vengeance, often leaving her unable to marry and with difficulties in finding work to feed herself. In cases where the private sphere is a key site of gender discrimination and subordination, addressing discrimination means moving beyond the public/private dichotomy, where the family is categorized as 'private' and beyond the reach and responsibility of the State, towards taking concrete action to change perceptions of gender relations within the private sphere.

Continued discrimination in the workplace also means that the incomes of women are still less than those for men, leaving them less able to feed themselves and their families, particularly in the case of female-headed households. While women are increasingly being incorporated into the workforce, the terms of this incorporation are often exploitative, particularly in the low-skill, low-wage sectors. Increasing deregulation and the relaxation of labour laws under neoliberal policy strategies also make it harder for women to demand better wages and conditions, adding to the growing feminization of poverty. At the other end of the spectrum, much of women's work in the home and in agriculture is still not recognized as a productive activity, and this invisible labour is rarely remunerated. As a result, women are frequently economically dependent on men, which reinforces their lack of power and is often the reason that violence of different forms against women is often unreported. During our visit to Brazil[7] we also found that gender discrimination often intersects with other forms of discrimination, such as race. In Brazil, for example, poverty and hunger is predominantly black.[8] The level of poverty for Afro-Brazilians is double that for whites. Afro-Brazilian men earn on average less than 42 per cent of the salary earned by white Brazilians. Yet the salaries of Afro-Brazilian women are significantly lower than that as they suffer from double discrimination of both gender and race.

Women also face great difficulties in gaining secure access to and control over other resources, such as land, water and credit, as they are often not recognized as producers or juridical equals. Access to credit and secure land tenure is often denied to women because they are not officially recognized by government authorities as food producers or agricultural workers. Without access to productive resources, a woman's economic independence and ability to feed herself and her family is limited. Again, according to FAO, while the proportion of women heads of rural household continues to grow, reaching more than 30 per cent in some developing countries, less than 2 per cent of all land is owned by women.[9] Customs and traditions in many parts of the world limit women's equal access to productive resources. In some countries, however, this discrimination is codified in customary law.

During the mission to Niger,[10] we found that Niger has three coexisting and complex legal systems – modern law, customary law and Islamic law. This pluralist system shows the rich legal heritage of the country, but is also a challenge to women's right to food. Customary law, in a syncretic mix with Islamic law, tends to be applied at community and family levels, but this gives women far less rights than the coexisting modern law, particularly with respect to inheritance rights. For example, custom permits child marriage of young girls, which, if consummated at too early an age, can have serious health effects, tearing apart their organs and resulting in a condition called fistula which causes incontinence. This leads to their repudiation by their husbands, leaving them with little means of survival, often unable to feed themselves. We were also concerned by the large number of reservations that the Government of Niger has entered upon its accession to the Convention on the Elimination of All Forms of Discrimination against Women on the grounds of culture and custom, but which renders effectively meaningless much of the protections offered by the Convention.

Clearly, there is a need to protect culture and difference, but that should not lead to the persistence of discrimination against women.

Gender blindness in policy development can also lead to the persistence of women's inequality and disproportionately affect their right to food. Policies of structural adjustment, deregulation and privatization often appear to be gender neutral, but their impacts on men and women are very different. The costs of economic restructuring, for example, are often disproportionately borne by women. It is vital to examine the gender-differentiated effects of economic restructuring under the current dominant economic model supported by the World Bank, the International Monetary Fund and the World Trade Organization, which calls for a downsizing of State responsibility for social policy. While social policy used to revolve around issues of redistribution, universal provision and reducing levels of inequality, it now focuses on targeting the 'poorest of the poor'. This aims to 'reduce poverty and destitution, but is unconcerned about the overall distribution of income and wealth within society'.[11] As many women's rights advocates have pointed out, substantive equality for women will never be reached unless the State takes concrete positive action to improve the position of women relative to men. Formal equality of human rights is not enough; in fact, formal equality of rights will even generate inequality, if initial starting points and different disadvantages of men and women are not considered. The downsizing of the State reduces the capacity of the State to take positive action, despite the fact that under human rights treaties, most Governments have signed up to international human rights commitments to respect, protect and fulfil the right to food of women – that is, to take concrete positive action to address the issues of discrimination facing women and to ensure their substantive equality.

The right to food places obligations on the State to respect, protect and fulfil the right to food. Undertaking these obligations must be understood in a way that respects gender difference, understands existing obstacles facing women and seeks to improve the situation. In the first instance, the obligation to respect the right to food for women means that the State is obliged to refrain from doing anything that impedes women's existing access to food, water, land, income or other resources. The obligation to protect the right to food for women means that the State is obliged to protect women from all forms of discrimination by non-State actors, including discrimination in the workplace, in the private sphere, and in access to resources. The obligation to fulfil the right to food for women means that Governments have a positive obligation to create an enabling environment to ensure that women have sufficient access to resources to be able to feed themselves and, in the final resort, to support women who, for reasons beyond their control, cannot feed themselves. This positive obligation means that the State must take concrete positive action to improve the substantive equality of women and to challenge norms, traditions and customary laws that legitimate discrimination and violence against women, including within the family and within the household, particularly in relation to the allocation of food.

3.1.2 International instruments protecting women's right to food

Enormous progress has been made across the world in the last decade in developing legal instruments to address discrimination and protect women. This section looks at some of the international instruments which protect women's right to food, highlighting articles that can be used to improve the protection of women's right to food. The following section, however, will move on to look at the continued difficulties in relation to gender and the right to food.

Women's right to food is protected, both explicitly and implicitly, in a wide range of international and regional human rights instruments. The strongest protection of the human right to food is found in the International Covenant on Economic, Social and Cultural Rights (Articles 3 and 2(2)), which also contains guarantees of non-discrimination and of equal enjoyment for women of these rights. The right to food requires that governments respect, protect and fulfil the right to food for their citizens and an interpretation based on gender must recognize that this could imply taking specific and different actions for women. General Comment No. 12 of the CESCR, the authoritative definition of the right to food, also states that government policies to realize the right to food:

> [S]hould give particular attention to the need to prevent discrimination in access to food or resources for food. This should include: guarantees of full and equal access to economic resources, particularly for women, including the right to inheritance and the ownership of land and other property, credit, natural resources and appropriate technology; measures to respect and protect self-employment and work which provides a remuneration ensuring a decent living for wage earners and their families (as stipulated in article 7 (a) (ii) of the Covenant); maintaining registries on rights in land (including forests). (paragraph 26)

Women's rights are most fully protected in the Convention on the Elimination of All Forms of Discrimination against Women. Although the Convention does not explicitly refer to the right to food as such, it does protect women's equal access to land, credit, income and social security or safety nets, which are all essential elements of the right to food. As one example, Article 14(g) demands equal treatment in land and agrarian reform. Article 16(h) ensures equal rights in terms of the ownership of property. A useful resource on women's rights to land and other resources is the document published by FAO entitled *Gender and Law – Women's Rights in Agriculture*,[12] which gives a full overview of different rights of women under different legal systems around the world, at both international and national levels. During times of armed conflict, special protection is also granted to women and their right to assistance, including food, under international humanitarian law.[13]

Women's rights are also strongly protected under provisions on equality and non-discrimination in many international legal instruments, including the conventions of the International Labour Organization.[14] At the national level, numerous laws also prohibit discrimination and provide for equality of women, and States are required to act with due diligence to prevent, investigate and punish discrimination and violence against women committed by the State or private actors.[15] It should also be recognized that within the context of economic, social and cultural rights, including the right to food, the obligation of non-discrimination is an immediate obligation and is therefore not limited by the provision for progressive realization applied to other obligations under the International Covenant on Economic, Social and Cultural Rights (Article 2 (2)), but must be implemented immediately.

3.2 Children[16]

According to United Nations Children's Fund (UNICEF), more than 90 million children suffer from an acute stage of malnutrition, and most of them are born underweight. Undernourishment in the womb condemns these children to a life of stunted mental and physical development, a life in which they will be unable to concentrate even if they can go to school, a life in which they are condemned to be the poorest of the poor even when they become adults.[17] More than 400 million children also do not have access to clean drinking water, leaving them so vulnerable to water-borne disease that many do not live to see their fifth birthday. Many girls never get to go to school because they are forced to spend the whole day walking long distances to collect water for their families.

On World Food Day, 16 October 2006, the Executive Director of the World Food Programme (WFP), James Morris said:

> Every day some 18,000 children die of hunger and malnutrition. Yet there are no headlines and no public outcry. Instead these poor forgotten children die in silence, far from our sight in many countries of the world. This need not happen: we have every tool we need to solve hunger.[18]

There is no public outcry, because hunger and malnutrition in many parts of the world are still not treated as a human rights issue. Yet if an infant or child does not receive sufficient food and nutrition in their first days and first years, they will be condemned to limited physical and intellectual development, if they manage to survive.

3.2.1 The extreme vulnerability of children to hunger and malnutrition

About 5.6 million children die every year before they reach the age of five. In the Sahelian African country of Niger, one quarter of all children die before their fifth birthday. Millions more children suffer from stunted growth and limited intellectual development, as a result of the lack of adequate food and nutrition. About one in every four children around the world is underweight for their age, more than 96 per cent of low birth weight babies are born to underweight mothers in the developing world, reflecting a generational cycle of undernutrition, the consequences of which are passed along to children by mothers who are themselves in poor health and undernourished.[19] Although there has been some recent progress in reducing global levels of malnutrition, it is a concern that the Millennium Development Goal to halve the number of underweight children by 2015 will not be met.[20]

Malnutrition causes more than half of all deaths of children under five years old. About 100 million children still lack sufficient vitamin A, essential for immune system functions and their survival, growth and development.[21] Millions suffer from iodine deficiency disorders, which prevent normal growth in the brain and nervous system, yet it is easily preventable through the simple iodization of salt. Iron-deficiency anaemia seriously affects the intellectual development in young children. Undernutrition is also closely linked to diarrhoea and other water-borne diseases.[22] Unsafe water and a lack of basic sanitation and hygiene every year kill more than 1.5 million children. Around the world approximately 125 million children under five years of age have no access to an improved drinking water source, and around 280 million children under five have no access to improved sanitation facilities.

3.2.2 Children's right to food under international law

The Universal Declaration of Human Rights protects the right of every human being 'to a standard of living adequate for the health and well-being of himself and his family, including food, clothing, housing and medical care and necessary social services' (Article 25). The International Covenant on Economic, Social and Cultural Rights recognizes the right of everyone to an adequate standard of living 'including adequate food' and the fundamental right of everyone to be free from hunger (Article 11).

Although all international human rights instruments apply both to children and adults, it is the Convention on the Rights of the Child which is the main international human rights treaty specifically aimed to protect and promote children's rights, including children's right to food. Article 27 recognizes the right of every child to a standard of living adequate for the child's physical, mental, spiritual, moral and social development. Article 24 provides that States parties should take appropriate measures to combat disease and malnutrition, through, *inter alia*, the application of readily available technology and through the provision of adequate nutritious foods and clean drinking water, taking into consideration the dangers and risks of environmental pollution. Article 6 states that '1. States Parties recognize that every child has the inherent right to life; 2. States Parties shall ensure to the maximum extent possible the survival and development of the child.' International humanitarian law also provides for a series of measures to protect the specific needs of children during armed conflicts.[23]

Children's right to food can be understood within the framework laid out by the CESCR that requires States to respect, protect and fulfil the right to food of all members of their population, without discrimination. This implies that the right to food is not only a positive right, it is also a negative right that aims to prevent discrimination and violations of children's existing access to adequate food.

The prohibition of discrimination

The prohibition of discrimination requires Governments not to discriminate against children in their access to food, nor to the means and entitlements for its procurement, on the grounds of race, colour, sex, language, age, religion, political or other opinion, national or social origin, property, birth or other status. Yet discrimination against children is still frequent between rural and urban areas or within different communities in one country. Children living in rural areas are twice as likely to suffer from malnutrition as those living in urban areas in almost all developing countries.[24] In South Asia, girls are more likely to be underweight than boys.[25] In India, Dalit children are discriminated against in multiple ways that affect their right to food.[26] These disparities, whether they are the direct or indirect consequences of governmental policies and practices, constitute violations of the prohibition of non-discrimination in the enjoyment of children's right to food.

The obligation to respect

The obligation to respect the right to food requires that governments refrain from taking any action that would negatively affect children's existing access to adequate food and water. This includes avoiding taking measures to forcibly evict from their land and means of livelihoods millions of families, including their children. States' agents should also refrain from destroying or encouraging the destruction of food crops, water supplies and health services, and engaging in forced displacement of families and communities including during armed conflicts, as this takes a heavy toll on children. Privatization of public water systems very often leads to the violation of the right to clean drinking water for the poorest segment of the population.

The obligation to protect

The obligation to protect requires measures by the State to ensure that third parties, including enterprises or individuals, do not deprive children of their access to adequate food. One clear example of measures that governments can take to protect the right to food of children involves regulating marketing practices on breast milk substitutes. The International Code of Marketing of Breast-milk Substitutes protects against inappropriate marketing strategies that try to convince women that substitutes are better than breast milk. The International Code was adopted as a 'minimum requirement' for all countries under resolution 34.22 of the World Health Assembly (WHA). Breastfeeding in the first six months of life is of great benefit as it helps to stimulate babies' immune systems, and protect them from diarrhoea and acute respiratory infections. Substituting breast milk carries high risks of infection, especially when substitute milk has to be mixed with contaminated water.

The obligation to fulfil (facilitate and provide)

The obligation to fulfil the right to food requires governments to take steps to address hunger and poverty of children. This obligation is made up of two positive obligations – the obligations to *facilitate* and the obligation to *provide*. The obligation to facilitate means that the State must facilitate and actively engage in activities intended to strengthen families, parents and caregivers' access to and utilization of resources and means to ensure their livelihood, including food security. This will enable parents and caregivers to fulfil their responsibility of providing access to adequate and sufficient food to their children. In addition, whenever children or their families are unable, for reasons beyond their control, to enjoy the right to food by the means at their disposal, States have the obligation to provide that right directly. School meal programmes are one example of measures to fulfil the right to food. The examples of India, South Africa, Cuba and Brazil are welcome, as these have been at the forefront of efforts to make school meals an entitlement. Governments must also ensure that care and other institutions are able to provide for adequate and nutritious food to those children who remain in their care. This obligation also applies for children who are victims of natural or other disasters. In emergencies, relief programmes that provide food and nutrition must take special care to meet the special needs of children.[27] In this regard, there was a welcome revision of the 2001 operational guidelines for emergency relief staff and programme managers produced by the Interagency Working Group on Infant and Young Child Feeding in Emergencies.

3.2.3 Child combatants in armed conflicts and the right to food

The protection of children's right to food is fundamental in the fight to eliminate childhood malnutrition and early mortality, and also in the fight against child labour, including forced recruitment of children into armed forces. In Zambia, the official in charge of reducing child labour has declared that 'I've heard children who work as prostitutes say they would rather die from AIDS, because it is slower than dying of hunger.'[28]

The shocking number of children fighting in wars around the world is also a result of hunger and poverty.[29] Ten years after the seminal report of Graça Machel on the impact of armed conflict on children,[30] it is time to review what role hunger and food insecurity play in creating an environment which leads children to become involved in armed groups.

In 2006 the United Nations estimated that more than 250,000 children were actively involved in armed conflict in government armed forces, government militias and in a range of armed opposition groups.[31] Children are recruited to fight in wars in all regions of the world, from Africa (including Angola, Burundi, Côte d'Ivoire, the Democratic Republic of the Congo, Liberia, Sierra Leone, Somalia and Uganda) to Asia (including Afghanistan, Myanmar and Nepal) and in Latin America, where the phenomenon is prevalent in Colombia. Europe has also seen the problem of child soldiers during the conflicts in the Balkans, including in Kosovo.[32]

Thousands of children make decisions to enlist in armed groups as a result of hunger, malnutrition and food insecurity, yet this is rarely discussed in debates over this problem.[33] Although many children are forcibly recruited, the majority of child soldiers are adolescents between the age of 14 and 18 who 'volunteer' because they are desperately in need of food and income, with which they can support themselves and their families.[34] In Guinea, research showed that almost 10 per cent of child soldiers declared having joined armed groups in order to obtain food or other benefits. During the Liberian conflict, children also joined voluntarily to obtain food for themselves and their families. Similarly, in many of those regions affected by conflict in the Democratic Republic of the Congo and Uganda, children who enlisted came from the poorest families earning less than one dollar per day.[35]

Many young people decide to enlist as a means of covering basic necessities for them and their families, especially when livelihoods have already been eroded by war.[36] Many children and young people decide to join armed groups because they feel responsibility for contributing to supporting their families, especially when family breadwinners are killed, injured, imprisoned or disappear. Evidence from Nepal, for example, seems to indicate that children from very poor households headed by a single parent were more at risk of being recruited by Maoists on account of food insecurity.[37]

However, taking up arms or carrying out other duties for armed groups does not necessarily and automatically entail an improvement in children's food security situation. At times armed groups promise rewards in the form of money, food and clothing to persuade young people to join, but these promises are often not kept. In a study of 2006, it was found that children were told by the commanders that they had to provide food or means to acquire it by themselves, a clear encouragement to looting families and communities.[38] Frequently, child combatants went hungry and died of starvation, as Josephine from northern Uganda, recounted:

> Sometimes we would go on an empty stomach for days. We had not food and were eating only wild leaves and wild fruit...Sometimes we had one handful of beans for 10 people. Hunger kills many children, including the children of the commanders.[39]

The international community, especially NGOs from Sweden, the United States of America and Norway, have made impressive efforts to focus on the elimination of recruitment of children in armed conflicts. In 2005, the Security Council adopted a far-reaching resolution on conflict-affected children, calling for compliance with protection standards and norms and creating a Working Group with the aim of monitoring such compliance.[40] On the ground, collaboration between United Nations agencies, particularly UNICEF, governments, regional organizations, NGOs and civil society has produced significant progress, including raising global awareness, strengthening the international human rights system so as to enhance protection for children's rights and integrating this issue within the United Nations.[41] The International Criminal Court has also issued arrest warrants for five senior members of the Lord's Resistance Army (LRA) and the founder and leader of the Union of Congolese Patriots in the Ituri region of the Democratic Republic of the Congo for forcibly enlisting and using children under the age of 15 in conflicts.

The international legislative framework to protect children from the impact of armed conflicts has also been considerably strengthened with the entry into force in 2000 of International Labour Organization Convention No. 182 on the Worst Forms of Child Labour (1999), which stipulates that States must take immediate action to prohibit and eliminate the worst forms of child labour, including forced or compulsory recruitment of children for use in armed conflict, and by the entry into force in 2002 of the Optional Protocol to the Convention on the Rights of the Child on the involvement of children in armed conflict. These developments reflect significant advances in the efforts to eliminate child recruitment. However, these efforts are not always focusing on the root causes of child recruitment, which are hunger and lack of schooling.

There is an urgent need to recognize the link between hunger and food insecurity, and child recruitment into armed conflict. Concrete measures must be taken by Governments and the international community to respect, protect and fulfil children's right to food in order to remove the root causes of conflict and child recruitment. During conflict situations, if security permits, there must be a focus on ensuring adequate food and nutrition of all children, including through promoting measures such as universal school meals to keep children in school or food for vocational training programmes for adolescents. Special programmes must address the basic needs for food and safe drinking water for the 140 million children under age 12 who have no regular access to school. However, eradicating hunger and ensuring adequate access of all people to productive resources will be the key to eradicating child recruitment into armed conflict.

3.3 Farmers and peasants[42]

3.3.1 Rural poverty and access to land

Hunger, like poverty, is still predominantly a rural problem. The United Nations Millennium Development Project's Task Force on Hunger has shown that 80 per cent of the world's hungry live in rural areas.[43] Of the 1.4 billion people who suffer from extreme poverty in the world today, 75 per cent live and work in rural areas.[44] The majority are smallholder farmers who depend mainly or partly on agriculture for their livelihoods. Many rural people suffer from hunger because either they are landless, they do not hold secure tenure or their properties are so small that they cannot grow enough food to feed themselves. Most of them cannot produce enough to feed themselves usually because they do not have sufficient access to productive resources such as land, water and seeds. Two thirds of these smallholder farmers live on remote and marginal lands under environmentally difficult conditions, such as mountainous areas or areas threatened by droughts and other natural disasters (fertile lands are concentrated in the hands of wealthier farmers). Another 22 per cent of those suffering from hunger are landless families who survive as poorly paid landless labourers. Another 8 per cent of the hungry in rural communities live from fishing, hunting and herding activities. Approximately 20 per cent of the hungry live in urban areas – but with migrants from rural areas increasing as conditions in rural areas become increasingly more difficult and unsustainable, urban hunger is rising fast.

Rural poverty is often closely linked to extreme inequality in access to land.[45] Access to land is often fundamental for ensuring access to food and to a livelihood, and therefore freedom from hunger. Yet in many countries, land ownership is highly concentrated. In some cases, part of this land may even be left unproductive. In Brazil, for example, 2 per cent of landowners own 56 per cent of all private land, and much of this land is unused, or used minimally as pastureland.[46] Although land concentration is often the result of the historical legacies of colonialism, slavery and exploitation, these historically produced inequalities often persist today, given the resistance of landholding elites to redistribution and agrarian reform programmes. The persistence of extreme concentration of land ownership and high levels of inequality has particularly damaging effects in most of the developing countries, where land (together with labour) is the fundamental factor of production.

More than 65 per cent of the hungry live on small plots of land and produce crops for subsistence and for sale on local markets. Many face problems because they live in remote lands or marginal lands that are vulnerable to drought and natural disasters. Good fertile land tends to be concentrated in the hands of wealthier landowners. For example, most of the fertile lands of central Guatemala are part of huge plantations while the majority of indigenous people are left to cultivate the steep slopes of Guatemala's mountainous regions.[47] Another 20 per cent of the hungry are not small farmers, but landless labourers dependent on agricultural labour, paid pitiful wages that are insufficient to feed their families. With the situation deteriorating in rural areas, migrants are moving to urban slums and urban hunger is rising fast with 20 per cent of the hungry now living in urban areas but unable to find livelihoods that can feed their families.

Approximately 100 million agricultural households, or 500 million people, are landless in less developed countries.[48] These 500 million landless people are among the poorest on earth. They constitute high proportions of the agricultural population of India, Bangladesh, Pakistan, the Philippines, Indonesia, South Africa, Kenya, Zimbabwe, Malawi, Brazil, Guatemala, Honduras and several other countries.[49] Most of these people work as tenant farmers or agricultural labourers, lacking ownership or owner-like tenure on the land that they farm. Tenant farmers usually have to pay high rents and have little security of possession from season to season. Agricultural labourers usually work for extremely low wages and often have to migrate from one insecure, informal job to another.[50]

3.3.2 Agrarian reform

Agrarian reform programmes, when they have contributed to genuinely transformative change, have been very successful in reducing poverty and inequality in many countries. These reforms have proved most successful when land reform radically reduces inequalities in land distribution and is accompanied by sufficient access to other inputs, and when political obstacles to reform have been overcome. Secure property titles, accurately maintained land records, and efficient and fair land administration bureaucracies that are adequately funded and not corrupt have also been essential elements in successful reforms.[51] It is also clear that in agrarian reform, land in itself is not enough. Often the quality of land is just as important for a viable livelihood as the quantity. Access to land must also always be accompanied by sufficient access to other inputs, including water, credit, transport, extension services and other infrastructure.

While the 'death' of agrarian reform was proclaimed in the 1970s, and few efforts were made to conduct land reform programmes in the 1980s and early 1990s, more recently land reform has come back onto the international agenda.[52] In the Rome Declaration on World Food Security and World Food Summit Plan of Action,[53] land reform constituted a key part of stated commitments. In the Conference Declaration of the International Conference on Agrarian Reform and Rural Development organized by FAO and the Government of Brazil and held in Porto Alegre, Brazil from 7 to 10 March 2006,[54] 95 States recognized that one important way to ensure the fulfilment of the right to food was to establish appropriate land reform to secure access to land for marginalized and vulnerable groups, and to adopt adequate legal frameworks and policies to promote traditional and family agriculture.

Social movements have been a key force behind this re-emergence of land reform. As FAO points out, 'first and foremost land reform is back on the agenda because rural populations have put it there'.[55] Landless movements across the third world, and highly visible land conflicts in Zimbabwe, South Africa, Colombia, Brazil, Mexico, the Philippines, Indonesia and elsewhere, have brought land reform back to centre stage.[56] NGOs fighting hunger, such as Food First and the Food First Information and Action Network, argue that 'access to farm land is a fundamental human right for rural peoples, and that grossly inequitable distribution of land is one of the most common underlying causes of poverty and destitution in much of the world'.[57] A report of FAO recognizes that there are now 'new demands on the social contract between rural citizens and their government the demand for rights. ... Indeed, most of the land reform movements generated at the grass roots are an assertion of the rights already guaranteed in national law and legislation, but never effectively applied.'[58]

Land reform is back on the agenda also because there has been greater recognition of its economic and political benefits. According to the International Fund for Agricultural Development (IFAD), land reform has demonstrably reduced poverty where it has been conducted successfully, and greater equality in landholding is associated with faster overall growth.[59] It also helps to reduce vulnerability to famine and hunger. It is now also increasingly clear that agricultural productivity is greater on small farms than on larger ones. Although large farms can benefit from economies of scale, it is a myth that small farms are less productive. According to a World Bank report, 'data show a deep decline in income per acre as farm size increases, with productivity of the largest size category less than half that of the smallest'.[60] Farmers with ownership or secure tenure are also more likely to invest in their land, which improves environmental conservation. The World Bank has also recognized the importance of reducing inequality around the world, and suggests that States must engage in active measures of redistribution, such as land reform, 'a classic form of redistribution that can be very effective'.[61]

Small-scale farms tend to use more labour than high-technology, mechanized large farms, thereby generating greater agricultural employment. This in turn generates improved non-agricultural opportunities, as a broad base of agricultural families benefiting from land reform receive higher incomes and enter the marketplace to purchase a range of locally produced goods and services.[62] Many studies argue that only land reform holds the potential to address chronic unemployment in many developing countries.[63] As small farms employ more labour and are less highly capital intensive, only land reform will be able to reduce rapid urbanization and reverse migration from rural areas to urban areas. In Brazil, a study by the Brazilian Institute of Social and Economic Analysis calculated that the cost to the Brazilian Government of maintaining people in the urban slums, or favelas – including services and infrastructure – would exceed in one month the yearly cost of legalizing land occupations through purchase and expropriation of the land.[64] The potential costs of agrarian reform should therefore be weighed against other costs, including urban unemployment and increasing social conflicts.

It is now widely agreed that land reforms in Japan, the Republic of Korea, Taiwan Province of China, China and Cuba have had a significant impact on reducing poverty and hunger and increasing economic growth.[65] In India, the states with the steepest declines in poverty from 1958 to 1992 were those that implemented land reform.[66] In general, based on the evidence of agrarian reforms instituted in more than 60 countries since the end of the Second World War, land reform has worked when reforms have been genuinely transformative and genuinely redistributive, when quality land has really been distributed to the poor and when rural power structures have been broken. In contrast, reforms that have given only poor-quality land to beneficiaries or have failed to alter the rural power structures that work against the poor have failed to have a significant impact on inequality, poverty or hunger.[67] In much of Latin America, for example, while land reform programmes have benefited a substantial number of poor rural families, in many countries they have not been transformative, as governments have been unable or unwilling to implement the extensive reforms seen in Asia (with the exception of Cuba and new reforms in Venezuela). Latin America still has one of the most inequitable distributions of land in the world.[68]

Access to land and agrarian reform must form a key part of the right to food. The legal basis for this is already clear in the text of the International Covenant on Economic, Social and Cultural Rights. Under Article 11, paragraph 2(a), States are committed to 'developing or reforming agrarian systems in such a way as to achieve the most efficient development and utilization of natural resources'. Given that it is becoming increasingly understood that small farms are more efficient than large ones and better protect the environment,[69] this can be understood as promoting agrarian reform to encourage small-scale farming. General Comment No. 12, the authoritative interpretation of the right to food by the CESCR, clarifies that the right to food requires physical and economic access to resources. The General Comment recognizes that access to food comes from either access to income or access to productive resources such as land. It argues that vulnerable people, including landless people, need special attention and that indigenous peoples and women should be entitled to the right to inheritance and ownership of land. It is also clear that governments must respect, protect and fulfil access to land. The governments' obligation to respect the right to food means that the State should not take any action that would affect access to food. Therefore, eviction from land without adequate compensation would constitute a violation of the right to food.[70]

The rights of women to land and property are also protected in the Convention on the Elimination of All Forms of Discrimination against Women. Article 14.2 prohibits discrimination against women in rural areas and calls for equal treatment in land and agrarian reform. Article 16.1(h) calls for equal rights in terms of the ownership of property. Nonetheless, despite enjoying legal and often constitutional rights in many countries, women still face severe obstacles to the inheritance, purchase and control of land, even though it is now widely agreed that women produce 60–80 per cent of food crops in developing countries and play a crucial role in the food security of households. In addition, land distribution programmes still often assume that recipients will be men, not women. This must be changed if agrarian reforms are to be successful. Traditional forms of land tenure and use rights must also be better recognized and understood. The rights of indigenous peoples to land are protected by Articles 13–19 of the 1989 International Labour Organization Convention No. 169 concerning Indigenous and Tribal Peoples. Indigenous rights to land are also included under the right to food in General Comment No. 12 of the CESCR. There is also now a Declaration on the Rights of Indigenous Peoples, which will give greater protection to indigenous rights to land. It is clear that land traditionally occupied and used by indigenous populations has frequently been appropriated, often through various forms of violence or discrimination, and that ways of guaranteeing effective protection for their rights of ownership and possession are fundamental.

Property rights are generally granted clear protection under the constitutions and legislation of many countries. In many cases, however, a severe tension exists between the protection of property rights and the call for the right to land, access to land or agrarian reform. Protecting property rights can mean protecting large, concentrated landholdings, and therefore can constitute a challenge to agrarian reform. This legal tension is resolved in different ways in different countries. In Article 5 of the Constitution of Brazil, for example, property rights are protected, but only to the extent that property fulfils its social function as defined in Article 186. If the ownership of land does not meet this social function (which usually means that it is not being actively cultivated), then it may be expropriated by the State for the purpose of agrarian reform. Expropriated land must be given to rural labourers or to rural farmers who do not have access to sufficient land to feed themselves.

Nonetheless, there are still problems in enforcing these distinctions between property rights and the right to land. For example, in Brazil there still remain significant problems in translating constitutional obligations into practice.[71] The pace of implementation of agrarian reform and the persistent resistance of the landholding elites in some regions of the country have led to the emergence of one of the most important peasant movements to emerge in recent history, the Landless Workers Movement. The reasons for the slow pace of agrarian reform are multiple, but there are some that stand out. In some regions, for example, a quasi-feudal system persists, by which elites control vast tracts of land in order to maintain political power, although the land is often uncultivated. The Landless Workers Movement has increasingly tried to occupy land that is uncultivated and pressed for the application of the constitutional provision to allow the expropriation of land. However, the conservative judicial system often tends to rule in favour of the property rights of landholders and against the land rights claimed by the peasants, even when land is uncultivated, thus failing to recognize the social function provision of the Brazilian Constitution. Protests calling for agrarian reform are often repressed with force. While agrarian reform is understood as a duty of the Government, increasingly it is not seen as a right that rural workers can demand themselves.

For the people of the Landless Workers Movement, what is often at stake is not just the means of subsistence, but also the means to maintain a dignified life.[72] It is important to recognize, however, that in many countries large, land-owning farmers are not necessarily personally responsible for past land theft or appropriation, which may be rather the result of long historical processes. Therefore, it is important to recognize the property rights of these farmers and consider appropriate forms of compensation, while also recognizing the claims to land of the poor. In Zimbabwe, for example, rapid evictions and the lack of compensation are unlikely to promote sustainable land reform, particularly in the context of impending famine.

Despite the re-emergence of land reform on the international agenda, there are a number of contradictions that reflect the 'schizophrenia' in the United Nations system.[73] In the 1996 Declaration of the World Food Summit, land reform constituted a key part of stated commitments. Yet land reform is noticeable in its absence from the 2002 final Declaration of the World Food Summit: five years later. While the IFAD and FAO broadly support agrarian reform models that promote transformative, redistributive reform, agencies such as the World Bank are, in contrast, promoting new models of agrarian reform that emphasize the market and are compatible with the 'Washington consensus', a paradigm that is 'inherently opposed to policy interventions aimed at achieving social equity'.[74]

The World Bank's current 'market-assisted' or 'negotiated' models of land reform seek to overcome elite resistance to land reform by offering credit to landless or land-poor farmers so that they can buy land at market rates from large landholders, with the State playing a part only in mediation and the provision of credit.[75] These models have been bitterly criticized by NGOs and social movements that claim that they are undermining more transformative programmes of agrarian reform (e.g. in Brazil).[76] There are also concerns that offering credit to small farmers to purchase land at market prices cannot result in transformative, redistributive reform, as landowners benefit from often inflated prices for often low-quality land, while poor farmers are frequently left with debts that they can never fully repay. This model shifts the logic of agrarian reform away from a concept of a right to land and redistribution, towards the view that access to land is possible only through the purchase of the land at market prices, despite a context of historically produced inequities.

We saw the limits of the 'market-assisted' model during our mission to Guatemala.[77] Despite the fact that the Government is making impressive efforts to change the situation, Guatemala remains one of the most inequitable countries in the world. Land ownership is highly concentrated: 2 per cent of the population owns up to 70–75 per cent of agricultural land, while 90 per cent of small farmers survive on less than one hectare. This situation is the result of a long history of land expropriation from indigenous people, exacerbated by a 36-year civil war (1960–1996) during which military and landowners forcibly controlled more land. In this particular context, the promotion by the World Bank of a market-based redistribution of land, concretized by the creation of a land fund, FONTIERRA, to provide credit for land purchases, is particularly ineffective. It precludes the adoption of more important measures required under the Peace Accords of 1996, including the creation of an effective land registry system, the elaboration of an agrarian code recognizing indigenous forms of land ownership and the establishment of an agrarian jurisdiction to resolve land disputes.

There are also concerns that many of the programmes for tenure reform undertaken by the World Bank and others – mapping, cadastres, land registers and individual title – have been implemented without trying to respond to local customary and traditional forms of land tenure, but rather with the aim only of creating conditions for functional land markets. This has frequently resulted in massive and progressive sales of land, the reconcentration of property and an increase in social conflict (as in, e.g. the case of Egypt).[78]

The current market-fundamentalist macroeconomic model has also created environments in which small-scale agriculture is becoming unviable, making agrarian reform less viable. Trade liberalization and policies of structural adjustment in the agricultural sector have brought small-scale agriculture (in developing countries, though not in developed countries that maintain subsidies) into direct competition with imports from markets where world prices are artificially low as a result of subsidies. The withdrawal of the State from the delivery of extension services and production support has also contributed to the further exclusion of marginalized groups from access to productive resources, as was evident in Niger.[79] Despite past criticism by the Special Rapporteur and many NGOs and social movements who claim that this undermines more transformative programmes of agrarian reform,[80] the practice continues.

What is important to realize is that the loss of viability of small-scale agriculture is not an inevitable historical process, but is man-made. It is clear that granting access to land for small-scale farming is more productive, more ecologically viable and more socially sustainable than the current economic model being imposed. There is an urgent need to look at the concept of food sovereignty being proposed by NGOs, which challenges the existing model, and in which access to land and agrarian reform play a prominent role in reducing poverty and hunger.

Access to land is an essential element of the right to food. Extreme inequality in the distribution of land is a key factor in the persistence of hunger and poverty. Agrarian reform that is truly transformative and redistributive has proved to be fundamental in reducing poverty and hunger in many countries, and can be a key to generating economic growth that benefits the poorest. Agrarian reform is often recognized as a constitutional or legal right under national law, yet it is difficult to implement, given the resistance of the elites and an economic model that is inherently opposed to policy interventions directed towards greater social equity. The emerging model of 'market-assisted' land reform, which fits into the predominant neoliberal model, is unlikely to have the same effects on hunger and poverty as the radical, redistributive and transformative model. In a context of rapid urbanization, mass urban unemployment and the resulting increase in social conflict and crime, it is increasingly urgent that agrarian reform be viewed as a viable alternative and be supported by macroeconomic policy.

Although agrarian reform can be costly, its costs will be less than those of rapid urbanization and mass urban unemployment, and less than the cost of the brutal, repressive police forces that are often used to suppress the instability and insecurity that they create. Meeting the right to food is an obligation of Governments, and we believe that the right to land, and transformative and genuinely redistributive land reform, must be a fundamental part of Government obligations under the International Covenant on Economic, Social and Cultural Rights to meet the right to food.

3.4 Fisherpeople[81]

An emerging issue of concern regarding equitable access to productive and natural resources for the poor is the situation of fish-farming communities that traditionally survive through their access to local fishing grounds (both inland and coastal). In the drive to industrialize, privatize and orient fish production towards exports, poor fishing and fish-farming communities are often left behind, if their rights over these resources are not protected. Although some employment may be gained by the global restructuring and industrialization of the fishing industry, poor and marginalized people may be displaced from their livelihoods if these changes work to effectively deny their access to resources. From the perspective of the right to food, it is essential to protect access to sustainable fishery resources for poor and marginalized communities, especially where this provides their primary means of livelihood and where few alternative opportunities exist.

3.4.1 Linkages between fisheries and the right to food

Fisheries provide both food and livelihoods, particularly for poor and marginalized communities living in coastal areas, but also inland communities dependent on freshwater fishing or traditional methods of raising fish. The right to food of these communities is therefore closely linked to their access to and control over fishing resources. It is extremely important to ensure that fishing communities have secure rights of access to sustainably managed fishing resources.

Fish, as food for consumption, is an important part of the right to food. More than one billion people worldwide rely on fish as their major source of animal protein.[82] In some of the less developed areas of the world, fish is often the most important source of animal protein in poor people's diets. Fish accounts for 23.1 per cent of total animal protein intake in Asia and 19 per cent in Africa, and this average figure is higher for coastal and fishing communities.[83] Fish is an important source of protein, but also provides vitamins A, D, B1 and B2, iron, phosphorus and calcium, iodine, fatty acids – all nutrients that are essential for physical and mental development, especially for young children.

Fisheries also provide a livelihood for millions of poor people. It provides employment and income from fishing or fish farming, processing and marketing fish. It is estimated that 35 million people are directly engaged in fishing and fish farming, and approximately another 100 million people work in fisheries-related occupations. Around 97 per cent of all fishery workers live and work in developing countries – the majority in Asia (85 per cent), followed by Africa (7 per cent) with far fewer employed in Europe, North America and South and Central America (about 2 per cent each).[84] Most of these people work in small-scale artisanal or subsistence fisheries to provide nourishment for their families and communities. Millions of people around the world therefore depend in some way on fishing and fish farming livelihoods for their income, making it paramount that they have secure access to these resources and that these resources are not overfished, but used at sustainable levels.

3.4.2 Challenges to the right to food for fishing and fish-farming communities

Global fish production has rapidly expanded in the last 40 years, reaching 130 million tons in 2000, up from 40 million tons in 1961. There are two types of fish production – fish captured in the wild from the sea or inland waters (capture fisheries), and fish farmed in the sea or inland waters (aquaculture). Of global fish production, most fish is still captured at sea (66 per cent) with some fish caught inland (7 per cent); however, fish farming is rapidly expanding and now makes up 27 per cent of global production (11 per cent at sea, 16 per cent inland).[85] In the face of this rapidly increasing global fish production and the growing overexploitation of marine fishing resources,[86] there have been a number of changes in the global and local fisheries management.

Marine fishing

In the past, access to global marine fishing resources was generally based on open access or traditional customary rules. Over the last decades, however, in order to overcome conflicts between countries and between fisheries – industrial versus artisanal, export-based versus subsistence – and the overexploitation of marine fish stocks, there have been attempts to regulate access to fishing resources through the United Nations Convention on the Law of the Sea of 1982 and several subsequent agreements. While these agreements have aimed at protecting equity in access to marine fishing and some agreements have aimed to protect artisanal fishing livelihoods, in practice, this has not always worked and there remain inequities in practice between developed and developing countries.

The Convention on the Law of the Sea guarantees the rights of countries to their own fishing resources in their territorial waters and exclusive economic zone. National jurisdictions now cover nearly 99 per cent of the world's fishery resources. Each country is obliged to calculate an 'allowable catch' (the level of sustainable harvest) and is obliged to avoid overexploitation of its own resources. Each country is bound, if it does not have the capacity to fish all its allowable catch, to give access to other countries. However, the terms of this access are supposed to be regulated in ways which first consider national interests and local livelihoods, then consider the needs of regional countries, especially landlocked and geographically disadvantaged countries and only finally other countries. This Convention attempts to strengthen the rights of countries to their own fishing resources.

Subsequent agreements accord special recognition of the needs of poorer countries and the need for protection to artisanal and small-scale fisheries. These include the Agreement for the Conservation and Management of Straddling Fish Stocks and Highly Migratory Fish Stocks[87] and the FAO Code of Conduct for Responsible Fisheries of 1995. The FAO Code of Conduct, in its Article 6, paragraph 18, states:

> Recognizing the important contributions of artisanal and small-scale fisheries to employment, income and food security, States should appropriately protect the rights of fishers and fishworkers, particularly those engaged in subsistence, small-scale and artisanal fisheries, to a secure

and just livelihood, as well as preferential access, where appropriate, to traditional fishing grounds and resources in the waters under their national jurisdiction.

There are now many agreements and organizations set up between countries to try to implement these principles and protect artisanal and small-scale fisheries. For example, in Asia, the Bay of Bengal organization tries to protect fishers in member countries (Bangladesh, India, Maldives and Sri Lanka). In Africa, a Sub-Regional Commission on Fisheries brings together Cape Verde, the Gambia, Guinea, Guinea-Bissau, Mauritania and Senegal. In Latin America, another organization (the *Organización Latinoamericana de Desarrollo Pesquero*), with members from almost all South and Central American countries, has initiated a project focused on artisanal fisheries.

However, many of these valuable efforts to improve equity of access to fishing resources between developed and developing countries are undermined by policies and activities of developed countries, including subsidies. Subsidies are estimated to total at least US$ 15 billion annually.[88] About 90 per cent of total subsidies are granted by Japan, the European Union (EU), the United States of America, Canada and the Russian Federation to their fishing fleets and fishing industry. In the past, these subsidies have led to the overexploitation of marine resources in developed countries.[89] This has led them to demand greater access rights to the fishing resources of developing countries, and subsidies have permitted the growth of fishing fleets capable of travelling long distances. The United Nations Environment Programme (UNEP) has reported, for example, that the EU paid US$ 230 million in subsidies to its fishing fleets to enable them to take advantage of fishing rights obtained in the Argentine exclusive economic zone.[90]

Inequities in bilateral fishing negotiations also sometimes mean that international agreements fail to take account of equity concerns, the potential impact on poor fishing communities or the ways in which such agreements might undermine the efforts of regional and subregional organizations to protect artisanal and small-scale fisheries. In a fishing agreement with Senegal, for example, the EU managed to obtain fishing rights over species that are endangered or locally used, which has allegedly threatened the food security of thousands of local fishing communities.[91] Guidelines for negotiations, such as those in World Wildlife Fund (WWF) *Handbook for Negotiating Fishing Access Agreement*, should therefore be taken into account in this context.

Poorer countries often do not have the capacity to monitor fishing in their territorial waters and therefore can lose out to illegal fishing (both large- and small-scale operations). According to FAO, illegal, unreported and unregulated (IUU) fishing is increasing in both intensity and scope, and is seriously undermining national and regional efforts to sustainably manage fisheries'.[92] Many NGOs point to the fact that poorer countries, in particular, often do not have the capacity to monitor fishing in their territorial waters and exclusive economic zones and therefore lose out to illegal fishing. NGOs have suggested that the inability of countries to monitor their waters is partly due to globalized economic policies, which restrict the capacity of the State to undertake monitoring activities. The International Collective in Support of Fishworkers argues that 'neo-liberal policies that support decentralization and the withdrawal of the State are also a matter for concern. Cutting back of State participation has also meant that fewer resources are now available for monitoring, control and surveillance (MCS) activities'.[93]

At the more local level, global policies driving privatization and an export orientation for marine fishing sometimes end up depriving local people of their traditional rights of access to fishing resources. In the past, open-access fishery resources or those regulated through traditional or community access systems allowed local people access to fishing resources, although these rights were not formally codified. However, on the basis that these open-access systems have suffered from overexploitation, recent attempts to control overexploitation have sometimes ended up restricting the access of artisanal and subsistence fishers, effectively punishing them, even though it is often large-scale fishing that is most responsible for overfishing. For example, attempts to regulate access through replacing regulation with the individual transferable quotas (ITQ) system has amounted to an effective privatization of fishing resources. If the initial design fails to include and protect the poor, this can result in the exclusion of traditional fishing communities from access to their marine resources. Although the ITQ system need not exclude small artisanal and subsistence fishers, in practice, it has favoured commercial fishing at the expense of these groups, whose methods are considered inefficient. Some argue that the ITQ system has been used to systematically shift control over fishing resources from the poor to the rich.[94] It is possible to allocate quotas to traditional fishers, which can strengthen their property rights, but only if quotas are allocated fairly and there are safeguard mechanisms in place to ensure that the poor can maintain their quotas and also to ensure against monopolization of ownership. There are examples in which reallocation of rights has strengthened the access of poorer communities, such as the reallocation of Canadian salmon fishery to indigenous peoples, which show how allocation systems can be designed specifically to protect the rights of marginalized communities. However, many argue that reallocation processes are often inequitable in practice:

> People with higher incomes have a disproportionately large claim to the world's fishery resources. It is not only a matter of the rich outbidding the poor in the marketplace. It is also a matter of the rich controlling much of the supply process, including its regulation.[95]

According to one study, for example, the Government of Chile instituted a 'transitory fishery law' in 2001 that established the quota system. Under the new allocation system, the industrial sector was able to obtain the great majority of the quotas at the expense of the poor. In the case of one fish, horse mackerel (*Trachurus murphyi*), it is reported that the industrial fishery sector obtained 98 per cent of the annual quota. Yet this fish is an important resource for local artisanal fishers and an important source of food security, while the industrial fishery uses the fish to transform into animal feed.[96]

The NGO Foodfirst Information and Action Network (FIAN) has reported cases of alleged violations of the right to food affecting indigenous fishing communities in the Russian Federation. FIAN reports that, under new regulations on access to fishing resources, the Aleut community on Bering Island has not been granted adequate fishing quotas to maintain the food security of the traditional fishing community.[97] FIAN also highlights another case on Sakhalin Island where indigenous communities were not granted any fishing quota for subsistence consumption of Siberian salmon (*keta*), or humpback salmon (*gorbusha*), even though these species make up their basic source of traditional food and they depend on fishing livelihoods, given persistent high unemployment in the area.[98] Another case alleges that, in the waters of the Nyiskii gulf on the north-east coast of Sakhalin, the local salmon has been decimated by seismic-prospection submarine explosives used in the search for oil by corporations, including transnational corporations Esso and BP, without consultation or compensation to local communities. Under the right to food, Governments have an obligation to protect communities from the negative impact of non-State actors, such as corporations, on their food security and should institute compensation where this right has been violated.

In another case, non-governmental fishing organizations in South Africa have reported that the Government's new fisheries policy, under the Marine Living Resource Act 18 of 1998, which officially aimed to design an equitable fishing policy, has worked in practice to exclude a large number of artisanal and subsistence fishers in the Southern and Western Cape from their previous access to fishing resources. NGOs have argued that, under the new law, there was no recognition of 'artisanal fishers' as a separate category of fishers, as they were subsumed in the category of the commercial sector, which the fishing organizations allege did not meet the very different needs of the artisanal fishers. With the adoption of an ITQ quota system, they suggested that the fishing resources had been to some extent privatized out of the hands of the fishing communities. They argued that a large number of traditional artisanal and subsistence fishers were not granted quotas and had therefore lost access to their traditional fishing resources. They could not undertake fishing without breaking the law, even if they had fished for their families' consumption. It was also alleged that a shift towards export orientation required that certain fish, such as abalone, be sold to private industrial processing companies to be sold on export markets and could not be sold on local markets. This affected the community-based trade in fish that supported the broader fishing community. They have alleged that, as a result of the new law, food insecurity among the fishing communities increased, particularly given that relatively few fishers were finding new jobs in the industrialized fishing sector. The fisherfolk had held public hearings to discuss their plight and in 2004 they brought a case to the High Court of Cape of Good Hope to challenge their effective exclusion from access to fishing resources.[99] The Court examined the case and the Government and the fishermen reached a friendly agreement, which took a number of months. It allowed 1000 fishermen to have immediate access to the sea. In a judgement in 2007, the Court took responsibility for ensuring the implementation of the agreement and it obliged the Government to review the law while respecting the right to food in this context.[100]

With the shift towards the export orientation of the fish industry, developing countries account for half of global fish exports and their net export trade increased from US$ 10 billion in 1990 to US$ 18 billion in 2000 (more than the net export value of coffee, bananas, rice and tea taken together).[101] However, it is not clear whether the income gained from these exports is generally benefiting poorer fishing communities, given the simultaneous shift towards the privatization of fishing resources, which has not always improved the access rights of the poorest. It is suggested that the shift to export orientation of fish economies in Asia, for example, has 'led to the marginalization of communities that had been traditionally involved in fishing and fish processing'.[102]

Fish farming

In response to the overexploitation of marine fishing resources, the fish industry is moving increasingly towards fish farming (aquaculture) for the further expansion of global fish production. Aquaculture production has rapidly grown in the last decades, reaching 35.6 million tons in 2000, compared to 1.9 million tons in 1961. At the current rate, it is estimated that fish farming will overtake fish capture by the year 2020.[103] Most fish farming is located in developing countries (with 84 per cent of global production in low-income food deficit countries), particularly in China, India, the Philippines and Indonesia. Fish farming is frequently promoted on the promise that it will relieve pressure on wild fish stocks and improve food security and provide livelihoods for the poor. However, fish farming does not automatically relieve exploitation of marine stocks – given that many farm fish are, ironically, fed with marine fish.[104] And, while it has promoted food security in some countries, such as China, where fish farming remains small-scale and most fish is consumed locally, this is generally not the case where fish farming that is industrial in scale and export-oriented.

Although traditional, low-technology methods of fish farming have been practised for many centuries by inland and coastal communities to supplement food security, particularly in Asia, these traditional methods are very different from new industrialized methods of fish farming. In India, Bangladesh and Thailand, for example, there is a tradition of rice/shrimp rotation, with rice grown for part of the year and shrimp and other fish cultured on land the rest of the year. No chemicals, antibiotics or processed feed are used in this method, which is low-yield but sustainable over the long term.[105] New industrial methods of fish farming, on the other hand, use highly technical methods based on intense production, dense stocking rates with artificial feed, chemical additives and antibiotics to improve production 'efficiency'. These new methods require high capital investment, which often excludes poorer farmers from engaging in this kind of production. Although these new methods are often promoted in the name of reducing hunger, in practice this type of farming rarely benefits the poor. According to one study on shrimp farming:

> Like the earlier Green Revolution, the Blue Revolution is frequently promoted as a way to help feed the world's hungry by increasing the supply of affordable food. The results of the Blue Revolution have been exactly the opposite...One of the most critical social problems identified by local peoples as part of expansion of the Blue Revolution is the loss of communal resources – including mangrove areas, estuaries, and fishing grounds – that local people depend on for both subsistence and commercial economic activities. Commercial shrimp farming has displaced local communities, exacerbated conflicts and provoked violence involving property and tenant rights, decreased the quality and quantity of drinking water, increased local food insecurity and threatened human health.[106]

In a landmark case in India on shrimp farming and its impact on livelihoods, the Supreme Court of India found that damage caused by shrimp farming had resulted in the loss of land for subsistence farming in favour of export shrimp production, the loss of access to the beach, important as landing grounds for fish catch, and the loss of access to safe drinking water with inadequate drainage systems contributing to 'skin, eye and waterborne diseases in the contiguous population'.[107] In addition, shrimp farming had not resulted in increased employment and the damage caused to local livelihoods and ecology was considered to be greater than the total earnings from shrimp farming. The case suggests that both local marine fishers and agricultural farmers had lost livelihoods and subsistence food production as a result of the expansion of shrimp production, through both the takeover of land and the environmental impacts.

Although it is clearly true that fish farming can create employment, especially where it is practised on a small scale, NGOs have challenged the generalized claim that industrialized fish farming brings more employment for the poor, showing how it often displaces other local livelihoods that generate far more employment. For example, in India, shrimp production has displaced rice production by small farmers along coastal stretches and total levels of employment have fallen. While rice production employs on average 76 workers per hectare, shrimp production employs only 26 workers per hectare. According to the activist Vandana Shiva, in Tamil Nadu total export revenue from shrimp production (US$ 868 million) came at the expense of job loss and environmental destruction totalling an amount far greater (US$ 1.38 billion).[108]

3.4.3 A right-to-food approach to fisheries

The right to food is a human right, under which governments have a legal obligation to guarantee economic and physical access to food for everyone. The right to food implies obligations on governments to ensure that all people have physical and economic access to an adequate quantity and quality of food, without discrimination. It also requires governments to comply with the obligation to respect, protect and fulfil the right to food.

In relation to fisheries, the obligation to respect means that the state should not take actions that arbitrarily deprive people of their existing access to adequate food. The obligation to protect means that the state should enforce appropriate laws to prevent third parties, including powerful people and corporations, from depriving individuals of their access to adequate food. Finally, the obligation to fulfil (facilitate and provide) means that the state should take positive actions to identify vulnerable groups and should elaborate and implement appropriate policies and programmes to ensure their access to adequate food by facilitating their ability to feed themselves. As a last resort, the government is also required to provide adequate food to those who cannot feed themselves, for reasons beyond their own control. It is also fundamental that participation, accountability and access to effective remedies be ensured at all times and at all levels of the implementation of the right to food. Governments are obliged to ensure the progressive realization of the right to food.

It is vital that changes in the fishing industry do not precipitate an increase in food insecurity and a reduction in the physical or economic accessibility of food for the fishing communities or other surrounding communities. This would amount to a regression in the realization of the right to adequate food. The obligation of Governments to the progressive realization of the right to food means that people's standard of living and level of food security should consistently improve, not deteriorate.

The obligation to respect the people's *existing* access to food is frequently being violated, not only through direct actions, but also through policies that have failed to protect artisanal and subsistence fisheries. Human rights and social impact assessments should be carried out before instituting legislative and policy changes in the fishing industry in order to measure the impacts if fishers lose their access to their traditional fishing resources, such as in the cases mentioned above in Chile, South Africa and the Russian Federation. To deprive people of livelihoods and their access to food, without compensation or in an arbitrary or discriminatory way, is a clear violation of the obligation to respect people's *existing* access to food. This is particularly the case when there is no alternative employment, especially if or when the new fisheries industry structure fails to provide employment equal to that lost through the restructuring. Rights of access should be secured and compensation offered in cases where reallocation leaves traditional fishing communities with no access to their traditional resources.

The obligation to protect the right to food is also often violated. In the case mentioned above for the Russian Federation, for example, the local salmon has been decimated by seismic-prospection submarine explosives in the search for oil by corporations, including the transnational corporations Esso and BP, in the waters of the Nyiskii gulf on the Northeast coast of Sakhalin, without any consultation or compensation to local communities. This amounts to a violation of the obligation to protect the right to food.

The obligation to fulfil the right to food is also frequently being violated. This obligation is violated when there are no policies and programmes in place to improve the livelihoods of fishing and fish-farming communities, and to secure their access to resources, especially if the industry changes leave poor marginalized communities with no alternative livelihoods or employment. As a last resort, the Government must provide assistance and safety nets to those who cannot feed themselves. However, ensuring livelihoods so that people can feed themselves in dignity must take priority. Numerous positive examples already exist that show that it is possible to support artisanal and subsistence fishers. Brazil, for example, has adopted a comprehensive Programme for the Support and Development of Artisanal Fisheries. At the regional level, Latin American countries are currently in the process of establishing a 'regional project for artisanal fisheries' that will support artisanal fisheries in all the countries of the region. These will help to ensure that traditional fishing communities are not simply left behind.

3.5 Indigenous people[109]

Indigenous peoples also face exclusion and discrimination that impact upon their right to food, despite the commitments to protect the economic, social and cultural rights of indigenous peoples set out in the United Nations Declaration on the Rights of Indigenous Peoples, adopted by the

General Assembly in September 2007.[110] Indigenous peoples encompass approximately 5000 distinct peoples and some 350 million individuals, the vast majority of whom live in developing countries. It has long been understood that due to long historical processes of colonization, exploitation and political and economic exclusion, indigenous peoples are among the most vulnerable to poverty, hunger and malnutrition. Various studies have, over an extended period of time, established that the living standards for indigenous peoples 'were at the bottom of the socio-economic scale' and that 'indigenous peoples the world over are usually among the most marginalized and dispossessed sectors of society'.[111] This problem continues to be a cause for alarm as a result of continued discrimination in access to productive resources.

Over the years, a number of indigenous organizations have expressed, at the annual sessions of the Working Group on Indigenous People and at the Permanent Forum on Indigenous Issues, their deep concerns over the obstacles and challenges that their communities face in fully enjoying their right to food. As was stated in the Declaration of Atitlán, at the First Indigenous Peoples' Global Consultation on the Right to Food in April 2002 in Guatemala:

> the denial of the Right to Food for Indigenous Peoples not only denies our physical survival, but also denies us our social organization, our cultures, traditions, languages, spirituality, sovereignty, and total identity; it is a denial of our collective indigenous existence.

In international law, the right to adequate food and the fundamental right to be free from hunger apply to everyone without discrimination, yet the right to food of indigenous peoples is frequently denied or violated, often as a result of systematic discrimination or the widespread lack of recognition of indigenous rights. The levels of hunger and malnutrition among indigenous peoples are often disproportionately higher than among the non-indigenous population, and yet they often do not benefit from programmes designed to fight hunger and malnutrition or to promote development. Moreover, inappropriate development efforts often intensify the marginalization, poverty and food insecurity of indigenous peoples, failing to recognize indigenous ways of securing their own subsistence and ignoring their right to define their own path towards development. In its report to the Economic and Social Council, the Inter-Agency Support Group on Indigenous Issues expressed concern that the universality and simplicity of expression of the Millennium Development Goals may lead to homogenization instead of equality in respect of the enjoyment of human rights, if the specificities of indigenous peoples is not acknowledged and addressed.[112]

One of the earliest international studies on the vulnerability of indigenous people was carried out in 1953 by the International Labour Organization

(ILO), which found that the living standards of indigenous populations were extremely low, considerably lower than those of the non-indigenous population.[113] Three decades later, the Special Rapporteur of the Sub-commission José Martínez Cobo found that indigenous peoples were at the bottom of the socioeconomic scale.[114] The Special Rapporteur on the situation of human rights and fundamental freedoms of indigenous people also found that 'indigenous peoples the world over are usually among the most marginalized and dispossessed sectors of society'.[115] A research project undertaken by ILO study found that many poverty reduction strategies do not take indigenous peoples into account in the process or in the strategies proposed.[116] In a study published in 1994, the World Bank found that 'poverty among Latin America's indigenous population is pervasive and severe' and that 'the living conditions of the indigenous population are generally abysmal',[117] and in an update carried out in 2004, found that little progress had been made.[118]

Another study undertaken by the Inter-Agency Support Group for the Permanent Forum on Indigenous Issues[119] shows that despite widespread awareness of the vulnerability of indigenous peoples, there is a lack of disaggregated data on the situation of indigenous peoples and therefore often little information available about the exact extent of hunger and malnutrition. The general lack of information gathering often reflects the reluctance of Governments to recognize the issues faced by their indigenous populations. Only recently has data started to be collected. In Guatemala for instance, where the Government has made important efforts to disaggregate statistics, it is clear that indigenous peoples face much higher levels of poverty and malnutrition than the rest of the population. While half of all Guatemalan children under the age of five are stunted, malnutrition is much higher among indigenous children, with 70 per cent stunted in their growth compared to 36 per cent of non-indigenous children.[120]

Understanding what the right to food means to indigenous peoples is however far more complex than merely examining statistics on hunger, malnutrition or poverty. Many indigenous peoples have their own particular conceptions of food, hunger and subsistence. In general, it is difficult to conceptually separate indigenous peoples' relationships with food from their relationships to land, resources, culture, values and social organization. Food, procurement and consumption of food are often an important part of culture, as well as of social, economic and political organization. Many indigenous peoples understand the right to adequate food as a collective right. They often see subsistence activities such as hunting, fishing and gathering as essential not only to their right to food, but to nurturing their cultures, languages, social life and identity. Their right to food often depends closely on their access to and control over their lands and other natural resources in their territories. For many traditional communities, especially those living in remote regions, access to hunting, fishing and gathering grounds for their subsistence livelihoods is essential for ensuring their adequate nutrition, as they may have no physical or economic access to marketed food. As a study on the food security of Inuit peoples of Alaska shows, 'the legal protection of subsistence is a prerequisite to Inuit food security for nutritional, cultural and economic reasons'.[121] The loss of access to traditional subsistence activities has left some indigenous communities dependent on cheap fast food, suffering from high levels of diabetes and other nutritional problems.[122]

3.5.1 Key issues facing the right to food of indigenous peoples

The lack of recognition of rights to land and resources

The realization of indigenous peoples' right to food often depends crucially on their access to and control over the natural resources in the land and territories they occupy or use. Only then can they maintain traditional economic and subsistence activities such as hunting, gathering or fishing that enable them to feed themselves and preserve their culture and distinct identity. Yet for centuries, indigenous peoples have been dispossessed of their land, resources and access to water and that trend continues even today. While indigenous land rights are largely vested on the community as such, with land being divided into individual or family holdings only for the purpose of economic use, this traditional form of ownership and possession has been under pressure for a long time, starting with colonization. Attempts have been made to break collective control of land and to allow for the privatization of land and its subsequent transfer onto the market. In Guatemala for example, communally held indigenous lands (*ejidos*) were nationalized or privatized as individual holdings in the 1800s, with the deliberate aim of consolidating the land into large coffee plantations. As the best coffee was cultivated at an altitude between 800 and 1500 metres, many indigenous people were displaced from their lands and forced to relocate to steeper, less fertile ground for their subsistence farming.[123] More recent land reform processes aimed at facilitating and encouraging foreign investment are further undermining traditional indigenous forms of ownership over land, water and other resources. However, as the Special Rapporteur on the situation of human rights and fundamental freedoms of indigenous people has noted, 'land, territory and resources constitute an essential human rights issue for the survival of indigenous peoples'.[124] In August 2001, for example, the Mayagna community of Awas Tingni won a case in the Inter-American Court of Human Rights, which ruled that the Government of Nicaragua had violated the community's property rights in granting their land to a foreign timber company, and imposed that the State recognize, demarcate and issue title for the land belonging to the Mayagna community.[125]

Appropriation of resources – intellectual property rights

For centuries, indigenous peoples have been dispossessed of their lands and resources, often through the imposition of colonial laws. Today, a similar pattern continues as indigenous peoples continue to lose even their genetic resources and indigenous knowledge. Indigenous peoples are concerned that recent developments in international intellectual property rights regimes represent a threat to indigenous access to and control over plant and animal genetic resources, as well as to community knowledge gained over generations. Concern is rising among indigenous communities and farmers about 'bioprospecting' and the appropriation or 'biopiracy' of their traditional knowledge and folklore, particularly about the curative and nutritive properties of plants and animals. Indigenous peoples see the World Trade Organization (WTO) Agreement on Trade-Related Aspects of Intellectual Property Rights (TRIPS) as a framework for the appropriation of traditional knowledge by agrochemical industrialists and researchers in industrialized countries. They want to be consulted about the ways their knowledge is used, and to equitably share in any benefits.[126] They are particularly concerned about developments in biotechnology and intellectual property protection that could deprive indigenous farming communities of their access to and control of seeds and livestock breeds, allowing intellectual property protection to 'inventions' that will later require pay for its use. In 1994 for example, two researchers of the Colorado State University obtained a US patent on quinoa, a high-protein grain traditionally used by Andean indigenous peoples in Bolivia and Ecuador. Indigenous peoples were frustrated that researchers in the United States could be granted the status of 'inventors' of quinoa and given exclusive control over a traditional Bolivian variety. In 1998, Bolivia's National Association of Quinoa Producers (Asociación Nacional de Productores de Quinoa – ANAPQUI) managed to have the university surrender the patent.[127]

Negative impacts of inappropriate development

Development projects in lands and resources owned or controlled by indigenous can also threaten the right to food of indigenous communities. As the Special Rapporteur of the Sub-commission on the Promotion and Protection on Human Rights, Erica-Irene Daes, noted in her final working paper on indigenous peoples and their relationship to land,[128] that 'economic development has been largely imposed from outside, with complete disregard for the right of indigenous peoples to participation in the control, implementation and benefits of development'. Development projects are often carried out without the free, prior and informed consent of those affected, and can threaten the right to food through the destruction or loss of ancestral territories and resources or displacement. This often happens in the case of large-scale commercial exploitation of the resources on indigenous territories – including mining for minerals, oil or gas, logging, building dams and highways, or expanding industrial agriculture on indigenous lands, which can seriously threaten the right to food. Authorities rarely assess the likely impact of such projects nor do they take timely corrective action, despite legal obligations under the ILO Convention No. 169 concerning Indigenous and Tribal Peoples in Independent Countries. In a case in Malaysia, the Malaysian Court of Appeal did award compensation to the Jakun tribe, an Orang Asli population, after the state government had appropriated more than 53,000 acres of ancestral lands in the southern state of Johor for the construction of a dam to supply water to Johor and Singapore, without consulting the local communities or sharing the benefits with them.[129] In the Declaration of Atitlán on the right to food, the representatives of indigenous communities criticized the dominant model of economic development based on globalized free trade, industrial agriculture and unsustainable development, for undermining alternative modes of subsistence and violating their right to food.

Lack of access to justice

A critical element for the possibilities of indigenous peoples to enforce their right to food is their access to the judicial system. Even where indigenous do have access to justice, it is often limited by geographical distance, discrimination and prejudice, and the non-recognition of indigenous customary law and legal authorities. Often, the implementation of laws protecting indigenous rights is insufficient and indigenous themselves lack sufficient knowledge about the laws and institutions designed to protect their rights, a situation that results in third-party interests finding it easy to dispossess and exploit them. Indigenous peoples are also critical of the repression that often characterizes the relationship between Governments and indigenous communities, even when they have resolved their cases. In a case reported to us, it was alleged that a group of 86 peasant families has been forcibly evicted from their land *El Maguey* farm (Fraijanes) in Guatemala, with their crops and irrigations system destroyed repeatedly by the police and the army over the last 2 years, despite the recognition that they own the land in a Governmental Agreement dated 7 April 2003 and a Constitutional Court decision dated 4 May 2004.[130] Also of concern are reports of the use of food as an instrument of political or economic pressures, particularly in situations of conflict. In Colombia, for instance there are serious concerns about blockades that prevent food reaching indigenous communities, threatening their food security and forcing them into the conflict.[131]

3.5.2 Legal framework governing the right to food of indigenous peoples

The international framework for the protection of the rights of indigenous peoples is still relatively weak. Until recently, the only international instrument offering specific protection was ILO Convention No. 169. This Convention is important, protecting indigenous peoples' right to food, as well a broad range of civil, political, economic, social and cultural rights. Articles 13–17 provide special protection of indigenous peoples' rights to land and territories, and their right to participate in the use, management and conservation of these resources, requiring their participation and consultation before any exploitation of resources located on indigenous lands and prohibiting the displacement of indigenous communities.

At its first session, the Human Rights Council adopted the United Nations Declaration on the Rights of Indigenous Peoples,[132] which is particularly relevant for the right to food. As we have seen, the United Nations Declaration on the Rights of Indigenous Peoples was then adopted by the General Assembly in September 2007, which offers the possibility of greater protection for indigenous peoples, going beyond the ILO Convention. The Declaration recognizes that indigenous peoples have the right to the full enjoyment, as a collective or as individuals, of all human rights and fundamental freedoms as recognized in the Charter of the United Nations, the Universal Declaration of Human Rights and international human rights law. It also recognizes their right to self-determination and rights over land and resources, acknowledging the historical injustices of colonization but also addressing contemporary threats posed by economic globalization, offering protection of traditional knowledge, biodiversity and genetic resources, and setting limits on the activities of third parties on the territories of indigenous communities without their consent. This new instrument, even if it is not a treaty, represents an important new tool that indigenous peoples can use to claim their rights, including their right to food, and seek appropriate remedies in case of violations.

Broader human rights instruments also offer protection to all peoples, including indigenous peoples. The International Covenant on Economic, Social and Cultural Rights protects the right of everyone to food in Article 11. The CESCR, in its General Comment No. 12 stresses their right to food and highlights that 'particular vulnerability is that of many indigenous population groups whose access to their ancestral lands may be threatened' (paragraph 13). The Committee also outlined that the right to adequate food implies that food is available, accessible, adequate and *culturally* acceptable, which means that food should correspond to the cultural traditions of the people. This has special implications for indigenous peoples, for whom culturally appropriate foods derive from subsistence-based activities, such as hunting, gathering or fishing, with implications in terms of maintaining their livelihoods. Even in communities that are closely integrated into the mainstream economy, imported foods are sometimes too expensive or non-nutritious and subsistence activities play an important part in maintaining their food security, as well as their culture and identity. The general comment outlines the obligations of States to respect, protect and fulfil the right to food and demands that food should never be used as an instrument of political or economic pressure.

Of special importance to the right to food of indigenous peoples is common Article 1 of both human rights covenants, which recognizes the rights of all peoples to self-determination and the right to freely pursue their economic, social and cultural development. Moreover, paragraph 2 of the article also stipulates that in no case may a people be deprived of its own means of subsistence. The prohibition of discrimination, contained in Article 2 of the International Covenant on Civil and Political Rights, is also of crucial importance for indigenous peoples. Non-discrimination sometimes requires affirmative action and measures in favour of indigenous peoples to compensate or redress traditional imbalances and marginalization. Other human rights instruments protecting women and children are also relevant to indigenous peoples. Control over and preservation of plant and animal genetic resources is today crucial for the economic interests of indigenous peoples and their long-term food security. Article 8 of the Convention on Biological Diversity in conjunction with the International Treaty on Plant Genetic Resources for Food and Agriculture provide a legal framework for the protection of those rights.

3.5.3 Government obligations vis-à-vis the right to food of indigenous peoples

The right to food of indigenous peoples can be understood within the framework laid out by the CESCR that requires States to respect, protect and fulfil the right to food of all members of their population. This implies that the right to food is not only a positive right; it is also a negative right that aims to prevent violations of indigenous people's existing access to food.

The obligation to respect

The obligation to respect the right to food requires that governments refrain from taking any action that would negatively affect peoples' existing right to food. This entails refraining from acts such as dispossessing or displacing people from their land, where their land is their primary means of subsistence. It also means refraining from realizing development projects that may obstruct or destroy traditional access to subsistence resources, such as hunting or fishing, where this constitutes indigenous peoples' main means of feeding themselves. It also means that governments must never engage in killings and repressive actions against indigenous peoples, where they are engaged in peaceful protest to protect their right to food, land and resources.

The obligation to protect

The obligation to protect the right to food requires governments to ensure that third parties (such as powerful landowners or corporations) do not take any actions that negatively affect indigenous peoples' right to food. This means that governments must regulate or control powerful third parties to prevent abuses of the right to food of indigenous peoples. Third parties should be prevented from displacing indigenous peoples from their lands and resources. In cases where a government grants concessions to corporations for the exploitation of resources on indigenous lands, it should adhere to the principle of free, prior and informed consent of indigenous peoples to ensure that they agree to and benefit from the exploitation of their resources and that their food security is not threatened. This requires also ensuring mitigating the human and ecological costs of environmentally damaging projects, such as gold mining, to ensure that traditional food, water and other subsistence resources are not destroyed or poisoned.

The obligation to fulfil

The obligation to fulfil (facilitate and provide) the right to food requires governments to take steps to address the marginalization, hunger and poverty of indigenous communities, with respect to indigenous peoples' own priorities, in order to ensure their integrity and cultural survival. This obligation comprises two positive obligations – the obligations to *facilitate* and the obligation to *provide*. The key obligation to facilitate indigenous peoples' right to food requires governments to take positive actions to facilitate the capacity of indigenous communities to feed themselves, such as formally recognizing and demarcating indigenous territories to enable them to carry out subsistence activities. Governments also have an obligation to respect the right of indigenous peoples to determine how best to improve their food security and to pursue their own priorities for development. Governments are always required to prevent starvation and ensure access to food, by facilitating the provision of marketed food where necessary and providing emergency food in situations of crisis. The obligation to fulfil also includes an immediate obligation to take action against discrimination against indigenous peoples in terms of access to land, employment and other productive resources. This requires not only overturning de jure legal institutions of discrimination, but also addressing de facto discrimination against indigenous peoples that contributes to their hunger and malnutrition.

3.6 Refugees from hunger[133]

In many regions of the world, particularly in Africa, famine, destitution and chronic hunger are forcing people to leave their homes, land and even their countries. For example, tens of thousands of young Africans flee their countries, risking their lives to try to reach Europe every year. Hunger and famine are due not only to drought, but also to economic problems as well as political problems of corruption and mismanagement. Today, most Governments treat people crossing their borders without permission as criminals, even if they are fleeing from life-threatening consequences of hunger and severe violations of their human right to food. It is also due to the hypocritical policies of developed countries on agriculture and climate change, which are further contributing to hunger, poverty and inequality in developing countries. Famine and food are often used as a weapon of war against certain groups of people who are forced to flee for their lives. Yet hunger and violations of the human right to food are still not seen by the international community as legitimate reasons or sufficient legal grounds for people to flee their countries. People fleeing from hunger and famine and crossing borders, especially if they try to flee to developed countries, are treated as 'illegal migrants', arrested and held in often appalling conditions in detention and processing centres. Refused asylum, they are usually forcibly deported home, even when their lives remain at risk from famine and chronic hunger.

The vast majority of people who flee from hunger and famine do not cross international borders, but remain within their own countries, displaced from their places of origin, usually living in the mega-slums of the developing world.[134] But millions of people do cross international borders and some try to reach developed countries to escape pervasive hunger, especially people living in sub-Saharan Africa. It is estimated, for example, that about two million such people try to enter the EU illegally every year and about 2000 of them drown in the Mediterranean Sea. They try to reach the Canary Islands from Mauritania or Senegal, or to cross the Straits of Gibraltar from Morocco. According to the Government of Spain, 37,685 African migrants reached Spanish shores in 2005. Another 22,824 migrants reached the islands of Italy or Malta, leaving from the Libyan Arab Jamahiriya or Tunisia.[135] African migrants also try to reach Greece through Turkey or from Egypt. During 2006, the Spanish authorities detained at least 28,000 people arriving in the Canary Islands after a dangerous journey across the open sea in overcrowded open fishing boats.[136] Many arrive in a terrible condition, too weak to walk or stand and chronically undernourished. Yet most of them are detained and held in processing or detention centres, before being forcibly repatriated to their own countries.

Nobody knows how many thousands of people die while trying to make the journey, but bodies regularly wash up on the beaches or fishermen catch them in their nets. On 18 December 2006, the international press reported that over 100 refugees drowned in one day off the coast of Senegal on their way to Spain.[137] However, there are no official records. As Markku Niskala, Secretary General of the International Federation of the Red Cross has said: 'This crisis is being completely ignored: not only does no one come to the help of these desperate people, but there is no organization that even compiles statistics that record this daily tragedy.'[138]

If they survive the risks of crossing the seas, they face violence and human rights violations when they reach the shores of developed countries, as came to be highlighted by the outrageous tragedies that occurred in Ceuta and Melilla in 2005. On the night of 28 September 2005, at least five African men were shot dead, when several hundred people trying to enter Spanish territory by climbing over two razor-wire fences separating

Ceuta from Morocco, were confronted by law-enforcement officials.[139] On 6 October 2005, another six men were shot dead on the Moroccan side of the border. Amnesty International called for an independent international investigation into these events, as well as into further reports that a number of people had been injured as a result of ill-treatment and use of excessive force by Spanish and Moroccan security forces in Ceuta and Melilla.[140] Amnesty International also expressed serious concern about deportations from Spain to Morocco after Médecins Sans Frontières reported that it had discovered more than 500 people abandoned in the desert on the Morocco-Algeria border by the Moroccan police, without any food or water.[141]

This tragedy of African refugees from hunger was a key focus of the World Social Forum on Migration held in Madrid on 21–24 June 2006, and is also a focus of Africa's own extremely diverse and dynamic civil society, including during the African Social Forum held in Bamako (22–25 January 2005) and the World Social Forum held in Nairobi (19–23 January 2007). Special days of commemoration for the bloody events at Ceuta and Melilla were focused on the theme of 'Globalization and African migration' (29 September to 7 October 2006 at Bamako). In the words of Aminata Traoré, former Minister of Culture of Mali and one of the most prominent writers of French-speaking Africa:

> The human, financial and technological resources that Europe's 25 countries have deployed against the inflow of African migrants, in fact, signify a real war between this world power and these young, defenceless, rural and urban Africans, whose right to education, right to economic information, right to work and right to food have been denied in their own countries under structural adjustment. Victims of macroeconomic decisions and choices, through no fault of their own, they are chased, tracked down and humiliated if they try to flee. The dead, the injured and the handicapped of the bloody events of Ceuta and Melilla in 2005, as well as the hundreds of lifeless bodies that wash up on the beaches of Mauritania, the Canary Islands, Lampedus or elsewhere are also drowned by this forced and criminalized migration.

The response of the EU to African refugees from hunger is increasingly to militarize immigration procedures and border patrol. Rapid reaction teams of border guards are acting a new institution called Frontex. Frontex's 'Operation Hera II' involved patrol boats, aeroplanes and helicopters from Spain, Italy, Finland and Portugal operating along the borders of Mauritania, Senegal and Cape Verde to intercept boats and return them immediately to shore.[142] European Governments seem to believe that it is possible to address the drama of migration as a military and police problem. Refugees from hunger face ill-treatment in other regions also. The thousands of people who have been fleeing famine and food shortages in the People's

Democratic Republic of Korea by crossing the border to China have often faced immediate deportation. Nationals of the People's Democratic Republic of Korea who are caught while crossing the border or who are deported by the Chinese authorities are very likely to be subjected to ill and degrading treatment,[143] including forced labour in prison camps in their country of origin.

The European and Chinese governments and China are not alone in their approch toward migration as a military and policing problem. Hundreds of thousands of Mexicans and other Latin Americans attempt to cross the border into the United States. When tens of thousands of people were arrested trying to cross illegally the border during 2005 and 2006, President Bush signed into law the Secure Fence Act which included plans to build a 1125 km fence to prevent people from illegally crossing the border.[144] Australia has also been criticized for the tightening of its migration and asylum policies.[145]

3.6.1 Fleeing from hunger

Hundreds of millions of people have been forced from their homes and lands for numerous reasons, but few have managed to cross international borders to another country. Currently there are millions of migrants who have moved within their own countries (whether through forced or voluntary migration), there are only about 190 million international migrants, living and working in a country other than their country of birth, which is only about 2.9 per cent of the global population.[146] There are even fewer refugees, with the Office of the United Nations High Commissioner for Refugees (UNHCR) estimating that, at the end of 2000, there were 9.2 million refugees around the world (defined as those who have crossed an international border fearing persecution). The vast majority of these refugees have left their countries, but remains in neighbouring countries in Africa or Asia. Only about 800,000 refugees are actively seeking asylum and refugee status in North America, Europe as well as in developing countries in 2006.[147] Many countries are setting up more barriers to reduce those eligible for asylum.[148]

According to the 1951 Convention relating to the Status of Refugees, all Governments are obliged to grant refugee status to those who qualify for international protection. Refugees are those who have to flee due to a 'well-founded fear of being persecuted for reasons of race, religion, nationality, membership of a particular social group or political opinion' (Article 1). According this understanding, refugees are different from other migrants in that they are forced to leave their homes because of a change in their social environment which makes it impossible to continue their lives as they have known it before, usually involving a coercive force and political persecution. However, there is no such protection for other people who voluntarily leave their homes in search of a better life or better livelihood in another country. According to the UNHCR, an 'economic migrant' is a person who voluntarily leaves their country, on the basis of economic, rather than political reasons, in order to take up residence elsewhere.[149] It is the voluntary and economic nature of this choice that defines someone as an economic migrant. Economic migrants may be accepted into another country, but this is at the discretion of each country's migration policy and is usually based on the country's own national interest. Unlike refugees, States have no legal responsibility to accept economic migrants because it is believed that they have not been forced to leave their countries.

Many migrants do choose voluntarily to leave their homes and lands in search of a better life in another country. In a world where the richer countries are getting richer and the poorer are getting poorer, migration is an obvious response. A study by the World Institute for Development Economics Research (WIDER) of the United Nations University, shows how extreme global inequality has become, with most of the world's wealth heavily concentrated in North America, Europe and high-income Asia-Pacific countries, including Australia and Japan.[150] People in these countries collectively hold almost 90 per cent of the world's total wealth, while the poorer half of the world's population owns barely 1 per cent of global wealth.[151] However, in a world where the poor and hungry are getting even poorer, there are increasing numbers of people who have little choice but to leave their homes and lands in order to survive, and it is becoming more difficult to distinguish between economic migrants and refugees.[152]

If migrants are fleeing from famine, chronic hunger and deprivation, then we must call into question whether such migration is 'voluntary'. Millions of people living in Africa, especially sub-Saharan Africa, regularly face famine and growing destitution. Sub-Saharan Africa is the only region of the world where levels of hunger have been constantly increasing since 1990. Between 1990 and 2008, the number of chronically undernourished people is estimated to have increased from 169 million to 236 million people.[153] It is the developing region with the highest proportion of people living in hunger – one third of the population does not get the minimum amount of calories every day that is necessary to sustain healthy life. In the poorest countries, more than 35 per cent of the population goes hungry every day, even during normal times when there is no drought or famine. Hunger has increased most in countries torn apart by conflict over the 1990s, including Burundi, the Democratic Republic of the Congo, Liberia and Sierra Leone. This has been particularly severe in the Democratic Republic of the Congo, where the number of victims of undernutrition rose from 31 to 72 per cent of the Congolese people. These close links between hunger and conflict are often exacerbated when food and famine have also been used as weapons of war in many African countries, against certain groups or communities.[154] It is difficult to suggest that mass population movements precipitated by famine, just as by conflict, are voluntary.

Environmental degradation, desertification and global climate change are also exacerbating destitution and desperation, especially in the highly arid countries of Sahelian Africa.[155] In 1995 (the last time a comprehensive assessment was carried out), the United Nations estimated that there were already 25 million people forced to leave their homes for environmental reasons, mostly from sub-Saharan Africa.[156] However, the Intergovernmental Panel on Climate Change has estimated that, by 2050, there may be as many as 150 million 'environmental refugees'[157] – people forced to leave their homes and lands for environmental reasons linked to global climate change, including desertification and land degradation. Policies in developed countries are further exacerbating these effects – energy consumption in the North is contributing to global climate change, with the effects felt primarily in the South.[158] Agricultural policies in the North also have destructive effects on agricultural livelihoods and hunger in the South.[159]

Migration has always been a strategy to cope with hunger and famine in Africa,[160] but this has not been a matter of choice, but rather of necessity. People leave their homes and lands when they are desperate, when they cannot feed themselves and their families. Although most migration happens in neighbouring countries in Africa, in today's world no country can isolate itself from the effects of hunger; increasingly desperate people are trying to reach the shores of developed countries. Although the poor and hungry cannot always migrate if they cannot afford to pay boat passage or exploitative traffickers, many families gather together to pool all their resources to try to send just one person overseas. In the villages of Mali, for example, many people gather funds to send just one person to Mauritania or to Senegal to catch a boat to Spain. If that person succeeds, then the remittances they send home can feed several families. If they fail, however, then they can never return to their villages for the humiliation of loss and debt to their neighbours. Many thousands therefore stay in Mauritania or Senegal until they can make another attempt.

3.6.2 The need to recognize refugees from hunger

The rights of refugees are legally protected under the 1951 Convention relating to the Status of Refugees. Elaborated in the aftermath of the Second World War to protect people fleeing from communist countries, the objective of international refugee law was to protect people who had a well-founded fear of persecution, understood as severe violations of their civil and political rights. Legal developments at the regional level, in particular in Africa and Latin America, have broadened the concept to protect those escaping generalized violence, foreign aggression, internal conflicts, massive violation of human rights or other circumstances seriously disturbing public order. Many States in the past 50 years have also applied the Convention of 1951 to other asylum-seekers, such as the 'person considered worthy of receiving asylum for humanitarian reasons.' (Declaration on Territorial Asylum of the

Committee of Ministers of the Council of Europe, 1977). And UNHCR has in practice considerably broadened the categories of people of concern to it, to assist and protect today internally displaced persons (IDPs), stateless people or asylum-seekers.[161] Yet, violations of economic, social and cultural rights, including the right to be free from hunger, have never been really taken into account.

Every human being has the right to food and the fundamental right to be free from hunger. These rights have been recognized in Article 11 of the International Covenant on Economic, Social and Cultural Rights, as well as in many other international instruments, without any territorial or jurisdictional limitation. The legal consequences of this absence of territorial or jurisdictional limitations are clear: States have the obligations to respect, protect and fulfil the right to food of all people, living within their jurisdiction or in other countries.[162] In this particular context, this means that Governments have a legal obligation to help the refugees from hunger, regardless of their country of origin or status.

Today, however, most Governments treat crossing international frontiers to be free from hunger as an illegal act. This response is shameful. For those fleeing from hunger, the most appropriate response is to recognize that they have the right to seek asylum and to protection of temporary refuge, and in the long term, to recognize that they are refugees, entitled to international protection. To detain and then forcibly repatriate people fleeing from hunger to a territory where they will continue to suffer hunger and chronic undernourishment is unjustifiable. As the Office of the High Commissioner for Human Rights (OHCHR) rightly stated, 'there is little to distinguish between a person facing death through starvation and another threatened with arbitrary execution because of her political beliefs'.[163]

The existing legal framework of international human rights, humanitarian and refugee law does provide important protections, but these need to be seriously strengthened to cover the particular situation of 'refugees from hunger'.

Most people fleeing from hunger are refused entry and protection in other countries because they do not qualify as 'refugees' in the traditional and legal sense. All Governments are legally obliged to receive asylum-seekers and grant protection to refugees under international law, but the definition of 'refugee' is very limited. The 1951 Convention relating to the Status of Refugees is the key legal instrument defining who is a refugee, his or her rights and the legal obligations of States. According to the 1951 Convention and its 1967 Protocol, a refugee is a person who:

> [O]wing to well-founded fear of being persecuted for reasons of race, religion, nationality, membership of a particular social group or political opinion, is outside the country of his nationality and is unable or, owing to such fear, unwilling to avail himself of the protection of that country;

or who, not having a nationality and being outside the country of his former habitual residence as a result of such events, is unable or, owing to such fear, is unwilling to return to it.

Under the principle of non-refoulement set out in Article 33 of the 1951 Convention, all people granted refugee status must be protected from expulsion or return in any manner whatsoever to the frontiers of territories where their life or freedom would be threatened on account of one or more of the grounds referred to in the definition of a refugee. Accordingly, the Special Rapporteur on torture and other cruel, inhuman or degrading treatment or punishment, Manfred Nowak, urged all Governments to 'observe the principle of non-refoulement scrupulously and not expel any person to frontiers or territories where they might run the risk of human rights violations, regardless of whether they have officially been recognized as refugees'.[164]

Sadly, most people fleeing from hunger are not granted any of the protections that come with refugee status and the right of non-refoulement, even though they run the risk of grave violations of the right to food that amount to a threat to their life. There have been some legal developments that broaden the understanding of who qualifies as a 'refugee', but these are still limited.[165] One possible example could be that deprivation of food could amount to persecution of an individual where he or she was deprived of food because of persecution on the basis of race, religion, nationality, membership of a particular social group or political opinion. Persecutory acts could include discriminatory food distribution policies, forced and unlawful eviction from land, denial of food or severe restrictions on an individual's ability to earn a livelihood or to have access to means for procuring food for him/herself or his/her family for reasons of his/her political opinion, religion or any other of the five grounds. However, so far, few such cases have been accepted, which means that the vast majority of people fleeing from hunger are not treated as refugees under the 1951 Convention.

Most people fleeing across international borders to escape hunger and starvation are therefore treated as illegal 'economic migrants'. Under migration laws, economic migrants may be legally accepted into another country, but this is at the discretion of each country's migration policy and standard procedures and is usually based on the country's own national interest. No country is legally obliged to accept people who are defined as 'economic migrants', given that they have not been forced to leave their countries. Migrants are therefore not granted the same protections as refugees and have no right of non-refoulement that would protect them from being forcibly repatriated to their own countries.

However, to suggest that people fleeing from hunger and famine are simply 'economic migrants' and are not being forced to leave, but are simply choosing to seek a better life, is to fail completely to recognize the life-threatening situation that they face. It is absurd to suggest that people fleeing hunger and famine are fleeing 'voluntarily'. We insist on this crucial point: refugees from hunger should not be confused with other categories of 'economic migrants'. When an 'economic migrant' seeks a better life by migrating to another country, he does so voluntarily. The refugee from hunger, however, does not move voluntarily, but from a 'state of necessity'. He is forced to flee. Especially when famine strikes a whole country or a whole region (e.g. the 2005 famine in the Sahel zone of sub-Saharan Africa), refugees from hunger have no other choice but to flee across international borders. Hunger is an immediate threat to their lives and those of their families. They are fleeing out of a state of necessity, not out of choice.

The concept of a 'state of necessity' (*état de nécessité*) is a well-developed concept and one that is well established in common and civil law in many countries. For example, the French criminal code (Article 122–7) provides that a person may not be held liable for an act which would under normal circumstances constitute a crime if his/her conduct was necessary to avoid a threat or a danger to him/herself or a third person and if that conduct was proportionate to the seriousness of the danger. In the well-known case of Dame Ménard,[166] a mother was not sentenced for stealing bread because she acted out of a state of necessity, unable to allow her children to starve. Canadian criminal law similarly allows for a defence based on necessity. The rationale for this was clearly spelled out in the case of *Perka v. The Queen*, where the Supreme Court of Canada affirmed that 'a liberal and humane criminal law cannot hold people to the strict obedience of laws in emergency situations where normal human instincts, whether of self-preservation or of altruism, overwhelmingly impel disobedience'.[167] Fleeing across international borders cannot be considered an illegal act when people are fleeing from hunger and famine.

In relation to hunger and famine, it is not difficult to establish objectively such a state of necessity. Both WFP and FAO issue regular reports that identify regions where there are chronic food emergencies and even identify the number of people suffering from acute and chronic levels of malnutrition. On the basis of this concept, it would therefore be possible to allow for the protection of refugees from hunger by recognizing that they have the right to seek asylum and the right to receive the protection of temporary refuge. In the longer term, it is essential to take into account the most severe violations of economic and social rights, including violations of the right to food, in determining who is of refugee status.

On the basis of this concept, it is objectively possible to establish who is fleeing from hunger and famine, rather than for other reasons. The urgent next step is therefore to create a new legal instrument that will establish the status of 'refugees from hunger' and will provide them with the right of non-refoulement, so that they are not inhumanely deported back to countries in a state of famine. It is not possible to revise existing international instruments, including the 1951 Convention relating to the Status of Refugees, and therefore there is a need to develop a specially designed instrument that will protect people fleeing from hunger and other violations of the right to food.

States should consider the creation of a new legal instrument to protect people fleeing from hunger and violations of the right to food. Under this new legal instrument, they would be recognized as 'refugees from hunger' and granted, at the very minimum, the right of non-refoulement with temporary protection, so that they are not sent back to a country where hunger and famine threaten their lives. While Governments always bear the primary responsibility for ensuring respect of the right to food, if people flee their countries for their lives, receiving countries should not send them back to situations of hunger that threaten their lives. Criminalizing refugees from hunger will not make the problem go away. In today's world, no country can isolate itself from the effects of hunger, when millions of people are increasingly desperate. It is time that legal protection is extended to all people fleeing from hunger and severe violations of their right to food. Only by recognizing their obligations to the world's hunger refugees, will all Governments finally take seriously their responsibility for eradicating global hunger.

It is important today that this protection be enlarged to protect the refugees from hunger, to recognize that they have at least, but immediately, the right to seek asylum and the right to receive protection of temporary refuge. In the longer term, it is essential to take the most severe violations of economic and social rights into account in the determination of refugees, including violations of the right to food. To this end, States should consider the possibility of expanding the definition of refugees, either by revising the existing international instruments, or by adopting new instruments for the protection of all refugees, those fleeing to escape severe violations of civil and political rights as well as those fleeing to escape severe violations of economic, social and cultural rights.

4
The Right to Food in an Era of Globalization[1]

The primary obligations to respect, protect and fulfil the right to food of their people will always rest with national governments. However, in an age of globalization and increasing interconnectedness, with the gradual emergence of a single integrated world market and the progressive globalization of most commercial, economic and social relations between peoples, it is time to challenge the traditional territorial boundaries of human rights. With the simultaneous emergence of international organizations and private transnational corporations that often have greater economic and financial power than many States, particularly in the South, it is also important to challenge the idea that human rights are only about limiting arbitrary abuses of power by Governments against their citizens.

When other public and private actors are more powerful than States, human rights must be extended to limit their potential abuses of power against people. These powerful new actors, which include international organizations such as the World Bank, the International Monetary Fund (IMF) and the WTO and private actors such as transnational corporations (TNCs), must be made accountable. With power must come responsibility.

Four issues will be discussed in this chapter. The first is the issue of international trade and the right to food. The second is the issue of extraterritorial obligations – which refers to the human rights obligations of Governments towards people living outside of its own territory. The third is the human rights responsibilities of non-State actors, such as transnational corporations. The fourth is examining the human rights responsibilities of multilateral inter-State organizations such as IMF, the World Bank and WTO. The underlying principle for all four issues is the promotion of universal human dignity as enshrined in human rights.

4.1 International trade and the right to food[2]

4.1.1 Trade and food security

Today, agricultural trade is far from being free, and even further from being fair. Many developed countries continue to protect and subsidize the production of basic, staple foods. Many developing countries are becoming dependent on food imports, and are subjected to unfair competition from developed-country products sold at prices below the cost of production. This displaces local production of basic foodstuffs and farming livelihoods in those countries.[3] According to Peter Brabeck, President and Chief Executive Officer of Nestlé, the world's largest food and beverage company, 'In the industrialized countries, agricultural products are subsidized to the tune of US$ 1 billion per day (...). We cannot consume all these products and so we create mountains of butter and milk. After that we export them at extremely low prices to developing countries. The local farmers do not stand a chance [to sell their own products]. Why do all developing countries have these huge urban slums? Because their people can no longer find work in the countryside and must flee to the cities. Who is responsible? The agricultural subsidies.'[4]

Despite preaching the benefits of free trade in agriculture, the European Union, the United States of America, Japan and other industrialized countries heavily protect their agriculture in order to ensure the production of basic staple foods. In the European Union, 'the average European dairy cow has a bigger annual income than half the world's people', and it is estimated that 70 per cent of subsidies go to 20 per cent of Europe's largest farms.[5] In the United States, the 2002 Farm Bill authorized the spending of US$ 180 billion to be paid out over a ten-year period as 'emergency measures', mainly in support of staple cereal crops. In his address to the Future Farmers of America in Washington on 27 July 2001, President George W. Bush stated that:

> It's important for our nation to build – to grow foodstuffs, to feed our people. Can you imagine a country that was unable to grow enough food to feed the people? It would be a nation subject to international pressure. It would be a nation at risk. And so when we're talking about American agriculture, we're really talking about a national security issue.[6]

In the same speech, President Bush argued against 'the trade barriers, the protectionist tendencies around the world that prevent our [US] products from getting into markets'. Nobel Prize winner in Economics Joseph Stiglitz described the United States Farm Bill as 'the perfect illustration of the Bush administration's hypocrisy on trade liberalization'.[7] Civil society organizations criticized the Farm Bill as benefiting only rich, large farmers and agribusiness corporations – only farmers with incomes of US$ 2.5 million or more will not receive subsidy payments.[8]

Meanwhile, developing countries have been persuaded into unilaterally liberalizing their agricultural sectors, often under the programmes of the International Monetary Fund (IMF) and the World Bank, rather than the WTO Agreement on Agriculture, only to find that the promised benefits of 'free trade' in agriculture have not materialized. Instead, their farmers have often been devastated by artificially low prices created by the 'dumping' of subsidized agricultural products, as in the cases of Mexico and Zambia described below. The heavy production and export subsidies that OECD countries grant their farmers – more than US$ 340 billion per year (almost US$ 1 billion per day) – means that subsidized European fruit and vegetables can be found in a market stall in Dakar, Senegal, at lower prices than local produce. In terms of 'who is most to blame' for these losses, IFPRI argues that, of the total amount of agricultural trade displaced by industrialized country policies, the European Union countries are responsible for half. The United States is responsible for a third, with Japan and other high-income Asian countries causing another 10 per cent.[9] Although developed countries, including the European Union, made promises at the WTO Hong Kong conference in December 2005 to eliminate export subsidies that result in dumping, there has been little concrete progress so far.

For several developing countries that have liberalized their agricultural sectors, the experience has not been a positive one. While farming livelihoods have been devastated when opened up to competition for imports sold at below-cost-of-production, consumers have not always benefited from lower prices. Zambia, for example, undertook radical trade liberalization under a programme of structural adjustment in the 1990s, liberalizing well beyond its WTO commitments (lowering tariffs, eliminating subsidies for its staple crop, maize, and dismantling agricultural extension and marketing support systems). Such rapid changes left Zambian farmers without a way to sell their crops, particularly in more remote areas, as a vibrant private sector failed to emerge. An IMF evaluation recognized that the liberalization in agriculture caused hardship for poor Zambians, with maize consumption falling 20 per cent between 1990 and 1997 as a result of increased poverty.[10] At the same time, while farm prices for maize fell, maize prices paid by consumers increased.[11] In Mexico, where maize has been a traditional crop for thousands of years, the North American Free Trade Agreement has left Mexican farmers extremely vulnerable to competition from subsidized United States maize. A study by the United Nations Development Programme (UNDP) estimated that 700,000 to 800,000 livelihoods have been lost as a consequence of trade liberalization and the subsequent fall in maize prices.[12] Another study expects that up to 15 million Mexican farmers and their families (many from indigenous communities) may be displaced.[13] As was the case in Zambia, while the maize price for Mexican farmers fell by almost half, the consumer price for maize rose by 279 per cent in real terms.[14] Farming livelihoods have been devastated by lower prices, yet consumers have also suffered simultaneously from higher prices. The intended greatest beneficiaries of trade liberalization – the consumers – have not always benefited.

Consumers have not always benefited because public monopolies have often been simply replaced by private monopolies. A World Bank study examined why lower prices for consumers have not materialized, finding that since 1974 agricultural commodity prices have fallen, but consumer prices have increased.[15] The world price of coffee, for example, fell by 18 per cent between 1975 and 1993, but the consumer price increased by 240 per cent in the United States. The same study suggests that this seems to raise the suspicion of unfair trade in world commodity markets. Global commodity markets are increasingly dominated by fewer global transnational corporations that have the power to demand low producer prices, while keeping consumer prices high, thus, increasing their profit margins. Similar patterns occur at a smaller scale where, as even after the agricultural sector is liberalized, the number of private actors can be extremely limited. Consumers have often not benefited from the lower prices promised by free-trade advocates, either because a competitive private sector has failed to emerge or because of monopolistic practices by transnational agribusiness corporations increasingly in control of agricultural trade, processing and marketing.

This is the dynamic that leads to greater inequality as a few people or corporations get rich at the expense of the majority of farmers and consumers, in both the North and the South. The same dynamic is replicated between countries, and is one reason for the growing inequalities between developed and developing countries. Many commentators agree that the main beneficiaries of trade liberalization have been larger farmers and larger corporations, which have the capacities to take advantage of the economic restructuring. The poorest and most marginal people, especially rural peasant farmers, are increasingly being left behind.

A pattern of trade is beginning to emerge where the developed countries dominate the production of food staples like rice, maize and wheat, milk and meat, while poor, developing countries produce tropical cash crops, like coffee, cotton or flowers in order to trade to buy their food (tropical products on which the many developed countries still impose high, complex tariffs or tariff escalation). The 49 least-developed countries have shifted from being net food exporters to being net food importers over the last 30 years, and the costs of their food imports have risen from 45 to 70 per cent of their total merchandise exports, making it increasingly difficult for many of these countries to pay for their food imports.[16] This leaves these countries unable to produce their own food, but also unable to guarantee an income to buy their own food, leaving them increasingly vulnerable to food insecurity and severely affecting their ability to guarantee the realization of the right to food.

All this has left many countries and many people understandably distrustful of the promises of free trade for ensuring food security, particularly in the face of the 'do as I say, not as I do' positions of the northern, developed countries. The increasingly familiar story of trade talks collapsing is a symptom of the current inequities of the global trading system, which are being perpetuated rather than resolved under the WTO, given the unequal balance of power between member countries.

4.1.2 Trade liberalization and the right to food

Including the right to food in international trade negotiations is widely understood and believed by many experts and NGOs to be absolutely necessary.[17] Economic and social rights protect the basic human needs of all people. In today's world, it has become clear that the market by itself cannot guarantee the basic needs of the whole of society. Many people are left by the wayside. As some people in the world get richer and richer, certain others are getting poorer and poorer. According to the World Bank, average income in the richest 20 countries was 37 times the average in the poorest 20 countries in 2001, a gap which has doubled in the last 40 years.[18] The benefits of globalization and world trade have clearly not been equally distributed. Many individual people suffer from the unequal distribution of food and resources around the world. Action *contre la faim* writes: 'Many poor people around the world do not get enough to eat because food production is geared to cash payment.'[19] More people live in extreme poverty now than 20 years ago. The equation is simple: those who have money eat; those without money suffer from hunger, related illnesses and often die.

Many argue that international trade liberalization and globalization have been disastrous for food security and the right to food. They argue that the liberalization of agriculture, which has occurred mainly in developing countries (largely under programmes of structural adjustment rather than under WTO provisions), has produced increased hunger and malnutrition rather than safer food security. As Kevin Watkins of OXFAM wrote in the British newspaper *The Guardian* in November 1996 at the time of the World Food Summit: 'Free trade will never feed the world, on the contrary.'[20]

A report entitled 'Trade and Hunger'[21] claims that food security based on international trade is 'more mirage than fact' for the poorest in developing countries, on the basis of 27 case studies in different countries. The report argues that much of the agricultural trade liberalization in developing countries over the past 20 years has been based on the hope that agricultural production in developing countries would switch to high-value export crops, which would enable them to import food. However, this has not happened in many countries, which have struggled to find viable export crops, as commodity prices have fallen and they have laboured to find the funds to meet their food import needs. International trade does not automatically help countries to meet food shortages if they do not have foreign exchange to buy food imports.[22] Nor does it help when their farmers have to compete with cheap subsidized imports. Both producers and consumers suffer when liberalization allows unscrupulous traders and private monopolies to pay low prices to farmers and charge high prices to consumers.[23] The switch to export crops has also shifted government attention away from small-scale farm agriculture focused on food security. In Uganda, for example, the shift away from local food crops meant that people had less to eat.[24] In the case of Zambia, even the IMF has recognized that liberalization and adjustment reduced food consumption[25] or, in other words, left people struggling to find enough food to eat. It is those impacts on the daily lives of people that are left out of the picture of macroeconomic reform and protests are often silenced by violent repression.

It is clear that food self-sufficiency or food exports at the national level do not necessarily imply food security at the household level, in particular in developing countries, unless most of the farming is undertaken by small-scale farmers. The FAO State of Food Insecurity in the World Report 2008 argues that local production by small-scale farmers is the best way of ensuring food security at the household level in developing countries, because it both increases food availability and provides income and employment. Small-scale farming may be the only livelihood in many developing countries where there are few alternative forms of employment. It has also been argued that small farms are not backward, unproductive and inefficient, but can be more productive and more efficient and contribute more to economic development than large-scale industrialized agriculture.[26] Trade liberalization of agriculture across the world is resulting in an increasing concentration of agricultural production, however, benefiting large-scale farming and transnational corporations.[27] This is especially true for developing countries, but is also affecting family farms in developed countries as liberalization pushes their agriculture towards industrialization (including increasing use of biotechnology) and concentration (including corporate control of the food chain). Concentration moves production away from the site of consumption and away from local food security.

Although food aid is imperative to protect the right to food in situations of armed conflict and other disasters, it can act as a disincentive to produce in countries where production is still possible, thereby affecting the right of people to feed themselves. It is necessary to ensure that food aid policy does not disrupt local production and relates directly to the priorities of countries in need rather than to the needs of donor countries to remove their domestic surpluses.

Developed countries still tend to have more autonomy to control their local food security compared with developing countries. Developed countries have been slower to liberalize agriculture, despite promises made under the WTO Agreement on Agriculture to create a level playing field in the agricultural trading system in terms of market access, export subsidies and domestic support,[28] and despite promises made at the WTO Hong Kong conference in December 2005. Agriculture has continued to be protected and supported in many developed economies, while developing countries have had to liberalize under structural adjustment programmes (removing all subsidy support as well as drastically reducing import barriers to food imports well beyond what is formally required under WTO liberalization).[29] This has created an uneven playing field in which subsidies of developed countries act as a disincentive to agricultural production in developing countries.[30] In addition, under the WTO rules, it is almost impossible to reverse liberalization measures, even if they have had a disastrous impact on local-level food security.

Civil society organizations have called for WTO to recognize the primacy of human rights law over international trade law in the next round of trade negotiations.[31] Those NGOs claim that WTO agreements have had a negative effect on human rights. The Agreement on Agriculture has been blamed for terrible impacts on the livelihoods and food security of peasant farmers in developing countries, as those countries have been forced to liberalize and open up their markets without significant reciprocal liberalization of the developed countries in terms of market access, export subsidies or domestic supports. The Agreement on Trade-Related Aspects of Intellectual Property Rights has also been widely criticized. In particular, concerns have been expressed that the Agreement could be implemented in a way that limits the access of peasant farmers to seed for replanting. The Agreement also has been criticized for not actively protecting the cultural heritage and indigenous knowledge from patenting by external interests.[32] NGOs have also raised recent concerns that access to water will be negatively affected if water (the provision of drinking water) is included under the General Agreement on Trade in Services, although WTO disputes this in its article entitled 'The WTO is not after your water!'.[33]

4.1.3 Progress in international trade negotiations and the right to food

In the last decade, some States have begun to call for the right to food to be taken up in WTO negotiations, such as a proposal put forward by Norway, described below. A number of developing countries have also proposed concrete steps to protect their food security through the inclusion of a 'development/food security box' in the Agreement on Agriculture (see below). This issue is clearly extremely complex because food security is important to all countries, but it is the developing countries who face the greatest challenge as food security remains a daily struggle for many families there.

A proposal of Norway called for WTO commitments that do not conflict with States' obligations to respect the right to food. The proposal argued:

> The WTO policy reform must be undertaken in ways consistent with other relevant multilateral commitments, such as the Convention on Biological Diversity and commitments relating to the right to food. Since the Universal Declaration of Human Rights was adopted by the United Nations in 1948, a number of international legal instruments and recom-

mendations relating to nutritional concerns and the right to food have been developed, recognizing the fundamental right of everyone to be free from hunger and emphasizing the responsibility of the State in this respect.[34]

The proposal also argued that food security is a 'public good'. They suggested that the public good nature of agriculture demands that some levels of subsidy are needed to support local domestic production, but argued for tighter disciplines on export-oriented production. This was a concrete suggestion to ensure that subsidies are not used to subsidize the export sector (to avoid acting as a disincentive to the production of other countries):[35]

NTCs (non-trade concerns) often have public goods characteristics. While private goods can be exchanged in a market, NTCs often have public goods characteristics for which, by definition, functioning markets are lacking. Furthermore, the scope for market creation seems to be limited. While market creation is possible in certain cases, government intervention may be justified in order to correct the under-provisioning of NTCs with public good characteristics and to internalize externalities.

Contrary to most private goods for which international markets exist, NTCs, in general, cannot be ensured through trade, but need to be provided by domestic agricultural production. To some extent food security represents an exception, as both domestic production and a predictable and stable trading system contribute to increased food security. The domestic safeguarding of NTCs varies substantially from country to country, as well as within countries, depending on national priorities (i.e. demand side variations) and the cost levels that each country's agricultural sector is facing (i.e. supply side variations).

The 'public good' nature of food security is used to justify a minimum of domestic agricultural production in Norway for partial self-sufficiency (50 per cent) alongside trade. In the case of developing countries, however, the 'public good' nature of food security may be very different. If the capacity of a whole country to develop is severely restrained as millions of mothers give birth to millions of babies who are physically and mentally retarded, so that improving nutrition and reducing undernourishment could help lift a whole country out of poverty – is that not also a 'public good'?

A number of developing countries, namely, Cuba, Dominican Republic, El Salvador, Haiti, Honduras, Kenya, Nicaragua, Pakistan, Sri Lanka, Uganda and Zimbabwe, submitted a proposal calling for a 'food security box', which recognizes the specific food security needs and special situations of developing countries, although it does not mention the right to food.[36] The proposal called for exemptions under the 'box' that would give developing countries greater policy autonomy to protect the production of basic food staples. They argued that food security is fundamental for national security and propose a 'development box' based on the following basic objectives and policy instruments that aim to achieve them:

(a) To protect and enhance developing countries' domestic food production capacity, in particular in key staples;
(b) To increase food security and food accessibility for all, especially the poorest;
(c) To provide or at least sustain existing employment for the rural poor;
(d) To protect farmers who are already producing an adequate supply of key agricultural products from the onslaught of cheap imports;
(e) To ensure flexibility to provide the necessary supports to small farmers, especially in terms of increasing their production capacity and competitiveness;
(f) To stop the dumping of cheap subsidized imports on developing countries.

Non-governmental organizations further suggested that 'food security crops' should be defined as crops that are either staple foods in the country concerned or are the main sources of livelihood for poor farmers.[37] Of course, there would still be problems, if developing countries cannot afford to support local production of small farmers and if developed country protection continues to limit market access opportunities. However, the proposal made some concrete suggestions for steps towards changing the WTO Agreement on Agriculture so that it meets the food security needs of the developing countries and evens out the uneven playing field that currently exists. It made the following technical suggestions that instruments should be included that allow:[38]

- Choice of which products to liberalize. All developing countries should be able to use a positive list approach to declare which agricultural products or sectors they would like disciplined under the provisions of the Agreement on Agriculture. That is, only the products that are declared by a country are subject to the commitments of the Agreement;
- Re-evaluation of tariffs. Allow developing countries to re-evaluate and adjust their tariff levels. Where it has been established that cheap imports are destroying or threatening domestic producers, developing countries should be allowed to raise their tariff boundaries on key products to protect food security. Furthermore, the countries of the Organization for Economic Cooperation and Development that continue to have very high tariff peaks and escalations should drastically reduce those tariff levels, especially for products of interest to developing countries;

- Flexibility in levels of domestic subsidies. Developing countries should be allowed an additional 10 per cent on their de minimis support level, that is, bringing the level from 10 to 20 per cent;
- Protection against dumping. Dumping in any form must be prohibited. All forms of export subsidies (direct or indirect) by developed countries must be eliminated immediately;
- Protection against monopolies. Competition policy in agriculture must be addressed in the review. Developing countries must be given an easily accessible mechanism to protect themselves against the abuse of monopoly power and to seek compensation.

WTO negotiations must take into account these suggestions of the developing countries and must consider the need to protect the right to food. All economic policy changes must not endanger life through malnutrition, but guarantee at least a basic minimum that respects the right to food and the right to life. More attention must be paid to understanding that trade liberalization in itself does not automatically bring growth.[39] More attention must also be paid to the World Bank's understanding that economic growth does not necessarily benefit the poor, just as growth in itself does nothing to reduce pre-existing inequality.[40] Food security is best protected through small-scale farming and the principles of local food security.

If the right to food is not taken up by the WTO, we must search for other means of integrating human rights and the right to food into the rules of international trade. For example, it is important to look at the extension of human rights obligations to non-State actors. Unlike their member States, international organizations such as the WTO and the Bretton Woods institutions are not subject to international human rights law as such, because they are not parties to the international human rights treaties. However, this understanding is changing, as new work is being done on the obligations of non-State actors, including multinational companies. It is very important to examine developments in this field.

Another key area is the debate on the TRIPS Agreement. In the last decade, there were extremely important developments within the debate on HIV/AIDS and patents on medicines to treat epidemics. Developments in Brazil and South Africa suggested that there may be a victory of the right to health over the right to intellectual property patents. This is very relevant to the right to food, in terms of the long-running debate over biotechnology and patents covering seeds and genetic resources. The HIV/AIDS case could provide a useful framework for examining the situation in relation to questions over the TRIPS Agreement and concerns that patents on seeds limit the access of peasant farmers to seeds for replanting and effectively deny indigenous communities their cultural heritage and knowledge. The commitments undertaken by States in the International Treaty on Plant Genetic Resources for Food and Agriculture should also be respected.

4.2 Extraterritorial obligations of states to the right to food[41]

In the current context of globalization and strong international interdependence, the national Government is not always able to protect its citizens from the impacts of decisions taken in other countries. As S.I. Skogly has stated, the strict territorial application of human rights obligations is now outdated.[42] In such a globalized, interconnected world, the actions taken by one Government may have negative impacts on the right to food of individuals living in other countries. For example, international trade in agriculture is one clear case, as it is widely recognized that subsidies to farmers in developed countries have negative impacts on farmers and the right to food in developing countries if food products are 'dumped' on developing countries.[43] All countries should therefore ensure that their policies do not contribute to human rights violations in other countries.

The issue of extraterritorial obligations in relation to human rights has been debated mostly in relation to civil and political rights. Civil and political human rights instruments contain explicit territorial and jurisdictional limitations, and it has therefore been argued that extraterritorial obligations in relation to these rights do not exist at all. However, in spite of these explicit limitations, several monitoring bodies at the international and regional levels have nonetheless affirmed that human rights obligations cannot simply stop at territorial borders. The European Court of Human Rights, for example, held in the *Loizidou v. Turkey* case that 'responsibility of Contracting Parties can be involved because of acts of their authorities, whether performed within or outside national boundaries, which produce effects outside their own territory'.[44]

Unlike civil and political rights, the legal instruments on economic, social and cultural rights do not contain any territorial or jurisdictional limitations. On the contrary, there are explicit legal commitments to cooperate for the realization of economic, social and cultural rights of all individuals without limitations. It therefore cannot be argued that extraterritorial obligations toward these rights do not exist at all. Much work is currently being done by academic institutions and NGOs to better understand the definition and content of these obligations. This includes studies by the International Council on Human Rights Policy,[45] FIAN, Bread for the World and the Evangelischer Entwicklungsdienst,[46] 3D – Trade, Human Rights, Equitable Economy and Realizing Rights: The Ethical Globalization Initiative,[47] and by many academics, including S.I. Skogly,[48] F. Coomans and M.T. Kamminga.[49] There is also the work of the CESCR[50] and the Sub-

Commission for the Promotion and Protection of Human Rights, including the studies by Asbjørn Eide.[51] This work shows that States have responsibilities under international law towards people living in other countries, both through their own actions and through their decisions taken as members of international organizations.[52]

4.2.1 Legal framework for extraterritorial obligations

Since the creation of the United Nations, States have undertaken to cooperate to promote human rights, including the right to food. By the adoption of the Charter of the United Nations (Articles 55 and 56), the Universal Declaration of Human Rights (Articles 22 and 28), the International Covenant on Economic, Social and Cultural Rights (Articles 2 (1) and 11) and the Convention on the Rights of the Child (Articles 4 and 24 (4)), States have undertaken to cooperate for the full realization of all economic, social and cultural rights, including the right to food. As the CESCR has stated, international cooperation is therefore an obligation of all States.[53] States which do not have sufficient resources at their disposal to ensure economic, social and cultural rights, including the right to food, have an obligation to seek international support, and States which are in a position to assist others have an obligation to do so.[54] The Committee on the Rights on the Child has also stated that 'When States ratify the Convention, they take upon themselves obligations not only to implement it within their jurisdiction, but also to contribute, through international cooperation, to global implementation.'[55]

The right to food under the International Covenant on Economic, Social and Cultural Rights contains the most important and clearest commitment to cooperate. By adopting the treaty, States have undertaken to cooperate – without any territorial or jurisdictional limitations – to ensure the realization of the right to food and the fundamental right to be free from hunger (Articles 2, 11(1) and 11(2)).[56] Taking these commitments into account, the CESCR suggested a framework for extraterritorial obligations that mirrors the national obligations established under the right to food to respect, protect and fulfil the right to food of all individuals within its territory and subject to its jurisdiction, stating that: '

States parties should take steps to respect the enjoyment of the right to food in other countries, to protect that right, to facilitate access to food and to provide the necessary aid when required.'[57]

In the United Nations Millennium Declaration, as well as in the World Food Summit Declaration and Plan of Action (1996), States have further recognized their collective responsibility and have undertaken to halve, by the year 2015, the proportion of people who suffer from hunger and who are unable to reach or to afford safe drinking water.[58]

The CESCR and a number of scholars have argued that extraterritorial obligations should be framed in the same tripartite typology as States obligations at the national level, that is to respect, protect and fulfil the right to food.[59] Non-governmental organizations, such as FIAN, Bread for the World and the Evangelischer Entwicklungsdienst have adopted the same approach, although they have further clarified that the primary obligation to implement the right to food rests with the home Government, so another government cannot be obliged to guarantee complete implementation of the right to food in other countries, but only to assist, so a better formulation would be 'the obligation to support to fulfil' the right to food in other countries.[60] This clarification is important. It underlines that the principal obligation to guarantee the right to food is incumbent on the national government, but other States, if they have available resources, have a complementary obligation to help the national State, when it does not have the resources to realize the right to food of its population.

From our perspective, to fully comply with their obligations under the right to food, States must respect, protect and support the fulfilment of the right to food of people living in other territories. The obligation to respect is a minimum obligation which requires States to ensure that their policies and practices do not lead to violations of the right to food in other countries. The obligation to protect requires States to ensure that their own citizens and companies, as well as other third parties subject to their jurisdiction, including transnational corporations, do not violate the right to food in other countries. The obligation to support the fulfilment of the right to food requires States, depending on the availability of resources, to facilitate the realization of the right to food in other countries and to provide the necessary aid when required.

The extraterritorial obligation to respect the right to food

The extraterritorial obligation to respect the right to food requires States to ensure that their policies and practices do not lead to violations of the right to food for people living in other countries. The obligation to respect is a negative obligation which implies that governments must refrain from taking certain actions that have negative effects on the right to food. This obligation does not require any resources to be provided. It is rather simply the obligation to 'do no harm'. It also includes refraining from taking decisions within WTO, IMF or the World Bank that can lead to violations of the right to food in other countries.

To respect the right to food, States should refrain from implementing food embargoes which endanger the right to food of individuals in other countries. According to the CESCR, States should refrain at all time from food embargoes or similar measures which endanger conditions for food production and access to food in other countries or prevent the supply of water, as well as goods and services essential for securing the right to water.[61] Food and water should never be used as instruments of political or economic pressure.

States should also refrain at all time from policies of which the effects can be foreseen or that they are aware will have negative effects on the right to food. This means, for example, that Governments should not subsidize agricultural production that will be exported to primarily agrarian developing countries, as it can be seen in advance that the right to food of people living in those countries will be seriously negatively affected as their livelihoods will be destroyed and they will not be able to purchase food, even if the food is cheaper. In Mexico, for example, it is estimated that up to 15 million Mexican farmers and their families (many from indigenous communities) may be displaced from their livelihoods as a result of the North American Free Trade Agreement and competition with subsidized United States maize.[62]

States should also refrain from taking decisions within WTO, IMF or the World Bank that can lead to violations of the right to food in other countries. It is evident that decisions taken by a Ministry of Agriculture or a Ministry of Finance within WTO, IMF and the World Bank are acts of the authorities of a State that can produce effects outside their own territory. If these effects lead to violations of the right to food, then these decisions must be revised. In Niger, for example, the structural adjustment programme required by the IMF – such as the privatization of the national veterinary office – had detrimental consequences on the national pastoralist sector and on the right to food of nomad and peasant communities.[63]

The extraterritorial obligation to protect the right to food
The extraterritorial obligation to protect the right to food requires States to ensure that third parties subject to their jurisdiction (such as their own citizens or transnational corporations), do not violate the right to food of people living in other countries. This obligation does not undermine direct obligations that third parties, including transnational corporations, can have in relation to the right to food,[64] but rather puts a duty on the State to regulate its corporations and non-State actors in order to protect the inhabitants of other countries.[65]

With the increasing monopoly control by transnational corporations over all elements of the food chain, from the production, trade and processing to the marketing and retailing of food, as well as over the majority of water concessions worldwide,[66] it is becoming more difficult for less powerful national Governments to regulate transnational corporations working within their territory to respect human rights, making it essential that the often more powerful 'home' States engage in adequate regulation. In the process of water privatization, for example, steps should be taken by 'home' States to ensure that the policies and activities of transnational corporations respect the right to water of all people in the countries where they are working.[67]

Many countries have already made such commitments. For example, in the Guidelines for Multinational Enterprises of the Organization for Economic Cooperation and Development, OECD member States have already agreed that multinational enterprises of OECD should respect the human rights of those affected by their activities abroad (paragraph II.2). Other examples to protect human rights, including the right to food, in other countries, include tort laws in Australia, Canada and the United Kingdom of Great Britain and Northern Ireland, under which transnational corporations can be held responsible for complicity in human rights violations abroad. In the United States, the 1789 Alien Tort Claim Act has also provided a legal basis under which any transnational corporations (not only those based in the United States) can be held accountable for complicity with human rights violations in other countries.[68] The European and Australian Parliaments, which have called for regulation over the activities of their transnational corporations in other countries, also have taken this obligation into account.[69]

The extraterritorial obligation to support the fulfilment of the right to food

Governments also have a duty to support the fulfilment of the right to food in poorer countries. Developing States that do not possess the necessary resources for the full realization of the right to food are obliged to actively seek international assistance,[70] and wealthier States have a responsibility to help. This requires States, depending on the availability of their resources, to cooperate with other countries to support their fulfilment of the right to food.

The obligation to support the fulfilment is constituted by both the obligation to *facilitate* and *provide*. The obligation to facilitate realization of the right to food does not necessarily require resources or international aid. It rather requires that all countries should cooperate to provide an enabling environment that allows the realization of the right to food in all countries. As per Article 28 of the Universal Declaration of Human Rights, 'Everyone is entitled to a social and international order in which the rights and freedoms set forth in this Declaration can be fully realized.' For example, equitable trade rules would enable all countries to realize the right to food, both in their own countries and in other countries. Development cooperation, already undertaken by wealthier countries, must also help to create an enabling environment.[71] Wealthier governments already recognize their responsibility to facilitate the realization of the right to food in other countries. In the Monterrey Consensus of the International Conference on Financing for Development, in March 2002, States reaffirmed the goal of providing 0.7 per cent of gross national product for development assistance to developing countries and 0.15–0.20 per cent to least developed countries.[72] The representative of Japan, for example, made the following statement before the CESCR:

> Japan takes the basic position that human rights are a universal value and a legitimate international concern common among all human beings. Japan believes that development assistance should contribute to the promotion and protection of human rights. Examples of Japanese development assistance to promote economic, social, and cultural rights in other countries are as follows:... (c) Assistance to realize the fundamental right to be free from hunger. A citizen's fundamental right to be free from hunger can be ensured by stabilizing the agriculture, forestry and fishery industries in a country. From this point of view, Japan emphasizes assistance to develop agriculture and agricultural villages in developing countries through agricultural infrastructure projects such as irrigation and drainage projects, farm products research and test projects, dissemination of information related to cultivation, projects for organizing agricultural villages, and projects for agricultural product distribution. Japan also contributes to famine relief in the form of agricultural development assistance through general grants, marine grants, and disaster-relief grants.[73]

To support the fulfilment of the right to food, Governments also have an obligation to *provide*, which means to provide assistance, according to available resources, when individuals are suffering in another country, such as a situation of widespread famine. At the same time, emergency aid must always be provided in ways that do not destroy livelihoods or are incoherent with development objectives in order to avoid negative effects on the longer term realization of the right to food. Most Governments already recognize a responsibility to provide emergency assistance when this is required to support the fulfilment of the right to food in a situation, such as terrible famine or armed conflict.[74] The obligation to provide the necessary aid when required is particularly important in the context of disaster relief and humanitarian assistance. This has been recognized by States in the Voluntary Guidelines on the right to adequate food (guideline 16). As the CESCR stated:

> States have a joint and individual responsibility, in accordance with the Charter of the United Nations, to cooperate in providing disaster relief and humanitarian assistance in times of emergency, including assistance to refugees and internally displaced persons. Each State should contribute to this task in accordance with its ability. The role of the World Food Programme (WFP) and the Office of the United Nations High Commissioner for Refugees (UNHCR), and increasingly that of UNICEF and FAO is of particular importance in this respect and should be strengthened. Priority in food aid should be given to the most vulnerable populations.[75]

At the same time, all States should also ensure that food aid will be provided in accordance with their human rights obligations. Priority should be given to the most vulnerable populations, and human rights principles, including non-discrimination in the distribution of food aid, should be upheld at all time. As the CESCR underlined, food aid should also be provided in ways which do not adversely affect local producers and local markets, it should be organized in ways that facilitate the return to food self-reliance of the beneficiaries, and it must be safe and culturally acceptable to the recipient population.[76]

4.3 The responsibilities of international organizations concerning the right to food[77]

Given the powerful role that multilateral organizations such as IMF, World Bank and WTO play in determining economic policies, particularly in countries in the South, these organizations can have an important impact on human rights. There is no doubt, for example, that the programmes of economic reform imposed by IMF and the World Bank on indebted countries have a profound and direct influence on the situation of the right to food and food security in many countries. However, given that these organizations are intergovernmental organizations and that they are effectively directed by Governments to undertake such actions, it is a controversial question whether these organizations can be considered as autonomous legal subjects with obligations under international human rights law. For example, some authors think that WTO is merely a mechanism for negotiation between States and that member Governments are therefore accountable for all the rules and actions of WTO. Others think however, that organizations such as the World Bank and IMF, despite having State Governments on their executive council, still take autonomous actions and that it is important to consider the direct responsibilities of intergovernmental organizations as institutions in themselves.

4.3.1 Key impacts of international organizations on the right to food

The activities of the World Bank, IMF and WTO are in very different ways intimately related to policymaking as well as development projects, particularly in developing countries.

Many NGOs and civil society organizations have documented violations of the right to food that have occurred in the context of programmes and projects funded by the World Bank.[78] Typical cases include large development projects involving the constructions of dams in areas occupied by minorities or indigenous peoples who are forcibly displaced without due process and compensation. Other examples include projects financed by the World Bank in the mining or water infrastructure sectors that clearly carry adverse consequences for the human rights and even open violations of the indigenous' rights to their land, food and water. For example, the Kedung Ombo Project for a dam construction in Indonesia that started in 1985 with a loan approved by the World Bank and was completed in 1989, reportedly involved forced displacement without compensation and other related abuses. This project allegedly involved the displacement of nearly 12,000 people who lost their land and their means of subsistence as a result thereof. Another example is the implementation of a coal-mining project in Jarkhand, India, funded by the World Bank, which led to important involuntary resettlements and the destruction of many houses and sources of livelihood. In this case, despite clear recommendations made by the World Bank's own Inspection Panel in November 2002, the affected people had still not been adequately compensated and rehabilitated.[79]

The far-reaching policies of structural adjustment and poverty reduction strategies encouraged by the World Bank and IMF have significant impacts on the capacity of the nation State to meet its obligations in ensuring the right to food. Many NGOs and civil society organizations claim that the economic policies advocated by the World Bank and IMF through programmes such as structural adjustment programmes or poverty reduction strategies have had negative impacts on the right to food of large sections of the populations of many countries, particularly in Africa, but also in Asia and Latin America. Far from improving food security for the most vulnerable populations, these programmes have often resulted in a deterioration of food security among the poorest. The strong advocacy pursued by the World Bank and IMF for the drastic reduction of public spending, the privatization of public enterprises, trade liberalization and the flexibilization of financial, labour and land markets has had negative impacts on the right to food and other economic, social and cultural rights. One study on India, for example, suggests that when in July 1991 the Government introduced the budgetary reforms advocated by IMF, the resulting cuts in spending affected subsidies for staples and basic foodstuffs that supported the poorest. With the price of rice rising by 50 per cent and the revenue of workers falling dramatically, the three months following the introduction of the reform saw at least 73 deaths by starvation reported in the State of Andra Pradesh.[80] In Zambia, after a programme of rapid structural adjustment was introduced in the 1990s, an evaluation made by IMF itself recognized that the liberalization in agriculture had caused hardship for poor Zambians, with maize consumption falling by 20 per cent between 1990 and 1997 as the poorest could not afford enough to eat.[81] In most cases, the World Bank and IMF have not required that prior to introducing rapid adjustment measures safety nets be put in place that would support the poorest and most vulnerable populations, an omission which has resulted in the cases of starvation deaths in India and severe malnourishment in Zambia described above.

The rules of WTO, particularly the rules on trade in agriculture, also have a significant impact on the policies that Governments can choose in terms of maintaining their food security.[82] Much of the trade liberalization so far undertaken in agriculture, particularly in developing countries, has been required under IMF and World Bank programmes, and not WTO. Nonetheless, WTO has had an important impact through the way it 'locks in' and formalizes liberalization measures, leaving countries unable to reverse measures that might have significant negative impacts on food insecurity and malnutrition. The widely recognized inequities in the current WTO rules on agriculture, detailed in reports such as *Rigged Rules and Double Standards* published by Oxfam also severely affect small farmers and put developing countries at a serious disadvantage compared to developed countries.[83] The heavy production and export subsidies that OECD countries give to their farmers of more than US$349 billion per year (almost US$1billion per day) means that you can find subsidised European fruit and vegetables on a market stall in Dakar, Senegal at prices cheaper than local produce. Although developed countries, including the European Union, made promises at the WTO's Hong Kong conference in December 2005 to eliminate export subsidies that result in dumping, there has been little in concrete progress so far, and the WTO continues to enforce rules that are inequitable.

4.3.2 The legal framework: international organizations and the right to food

This section outlines a legal framework for the responsibilities of these international intergovernmental organizations, based on the three levels of obligations *to respect, protect* and *support the fulfilment of* the right to food. As with the previous section on extraterritorial obligations, this section draws on work that is currently being done by academic institutions and NGOs to better understand the definition and content of these responsibilities of international organizations in relation to human rights, some of which focusing on the right to food. This includes studies by the International Federation of Human Rights Leagues,[84] 3D – Trade, Human Rights, Equitable Economy and FORUM-ASIA,[85] FIAN[86] and by many academics, including S. I. Skogly,[87] A. Clapham,[88] M. Darrow[89] and B. Ghazi,[90] as well as the CESCR[91] and the Sub-commission for the Promotion and Protection of Human Rights.[92]

A number of these studies have pointed out that these institutions are bound directly by human rights norms in two ways. First, through customary law under which there are direct obligations to human rights standards[93] and secondly through the responsibility of international cooperation that is enshrined in Article 2 (1) of the International Covenant on Economic, Social and Cultural Rights, as well as in Article 11 on the right to freedom from hunger.[94] Most intergovernmental organizations are also bound to respect the principles of the Charter of the United Nations through their relationship agreements with the United Nations. This issue of the direct obligations of intergovernmental organizations is extremely important.

There is no question today that international organizations such as the World Bank, IMF and WTO have legal personality under international law.[95] In its advisory opinion on Reparation for Injuries Suffered in the Service of the United Nations, the International Court of Justice, in 1949, interpreted an international organization as a subject of international law and capable of possessing international rights and duties. As subjects of international law, international organizations are thus bound by any obligations incumbent upon them under general rules of international law, under their constitutions or under international agreements to which they are parties.[96] It is clear that international law is binding on international organizations such as the World Bank, IMF and WTO, including as concerns the human right to food.

In its resolution on the right to food,[97] the UN General Assembly supported this view and requested all international organizations, within their respective mandates, to take fully into account the need to promote the effective realization of the right to food for all (paragraph 9) and invited:

> all relevant international organizations, including the World Bank and the International Monetary Fund, to promote policies and projects that have a positive impact on the right to food, to ensure that partners respect the right to food in the implementation of common projects, to support strategies of Member States aimed at the fulfilment of the right to food and to avoid any actions that could have a negative impact on the realization of the right to food. (paragraph 16)

In many instances, international organizations, particularly IMF and the World Bank, have disputed their responsibilities towards human rights, on the ground of three main arguments. First, they argue that they are multilateral organizations, directed to take action by Governments and therefore do not have autonomous responsibilities in relation to human rights. However, it is clear that these organizations are not only driven by the decisions of their member States, as they have important autonomous decision-making powers. The World Bank is governed by a Board of Governors representing all member States, but its day-to-day business is run by a Board of Executive Directors, with five out of 24 members appointed by the largest shareholders (the United States being the largest with over 15 per cent of shares, giving it a practical veto power in decision-making at the Bank). Although it has been claimed that the World Bank Group is 'owned by its shareholders', the fact that the Board of Executive Directors and the largest shareholders control the activities of the organization suggests that it does take autonomous decisions in its actions. Similarly, although the highest governing body in IMF is the Board of Directors, which represents the whole membership, daily management rests with an Executive Board and autonomous decisions can also be taken by this Executive Board.

In WTO, on the other hand, it is clear that most decisions are taken by the Ministerial Conference or the General Council, both made up of Member States. For this reason it has often been characterized as a 'member-driven' consensus-based organization, driven in other words by Governments, with no separate legal identity of its own.[98] But WTO does also have its own organs and agents through which it operates. The secretariat, for example, has a large margin of discretion to facilitate the implementation, administration and operation of the agreements and to this end is engaged in wide-ranging technical assistance projects. Some of its organs, such as the Dispute Settlement Body (DSB) are also required to achieve decisions, including interpretations of WTO law, that are essential to the organization. As an international organization, WTO should thus also be bound by international human rights, including the right to food.

Secondly, according to the principle that international organizations have only rights and duties commensurate to their functions and powers,[99] the World Bank and IMF have argued that their constitutive instruments (Articles of Agreement) preclude them from using political considerations in their activities. However, the suggestion that this precludes them from dealing directly with human rights is not well founded. Relevant provisions (for instance Article IV, section 10, of the Articles of Agreement of the Bank) can be interpreted so as to allow those institutions to integrate human rights considerations into their activities.[100] Furthermore, in accordance with the same principle of functional legal personality, the World Bank, IMF and WTO all carry out activities and perform functions that have an important, and sometimes crucial, influence on the realization of the right to food and other rights in member States. In carrying out those functions these organizations should therefore be bound to ensure respect for human rights, including the right to food, in a way commensurate to their power.

Lastly, IMF and the World Bank have argued that they do not have responsibilities in the field of human rights because they are organizations and not States, and in that capacity have not ratified the respective human rights treaties.[101] It would therefore follow that as IMF, the World Bank and WTO have not ratified the International Covenant on Economic, Social and Cultural Rights, they would not be bound by obligations in respect to the right to adequate food. However, such an argument overlooks the widely recognized view that human rights find their source not only in treaties but also in customary international law. The obligation to realize the right to adequate food has become today part of customary international law, given the almost universal ratification of treaties that contain it (in particular the International Covenant and the Convention on the Rights of the Child) and the constant practice of States in reaffirming the right to food and the fundamental right to be free from hunger at the World Food Summits in 1996 and 2002 and other international conferences, as well as in the General Assembly and the Commission on Human Rights.[102] There is no reason to assume that international economic organizations are not bound by general international law on the right to food and other human rights. Furthermore, as in the case of the European Union, international organizations are bound by general principles of law recognized by civilized nations, which can be drawn from national legal systems.[103] Many national constitutions recognize the right to food or require the interpretation of their provisions to be in accordance with international human rights law where the right to food is fully recognized. Finally, most member States of these international economic organizations have ratified at least one human rights treaty in which the right to food is contained. Clearly, international organizations cannot be free to do what their constituents are not permitted to do.

In its resolution 2005/17 on globalization and human rights, the Commission on Human Rights affirmed the need for multilateral institutions 'to recognize, respect and protect all human rights'. In their final report, the Special Rapporteurs of the Sub-commission for the Promotion and Protection of Human Rights J. Oloka-Onyango and Deepika Udagama noted that 'reiteration of the legal obligation of international organizations such as the WTO, the World Bank and the IMF is deemed necessary in order to emphasize the point that these institutions must, at a minimum, recognize, respect, and protect human rights'.[104] However, as many others have suggested, these organizations would also have obligations to positively promote and assist States in their efforts to protect and realize the right to adequate food of their populations.[105] As the CESCR has argued:

> International organizations...have a strong and continuous responsibility to take whatever measures they can to assist governments to act in ways which are compatible with their human rights obligations and to seek to devise policies and programmes which promote respect for those rights. It is particularly important to emphasize that the realms of trade, finance and investment are in no way exempt from these general principles and that the international organizations with specific responsibilities in those areas should play a positive and constructive role in relation to human rights.[106]

In order to fully comply with their obligations under the right to food, international organizations must respect, protect and support the fulfilment of the right to food by their member States.

The obligation of international organizations to respect the right to food

The obligation to respect is a minimum obligation, which requires international organizations to ensure that their advice, policies and practices do not lead to violations of the right to food.[107] This means that, at least with regard to the World Bank and IMF, international organizations should have minimum negative obligations to respect or not to do harm in relation to the realization of the right to food. This prohibition of doing harm seems to be universally recognized. This means that these organizations should not promote 'development' projects that would result in forced displacement or the destruction of sources of livelihood, especially in cases without proper compensation and rehabilitation for the affected populations. It also means that actions and decisions of the World Bank, IMF and WTO should not increase people's food insecurity in a given country, including the poorest people. Adjustment measures should not be implemented without carrying out impact studies for vulnerable groups, and putting in place necessary safety nets in advance, to ensure that they will not result in starvation or chronic malnutrition. WTO would also have to take due account of the human rights obligations of its members and should advise against the adoption of trade policies that may have negative impacts on the right to food.

The obligation of international organizations to protect the right to food
The obligation to protect requires international organizations to ensure that their partners, whether states or private actors, including transnational corporations, do not violate the right to food, including in cases where concessions and contracts are granted, or in common projects that could threaten people's livelihoods and food security. Those organs of WTO that have decision-making power, such as the DSB, should protect the right to food in judicial decisions, and should ensure that interpretations of WTO law are compatible with the human rights obligations of its member States regarding the right to food.

The obligation of international organizations to support the fulfilment of the right to food
The obligation to support the fulfilment of the right to food requires that international organizations facilitate the realization of the right to food and help to provide necessary assistance when required for all people, indigenous, minorities and vulnerable groups. This should include facilitating the capacity of all people to feed themselves, as well as helping to ensure emergency support when they cannot feed themselves for reasons beyond their control. In developing countries, where up to 80 per cent of the population may depend on agriculture, small-scale agriculture should form the basis of food security strategies, as non-agricultural employment is often inadequate to absorb all those forced out of agriculture. WTO should also ensure that trade rules adopted are raising the standard of living in all countries, and not permit the persistence of current inequities in rules on agricultural trade.

4.4 The responsibilities of private actors regarding the right to food: transnational corporations[108]

4.4.1 The impact of transnational corporations on the right to food

In an era of globalization, private actors, particularly large transnational private corporations, have become more powerful than nation states. Yet as the report of the Secretary-General on the impact of the activities and working methods of transnational corporations (TNCs) in 1996 stated, 'the global reach of TNCs is not matched by a coherent global system of accountability'.[109] Despite wielding greater power than ever before, transnational corporations are trying to avoid being held accountable to human rights.

According to UNDP *Human Development Report, 2002*, 'global corporations can have enormous impact on human rights – in their employment practices, in their environmental impact, in their support for corrupt regimes or in their advocacy for policy changes'.[110] As financially powerful lobbying groups, corporations can exert great control over laws, policies and standards applied in their industries, which can result in looser regulation and negative impacts on health, safety, and the price and quality of food.

The top 200 corporations control around a quarter of the world's total productive assets. Many transnational corporations have revenues far exceeding the revenues of the Governments of the countries in which they are operating. According to the United Nations Conference on Trade and Development (UNCTAD), 'Twenty-nine of the world's 100 largest economic entities are transnational corporations (TNCs).'[111] Concentration has produced huge transnational corporations that monopolize the food chain, from the production, trade, processing, to the marketing and retailing of food, narrowing choices for farmers and consumers. Just 10 corporations (which include Aventis, Monsanto, Pioneer and Syngenta) control one-third of the US$ 23 billion commercial seed market and 80 per cent of the US$ 28 billion global pesticide market.[112] Monsanto alone controls 91 per cent of the global market for genetically modified seed.[113] Another 10 corporations, including Cargill, control 57 per cent of the total sales of the world's leading 30 retailers and account for 37 per cent of the revenues earned by the world's top 100 food and beverage companies.[114] In South Africa, Monsanto completely controls the national market for genetically modified seed, 60 per cent of the hybrid maize market and 90 per cent of the wheat market.[115] The participation of private sector corporations in food, agriculture and water sectors may improve efficiency, but concentration of monopoly power also brings a danger that neither small producers, nor consumers will benefit.

There is also the growing power of transnational corporations over the supply of water, as this is increasingly liberalized across the world. The privatization of water services have already been carried out in various parts of the world, including Argentina, Bangladesh, Bolivia, Colombia, Côte d'Ivoire, Hungary, Indonesia, Madagascar, Mexico, Morocco, Nepal, Nigeria, Pakistan, the Philippines, Senegal, Sri Lanka and Tunisia. In many cases, this has largely been because private sector participation in water services has been made a precondition for the provision of loans and grants to developing countries by the IMF and the World Bank. Just two companies, Veolia Environnement, formerly Vivendi Environnement, and Suez Lyonnaise des Eaux, control a majority of private concessions worldwide.

Evidence on water privatization suggests that, while in some cases it can bring increased efficiency it often means higher prices which the poorest cannot afford. The case of Cochabamba, Bolivia, is now famous (see further below).[116] A study on the privatization of water services in Manila to *Ondeo/Suez Lyonnaise des Eaux*[117] shows that this has had some positive effects, with one million more people being connected to the network between 1997 and 2003, but the price also rose by 425 per cent, making it too expensive for the poor. The study suggests that the poorest are doubly discriminated against because the price is at its highest in poorest communities and water quality has deteriorated rapidly in the poorest parts of the city. The lack of effective regulation frequently results in outcomes that are not beneficial to the poor. The study concluded that there was no independent mechanism for accountability and affected populations were not able to participate in the process. Another study on water privatization in Bolivia[118] concluded that deficient legislative and regulatory frameworks and accountability mechanisms, as well as limited user participation and access to information, were the main causes of the failure of the privatization process, together with the fact that the concessions contracts did not prioritize poor regions. The same conclusions have also been presented by WaterAid and Tearfund, in a study funded by the Department for International Development of the Government of the United Kingdom, on the effects of water privatization in 10 developing countries.[119]

In another example, the design of genetically modified seeds has largely been about creating vertical integration between seed, pesticides and production to increase corporate profits. FAO Assistant Director General Louise Fresco revealed that 85 per cent of all plantings of transgenic crops are soybean, maize and cotton, modified to reduce input and labour costs for large-scale production systems, but not designed 'to feed the world or increase food quality'.[120] No serious investments have been made in any of the five most important crops of the poorest, arid countries – sorghum, millet, pigeon pea, chickpea and groundnut. Only 1 per cent of research and development budgets of multinational corporations is spent on crops that might be useful in the developing world.[121] A report by NGO ActionAid which examined the evidence in Africa, Asia and Latin America concluded that 'the expansion of GM is more likely to benefit rich corporations than poor people'.[122]

Although it is generally agreed that genetically modified seeds can in some conditions bring higher yields, NGOs are concerned that increasing control over seeds by a few agro-alimentary corporations will eventually reduce competition, reduce choice and may lead to higher prices for seeds. Many organizations, including FAO, are also concerned that current biotechnology research is driven by commercial imperatives and does not focus on the food security needs of the poorest.[123] It is widely agreed that hunger persists, not because a shortage of food supply, but rather because of very low incomes and unequal access to land, water, credit and markets. NGOs and farmers are particularly concerned by technologies that prevent seeds from regenerating and by the use of intellectual property rights over seeds, which require farmers to purchase new seeds every year, threatening their independence and capacity to generate their own seed stocks. Although it is clear that the patent rights of corporations must be protected, the rights of small farmers must also be protected.[124] And, as Oxfam has pointed out, the rights of consumers must simultaneously be protected, through regulation, labelling, precautionary approaches and legislation on company liability for potential harmful effects on people or the environment.[125]

As another example, several NGOs raised concerns that, as one of the largest food processing corporations in the world, Nestlé dominates the market for breastmilk substitutes in many countries around the world, yet some of its marketing practices violate the internationally agreed International Code of Marketing of Breastmilk Substitutes. They allege that some Nestlé advertising has been found to discourage breastfeeding and to promote bottle feeding, which runs contrary to the Code.[126] United Nations agencies, including UNICEF, have expressed similar concerns.[127]

It is often assumed that corporations are neutral providers of goods and services and that market forces have everyone's interest at heart. However, it is becoming increasingly clear that monopoly control of the food system by transnational corporations can be directed towards seeking monopoly profits, benefiting the companies more than the consumer. The actions of transnational corporations can sometimes directly violate human rights standards, including the right to food. Despite the fact the transnational corporations increasingly control our food system, there are still relatively few mechanisms in place to ensure that they respect standards and do not violate human rights. There is no existing 'social contract' between individuals and TNCs. Over the centuries, human rights standards were developed to ensure that Governments do not abuse their power but, in an age where corporations are now more powerful than Governments, it is becoming imperative to extend the scope of application of human rights norms to ensure that corporations do not abuse their new-found power.

4.4.2 Holding corporations accountable for human rights violations

Under the traditional application of human rights law, it is not well understood how a corporation could be held to account for human rights violations. However, new developments are occurring within human rights law.[128] It is now increasingly understood that there are two key ways of holding corporations to respect human rights – one indirect, the other direct. Corporations can be held to account indirectly, by Governments which have a duty to protect their people and people living in other countries against any negative impacts on the right to food of third parties. From this perspective, Governments are responsible for regulating and preventing the activities of corporations that violate human rights. However, it is increasingly becoming understood that corporations can also be held to account for human rights directly, through the development of direct human rights obligations, intergovernmental instruments and voluntary codes of conduct. As a result of new developments in human rights law, it is becoming increasingly clear that transnational corporations have direct obligations to respect human rights and to avoid complicity with human rights violations carried out by others.

Indirect obligation of the State to protect the right to food

The right to food imposes three levels of obligations on the State: the obligations to respect, protect and fulfil the right to food. It is the obligation to protect the right to food which is the most important obligation in this context, because it implies that Governments must regulate corporations to ensure that they do not commit violations of human rights.

So what does the obligation to protect mean? According to the Maastricht Guidelines:[129]

> The obligation to protect includes the State's responsibility to ensure that private entities or individuals, including transnational corporations over which they exercise jurisdiction, do not deprive individuals of their economic, social and cultural rights. States are responsible for violations of economic, social and cultural rights that result from their failure to exercise due diligence in controlling the behaviour of such non-state actors. (paragraph 18)

The CESCR underlined in its General Comment No. 12 on the right to food that 'the obligation to protect requires measures by the State to ensure that enterprises or individuals do not deprive individuals of their access to adequate food' (paragraph 15). 'As part of their obligations to protect people's resource base for food, States parties should take appropriate steps to ensure that activities of the private business sector and civil society are in conformity with the right to food' (paragraph 27). In relation to water, which is inherently linked to the right to food,[130] the Committee clarifies in *General Comment No. 15* that the obligation to protect includes 'adopting the necessary and effective legislative and other measures to restrain, for example, third parties from denying equal access to adequate water; and polluting and inequitably extracting from water resources, including natural sources, wells and other water distribution systems' (paragraph 23). For the Committee, water is a public good fundamental for life and health (paragraph 1). Therefore, where water services (such as piped water networks, water tankers, access to rivers and wells) are operated or controlled by third parties, an effective regulatory system must be established which includes independent monitoring, genuine public participation and imposition of penalties for non-compliance (paragraph 24).

The most important way to ensure respect for the rights to food and water is to put in place effective domestic legislation to protect people from violations by third parties, including transnational corporations – laws and regulations that protect access to land, drinking water, water for irrigation and a minimum income, and that prohibit interference with people's family or community means of subsistence and so on – and provide effective administrative and judicial remedies.

Governments also have a responsibility to monitor and regulate the activities of their transnational corporations abroad. This means that 'home' States should put in place effective domestic regulation and monitoring mechanisms and provide effective remedies for violations of the right to food if these occur.

Finally, home States have the obligation not to pressure the host State not to regulate the activities of transnational corporations. This has been taken into account, for example, in the Guidelines for Multinational Enterprises of the Organization for Economic Cooperation and Development by which OECD Member States agreed that enterprises should 'respect the human rights of those affected by their activities consistent with the host government's international obligations and commitments' (paragraph II.2), and that 'Governments have the right to prescribe the conditions under which multinational enterprises operate within their jurisdictions, subject to international law' (paragraph I.7). By this agreement, OECD Member States shall use their influence to protect human rights, including the right to food, with regard to the activities of transnational corporations in host States.

Monitoring the indirect obligations of the State to protect the right to food

There are a number of monitoring mechanisms that can be used to ensure that Governments protect the right to food and water by monitoring and regulating the activities of transnational corporations. This includes national and regional courts and human rights institutions, as well as international mechanisms, such as the CESCR, and the special procedures of the Commission on Human Rights.

At the national and regional levels, the obligation to protect human rights is well established in the jurisprudence.[131] For example, one illustrative case of the failure by the State to protect the right to food was the decision by the African Commission on Human and Peoples' Rights, which monitors the African Charter on Human and Peoples' Rights, on communication 155/96, concerning the case brought by the Social and Economic Rights Action Center and the Center for Economic, Social and Cultural Rights against Nigeria at the thirtieth ordinary session of the Commission held in Banjul from 13 to 27 October 2001. This case argued that the Government of Nigeria had failed to regulate or monitor the activities of the oil consortium (Nigerian National Petroleum Company and the Shell Petroleum Development Corporation) in Ogoniland. In its decision, the African Commission found several violations of the African Charter, including violation of the right to food of the Ogoni people. The African Commission ruled that

> Governments have a duty to protect their citizens, not only through appropriate legislation and effective enforcement but also by protecting them from damaging acts that may be perpetrated by private parties.... the right to food requires that the Nigerian Government...not allow private parties to destroy or contaminate food sources, and prevent peoples' effort to feed themselves.

In its conclusions, the African Commission appealed to the Government of Nigeria to ensure protection of the people of Ogoniland, including ensuring adequate compensation to victims of the human rights violations, ensuring relief and resettlement assistance to victims of Government-sponsored raids, and ensuring that any further oil development is monitored by effective and independent oversight bodies for the petroleum industry. This courageous decision must be implemented and should be seen as an example to follow in other similar cases.

Another important example is a case brought to the Inter-American Commission on Human Rights. In 1990, a petition on behalf of the indigenous Huaorani people living in the Oriente region in Ecuador alleged that oil exploitation activities by the Government's own oil company, Petro-Ecuador, and by Texaco, contaminated the water they use for drinking and cooking and the soil in which they cultivate their food. Following a report issued by the Center for Economic and Social Rights,[132] the Inter-American Commission conducted a country visit to Ecuador in November 1994, and in its final report presented in 1997, stated that access to information, participation in decision-making and access to judicial remedies had not been guaranteed to the Huaorani people, and that oil activities in Ecuador were not regulated enough to protect indigenous people.[133]

Case law also exists at the national level, including in South Africa where the Constitution (Articles 7 and 27) obliges the State to protect the right to food, and in India where the Supreme Court stated that the Union and all the state governments shall protect the right of the workers to have access to medical facilities and drinking water.[134]

At the international level, the CESCR is an important mechanism that can help to ensure that Governments do protect their citizens through adequate regulation. An NGO shadow report to the CESCR on the negative impacts of water privatization on the poorest, led to a recommendation from the Committee that the Government of Nepal ensure that projects involving privatization of water supply provide for continued, assured and affordable access to water by local communities, indigenous people, and the most disadvantaged and marginalized groups of society, with adequate regulation and accountability built into the privatization process.[135]

The Office of the Special Rapporteur is another available mechanism mandated to receive communications from various organizations including NGOs, regarding the activities of transnational corporations and the obligations of States to protect the right to food.

Direct obligations of transnational corporations to respect the right to food

States have the primary responsibility to promote and protect human rights, and, as the European Court of Human Rights stated, a State 'could not absolve itself of responsibility by delegating its obligations to private bodies or individuals'.[136] However, transnational corporations should be bound to respect human rights as well as the national law of the host State in which they operate and of the home State in which they are based. It is also becoming increasingly clear that, under international law, intergovernmental organizations' instruments and voluntary commitments, transnational corporations can be held responsible for promoting and securing human rights.

The Universal Declaration of Human Rights proclaims that the obligation to promote respect for human rights and to secure their universal and effective recognition and observance is addressed not only to States but also to 'every individual and every organ of society'. This must include transnational corporations. This interpretation has been confirmed by the General Assembly (in its resolution 42/115) and by the Commission on Human Rights in its resolution 1987/18, in which transnational corporations were urged to ensure that their activities did not adversely affect the process of implementing human rights in developing countries (paragraph 4).

Transnational corporations have direct obligations, at a minimum, to respect the right to food in all their activities and to avoid complicity in violations of the right to food carried out by others, including host

Governments. As the CESCR states in its *General Comment No. 12* on the right to food:

> While only States are parties to the Covenant and are thus ultimately accountable for compliance with it, all members of society – individuals, families, local communities, non-governmental organizations, civil society organizations, as well as the private business sector – have responsibilities in the realization of the right to adequate food. (paragraph 20)[137]

In many cases, transnational corporations have chosen themselves to abide by human rights, adopting human rights policies and Codes of Conduct. In 1999, OECD inventoried 233 codes of conduct, issued mostly by individual corporations.[138] Several companies now have their own policies on human rights. The Shell Corporation, for example, now has a policy on how to protect human rights and when to speak out about human rights violations. Reebok has a policy on child labour, and Nestlé has incorporated into its corporate business principles the standards set out in ILO conventions, the Global Compact principles and the International Code of Marketing of Breastmilk Substitutes. While some of these policies amount to little more than improving their public image, in some cases, corporations are taking real action to respect human rights. Civil society can also help to improve the enforcement and implementation of principles that corporations have signed up to by monitoring their compliance with human rights principles. The voluntary guidelines on the right to food, adopted in November 2004 within the FAO, should also serve to strengthen the framework governing the responsibilities of corporations with respect to the right to food.

Numerous codes of conduct have also been developed at the international level which strengthens accountability for human rights, including the OECD Guidelines for Multinational Enterprises (revised in 2000) under which all Adhering Governments (the OECD States, Argentina, Brazil and Chile) are bound to establish national contact points to handle complaints of violations by a transnational corporation and the 1977 ILO Tripartite Declaration of Principles Concerning Multinational Enterprises and Social Policy. According to the ILO Tripartite Declaration transnational corporations

> should respect the sovereign rights of States, obey the national laws and regulations, give due consideration to local practices and respect relevant international standards. They should respect the Universal Declaration of Human Rights and the corresponding International Covenants adopted by the General Assembly of the United Nations as well as the Constitution of the International Labour Organization and its principles. (paragraph 8)

Others include the International Code of Marketing of Breastmilk Substitutes adopted by the World Health Organization (WHO) and UNICEF and the Code of Ethics for International Trade in Food adopted by the Codex Alimentarius Commission. The Secretary-General's Global Compact initiative, by which transnational corporations can commit themselves to 'support and respect the protection of internationally proclaimed human rights within their sphere of influence' and 'make sure that they are not complicit in human rights abuses' is also an important initiative. Unfortunately however, TNCs refused in June 2004 to adopt any monitoring mechanism that could hold these corporations accountable to their Global Compact promises.

In 2003, a new set of instruments has been proposed to create a strong and coherent system of accountability at the international level – the Norms on the Responsibilities of Transnational Corporations and Other Business Enterprises with Regard to Human Rights, adopted by the Sub-Commission on the Promotion and Protection of Human Rights on 13 August 2003.[139] Based on existing international human rights instruments, these Norms state that 'Within their respective spheres of activity and influence, transnational corporations and other business enterprises have the obligation to promote, secure the fulfilment of, respect, ensure respect of and protect human rights recognized in international as well as national law' (paragraph 1). According to the Norms, transnational corporations:

> shall respect economic, social and cultural rights as well as civil and political rights and contribute to their realization, in particular the rights to ... adequate food and drinking water ... and shall refrain from actions which obstruct or impede the realization of those rights. (paragraph 12)

This was an important attempt to extend human rights, including the right to food, beyond the State-centric paradigm. It also tried to extend the obligations beyond the parent company to include all the suppliers to ensure that companies cannot deny obligations on the basis that they are not operating directly, but have contracted out much of their production or activities to local suppliers (paragraph 15).

The adoption of the Norms by the Sub-Commission was welcomed by several NGOs but it was severely criticized by transnational corporations and other business enterprises, including the United States Council for International Business (USCIB).[140] The Sub-Commission decided to transmit the Norms to the Commission on Human Rights for consideration[141]; however the Norms were never adopted by the Commission on Human Rights or the Human Rights Council. Yet, it should be remembered, as Sir Geoffrey Chandler, Founder-Chair of Amnesty International UK Business Group, 1991–2001, and a former Director of Shell International noted, that the Norms 'were the subject of four public hearings in Geneva in 2000, 2001,

2002 and 2003 and of meetings during March 2001 and 2003 at which representatives of business, unions, NGOs, and the academic world were involved in re-shaping the document'. As Sir Geoffrey Chandler also stated 'The Norms (...) represent an opportunity for companies, not a threat – an opportunity to assist and profit from a safer and more prosperous world.'[142]

Monitoring TNCs and their direct obligations to respect the right to food

There is increasing scope for holding corporations accountable for their human rights obligations through mechanisms at the international level, as well as the national level. At the international level, these mechanisms are still quite weak. For example, there is no monitoring or enforcement mechanism in place for the Global Compact initiative, and the Norms have not been adopted.

Mechanisms at the national level tend to be stronger because national courts can be, and have been, used. As we saw above, examples can be found in court decisions from Australia,[143] Canada[144] and the United Kingdom of Great Britain and Northern Ireland,[145] in which transnational corporations were held responsible (under tort law) for complicity in human rights violations abroad. In the United States, the 1789 Alien Tort Claim Act has provided a legal basis under which any transnational corporations (not only those based in the United States) can be held accountable for complicity with human rights violations in other countries.[146] In India, the Supreme Court has ruled in several cases that corporations must respect human rights.[147] In South Africa this is now possible, given that the Constitution demands respect of human rights and treats corporations as a juridical person. Useful lessons could also be drawn from Uganda and Namibian experiences, where privatization has been accompanied by an extension of the ambit of human rights institutions, including their respective national ombudsman's office and human rights commission to monitor the activities of the privatized entities.[148]

5
The Right to Food in Situations of Armed Conflict[1]

During situations of armed conflict, more people die directly from starvation and malnutrition than from bullets and bombs. Victims are almost inevitably young children, who are extremely susceptible to malnutrition and suffer most as food security is destroyed. Sometimes starvation is used as a political weapon, when crops are destroyed or poisoned and relief supplies are blocked. Sometimes populations are displaced from their homes with the explicit aim of depriving people of resources with which to feed themselves. Very often, vulnerable groups – women, children, prisoners of war, detainees – who have no means to feed themselves are left to starve.

The International Committee of the Red Cross (ICRC) was the first organization to systematically defend and develop the concept of humanitarian law: founded in the aftermath of the Battle of Solferino in 1859, it is today the promoter and guardian of that law. The ICRC argues that armed conflict is one of the key reasons for the lack of food and violations of the right to food, yet the international debate on the right to food has made little reference to international humanitarian law.[2] The ICRC argues that humanitarian law contains many provisions that relate to the protection of access to food in armed conflict situations and must therefore be seen as an essential component of the legal framework that protects the right to food.[3]

5.1 The protection of the right to food under international humanitarian law

The protection of the right to food by international human rights law continues in times of armed conflict.[4] But in these situations, international humanitarian law complements the protection of the right to food.

The bulk of contemporary international humanitarian law rules are contained in the four Geneva Conventions of 1949 and in the two Additional Protocols of 1977. International humanitarian law also includes several treaties that prohibit or regulate the use of certain weapons, for example, the 1997 Convention on the Prohibition of the Use, Stockpiling,

Production and Transfer of Anti-Personnel Mines and on their Destruction ('the Ottawa Convention'),[5] which bans the use of anti-personnel mines. The Rome Statute of the International Criminal Court, adopted on 17 July 1998,[6] contributes to the better implementation of international humanitarian law.

International humanitarian law is designed to protect people and property and to limit the use of certain methods and means of warfare. Its primary objective is to protect persons not taking or no longer taking part in hostilities, such as civilian populations, the wounded or prisoners of war. Women and children are automatically covered as persons not taking part in the hostilities and are given special protection by the conventions and protocols. In contrast to economic, social and cultural rights, international humanitarian law is not subject to progressive realization, but must always be implemented immediately. It also binds both State and non-State actors and there cannot be any derogation from its rules. A basic principle is that parties to an armed conflict must at all times distinguish between the civilian population and combatants and between civilian objects and military objectives and direct attacks only against military objectives. The logic of humanitarian law is to ensure that civilian populations, who do not play a part in the conflict, should never be victims of war.

While international humanitarian law does not mention the 'right to food' as such, many of its provisions are aimed at ensuring that people are not denied access to food during conflict. Some of these rules are preventive in nature, other rules apply to relief and humanitarian assistance once prevention fails, and further rules provide for access to food by specific categories of people. Preventive rules include the prohibition of starvation of civilians as a method of warfare, the prohibition of the destruction of crops, foodstuffs, water and other objects that are essential to the survival of civilian populations, and the prohibition of forced displacement.

5.1.1 Prohibition of starvation of civilians as a method of warfare

The starvation of civilians as a method of warfare is prohibited in both international and non-international armed conflict.[7] That prohibition is violated not only when denial of access to food causes death, but also when the population suffers hunger because of deprivation of food sources or supplies. The prohibition of starvation is elaborated upon in provisions prohibiting attacks against or destruction of items necessary for the survival of the civilian population, including foodstuffs and drinking water.[8] The Second Additional Protocol to the Geneva Conventions of 12 August 1949, relating to the Protection of Victims of Non-International Armed Conflicts, stipulates in Article 14:

> Starvation of civilians as a method of combat is prohibited. It is therefore prohibited to attack, destroy, remove or render useless, for that purpose,

objects indispensable to the survival of the civilian population, such as food-stuffs, agricultural areas for the production of food-stuffs, crops, livestock, drinking water installations and supplies and irrigation works.

Physical destruction includes the destruction of crops by chemical defoliants or the pollution of water reservoirs. Violations would also occur if landmines were to render agricultural areas useless. Under the Rome Statute of the International Criminal Court, intentionally using starvation of civilians as a method of warfare by depriving them of objects indispensable to their survival is considered a war crime in international armed conflict.[9] One example of this occurred when, from April 1992 to June 1995, units of the Yugoslav Federal Army and Serb militias besieged the town of Sarajevo, imposing a food blockage and causing thousands of deaths.[10]

5.1.2 Forced displacement

The prohibition of forced population displacement also seeks to prevent situations of hunger and starvation during armed conflict. Forced displacement is prohibited under Article 49 of the Geneva Convention relative to the Protection of Civilian Persons in Time of War, of 12 August 1949, which prohibits individual or mass forcible transfers of civilians in situations of occupation, except in cases of necessity for the safety of the population or for imperative military reasons. In such cases, evacuation must be effected in a way that guarantees satisfactory 'nutrition'. Similar provisions are made for non-international conflict.[11] Unlawful displacement constitutes a war crime under the Rome Statute of the International Criminal Court in both international and non-international armed conflict.[12]

5.1.3 Rules for specific categories of person

Numerous rules for specific categories of person are also provided for under international humanitarian law and ensure that those who cannot feed themselves are adequately supplied with food and have the right to relief. Categories include prisoners of war, civilian internees and detainees. Special provisions also exist for women and children.

Mothers and pregnant women are afforded special protection under international humanitarian law. Special protection is also provided for pregnant women in occupied territory. Article 89 of the Fourth Geneva Convention provides that women must receive nutritional supplements proportional to their physiological needs. Other articles cover special attention which must be given to women in humanitarian operations. The special protection to be accorded to mothers is essential for the respect of the right to food in armed conflict. To ensure adequate food for women in armed conflict is to protect them and the future health of their children. A State which detains prisoners of war must give them adequate food and water during their captivity and subsequent transfer.[13] And it must, during their internment, ensure that food and water are of adequate quantity, quality and variety.[14] The State is bound by the same obligations concerning civilian prisoners.[15] These people do not participate in the armed conflict; they are innocent, and therefore must be totally protected against the effects of the war.

5.2 Principles and rules for humanitarian assistance

This section looks particularly at the question of humanitarian assistance. Humanitarian food aid in periods of war should be distinguished from food aid in periods of peace. Here we outline the key principles and the most important rules which govern international humanitarian assistance in all situations of armed conflict. These principles, which relate to the neutrality, impartiality and humanity of humanitarian aid, are fundamental and must be applied by all.

5.2.1 Principles of humanitarian assistance

The United Nations has clearly outlined key principles which must be applied to humanitarian assistance. The General Assembly has stated that: 'Humanitarian assistance must be provided in accordance with the principles of humanity, neutrality and impartiality.'[16] These principles have also been recognized by the International Court of Justice in 1986 in an important case, *Nicaragua v. United States*.[17] For the United Nations, humanitarian assistance must be coordinated by the United Nations, even if it is provided by other actors – the States concerned, United Nations agencies, the ICRC, NGOs and others.[18] The first aim of all actors providing humanitarian assistance must be the same: to ensure assistance (food or other assistance) which is neutral, impartial and provided with strictly humanitarian motives, as rapidly as possible to all people in need.

These same principles have also been emphasized by the ICRC, the organization charged with implementing and developing international humanitarian law and providing humanitarian assistance in situations of armed conflict. To ensure effective relief action, the ICRC calls upon States:

> To recognize the need for the [Red Cross] Movement to maintain a clear separation between its humanitarian action, on the one hand, and actions of a political, military or economic nature carried out by governments, intergovernmental bodies and other agencies during humanitarian crises, on the other hand, bearing in mind the need for the Movement to maintain, in its humanitarian work, its independence, impartiality and neutrality.[19]

Acknowledging that even a perception of bias endangers the safety of aid personnel and compromises their effectiveness, the ICRC rejects any direct involvement of military forces in relief operations, even armed escorts.[20] Indeed, one of the founding principles of humanitarian relief is that:

> Military operations should be clearly distinct from humanitarian activities. Particularly at the height of hostilities, military forces should not be directly involved in humanitarian action, as this would or could, in the minds of the authorities and the population, associate humanitarian organizations with political or military objectives that go beyond humanitarian concerns.[21]

5.2.2 Rules of humanitarian assistance

International humanitarian law contains many rules which protect the right to food for populations caught in armed conflict. These rules cover both the rights of affected civilians to receive aid and the rights of humanitarian agencies to deliver it.

Humanitarian law is very clear in a situation of an international armed conflict. The parties to the armed conflict have a duty to ensure that all the basic needs of the civilian population, such as food and water, in the territory under their control are met as far as possible. Parties to the conflict have the primary role in providing assistance to the civilian population living on the territory they control. If these entities cannot provide this assistance, if people lack access to food and water, they should allow entry of the ICRC or any other impartial humanitarian organization to undertake relief actions. They must also allow the free passage of essential relief supplies intended for civilians. They must authorize and facilitate impartial humanitarian relief operations and ensure the safety of medical and humanitarian personnel.[22] States must facilitate and protect these operations, and must not divert or obstruct the passage of humanitarian assistance.

States are required to allow free passage of certain goods for specific categories of people, even if those people belong to the adversary State. The rule was designed to deal primarily with humanitarian assistance in blockade situations and requires free passage of essential foodstuffs for children and pregnant women, although stringent conditions are attached.[23] This was extended under the First Additional Protocol, Article 70, paragraph 1, which covers relief for any civilian population lacking adequate supplies, including food, as long as relief actions are humanitarian and impartial. This is subject to the agreement of the State, but that agreement is expected and a State cannot refuse aid, except in exceptional conditions. Only the minimum is required: to allow the free passage of humanitarian assistance. To refuse is a violation of the right to food, if civilians die of hunger. Indeed, impeding relief supplies is a war crime under the Rome Statute of the International Criminal Court.[24]

When humanitarian assistance is provided by impartial organizations, all States, because they are parties to the conventions and protocols, and the parties to the conflict have specific obligations. All States must 'allow and facilitate rapid and unimpeded passage of all relief consignments, equipment and personnel...'[25] and they must 'encourage and facilitate effective international coordination of the relief actions'.[26] They must not in any way 'divert relief consignments from the purpose for which they are intended nor delay their forwarding, except in cases of urgent necessity in the interest of the civilian population concerned'.[27] In addition, parties to the conflict must also 'protect relief consignments and facilitate their rapid distribution' because they are in the country.[28]

There are also a series of provisions that relate to relief assistance to civilians in occupied territories, under the Fourth Geneva Convention (Articles 55 and 59, paragraph 1) and the First Additional Protocol (Articles 68–71). The 'occupying Power' has the duty to ensure food for the population and must bring in necessary foodstuffs, medical stores and other articles, or allow relief, if the resources of the occupied territory are inadequate.[29] If the State cannot ensure this assistance and the civilian population is not adequately provided with the supplies mentioned, 'relief actions which are humanitarian and impartial in character and conducted without any adverse distinction shall be undertaken, subject to the agreement'.[30] In relief operations, there are also several rules which provide special protection for women and children in situations of armed conflict. Children, mothers expecting babies and those breastfeeding their babies must benefit from a special protection in humanitarian relief actions.[31] This special protection means the provision of all food and medicines essential for their survival.[32]

Humanitarian law is less complete in the situation of a non-international armed conflict, because there are fewer clear obligations required of States.[33] However, there are clear rules that allow the humanitarian intervention of impartial humanitarian organizations, such as the ICRC, subject to the consent of the parties to the conflict. This is extremely important because it is the only way for the populations who are suffering to obtain the supplies essential for their survival. Article 3 common to the Geneva Conventions is very important. It contains the right of humanitarian organizations to offer their services. It states that an 'impartial humanitarian body, such as the ICRC, may offer its services to the Party to the conflict'.[34] This is the basis on which the ICRC can obtain access to the victims of an internal armed conflict. Protocol II, Article 18, paragraph 2, says that if

> the civilian population is suffering undue hardship owing to a lack of the supplies essential for its survival, such as food-stuffs and medical supplies, relief actions for the civilian population which are of an exclusively

humanitarian and impartial nature and which are conducted without any adverse distinction shall be undertaken subject to the consent of [the parties to the conflict].

5.3 Enforcement mechanisms for international humanitarian law

Although there are still many violations of international humanitarian law in situations of armed conflict, there has been substantial improvement in the development of enforcement mechanisms to ensure the implementation of international humanitarian law. These enforcement mechanisms should improve the respect for the right to food in armed conflict.

In the last decade, the most important development was the establishment of the International Criminal Court (ICC), in accordance with the Rome Statute adopted in 1998. This means that it is now possible to bring war criminals who let their populations starve to death during armed conflict (international or non-international) to justice and punish them. Prior to the establishment of the ICC, important steps forward in enforcing international criminal law had already been taken through the establishment of international criminal tribunals for the former Yugoslavia and Rwanda.

There are also several different ways of ensuring respect of humanitarian law. States parties to the Geneva Conventions and the First Additional Protocol are obliged 'to respect and to ensure respect' for humanitarian law in international armed conflict.[35] States can call a meeting of all States parties in order to make one State respect any one of these laws. States can also put economic and diplomatic pressure, alone or in cooperation with the United Nations, on a State which does not respect international humanitarian law.[36]

In the case of a violation of the rules of international humanitarian law, the General Assembly and the Security Council can also take action. For example, in 1988, the General Assembly adopted a resolution in the situation of the Sudan in which it called on all States to provide assistance.[37] Resolutions of the General Assembly are, however, only recommendations and are not legally binding. But the Security Council can adopt a binding resolution, if it takes action under Chapter VII of the Charter of the United Nations. After having determined the existence of a threat to or breach of the peace, it can decide what measures can be taken to maintain or restore international peace and security.[38] The fact that a State does not permit humanitarian or food assistance into its territory or starves its civilian population is not a priori considered a threat to the peace or a breach of the peace. However, the Security Council can determine that there is a threat to the peace and can decide what action should be taken. This is what happened in Somalia and in the Republic of Bosnia and Herzegovina in 1992. Sometimes the situation of famine itself can provoke a threat to peace.

In Somalia, the Security Council determined 'that the magnitude of the human tragedy caused by the conflict in Somalia, further exacerbated by the obstacles being created to the distribution of humanitarian assistance, constitutes a threat to international peace and security'. The Security Council demanded 'that all parties, movements and factions in Somalia take all measures necessary to facilitate the efforts of the United Nations, its specialized agencies and humanitarian organizations to provide urgent humanitarian assistance to the affected population'.[39] In the case of Bosnia and Herzegovina, the Security Council determined that the hostilities were a breach of the peace and initiated actions, including establishing security corridors for humanitarian access.[40] In 1999, the Security Council reaffirmed this idea, and expressed its willingness to respond to situations of armed conflict where humanitarian assistance to civilians is being deliberately obstructed.[41] In this situation the Security Council can act to impose food assistance and to stop the use of starvation as a weapon of war.

Part II
The Right to Food in Practice: Country Missions in Africa, Asia and Latin America

From 2001 to 2007, we conducted 11 official country missions to 10 countries, in Niger (2001 and 2005), Brazil and Bangladesh (2002), the Occupied Palestinian Territories (2003), Ethiopia and Mongolia (2004), Guatemala and India (2005), Lebanon (2006), Bolivia and Cuba (2007).[1]

In each of these country missions, the focus was to examine the progress in realizing the right to food over time, monitor the situation of vulnerable groups, especially those that suffer from discrimination, as well as to monitor compliance with the obligations to respect, protect and fulfil the right to food.

The objective of this second part of the book is to present the right to food in practice, by highlighting the results of these 11 missions in Africa, Asia and Latin America. For each country mission, we look at the situation of food insecurity in the country. We then analyse the situation from the perspective of the right to food. For the analysis of the right to food in practice, it is important first to look at the country's commitment to human rights, particularly the right to food. One section therefore examines the legal framework governing the right to food in the country, including obligations under international covenants and conventions, as well as its obligations under national legislation. The Government's policies and action can then be judged against the commitments which they have made to legally binding standards, at the international and domestic level. The next section moves on to look in detail at the policy framework governing the response to food insecurity and the right to food in the country. Then, we outline the main findings and concerns regarding the realization of the right to food. Where government actions and policies have failed to meet the goal of fulfilling the Government's obligations at the international and national level, the reasons why are examined along with the obstacles to realizing the right to food. Finally, the last section of each chapter presents the conclusions and recommendations that were presented by Jean Ziegler to the United Nations.

6
Niger

At the kind invitation of the Government of the Republic of Niger, we (Jean Ziegler and Sally-Anne Way) conducted a first country mission to Niger from 27 August to 3 September 2001. We (Jean Ziegler and Christophe Golay) then undertook an emergency mission to Niger from 8 to 12 July 2005, to raise awareness about the dramatic food situation prevailing in the country (see below).

6.1 First mission to Niger

During our first mission in 2001,[2] we had the honour to be received by the Prime Minister of Niger, Hama Amadou, the Minister of Rural Development, the Minister of Water Resources, the Minister of the Environment and Fight against Desertification, the Minister of Trade and Industry, and the Minister of Animal Resources, and representatives of the National Committee for Early Warning. We met with members of parliament, as well as with the President and other members of the National Commission of Human Rights and Fundamental Freedoms. We also had the honour to be received by leaders of the opposition, notably Mahmadou Issoufu, former Prime Minister, leader of the Parti nigérien pour la démocratie et socialisme (PNDS) and member of the Socialist International, and Massoudou Hassoumé, leader of the opposition in parliament. We held talks with the country representatives of United Nations agencies, including the FAO and the WFP, multilateral and bilateral organizations and NGOs, and with Niger's very vibrant civil society who provided a great insight into Niger. The programme included two field visits, one to Gaya and Dosso in the southern agricultural zone of Niger, and one to Maradi and Dakoro in the central agro-pastoral zone, which gave us a valuable opportunity to hold meetings with local government authorities, NGOs, representatives of civil society, and with communities of Nigerien farmers and pastoralists. The offices of DDC-Niamey and Gaya and the offices of CARE International in Niamey, Maradi and

Dakoro were particularly generous in organizing the visits, which gave the mission the opportunity to witness the impressive efforts of local communities, NGOs, United Nations organizations and State agencies to address the problem of hunger in Niger.

Although the situation of food security in Niger is precarious and the threat of famine frequent, Niger is a country that is not a very high priority for the international community. The scale of poverty and food insecurity in Niger, which is a threat to social cohesion and stability and may provide the basis for increasing Islamic fundamentalism in the region, should make it a priority for the international community. Over 80 per cent of the population is touched by food insecurity. Over 4.2 million people suffer from chronic malnourishment. Things may change, but only if the right to food becomes a key priority in economic, political and social policies, both in Niger and in the international community.

Niger is a country inhabited by some of the greatest civilizations of humanity – the Songhai, the Djerma, the Hausa, the Tuareg, the Peul – whose earlier riches were based on dominance of the trans-Saharan caravan trade. The people of Niger are men and women of great dignity, courageous and hardworking. Yet, like other countries of the Sahel, Niger has been in economic and environmental crisis, with only brief respites, for much of the twentieth century. Since the 1970s, recurring drought and famine have become more severe. Not only is Niger's climate harsh and unforgiving, but the international climate is also not conducive to resolving the fundamental problems of the Sahel.

6.2 Food insecurity and the right to food in Niger

6.2.1 Threats of famine

The threat of famine in Niger precipitated our first mission in 2001. Ambassador Seydou, head of the delegation of Niger to the 57th session of the Commission on Human Rights, requested us, on behalf of the Government, to visit Niger. The year 2000 had seen the worst harvest since the one preceding the great famine of 1984, leading to hunger over the following months. Stocks of food (particularly the staple food, millet) were critically low across the country, both in regions traditionally in surplus and in those often in deficit. This provoked speculation on the part of grain merchants, who withheld stocks to drive up the prices. Sharp price increases (double or triple the normal price for a bag of millet) made it very difficult for poor farmers and pastoralists with little money to pay for food. NGOs informed us that many people were displaced, particularly from the regions of Diffa, Zinder, North Maradi, Tillabéry and Boboye, migrating to the cities in search of food. The local and national press carried articles about starving people reduced to breaking down termite hills to steal single grains of millet from the insects.

The Government publicly registered a food deficit of 160,000 tonnes for the year 2000/2001 and appealed to the international community for help to fill the food gap. With the donor community, the Government initiated an important programme based on the sale of food staples at a moderate price (called simply *prix modéré* in Niger). Under this programme, the Government bought food from the grain merchants and delivered it to the villages to be sold in small quantities to the poorest and most vulnerable at a moderate, subsidized, price. At the time of our visit, the government action appeared to have averted famine, although there was some criticism that the response had been slow in coming. It appeared that the next harvest would be sufficient to avoid the risk of famine in the following season. The rains had already started and the millet was springing up from the vast sands of southern Niger.

6.2.2 Overview of food insecurity situation

Nonetheless, Niger suffers from chronic food and nutrition insecurity. Food insecurity, hunger and malnutrition are closely linked to poverty, which heightens vulnerability to food crises. The country is a vast and landlocked area of 1.2 million km². Much of its land is desert or semi-arid; only 3 per cent is totally cultivable. It is the second poorest country in the world, barely above wartorn Sierra Leone in the UNDP Human Development Index, and getting poorer. Of a total population estimated to be around 11 million people, 4.2 million people suffer from chronic malnourishment, 80 per cent suffer from food insecurity and 61 per cent live in grinding poverty.[3] Almost 50 per cent of Niger's children under five are underweight[4] and nearly one out every three children suffers from chronic malnutrition. The mortality rate for children under five is 28 per cent, the third highest in the world. This terrible statistic means that one out of every four children dies before the age of five.

Deficiencies in micronutrients, especially vitamin A, iron and iodine, have severe consequences for the growth and potential of Niger's children, women and men. The average vitamin A clinical deficiency rate is 2.6 per cent for each child (much worse than the threshold of 1 per cent recommended by the WHO) and the rate of blindness is 2.2 per cent.[5] Rural areas are more severely affected than urban areas – severe malnutrition in children is twice as high in rural areas.[6] Both health and education also remain challenges – 85 per cent of the population is illiterate and even this figure disguises considerable gender disparity as 92 per cent of women are illiterate compared with 77 per cent of men. There are also gender disparities in access to and rights over food and water for women. In terms of access to water, the Ministry of Water Resources informed us that 52 per cent of the urban population and 90 per cent of the rural population do not have access to treated water.

The great majority of people in Niger depend on the land for their survival. Four out of five Nigeriens live in rural areas, two thirds in absolute poverty. Most people eke out a livelihood as subsistence farmers or pastoralists (or a mix of the two) – interrupted by long periods of migration to neighbouring countries to seek paid work. Food security is tightly bound to agriculture, which provides the bulk of most people's food, income and employment. Life is lived at the mercy of the rain. Food security depends on the rains, which are volatile and unpredictable and which vary widely from season to season and from year to year. If the rains do not come, or if they come as sudden violent flash floods that ravage the landscape, Niger is threatened by famine – the millet crop fails and animals die as the pasture dries up. Two major droughts have occurred during the past 30 years, in 1973 and 1984.

Most of the people are therefore affected by food insecurity, especially in rural areas. Most people experience seasonal hunger during the *soudure*, the period between June and September before the harvest, after the previous year's harvest has run out and when cereal prices are at their highest. Most people do not receive adequate food, in terms of quantity and quality, on a daily basis, which results in stunted physical and mental development, emaciation and low resistance to diseases, particularly among children. Finally, most of the people of Niger are vulnerable to food insecurity which can develop into generalized famine as a result of natural catastrophes, such as drought, which occur frequently. A large section of the population also suffer from nutrition insecurity, given the nutritional deficiencies and the lack of consumption of fruit, vegetables and protein, particularly among the poorest. It is the combination of all these kinds of food and nutrition insecurity that results in chronic malnourishment and food insecurity across Niger.

Traditional methods of reducing vulnerability to famine included leaving fields fallow for farmers and nomadic mobility for pastoralists. However, these traditional practices have become increasingly difficult in the face of desertification, declining yields, population growth and earlier policies of sedentarization and limits on the movement of pastoralists. Traditionally, growth in agricultural production has relied on extension, rather than intensification, which means increasing the area of cultivation rather than using fertilizers and high-yield inputs, largely because of poverty and climatic risks. However, with the growth of the population, increasing the area of cultivation is becoming more difficult and land shortages and conflicts have contributed to violence among and between farmers and pastoralists. As a result of extension onto less fertile land, combined with the effects of land degradation and decline of soil fertility, agricultural yields have fallen. As grain yields have fallen, farm families have been deprived of their historic survival mechanism of storing grain in surplus years to weather years of poor harvests. Now, in years of poor rainfall, they are forced to buy grain in a market where grain prices soar when availability falls, partly due to speculation. With few cash crops, many farmers are forced to sell their food crops for the cash to pay for necessities. Less food is therefore available for family consumption.

The level of vulnerability differs from region to region and between modes of production. The mode of agricultural production is defined by the level of rainfall. Most of the population live in the Niger River Valley in the south-west and along the Niger-Nigeria border where there is just enough rain to allow for agriculture, most of the time. Further north, the climate gets drier and, in the Sahara desert, arid. This land is not cultivable and much of it is suitable only for pastoralism (livestock rearing). Agriculture is primarily constrained by the lack of water, but also by declining soil fertility and desertification, sudden floods, pests, weeds (including hyacinth in the waters of the River Niger, which strangle rice plants), the high price of imported inputs, lack of roads and markets, the growing population and extreme poverty. Farmers and pastoralists struggle to meet even their subsistence needs. Migration on both a seasonal and permanent basis to neighbouring countries, particularly Côte d'Ivoire, Benin and Nigeria, is a clear consequence of the lack of food security in Niger. Only a tiny proportion of the people of Niger have access to paid jobs in the country, given the low level of development, lack of industrialization, small domestic market and lack of resources to invest in the economy.

The most vulnerable groups are subsistence farmers with inadequate, low-quality land and no livestock, herders with fewer than three animals, pastoralists who have lost their herds and become shepherds of other people's small animals, agro-pastoralists in the process of sedentarization who have limited land and few animals, and households headed by women. Other particularly vulnerable groups include the handicapped who line the streets of Niamey. We were particularly concerned to hear about extremely vulnerable women, repudiated by their husbands, who lie hidden in hospices because of a condition called obstetrical fistula (often the result of early marriage and childbirth at an immature age, which compounded with malnutrition, can lead to serious complications, including the loss of control over their bodily functions). Due to time constraints during the mission we were unable to examine issues of discrimination against particular groups, ethnic, religious or otherwise, in Niger, but this could also be a source of vulnerability.

Since the end of a short uranium boom in the 1970s, the economy of Niger has relied heavily on subsistence, rain-fed agriculture (only 15 per cent of agricultural production is commercialized). Its natural disadvantages, combined with a lack of adequate transport infrastructure and no connecting rail line to sea ports, some more than 1000 km away, drives up the costs of imports and exports. Like other countries of the Sahel, Niger has been in economic and environmental crisis, with only brief respites, for the last 30 years. The collapse of uranium prices in the 1980s created a large debt burden and since the 1970s, recurring droughts and famine have become harsher. Frequent droughts have increased the fragility of the economy as well as the landscape. Although the discovery of gold and oil in the 1990s revived hopes for the economy, exploitation of these resources has still not proved sufficiently viable to provide adequate financial resources for the Government. Social unrest, including the Tuareg and Toubou rebellions, and political instability since 1989, including two military coups d'états in 1996 and another in 1999 which interrupted the democratic transition from the military regime, have compounded these economic problems. Democracy is now stronger, but the cohabitation of the various political forces remains uneasy and the continuing presence of the army adds to the existing tensions. Extreme poverty and the precarious food security situation is a source of social instability and rising Islamic fundamentalism. However, the transition to democracy and the birth of a civil society in the early 1990s are extremely important developments for the human rights context. We were particularly impressed by the freedom and vitality of public debate.

6.3 Legal framework for the right to food in Niger

6.3.1 International obligations

Niger has ratified the International Covenant on Economic, Social and Cultural Rights, which protects the right to food (Article 11). However, at the time of our mission, Niger had not yet submitted its initial report to the CESCR, due in 1988. It has also ratified all other relevant major international treaties relevant to the right to food, including the International Covenant on Civil and Political Rights (Article 6), the Convention on the Rights of the Child (Articles 24 and 27) and the Convention on the Elimination of All Forms of Discrimination against Women (Articles 12 and 14). At the regional level, the Government is committed to the right to food through the African Charter on Human and Peoples' Rights (Articles 16 and 60). This means that under the right to food, the Government of Niger has the obligation to respect, protect and fulfil the right to food, without any discrimination.

During our mission, we expressed concerns that Niger acceded to the Convention on the Elimination of All Forms of Discrimination against Women with a large number of strong reservations to various articles protecting the rights of women, including Articles 2 (d) and (f), 5 (a), 15 (4), 16 (1) (c), (1) (e) and (1) (g), and 29.[7] The reservations mean that discrimination against women in Niger may be allowed to persist under the guise of custom and Islamic law. While it is recognized that cultural change must come about within a country, rather than be imposed from the outside, the Government must promote respect of the rights of women to ensure that the situation of women evolves just as it has around the world under different cultural and religious systems.

6.3.2 National obligations

Under the Constitution of the Fifth Republic (1999), Niger has committed itself to protect the security and integrity of the person, and thereby a range of economic, social and cultural rights. The right to food is not explicitly mentioned in the Constitution. However, several agencies and NGOs drew attention to a number of articles that can be understood as relevant to the right to food as they protect the integrity of the person, for which access to food and water is fundamental. For example, Title II, Article 11 states: 'Everyone has the right to life, to health, to liberty, to security, to physical and mental integrity, to education and to instruction under the conditions defined by the law.'

Article 21 protects the right to property and prohibits the State from requisitioning property without adequate compensation. Article 18 also gives the State special responsibilities to provide protection to vulnerable groups, including mothers and children, young people, old people and handicapped persons.

There are no national laws specifically protecting food security, nor national framework legislation that makes the right to food a priority. Framework legislation is important as it would provide an overarching framework that articulates the right to food as a national priority and a point of departure to begin the harmonization and revision of diverse laws and sectoral policies so that they all comply with obligations under the right to food. There are, however, many policies that the Government has put in place aimed at food security; these are outlined in the next section.

There is also legislation which sets legal standards in relation to food and water quality, which are relevant to the right to food. For example, Ordinance No. 93-013 of 2 March 1993 sets out the Public Hygiene Code governing the production and distribution of food and water. We met with one NGO fighting for stronger consumer rights, the Association for the Defence of Consumer Rights (ADDC). Work on the protection of consumers is important in the context of weak enforcement of this type of legislation in practice. The work of NGOs such as ADDC is very important for monitoring the implementation and adequacy of legislation in place.

In terms of access to water, the legal framework is broad. Ordinance No. 93-014 of 2 March 1993 sets out a framework for managing water resources. Under Ordinance No. 93-015 of 2 March 1993, Guiding Principles of the *Code rural* have been adopted authorizing the establishment of a land commission for each arrondissement to manage land and water issues. These principles outline rules for equal access by the rural population to national resources and for the management of conflicts over these resources. The *Code rural* is an important document which aims to harmonize and integrate all existing laws and rules governing access to natural resources into one document, as part of an effort to reduce conflicts between pastoralists and farmers.

It should be noted here that Niger has several coexisting and complex legal systems, which have implications for the implementation of human rights, including the right to food. The law of Niger includes three different legal systems: modern law (the *code civil* based on the Napoleonic tradition), which is written; traditional customary law, which is based on oral tradition; and Islamic law, which is based on oral tradition and interpretations of the texts of the Koran. Customary law is based on the pre-Islamic traditions and culture of Niger, and varies between regions and ethnicities. Islamic law is based on prescriptions that govern daily life and stipulate religious obligations, such as prayer. In practice, customary law and Islamic law have become indistinguishable from one another in a syncretic mix. This pluralist system shows the rich legal heritage of the country, but is also a challenge to the implementation of human rights, including the right to food, particularly for women.

6.3.3 Access to justice and human rights institutions

An extremely important step in the realization of human rights has been the establishment, on 19 November 1999, of the National Commission of Human Rights and Fundamental Freedoms, charged with the promotion and protection of human rights. The strong mandate of the Commission, as defined in Article 33 of the Constitution, is to realize the rights and liberties protected in the Constitution. Law 98-55 of 29 December 1998 sets out the principles for the operation of the Commission in line with the international guidelines for national institutions for the promotion and protection of human rights (Paris Principles).

We met with the President and other members of the Commission and were encouraged by the strength of the Commission's mandate. Economic, social and cultural rights are included, as well as civil and political rights. Anyone whose rights have been violated can submit a complaint to the Commission for remedy, including in cases of violations of the right to food. Important investigations into human rights violations have been initiated following appeals made by human rights organizations. These include the initiation of one investigation relevant to the right to food – the case of the 425 children in Tibiri who became handicapped as a result of drinking contaminated tap water (see details below). The Commission has also established a Sub-commission to deal with issues under economic, social and cultural rights, and members expressed an interest in working on the right to food. The President of the Commission asserted that part of the work of the Commission would be to integrate economic, social and cultural rights into the work of the government ministries involved in development. The Commission has experienced problems in securing adequate finance and establishing its independence from governmental authorities, both of which are vital if the Commission is to be effective.

The democratization process that began at the beginning of the 1990s has favoured the creation of national NGOs, including human rights organizations. We met with one of the main human rights NGOs in Niger, the Niger Association for the Defence of Human Rights (ANDDH). This association was established in 1991 and its activities include the promotion of the realization of human rights, including economic, social and cultural rights, rule of law and awareness-raising of rights through the establishment of legal clinics and the training of paralegals to staff these clinics. The clinics offer legal advice and disseminate information on human rights and the rule of law, activities that are extremely important for broadening understanding of human rights, particularly for a population that is largely illiterate. It is also particularly important in the context of legal pluralism in Niger, with its competing sources of law and obligation.

We were invited to see important projects which had been put in place to disseminate information about human rights through radio and television. One of these projects was 'Radio Gaya'. This very informative and courageous radio station is heard all over the south of Niger and also in northern Nigeria, reaching approximately 40,000 people. It is one of the strong and independent media sources that disseminate information about human rights, as well as announcing food crises and important information on the response of the Government, including the proposed arrival date of food aid. This can greatly help in ensuring that national and local authorities are held to account by the population. One woman reported that, hungry during the *soudure*, she had taken part in a food-for-work project to build a mini-dam but never received the millet she was promised, and the cash payment arrived only after a long delay.

Few people, particularly in rural areas, have any access to a system of justice based on modern law with magistrates and judges. Most local-level disputes (such as conflicts over land and divorce) are settled in a traditional court and decided on the basis of a mixture of Islamic and traditional customary law rather than modern law, although theoretically these are bound to stay within the laws of the State. Although only the magistrates and judges at the courts have formal adjudicating powers, and traditional chiefs have formal conciliatory powers, in practice the powers of the traditional chiefs are often understood as adjudicatory. Traditional authorities play a large and generally beneficial role. We were received by the Djermakoye, the King of the Djerma, who has immense influence and who 'holds court' every day to reconcile conflicts among his people.

6.4 Policy framework for addressing food insecurity

6.4.1 Government policies and institutions

There are a number of government policies and institutions in place to address food crises and food in security, although these do not adopt an explicitly rights-based approach.

The key Government policy for the management of food crises is to maintain a permanent National Food Security Stock (of 40,000 tonnes), a National Fund for Food Security (a financial reserve capable of purchasing another 40,000 tonnes of food), and a Common Donor Fund (which finances small projects for food security, such as the construction of cereal banks or small dams).

A Food Crisis Unit, in the Cabinet of the Prime Minister, has responsibility for monitoring the implementation and realization of action taken in food crises. The early-warning system includes the National Committee for Early Warning and Disaster Management which is responsible for collecting statistical information on the food situation and the nutritional status of the population, and for issuing early warnings of potential food crises. Both of these institutions are located in the Office of the Prime Minister. In addition, a Joint State-Donor Commission has been established to monitor national food security and to coordinate responses to crisis situations between the Government and donors. The National Office for Basic Foodstuffs of Niger (ONPVN), is also an important institution in the management of food crises, being responsible for maintaining the food stocks and distributing food aid. The ONPVN trucks are also used to deliver food and seeds in emergencies. However, the transport section was slated for privatization when we undertook our mission, and there were concerns that it will become more difficult to deliver food in the future, particularly to remote areas, as private trucks will not venture into areas which are difficult and expensive to reach.

At the time of the food crisis that followed the poor harvest of 2000, the Government, in cooperation with the Joint State-Donor Commission, decided to initiate a programme of selling food staples at moderate prices. The *prix modéré* programme was an extremely important initiative and it appeared to have averted a potential famine in Niger in 2001, although there was some criticism from several sources which is elaborated below. Under this programme, the Government bought cereals from the grain merchants and delivered them to the villages of Niger to be sold in small quantities to the poorest and most vulnerable at a moderate, subsidized price. Controlling the quantities was aimed at ensuring that the cheaper food did go to the poorest, rather than the better-off, thereby avoiding inequities in its distribution. The food was distributed through the logistical resources of ONPVN, using its stocks and trucks. Cereal banks in villages were used as distribution points and the sales were managed by members of the community. We visited distribution points on field visits. The *prix modéré* programme could serve as a useful model for other countries in similar situations.

Another important element of the Government's response to the food crisis was the initiative to promote off-season agriculture through the development of irrigated cultivation under a special programme sponsored by the President and development projects financed by the donor community. The promotion of off-season agriculture and the harnessing of water resources is fundamental in such an arid country.

To address general food insecurity, policy responses are wide-ranging and cover the spectrum of development policies. During our mission, we were informed that food security had been a priority in government policies for rural development, economic growth and poverty eradication. In 2000, the Government instituted a specific policy on food security. The Operational Strategy for Food Security 2000, adopted by decree 2000-281/PRN/PM of 4 August 2000, was the first national document to specifically address food security.[8] One of the key principles of this document is that food security of the population of Niger constitutes a public service. This means that food security is considered as a key objective of the State. The policy document recognizes that '[i]n effect, the experience of Niger, like that of other Sahelian countries and numerous other countries in the world, shows that the forces of the market cannot by themselves ensure the food security of the whole of the population at all times in all places'.[9] This means that the policy conceives of ensuring food security as a public function, in view of failures of the market to provide food, particularly in periods of crisis, giving the State a clear role in preventing starvation. This is an important principle and one which must be observed. The National Plan of Action for Nutrition (1997) is also a key policy document.

The Government has formed the Committee on National Food Security (CNSA), which coordinates multisectoral programmes and strategies related to food security in the country and develops the National Programme for Global Food Security. Its aim is also to follow up on World Food Summit 1996 commitments. Policies have been designed in close consultation with partners such as FAO, including the Special Programme for Food Security in Niger which is managed by the Ministry of Rural Development. A Thematic Group on Food Security has also been established comprising the United Nations agencies and other partners. This is aimed at ensuring coherence and cooperation between the different agencies and supporting the Government in the preparation of the National Programme for Global Food Security.

In the face of frequent drought and the arid climate, government initiatives on water include the Policy and Strategies for Water and Purification and the Short-, Medium- and Long-Term Action Plans of May 2001 of the Ministry of Water Resources. These set out the guiding principles governing the use of water resources for all purposes, and specify the institutions responsible. Despite being a mostly arid country, Niger does have significant potential for harnessing water resources, but this has been little utilized. Surface waters include the Niger River (30 million m^3 per year, of which only 1 per cent is exploited), 1000 temporary lakes from rain run-off, and subterranean aquifers (2 million m^3 of renewable water of which 20 per cent is exploited and 2000 million m^3 of non-renewable water, some of which is exploited by mining activity in the north of the country). The main constraint to utilizing water resources is the question of financing for investment.[10] A comprehensive programme to address desertification and drought has also been established.[11]

Government policies also include a commitment to promote the building of small dams in villages, and the promotion of off-season cultivation of gardens using the rain run-off collected. This is important for extra income and for encouraging nutritional variation in diet, although most off-season vegetables grown tend to be sold as cash crops, as there is lack of knowledge about nutrition. Policies also include encouraging the establishment of cereal banks within villages to reduce reliance on the market in times when prices are very high. Cereal banks allow a community to manage its own food security, as it can store its own stocks of grain. Under guarantee systems, communities can sell their crops for cash to the cereal bank and then buy them back at the same price, often for a much cheaper price than on the market.

6.4.2 Non-governmental organizations and associations

As noted above, the democratization process that began at the beginning of the 1990s has favoured the emergence of a series of very vivid, competent and highly motivated national NGOs and associations, including many organizations that work on food security from different perspectives. We met most of these organizations, as well as the associations of farmers, the *Platforme paysanne*, and of pastoralists, the *Association pour la redynamisation de l'elevage* (AREN). Activities of these organizations include promotion and financing of cereal banks, promotion of marketing strategies, provision of credit, financing of water resources, nutritional education, conflict resolution between farmers and herders, support to local communities in claiming rights, such as the right to land, through the adoption of legislative and regulatory texts (e.g. the *Code rural*). The emergence of NGOs within Niger is an important force for positive action, and the strength and commitment of these organizations are impressive. It is clear, however, that these organizations will need donor support and capacity building to carry out their activities effectively.

Some of these NGOs work from a rights-based perspective on food issues, for example, the national NGO ADDC, which works on consumer rights, and the international NGO CARE International, which is initiating a rights-based approach in all its activities. Most other organizations, including the State and United Nations agencies, tend to approach food security through the prism of three essential elements – the availability, accessibility and utilization of food, particularly for the most vulnerable groups. These elements of food security are all included in the right to food. What a rights-based approach adds is setting specific responsibilities and holding the relevant parties accountable for the lack of action or any violations in relation to these responsibilities.

6.5 Main findings and concerns regarding the realization of the right to food

6.5.1 Progressive realization

Like other economic, social and cultural rights, the right to food is qualified to the extent that it must be achieved progressively and to the maximum of available resources.[12] The principal obligation is to take steps to achieve *progressively* the full realization of the right to adequate food. If regression occurs, an analysis of the reasons why and the obstacles to the realization of the right to food is needed. In the case of Niger, the level of available resources is extremely limited and it is difficult to take any positive action with respect to the right to food. Niger is an extremely poor country and, despite the cultural richness and the vitality of its social and political forces, Niger has few development options.

We were particularly concerned that the situation of food security in Niger is one of regression, rather than progression. Hunger and terrible poverty have become chronic and endemic. The situation is worsening and Niger's vulnerability to famine is increasing. From discussions with United Nations agencies and NGOs, it is clear that since 1970, which marked the end of a period of structural surplus in food production, the situation has declined and Niger now has a structural deficit in that regard. A graph provided by CARE International shows that cereal production is becoming increasingly erratic and food deficits increasingly severe. That cereal availability is clearly falling behind the needs of a growing population is clearly the result of a serious decline in yields, given land degradation in Niger, among many other factors and obstacles which are analysed below. This means that food crises have become a structural problem, rather than unpredictable, momentary.

The lack of financial resources makes it difficult for the Government to halt this regression. The poverty of the people of Niger also heightens their vulnerability to food crises. Many people in Niger believe that the real issue is poverty and underdevelopment, which heighten their vulnerability to, and can even provoke, crises. From discussions with United Nations and other organizations, it is clear that emergency food aid during periods of crisis does not necessarily solve the problem; investing in development is needed. For example, investing in mass irrigation programmes would reduce reliance on erratic rainfall; reducing poverty would increase assets which would help buffer crises. In this regard, we were encouraged by efforts to implement small irrigation schemes and build mini-dams, which will help in part to reduce the reliance of the poor on the mercy of the rain. Promoting off-season agriculture that is irrigated will also help.

In terms of the legal framework governing the right to food, we were encouraged by signs of growing dissemination of information about human rights, including economic, social and cultural rights. We were particularly encouraged by the establishment of the National Commission of Human Rights and Fundamental Freedoms with the mandate to protect economic, social and cultural rights, including the right to food. However, we were concerned to note the difficulties faced by the Commission. These included a stark lack of resources and the difficulty of ensuring its independence. According to several sources, the Commission's mandate and the Paris Principles have not been fully respected, despite the individual strengths and competence of the President and other members. These factors have significantly affected its functional capacity. In its annual report for 2000, the Commission stated that a lack of understanding of the functioning of an administrative institution independent of political power hindered its activities.[13] The Government, and the military authorities, attempted to halt an investigation into a case of torture, courageously initiated by the Commission. Subsequently, the Government announced that it would appoint two government representatives to the Commission and that it would reduce the mandate of the Commission from four to two years, although no action had yet been taken after protests by NGOs and international organizations. These difficulties represent some reversal of the progress made in the human rights field by the Government of Niger. The independence of the Commission should be fully restored and the Paris Principles respected, and the Commission should be adequately financed.

We were also concerned by some signs of regression with respect to the rights of women. This is important in the context of the right to food, given the extremely important role played by women in maintaining food security. In particular, we noted signs of a possible shift within Niger to the practice of Islamic Shariah in some regions and stricter interpretations of Islamic law, which run contrary to the traditional tolerance of Niger's 95 per cent Muslim population, despite the energetic efforts of the Government to combat fundamentalism. We were concerned to note the widespread rejection (on the grounds of both custom and Islamic law) of the long-standing draft Family Code which would give greater rights to women. The adoption of such a code has long been planned to harmonize the existing multiple sources of law.[14] However, a campaign by Islamic militant groups against the Code was orchestrated and prevented its adoption in 1994. Reportedly, women who supported the Code were threatened with physical harm. During our mission, State sources suggested that the Government was interested in reopening the debate on the Family Code but strong Islamic forces were still ranged against it.

6.5.2 Violations of the right to food

The Government is required to respect, protect and fulfil the right to food. Specific violations of these obligations should be documented, as for other violations of human rights. However, it is sometimes difficult to find fully documented cases of violations of the right to food, in many parts of the world and also in Niger.

With regard to specific cases of violations, attention was drawn particularly to the case of the tragic poisoning by tap water of hundreds of children in Tibiri, 720 km from Niamey. As a result of the poisoning, it has been documented that 425 children have contracted skeletal fluorosis, a disease which causes terrible deformities of the bones and leaves children paralysed.[15] They are disabled for life and every movement is painful. This is reportedly owing to extremely high levels of fluoride in the water provided by the national water company since 1984. The water is said to have contained 4.77–6.6 milligrams of fluoride per litre, far over the maximum of 1.5 milligrams per litre recommended by the World Health Organization. At the time of our mission, this case was being taken to court by the Niger ANDDH to seek compensation for the children from the SNE. The national Human Rights Commission had also said that it will be pursuing an investigation into this case. It important to reduce impunity in these kinds of cases and to allow for remedy to be sought in the courts.

The provision of water has now been privatized, but it is extremely important that the Government ensure that water quality standards are maintained. The Government should also ensure that avenues of recourse and remedy are open in case of a similar catastrophe. In meetings with the management of the newly privatized water company (Vivendi), another concern expressed was the cleanliness of the water that is sold by water sellers. Even if the company maintains high standards, water is generally distributed to water points in the cities. Water sellers purchase water at the tap and then distribute it further, but there are reportedly no checks to ensure the adequate hygiene of the containers that they use. The Government must also ensure that water is not priced at a level which makes it inaccessible to the poorest people.

Our attention was not drawn to specific, documented cases of violations in terms of access to food. However, we noted the delay in response to the food crisis of 2001, with problems of inefficiency adding to late arrival of the food aid. For example, in the subprefecture of Gaya, in southern Niger, local communities informed us that food and seed assistance was due to arrive in June 2001, but did not arrive until August 2001. Criticisms of the programme of *prix modéré* from several sources also suggested that the quantities provided to each village were insignificant compared to the needs and some people questioned whether the total amount designated for each community really arrived. Some people also criticized the 'moderate' price as still out of reach of the poorest – many people earn less than CFA 500 per day and a sack of cereal sold at the *prix modéré* cost CFA 10,000. We were also particularly concerned about allegations of misappropriation of food stocks collected for the programme of *prix modéré* in some regions. For example, we heard that a subprefect was alleged to have misappropriated important quantities of these food stocks. However, we were also encouraged to hear that the case is being pursued through the judicial process. We also visited a food distribution point on one field visit, and were impressed with the level of local participation of community members, together with State authorities, in the control and distribution of food stocks. However, we are concerned that the local hierarchies may still allow corrupt practices to take place. It should be ensured that the mechanisms put in place are strong and independent.

It was also of particular concern to hear the views of some sources who criticized the fact that the government institutions established to manage food crises, specifically the Food Crisis Unit and the National Committee for Early Warning and Crisis Management, are located in the Office of the Prime Minister. This has resulted in some confusion, for example, the early-warning system did give an initial alert, but the warning was later withdrawn. In the view of these sources, these institutions should be totally independent. We can agree with this view, as we were concerned that different organizations had different understandings of the severity of hunger in this critical period. There is clearly a need to improve the accuracy, analysis and transparency of the use of early warning data to improve coordination between the different institutions responsible for response to food crises.

Speculation on the food markets can also severely affect access to food, as millet prices soar during the most difficult periods. We were concerned to hear allegations that grain merchants deliberately withhold stocks of food from the market during times of difficulty. These price rises are not passed on to the farmers from whom the grain merchants purchase the crops. We were informed that the merchants tend to buy the crops at very low prices at harvest time, when farmers are most in need of cash to pay for necessities. The grain merchants then hold on to the stocks until prices are at their highest. There is clearly a need to limit this kind of speculation.

6.5.3 Obstacles to the realization of the right to food

Not only is Niger's climate harsh and unforgiving, but the international climate is also not conducive to resolving the fundamental problems of the Sahel. There are a number of obstacles to the realization of the right to food – both endogenous and exogenous.

Climatic constraints are a serious obstacle to food security in Niger. The arid climate, droughts and floods, combined with pests, make food security difficult to achieve. For the millet to grow it must rain several times over the agricultural season from June to October. If the rains do not come, then the newly planted millet withers and dies. Sometimes the rain comes, but as sudden, violent floods which ravages the dry landscape. Changes in rainfall patterns over recent years have left Niger with less rain than before in each of its three climatic zones (Saharan, Sahelian and Sudano-sahelian), which has precipitated greater migration of people from the north to the southern regions. Desertification and declining soil fertility are also accelerating, adding to these problems. Most of Niger's soils are already poor in nutritive elements and organic matter. According to the Ministry of the Environment, in one generation of 30 years, the productivity of the land has fallen from 600 kilos of millet per hectare to 250 kilos per hectare. Desertification is the result both of lower rainfall and of farming practices which have reduced the use of fallow and promoted sedentarization in areas better suited for pastoral activities.

The failure to harness water resources, both for irrigation and for drinking water (for people and for livestock) is also a clear obstacle to food security in Niger. Only 10 per cent of cultivation is irrigated. Although there are water resources available in Niger, as noted above, these have been little exploited. The reason is the severe shortage of financial resources to invest in irrigation given its immense costs, particularly on a large scale. There have been impressive efforts at promoting small-scale irrigation and providing wells in some villages, but these have been limited. The cost of a well depends on its depth, and the water line is much lower in some regions than in others: in some regions the water line is at six metres, while in others it can be as low as 80 metres. Much foreign aid is now financing small-scale irrigation projects. However, in the past, there has been little financing given that irrigation is extremely expensive in relation to the high costs of production relative to price. As food crops cannot be produced profitably under irrigation in Niger, irrigation has not been considered a priority, even though it is clearly essential for ensuring people's food security.

The lack of infrastructure and markets for Niger's agricultural produce is another severe obstacle. The lack of infrastructure constrains delivery of food and seed aid. As a landlocked country, with no railway and a road network only 8 per cent of which is paved (and much of that is pitted, as anyone who has driven on Niger's roads has observed), transport costs are extremely high. At independence Niger had no rail infrastructure for access to the sea or across the country. It had only 10 km of paved road, plus one bridge across the River Niger. This has clearly improved since, but not very much. One result is the high cost of factors of production, such as fertilizer, which is therefore not very much used by poor farmers. Combined with the lack of credit in local financial markets, there is little room for intensification of agriculture in such a situation of poverty.

The fast growth of the population in Niger is also a concern: with a high annual rate of 3.3 per cent, the population increased from 4.8 million in 1975 to approximately 11.2 million in mid-2001. However, in Niger, population growth should be understood within a context of extremely high infant mortality – one out of every four children dies before the age of 5. Moreover, large families are often believed to be one of the best ways of ensuring food security, as it widens the networks of social support and access to resources.

However, the increase in population has put further pressure on land and other resources.

Conflicts over land and water are increasing, between pastoralists and crop farmers. The complementarity between pastoralists and farmers has been lost, as farmers tend their own small animals and are less eager to allow pastoralists to graze their herds in the fields after the harvest. There are also conflicts – sometimes fatal – between pastoralists, often over access to water, and also between farmers. All these issues are addressed in the *Code rural*, which sets out clear rules for access to resources and sets up clearly marked corridors and areas of pasture so as to minimize conflict. However, the means to implement the *Code rural* are sorely lacking, and the land commissions set up to ensure implementation and manage conflicts exist only in some *arrondissements* and have not been able to act effectively. Criticism of the bias towards agriculture in the *Code rural* has given rise to calls for a new *Code pastoral* which would focus more attention on the different and very specific problems of the nomadic and semi-nomadic pastoralists. The Government and some organizations in Niger have also undertaken pioneering work in establishing fixed pastoral corridors and grazing lands, marked by solid white and red stakes, in an impressive effort to reduce conflicts between pastoralists and farmers.

With poverty and social tensions increasing, we also noted a worrying trend towards Islamic fundamentalism. Niger is 95 per cent Muslim and has long been an Islamic country, but the modern form of Islam in Niger has generally been a tolerant one and the State is secular. However, the influence of Islamists is increasing, having negative effects in terms of, for example, discrimination against women. There are clear tensions between traditional Islamic norms and international human rights standards – this is recognized around the world. Traditional practices such as unilateral repudiation or divorce by the husband, polygamy and child marriage are practised in Niger. However, in many other Muslim countries these practices are disapproved of and legal reforms have been instituted. Given the role of women in ensuring food and nutrition security of the family, any form of discrimination should not be allowed to persist. It was encouraging to hear that a law to penalize early marriage is in preparation, and a law criminalizing female genital mutilation is now before the Assembly.

We met with a number of human rights organizations and women's organizations which raised concerns about promoting human rights in the context of legal pluralism. The plurality of the legal system in Niger is part of the rich legal heritage of the country, but is also a challenge for the implementation of human rights, including the right to food. They pointed to the difficulties of disseminating information about human rights in a situation where most people do not have access to a modern court of law, with a law based on written standards. For many people, the fact that the law is not written means that it is impossible to know with certainty what is authorized and what is forbidden under the law. As the Koran and the Islamic texts do not express a detailed legal code, but often use metaphors and parables, they can be interpreted in manipulative ways. The multiplicity of sources is often to the disadvantage of women. Customary/Islamic law is applied primarily in matters concerning women, especially the family, marriage, divorce and conflicts over land. This is particularly a problem for women, as both customary law and Islamic law legitimize their subordination in certain ways. It is for this reason that the Government made many reservations on accession to the Convention on the Elimination of Discrimination against Women. The illiteracy of women in Niger, and the consequent inaccessibility of legal discourse, is also an obstacle to improving women's knowledge about their rights and about nutrition in Niger.

In terms of exogenous obstacles, Niger suffers from a heavy burden of external debt which severely constrains the amount of financial resources available to spend on social services, including the maintenance of food security. During the uranium boom years in the 1970s, the Government borrowed heavily, mainly to finance investments in mining and infrastructure. Many public investments which the country was encouraged to make during that time were made with borrowed money, and Niger has since been trapped in debt. In the mid-1980s and 1990s Niger's debt service approached about half of the Government's total revenue. In January 1994, the CFA franc was devalued, doubling Niger's dollar-denominated debt overnight. In 2000, total external debt stood at US$ 1.62 billion. Niger was then qualified for the Heavily Indebted Poor Countries (HIPC) initiative, under certain conditions. These include a cut in the size of the public-sector salary bill, measures to privatize more State utilities and a reduction in the number of education-sector employees. These measures will have severe social costs in a country where virtually all employment is in government service, as even after 15 years of structural adjustment there have not been adequate efforts to generate a strong private sector. In a country where illiteracy is at extremely high levels (92 per cent of women and 77 per cent of men are illiterate – including many people within the lower cadre of the government administration), restricting the education sector even further will leave Niger even more marginalized.

Similarly, the IMF imposes draconian adjustment in the agricultural sector. Niger has wealth of 20 million head of cattle, sheep and camels, which are historically much sought after and exported widely. The animals constitute essential revenue for millions of nomads and peasants. But the privatization of the national veterinary office has produced disaster: these people can no longer afford the prices of vaccinations, medicines and vitamins charged by the commercial traders. Although there are still veterinary assistants, they are far from covering the need in Niger, and people are required to pay not only for their services, but also for their transport, which, given the inadequacies of the transport network in Niger, is extremely costly. In 2001, the privatization of the transport section of the ONPVN was also slated, which threatened the right to food. ONPVN trucks transport emergency food and seeds in times of famine, but after privatization, companies operating under the logic of the market will not venture into the remote areas on bad roads. The end result is that many villages risk not receiving any help. A final example: under adjustment, there is no longer a central laboratory to issue health certificates for animals as demanded under the rules of the World Trade Organization. Without certificates, buyers force the prices of the animals on the market lower, leaving pastoralists and farmers even poorer.

Policies of economic stabilization and structural adjustment have shown their limitations in Niger, given the failure of a vibrant private sector to emerge. Adjustment efforts have concentrated less on stimulating the growth of a national capitalist private sector and rather more on reducing the public sector. Thus, the negative effects have outweighed the positive effects. The withdrawal of the State, under programmes of adjustment and austerity, has further limited development within the social sectors, including health, education and food security. This suggests that there is an urgent need for deepening reflection on the economic role of the State in an economy which is so underdeveloped. Economic liberalization is unlikely to generate significant growth in the absence of infrastructure in the country. Economic liberalization in Niger has not particularly improved its minimal participation in the global economy. This is partly because of its high transport costs and its low capacity for production, but also because the only products it has to offer as exports are uranium and agriculture. While these are important sources of revenue (particularly uranium and the export of livestock), Niger is not very integrated into the world economy, as there is little else to export. Devaluation of the franc zone was not a measure that significantly helped Niger's exports, given its heavy dependence on trading partners already within the franc zone. Although Niger does export to its huge neighbour Nigeria, most of this trade is carried out in the informal sector. Effectively excluded from the international market, there is little that Niger can do with a small domestic market, with minimal infrastructure and expensive transport. There is little the country can produce that is likely to prove a 'comparative advantage', when Niger is subject to far more constraints even than its close neighbours.

This is not to ignore that there have been some economic successes, including Galmi onions which now have 70 per cent of the market share in Côte d'Ivoire. The European markets have also been penetrated by local providers of gum arabic, which has also generated a local forestry sector. There are also many small initiatives, some undertaken by NGOs, that have shown success, as we witnessed on our field visits. These include the projects undertaken by the Swiss cooperation agency in Gaya and Dosso, including the cultivation of off-season crops such as manioc, sugar cane, maize and onions, which allow some diversification of income, and community efforts to combat desertification and to establish community cereal banks. We also recognize that there are several important projects initiated by the World Bank to combat poverty, such as the promotion of small-scale irrigation.

However, a key obstacle to the realization of the right to food in Niger is the profound internal contradictions operating in the United Nations system.[16] On one hand, the United Nations agencies emphasize social justice and human rights, including the right to food. United Nations agencies, including FAO, UNDP, UNICEF, WFP and many others, do excellent work in promoting development. On the other hand, the Bretton Woods institutions, along with the Government of the United States of America and the World Trade Organization, oppose the right to food in their practice by means of the Washington Consensus emphasizing liberalization, deregulation, privatization and the compression of State domestic budgets, a model which in many cases produces greater inequalities. The mission to Niger showed these contradictions clearly at work. Niger is a country in extreme poverty, but the IMF still imposes draconian structural adjustment. The country has little room to manoeuvre within the constraints imposed by the IMF and the World Bank. All other donor financing, including funds to feed the population in times of crisis, depends on the fact that the Government has an agreement in place with these Bretton Woods institutions. The key obstacle to food security in Niger is, therefore, the difficulty of mobilizing finances.

6.6 Conclusions and recommendations

In his report on the mission to Niger, presented to the Commission on Human Rights in March 2002, Jean Ziegler presented the following conclusions and recommendations.

He believed that the Government of Niger was doing what it can within the limits of its resources to progressively realize the right to food. However, he recommended that:

(a) Urgent attention must be paid to the regression with respect to food security and the increasing vulnerability of the people of Niger to famine. Investing in development to reduce this vulnerability must be given priority;
(b) It must be ensured that remedies for violations of the right to food and water can be sought in the courts in order to reduce impunity for these violations. This should include judicial action, for example in cases of misappropriation of food stocks or poisoning of drinking water. Action should be taken against speculation on food markets, when this is deliberately orchestrated for the purpose of increasing profits during a time of famine;
(c) The independence of the Food Crisis Unit and the National Committee for Early Warning and Crisis Management must be established to ensure

the accuracy, analysis and transparency of the use of early-warning data and to promote a rapid response to food crises;
(d) The independence of the National Commission on Human Rights and Fundamental Freedoms must be fully restored and the Paris Principles respected, and the Commission must be adequately financed;
(e) Given the vital role that women play in ensuring food security, the implementation of legislation to protect the right of women to be protected against discrimination is a priority. This could be based on the existing draft Family Code or new protective legislation. Laws against early marriage, female genital mutilation and other discriminatory traditional practices should be implemented;
(f) The *Code rural* should be fully implemented and adequate financing sought for the establishment of land commissions to properly secure land tenure and manage conflicts. The *Code pastoral* and the concerns of pastoralists should be given equal priority to the concerns of farmers;
(g) The harnessing of water resources for drinking water and irrigation must be given priority to ensure food security, particularly of rural people. Priority must also be given to improving transport infrastructure and markets for Niger's agricultural produce. The problems of desertification and declining soil fertility must receive adequate attention and financing to ensure that agricultural yields do not continue to fall, thereby further increasing food insecurity;
(h) The privatization of ONPVN should be resisted, unless other measures are put in place to ensure that emergency food aid will be transported to isolated villages. An adequate veterinary public service should be re-established;
(i) The international community must focus on reducing the current external debt of Niger. The HIPC Initiative must be fully implemented to ensure that Niger's debt burden is reduced, but without conditions that severely paralyze the social sectors of health, education and food security;
(j) The profound internal contradictions in the United Nations system must be resolved so that they do not become an obstacle to the realization of the right to food for countries such as Niger. There is an urgent need for deepening reflection on the economic role of the State in an economy which is so underdeveloped, and to find ways of ensuring that States, including Niger, are able to meet their binding international and national obligations with respect to the right to food.

6.7 Emergency follow-up

We (Jean Ziegler and Christophe Golay) conducted an urgent mission to Niger from 8 to 12 July 2005.[17] The objective of the mission was to raise awareness about the dramatic food situation. We were accompanied by a United Nations television team, which did an efficient work in generating a reaction by the international community. Despite numerous appeals by the Government and the United Nations agencies since November 2004, there was little response to the crisis until August 2005. At a press briefing on 24 May 2005, the Under-Secretary-General for Humanitarian Affairs and Emergency Relief Coordinator Jan Egeland described Niger as 'the number one forgotten and neglected emergency in the world'.

During our mission, we witnessed the gravity of the situation. Almost a third of the population, around 3.6 million people, including 800,000 children, were facing acute malnutrition, and in some regions vulnerable people, in particular infant children, were already dying from starvation. According to the Government's surveillance of the hunger situation in July 2005, only 19 out of 106 zones were in a satisfactory food situation, the situation in all other zones being critical or extremely critical. During visits to Ouallam and Tondikiwindi, we saw evidence that thousands of farmers were reduced to subsisting on seeds gathered from termite mounds and roots and poisonous fruits called Anza. Most men had left the fields to try to find work and their undernourished wives were too weak to work in the fields, threatening the next harvest of millet that is not due before October, and only then if the rains come. We also visited the Saga Emergency Feeding Center operated by the Mother Theresa Sisters on the outskirts of Niamey, where we received reports that undernourished children were dying from hunger every week.

We met with the President and the Prime Minister, as well as with the directors of the Food Crisis Unit, the Office for Food Production in Niger and the Early Warning System. We found that the Government had already taken action to address the emergency situation, selling food reserve stocks at reasonable prices, promoting the use of grain banks, and providing fodder to farmers. We urged the Government to begin free distribution of food aid to vulnerable groups, especially children, pregnant women and elderly people, and to guarantee free access to health units for undernourished children, as cost-recovery policies did not make sense in an extreme emergency. The Government agreed that it would do this as far as possible with its limited resources. We found that the role of the United Nations agencies (including UNICEF, FAO, WFP, UNDP, WHO and the World Bank) and international NGOs (Médecins Sans Frontières (MSF), Action against Hunger, Oxfam, World Vision, Plan International) was also critical, although their resources were limited.

We were concerned that the response of the international community was extremely slow. Of the US$ 16.2 million requested in the urgent appeal launched by the United Nations in May 2005 to cover basic essential needs, only $3.8 million had been received. Even the appeal by the Prime Minister on 28 May 2005 generated a slow response. However, it was encouraging that, with increased media attention, the response has been swifter since August 2005. Media coverage by a United Nations television team and the United Nations Secretary-General's urgent visit did much to raise public awareness of the crisis. This finally generated an international response in July and August 2005. The Arab States, including Algeria, Morocco, the Libyan Arab Jamahiriya, Saudi Arabia and Dubai, sent emergency food aid and promised funds. The European Union, France, Sweden, Norway, Switzerland, Belgium, Denmark, Germany and the United States of America also sent emergency aid and announced that they would contribute US$ 10 million. Venezuela alone announced that it would contribute US$ 3 million. Cuba increased its medical assistance programme, providing further qualified doctors, to treat those suffering from malnutrition.

In a press release issued on 13 July 2005, Jean Ziegler emphasized that the right to food is a human right, and called on all Member States to honour their obligations to ensure the right to food of Niger's population. He insisted that when a country does not have enough resources to fulfil the right to food of its population, it has a legal obligation to actively seek international assistance and cooperation, and other States have an obligation, depending on the availability of their resources, to facilitate the realization of the right to food through development cooperation and to provide emergency aid when required. He recalled that national Governments have the primary obligation to respect, protect and fulfil the right to food of their populations. However, all Member States also have extraterritorial obligations to respect, protect and support the fulfilment of the right to food of people living in other countries. This means ensuring adequate provision of food aid, but it also means addressing the underlying factors that produce repeated famine.

The food crisis of 2005 was the result of both unfavourable economic trends and structural shortcomings. Its immediate causes were the drought and the locust invasion that destroyed many crops in 2004, impeding pasture and cereal production; but its more profound causes were the lack of development, withdrawal of the State from agricultural and pastoral extension services (after privatization) and pervasive chronic food insecurity, which means that any crisis quickly turns into catastrophic famine (see above).

The food crisis of 2005 highlighted that immediate provision of free food aid is essential to avert famine. But addressing the underlying structural causes of hunger is also essential to limit vulnerability to future famines and to fully realize the right to food of the people of Niger.

7
Brazil

7.1 Introduction

At the invitation of the Government of Brazil, we (Jean Ziegler, Sally-Anne Way and Christophe Golay) conducted a country mission to Brazil from 1 to 18 March 2002.[1] We were honoured to be received by the President of Brazil, Fernando Henrique Cardoso, the Minister of Foreign Affairs, Celso Lafer, the Ministers of Finance, Education, and of Development, and senior members of the Ministries of Health, Agrarian Reform and the Secretaries of State for Social Assistance and for Justice. We were also honoured to be received by the Presidents of the two chambers of the National Congress, members of the Human Rights Commission of the Chamber of Deputies, and Dr. Ruth Cardoso of *Comunidade Solidaria*. At the state level, we were received by authorities including the governor of Rio de Janeiro, the mayor of Sao Paulo and the governor of Pernambuco. We met with NGOs and social movements, some of whom had arranged regional non-governmental organization meetings and field visits during the mission. In particular, we met with MST (Landless Workers Movement), Brazilian Forum on Food and Nutritional Security, MNDH (*Movimento Nacional para Direitos Humanos*), GAJOP (Center for Judicial Counsel for Grassroots Organizations), CPT (Pastoral Land Commission), FIAN, Rede Social, FASE (Federation of Organizations for Social and Educational Assistance), IBASE (Brazilian Institute for Social and Economic Analysis) and CESE (Ecumenical Coordination of Service). We also met with the *Ordem dos Avogados* and the Federal Public Prosecutor's Office.

The Institute for Applied Economic Research (IPEA), the Secretary of State for Human Rights and the Ministry of Foreign Affairs produced a very valuable document detailing the Federal Government's activities in relation to the right to food, which greatly facilitated our work in Brazil. The Government organized a National Workshop on the Right to Food in Brasilia, in collaboration with civil society, and the Federal Government established a new initiative to create a National Council for the Implementation of the Right to Food, within the Ministry of Justice.

We visited Brasilia, Recife, Petrolina, Salvador, Sao Paulo and Rio de Janeiro and field trips were made to rural areas outside of these urban centres, including the poorest regions of the North-East. During our mission, we recognized the important efforts of the Brazilian Government and civil society to fight hunger, but also recorded the serious situation of malnutrition and hunger that still existed in Brazil.

In this chapter of the book, we analyse the situation of hunger and the right to food in Brazil at the time of our mission, in 2002. In January 2003, the newly elected President, H.E. Luiz Ignacio Lula da Silva, declared that the fight against hunger will be the first priority of his presidency. Since then, the Government of Brazil has taken important steps to fight against hunger and malnutrition. These steps, which have been analysed in detail elsewhere,[2] include the adoption of the Zero Hunger strategy in January 2003, based on four pillars: increasing access to food, strengthening family-based agriculture, promoting income generation and empowerment and providing food assistance. They also include the creation of a National Council of Food and Nutrition Security in 2006, as a forum for discussion between the government and the civil society, reporting directly to the President, with the aim of coordinating the policies of various governmental institutions and the efforts of civil society and representatives of the most vulnerable groups.[3] On 15 September 2006, the Brazilian Congress passed a law creating the national system of food and nutrition security, which sanctioned the system put in place by the government and recognized the right to food and related obligations of the State.[4] And on 3 February 2010, the Constitution of Brazil was amended to include the right to food within the social rights enshrined in its Article 6.[5]

7.2 Overview of hunger and poverty in Brazil

There was some important progress in reducing malnutrition, hunger and poverty in Brazil over the 1990s. According to government figures presented to us, levels of poverty had decreased as had child malnutrition[6] and child mortality from malnutrition-related diseases.[7] Broader social developments also showed improvements, particularly in education and eradicating illiteracy. Brazil had improved its position in UNDP's Human Development Index and in 2002 it ranked in 73rd position out of 162 countries, but remained behind much of Latin America, including Mexico, Venezuela and Colombia.[8] There was also substantial progress in increasing levels of food production, and Brazil is now one of the world's leading exporters of food products. It produces more than enough food to feed its population of 170 million people.

However, despite this progress, millions of Brazilians continue to suffer from hunger and malnutrition. According to the Government, 22 million people in Brazil lived below the extreme poverty line in 2002, which means that they cannot afford to buy a food basket that meets a minimum calorie intake for one individual per day.[9] According to the PT (the Worker's Party), 44 million Brazilians suffered from hunger and malnutrition.[10] According to Dom Mauro Morelli, an important Catholic bishop who has dedicated his life to the poor in Brazil, there were 53 million hungry people in Brazil in 2002.[11] Malnutrition and deficiencies in micronutrients, such as vitamin A, iron and iodine, continue to have severe consequences on the growth and potential of Brazil's children, women and men. More than 10.5 per cent of children suffer from stunted growth.[12] Malnutrition leaves schoolchildren unable to concentrate at school and leaves adults too weak to work. In the soup kitchens of the Catholic Church and other charities in Brazil, we met with many people, mainly women and children, who could barely walk and whose ravaged skin and hair bore all the signs of severe undernourishment and malnutrition.

The question of hunger and malnutrition in Brazil is not a question of the availability of food. It is rather a question of *access* to food - poor people simply do not have enough money to buy food or do not have enough land or other resources to grow their own food. According to the FAO, there is more than enough food produced in Brazil to feed all Brazilians.[13] Brazil is now a highly developed economic power and the tenth largest economy in the world, but it is also a country with millions of poor, hungry people, effectively excluded from this powerful economy.

In the rural areas, the hungry and malnourished are landless labourers who often earn pitifully low wages and the small farmers who struggle to survive from the land. In many regions of the country, vast tracts of fertile agricultural land lie uncultivated, while nearly 4.8 million rural 'landless' families (renters, sharecroppers, squatters or small farmers) struggle to survive on properties smaller than five hectares, and would benefit from larger landholdings to cultivate food crops.[14] Landownership is extremely unequal – 2 per cent of landowners own 56 per cent of all available land, while the smallest 80 per cent of landowners own only 12 per cent of the land between them.[15] According toInstitute for Colonization and Agrarian Reform (INCRA), there are nearly 100 million hectares of uncultivated land in Brazil. Export-oriented agriculture has accelerated the problem of landlessness and the increasing concentration of the land is pushing more people to the cities. For these reasons, the land question continues to be an emotive driving force for social change in Brazil.

In urban areas, the hungry and malnourished are the street children, the homeless and millions of Brazilians who live in the *favelas* (slums) of the mega-cities, particularly women and children. Extreme urban misery, poverty and hunger are closely linked to the problem of the rural poverty and landlessness. Rapid urbanization has been the result of a continued concentration of land, the loss of farming livelihoods and the search for employment and better conditions of labour in the cities. But in the crowded *favelas* of Brazil's mega-cities, unemployment is a widespread, structural problem. Unemployment has increased from 5 per cent in 1994 to 7.7 per cent in 2001, yet this reflects only the formal sector.[16] Most people do not have regular jobs and struggle to feed themselves and their families by doing 'piecework' (bits of work wherever and whenever they can find it). Extremely low wages, even for permanent work, are the key source of food insecurity. Poverty and misery contribute to high levels of urban criminality. Many poor young men end up in prison, some driven to petty crime or involvement with the drug mafias. Conditions in Brazil's urban *favelas* are sometimes terrible: overcrowding (including up to 12 people living in one small room, as we saw in Sao Joao de Meriti) contributes to problems of domestic violence, child sex abuse, as well as unsanitary and unhygienic conditions for the preparation and consumption of food. In the slums of Alagados, Sao Salvador de Bahia, where huts are built on stilts over the water for lack of space on the land, human waste pollutes the waters below for lack of any proper sanitation. In Brasilia, thousands of people live in an 'illegal settlement' on the municipal rubbish dump, making a desperate living from other people's waste.

There are vast disparities between regions. The poorest region is the North-East, particularly Maranhão and Bahia.[17] Malnutrition levels are much worse in the North-East (17.9 per cent of children are stunted) than in the South (5.1 per cent). More than 80 per cent of families in rural areas and 10 per cent of families in urban areas still do not have permanent access to clean, safe drinking water.[18] Poverty and hunger in Brazil is also predominantly black.[19] Over 45 per cent of the population define themselves as black or Afro-Brazilian, and many black groups are now challenging the 'myth' of Brazil's 'racial democracy'. The level of poverty for blacks is double that for whites, black illiteracy levels are two and a half times that of white illiteracy and the difference in incomes is vast – blacks earn on average only 42 per cent of a white salary. Gender discrimination is also linked closely, with poverty most keenly felt by women, who often have incomes far lower than men. Afro-Brazilian women suffer double discrimination – their incomes are even lower than those of white women.[20]

The key issue in Brazil is the vast inequities in the distribution of resources. As Brazil's President, Fernando Henrique Cardoso, said in 1994 'Brazil is no longer an underdeveloped country; but it is an unjust country.'[21] Brazil is one of the most unequal countries in the world[22] and the Government recognizes the result: 'a perverse social symmetry, where the richest 10 per cent appropriate 50 per cent of family incomes, mirroring the fact that the poorest 50 per cent possess only 10 per cent of income'.[23] Although Brazil is categorized as an upper-middle income country in terms of per capita income, it still has levels of poverty, undernourishment and malnutrition that are far higher than most other middle-income countries.[24]

7.3 Legal framework for the right to food in Brazil

7.3.1 International obligations

Brazil has ratified without reservations all the major international conventions relevant to the right to food. Brazil is party to the International Covenant on Economic, Social and Cultural Rights, the most important human rights instrument for the right to food. The Government has also committed itself to a number of other treaties relevant to the right to food, including the International Covenant on Civil and Political Rights (see Article 6), the Convention on the Rights of the Child (see Articles 24 and 27 on child nutrition) and the Convention on the Elimination of All Forms of Discrimination against Women (see Articles 12 and 14). The Government is also committed to addressing the right to food through regional instruments, including the Additional Protocol to the American Convention of Human Rights (see relevant Article 12). This means that the Government has committed itself to respect, protect and fulfil the right to food.

7.3.2 National constitutional norms

In 1988, at the end of almost 20 years of military dictatorship, Brazil adopted one of the most progressive constitutions in the world. The groundbreaking Constitution, notable for its inclusion of economic, social and cultural rights, reflects the broad participation of Brazilian civil society in drawing up a vision for Brazil's future. The preamble of the Constitution places a primary focus on ending inequality and promoting social rights. The 'fundamental objectives' of the Federative Republic of Brazil are defined in Article 3 as: '

To build a free, just and solidary society [and] to eradicate poverty and substandard living conditions and to reduce social and regional inequalities.'

The Brazilian Constitution did not make specific provision for the right to food per se in 2002, but it did provide for a wide range of 'social rights', and it was possible to derive the right to food from other rights in the Constitution (e.g. rights to a minimum wage, agrarian reform, social assistance, education, non-discrimination and the right to life). In 2003, an important new amendment was discussed, originally proposed by Senator Antonio Carlos Valadares, to include the right to food as a social right under Article 6.[25] During our mission, we recommended the adoption of this proposal, and also of the proposal of Senator Eduardo Supplicy to legislate for a basic minimum income for all Brazilians.

Agrarian reform figures prominently in the Constitution, with a specific provision that allows land expropriation for land redistribution. Expropriation is allowed in specific cases where the 'social function' of land is not being fulfilled, for example where land is not being actively cultivated. Under the Constitution, providing school lunches is also included as an important element for ensuring school attendance.[26] Under the

Constitution, the Government is also committed to non-discrimination and special protections for vulnerable groups, indigenous peoples and Afro-Brazilians, including issuing property titles to the Quilombo communities (originally clandestine communities of escaped slaves).[27]

Brazil's Constitution is also special in that it allows for the immediate recognition of international treaties in Brazil's national law. Under Article 5 of the Constitution, the rights and guarantees in international treaties to which Brazil is party, are considered part of national law.[28]

7.3.3 Access to justice and human rights institutions

Article 5 of the Constitution provides that all fundamental rights and guarantees (which include all human rights under the Brazilian Constitution) can be immediately applicable. This means that the Constitution provides a framework for the right to food to be justiciable; violations of the right to food could be brought before a court of law and Brazilian judges could base their competence directly on international instruments. In practice, however, this is rarely applied, and Brazil's relatively conservative judicial system generally still does not consider economic, social and cultural rights as justiciable, unlike advances being made in other countries.[29]

Significant progress has been made in setting up human rights institutions and in opening up Brazil's human rights record to international scrutiny. In 1996, a National Programme for Human Rights was adopted and a new institution created to monitor its implementation – the State Secretariat for Human Rights, based within the Ministry of Justice. This represents significant progress, although Brazil still does not have a fully independent human rights institution that operates in line with the Paris Principles. In 2002, a new updated national programme was adopted which includes greater emphasis on economic, social and cultural rights. The programme specifically recognizes the right to food and outlines a series of measures which must be implemented (in Articles 442–457) including cutting regressive taxes on essential food to reduce food prices and to make food more accessible to the poor.[30]

The institution of the Federal Public Prosecutor (the *Ministerio Publico Federal*) has an independent mandate guaranteed under the Constitution to investigate the actions of Government and to ensure compliance with constitutional obligations. Public prosecutors, at both the federal and the state level, can initiate 'civil suits' (similar to 'class actions'), on human rights violations, including cases of economic, social and cultural rights, and have special responsibility to protect indigenous peoples' rights. However, we were concerned that a shortage of resources and the small number of public prosecutors, at federal and state level, make it difficult for the Public Ministry to fulfil its very broad mandate. Of the 600 federal public prosecutors, only around 100 were working on issues of economic, social and cultural rights, making it often difficult to put real focus on the issue of the right to food.

7.4 Policy framework to address food insecurity and the right to food

7.4.1 Government policies for food security and the right to food

At the time of our visit, Brazil had no overarching national policy on food security or the right to food. However, a wide range of different policies and programmes had been placed to address poverty, hunger and malnutrition, even though these were not articulated within an overarching framework of the right to food or food security. Some of the policies and programmes had, however, included important references to the right to food, including for example, the national policy on food and nutrition of the Ministry of Health, partly as a result of NGO advocacy on the right to food.

During our visit, President Cardoso announced an important new initiative: the creation of a new 'National Council for the Promotion of the Human Right to Food in Brazil' (CNPDA) within the Ministry of Justice, to be composed of representatives of both Government and civil society. This was seen as an important initiative and we recommended that this Council should be given a strong mandate for monitoring the implementation of Brazil's obligations with respect to the right to food.

President Cardoso also presented the Special Rapporteur with a valuable document outlining the range of different government policies and programmes relevant to the right to food, entitled 'Food and nutrition security and the right to food in Brazil: Document elaborated for the visit to Brazil of the Special Rapporteur on the right to food of the United Nations Commission on Human Rights'.[31] The document is important as the Government has based it on the understanding of the right to adequate food articulated in General Comment No. 12 (1999) of the CESCR. It shows how policies and programmes of different ministries and departments can be brought together under an overarching framework of the right to food.

The government report brings together a list of the following government policies and programmes, all of which it believes are relevant to the right to food:

(a) ensuring availability of food;
(b) improving accessibility of food;
  - employment generation;
  - minimum wage;
  - agrarian reform;
  - supporting small-scale farmers;
  - minimum income programmes (elements of a safety net), including innovative income-transfer programmes (*Bolsa Alimentaçao, Bolsa Escola*); *Merenda Escolar*;
(c) nutrition programmes;
(d) public health and food safety programmes;

(e) assistance to vulnerable social groups, reducing discrimination; and
(f) increasing total social spending.

The government report recognizes that accessibility of food is the key issue in Brazil.[32] It shows that there is enough food produced in Brazil to feed all Brazilians, but recognizes that 22 million Brazilians do not get enough to eat each day. Government programmes therefore focus on improving access to food. In summary, these include employment-generating programmes, better enforcement of the legally established minimum wage, better support for small-scale farming and a broader and faster programme of agrarian reform to meet constitutional obligations to redistribute land to the landless.

These programmes were welcome developments, but during our visit we became aware of concerns that unemployment levels were rising in Brazil and the minimum wage (R$ 180 per month in March 2002) was too low to guarantee access to adequate food and was sometimes not enforced. The new emphasis on speeding up agrarian reform was extremely important, but we also became aware of problems in its implementation, given that it was proceeding too slowly and only a small proportion of social spending went on land reform. Given the lack of adequate support in terms of credit, tools and infrastructure and the often poor quality land, it was also difficult for a real agrarian reform to succeed. Concerns had also been raised by social movements and NGOs that a World Bank-backed market-based agrarian reform being simultaneously implemented was undermining the existing process of agrarian reform provided for in Brazil's Constitution. Similarly, support for small-scale farming had been insufficient and national agricultural policy seemed to predominantly focus on export-orientated, large-scale agriculture.

The government report also outlines a number of innovative programmes that the Federal Government introduced to combat poverty, hunger and malnutrition and to change patterns of clientelism, whereby regional elites and local governments often exercise control over resources at the expense of targeting programmes towards the poor. These innovative programmes constituted elements of a safety net, attempting to provide a basic minimum income for poor families, through cash transfers to ensure families can buy enough food. These programmes included the *Bolsa Alimentaçao* (food bonus) and the *Bolsa Escola* (school bonus), and another programme *Merenda Escola* (school lunch) which tried to improve access to food. During our visit, we concluded that the design of these programmes could provide valuable examples that could be drawn from in other regions of the world, although we noted that there were also some problems in the practical implementation of these programmes. The positive initiatives put in place by the Federal Government could still be limited in their effectiveness by resistance of municipal and state governments and local elites and by a lack of adequate resources.

The *Bolsa Alimentaçao*, for example, was an innovative programme that provided R$ 15 per month income support to poor mothers with children (aged six months to seven years) who were considered to be at nutritional risk. A direct payment was made to the mother who could withdraw the cash from a bank. Part of the aim of this cash transfer system was to reduce the possibilities for corruption and clientelism[33] by some municipal authorities, which existed with the distribution of food baskets. In the past, distribution of *cesta basicas* (food baskets) had sometimes been used as a way of maintaining political power and buying votes and loyalty, and did not always go to the most vulnerable families. The new system aimed to overcome clientelism by giving money directly to the families. However, in practice there remained problems in implementation because the registration process had to be carried out by the municipal authorities, and there was no monitoring mechanism to ensure that those registered were the most vulnerable families. In addition, no time limit had been set and the *cadastro* (register) had not yet been completed in many municipalities, partly through lack of resources. While an innovative programme, the *Bolsa Alimentaçao* programme so far still had a low coverage, reaching only around 300,000 out of a target of three million poor families. In terms of the impact on poor families, it must also be recognized that the payment of R$ 15 per child per month had a relatively modest impact on overall levels of malnutrition and poverty, although it did provide some extra income to purchase food.

The innovative *Bolsa Escola* programme also provided R$ 15 per child (aged 6–15) in income support to families in order to encourage families to send children to school. This had had an important impact on reducing the prevalence of child labour and also added to incomes to purchase food. However, in practice, this programme was also limited to the extent that it had not yet been widely implemented across Brazil's municipalities and adequate resources had not been made available. It was reported that only 29.1 per cent of the funds allocated in the 2001 budget for *Bolsa Escola* were spent during the year[34] (partly as a result of strict IMF requirements to maintain a primary budget surplus to support repayment of Brazil's US$ 274 billion debt).[35] There were also difficulties in targeting these kinds of programmes towards the poorest, given that a condition of participation is an address and fixed residence. In Brasilia, we visited extremely poor families living in makeshift cardboard huts off the edge of a main road, who had no access to any government programmes because they lack a fixed residence (and who are reportedly frequently evicted by the authorities).

Another innovation by the Brazilian Government was the universalization of the *Merenda Escolar* (school lunch) programme.[36] Under this programme, every child at school in Brazil was entitled to one meal a day in school. Funds were provided by the Federal Government to the municipalities, who made the funds available to schools. Nonetheless, in practice, we found that in some examples the funds made available were insufficient. One school that we visited in the Alagados of Salvador was only able to feed all the children the *Merenda Escola* because it received funds not only from the Federal Government programme, but also from local church and civil society organizations.

The Government report also outlines a variety of other important programmes to combat malnutrition, including nutrition education, promotion of maternal breastfeeding and the setting of standards for and monitoring of food quality and hygiene. It also describes new government programmes to combat discrimination in Brazil, including the establishment of a National Council on the Rights of Women, a National Council to Combat Discrimination and affirmative action programmes for Afro-Brazilians. These were positive advances, although we were concerned to hear from leaders of the Afro-Brazilian movement in Salvador and Bahia, including Ile Aye, the Centre of Afro-Asian Studies in the Federal University in Bahia, the leaders of *candomblé* and representatives of the Domestic Servants Union, that little impact of these new programmes had yet been seen on the ground. These leaders spoke of the continued discrimination suffered by Brazil's Afro-Brazilians, including discrimination in employment and access to resources, and the black population remains the poorest of the poor. While there had been some progress on recognizing the lands of black Quilombo communities, there still had been no official census of Quilombo communities making it difficult to delineate their lands.

It should be noted here that the government document provides a summary of *Federal* Government programmes and policies to address the right to food. However, responsibility for social policy is shared between the federal, state and municipal authorities.

We were able to visit some positive programmes initiated at the level of state governments. For example, in the state of Rio de Janeiro, a *restaurante popular* had been set up by the Governor, at which anyone can cheaply eat a nutritious meal for R$ 1 in central Rio. Other initiatives included the distribution of the *sopa da cidadania*, a vitamin-enriched soup, and a programme to ensure babies were registered for their identity documents at birth. In the state of Rio de Janeiro, 9 per cent of the population (1.26 million people) did not have a birth certificate in 2002. We were concerned to learn that, in Brazil as a whole, 20 million Brazilians were not registered, which means that they had no legal identity as citizens and consequently little access to social programmes or to justice. We also welcomed initiatives of the state authorities of Rio Grande do Sul. The model of *participatory budgeting* used in Rio Grande do Sul, notably in Porto Alegre, should serve as an example for other states in Brazil and other countries around the world.

7.4.2 Activities of non-governmental organizations and social movements

Brazil has an extremely strong and vibrant civil society, with a strong history of working on issues of food and nutrition security, as well as economic, social and cultural rights.

During the 1990s, a mass anti-hunger movement named *Açao Cidadania contra a Fome e Miseria e pela Vida* (Citizens' Action Against Hunger and Poverty and for Life) grew out of the social 'Movement for Ethics in Politics'. They campaigned that hunger in a country as rich as Brazil amounted to corruption and that extreme socioeconomic inequality was an obstacle to Brazil's ongoing democratization. At its height, Citizens' Action mobilized more than 30 million people, almost 20 per cent of Brazil's population, in more than 7000 local committees undertaking many different activities: food distribution, capacity-building, urban vegetable gardens, income and job-generation projects, professional training, reintegration of street children, support for agrarian reform, literacy programmes, popular education, as well as many other activities. This mass mobilization also led to the establishment of a government institution to deal with hunger and malnutrition, the Council for Food Security (CONSEA), but social movements and NGOs were frustrated by the abolition of this Council when President Cardoso came to power.

National preparations for the 1996 World Food Summit provided fertile ground for the meeting of different NGOs working on food security, nutrition and human rights issues, which ultimately resulted in the convergence on a new local concept of the 'right to food and nutrition security', recognizing the socioeconomic and nutritional aspects of the right to food. In 2002, human rights organizations, led by GAJOP, appointed a series of national special rapporteurs (based on the model of the international human rights system), including a national Special Rapporteur on the Right to Food to report domestically on the right to food.

There are also a number of other strong social movements whose activities are closely linked to the right to food. The MST, or Landless Worker's Movement, one of the strongest peasant movements in the whole of Latin America and the base of the global *Via Campesina* peasant movement, has long been fighting for agrarian reform and right to land to enable people to feed themselves. This movement has emerged out of frustration at the extreme concentration of land in the huge estates of rich landowners (*latifundios*), the practice of *grillagem* (land-grabbing) and the ongoing process of the modernization and liberalization of agriculture, which is pushing even more peasants off their land. As land translates into social and economic power in Brazil, many landowners continue to control vast tracts of land that lie uncultivated. Frustrated by the sometimes slow action of Government to meet constitutional promises to expropriate land which does not serve to fulfil a 'social function', MST have taken the initiative to occupy uncultivated lands and cultivate it themselves. Vibrant and hardworking communities have been set up in occupied land (*accampamentos*) and over the years, the MST has been successful in gaining legal title to some of this land (*assentamentos*). We visited *accampamentos* and *assentamentos* in the region of Petrolina in Pernambuco. We were also concerned by the lack of action by the authorities to re-appropriate clearly uncultivated land in the particular case of Usina Alianca. We believe that agrarian reform must play a fundamental part in meeting the right to food in Brazil and believes that the role of MST is overall a beneficial one. We were concerned by campaigns to discredit the MST and to reduce their ability to take action. During our visit, we recommended that a May 2000 law stipulating that rural property that has been occupied will not be inspected for agrarian reform purposes for two years following the end of the invasion, should be revoked.[37]

A vast number of organizations are working on a range of projects in different regions of Brazil. In Juazeiro, in the semi-arid region of Bahia, we visited the Diocese, which is working with Caritas Brazil, CPT, FIAN, CRS and ASA (Coordination of the Semi-Arid Region) to build small water tanks to conserve rainwater as desperately needed drinking water for families in this arid region. We were concerned at reports that local authorities, including municipal *prefeitos*, have attempted to obstruct or prohibit the efforts of civil society to construct these water tanks. Water, like food, has long been used as a means of power and control in Brazil, with elites ('elites' defined as the political and economic classes who traditionally hold power in Brazil, as per Bastide)[38] providing water and food in return for loyalty and votes – such as providing a water truck from time to time. Elites are therefore unwilling to lose their hold over local populations that they maintain through giving favours. In some regions, these persistent forms of clientelism continue to undermine the understanding of rights as also belonging to the poor.

In Sao Joao de Meriti, one of the most highly populated municipalities of Baixada Fluminense on the periphery of Rio de Janeiro, we were presented with a survey conducted by social and church organizations showing that 25 per cent of Sao Joao de Meriti's children were at nutritional risk, and 6.6 per cent were found to be severely malnourished. We attended a meeting in which Dom Mauro Morelli proposed a 'municipal plan for combating child and mother malnutrition and for the rights of the child' to the *Prefeito* Antonio de Carvalho. We urged *Prefeito* Carvalho to implement this plan. We were also impressed by the work of many other organizations across Brazil. We visited soup kitchens, which were providing the only means of survival for malnourished people, and other projects aimed at improving nutrition such as the promotion of *multimistura*, a mix of locally available nutritionally rich plants, used to enrich daily food.

7.5 Main findings and concerns regarding the realization of the right to food

7.5.1 Progressive realization

Like other economic, social and cultural rights, the right to food is qualified to the extent that it must be achieved progressively and to the maximum of available resources.[39] The principal obligation is to progressively achieve the full realization of the right to adequate food.

During our mission, we welcomed the positive progress that had been made in Brazil in reducing child malnutrition and child mortality and in reducing poverty and undernourishment over the 1990s. However, given the level of resources in Brazil, we concluded that more progress could have been made in addressing poverty and inequality in general. While poverty had certainly decreased over the 1990s in relative terms, much of this reduction had been due to the fact that poverty was at exceptionally high levels in the early 1990s as a result of inflation. The control of inflation had an important impact on reducing poverty that arose out of hyperinflation. However, government programmes seemed to have had relatively small overall impacts on reducing underlying structural poverty and hunger. In absolute terms, more people were suffering from poverty in 2002 than 20 years ago (54 million compared to 52 million).[40] Brazil remained one of the most unequal countries in the world, and economic growth had benefited the rich more than the poor, as the result of this persistent inequality.[41]

Brazil also had unusually high levels of poverty and hunger compared to other countries with a similar GNP. We were therefore concerned that Brazil had not used the *maximum available resources* to address the situation of hunger and malnutrition. According to the World Bank 'theoretically and in aggregate, Brazil has the resources necessary for solving its poverty problems'.[42] While total federal social spending in Brazil increased over the 1990s, it was not well targeted towards the poorest. The World Bank estimated that only 14 per cent of social spending went to the poorest.[43] Spending on the programmes that benefit the poorest (e.g. *Bolsa Alimentaçao*) was very low. Most of social spending was on pensions, health and unemployment insurance, which are important but still mainly benefit the better-off. Strong resistance from Brazil's elite and middle classes to social spending reform makes it difficult to reorient social spending towards the poor, perpetuating and deepening existing social inequalities. Resistance to tax reform also means that it is difficult to increase the resources available for redistribution. During our visit, we also recognized that fiscal constraints imposed by the IMF means that some of the funds allocated for social projects cannot be spent.

In terms of the legal framework governing the right to food, we were encouraged by progress in the protection of the right to food, through the establishment of the National Council and the second National Programme of Human Rights. However, we were concerned to note that economic, social and cultural rights were not considered justiciable by Brazil's often conservative judiciary. We were also concerned to note effective regression in the institutional protection of the right to food that had resulted from discontinuities in government policies, notably the abolition of CONSEA in 1994 by the Cardoso government. We were also concerned by the continued structural weaknesses in Brazil's judicial system which leaves access to justice of the poor problematic.

7.5.2 Violations of the right to food

In Sao Paulo, we made unannounced visits to prisons and police stations to examine the right to food of prisoners and detainees. In the prisons, but particularly in the police station lock-ups (where 10,000 prisoners are held), there were clear and shocking violations of the right to food. For example, at the 44th Distrito Policial, in each tiny cell (four by four square metres), up to 32 persons were being detained in conditions of extreme overcrowding and unhygienic squalor, deprived of all human dignity. Although prisoners were provided with daily food, conditions for the consumption and storage of food were appalling. Food was kept in unsanitary conditions beside a single toilet. No drinkable water was available in the cells, and it was reported that detainees had to buy water from guards at a high price. Legally, prisoners cannot be detained in police stations for more than 48 hours without a court hearing, but some pre-trial detainees had spent more than a year in these cells. Others had been sentenced, but had not been transferred to prisons because of lack of prison space. Some had even finished their sentences, but were not let out, given slow, inadequate bureaucratic judicial and administrative procedures. At our request, a delegation of the Commission of Human Rights of the *Ordem dos Avogados* in Brazil subsequently visited the police station and also characterized the situation as terrible.[44] We then wrote to the Brazilian authorities, asking them to respond to its appeal regarding conditions in the police *delegacias*.[45]

A vast number of allegations of human rights violations had been recorded in relation to the fight for land of the rural landless workers.[46] Often land occupations were met with violent repression and killings, both by private forces of landowners and by police forces. *Comissão Pastoral da Terra*, or Pastoral Land Commission (CPT), a Catholic organization which works with landless workers, believed that a climate of impunity enjoyed by landowners, a fragile justice system and the collusion of local political authorities continued to encourage serious human rights abuses of landless activists. CPT presented a report to us recording that between 1988 and 2000, a total of 1517 rural peasants were killed in Brazil.[47] In the year 2000, CPT alleged that 21 rural workers were murdered, 98 were victims of attempted murder,

82 were victims of murder threats, 27 were tortured, 95 were physically aggressed, 365 were put in jail; 6852 families were forcibly evicted, 11,947 were victims of threats of eviction, 2108 people were victims of destruction of their houses.[48]

The international NGO FIAN reported particularly high levels of violence in the state of Pará, alleging that just in that state, more than 700 rural workers, landless activities, union leaders, lawyers, and members of the parliament were killed with impunity between 1971 and 2001.[49] One of the cases to have remained etched in the consciousness of most Brazilians is the 1996 massacre of 19 landless peasants at Eldorado do Carajas in Pará. Pressure from civil society led to the case finally being brought before a civil court in 2002. Since then, a sentence has been handed down to one out of the three police officers in charge of the operation to clear landless demonstrators. However, the other people involved have not been brought to justice. There is an urgent need, in this kind of cases, for trials to be held at the federal, rather than state level, so that political pressure does not affect the independence of judicial decision.[50]

Other human rights abuses also continued to be prevalent in Brazil. CPT reported allegations of continued existence of forced labour. Between January 2001 and November 2001, 2215 people were identified as working in slavery-like conditions.[51] CPT defined this as workers who are deprived of their fundamental liberty and kept captive in degrading working conditions, either through withholding of identity documents, debt, through the capture by armed militias. We commended the Government for establishing an Executive Group for the repression of forced labour and a Special Group for mobile inspection, and recognized that forced labour has decreased in Brazil.[52]

We also received a document on extreme poverty from the Brazilian Platform for Economic, Social and Cultural Rights, alleging 64 cases of violations of the right to food and housing.[53] Most of these cases related to the extreme poverty in which many individuals and families live in all parts of Brazil. They were testimonies to the suffering of Brazilians from an economic policy that is failing to allow Brazilians to feed themselves.

In another document submitted to us,[54] FIAN signalled that nearly 5000 smallholders and workers out of 47 communities might soon be expelled from their land through the construction of the Irapé dam in Alto Jequitinhonha. It was alleged that the 205-metre-high dam will submerge nearly 14,000 hectares in 7 municipalities. Compensation for displacement being proposed by the state company was reportedly inadequate. We called on the state and Federal Government to review this project and to follow the Guiding Principles on Internal Displacement and the World Bank Guidelines on Resettlement for all cases of forced displacement.

7.5.3 Obstacles to the realization of the right to food

There are a number of key obstacles to achieving the full realization of the right to food in Brazil that we observed in 2002 and which remain true in 2010.

The first obstacle to fully realizing the right to food is the clash of development paradigms in Brazil and the conflict this generates between the Government and many civil society organizations. The Government of Fernando Henrique Cardoso, as well as the Government of Luiz Inácio Lula da Silva, have mostly focused on a neoliberal market model, which has favoured economic growth, but has failed to significantly reduce inequality. This agricultural model, focused on liberalization and exports, has increased Brazil's production and made it one of the world's leading exporters, yet millions of Brazilians do not have access to enough food each day. Much of civil society is driven by an alternative vision of social justice and the elimination of hunger and social inequality. Many NGOs have recorded that the benefits of economic growth are failing to trickle down to Brazil's poor, largely because of existing high levels of inequality. Wages are often very low, and productivity and profit gains are not being passed on to workers. Joao Pedro Stedile, one of the MST's most prominent leaders, argues that this market model is producing greater hunger, poverty and marginalization. This agricultural policy and the landless problem are intimately linked with extreme urban misery, as people are forced to migrate to the cities, feeding into the vicious circles of violence, repression and human rights abuses in both rural and urban areas.[55]

Growth in agricultural production has not eradicated hunger. Nor has economic growth been enough to improve access to food, suggesting that the market model has proved insufficient to guarantee the right to food. Export orientation of agriculture and the import of cheaper food crops have also failed to feed all the poor. A trade-based strategy for food security is therefore not the answer to persistent hunger and malnutrition in Brazil. Although insufficient access to European and North American markets constitutes a clear obstacle to Brazil's further agricultural development, if this access is improved few of the benefits of greater agricultural exports are likely to trickle down to Brazil's hungry. Add-on social safety net programmes, while important, have also been unable to fully protect the right to food given limits on social spending and resistance to reform. Social spending has been cut back under IMF demands to maintain a primary surplus in order to prioritize the payment of Brazil's debts, leaving discrepancies and a lack of transparency between the 'funds allocated' to projects and the funds actually spent on social projects. In this sense, Brazil's debt and the IMF's stringent demands for fiscal surpluses also constitute an obstacle to realizing the right to food in Brazil.

In some regions, quasi-feudal structures and clientelistic relations between the poor and the powerful Brazilian families still constitute an obstacle to the realization of the right to food. The instrumentalization of food and water in order to maintain power and buy votes persists. The halting progress of land reform, lack of limits on land concentration and lack of implementation of tax reforms and social spending reforms is largely due to the resistance of some segments of the middle and upper classes, including some members of Congress. The relatively low levels of tax received from the rich in Brazil also constitutes an obstacle to increasing social spending and the resources available for implementing the right to food.[56]

A certain climate of impunity for human rights abuses also constitutes a serious obstacle to the realization of the right to food. Structural weakness and occasional corruption within the legal system mean that those who have political connections sometimes benefit from impunity. The poor often live in fear of the conservative judicial system and are reluctant to use the courts to redress even the most basic violations of human rights. The slowness of the courts and the very low ratio of judges – one per 25,000 people – also contribute to this ineffectiveness. Although under Brazil's Constitution, economic, social and cultural rights are justiciable, in practice, Brazil's conservative judiciary does not take this into account and therefore it is difficult to seek remedy for violations of the right to food. A misunderstanding of human rights as 'bandit's rights' by some sectors of society, which portrays human rights as only belonging to convicted criminals and therefore not worthy of support, also limits the realization of human rights.

Brazil's laws and decrees do not generally provide for effective remedy, either administrative or judicial, in cases where the policies are not implemented effectively or reaching the hungry and the poor. For example, the legislation on safety-net programmes (like the *bolsas* or the *fome zero* programme) does not provide a mechanism for monitoring, control or remedy. In a rights-based approach, effective monitoring mechanisms should be incorporated into the regulatory and legal framework to ensure that programmes are implemented and do reach their intended beneficiaries within a specified time limit.

7.6 Conclusions and recommendations

In his report on the mission to Brazil, presented to the Human Rights Council in March 2003, Jean Ziegler presented the following conclusions and recommendations.

Brazil has made important advances in terms of the protection of the right to food at the legal level and has designed several innovative programmes to address poverty, hunger and malnutrition. However, there remain problems in implementation of these programmes. The Brazilian Government should use a greater proportion of resources to meet its obligation to progressively realize the right to food. Jean Ziegler recommended that:

(a) The mandate of the new National Council for the Promotion of the Human Right to Food in Brazil should include monitoring the realization of the right to food. It should follow the Paris Principles and be independent with effective participation of civil society;
(b) A national law on the right to food should be elaborated to improve the protection of the right to food in Brazil and improve justiciability. Better understanding of all human rights, including the right to food, must be promoted across Brazil. Legislation on programmes related to hunger and malnutrition should include time limits for implementation and effective remedies (for example for the *bolsa* programmes) to promote government accountability and ensure that they reach the most vulnerable families. The proposed amendment to Article 6 of the Constitution to include the right to food as a social right should be passed;
(c) Impunity for human rights violations must be addressed. Independence of national human rights institutions and the judicial system should be promoted. In cases where local authorities may be implicated in human rights abuses, cases should be tried at the federal level. Adequate resources for institutions, including the public prosecutor, should also be ensured. The number of federal public prosecutors should be increased to enhance capacity to investigate violations of the right to food. Improved judicial and administrative mechanisms of redress and accountability should be instituted. Implementation of the right to food should include better access to effective mechanisms for redress and accountability for the poor. Discriminatory practices within the judicial system and the lack of access of the poor to justice should be eliminated;
(d) More resources should be made available for addressing poverty, hunger and malnutrition. Reducing poverty and inequality will be important for public security, and will be more effective and less costly than a brutal, repressive law enforcement apparatus. There should be an end to the system of imprisonment in police stations for periods longer than 48 hours without a court hearing, to ensure compliance with both national and international standards. Actions to improve the often inhuman and unsanitary conditions of prisoners should be taken immediately;
(e) The current economic model should be reviewed to examine the impacts of macroeconomic policy and trade liberalization on poverty and social inequality. It should be ensured that the benefits of economic growth are more evenly distributed. Tax reform should be implemented to reduce the emphasis on regressive taxation, particularly tax on food consumption;

(f) Agrarian reform should be implemented more rapidly. Expropriation and granting land titles should be speeded up. The projected law on limiting the size of landholdings should be implemented. Efforts to prevent *grillagem*, or land-grabbing, should be intensified. Resistance of some quarters of the political and economic elite to agrarian reform should be challenged, by offering compensation for land but without resorting to market-based mechanisms of land reform if these do not promote effective redistribution. The May 2000 law which stipulates that rural property that has been occupied will not be considered for agrarian reform purposes, should be revoked. Small-scale agriculture should be supported;

(g) More resources should be made available to enable the extension of the coverage of social safety net programmes, including *Bolsa Alimentaçao* and *Bolsa Escola* should be extended. Adequate resources should be provided for conducting cadastral surveys and a time limit set for a rapid and fair implementation. The level of the minimum wage should be enforced and raised to a level adequate to meet minimum daily food needs;

(h) Reform of social spending should be pursued to ensure that more resources are targeted towards the poorest. It should also be ensured that IMF requirements for budget surpluses do not limit the 'available resources' in ways that prevent the realization of the right to food in Brazil. Social programmes should not be disproportionately penalized by IMF budget restrictions;

(i) Efforts to challenge relations of clientelism and the instrumentalization of food and water as a mechanism of maintaining political and economic power should be stepped up. Sustainable, community-controlled access to water for the poor in Brazil's semi-arid region should be made a priority to eliminate clientelism. Government authorities as well as other political and economic elites should be held accountable if enforced control of resources, including land, food and water affects the right to food and water of the poor;

(j) The initiative of non-governmental organizations to appoint national special rapporteurs on human rights issues, including a special rapporteur on the right to food, should be granted the support to operate effectively;

(k) The Government of Brazil should defend the right to food in the ongoing trade negotiations under the framework of the WTO. The right to food and the concept of food sovereignty[57] should be used to ensure the primacy of the people's right to food and food security;

(l) Finally, the important progress accomplished by the Federal Government in its fight against hunger and malnutrition must be recognized. However, the persistence of hunger and malnutrition in a country so powerful and rich in economic resources as Brazil should not be tolerated. State obligations to fulfil the right to food should be reviewed in the context of the overall level of state resources. In a country with such an abundance of resources, it should be possible to ensure the right to food of all Brazilians. As Jean-Paul Sartre has said, 'Time is not an abstract entity, it is human life.' The silent daily suffering of so many millions of hungry and malnourished Brazilians must be stopped.

8
Bangladesh

8.1 Introduction

We (Jean Ziegler, Sally-Anne Way and Christophe Golay) conducted a country mission to Bangladesh from 23 October to 4 November 2002.[1] We had the honour in Bangladesh to be received by the State Minister of Foreign Affairs, the Minister for Foreign Affairs, the Foreign Secretary and the Ministers of Agriculture, Disaster Management, Women and Children's Affairs, and Water. We also had the honour to be received by the then former Prime Minister and Leader of the Opposition – Prime Minister again since March 2009 – Ms. Sheikh Hasina, as well as the former Minister of Agriculture, Ms. Begum Matia Chowdhury, and a former diplomat, Mr. Waliur Rahman. We were also received by Dr. Mohammed Yunus of the Grameen Bank, and by Mr. Fazle Hossain Abed of BRAC (originally the Bangladesh Rural Advancement Committee) whose activities across Bangladesh are remarkable. We were received by many of Bangladesh's numerous and vibrant NGOs, which shared their own insights at two large round-table conferences on the right to food in Bangladesh. The programme included field visits to the districts of Jessore and Khulna to the East, to Jamalpur and to Rajshahi, poorer areas of the North, which gave the mission a valuable opportunity to hold meetings with local government authorities, representatives of civil society and to visit field projects.

Born as a nation in 1971 under the leadership of Sheikh Mujibur Rahman, after a bloody struggle for independence, Bangladesh is today endeavouring to modernize and consolidate its democracy. A country in which 90 per cent of the population is Muslim, the State remains predominantly secular and its Islam is a tolerant and moderating influence. The region of Bengal (of which Bangladesh is part) is home to some of the greatest poets of recent history; Rabindranath Tagore, Kazi Nazrul Islam and Lalan Shah, among others. The Bengali culture is rich and vibrant. Although Bengal was once the richest region of South Asia, dominating international trade in textiles, today Bangladesh is amongst the poorest nations. Today Bangladesh is the most densely populated nation in the world, with more than 130 million people in a land of only 144,000 km². Its land is very fertile, but Bangladesh suffers from being one of the most disaster-prone countries in the world – not only frequent floods, but also droughts, tornadoes, earthquakes and epidemics. Despite recent progress, food insecurity remains a constant threat for millions of Bangladesh's poor.

8.2 Hunger and poverty in Bangladesh

8.2.1 Overview of food insecurity in Bangladesh

Hunger, malnutrition and poverty are widespread in Bangladesh and millions of people struggle to meet their basic food needs every day. Half of the population, 65 million people, is too poor to be able to afford enough food to sustain a healthy and productive life. Nearly a third of the population lives in grinding poverty on less than US$ 1 per day.[2] The average Bangladeshi diet is 15 per cent deficient in energy[3] and levels of malnutrition are amongst the highest in the world.

Many of Bangladesh's men, women and children are profoundly affected by macro and micronutrient deficiencies. Every year, 30,000 children become blind due to vitamin A deficiency. Over half the population is affected by iodine deficiency, including 80 per cent of children. The effects of malnutrition are also compounded by inadequate utilization of nutrients, given difficult conditions in terms of access to water, sanitation, health services.[4]

However, it is women who are most profoundly affected by malnutrition in Bangladesh. Malnutrition levels show a marked gender disparity – far more girl children are underweight and stunted than boy children. This is largely due to patterns of discrimination against women and girls, given the custom that women eat last, which means that they often eat least. The implications of gender discrimination are broad, given the essential role that women play in food production and in assuring the nutrition of the household. It is also increasingly being recognized that high rates of maternal malnutrition have impacts on society as a whole, as underweight mothers are more likely to give birth to underweight babies.

One out of five Bangladeshi children dies before his or her fifth birthday, two thirds from malnutrition-related illnesses.[5] Half of all children below the age of five are underweight and stunted in their growth. This is predominantly due to the vicious circle of hunger that is passed on through the generations, as malnourished mothers give birth to malnourished babies. Over 45 per cent of all mothers are malnourished and underweight and 30 per cent of all babies are born underweight. This has terrible implications: as we now know, malnourishment in the womb, combined with childhood malnourishment, fundamentally affects not only the physical growth of children, but also mental growth, learning abilities and life possibilities.

The great majority of people in Bangladesh still depend on agriculture to make their living. More than 80 per cent of the population, or over 100 million people, live in rural areas, over half in absolute poverty.[6] Malnutrition in rural areas is higher than in urban areas. Only a very small proportion of rural people (less than 10 per cent) have enough land to survive. More than two thirds of rural people are now landless (own less than 0.2 hectares), and landlessness is increasing rapidly, due to demography and inheritance laws that divide holdings into ever smaller plots, but also to land-grabbing by powerful people. The landless work as agricultural labourers, often for pitiful wages. Many of the rest are sharecroppers who work the land of absentee landlords in exploitative relationships where 50 per cent of the crop must be passed back to the landlord. Around two million people live on the 'char' lands of Bangladesh (sandbank islands created by the floods), constantly under pressure from river erosion and flooding. Seasonal crises of hunger are still experienced in the northern, more arid regions of Bangladesh, particularly during the *monga*, lean season between crops when no agricultural work is available for landless labourers. At the time of our visit, the local newspapers were carrying reports of starvation deaths in the regions north of Rajshahi, although we did not see any evidence of starvation on our visit to this district. Increasing landlessness is contributing to migration to urban areas in search of work, with many people living in the terrible conditions of Dhaka's slums.

Food security and nutritional levels in Bangladesh are affected by frequent natural disasters, when availability and access to adequate food is temporarily or permanently disrupted or destroyed. Bangladesh's lands are located on the fertile alluvial plains of the deltas of three of the greatest rivers of Asia, the Ganges (called the Padma in Bangladesh), the Brahmaputra (the Jamuna) and the Megna, which all flow out to sea through Bangladesh. Annual floods are a normal part of life in Bangladesh and critical to the fertility of its land, but can also become a threat to food security. Around one third of the land is under water during the good times of the year, and during the annual flood season up to 70 per cent of land may be submerged for two months. It is when the floods are greater than normal or last for longer than normal that disaster threatens. In 1998, for example, 75 per cent of the country was covered in water for more than four months – far longer and in far greater quantities than normal. This led to the devastation of crops and substantial shortfall in food production levels. However, despite dire predictions of starvation and death, not one person is believed to have died of hunger during that flood, largely as a result of the efficiency of the Government and private response that made food available during the floods.

8.2.2 Progress

It is fundamental to recognize the progress made in Bangladesh despite so many climatic and other challenges. Today, Bangladesh does not deserve the label of 'basket-case' accorded to it in the 1970s. Bangladesh has managed to overcome the shadow of famine[7] and from 1990 to 2000, the number of Bangladeshis suffering from poverty has fallen by 10 per cent.[8] Between 1996 and 1999, the proportion of underweight children fell by 8 per cent and those with stunted growth fell by 7 per cent.[9] Broader social development improvements have also been made, including great steps forward in improving education, particularly in increasing enrolment of girls in school, which will have a fundamental impact on gender relations in the future.

Successive Governments have been successful in raising food production and since 1996 Bangladesh has managed to achieve self-sufficiency in the production of cereals, significantly improving the aggregate availability of food, although access to food still remains a key problem. In some parts of Bangladesh, with the extension of irrigation, it is now possible to grow three crops of rice a year. Public sector investments in agricultural research and extension and improvements in small-scale irrigation, have led to substantial increases in wheat and Boro rice production. The shift towards Boro cultivation of rice (in the dry season) has reduced dependence on flood-susceptible, deepwater Aman cultivation (in the monsoon season). This has reduced the length of time between harvests, diminishing the vulnerability of people in areas where this has been possible. Important strides have also been made in extending the physical infrastructure (storage for food crops, roads, bridges, telecommunications, electricity), all of which has played an important role in reducing vulnerability to food crises, by improving accessibility to rural communities. However, although rice production has generally increased, the production and consumption of other crops are low – the diet of most Bangladeshis is predominantly cereal-based and does not include enough vegetables and protein, partly as a result of poverty and partly as a result of a lack of knowledge of nutrition principles.

In terms of access to safe drinking water, which is an essential part of healthy nutrition, the installation of millions of tubewells across Bangladesh constituted progress until arsenic contamination of these tubewells prompted their reconsideration. Millions of small-scale tubewells have been sunk in Bangladeshi villages, which have provided access to water for many millions of people for both drinking water and irrigation. This has brought with it some great advances: using drinking water from groundwater, rather than surface ponds, has radically reduced the prevalence of waterborne disease, including diarrhoea, which was one of the major causes of premature death, especially of small children and babies. Increased availability of water for irrigation purposes has improved food security by enabling agriculture outside of the rainy season and significantly improving productivity.

However, unforeseen in the development of tubewells was the terrible problem of arsenic contamination of the groundwater. The water of many of Bangladesh's village tubewells has been examined and identified as being contaminated by arsenic. Thousands of people have begun to suffer the effects of arsenic poisoning, a disease that poisons the body over 5–10 years, eventually destroying internal organs and evolving into cancer. The arsenic is believed to be naturally occurring in rock, washed down in the great rivers from the Himalayas and other watersheds into the flat delta which is Bangladesh. The concentration of arsenic is high compared to other regions. Drinking water from tubewells in some regions has been found to be contaminated with arsenic, and approximately 21 million people are already showing symptoms of arsenic poisoning. Out of 64 districts, 59 have been found to have arsenic at levels higher than the national standard. This suggests that serious and urgent action is required. During our mission, we were encouraged that the Government had instituted programmes to raise awareness and has trained 2000 doctors and 15,000 fieldworkers to deal with this crisis.

8.3 Legal framework for the right to food in Bangladesh

8.3.1 International obligations

Bangladesh has ratified all the major international human rights instruments relevant to the right to food, although it has made some important reservations. Bangladesh is party to the International Covenant on Economic, Social and Cultural Rights, which is the main instrument protecting the right to food. It therefore has committed itself to respect, protect and fulfil the right to food, without any discrimination.

Bangladesh has also ratified the other instruments relevant to the right to food, including the International Covenant on Civil and Political Rights (Article 6), the Convention on the Rights of the Child (Articles 24 and 27) and the Convention on the Elimination of All Forms of Discrimination Against Women (Articles 12 and 14). However, there are a number of reservations made to this Convention which effectively deny equal status for women in Bangladesh. During our mission, we were encouraged that the Ministry for Women's and Children's Affairs was working towards the lifting of these reservations. We also discussed this issue with the Minister of Foreign Affairs who agreed that these reservations should be reconsidered. We were also encouraged that the Government of Bangladesh has submitted reports to both the Committee on the Elimination of Discrimination against Women and the Committee on the Rights of the Child.

However, we were concerned that Bangladesh had not submitted regular reports on the implementation and realization of the rights guaranteed in this International Covenant on Economic, Social and Cultural Rights, although the Government said that these reports were being prepared. We are also concerned that Bangladesh had failed to pass enabling legislation that would accord the International Covenant the force of law.

8.3.2 National obligations

In 1972, upon emerging as a sovereign, independent State, Bangladesh adopted a very progressive Constitution, which includes both civil and political rights and economic, social and cultural rights. Civil and political rights are directly justiciable, although economic, social and cultural rights are defined as fundamental principles of State policy, but are not automatically justiciable. Specific provision for the right to food, as one of the fundamental principles of State policy is in Article 15 (a) of the Constitution which states that: 'It shall be a fundamental responsibility of the State to attain, [...] a steady improvement in the material and cultural standard of living of the people, with a view to securing to its citizens [...] the provision of the basic necessities of life, including food, clothing, shelter, education and medical care'.

Although the right to food is not directly justiciable,[10] its inclusion as a fundamental principle of State policy is important because it serves to guide interpretation of fundamental rights, including the right to life protected by Article 32.[11] The courts are increasingly using the 'fundamental principles' to interpret the meaning of the 'fundamental rights', as evidenced by a number of decisions of the Supreme Court. For example, according to the Supreme Court, the right to life under the Constitution 'not only means protection of life and limbs necessary for full enjoyment of life but also includes, amongst others, protection of health, and normal longevity of an ordinary human being'.[12] In a landmark case on housing, the Supreme Court stated in 1999, that fundamental rights include the right to livelihood, and that the Constitution 'both in the Directive State Policy and in the preservation of the fundamental rights provided that the State shall direct its policy towards securing that the citizens have the right to life, living and livelihood'.[13] This represented a significant advance in terms of the justiciability of economic, social and cultural rights in Bangladesh (although there remain problems with the enforcement of the judgement). It also meant, by extension, that the right to food can be considered to be justiciable, as a case can be brought under the basis of the overarching right to life.[14]

The right to drinking water is also protected by Articles 15 (a) and 32 (right to life) of the Constitution, and by Article 18 (1), which states that 'The State shall regard the raising of nutrition and the improvement of public health as among its primary duties'. The Constitution of Bangladesh also provides for a wide range of 'social rights' that are relevant to the right to food, including the right to social security and the right to work. Women, children and minorities are also granted special protection by the Constitution, as well as national laws. Disabled people, who are estimated to be more than 10 per cent of the population, are also protected by the obligations of non-discrimination and equal protection before the law. Although women are protected by the Constitution and national legislation, this is still insufficient to protect against discrimination, as it has been noted that 'the prevailing legal system is paternalistic towards women to the extent that the protection of women actually amounts to protection of a man's property.'[15]

The right to land is not explicitly guaranteed in the Constitution. National legislation which governs access to land is often contradictory and, according to many NGOs, fails to protect the land rights of the poor and indigenous people in Bangladesh. A wide range of national legislation is in place regarding food safety, although this is still fragmented and does not fully reflect international standards (such as the food code, or Codex Alimentarius). Implementation appears to be ineffective, partly as a result of the lack of coordination between the different ministries responsible.[16] With respect to the legal framework governing water resources, this is also fragmented and no one ministry appears to have responsibility for governing and managing groundwater resources. This is an important lacuna in the administrative and legal framework, particularly given the problems that have arisen with respect to arsenic contamination of groundwater.

8.3.3 Access to Justice and human rights institutions

During our visit, we were concerned that, despite advances in justiciability, there remain difficulties in enforcing national legislation and in ensuring the implementation of court decisions. Bangladesh's poor have insufficient access to justice to protect their rights. The high costs of going to court, long delays in court proceedings, lack of legal aid and the lack of full independence of the judiciary, have made the judicial system virtually inaccessible for the vast majority of the poor and disadvantaged.[17] We were encouraged by the fact that public-interest litigation is now possible in Bangladesh, given that in 1997 the Appellate Division of the Supreme Court of Bangladesh recognized the rights of persons who may not be 'personally aggrieved' to file cases in court for redress of others.[18] This allows public-interest litigation, extending the basis for initiating legal proceedings directly to the High Court under Article 102 of the Constitution (writ petition only). It will certainly serve as one possible means of improving the protection of the right to food, if public-interest cases can be brought before the courts. A new law had also been enacted to introduce an alternative dispute resolution mechanism, with the aim of reducing the number of outstanding civil suits in the judicial system.

During our mission, we underlined that an extremely important step in the realization of human rights would be the establishment in Bangladesh of a national human rights institution. The establishment of such a commission has been under discussion in Bangladesh since 1995, but little progress has been made towards making this institution a reality, despite numerous public commitments of the previous and current Governments. Draft legislation was elaborated in 1997 and approved by the Cabinet in 1999, but it remained under review at the time of our mission. A Cabinet committee had finalized the Human Rights Commission Bill which was under consideration of the Cabinet. We were concerned that in September 2002, certain changes to the legislation were made which were not consistent with international standards of the Paris Principles. In order to have credibility, the National Human Rights Commission will have to be independent of Government and have adequate powers to monitor human rights, as well as be adequately equipped and financed and accessible. It will also be fundamental that the National Human Rights Commission is given a strong mandate to monitor the realization of economic, social and cultural rights, including the right to food.

Another human rights institution that will be important is the role of the Ombudsman, as provided for in the Constitution. However, although we welcomed the gazetting of the Ombudsman Act of 1980, we were concerned that an office was still not operational, nor an Ombudsman appointed, although the Government issued a notification for the office to be established effective from 6 January 2002.

In the absence of strong human rights institutions, the importance of Bangladesh's NGOs working on the monitoring of human rights must be underlined. During our visit, we met with representatives of the Human Rights Council, which represents 200 activist human rights organizations, which are advocating for the National Human Rights Commission, monitoring electoral processes and investigating violations of human rights. There are few organizations specialized in monitoring economic, social and cultural rights, but this is increasingly becoming a part of the work of human rights organizations. A number of very effective organizations are also working on the promotion of women's rights, and we were encouraged that many of these organizations have worked with Islamic religious leaders who have helped to promote community awareness of women's rights and other issues, such as the elimination of child marriage, acid-throwing and other acts of violence against women.

We have also learned of the work of organizations such as Bangladesh Legal Aid and Services Trust (BLAST) and the Madaripur Legal Aid Association (MLAA), which are doing important work in providing the legal aid to the poor to improve access to justice and in arranging mediations to resolve disputes.[19] It should be noted here, that although access to the formal court system remains difficult, many disputes are settled at the local level through informal courts for conciliation (salish) or village courts, which are headed by local leaders and village authorities. These include disputes such as those involving land, dowry and inheritance issues. Although modern law, based on English law, is applied in the official court system, Islamic law is often applied in the salish and village courts. We were encouraged to hear that NGOs are also working with the salish and village courts to raise awareness of human rights and gender issues, particularly where the precepts of Islamic law are inconsistent with national Bangladesh law.

8.4 Policy framework for the right to food

8.4.1 Government policies and institutions

The Government of Bangladesh has a wide range of policies and institutions in place to address food security and food crises, although these do not generally adopt an explicitly rights-based approach. With a history that has included the great Bengal famine of 1943, which killed 3–5 million people, and the famine of 1974, which killed 150,000 people, the concern to avoid famine is strongly etched in national political consciousness. This concern still plays a powerful part in Bangladesh's political logic and underlies much of Government policy on food security.

The key element of Government policy is the Public Food Distribution System (PFDS), a system dating back to the great Bengal famine when it was set up to distribute food to the poorest from Government-held foodstocks. The PFDS and Government-held foodstocks have long played an important role in ensuring food security and crisis management in Bangladesh. More recently, PFDS has been undergoing a period of considerable change, shifting towards a more market-orientated approach and away from universal distribution to a targeted 'safety-net' programme for the most needy, as well as reducing Government foodstocks and deregulating the import of foodstocks by the private sector to enable commercial imports. PFDS is now fundamentally constituted by a range of safety-net programmes for the very poorest, which distribute foreign food aid. These programmes include Food for Work, Food for Education and the Vulnerable Group Development programme. Food for Work provides wheat in exchange for work in rural infrastructure projects. Food for Education initially provided wheat, and then wheat and rice, to poor children in return for regular primary school attendance. The Vulnerable Group Development project provides food grain training ration, providing nutrition, skills and literacy training for 400,000 poor women each year. Other programmes, including the Vulnerable Groups Feeding (VGF) programme, form part of disaster response, rather than part of the safety-net programmes. During the floods of 1998, for example, the VGF programme is considered to have played a very important role in stabilizing the situation of hunger in the country.

Given frequent floods and other natural disasters which destroy crops and render many people homeless, the Government of Bangladesh maintains public foodgrains stock to respond quickly to emergency situations. The Ministry of Food procures and holds foodgrain stocks to cover at least three months of emergency relief, and the Ministry of Relief and Disaster Management is responsible for distribution. It provides rice, cash grants and provision for shelter and it implements immediate measures to rehabilitate infrastructure and generate income by providing food-for-work programmes. The Ministry of Relief and Disaster Management is also responsible (in collaboration with donors and NGOs) for providing training in disaster preparedness to ensure that villagers move to safer places during floods or cyclones. Shelters have been constructed in many areas and we saw instructions for their use painted on the walls of one slum dwelling of Dhaka, a positive element in raising awareness and reducing the loss of life during disasters.

Following the 1998 floods, the Government set up a comprehensive food security policy, with the collaboration of WFP and FAO. This policy is important because it outlines the responsibilities of the Government in assuring the different elements of food security: availability, access and the utilization of food (including nutrition). The Ministry of Food is responsible for promoting the availability and access to food, while nutrition and the utilization of food is primarily the responsibility of the Ministry of Health. Clear policies have been outlined with respect to improving availability, enhancing accessibility and promoting nutrition. A focus has been put on improving food availability, targeting food grain self-sufficiency and increasing domestic production of rice, although there is still a need for diversification of production, including increasing vegetable production. The availability of foodgrains (rice) has improved greatly, but access to food is still the fundamental problem and the policy recognizes that chronic food insecurity is reflected in the severe malnutrition levels particularly of women and children. One way in which access is addressed is through the food aid programmes outlined above. A key principle within this overall policy is also that disaster management must form an essential part of planning for food security, given the great risks of transitory food insecurity, created by floods, droughts or other disasters, for millions of people in Bangladesh. However, in some regions in the North, emergency food relief has to be provided every year, suggesting that this is a problem of structural hunger, rather than transitory food insecurity. It is also clear that in order to improve access to food, emphasis should not only be put on food aid programmes, but also on the importance of generating wage employment within the economy, not only relying on microenterprises.

Improving nutrition is also a key aim of the Government. The Bangladesh Integrated Nutrition Project (BINP) which operated from 1996 to 2003 in cooperation with the NGO BRAC, has resulted in important improvements in the nutritional status of young children and mothers in 59 out of 464 *upazilas* where it has been piloted. This project has now been scaled up to the National Nutrition Programme (NNP), although at the time of the visit, it was not operational as the disbursement of funds provided by the World Bank had stalled due to disagreements over procurement policies.

In terms of broader strategies to address poverty in Bangladesh, we were encouraged by the rights-based approach taken in Bangladesh's interim

Poverty Reduction Strategy Paper (I-PRSP). It highlights 'the need for progressive realization of rights in the shortest possible time', including the realization of economic, social and cultural rights.[20] This proposes a comprehensive approach to measure progression and regression in targets set in Bangladesh's poverty reduction strategy and in broader commitments made at the World Food Summit of 1996 and in the Millennium Development Goals. This includes monitoring some important commitments with respect to hunger, malnutrition and poverty, including for example the commitment to eradicate hunger, chronic food-insecurity and extreme destitution, to reduce the number of people living below the poverty line by 50 per cent, to reduce the proportion of malnourished children and child mortality rates and to eliminate gender disparity that exists. We were concerned, however, by some reports during our visit that the PRSP process has been less participatory than expected and urged that the full participation of civil society in finalizing the strategy be facilitated.

The Government has also put in place a National Policy for Safe Water Supply and Sanitation; 97 per cent of the population had access to water in 1998 (95 per cent from tubewells).[21] However, this is now threatened by the arsenic problem. The presence of arsenic was first detected in Bangladesh tubewells in 1987 and the first identification of persons with physical manifestations of arsenicosis in 1994.[22] According to estimates, about 21 million people are affected by arsenic contamination, but this is based on using the standard set in Bangladesh which registers water as contaminated if there is more than is 0.05 mg of arsenic per litre of water. If the WHO international standard of 0.01 mg/litre is used, then an estimated 42 million people may be affected.[23] According to the Dhaka Community Hospital, these numbers may even be higher. The Department of Public Health Engineering, which is responsible for ensuring the safety of groundwater, used for drinking water, working with the Ministry of Local Government, UNICEF and important NGOs including BRAC, Grameen Bank and the Dhaka Community Hospital (DCH), have started to test Bangladesh's 4 million wells.

We visited a number of villages in the different regions where the testing of tubewells had been carried out, with tubewells marked green if safe for drinking or red if contaminated with arsenic. For example, we visited Comilla District to examine the arsenic problem of the village's 58 tubewells, all of which were contaminated. However, it will take a very long time to test so many wells and it appears that arsenic travels in the water, so tested wells are not stable. In some critical places such as school yards, tubewells have not been tested and are still being used by hundreds of schoolchildren who are thus being exposed to unreasonable and avoidable health risks, as for example in a Government primary school in Jessore we visited. It is of particular concern that there seems to be no one institution with overall responsibility for regulating the use of groundwater, even given the fact that overexploitation of groundwater and the lack of regulation and monitoring is one element of the arsenic problem. Although the Ministry of Public Health has responsibility for groundwater in relation to drinking water, there seems to be no one institution that monitors both drinking water and irrigation consumption. Allocating core responsibility and ensuring coordination is urgent in ensuring faster mitigation of the arsenic catastrophe.

8.4.2 Non-governmental organizations and associations

The strength and competence of civil society in Bangladesh is unique, particularly with regard to larger non-governmental development organizations. Born out of the history of liberation and the great famine and poverty of the first years of independence, the NGOs that emerged became major actors in national development. It is estimated that there are about 19,000 NGOs in Bangladesh, including some of the largest in the world, such as BRAC, Proshika and the Grameen Bank. BRAC has a staff of 30,000 people and many of its programmes are on a scale equal to Government programmes. Many of these large NGOs have activities based on microcredit, invented by Dr Mohammed Yunus of the Grameen Bank, but the activities of organizations such as BRAC concentrate also on a broad spectrum of development programmes, including food security, nutrition and employment promotion programmes. We had the honour to meet with Mr Fazle Hossain Abed of BRAC and Dr Yunus of the Grameen Bank and had the opportunity to visit integrated horticultural and nutrition projects and gardening and forestry projects, as well as learn about education projects and microcredit lending and arsenic mitigation projects during our visits outside Dhaka and to the regions of Jessore to the East, to Jamalpur and to Rajshahi in the North. A number of organizations working on development and food security issues are now making links with the NGOs working on human rights issues, which should encourage work on specific issues of economic, social and cultural rights, including on the right to food.

8.5 Main findings and concerns regarding the realization of the right to food

8.5.1 Progressive realization

We were very encouraged by the important *progress* that Bangladesh has made in overcoming the threat of famine and mass starvation that haunted its past, despite being faced with so many climatic and other challenges. Improved disaster management and raising levels of cereal production to self-sufficiency levels has significantly reduced chronic food shortage and insecurity and contributed to the progressive realization of the right to food.[24] Progress has been made in reducing malnutrition, particularly of small children. The numbers of underweight infants has fallen from 72 per cent in 1985 to 51 per cent in 2000 and infants with stunted growth has fallen from 69 per cent in 1985 to 49 per cent in 2000.[25] Child mortality levels have also fallen, from 94 deaths per 1000 live births in 1990 to 66 in 2000, which means that fewer children are dying from malnutrition or malnutrition-related diseases before their fifth birthday. From 1990 to 2000, the number of Bangladeshis suffering from poverty has fallen by 10 per cent.[26] Progress in broader social developments has also been made, as noted above.

However, we were also concerned by signs of *regression* in the realization of the right to food. Levels of inequality began rising over the 1990s, with growing disparities between urban areas and poorer rural areas. Gender disparity in nutrition not only continues to persist, but deteriorated in the 1990s. Government statistics show that girls are increasingly likely to be more underweight and stunted than boys, with the most severe cases of malnutrition. Maternal malnutrition also continues to be very high, particularly in rural areas.[27] In general, around half of the babies born in Bangladesh are underweight at birth, compared with one sixth of babies born in Africa and under 10 per cent in Europe and the United States, a significant difference which seems to be largely due to the persistence of social discrimination against women and the fact that women eat last and eat least.

In terms of access to water, considerable progress has also been made in improving access to water across Bangladesh through millions of small-scale tubewells for both drinking water and irrigation. Using tubewells instead of surface ponds has radically reduced the prevalence of waterborne disease, including diarrhoea, which was one of the major causes of premature death, especially of small children and babies. Increased availability of water for irrigation purposes has improved food security, enabling agriculture outside the rainy season and improving productivity. However, we reiterate our concern about arsenic contamination, which represents a regression in terms of access to fresh and safe drinking water. The poisoning of tubewell water by arsenic is a phenomenon that must be urgently addressed if Bangladesh's progress in social development is to be adequately realized. It should be recognized as well that high levels of malnutrition increase susceptibility to arsenic poisoning, which means that many Bangladeshis are at high risk, particularly women. There is also growing concern about the possible uptake of arsenic into the food chain, through the use of contaminated irrigation water. It has been demonstrated in a few studies that there is a risk that if crops, especially fruit, leaf vegetables and tubers, are irrigated using arsenic-contaminated water, then the arsenic may become present in the food produced. More broad-based and comprehensive studies will be needed to establish if this is the case. The urgency for dealing with the arsenic issue is therefore clear. There is an urgent need for immediate simple solutions that can be replicated across millions of villages, such as the provision of tanks to collect rainwater.

In terms of the general environment for human rights, we were encouraged by the electoral pledge of the then Prime Minister Khaleda Zia to establish the National Human Rights Commission and the Office of the Ombudsman, but disappointed by the lack of action so far taken towards their establishment. We would warn against moves to water down mandates, including the recent proposal to exempt the armed forces from the oversight of the Human Rights Commission. This is particularly important, given that, at the time of our visit, the launch of 'Operation Clean Heart', under which the Army had been brought in to restore the law-and-order situation in the country, had given rise to reports of human rights abuses. We emphasize that all elements of the Government and the armed forces should be trained in, and should respect, fundamental human rights.

8.5.2 Violations of the right to food

The Government of Bangladesh is obligated to respect, protect and fulfil all human rights, including the right to food. Specific violations of these obligations should be documented and treated as human rights violations, although few organizations in Bangladesh are yet working to monitor and document violations of the right to food.

With respect to specific cases of violations, our attention was drawn to one particularly worrisome case. This concerned the procurement of wheat in July 2002 by the Government for the creation of emergency grain stocks, which appeared to involve corruption in procurement and resulted in severe health impacts. These constituted a violation of the obligation to respect the right to food. As a part of its support and subsidy scheme to poor farmers and to create a buffer stock in line with existing policy, the Government apparently procured 100,000 metric tonnes of wheat at a cost of Tk 1 billion from local farmers. However, it was later alleged that this procurement was not from local Bangladeshi farmers as was required, as there was no production of wheat anywhere in Bangladesh at that time. Instead, it was alleged that the funds were largely misappropriated and low-cost, poultry grade feed was imported from India, but disguised as wheat from Bangladesh. In places where this wheat, which was unfit for human consumption, was later distributed, it is alleged that major health problems resulted, including diarrhoea. The misappropriation of funds which were supposed to support the right to food, apparently implicated senior Government officials. Although the Government took action to remove some officials responsible from their posts, no legal action was taken and no action was taken against senior officials, suggesting that impunity from the law for corrupt practices persists.

A number of other organizations raised serious concerns with regard to very different issues, although these had not been documented as violations of the right to food. Many NGOs were concerned that 'fisheries' programmes, such as shrimp farming, was resulting in displacement of poor farmers by powerful landowners, without any compensation to poor farmers or legal resort for them to recover their lands or to seek justice for violent attacks against them. We observed numerous serious violations of the right to food in Bangladesh, but given the lack of organizations working specifically on the right to food, there remains a lack of fully documented cases. We therefore urged greater documentation of violations of the obligations to respect, protect and fulfil the right to food, in order to reduce impunity and improve accountability.

8.5.3 Obstacles to the realization of the right to food

Bangladesh has made progress in overcoming the threat of famine and realization of the right to food, but there remain obstacles to the full realization of the right to food.

Natural disasters and climatic constraints are serious obstacles to establishing food security. Considerable progress has been made in reducing vulnerability to disasters and there have been improvements in disaster management and in addressing post-disaster transitory food insecurity. However, there remain problems of structural hunger, particularly in the more arid North and serious malnutrition and undernourishment remain common. The emergence of the problem of the natural disaster of arsenic contamination is also an obstacle to ensuring safe and healthy nutrition. The interlinkages between malnutrition and susceptibility to arsenicosis must be recognized.

Access to land and the lack of availability of land, as well as the illegal acquisition of land by powerful people is also an obstacle to food security. After the abolition of the *zamindari* (feudal landlord) system in 1950, certain categories of land were converted into *khas* land (fallow Government-owned lands) and subsequent land laws guaranteed access to *khas* land for poor and landless farmers. In practice however, much of this land is acquired by powerful people and the land registration and recording system lacks transparency and accountability. Over 70 per cent of criminal cases and civil litigations in rural Bangladesh relate to land disputes. Minority rights to land, including the rights of the Adivasi minorities of the Chittagong Hill Tracts, and the rights of ethnic and religious minorities to plain lands lack full protection under modern land laws, although a Land Commission for the Chittagong Hill Tracts areas should soon be operative. We met with one indigenous tribe during these field visits, among which only two families in the whole community still retained ownership of their lands. Under Islamic law, women have a right to only half the land to which their male siblings are entitled, although many women in Bangladesh considered that Islamic law was better than the Hindu tradition, which accords no land to women in inheritance custom.

Gender discrimination remains a powerful obstacle to the realization of the right to food in Bangladesh, with women more malnourished than men. Although women are protected and guaranteed equality by the law, existing social values, reinforced by religion, permit discrimination against women. The fact that women eat last and eat least reflects an unequal distribution of food within the household which should be understood as another form of violence against women. It should also be recognized that the malnutrition of women is a contributor to the low birth weight and high mortality of infants, both girl and boy children. The best way to ensure that babies are not born underweight is to ensure the health and nutrition of women. Other forms of discrimination encourage violence against women and contribute to and reinforce the undervaluation of women, including dowry-related violence, child marriage and 'acid-throwing' where women are intentionally disfigured by acid thrown in the face as vengeance for refusal of marriage proposals. Important work is being done by both the Government and NGOs to address these issues, but more still needs to be done.

Poor governance and mismanagement is also an obstacle to the realization of the right to food. It is widely alleged in Bangladesh, and by different international NGOs, that corruption is widespread in some institutions and authorities. At the time of our visit, a number of important development projects were stalled and the funds not disbursed by the World Bank, as a result of disagreements over procurement practices, including important National Integrated Nutrition Project and the Arsenic Mitigation Project. Leakages in funds and food aid provided for the poor are said to be frequent, and there is corruption alleged in procurement. Access to resources is also becoming increasingly controlled by powerful criminalized groups (Bangladesh's 'musclemen'), often linked into the Government structure through patron–client politics, contributing to the fragile law-and-order situation. Bangladesh's developing democracy is characterized by confrontational politics, which, together with the lack of accountability within the political and legal system, make it difficult to establish a solid system of governance. However, the Cabinet has decided that an Anti-Corruption Commission will soon be established.

Impunity is also an obstacle for the realization of all human rights, including the right to food. While the importance of restoring the law-and-order situation is clear, Operation Clean Heart, which began on 17 October 2002, entailed serious violations of human rights which must never be repeated, including the deaths in army custody of up to 40 people, allegedly due to torture. While efforts must be undertaken to restore and maintain respect for the rule of law, these must always be done within a framework of norms and standards which do not further exacerbate the situation of instability in the country and further violate human rights. Ad hoc practices, inconsistent with international human rights law, lead more to a breakdown in the physical integrity and security of the person, create fear and a climate of impunity, and take away the conditions for people to live and prosper in dignity rather than resolve the problem over the long-term. Parliament's enactment of the Joint Drive Indemnity Bill 2003 on 23 February 2003, which gave immunity from prosecution to the armed forces for actions carried out during Operation Clean Heart from 16 October 2002 and 9 January 2003, was a case in point.

Creating a climate of impunity is an obstacle to the cause of human rights in Bangladesh. The delays in setting up an independent human rights institution also constitute an obstacle to creating a strong environment for human rights. The lack of access to justice for the poor, with the lack of independence of the judiciary and the delay in fully separating the judiciary from the executive, also constitute obstacles, although a Cabinet Committee has been appointed to review the separation of the judiciary from the executive.

There are also a number of exogenous obstacles to the implementation of the right to food. We were concerned that the reform of the Public Food Distribution System, under the structural adjustment programme, was placing significant pressure on the Government to reduce public food stocks. Maintaining some form of Government capacity to respond to disasters, such as foodstocks or a cash reserve, is clearly fundamental in a country which suffers so frequently from natural disasters. Structural adjustment has been implemented gradually in Bangladesh, but many argue that it has not been effective in raising real wage rates to combat poverty. Patterns of increasing inequality and land concentration are beginning to be seen. The generation of employment, in both urban and rural areas, remains a key problem, particularly when changes in the textile quota system are likely to have devastating impacts on employment in the sector, particularly for women.

In terms of water policy, another important issue in Bangladesh is the sharing of the water of the great rivers of Asia that flow through it. Although Bangladesh often suffers from floods, as the rivers coming down from India, Nepal and Bhutan overflow with the meltwaters of the Himalayas, it is also a country that is dependent on vast water resources for food crops. More than 90 per cent of surface water in Bangladesh originates outside its territories which gives rise to uncertainties in the availability of water in Bangladesh, as water flowing into Bangladesh can be diverted by upper riparian countries.[28] The sharing of the Ganges River waters has been a major point of contention between Bangladesh and India for more than two decades. It is imperative that upper riparian countries reach agreements with Bangladesh over the fair sharing of water resources, acknowledging the effects of dams on the lower riparian nation of Bangladesh and according priority to drinking water and water required for food production. Some progress has been made in addressing this obstacle. An historic treaty between the two countries was signed in December 1996 which requires equitable sharing of the Ganges water and allows Bangladesh access to this water during the dry seasons,[29] but agreements on the sharing of water in the other rivers have still not been made.

8.6 Conclusions and recommendations

In his report on the mission to Bangladesh, presented to the Human Rights Council in March 2004, Jean Ziegler presented the following conclusions and recommendations.

The Government of Bangladesh has made important progress in realizing the right to food, in line with its human rights obligations. However, it is still clear that more could be done within available resources to improve the situation of the hungry and malnourished within the country. In particular, Jean Ziegler recommended that:

(a) Impressive progress has been made in reducing vulnerability to famine, particularly by increasing levels of production so as to reach self-sufficiency in cereal production. It is clear, however, that, given persistent widespread malnutrition and poverty in Bangladesh, there is also a need to increase the focus on access to food by the poorest and to address problems of structural hunger. This should be done through measures that include food aid, but also go beyond food aid to ensure a consistent and sustainable improvement in the access to food. In addition to the availability of and access to food, the right to food also relates to dietary needs; a public campaign to improve knowledge about nutrition should also be part of improving the realization of the right to food. Progress towards meeting goals set under international and national commitments should be monitored to ensure that the timetables for action are respected;

(b) An emergency reserve of food stocks or cash should always be maintained in order to provide an immediate response to the frequent disasters. It is fundamental that the Government retain a capacity for emergency relief response and that resources can be made immediately available, without relying only on the private sector in case of flooding or other disasters;

(c) Urgent action must be taken to address the arsenic problem. This should include preventive measures as well as measures for treating those suffering from arsenicosis. The recommendations for immediate action that emerged from the International Workshop on Arsenic Mitigation held in Dhaka in January 2002 should be implemented. There is a clear need for national legislation on water quality and supply, and for regulatory, monitoring and implementation mechanisms to be instituted. The responsibilities of the different ministries and government departments should be clearly formulated, in particular to ensure a coherent and comprehensive regulatory framework for groundwater utilization. The Bangladesh standard for arsenic contamination should also be brought into line with the international standards as set by the WHO, a process that could be led by the WHO office in Dhaka;

(d) There is an urgent need for a public information campaign on arsenic that makes suggestions for immediate and low-cost solutions that Bangladeshi villages can put immediately into effect, in addition to continued studies and discussions regarding longer term solutions to the problem. In the immediate term, one of the best solutions appears to be the collection of rainwater to use as drinking water by building small family cisterns to collect rainwater. Remedial action will be possible, given that Bangladesh benefits from high rainfall and has abundant access to surface water; however, it will require immediate and strong political will on the part of the Government. Places such as schools and hospitals should be tested immediately to ensure that children and others are not unnecessarily exposed to arsenic contamination;

(e) More work needs to be done to challenge patterns of gender discrimination, given increasing disparities in malnutrition rates between men and women, girls and boys. There is a particular need to understand that underweight mothers will have an affect on the health of the whole society, as malnourishment in the womb can severely affect the physical and mental growth of babies. Patterns of discrimination whereby women eat last should be challenged, particularly where this implies that they also eat least, and they should be understood as a form of violence against women. The implementation of legal protections in place to protect women should be strengthened, including protection against other forms of violence against women such as acid-throwing or child marriage. The Government should withdraw its reservations to the Convention on the Elimination of all forms of Discrimination against Women. More attention should be paid to implementing the laws and bridging the gap between laws and practice, the Government must show strong political will in support of women's rights to help eradicate the violence and discrimination against women in Bangladesh;

(f) Existing legislation on land issues should also be reviewed, revised and harmonized in order to improve protection of the land rights of the poorest, minorities and women, including improving access to *khas* (fallow Government-owned) land and challenging the illegal acquisition of land by powerful people. The review should include the Land Reform Act as it relates to sharecropping and leasing practices, with a view to improving the situation of tenant farmers. The land registration and recording system should also be made more reliable, transparent and accountable, and brought under the responsibility of the Land Ministry. A separate land tribunal or land court could be established to improve the settlement of disputes over land;

(g) Remedies for violations of the right to food and water must be available through the courts in order to reduce impunity for these violations. This should include judicial action, or other forms of accountability, in cases of misappropriation of food stocks, or mismanagement in procurement methods, or illegal forced displacement without compensation. The proposed Anti-Corruption Commission should also be established to improve transparency and accountability, particularly in food distribution and procurement;

(h) Access to justice for the poor should be improved. The independence of the judiciary and the enforcement of court decisions, as well as existing national legislation, should also be addressed so as to improve accountability. Efforts must be made to reduce impunity for human rights violations and decisions of the executive branch should not contribute to violations of human rights. Parliament also has a role in promoting and protecting human rights. Even in a difficult law and order situation, it is fundamental to respect human rights and the rule of law. This is also vital for the external perception of Bangladesh's and will ensure the continued positive perception of Bangladesh's international peacekeeping troops. The Government should take into account the very serious observations and recommendations made in the report 'Human security in Bangladesh: in search of justice and dignity', drafted under the auspices of the UNDP in September 2002;

(i) The long-promised national human rights commission should be established, as should the human rights ombudsman, to strengthen the human rights situation in Bangladesh. The independence of these institutions must be ensured and they should be set up in accordance with the Paris Principles. Changes made to the mandate of the proposed commission, including the exclusion of the armed forces from its supervision, should be reviewed and revised in the light of the Paris Principles. Both institutions should also be given a strong mandate to monitor and promote the realization of economic, social and cultural rights, including the right to food;

(j) Finally, it is imperative that India and Bangladesh conclude arrangements for the fair sharing of water resources, including water in the rivers other than the Ganges, which cross the boundaries between India and Bangladesh, as envisaged in the 1996 treaty. These agreements should acknowledge the effects of dams, but also of floods, on the lower riverine nation of Bangladesh. The rights of Bangladesh under international watercourse law should be recognized by India.

9
The Occupied Palestinian Territories

9.1 Introduction

We (Jean Ziegler, Sally-Anne Way and Christophe Golay) carried out a mission to the Occupied Palestinian Territories (OPT) from 3 to 12 July 2003.[1] The mission was welcomed by the Government of Israel in a letter dated 23 May 2003. The mission was carried out during a moment of hope when negotiations for the 'road map' were making progress and the ceasefire was holding. The road map process, an outline for peace in which the United Nations has played a vital role as a participant in the Quartet, holed the promise of bringing an end to the terrible suffering of both Israelis and Palestinians.

During the mission, we expressed our deep sympathy and compassion for all those killed and injured in the violence. In 2003, both the Palestinian and the Israeli populations were living through a horrifying tragedy. Israelis lived under the threat of suicide attacks by Palestinian bombers. Palestinians also lived in fear as women and children were often killed in their homes or in crowded streets by Israeli military operations targeting Palestinian leaders. Since the start of the second intifada in September 2000, 820 Israelis and 2518 Palestinians had reportedly been killed, many of them innocent women and children.[2] Thousands of Israeli and Palestinian civilians had been severely injured.

Our visit was undertaken in accordance with the mandate of Jean Ziegler and in response to the emergence of a humanitarian crisis in the OPT. The objectives of the mission were to gain a greater understanding of the reasons for the emerging food crisis in the Territories, a crisis which seemed absurd in a land so fertile. The mission aimed to examine the malnutrition among the Palestinians from the perspective of the right to food. It was not within the mandate of the mission to examine malnutrition in Israel, as while malnutrition did exist among the poorest Israelis, it was not at crisis levels.

We were received by officials of the Government of Israel in Tel Aviv and Jerusalem. We met with the Deputy Director-General of the Ministry for

Foreign Affairs and with officials from the Ministry of Defence, including the Deputy Coordinator of Civil Activities in the Gaza Strip and the West Bank, Mr Camil Abu Rukun. We also met with Mr Yossef C. Dreizin, Director of the Water Planning Division of the Water Commission. We also had the opportunity to meet distinguished opposition party leaders in the Israeli parliament. However, while granted these meetings, we were not granted free movement in the West Bank and Gaza Strip and we were frequently held up at military checkpoints, despite advance coordination of all travel. At a checkpoint in Qualqilya, an Israeli soldier deliberately took aim with his weapon at very short range at our vehicle. Fortunately, the soldier did not fire his weapon, but we noted that these types of incidents were occurring far too frequently.

We were received by the Palestinian National Authority in the West Bank and the Gaza Strip, including the Chairman of the Palestinian National Authority, Yasir Arafat, and Chief Palestinian Negotiator, Saeb Erekat, as well as the Ministers of Health, Housing and Agriculture. We also met with representatives from the Ministry of Labour, the Palestinian Water Authority and the Negotiation Unit of the Palestine Liberation Organization and with distinguished members of the Palestinian Legislative Council. The mission also met with Dr Said Zeidani, Director of the Palestinian Independent Commission for Citizens' Rights. In the different areas of the West Bank and the Gaza Strip, the mission met with local authority leaders, village and town mayors, unionists and academics.

In Jerusalem, we held meetings with senior representatives of the Office of the United Nations Special Coordinator in the Occupied Territories (UNSCO), the United Nations Relief and Works Agency for Palestine Refugees in the Near East (UNRWA), FAO, WFP, UNDP, the Office for the Coordination of Humanitarian Affairs (OCHA), UNICEF, the United Nations Fund for Population Activities (UNFPA), the United Nations Security Coordinator (UNSECOORD) and the World Bank, and met UNRWA Commissioner General Peter Hansen in Geneva.

We also met with international, Israeli and Palestinian NGOs in Tel Aviv, Jerusalem, the West Bank and the Gaza Strip. We met with international organizations, including Action Against Hunger, Oxfam, Care International, Save the Children, Terre des Hommes, Physicians for Human Rights and Habitat International Coalition, working to relieve the crisis in the OPT. We also met with Israeli and Palestinian organizations, including B'Tselem, Rabbis for Human Rights, the Mandela Institute, LAW, the Public Committee against Torture, the Palestinian Hydrology Group, the Palestinian Agricultural Relief Committees and the Applied Research Institute-Jerusalem. It is these NGOs that bring hope, as it is mainly through their work that vital bridges were being built between Israelis and Palestinians.

We travelled in the West Bank and the Gaza Strip, the territories that together make up the OPT, occupied and under Israeli military administration since 1967. They have an area of around 5800 km² in which more than 3.5 million Palestinians live. The Gaza Strip is one of the most crowded places on earth with one of the highest population densities: 1.3 million people in an area of 360 km², 83 per cent of whom live in refugee camps. We travelled in the Gaza strip, visiting Beit Hanoun, Jabalia, Khan Younis and the border areas of Rafah. We also travelled widely in the West Bank, visiting, among other places, Jerusalem, Bethlehem, Ramallah, Jericho, Qalquilya and Tulkarem, where the huge fence/wall (called the 'security fence' by the Israelis and the 'apartheid wall' by the Israeli opposition and Palestinian activists), was being built. We also visited Meggido prison, an Israeli institution holding Palestinian detainees, and a Palestinian prison holding Palestinian detainees in Jericho. During these trips, we had the opportunity to speak with a wide variety of Palestinian men and women, including Palestinian farmers, merchants and academics.

9.2 Malnutrition and food insecurity in the Occupied Palestinian Territories

9.2.1 On the verge of humanitarian catastrophe

The OPT was on the verge of humanitarian catastrophe, as the result of extremely harsh military measures that the occupying Israeli military forces had imposed in response to the outbreak of the second intifada in September 2000.

Malnutrition levels among Palestinians had increased rapidly since September 2000. A study by John Hopkins University/Al-Quds University, funded by the United States Agency for International Development (USAID), reported that 'the Palestinian Territories, and especially the Gaza Strip, face a distinct humanitarian emergency in regard to acute moderate and severe malnutrition'.[3] The report of the Personal Humanitarian Envoy of the Secretary-General, Catherine Bertini also regarded the increase in malnutrition as an indicator of a growing humanitarian crisis.[4] Over 22 per cent of children under five were suffering from malnutrition (9.3 per cent suffering from acute malnutrition and 13.2 per cent suffering from chronic malnutrition) in 2002.[5] Around 15.6 per cent of children under five suffered from acute anaemia,[6] which for many will have permanent negative effects on their physical and mental development. Severe malnutrition reported in Gaza was then equivalent to levels found in poor sub-Saharan countries, an absurd situation as Palestine was formerly a middle-income economy. Food consumption had fallen by 25–30 per cent per capita. This had been attributed largely to job losses (65 per cent) and curfews (33 per cent).[7] Food shortages, particularly of proteins, had been widely reported.[8] More than half of Palestinian households did eat only once per day.[9] Many Palestinians who we met spoke of trying to subsist on little more than bread and tea.

A 2003 World Bank report pointed to economic crisis in the OPT.[10] The economy had almost collapsed and the numbers of the extreme poor had tripled. Around 60 per cent of Palestinians lived in acute poverty (75 per cent in Gaza and 50 per cent in the West Bank). Gross national income per capita had fallen to nearly half of what it was two years before.[11] Even when food was available, many Palestinians were not able to buy it. Around 50 per cent of Palestinians had been forced into debt to buy food[12] and over 50 per cent of Palestinians were then completely dependent on food aid, yet humanitarian access remained problematic.

9.2.2 Causes of the food crisis

Closures and movement restrictions

An unprecedented level of restrictions on the movements of Palestinians inside the Occupied Territories was depriving Palestinians not only of their freedom of movement, but also of their right to food. The extensive imposition of curfews, road closures, permit systems, security checkpoints and 'back-to-back' truck off-loading systems, which required that most trucks be off-loaded on one side of a checkpoint and reloaded onto another truck on the other side, imposed by the occupying military forces were producing the humanitarian crisis. The USAID-funded study argued that 'The onset of the Intifada in September 2000 and the subsequent Israeli military incursions, closure and curfews have devastated the Palestinian economy and undermined those systems the Palestinian civilian population relies on for basic needs, including food and health'.[13] The World Bank agreed that 'the proximate cause of the Palestinian economic crisis is closure'.[14] Restrictions on movement meant that many Palestinians were not able to feed themselves: they were not able to go to work, go to harvest their fields or go to buy food. For many Palestinians, the inability to feed their families was leading to a loss of human dignity, often heightened by bullying and humiliation at checkpoints.[15]

Closures prevented movement between the Palestinian areas and Israel, but also within the OPT. Roads were closed between nearly every village and town in the OPT, using checkpoints manned by soldiers or by physical barriers such as concrete blocks and deep trenches. Journeys that would have taken a few minutes then took several hours or days. We saw that it was sometimes possible, in going from one place to another, to take a long way around through mountains if one was fit and able to walk, but not if one was old, weak, hungry or sick. The movement of goods was controlled by the back-to-back off-loading system. With numerous checkpoints, this dramatically increased the cost of transporting food and agricultural produce.[16] Permission to cross at checkpoints for agricultural produce and other food could be refused for days. At various checkpoints in the West Bank, we saw truckloads of fruit and vegetables rotting under the sun.

Every Palestinian had to have a permit to travel any long distance or to work in Israel. At the outbreak of the intifada, permits were revoked and more than 100,000 Palestinians lost jobs in Israel, severely affecting economic access to food. The Government of Israel had taken steps to reissue 32,000 permits, but movement restrictions made it difficult for Palestinians even when they had permits.[17] Palestinians were required to apply for permits to travel from one West Bank town to another, but permits were frequently refused without explanation, making it difficult to find work even in the OPT.[18] Curfews, sometimes imposed for days at a time, had kept populations of whole towns inside their homes under virtual house arrest.[19] These measures made life unbearable and were seriously threatening the food security of all Palestinians.

Water shortages in the OPT were also very serious. With the system of checkpoints and road closures in place, it was reported that water tankers could not always reach villages or were not permitted to cross checkpoints, leaving communities without water for days at a time.[20] It was reported that the situation was most serious for the approximately 280 rural communities in the OPT that had no access to wells or running water and were completely dependent on water delivered by municipal and private water tankers that frequently had to be purchased from the Israeli water company, Mekorot. The price of such water had reportedly risen by up to 80 per cent since September 2000 as a result of the increase in transport costs due to closures, the quality of most water brought in by tanker no longer met World Health Organization drinking water standards[21] and reports of water-borne diseases continued to rise as a result of increased dependence on poor quality water resources.[22]

Destruction, expropriation and confiscation of Palestinian land

Since the outbreak of the second intifada, an unprecedented level of destruction and confiscation of Palestinian land, water, infrastructure and other resources was also depriving many Palestinians of their right to food and water. The tearing up of farms wells and wide swathes of agricultural field had contributed to the collapse of agriculture. In Beit Hanoun in the Gaza Strip, we saw the devastating destruction of agricultural infrastructure, and farm buildings and the razing of hundreds of olive and citrus trees after a military incursion. We saw the destruction of homes and livelihoods in Khan Younis and in Rafah. We saw the bulldozers of the occupying forces still at work in Rafah in the place where Rachel Corrie, the American peace activist, was killed by an armoured bulldozer while trying to save a Palestinian home from destruction in March 2003.[23]

The expropriation and confiscation of vast swathes of Palestinian agricultural land and water sources was also threatening the right to food. Land was being confiscated to build the fence/wall on the western side of the OPT (see below) and in Jerusalem, including the sections that bisect towns such as Abu Dis and Sawahreh. Gideon Levy wrote that the wall that cuts Abu Dis in half amounted to 'collective abuse bearing no relation to its declared purpose'. The soldiers allowed people to climb over the wall if they could. 'An entire town scales the wall to get to school, to the grocery store, to work – day after day, evening after evening: old folks, young folks, women and children'.[24]

Land was also confiscated for the extension of settlements, the building of settler-only roads and the building of security buffers around the settlements. On 21 May 2003, for example, the Housing Ministry advertised a tender for the construction of 502 new apartments in Maale Adumim.[25] The occupying force was gradually taking greater control over more Palestinian land, following the planned map of settlement and the by-pass road construction which aimed at ensuring the continuous rule of Israel, both directly over the confiscated land which was declared 'State land', and indirectly by encircling almost every single Palestinian community by settlements and 'fire areas' or military training grounds.[26] Settler-only roads cut through Palestinian territories, slicing the area up and operating as another form of closure which prevented movement of Palestinians. Many international, Israeli and Palestinian NGOs argued that the ongoing confiscation of Palestinian land amounted to a slow dispossession of the Palestinian people, depriving them of their means of subsistence.

Impeding humanitarian aid

The Government of Israel has an obligation under international law to ensure the basic food and water needs of the occupied population and to provide assistance when necessary. Nonetheless, at the time of our visit, it was the United Nations and other international and non-governmental agencies that had to step in to provide food aid to the Palestinians. At the time of the mission, UNRWA was providing food aid to 127,000 families in Gaza and 90,000 refugee families in the West Bank. The World Food Programme (WFP) was providing emergency support to half a million Palestinians in cooperation with the ICRC, which had exceptionally extended its food aid programme. The Government of Israel informed us that efforts were being made to assure humanitarian access for food and water. The August 2002 visit of Catherine Bertini, the Secretary-General's Personal Humanitarian Envoy, was intended to secure specific commitments from the Government of Israel to facilitate access to humanitarian aid. However, many humanitarian organizations stated that their access was frequently restricted or denied through checkpoints, closures and the back-to-back truck off-loading system. Although the Bertini visit had resulted in some improvements in humanitarian access, the commitments made by the Government of Israel to Catherine Bertini (the 'Bertini commitments') were still far from being fully respected.[27]

9.3 Legal framework governing the right to food in the Occupied Palestinian Territories

Under international human rights and humanitarian law, the Government of Israel, as occupying Power, has the responsibility to ensure the basic needs of the civilian Palestinian population and to avoid violating the right to food.

9.3.1 International law status of the Occupied Palestinian Territories in 2003

Under international law, the West Bank, East Jerusalem and the Gaza Strip were defined as 'occupied territory', and Israel as the 'occupying Power' in 2003, as confirmed by the United Nations Security Council (resolution 471 (1980)). The Oslo process had not changed the status of the Occupied Territories, as the Security Council (resolution 1322 (2000)), the General Assembly, the ICRC and the High Contracting Parties to the Fourth Geneva Convention had reaffirmed.

Both international human rights and humanitarian law were applicable in the OPT, although the Government of Israel contested this. Israel contested the (de jure) application of the Geneva Convention relative to the Protection of Civilian Persons in Time of War (but agreed nonetheless to apply its humanitarian provisions de facto) and of human rights law.

However, most countries and United Nations bodies had agreed that international humanitarian law did apply. The Security Council, the General Assembly, the ICRC, High Contracting Parties to the Geneva Convention, as well as the Commission on Human Rights had repeatedly reiterated that the Fourth Geneva Convention applied de jure to the situation of the OPT. According to the Israeli High Court,[28] the only regulations that applied were the Regulations concerning the Laws and Customs of War on Land annexed to the Hague Convention No. IV of 1907 of which Articles 42–56 relate to occupied territory, as these were part of customary international law. However, the Fourth Geneva Convention also forms part of customary international law, as confirmed by the International Court of Justice[29] and the Security Council, as does the Geneva Convention relative to the Treatment of Prisoners of War.[30]

United Nations bodies had also repeatedly reaffirmed the applicability of human rights law in the OPT, including the Security Council (resolution 237 (1967)), Special Rapporteur of the Commission on Human Rights on the situation of human rights in the OPT, John Dugard (see E/CN.4/2002/32) the CESCR and other treaty bodies. This was also reaffirmed in the 1995 Israeli-Palestinian Interim Agreement on the West Bank and the Gaza Strip (Article XIX). The General Assembly had repeatedly reaffirmed the Palestinian people's right to self-determination,[31] which means that Palestinians should be able to freely dispose of their natural wealth and natural resources, and in no case be deprived of their means of subsistence.[32]

9.3.2 Obligations of the Government of Israel

The Government of Israel was the occupying Power with certain defined obligations under international humanitarian law. Humanitarian law aims to ensure access to adequate food and water in times of conflict and for occupied populations.

The first obligation of Israel as the occupying Power was to respect access to food and drinking water of the Palestinian population. According to humanitarian law, private property cannot be confiscated (The Hague Regulations, Article 46), collective punishment and annexation are prohibited (Fourth Geneva Convention, Articles 33, 47), requisitions cannot be demanded, except for military needs (The Hague Regulations, Article 52), and any destruction of property belonging to individuals or collectively to private persons, or to the State, is prohibited (Fourth Geneva Convention, Article 53) unless such destruction is rendered absolutely necessary for military operations.

As the occupying Power, the Government of Israel also had the obligation to provide food and water if the resources in the territories were inadequate. The occupying Power should assure the food and water supplies of the population and bring in necessary foodstuffs (ibid. Article 55). If this is not possible, then the occupying Power must allow access for impartial humanitarian organizations (ibid. Articles 23 and 59), but this does not in any way reduce the obligations of the occupying Power (ibid. Article 60).

Humanitarian law does take military necessities into account. The occupying Power is not prohibited from taking measures – military or administrative – to ensure the security of its military forces and civilian administration in the occupied territory, as long as the measures taken are absolutely necessary for military operations, are proportional and do not prevent the occupying Power from respecting its obligations, including the obligation to assure the basic needs of the inhabitants of the occupied territory. However, according to humanitarian law, the occupying Power does not automatically have the right to take measures related to the security of its civilians living in settlements in the occupied territory, because the establishment of settlements is in itself illegal, as outlined under the sixth paragraph of Article 49 of the Fourth Geneva Convention. This has been reaffirmed repeatedly by the United Nations General Assembly, the ICRC, the High Contracting Parties to the Geneva Conventions and the Security Council.

The State of Israel has ratified all the principal instruments for the protection of human rights that protect the right to food, including the International Covenant on Economic, Social and Cultural Rights (Article 11), without reservations on the applicability of these conventions in the occupied territories. It should also respect the Universal Declaration of

Human Rights (Article 25), which in many respects has become part of customary international law. The CESCR, along with other treaty bodies and legal experts, has insisted on the facts that Israel's 'obligations...apply to all territories and populations under its effective control'.[33] A State is also accountable for the actions of its authorities in territories outside of its de jure jurisdiction, including in occupied territories,[34] and the International Covenant on Economic, Social and Cultural Rights does not include a territorial limitation clause. As noted above, the Covenant states that '[i]n no case may a people be deprived of its own means of subsistence' (Article 1).

Under the Oslo Accords, an important part of the responsibilities of the Government of Israel in the OPT was transferred to the Palestinian Authority.[35] However, the situation had evolved since September 2000, and the occupying forces had retaken control over most of the OPT within these areas. The vast majority of the OPT was under the effective control of the occupying army, as was entry and exit to areas under Palestinian administration, as we witnessed during visits to the Gaza Strip, Ramallah, Bethlehem, Jericho, Qalqilya and Tulkarem. In 2003, Israel therefore had the primary obligation to respect, protect and fulfil the right to food of the Palestinian population in the OPT, without discrimination.

9.3.3 Obligations of the Palestinian Authority

The Palestinian Authority is committed through the Oslo process to respect human rights, including the right to food.[36] Under the Oslo process, certain responsibilities were transferred to the Palestinian Authority in Areas A and B in March 2000, including questions relating to food and water. However, given that since September 2000 the occupying Power had regained effective control of most of the OPT, including Areas A and B, the Palestinian Authority did not have the obligation to respect, protect and fulfil the right to food for the Palestinian population living in Areas A and B, except in the few areas where it exercised effective control and to the extent that resources were available.

For areas where it did have control, the Palestinian Authority was developing a National Food Security Strategy and was carrying out various social programmes, including supporting 36,000 families under the Special Hardship Cases programme of the Ministry of Social Affairs. We were concerned about numerous allegations of corruption in the use of the resources of the Palestinian Authority made by numerous Israeli and Palestinian commentators.[37] Nonetheless, with respect to the programme for Special Hardship Cases, the World Bank had stated that it was effectively managed and that there was little leakage of benefits.[38] The World Bank stated that the Palestinian Authority was undergoing reform and had managed as well as it could have had to deliver social services under the difficult circumstances of restrictions on the movement of staff and of its ministers.[39] However, we were concerned at reports, confirmed by NGOs, that numerous detainees in

Palestinian prisons complained of having received insufficient food. During our visit, we emphasized that the Palestinian Authority had the obligation to respect the right to food of the prisoners it detained, as outlined in the commitments made under the Interim Agreement (Article XI (1)) and the Wye River Memorandum (Article II (c) (4)).

9.3.4 Other key laws and institutions

The law governing the situation in the OPT is complex and includes elements of Ottoman law, the law under the British Mandate, Jordanian law in the West Bank and Egyptian law in the Gaza Strip, Israeli military orders, as well as more recent Palestinian laws and international law.

In 2003, according to the Emergency Regulations instituted by the Government of Israel in 1967, the Military Commander of the occupying Power had the competence to issue military orders that apply to the OPT. Using military orders, the occupying Power had taken control over water resources and thousands of acres of land throughout the West Bank and the Gaza Strip. The following four methods were used to take control of the land: (i) declaration and registration of land as 'State land', and of water resources as State property; (ii) requisitions for military needs; (iii) declaration of land as abandoned property and expropriation of wells used for irrigation; and (iv) confiscation of land for public needs. However, Article 43 of The Hague Regulations prohibits the occupying Power from altering the legal system in the occupied territory. Seizure of land for the establishment of settlements in the OPT is also a violation of the Fourth Geneva Convention, which prohibits the establishment of settlements, and any confiscation of private property in the OPT is in violation of The Hague Regulations. Moreover, the seizure of any property or resource of the Palestinian population or of the Palestinian Authority is a violation of the right of the Palestinian people to freely dispose of its natural wealth and natural resources, in accordance with its right to self-determination.

The Security Council in its resolution 465 (1980) determined that

> all measures taken by Israel to change the physical character, demographic composition, institutional structure or status of the Palestinian and other Arab territories occupied since 1967, including Jerusalem, or any part thereof have no legal validity and that Israel's policy and practices of settling parts of its population and new immigrants in those territories constitute a flagrant violation of the [Fourth Geneva Convention] and also constitute a serious obstruction to achieving a comprehensive, just and lasting peace in the Middle East. (paragraph 5)

The Oslo Accords were also important for understanding the land-, water- and settlement-related issues in the OPT. In terms of water issues, for example, the Government of Israel recognized Palestinian water rights in the West Bank and a Joint Water Committee was established to deal with water- and sewage-related issues there.[40] All decisions of the Joint Water Committee must be reached by consensus. In practice, NGOs suggested that the Government of Israel had vetoed the building of most new water drilling and sewage projects in the West Bank.[41]

9.4 Main findings and concerns

9.4.1 The humanitarian crisis

During our visit, we were gravely concerned by the rapid increase in the malnutrition and poverty levels in the OPT. The growing dependence of the Palestinian population on food aid, at the same time as restrictions on humanitarian access remain in force, was heightening the vulnerability of the Palestinian population. In discussions with us, the Israeli authorities recognized that there was a humanitarian crisis in the OPT. They did not dispute the statistics of increasing malnutrition and poverty of the Palestinians. However, they saw them as the regrettable, but inevitable, consequences of security measures that were necessary to prevent attacks on Israelis. We did not question the security needs of Israel, and understood the daily risks run by Israeli citizens. However, the measures being taken at that time were disproportionate because they were causing hunger and malnutrition among Palestinian civilians.

The Israeli Ministry of Defence and the Civil Administration officials informed us that they were taking measures in some circumstances to alleviate the humanitarian consequences of military action. The website of the Israeli Defence Forces listed such actions undertaken.[42] Nonetheless, we observed that these measures seemed to have had limited effects on alleviating the impacts of military measures. Only by lifting the closure regime could the humanitarian catastrophe have been averted. We were also gravely concerned at the continued destruction and confiscation of Palestinian land, water tanks and wells and other resources, as this foreclosed the possibility of an independent Palestinian State that could sustain a viable economy and agricultural sector.

9.4.2 Violations of the right to food

During our visit, we were also concerned by the numerous specific violations of the different obligations entailed under the right to food. As outlined in *General Comment No. 12*, these obligations include the obligation to respect, protect and fulfil the right to food.

Obligations to respect the right to food

The obligation to respect the right to food means that the occupying Power must not disrupt or destroy the Palestinians' existing access to food. It is an immediate (not progressive) obligation and requires the occupying Power to avoid negatively affecting existing availability and physical or economic access to adequate food and water.

Closures and curfews

The extensive imposition of closures, curfews and permit systems constituted a violation of the obligation to respect the right to food, as it threatened the physical and economic access to food, as well as food availability. The United Nations reported in June 2003 that 'due to movement restrictions, the distribution and marketing of food produce has been severely affected, thereby disrupting food supply stability and seriously affecting the economy of farmers/rural population.'[43] According to the USAID study, 'market disruptions from curfews, closures, military incursions, border closures and checkpoints affected [the availability] of key high protein foods, especially meat and poultry and dairy products, and in particular infant formula and powdered milk'.[44] Curfews had been a primary reason in the West Bank why people were eating less food, notably in Nablus, which was under curfew for 1797 hours from 21 June to 6 September 2002, and in Tulkarem, which was under curfew for 1486 hours during the same period, with Ramallah and Bethlehem also severely affected.[45] In discussions with UNRWA, we learned that despite a good harvest of 35,000 tonnes of olive oil in 2002, the Palestinians were only able to sell 200 tonnes, owing to restrictions on trade. External closures and the control by Israel over the import and export of Palestinian goods severely affected their access to international trade and therefore their ability to import food supplies when necessary.

Closures had also caused water shortages. Communities such as Burin, south-west of Nablus, had no independent water supply and were therefore completely dependent on water deliveries, which were severely disrupted by closures.[46] The village of Beit Furik, 10 km south-east of Nablus, received no water for at least nine consecutive days since no water tankers were allowed into the village.[47] A survey by the Palestinian Hydrology Group showed that 24 out of 27 villages surveyed experienced water problems as a result of curfews and closures.[48]

Destruction of Palestinian land, water and other resources

The direct destruction of livelihoods of Palestinians also amounted to a violation of the obligation to respect the right to food. Humanitarian and human rights provisions prohibit the destruction of objects necessary to the survival of the civilian population, such as water tanks, crops and agricultural infrastructure, as well as the broader economic and social infrastructure.

According to the World Bank, damage inflicted on agriculture had reached US$ 217 million and physical damage to the water and wastewater sector of about US$ 140 million.[49] The Palestinian National Information

Center (PNIC) suggested that between 29 September 2000 and 31 May 2003, the occupying forces uprooted hundreds of thousands of olive, citrus and other fruit trees, destroyed 806 wells and 296 agricultural warehouses, tore up 2000 roads and blocked thousands of others with concrete and dirt mounds.[50] The Palestinian Hydrology Group recorded the total or partial destruction between June 2002 and February 2003 of 42 water tankers and 9128 Palestinian roof-top water tanks. OCHA recorded, in Abu Nejeim, in the Bethlehem area, the severing of the water connections by the occupying army by digging up and destroying the pipes.[51] According to the Governorate of Northern Gaza, 3684 dunums of land were bulldozed with 95,000 olive and citrus trees, five water wells were destroyed, and many people were killed and houses destroyed during the incursions of the occupying forces between May and June 2003. The ministries and building of the Palestinian Authority had also been particular targets, making the delivery of social support difficult. The World Bank stated that damage to public infrastructure by the occupying forces amounted to US$ 251 million, including the 'widespread ransacking of Palestinian Authority ministry buildings and municipal offices'.[52]

Expropriation of Palestinian land, water and other resources
Expropriation of Palestinian land in the OPT constituted a violation of the obligation to respect the right to food when it deprived Palestinians of their means of existence and when it was for the establishment of settlements, as these are illegal under international law. Although the takeover of land was unilaterally legalized under Israeli military orders applied in the OPT, it still remained a violation of international law, including Article 43 of the Hague Regulations.

NGOs pointed out that in 1999, 44 new settlements or outposts were built in the West Bank. In 2001, 34 settlements were established and 14 further settlements approved by the Government of Israel. According to the non-governmental organization ARIJ, the total area that had been confiscated or designated military zones in the Gaza Strip amounts to 165.04 km^2, or 45 per cent of the Gaza territory. In the Gaza Strip, there were reportedly 6429 Israeli settlers who used this 45 per cent of the land, compared with over 1 million Palestinians on the remaining 55 per cent of the land. This resulted in a population density for the Palestinians that was one of the highest in the world, and almost 100 times greater than that of the Israelis.

Although three very important fresh water aquifers were located beneath the OPT, there was an extremely inequitable distribution of water resources. The Palestinian entitlements to water included the West Bank (western, north-eastern and eastern) and Gaza aquifers, and the Jordan River. However, statistics for daily per capita water consumption suggested that Israelis received and used five times more water than Palestinians.[53] In the year 2002, Palestinians used 70 litres, compared to 350 litres for Israelis in

Israel and in the settlements. According to Oxfam, the occupying Power extracted more than 85 per cent of the water from the West Bank aquifers. Irrigated farmland along the Jordan River had been declared a closed military area which Palestinians cannot use. In discussions with the Water Commission of Israel, officials informed us that the Government of Israel had offered the Palestinians access to a desalinization plant to take water from the Mediterranean. However, it did not appear to be economically viable to bring water from the sea, when aquifers and surface water already existed in the Palestinian Territories. The transport of water would be extremely expensive and physically difficult, particularly given movement restrictions and the construction of the fence/wall.

The fence/wall

The fence/wall is a huge barrier, sometimes a fence, sometimes a concrete wall, over 8 m high (around Qualquilya), which does not follow the 1967 border between Israel and the OPT. The building of the fence/wall led to violations of the obligation to respect the right to food because it cut off Palestinians from their agricultural lands, wells and means of subsistence.[54]

In 2003, the Israeli human rights organization B'Tselem evaluated that 36 communities (72,200 Palestinians) would be separated from their lands that lied west of the barrier; 19 communities (128,500 people) would be almost completely imprisoned by the winding route of the wall, including 40,000 people who would be trapped in Qualqilya; 13 communities (11,700 people) would be trapped in the land defined as a closed military zone between the wall and the Green Line, cut off from the OPT but forbidden from entering Israel.[55] We visited a village of 3500 inhabitants situated in the hills of Qualqilya, in the region of Tulkarem. The mayor's office overlooked the fields of olive and citrus trees and tomato greenhouses, but all these lay on the other side of the fence/wall. Although one gate had been built in the wall, it had not been possible to use it. The mayor recounted that 'the families have tried numerous times to reach their olive fields, but the soldiers set dogs on them, fired shots and beat young women and men, so that now no one tries to risk it'.

It was evaluated that the first phase of the fence/wall would confiscate 2875 acres of land just for the 'footprint'.[56] The land confiscated was some of the most fertile land in the OPT. By constructing the fence Israel would also effectively annex most of the western aquifer system (which provides 51 per cent of the West Bank's water resources). With the fence/wall cutting communities off from their land and water without other means of subsistence, many of the Palestinians living in these areas would be forced to leave. It was estimated that 6000–8000 people had already left the area of Qualquilya. The Government of Israel informed us that legal procedures in place allowed every owner of land to file an objection to the requisition of their land. Yet, according to a report requested by the international donor community on the socioeconomic impacts of the fence/wall, every appeal against the requisitioning of land (numbering in the hundreds) made to the military Appeals Committee had been rejected, although in some cases the amount of land taken had been reduced.[57] The speed with which the occupying Power was building the wall (24 hours a day) made it difficult to allow for proper judicial process.

It was estimated that the planned second phase of the fence/wall, as outlined in official Israeli documents,[58] would cut right through the middle of the West Bank, from Salem to Bet-Shean, which would be a de facto annexation of the whole of the Jordan Valley by Israel. As described in the Israeli newspaper *Yediot Ahronot* in March 2003 and cited in *Between the Lines*, this wall would bite off almost half of the area remaining for the future Palestinian State and would thus eliminate all reasonable options for a settlement of the conflict in the coming years.[59] This would amount to a structural negation of the right to food, as it would effectively forestall the possibility of a viable Palestinian state.

Obligation to protect the right to food

The obligation to protect the right to food means that the responsible State must protect the civilian population in occupied areas from third parties attempting to restrict, deny or destroy people's existing access to food and water. Violations of this obligation to protect could include, in this case, impunity for settlers who shoot at Palestinians in their fields for harvesting. The Israeli non-governmental organization the Alternative Information Centre made regular reports on frequent settler violence against Palestinians and their right to food.[60] Amnesty International also recorded instances of violence that had not been investigated.[61]

Obligation to fulfil the right to food

The obligation to fulfil the right to food entails the obligation to facilitate people's capacity to feed themselves and, as a last resort, to provide food assistance to people who cannot feed themselves for reasons beyond their own control. As the occupying Power, the State of Israel bears a treaty obligation to facilitate and ensure the access to food of the civilian Palestinian population and to facilitate humanitarian access for impartial organizations providing emergency assistance.

Although the Government of Israel had improved levels of humanitarian access in some cases since the August 2002 visit by Catherine Bertini, substantial difficulties for humanitarian agencies remained. UNRWA reported in June 2003, 231 instances of excessive delay or denial of passage at checkpoints (186 incidents of delay, 41 incidents where access was denied and 4 incidents in which staff members were detained).[62] In December 2002, it was reported that the occupying army exploded a warehouse being used by WFP, destroying 537 tons of food aid largely financed by the European Commission.[63] In April 2003, it was reported that full closure was imposed on Gaza from 16 to 27 April and access for WFP and UNRWA was denied.[64] In its June 2003 monthly monitoring report on the Bertini commitments, OCHA reported that no unmanned barriers had been removed to facilitate movement of water tankers into villages and towns, but additional barriers of earth and concrete had been put up in Ramallah and Nablus governorates, as well as in Balta camp.[65]

The lack of provision of adequate food and water to Palestinians detained by the Government of Israel would also constitute a violation of the obligation to fulfil the right to food. The Israeli non-governmental organization the Mandela Institute, which monitored prison conditions, presented us with information about insufficient, poor quality food at Hawara camp, Qadumin, Kfar Atzen and Bet El. During our visit to Meggido prison, we noted that prisoners had to supplement their often insufficient portions of food by purchasing food from prison shops or by relying on family visits.

9.5 Conclusions and recommendations

In his report on the mission to the OPT, presented to the Human Rights Council in March 2004, Jean Ziegler made the following conclusions and recommendations.

The humanitarian catastrophe emerging in the OPT must be reversed. While Jean Ziegler recognized that the Government of Israel must protect the security of its own citizens, the consequences of the ways in which current security measures were applied in the OPT were entirely disproportionate in the sense that they jeopardized the food and water security of the great majority of the Palestinians. As Amnesty International had noted, it is not permissible to punish the whole population for the actions of a few of its members.[66]

Jean Ziegler agreed with Catherine Bertini that the humanitarian crisis was a man-made crisis. It was absurd that in what can be a comparatively wealthy economy given its fertile lands, Palestinian men, women and children were going hungry. As the occupying Power, the Government of Israel had obligations to ensure the right to food of the Palestinian people. The actions being taken in the OPT by the occupying forces violated the right to food. The level of restrictions on humanitarian access for the United Nations and NGOs, which limited the amount of food aid and water that can reach the Palestinian communities, also amounted to a violation of the right to food under international humanitarian law.

The effective 'encirclement' of certain communities, such as Qalquilya, by the fence/wall must be halted immediately. As Ethan Bronner wrote in the *International Herald Tribune*:

> Qalqilya is not only blocked off from Israel to its west. It is entirely surrounded by the barrier so it will be isolated from West Bank Jewish

settlements to its east. The result for Qalqilya is that it has become – there is no other word for it – a ghetto, a term with chilling resonance for Jews whose forebears were restricted to such areas across Europe not many generations ago.[67]

The confiscation of land, extension of settlements and settler-only roads, and the building of the fence/wall, where this deprived thousands of Palestinians of their lands, homes, crops and means of subsistence, was a violation of the right to food. The right to food requires the respect of Article 49 of the Fourth Geneva Convention which prohibits settlement. If there were no settlements, then there would be no need for the harsh internal closures that restricted movement inside the OPT. Avraham Burg, the distinguished former speaker of the Knesset, wrote: 'There is no middle path. We must remove all the settlements – all of them – and draw an internationally recognized border between the Jewish national home and the Palestinian national home.'[68]

In the short term, it was essential that access for food and water supplies be improved and humanitarian assistance not be blocked, restricted or harmed, but the Palestinian capacity for self-sufficiency must be protected to avoid complete dependence on food aid. Over the longer term, within the context of the road map and a two-State solution, serious consideration must be given to the viability of a future Palestinian State, to ensure that Palestinians are not left dependent on food aid forever. Palestinians are largely dependent on Israel for access to food and water and for international trade, which leaves them in a situation of extreme vulnerability every time political relations deteriorate. There is an urgent need to consider ways in which a future Palestinian State could have sustainable access to, and independent control over, its own food and water supplies. A viable Palestinian State will require a capacity to produce and to trade in order to create a viable economy and stable employment and thereby realize the right to food itself. This will require a land area that is not cut up into separate territorial areas and within which movement is not restricted. It will also require international borders to facilitate international trade.

In summary, Jean Ziegler recommended that the Government of Israel respect its *de jure* obligations under international human rights and humanitarian law. He specifically recommended that the Government of Israel:

(a) Take immediate action to end restrictions on humanitarian access. The Government of Israel should fully abide by the Bertini commitments, which should be made binding under the road map process. The Government of Israel should also ensure appropriate status for United Nations and NGO staff to enable access and allow humanitarian organizations to operate without excessive constraints on their movement or access to Palestinian populations;

(b) Take immediate action to ease the humanitarian crisis by ending the regime of closures and curfews where these are causing an increase in the malnutrition and poverty levels of the civilian Palestinian population;
(c) Immediately lift internal closures within the OPT, which restrict movement and inhibit the Palestinian civilian population's physical and economic access to food. It is imperative that the OPT not be reduced to complete dependence on international food aid;
(d) End the disproportionate destruction of Palestinian lands, wells and other resources, including the infrastructure for social services of the Palestinian Authority;
(e) Immediately stop the building of the fence/wall, in particular that encircling communities in Qalquilya and Tulkarem. The security fence should not be used as a mechanism for separating Palestinians from their land;
(f) Review the permit system and allow an increased number of Palestinians to return to their employment in Israel;
(g) Halt the confiscation and expropriation of land that is being used for the building of the fence/wall, settler-only roads, security buffers and the extension of settlements;
(h) Ensure the provision of adequate food and water for all prisoners and detainees in all detention facilities;
(i) The Israeli High Court should recognize the Fourth Geneva Convention as part of customary international law, which should be justiciable, as are the Hague Regulations of 1907;
(j) Review, with the Palestinian National Authority, the operation of the Joint Water Authority in order to ensure the fair sharing of the water resources under the OPT, in accordance with international law;
(k) Encourage international monitoring of the road map obligations by all members of the Quartet that drafted the road map – including the United Nations and the European Union – to ensure that the Government of Israel and the Palestinian Authority abide by their commitments. Monitoring should include a human rights mechanism charged with receiving, investigating and reporting on alleged violations of international human rights and humanitarian law, including the right to food.

Under the road map process, an urgent review must be undertaken of the potential for a viable Palestinian State. It must be ensured that the future State of Palestine has a viable territory and control over its own resources, so that it has the capacity to realize the right to food for the Palestinian population. It must also retain international borders in order to facilitate trade, especially the import and export of food products.

The Government of Israel should continue to cooperate with the United Nations Special Rapporteur on the right to food in the future by making a commitment to monitor violations of the right to food and the implementation of these recommendations over the long term. The Government of Israel is also encouraged to receive the visits of other special rapporteurs.

Finally, as most of the violations of the right to food stem from the occupation by the Government of Israel of the OPT, the occupation should be ended. As Ilan Pappe, Academic Director of the Research Institute for Peace and senior lecturer at Haifa University, has pointed out, 'The tedious and hackneyed truth remains that the end to violence of all kinds (including indiscriminate violence against the innocent) will come only with the end of the Occupation.'[69]

10
Ethiopia

10.1 Introduction

We (Jean Ziegler, Sally-Anne Way and Christophe Golay) conducted a mission to Ethiopia from 16 to 27 February 2004.[1] During this mission, we were honoured to be received by senior members of the Government, including Dr Alemu, State Minister of Foreign Affairs, Commissioner Simon Mechale of the Disaster Prevention and Preparedness Commission, the Minister of Water Resources and the Minister of Agriculture and Rural Development. We were also received by a wide range of international and national NGOs working on food security, the right to food and human rights issues. The programme included field visits to the Southern Nations, Nationalities and Peoples Region (SNNPR) and to the Tigray region. We were not able to visit the regions of Somali or Gambella, for security reasons. WFP organized the visit to SNNPR and the non-governmental Ethiopian organization REST (the Relief Association of Tigray, which developed out of the Tigray liberation movement) organized our visit to Tigray. These field visits provided the opportunity to understand the very complex and diverse realities of Ethiopia and enabled us to meet with regional government authorities and local representatives of civil society and NGOs. The objectives of the mission to Ethiopia were (a) to analyse the situation of famine, hunger and food insecurity, from the perspective of the right to food; (b) to learn from positive initiatives being taken in Ethiopia; and (c) to play a catalytic role in promoting the right to food in practice.

Ethiopia has very rich and ancient history. It possesses a unique culture and is one of the oldest Christian civilizations in the world, as well as one of the rare countries in Africa to have largely escaped European colonialism. It is a land of mountains, dominated by the vast highlands, the Great Rift Valley, and major rivers and lakes, including the Blue Nile, as well as the hot lowlands and dry desert regions. Altitudes reach from below sea level in the Danakil Depression (one of the hottest places on earth) to the cold mountainous summits reaching over 4000 m. Rainfall varies from up to 2000 mm in the high central plateau to less than 300 mm per year in the lowlands. Ecological diversity is mirrored by social diversity, with 83 languages and 200 dialects spoken by its 70 million people in a land of 1 million km^2. After the fall of Emperor Haile Salassie in 1974 and the end of the oppressive totalitarian dictatorship of the Derg regime of Colonel Mengistu Haile Mariam in 1991, Ethiopia embarked on broad political and economic reforms at the beginning of the 1990s.

Ethiopia is moving towards a decentralized system of 'ethnic federalism', constituted by a federal system of nine regional states and two special city administrations. The ruling coalition party of the Ethiopian Peoples Revolutionary Democratic Front (EPRDF) remains the dominant political power. The economy is moving towards a market economy, but has suffered severely as a result of the collapse in coffee prices and agriculture being inhibited by the lack of development of roads and marketing infrastructure. Over 85 per cent of the population remains dependent on small-scale agriculture or pastoralism for their livelihoods, but pervasive poverty, increasing destitution and chronic malnutrition leave many people highly vulnerable to drought. With the end of the Mengistu regime, the human rights environment has improved substantially, but the legacies of the past with regard to freedom of expression and access to information remain difficult to eradicate and processes of participation and accountability remain fragile in the decentralizing federal State. Nonetheless, the Government has committed to strengthening its democracy, establishing a national human rights commission and ombudsman to improve human rights accountability, and was very open to our visit. With the end of the war with Eritrea, government efforts and resources are again focused on eradicating hunger, yet are frustrated by the frequent recurrence of famine.

10.2 Famine and food insecurity in Ethiopia

10.2.1 Famine in Ethiopia in 2003

In 2003, Ethiopia suffered from a severe food crisis with 13.2 million people (one fifth of the population) reduced to surviving on food aid. The 2003 food shortage is believed to be the most widespread and severe emergency in Ethiopia's long history of famine, as it spread to the traditionally surplus food producing areas of SNNPR and several parts of Amhara.[2] The 2003 disaster precipitated an unprecedented national and international food aid response – the largest ever in Ethiopia's history. This prevented widespread deaths, in contrast with the earlier great famines 1973/74 and 1984/85 which together killed well over a million people. At the time of our mission, the situation had significantly improved, but the Government and donors still expected to provide food aid to 7.2 million people in 2004.[3]

Although Ethiopia has long suffered from famine, the impact of recurrent food shortages on Ethiopia's people has become increasingly severe.

Extreme poverty and lack of access to sufficient productive resources leaves most Ethiopians increasingly vulnerable: 'Against a backdrop of overwhelming rural poverty in households and the community, the margin of safety from climatic shocks has diminished'.[4] Increasing levels of destitution mean that most people do not have enough reserves in terms of nourishment or physical assets that can protect them from disaster. In addition to extreme poverty, a background of pervasive malnutrition also leaves people highly vulnerable and climate-related disasters such as drought can quickly turn into the catastrophe of widespread famine. As an Ethiopian scholar notes, 'Malnutrition is the nutritional landscape on which the footprint of recurrent famine is firmly etched.'[5] Destitution and malnutrition increase with each recurring disaster, and many people in drought-affected areas have not fully recovered since the terrible famine of 1984. This means that famine in Ethiopia today is as much about extreme poverty and chronic malnutrition as it is about the failure of the rains.

Disturbingly, the food shortage crisis in 2003 was caused not only by failure of the rains, but also by the constraints on development and the lack of sufficient rural infrastructure, roads, storage and markets.[6] It has been argued that up to half of the food shortage was due to the collapse in food prices the year before.[7] The food shortage may have actually begun well before the rains failed. In the 2003 season, farmers did not invest in agricultural inputs such as fertilizer and improved seed, partly because of rain conditions, but also because of the high financial losses they had experienced the year before, when farmers achieved excellent harvests but then could not sell their surplus crops because the crops could not be effectively transported to deficit areas; there was therefore a glut in surplus-producing areas. Grain prices collapsed by as much as 80 per cent in surplus areas, even as consumer prices escalated in deficit areas.[8] Many farmers, left heavily indebted for seeds and fertilizer, were unable to plant much the next year, contributing to the food shortage the following year.[9] Food shortages were therefore not only caused by droughts, but were exacerbated by many other factors linked to the lack of development.

With agricultural liberalization, agricultural trade is now private, rather than State run, but a strong private sector of traders capable of transporting food from surplus to deficit regions has not yet emerged, inhibited by the lack of adequate rural infrastructure, roads, storage and markets.[10] Linked to this problem is the issue that few donor resources are directed towards long-term development, but continue to be concentrated on providing emergency food aid. Ethiopia receives the highest amount of emergency aid in Africa (and in the world, after Bangladesh), yet it receives the lowest amount of development aid.[11] While emergency food aid has saved millions of lives, it has not contributed to Ethiopia's development. Indeed, there continues to be a concern that food aid may itself be disrupting the development of food markets and depressing domestic food production, leaving Ethiopia increasingly unable to feed itself.[12]

10.2.2 Overview of hunger and food insecurity in Ethiopia

Today, Ethiopia is one of the poorest and most food-insecure countries in the world. Nearly half of Ethiopians are undernourished, with 44 per cent living in extreme poverty, unable to guarantee enough food for themselves and their families every day.[13] Ethiopians have the lowest calorie intake in Africa, averaging approximately 1750 calories per person per day.[14] At least 58 per cent of deaths of children are directly caused by malnutrition and rates of child mortality increased between 1997 and 2000.[15] Half of all children under the age of five are underweight and stunted.[16]

Micronutrient deficiencies are also endemic, particularly deficiencies in vitamin A, iodine and iron, which affects the physical and mental growth of Ethiopia's children, women and men.[17] More than 76 per cent of rural Ethiopians and 69 per cent of all Ethiopians do not have sustainable access to safe and clean water. Women regularly travel as far as 15 km or more to fetch water for household purposes. The population is estimated to have doubled since 1980 to 70 million and more than 2 million people are now HIV positive (the third highest absolute number after India and South Africa). The number of literate people has fallen from nearly 80 per cent of adults in 1990 to less than 25 per cent in 2000. In the United Nations Development Programme Human Development Index of 2004, Ethiopia ranked as one of the poorest countries in the world, at 170 out of 175.[18] Even in years of good harvests, when there is no drought, it is estimated that 5–6 million Ethiopians are chronically food insecure and have to rely on 'emergency' food aid programmes to be able to feed themselves.

Chronic food insecurity persists in the country, which is predominantly agrarian. Poverty is significantly higher in rural areas than in urban areas. Over 85 per cent of Ethiopians live in rural areas and most are dependent on agriculture – on crop or livestock production, or on agriculture-related wage labour. Agriculture is still predominantly rain dependent and only 3 per cent of irrigable land is currently irrigated, contributing to high vulnerability to drought. Many of Ethiopia's farmers do not produce enough even for their own subsistence. Two thirds of households farm on less than 0.5 hectare, insufficient to support a family, and these holdings are becoming smaller and smaller given the fast rate of population growth. Farmers are concerned about the rapidly rising population, shrinking land plots, lack of small-scale irrigation, land degradation and soil erosion, pests and the high price of fertilizers, as well as poverty.[19] Greater poverty and destitution and the running down of reserves and local food safety nets – such as household enset (false banana) supplies in SNNPR or teff in Tigray – have left many people increasingly vulnerable to disasters. The collapse in international coffee prices has also devastated small-scale Ethiopian farmers in some regions – in

SNNPR we saw rows of coffee trees left unharvested because the value of the crop is so low. The poorest and most destitute are now dependent mainly on wage labour in other people's fields or homes.[20] With few opportunities for wage-labour or opportunities for off-farm employment to earn income, many people simply do not get enough to eat.

Nomadic pastoralism is better adapted to the drier areas of the lowlands, and is practised by the Afar and Somali peoples. Yet pastoral livelihoods are also becoming increasingly vulnerable, with pastoralists affected by the lack of water, land degradation and conflict with agriculturalists in competition for land and water, and poverty has been exacerbated by the collapse of the export market for livestock to Arab nations following an outbreak of Rift Valley fever.

Despite the precariousness of Ethiopian agriculture, its potential is impressive. Ethiopian farmers grow a vast range of crops including wheat, barley, teff, finger millet, maize, sorghum, enset, cassava and potatoes, sugar cane, many different pulses and coffee (although with the collapse in international coffee prices, more farmers are now switching to growing the narcotic khat for income). Ethiopia also has the greatest number of livestock in Africa: more than 35 million cattle, 39 million sheep and goats and 1 million camels.[21] The harnessing of water resources in agricultural and pastoral regions would greatly add to this potential. In Tigray, we were impressed by the development projects of REST to reduce land degradation and to develop irrigation through water-harvesting (ponds and shallow wells) or low-cost river diversion and treadle-pumps, in order to produce crops, including vegetables and spices, to improve nutrition and incomes for families on small plots of land.

Nonetheless, poverty is highest in rural areas, where the majority of the population lives. The poorest most food-insecure regions are Tigray, Amhara and SNNPR, although the pastoral regions, particularly Somali, are also increasingly vulnerable. Competition over resources is increasing. In some regions, particularly in the Somali region and more recently the Gambella region, armed conflict situations have also led to high food and water insecurity, particularly for those forced to flee from their homes who are often left without any kind of protection or assistance. Urban poverty is significantly lower than rural poverty, although there are a number of vulnerable groups, such as street children in the streets of Addis Abbaba and other urban centres.

Women are often the most vulnerable to hunger and poverty as a result of discrimination, especially in rural areas. In some regions of Ethiopia, traditional practices such as child marriage, inheritance practices and violence against women contribute to greater poverty and vulnerability of women and children.[22] Some marriages occur through abduction, a traditional practice whereby a young girl is raped by a man and his friends and then claimed cheaply in marriage. During our visit, we noted the extreme vulnerability and poverty of older single women, often working as servants in the homes of others. Women represent 50 per cent of the agricultural workforce, yet traditionally have no right to inherit the land they work on, and little access to credit, agricultural inputs or extension training.

10.3 Legal framework for the right to food

10.3.1 International obligations

Ethiopia has ratified the International Covenant on Economic, Social and Cultural Rights, which protects the right to food (Article 11). However, at the time of our mission, Ethiopia had not yet submitted its initial report to the CESCR, due in 1995.[23] It has also ratified all other relevant major international treaties relevant to the right to food, including the International Covenant on Civil and Political Rights (Article 6), the Convention on the Rights of the Child (Articles 24 and 27) and the Convention on the Elimination of All Forms of Discrimination against Women (Articles 12 and 14). Ethiopia is also bound by international humanitarian law, having ratified the Geneva Convention of 12 August 1999 and the Additional Protocols thereto of 1977. At the regional level, the Government is committed to the right to food through the African Charter on Human and Peoples' Rights (Articles 16 and 60). This means that under the right to food, the Government of Ethiopia has the obligation to respect, protect and fulfil the right to food, without any discrimination.

10.3.2 National constitutional norms

In 1994, after a three-year transition period following 17 years of the Mengistu dictatorship, Ethiopia adopted a very progressive constitution, which includes civil and political rights and economic, social and cultural rights. The Ethiopian Constitution 'for a Nation of Nations'[24] recognizes human rights in 31 of its 106 articles (Articles 14–44). Although it does not explicitly recognize the right to food, it recognizes economic, social and cultural rights, including the right of farmers and pastoralists to receive a fair price for their products, the right to equal access to publicly funded social services, and the obligation of the State to allocate resources to provide social services (Article 41). It also recognizes the right to life (Articles 14, 15 and 36), equality before the law (Article 25), freedom of association (Article 31), the equal rights of women and men (Article 35) and the right of access to justice (Article 37).

The right to food enshrined in international law is also part of Ethiopian law, by adoption and interpretation. According to Article 9 (4), 'All international agreements ratified by Ethiopia are an integral part of the law of the land'. In line with jurisprudence in other countries,[25] international conventions can be considered as directly applicable. According to Article 13 (2), human rights 'shall be interpreted in a manner conforming to the principles of the Universal Declaration of Human Rights, the International Covenants on Human Rights and international instruments adopted by Ethiopia'. As opined by the Human Rights Committee and well established in jurisprudence in other countries, the right to life could be broadly interpreted to include the right to food (Article 13 (2)).[26]

To address a legacy of inequality and discrimination, women are formally entitled by the Constitution to affirmative action and equal rights (Article 35 (3)). These include equal rights over property and land, including inheritance, and rights to equality in employment (Article 35 (7 and 8)). Federal legislation, including the 1997 Rural Land Administration Proclamation and the 2001 Family Code, as well as official policy outlines the de jure and de facto equality between men and women and the participation of women in the formulation and implementation of laws, policies, projects and programmes that concern and benefit them. However, these formal rights have not always been enforced in practice – women have hardly had access to information, and the application of regional and customary laws at local level often results in the continuation of de facto discriminatory practices. For Meaza Ashenafi, Executive Director of the Ethiopian Women Lawyers Association (EWLA), 'almost in all regions, women do not have any access to land whatsoever. They don't have the right to inherit, and the only option is to get married and have a husband. But when the husband dies, they are also kicked off their land'.[27]

Under the Constitution, ownership of land, as well as natural resources (including water), is exclusively vested in the State and in the peoples. It is defined as common property not subject to sale or to other means of exchange (Article 40 (3)). However, usufruct rights are set out for individuals and communities, including peasants, who have the right to obtain land without payment and who are protected against eviction from their possession (Article 40 (4)), pastoralists, who have the right to free land for grazing and cultivation as well as the right not to be displaced from their own lands (Article 40 (5)), and by private investors (Article 40 (8)). All expropriation of private property for public purposes gives all persons displaced or affected the right to commensurate monetary or alternative means of compensation, including relocation with adequate State assistance (Articles 40 (8) and 44 (2)).

Ethiopia has a federal system, which means that both the Federal Government and state members have competencies relevant to the right to food. The Federal Government has the power to formulate and implement national policies, strategies and plans in respect of overall economic, social and development matters (Article 51 (2)), and it may grant to states emergency, rehabilitation and development assistance and loans (Article 94 (2)). The state members have the power to administer land (Article 52 (2) (d)), to determine and collect fees for land usufruct rights and to levy and collect income tax from private farmers as well as from those forming cooperatives

(Article 97 (2) and (3)). According to the Constitution, all Federal and state legislative, executive and judicial organs at all levels have the responsibility and duty to respect and enforce human rights (Article 13 (1)), and any law, customary practice or decision of an organ of State or a public official that contravenes these human rights 'shall be of no effect' (Article 9 (1)). All organs of the State at all levels must respect, protect and fulfil the right to food, but the Federal Government retains the primary responsibility to ensure the right to food of every Ethiopian.

10.3.3 Access to justice and human rights institutions

Under the Constitution, Ethiopia committed itself to establishing a National Human Rights Commission and an Ombudsman to mediate human rights issues. This has been formalized through legislation drawn up in 2000, which represents significant progress towards improving the human rights environment and accountability.[28] At the time of our visit, these institutions were still not operational, but appointments of the Chair of the Commission and the Ombudsman have since been made, which is an important step in the right direction.

Ethiopia has a complex pluralistic legal system that includes customary and religious law at the local level. The majority of citizens in rural areas resolve their disputes at the *kebele* (local government) level, before religious, customary or social courts, most of which have no human rights knowledge and are traditionally composed of men. Even at the regional and federal levels, constitutionally recognized human rights and international conventions are rarely cited in legal arguments or court decisions and international conventions have not been translated in the working language of Ethiopia. Despite the constitutional right of access to justice, Ethiopia's poor still have inadequate access to justice, given the high costs of going to court, long delays in court proceedings, lack of legal aid and the lack of human rights knowledge, resources and independence of the judiciary at the *woreda* (district) level. In May 2002, the federal Minister for Capacity-Building acknowledged that the justice system was incapable of enforcing constitutional guarantees.[29] There is little access to information and to any effective forms of accountability and monitoring to ensure the effective implementation of laws, policies and programmes.[30]

In the continued absence of strong human rights institutions and judicial remedies, the importance of Ethiopia's NGOs working on the monitoring of human rights must be underlined. During our visit, we met the Ethiopian Human Rights Council (EHRCO) and EWLA. EHRCO mainly focuses on reporting violations of human rights in different parts of the country. EWLA is engaged in advocacy for law reform – including changes in the Family Code – and the provision of free legal aid to women. Other organizations, such as the Action Professionals' Association for the People (ASAP), are working with the religious, customary and social courts to raise awareness of human rights and gender issues at the *kebele* level. The University of Addis Ababa and the University of Mekelle were also establishing human rights resource centres. The Ministry of Justice was also in the process of establishing a similar centre to support the human rights training programme. Emphasis was also put on economic, social and cultural rights, which may contribute to the justiciability of the right to food.

The decentralization process in Ethiopia is important from the point of view of the right to food, as responsibilities are being devolved to the local levels. The administrative structure divides the 9 regions, or federal states, into 66 Zones, further divided into 556 *woredas* which include about 10,000 *kebeles*. It is generally clear, however, that at this stage in the process, governance at the local levels remains weak, given limited capacity, as well as the lack of full fiscal and political decentralization.[31] Regions and *woredas* still cover only 25 per cent and 45 per cent of their expenditure, respectively. Financial subsidies are therefore transferred from the Federal Government, leaving a high degree of control by higher levels of Government.[32] Although a formal decentralization has been carried out, the ruling EPRDF nonetheless retains political and economic control over the regions.

10.4 Policy framework for the right to food

10.4.1 Government policies and programmes

Ethiopia has a range of policies in place to fight against famine and food shortage, as well as strategies to improve access to food and drinking water. Although food-security policies are not explicitly based on the right to food, food security is a central priority of government policy.

The Disaster Prevention and Preparedness Commission (DPPC) is responsible for guaranteeing that Ethiopians do not suffer from starvation during famines, by ensuring the timely provision of food aid and other assistance. The DPPC operates an early warning system, coordinates appeals for food aid, and has the primary responsibility for all direct food aid distribution as well as food-for-work programmes through which the majority of food aid is distributed. It also works with an Emergency Food Security Reserve, which maintains stocks at seven sites around the country – Nazareth, Shashemene, Wolayita Sodo, Shinile, Kombolcha, Mekelle and Wereta. The DPPC has been very successful in averting widespread loss of life and the flight of starving Ethiopians into famine camps. However, the unprecedented crisis in 2003 precipitated an acknowledgement that food aid is not the answer and that there is an urgent need to focus on addressing the underlying factors of the increasingly devastating food shortages in Ethiopia.

At the time of our mission, the Government had just launched a major initiative: the New Coalition for Food Security.[33] This provides a framework for strategies aimed at ensuring food security, and has been agreed to by the Government, donors, the United Nations and civil society. The

Government suggests that this is a 'paradigm shift' in food-security policy in Ethiopia: the aim is to shift from a system dominated by the uncertainties of emergency aid towards a longer term development perspective. This distinguishes between predictable (chronic food insecurity) and unpredictable (emergency) needs in order to establish a long-term 'safety net' for the chronically food insecure, and take actions to enable people to build up their assets in order to reduce their vulnerability. This shift required donor resources to be committed in a predictable way for multi-year programming. The new approach places greater emphasis on the local purchase of food aid in times of surplus, which should in turn operate as a mechanism for stabilizing grain price volatility and promote the distribution of crops in surplus areas to deficit areas.

The New Coalition addresses the weaknesses in the emergency system. It introduces measures to improve health services (epidemics frequently kill more people than starvation during famines) and to establish a long-term safety net in order to reduce vulnerability to future famines. It also addresses longer term development objectives to improve availability and access to food, promoting small-scale water harvesting and irrigation, crop diversification and livestock management, and better marketing. It includes the specific needs of pastoral regions – building up livestock assets and improving veterinary health facilities. It also outlines plans for the resettlement of people from drought-prone areas, as well as building up off-farm employment opportunities. However, little attention is given to population issues and to highly vulnerable groups such as HIV/AIDS victims (although this is changing as the Government has outlined resource requirements for HIV/AIDS victims in 2004). The lack of an effective and implemented policy on population issues is a serious gap, given the high population growth rate of 2.8 per cent, and there appears to be a need for developing greater understanding of the links between population policy and food insecurity. Some of the Government's proposals have also proved controversial with foreign donors, including policies on land tenure reform, water harvesting, resettlement and agricultural modernization.

Land tenure reform is a key part of government strategy, but remains highly sensitive policy in the Ethiopian context. State ownership of land is enshrined in the Constitution, but there have been increasingly insistent calls for the privatization of land. State ownership of land has been criticized for reducing people's willingness to invest in land, preventing the consolidation of landholdings, giving the Government too much control over the peasant population, and preventing migration to the cities. However, the Government has resisted calls for the privatization of land, with a convincing argument that privatization would result in millions of landless peasants. It is clear that if land were privatized, farmers would be forced to sell their plots as soon as the next famine arrived. Given that there are few alternative forms of employment, millions of Ethiopians would be left in a situation of even greater poverty, not even able to subsist from their own production. The Government has therefore proposed strengthening land tenure rights through its Land Certification Policy. The aim is to give tenure security through a lease that can be held for 99 years and can be inherited by family members, but cannot be sold. The Government argues that this will avoid the total destitution of rural farmers. At the time of our visit, this policy was beginning to be implemented, but only in three regions – Tigray, Amhara and SNNPR. Many argue that the policy-making has not involved a nationwide referendum, which would ensure the adequate participation of the people. The important element is to ensure tenure security that will give people concrete rights over their land, even if they were to temporarily leave the land.

Water harvesting and small-scale irrigation development is a key part of the government strategy. Ethiopia has vast reserves of groundwater and surface water, but these have not yet been harnessed, even though this would significantly reduce Ethiopia's vulnerability to drought. The 15-year Water Sector Development Programme (2002–2016) outlines an ambitious plan to increase irrigated farmland from 200,000 to 470,000 hectares by 2016, and to increase access to drinking water from 74 per cent to 98 per cent of the urban population and from 23 per cent to 71 per cent of the rural population by 2016, through constructing wells, springs and other surface water works. Significant progress is already apparent in some regions. In Amhara and Tigray, for example, 70,000 ponds and tanks were constructed in 2002 alone. Nonetheless, the speed and scale of implementation has already given rise to certain problems. There are concerns that policy is being implemented in a top-down manner without adapting to local social and ecological situations. OCHA found that 'due to their small capacity, ponds and tanks are only economically viable if no other water source is present and has potential'.[34] In Gubalafto, Meket and North Wollo and in Tsebela *tabia* (village), Sastsadamba *woreda*, shallow wells or methods using river diversion may have been more appropriate and less expensive than open ponds, and would have avoided an increase in the incidence of malaria.[35] Little attention has so far been focused by the Government on methods of rainwater harvesting, despite successful results in NGO programmes as proposed by the Ethiopian Rainwater Harvesting Association – the Irish NGO, GOAL, uses rainwater harvesting in 165 school feeding centres throughout the country.

Resettlement is also part of the government strategy that aims to relocate 2.2 million people in three years. Farmers will voluntarily resettle from highly food-insecure *woredas* to more food-secure *woredas* (preferably in the same region). In return, the receiving *woredas* are offered improved basic services, such as storage facilities, health clinics and grain mills. However, resettlement remains a controversial policy, largely because of a history of forced resettlement schemes during the Derg era. Although the new resettlement programme is voluntary, participatory and allows for return, some suggest that these conditions are undermined by requirements to fill quotas for resettlement, although the Government confirmed that it is not imposing a quota system. Malaria has also turned into an issue, given that it is more prevalent in the low-lying areas targeted for resettlement. There are also concerns that resettlement will lead to conflict over traditional rights to resources or ethnic conflict, particularly if resettlement occurs in an interregional rather than intra-regional context. Donors are concerned that resettlement may leave people worse off than they were before. In one case of resettlement from Hadiya zone to Dawro zone in SNNPR, for example, resettlement was postponed when households had already sold off livestock and household assets, leaving people with little option but to move to look for work in nearby towns. There are also some cases where resettlement has occurred to sites with no existing infrastructure, no clean water and no tools for planting. It is clear that there is a need to incorporate mechanisms for monitoring and accountability into these programmes to remedy these problems, as well as to change the policy if resettlement does not have a positive impact on people's lives.

Increasing the availability and accessibility of food rests largely with the Government's long-established Agricultural Development-Led Industrialization strategy (ADLI). This forms a key part of the overarching framework for poverty reduction articulated in Ethiopia's Sustainable Development Poverty Reduction Programme (SDPRP). ADLI focuses on modernizing agriculture, as the key driver of economic growth and industrialization, and promoting employment. There has been progress under ADLI, with agricultural production levels increasing, particularly in the surplus harvests in 2001/02. However, the simultaneous liberalization of agriculture, including eliminating subsidies for fertilizer and the lack of markets, has limited the impact of ADLI. Critics have said that agricultural extension agents have to meet quotas to accelerate the adoption of improved seed and fertilizer use (which come from privatized companies, sometimes linked to the ruling party), although the Government confirmed that no quota system is in place. Many also criticize the focus on increasing production in high-potential areas, as this benefits the better off, while chronically food-insecure areas (as well as the pastoral, agropastoral and urban poor) are left behind. Others suggest that rural poverty will never be resolved while multiple taxes on farmers remain high and the costs of agricultural inputs keep farmers indebted.

10.4.2 Policies and programmes of the United Nations system in Ethiopia

The United Nations has a long history in Ethiopia, with most of the agencies present since the great famine of 1974. Today, the Country Team in Ethiopia is one of the largest and most competent in Africa, with 25 agencies represented, including WFP, FAO, UNDP, UNICEF, the IMF and the World Bank. The United Nations agencies work with the Government, within the framework of the New Coalition for Food Security, and the SDPRP, on projects that include food security, agriculture, industry and humanitarian and emergency relief. Development aid from multilateral and bilateral sources averaged US$ 1 billion per year from 1997 to 2003, although most of the assistance was provided in the form of humanitarian and relief assistance, predominantly food aid. A number of agencies, particularly UNICEF, are focusing their work around a rights-based approach to development.

During the mission, a number of agencies expressed concerns about the constraints on their work, given an historical bias towards emergency humanitarian assistance. The efforts of the agencies are often spent fighting famine, with little time and funds left to address the underlying problems of food insecurity, malnutrition and extreme poverty that lead to the repeat of crises from year to year. During the famine of 2003, the United States generously provided a record US$ 553.1 million in assistance, but US$ 471.7 million was provided as food. In March 2004, the Country Director of WFP called for the provision of greater cash assistance as part of humanitarian assistance.[36] Cash could be used to purchase grain locally and ensure support of the domestic agricultural development, in line with the new approach of the New Coalition for Food Security.

Non-governmental organizations

There are a large number of international and national NGOs in Ethiopia, mostly involved in emergency assistance and development projects. A number have begun to focus on a rights-based approach to development, although there are few working from the perspective of the right to food, with the notable exceptions of ActionAid and CARE.

Non-governmental organizations expressed particular concerns about constraints on their activities related to the control by the Government of their activities through registration and coordination processes. These processes require them to report all activities to the Government and limit the activities and regions in which they may work. The environment is particularly difficult for human rights organizations, of which relatively few exist in Ethiopia. We met with the Ethiopian Human Rights Council and with EWLA, which have had particularly difficult relations with the Government as a result of their work, often being accused of bias and partiality, as have organizations working for press and academic freedom. Several people alleged that farmers' associations and opposition parties sometimes have difficulties in holding meetings without having their members threatened and arrested by the police or the local authorities.

10.5 Main findings and concerns

10.5.1 Progressive realization

During our mission, we were encouraged to see that the fight for food security is the key priority of the Government of Ethiopia. Despite the legacies inherited from a history of feudalism, dictatorship and a difficult international trade environment, the Government has made important progress. Widespread deaths from famine have been averted, as evidenced by the 2003 crisis. There are many programmes and policies in place that seek to increase the availability of and access to food, as well as water. Agricultural production has increased (aside from famines) by more than 70 per cent since the 1980s. The Government has committed to increasing investment in agricultural development with 6.5 per cent of the budget allocated to support agriculture and food security programmes in 2002/03, to be doubled in the next years.[37] Official statistics show that overall poverty has fallen over the last decade, suggesting that some progress has been made towards reducing hunger and food insecurity.

However, we were concerned that the number of people in need of food aid has increased continuously over the last decade, which would suggest a regression in the progressive realization of the right to food. The food crisis in 2003 affected 13 million people – more than ever before. Food production is not keeping up with population growth. Rapid population growth has also increased vulnerability by diminishing landholdings and reducing access to land and other productive resources. In the face of extreme poverty and lack of resources, at least 5–6 million people depend on food aid every year, regardless of the rains or the harvest. Some studies have challenged the official statistics on the reduction of poverty, pointing to the increasing destitution.[38] The lack of access to productive resources of the poor therefore remains the key problem in Ethiopia.

The massive response to the 2003 crisis at the international and national levels was impressive and saved the lives of millions of people, preventing widespread famine. Nonetheless, food aid has not reduced the vulnerability of the Ethiopian people to future famines. As the Government and donors have come to recognize, food aid is not the answer. Saving lives is essential, but saving livelihoods and improving access to productive resources must be equally important for longer term development. Continued dependence on food aid will only be a recipe for continued disaster, and will not contribute to the progressive realization of the right to adequate food, which is primarily the right to be able to feed oneself in dignity.

We were encouraged by the improvements in the general human rights environment, although we continued to be concerned about abuses of power with respect to the right to food in some areas. We were encouraged by moves to establish a National Human Rights Commission and an

Ombudsman to mediate on human rights issues, although we were concerned that these institutions are still not fully operational. There is an urgent need for these institutions to monitor the progressive realization of the right to food in order to improve accountability of government policies and programmes and address possible violations of the right to food. The Government should also facilitate the important work of human rights organizations, which also provide a monitoring role as part of an effort to ensure the right to adequate food.

10.5.2 Violations of the right to food

During our mission, we were concerned to receive many documents detailing a number of violations of the right to food in different regions. In writing the report on the mission to Ethiopia, we took note of the view of the Government that the cases listed below are without basis in fact and that the information provided is politically biased.

In the highly sensitive political and ethnic context of democratic Ethiopia, it is not always clear to what extent allegations of violations are politically biased or motivated by political interests. At the same time, in a democratic State, it is essential that civil society, including opposition movements, should be heard. We note that most of the allegations detailed below relate to actions taken by local-level officials, not the central Government, but calls on the central Government to investigate and take remedial action where necessary and prevent future violations from occurring.

The documents we received detail allegations that include the use against opposition party members of threats to withhold food aid, credit or fertilizer, or even land scheduled for redistribution in the Southern Region. It was alleged that local officials at the *kebele* level in Innemai *woreda* (East Gojjam Zone) and in the South Gondar Zone withheld rural credit from one man and confiscated land from another.[39] In September 2002, local officials allegedly threatened and then evicted eight farmers from their land when they did not stop participating in meetings of the opposition party United Ethiopia Democratic Party in Masha *woreda*, Southern Region. Officials reportedly told the farmers that opposition party members were not entitled to have land.[40] On 1 February 2002, it was alleged that local officials threatened to withhold food assistance and remove people from their land at an All-Ethiopia Unity Organization (AEUO) meeting in Debre Tabor, Amhara Region.[41]

There were also allegations of the destruction and setting on fire of homes, livestock and food stocks of members of opposition parties, which amount to violations of the right to food. For example, on 10 November 2002 local *kebele* officials and militia in the Kuchit and Batay Farmers Association in East Gojjam reportedly set on fire the home of one AEUO member, destroying his house, livestock and food. There were also some concerns about the manipulation of government programmes, including the resettlement programme. For example, although the resettlement programme is entirely voluntary, human rights NGOs and opposition parties have suggested that local authorities in some areas were targeting opposition supporters for relocation by manipulating resettlement rosters.[42] There were also reports of farmers being evicted from their lands in order to provide the land to private investors, despite constitutional protections. In April 2001, in Abe Dongero *woreda* in East Wellega Zone of Oromiya, the *woreda* administrator allegedly ordered the forced eviction of approximately 250 Amhara persons from their land to make the land available to a business investor.[43]

During our visit in 2004, violence erupted in the Gambella Region between the Anuaks and the Nuer people over power-sharing and resource distribution. As many as 20,000 people were reportedly forced to flee to Pochalla in neighbouring Sudan, and human rights organizations documented the killing of 1000 members of the Anuak ethnic group as of 31 March 2004, allegedly by other ethnic groups and government military forces, as well as the burning and destruction of hundreds of homes and crops, leaving thousands of people without shelter and food.[44] However, according to government reports, the number of people killed in Gambella was significantly lower, with 56 killed, 74 injured and 410 houses burnt down. An investigating commission established by the Government confirmed that military forces were not involved, but had been deployed to detain 37 individuals considered to be responsible.

Discrimination against women remains a particular problem, despite the progress in addressing the legal framework at the federal level. The failure to strictly enforce existing legislation that addresses inequalities amounts to a failure to protect women against violations of the right to food, particularly in relation to inheritance and control over resources, including land. It is not acceptable that de facto discriminatory practices persist throughout the country, particularly when the Constitution affirms equality.

10.5.3 Obstacles to the realization of the right to food

Ethiopia is faced by numerous internal and external obstacles that affect the capacity of the Government to fully ensure the realization of the right to food.

Ethiopia is severely affected by its climatic variability and unpredictability, including drought, floods and land degradation. However, drought need not automatically lead to famine. As the experience of many countries shows, it should be possible to survive drought without succumbing to famine, if drought is treated as a regular occurrence and adequate investment is made in development and in reducing vulnerability to drought.

Food aid, while essential for saving lives, can also be an obstacle to the longer term realization of the right to food. While imported food aid is essential and while relief needs cannot be met through domestic production, it is essential to reduce dependence, purchasing food locally as far as possible to encourage local development over the long term. Government coordination of all food aid is essential, but the institutionalization of food aid within the Government and donor agencies may be an obstacle to the full realization of the right to food. Efforts should be focused on reducing food aid needs by addressing longer term development needs as well as population policy. Greater investment in longer term development, including in transport and marketing infrastructure, and building up an effective, independent private sector are essential to overcome local market failure. To ensure food security, transporting surplus crops to deficit areas should be made a priority, rather than developing export markets for surplus crops. Efforts should also be focused on the creation of employment in both rural and urban areas, increasing access to resources for the increasingly landless younger generations.

Although many cite the issue of State ownership of land as a key obstacle to achieving food security, the land question will not, on its own, reduce poverty and famine. Privatization would encourage the concentration of land and bigger farms, which might improve the availability of food but would clearly do little to increase access to food, as many Ethiopians are likely to lose their land, selling when faced with the next famine and, given the lack of alternative employment, many Ethiopians would become even poorer. Improving tenure security is essential to ensure that people can invest in their land, and to enable them to temporarily leave their land without it being redistributed. This would mean that they could search for alternatives, but would still retain their land as a key asset and as a safety net. Tenure security would also reduce arbitrary abuses of power. Accountability for such abuses should be strengthened to prevent violations, regardless of the system of land ownership or tenure.

The lack of participation in the design and implementation of policies and programmes is also an obstacle to the right to food, where this inhibits the adaptation of programmes to local social and ecological conditions. There is a need to incorporate the human rights principles of participation, transparency, accountability and non-discrimination in all programmes, including for women. Effective remedies and compensation should be provided where government policies may negatively affect people's right to food.

Ethiopia's debt burden remains a serious exogenous obstacle to the Government's capacity to ensure the right to food. At the time of our mission, we concluded that though it is one of the poorest countries in the world, debt service took up US$ 149 million in 2002. It means that Ethiopia paid around 12 per cent of its national revenue in debt service, double the 6 per cent it spent on food security and agriculture, one year before the food crisis of 2003. Although Ethiopia has qualified for the Highly Indebted Poor Countries initiative, the benefits are not clear, and the debt burden is unsustainable and an obstacle to the realization of the right to food.[45]

At the same time, it is difficult for Ethiopia to compete on the world economic stage, particularly when faced with inequities in the global liberalized economic system. For example, coffee originated in Ethiopia and has long been a part of the cultural heritage of Ethiopia, as well as its main export earner. More than 95 per cent of coffee in Ethiopia is produced by smallholder coffee farmers and has been a key source of income. Yet importing northern countries still retain high tariffs on processed coffee – which limits development that could occur through exporting the processed product. In the last years, world coffee prices have also collapsed. Farm gate prices are now lower than the cost of production, destroying livelihoods.[46] The Ministry of Finance estimates that Ethiopia has lost US$ 830 million in export revenue since the price crash.[47] Yet consumer prices for coffee sold by the large international brands have not fallen. Consumer prices are not translated into farm gate prices, suggesting monopolistic corporate practices. In some regions, coffee farmers have left their coffee unharvested, turning instead to the narcotic khat, and there is a risk that this may become Ethiopia's new key export earner. It is essential that the developed countries allow and enable development opportunities in Ethiopia.

Finally, Ethiopia also faces inequities in the water sharing of the Nile river, under a 1959 agreement between Egypt and the Sudan. Ethiopia contributes 86 per cent of the Nile waters, but uses less than 1 per cent.[48] The total irrigated land in the Ethiopian portion of the Nile basin is only 8000 hectares. We welcome the Nile Basin Initiative and the new cooperation between riparian States, which could lead to a new agreement on water-sharing. This should prioritize water necessary to ensure the right to food and water in all riparian countries.

10.6 Conclusions and recommendations

In his report on the mission to Ethiopia, presented to the Commission on Human rights in 2004, Jean Ziegler presented the following conclusions and recommendations.

The Government of Ethiopia is making important progress in the realization of the right to food. There are many programmes and policies in place that seek to increase availability and access to food, as well as water. There are also a number of innovative programmes, including the shift towards a permanent safety net, that are experiences to be shared around the world. Nonetheless it is not acceptable that nearly half of the Ethiopian population still do not get enough to eat every day and that more than two thirds of Ethiopians still do not have access to safe and clean water.

Jean Ziegler therefore recommended that:

(a) The shift from an emergency to a development perspective, as already begun with the New Coalition for Food Security, must be a key priority for food security and the right to food. Government will need to be supported in this effort by an increase in donor funding for long-term development in both rural and urban sectors to ensure food security;

(b) New Coalition programmes, including resettlement, must be implemented in ways that avoid potential negative impact on livelihoods and the right to food. Mechanisms for accountability and effective compensatory mechanisms should be built into all programmes. The safety-net programme must reach all those in need, with adequate resources provided from Government and donors to ensure that people are not left excluded;

(c) Effective programmes to address population growth, land degradation and land tenure must form part of food security planning, given that the smaller size of landholdings are unable to feed a family. Urban development and the creation of off-farm employment should also form an important part of food security planning;

(d) Land tenure must be secured to ensure that people have secure rights over their own land. Land certification provides an important alternative to the privatization of the land, in terms of food security and the rights of the poorest. However, land certification should be applied rapidly and consistently across the country to all farmers regardless of their gender or ethnicity;

(e) Dependence on imported food aid should be reduced. Local purchase of food aid should be prioritized, avoiding negative impacts on local production and consumer prices, providing a mechanism to manage price volatility and encouraging the distribution of crops from surplus regions to deficit regions;

(f) For longer term development, it is essential that priority be given to developing local markets before the development of export markets, otherwise dependence of imported food aid will remain even while Ethiopia exports food. This implies serious investment in roads, storage and marketing facilities;

(g) Programmes to harness water resources should be given priority in order to reduce long-term vulnerability to drought, especially shallow wells, river diversions and rainwater harvesting. The technologies chosen should be appropriate to the social and ecological environment. Everyone should have access to drinking water within 1 km from home;

(h) All government programme and policy designs should ensure appropriate levels of participation, non-discrimination, transparency and accountability;

(i) The National Human Rights Commission and Ombudsman institution should be made fully operational, independent from Government and accorded adequate resources, in accordance with the Paris Principles,

and should be given a mandate that includes monitoring compliance with the obligations to respect, protect and fulfil the right to food;
(j) The work of national and international NGOs should be facilitated. In particular, human rights organizations, organizations working for press and academic freedom, and farmers associations should be seen as an essential component of a democratic society and should be able to participate fully in policy processes;
(k) Resources, including land and food aid, should never be used as a political tool. All reported violations of the right to food should be investigated in a transparent process and remedies should be made available for substantiated claims. Access to effective remedies for all violations of human rights should be improved;
(l) Serious efforts should be made to address discrimination, particularly against women. This will require the implementation of federal law, especially the Family Code, throughout all regions of the country, and increasing access to basic education and information;
(m) Within the region, it is imperative that the Nile riparian States strengthen their cooperation for the fair sharing of the Nile river. Sharing water necessary for human consumption and for subsistence agriculture should be a priority;
(n) Finally, donor agencies should support the shift from emergency to long-term development funding. Donors should also ensure that their own countries' policies (such as on debt repayment or coffee tariffs) do not limit Ethiopia's opportunities for development and for ensuring the right to food.

11
Mongolia

11.1 Introduction

Mongolia issued a standing open invitation to special rapporteurs on 9 April 2004, and we (Jean Ziegler and Sally-Anne Way) were the first to visit the country.[1] During our mission, we were honoured to be received by the Acting Prime Minister of Mongolia, His Excellency Chultemiyn Ulaan, as well as senior members of the Government, including the Minister for Food and Agriculture, the Minister of Health, and senior officials from other relevant government ministries, including the Ministry of Social Welfare and Labour and the Ministry of Justice and Home Affairs. We also met with senior members of the Disaster Management Agency. We also met the municipal authorities in Ulaanbaatar. During the mission, we visited areas in Selenge province in the north and Dungobi province in the south.

We were received by a number of national and international organizations, and spent time with Mr. Dashdorj, the Commissioner, and other members of the Mongolian National Human Rights Commission. We also spent time with NGOs, including the Centre for Human Rights and Development in Mongolia, World Vision, Action Contre La Faim, and Save the Children Fund.

Mongolia is a beautiful country with rolling grassy steppes, permanently snowcapped mountains – the Taiga to the north and the Altai to the west – and in the south, the Gobi desert that stretches across a third of the country. It is a huge, landlocked country bordered by its vast neighbours, the Russian Federation to the north, China to the south and Kazakhstan to the west. It has one of the lowest population densities in the world, with only 2.6 million people for 1.5 million km^2. The short summers are dry and hot, but during the long, freezing winters, temperatures can drop below – 30° centigrade. Around 40 per cent of the population live in sparsely populated rural areas, leading a semi-nomadic lifestyle in round white felt tents or *gers* and herding camels, yaks, horses, sheep and goats on the open steppes. The other 60 per cent of the population are concentrated in urban areas and regional centres, with more than a third of the total population living in the capital Ulaanbaatar.

In the thirteenth century, the Mongol empire under Genghis Khaan and Kublai Khan stretched from Beijing to the Caspian Sea. Later under Chinese domination, Mongolia became an independent State in 1911, and then a communist republic closely tied to the Soviet Union in 1921. Heavily subsidized by the Soviet Union, Mongolia became partially urbanized and industrialized. Education, health services, social support and pensions were universalized and although living standards were low, extreme poverty was unknown in Mongolia until 1990. With the collapse of the Soviet Union and CMEA in the early 1990s, Mongolia lost its subsidies and its markets and the economy virtually collapsed. Mongolia suffered a brutal drop in income and living standards, rapidly declining from a middle-income country to a low-income one – 'from the Second World to the Third'.[2] Gross domestic product (GDP) fell sharply from US$ 1645 per capita in 1989 to US$ 393 in 2003.[3] Today, Mongolia is still consolidating radical political and economic reforms initiated in the early 1990s, when it embraced democracy and adopted a minimalist, laissez-faire economic model. However, the rapid shift towards a liberalized market economy has been accompanied by the emergence of extreme poverty and growing inequality. A process of de-industrialization has left the Mongolian economy dependent mainly on services, mining (especially gold and copper) and agriculture (especially cashmere), although agriculture is vulnerable to drought, land degradation and severe winters. Mongolia is now one of the least developed countries in Asia. While there are new signs of dynamism in the Mongolian economy, the benefits seem not to have yet reached those who are poor and hungry. Problems of food insecurity and chronic malnutrition persist as poverty deepens, despite high levels of multilateral aid and the efforts of the Government and international agencies.

11.2 Hunger and food insecurity in Mongolia

11.2.1 The harsh winters and dzuds

Between 1999 and 2001, Mongolia suffered from two extremely harsh winters and *dzuds* (a Mongolian word used to define any condition that stops livestock from grazing grass). This severely affected rural Mongolians who depend on the semi-nomadic livestock herding in the rolling steppes. Heavy snows and impenetrable ice cover prevented livestock from grazing and millions of animals, already weakened from poor pastures due to summer droughts and locusts, died from starvation. More than 3.5 million animals were killed in 2000 and another 4.7 million in 2001.[4] Over 10,000 herders were left without any livestock and thousands more Mongolian families lost most of their herd.

Despite the deaths of millions of animals, the *dzuds* did not result in famine, partly due to efforts to provide food aid and animal fodder. A study carried out in 2001 found no difference in the prevalence of acute malnutrition in children under five in provinces affected by the *dzud* compared to those that had not been affected.[5] Another study carried out in 2003 found that the stunting of children under five was significantly higher in *dzud*-afffected areas (38 per cent compared to 26 per cent), but concluded that this could be due to factors other than the *dzud*.[6]

However, the studies did raise concerns about the longer term nutritional impact of the *dzuds*, raising concerns that greater poverty and lost livelihoods would eventually translate into higher levels of chronic undernourishment.

It is important to understand that during the early 1990s, there was a 'return to the land', with many families driven back to rural areas to escape escalating urban poverty. Thousands of people lost their jobs in urban areas as the economy collapsed and State industry was dismantled during the brutal economic transition, and many turned to herding as the only alternative. The number of herders rose dramatically from 147,508 to 417,743 between 1990 and 1999 (an increase of 183 per cent in just one decade) and the urban population fell by 13 per cent between 1989 and 1998.[7] However, some of the new or returning herders proved ill-prepared for the difficulties and risks of pastoral life. Many people taking up herding concentrated around the water sources and *soum* (county) and *aimag* (province) centres, which led to problems of overgrazing and land degradation in areas close to population centres. Exacerbated by the massive death of livestock during the *dzuds*, many herders were eventually forced to return back to the city. Between 1995 and 2000, 75,000 Mongolians migrated to Ulaanbaatar.

However, inexperience and overgrazing were not the only factors that affected the sustainability of herding livelihoods. The withdrawal of the State from agriculture and a lack of investment in rural areas led to the absence of previously provided public goods – such as winter shelters, emergency fodder stocks, maintenance of water and wells and essential veterinary services – contributing heavily to increasing the vulnerability of individual herders to climatic disasters. The retreat to the land occurred at the same time as the breakdown in rural infrastructure. When the State-run livestock cooperatives (*negdels*) were dismantled, no alternative forms of collective management were established, and responsibility for maintenance of wells, shelters and emergency fodder stocks was left to individual herding families. Today, at least 60 per cent of the 35,000 engineered and deep-water wells created during the socialist period are inoperative.[8] It has proved difficult for individual nomads to manage such services alone. Reduced social services in rural areas has also meant that herders preferred to stay closer to population centres, where water, schools, health centres, markets and veterinary services are more easily accessible, but this has resulted in increased land degradation and overgrazing in areas close to population centres. Traditional patterns of mobility across the land that would prevent overgrazing have not been generally re-established. The costs of privatized veterinary services have also reduced accessibility leaving animals more vulnerable. All these changes have increased the vulnerability of herding families to Mongolia's severe winters and summer droughts.

11.2.2 Overview of hunger and food insecurity in Mongolia

According to FAO, Mongolia is the most food insecure country in Asia apart from Cambodia. More than a third of the population is undernourished, with 38 per cent of Mongolians unable to guarantee enough food for themselves and their families each day.[9] UNDP human development statistics show that undernourishment increased from 34 per cent to 38 per cent of the population between 1990 and 2000. Mongolia has levels of undernourishment similar to those of countries in sub-Saharan Africa, such as Kenya or Madagascar. The daily calorie intake per person in poor households is only 1784 kcals – well below the international standard of 2100 kcals and the Mongolian standard of 2731 kcals per day.[10] The national report on the Millennium Development Goals estimates that the poorest 20 per cent of the population would not have enough income to buy adequate food, even if all their income were spent on food. It reports that many people only get two thirds of the food they need – and far less in winter when food consumption falls by 30 per cent because Mongolians have to spend their money on heating fuel to survive the freezing temperatures.[11] One in every five Mongolian children is stunted and 6.4 per cent are underweight.[12] The number of infants with low birth weight increased from 6 per cent to 10 per cent between 1992 and 1999 and infant mortality remains high.[13] Over 13 per cent of children die before their fifth birthday due to malnutrition and related diseases.

Micronutrient deficiencies are also widespread, with iron deficiency affecting one in four children, and iodine deficiency one in seven. Anaemia has increased and rickets remains a problem.[14] Access to fresh drinking water is extremely unequal and about 40 per cent of the population do not have access to an improved drinking water source. Residents of the urban *ger* districts (urban shantytown districts surrounding Ulaanbaatar made up of the traditional Mongolian white felt tents or *gers*) face severe problems of access to safe water and pay far more for water from kiosks than apartment residents for running water.[15] Poor families spend over 70 per cent of their income on food,[16] and therefore have to make difficult choices between food, water, health, education or winter heating. The impacts of the economic transition has also been disproportionately borne by women, since in the privatization process, many assets, including livestock and property, were usually registered in the name of the male heads of households, leaving women without control over their assets.[17] It is estimated that 90 per cent of privatized property was registered under the name of the husband. Women have also been more heavily affected by the closure of health and education centres in rural areas, and are subject to increased domestic violence that has been generated by widespread unemployment, poverty and hunger.[18]

Although Mongolia's dry, short summers and harsh winters are not very conducive to crop agriculture, under the Soviet system of intensive, irrigated State farms, Mongolia was more than self-sufficient in grain production, and even exported wheat. However, during the brutal economic transition in the early 1990s, both the availability and accessibility of food declined rapidly. With the dismantling of State farms, food production fell by 75 per cent between 1990 and 2003 and Mongolia rapidly shifted from being a food-exporting to a food-importing country. At the same time, the dismantling of State-owned industry and the mass unemployment that ensued lead to a rapid rise in extreme poverty. According to the National Statistics Office, in 1991, the average calorie intake fell precipitously below the international minimum basic requirement of 2100 kcals/day. In 2005, the average calorie intake was back above the basic international standard (although it remained below the Mongolian national standard of 2731 kcals/day), but this average concealed patterns of undernourishment and overnourishment.[19] According to Government statistics, the extent of undernourishment is more severe in urban than in rural areas. The 1999 National Nutrition Survey showed that in rural areas poor families consume 58 per cent less than the national minimum requirement. In urban areas, poor families consume 68 per cent below the minimum requirement. However, economically better-off families consume well over the recommended nutrient intake.

The traditional Mongolian diet is based on the semi-nomadic lifestyle of livestock herding and largely consists of meat and dairy products. This diet is high in fat, but low in carbohydrates and vegetables. With an increasingly sedentary lifestyle, this type of nutrition is contributing to the increasing prevalence of cardiovascular diseases amongst higher income groups. However, amongst the poor, poverty is also producing a shift in diet, as many of the poorest, who are unable to afford meat, now eat bread or flour products instead.[20] A UNICEF study on children living in Ulaanbaatar's peri-urban districts found that many families cope with food shortages by eating only one meal a day, sometimes going without meals for two or three days a month, and many children now show serious signs of insufficient food intake.[21] It also suggests that official poverty statistics underestimate the extent of poverty in the *ger* districts, since many new migrants are not officially registered.[22] According to the World Bank, some people have been reduced to desperate strategies to cope – scavenging food from rubbish dumps, or even being forced into thieving in order to be able to feed their families, contributing to the rise in urban crime in Ulaanbaatar.[23]

Despite evidence of undernourishment and hunger, and the fact that Mongolia is recorded as having the most serious problem of undernourishment in Asia, we found no comprehensive study on the state of food insecurity in Mongolia. Although a number of studies on nutrition have already been carried out, these are not always comprehensive in measuring severe malnutrition[24] and have not gathered adequate information on undernourishment. We were concerned to find that there seemed to be no general agreement in Mongolia about the level of food insecurity and undernourishment in the country. A number of those we spoke with, particularly in the multilateral development banks, did not believe that Mongolia had a problem of undernourishment and suggested that the statistics were exaggerated. However, bringing together various available statistics and information on undernourishment, nutritional deficiencies and poverty statistics it seems that a problem of food insecurity and chronic undernourishment does certainly exist in Mongolia and needs to be urgently addressed. In its report on the Millennium Development Goals the Government recognizes that there is a problem, and poverty statistics would also appear to support the estimate on undernourishment. According to Government statistics 35.6 per cent of Mongolians live under the poverty line, which effectively means that they experience a systematic shortage of food because they cannot afford to buy sufficient food.[25] Six months after the conclusion of our visit, we received a communication from the Government of Mongolia stating that according to the III National Nutrition Survey, 2004, severe malnutrition among children under five had been reduced from 2.86 per cent in 1999 to 0.7 per cent in 2004. We had no possibility to check these figures against other findings of the FAO or UNICEF.

According to the 1998 Living Standard Measurement Survey, poverty levels are higher in urban areas (39 per cent) than in rural areas (32 per cent). Approximately 57 per cent of Mongolia's population live in urban areas, and poverty is concentrated in the *ger* districts on the outskirts of Ulaanbaatar, but also in *aimag* and *soum* centres, as a result of chronic unemployment and low wages. Food insecurity is heightened by job insecurity. Official unemployment stands at only 4.6 per cent of the workforce; however, alternative estimates suggest that at least 15 per cent and as many as 48 per cent are unemployed.[26] Many of the poorest eke out a living in small trade or services in the informal sector in urban areas. Some have left to follow the gold rush, working in difficult conditions mainly in the gold mines in Central Aimag. Many of the poorest are heavily dependent on the increasingly meagre benefits and pensions received by older members of the household[27] and may therefore be seriously affected by the reform of the social security and pension system that is currently being proposed. A survey in Ulaanbaatar found that poverty was actually lowest amongst those over 60,[28] probably because they received pensions. Poverty is often highest amongst new migrants to the city who may be denied access to social services if they are not registered. One survey recorded that one out of three adults from newly migrated families were unemployed, and nearly 35 per cent of recent migrants did not have enough food, stating that 'one out of three families does not have enough food at home'.[29]

Among the 43 per cent of the population that live in rural areas, some families also survive on pensions but most income is derived from the products of their herds. While rural families can live off their animals for food as well as produce income, this is becoming increasingly difficult as it is estimated that 55 per cent of herders now have less than 100 animals, considered the minimum for a sustainable livelihood. Very remote areas in Mongolia, particularly the western *aimags*, receive fewer resources and investment. Some groups, such as the Tsaatan minority of reindeer breeders, do not have adequate access to social services and live in conditions of extreme poverty and malnutrition. Food insecurity is heightened by climatic uncertainties, including drought and severe winters, but vulnerability increases with greater poverty. With massive losses of livestock and lack of investment in rural development, many rural families have been forced to survive by working for better-off families or migrating to the city to try to find work.

During our mission, we carried out visits to both urban and rural areas. In Ulaanbaatar, we met with large numbers of poorer Mongolians dependent on food canteens and soup kitchens. We also met with abandoned children brought into orphanages after being found living in underground heating pipe tunnels, drains and sewers. The number of street children has rapidly increased since the economic transition, as unemployment and economic insecurity have contributed to widespread social malaise and family breakdown. A six-year-old child we met in a State-run orphanage could neither walk nor speak as a result of severe malnutrition; others were also physically or mentally stunted. We bore witness to high levels of food insecurity and chronic malnourishment in the poor urban districts of Ulaanbaatar, but also saw the prevalence of poverty in rural areas, particularly among pastoralist families who have lost most of their herds. In discussions we had in Selenge *aimag*, we learned that new social classes have emerged, of landowners and landless labourers and tenant farmers. In Dungobi *aimag*, in the more arid south, life seemed even more difficult given the lack of investment in harnessing water resources to improve pastureland for fodder.

Access to water is increasingly difficult and highly unequal, and the quality and safety of drinking water is generally reported to have deteriorated since the economic transition. In Ulaanbaatar, 55 per cent of the population (mainly residents of the *ger* districts) have no access to the centralized water system and have to make use of distant water kiosks or water tanked in irregularly by trucks, which is much more expensive. Water consumption per person in the apartment blocks is of 240–450 litres a day, as opposed to 8–10 litres in the *ger* districts.[30] In Sukhbaatar district, Khoroo No. 11, for example, there are three water kiosks to meet the needs of more than 10,000 residents. Water supply does not cover needs, and sometimes children line up for two to three hours, only to find that the water has run out by the time they reach the beginning of the queue. In the summer, *ger* residents often use river water and natural springs, but in winter the water freezes and they therefore have no choice but to use kiosks, despite the high prices of water. There are also inequities in the use of water between private persons and corporations, in particular the mining industry. In discussions with UNDP it was said that reportedly, *ger* residents pay 84 times more for water than the mining corporations. Serious concerns are also being raised about the contamination of water resources, including deep wells and springs, by mercury from mining activities – given a weak regulatory environment and the focus on driving economic growth without environmental or social impact assessments. Access to clean water is therefore increasingly difficult, yet water is essential for life and an essential part of nutrition and therefore of the right to food.

11.3 Legal framework for the right to food in Mongolia

11.3.1 International obligations

Mongolia has ratified the International Covenant on Economic, Social and Cultural Rights, which protects the right to food in Article 11. It has also ratified a number of other international instruments relevant to the right to adequate food and adequate nutrition, including the International Covenant on Civil and Political Rights (Article 6), the Convention on the Rights of the Child (Articles 24 and 27) and the Convention on the Elimination of All Forms of Discrimination against Women (Articles 12 and 14). It means that under its international commitment to the right to food, Mongolia has the obligation to respect, protect and fulfil the right to food of its people, without discrimination.

With the exception of one report to the Committee on Discrimination against Women, all the periodic reports that Mongolia is required to submit on these Conventions were overdue when we undertook the visit.

11.3.2 Domestic constitutional and legislative framework

The Mongolian Constitution of 1992 guarantees democracy and fundamental rights and freedoms for the Mongolian people, including a range of economic and social rights. While the right to food is not explicitly recognized in the Constitution, there are a number of provisions that are closely related and which protect access to food for the most vulnerable.

Article 16, paragraph 5, recognizes the 'right to material and financial assistance in old age, disability, childbirth and childcare and in other circumstances as provided by law', which provides some protection for those groups and requires the Government to provide assistance to them, including food assistance. The right to food is also closely related to the right to work, to adequate livelihoods and to equal treatment. Article 14 of the Constitution enshrines the right to be treated equally before the law and the courts. Article 16, paragraph 14, recognizes the right of Mongolian citizens to have recourse to courts of law for the protection of rights or freedoms 'spelt out by the Mongolian law or an international treaty' and 'to be compensated for the damage illegally caused by other'. We were informed that recourse to courts was available for all rights in the Constitution, including economic, social and cultural rights. The Constitution declares that international treaties become effective as domestic legislation upon the entry into force of the laws on their ratification or accession, although it also states that 'Mongolia shall not abide by any international treaty or other instruments incompatible with its Constitution' (Article 10, paragraph 4), putting domestic law above international law. We share the observation of the Human Rights Committee that it should be clarified in the law that human rights contained in the Covenant should prevail over domestic law in case of any conflict.[31]

Mongolia's legislative framework also includes a number of other laws and regulations with direct relevance to the realization of the right to food. Among the most important is the Law of Food adopted in 1995 and amended in 1999. The purpose of the Law of Food is 'to ensure food necessities of the population, food safety and to regulate relations that arise between the Government, individuals and legal entities in connection with the food production and services'. However, the actual scope of the law is narrower than its declared objective. The law focuses mainly on food safety standards and partially on the food supply. It mentions the requirement to ensure nutritional quality of available food, but is silent on the critical issue of access to food and, does not recognize that all people living in Mongolia's territory are entitled to the right to food. Nor does it establish mechanisms of accountability.

The 1998 Social Welfare Law defines entitlements for 'extremely poor' citizens. A person is defined as 'extremely poor' if his/her earnings are 40 per cent below the poverty line and result in 'limited consumption'. Presumably 'limited consumption' refers to limited food consumption; but the National Human Rights Commission of Mongolia noted that the term 'limited consumption' has not been defined, resulting in ambiguity.[32] The Social Welfare Law is nevertheless an important complement to the Social Insurance Law in that it nominally covers people who are not entitled to pension under that law and provides them with some income. But these laws appear to have a limited coverage and are not always known to the potential beneficiaries. According to information provided to us by the Ministry of Labour, benefits provided for under the law amount to Tog 14,400, which is inadequate, the minimum living standard being of Tog 27,000 in Ulaanbaatar.

Legislation on land ownership and land use is particularly important for the right to food in Mongolia, given that almost half of the population depends on agriculture and related activities, especially herding. Current characteristics of land legislation in Mongolia were substantially crafted between 2000 and 2002 as part of the drive to economic reform and liberalization and came in response to pressures to provide better conditions for foreign investment in the food, agricultural and mining sectors. Two important laws were passed in 2002, the Law on Land and the Law on Allocation of Land to Mongolian Citizens for Ownership. These laws reserve land ownership for Mongolian citizens and provide rules on the allocation of land in the privatization process.

Grazing land remains excluded from private ownership, but land can be privatized for other uses both in urban and rural areas. So far, 0.9 per cent of the total land has been privatized. Land in urban centres was to be given to citizens without payment. Families in the capital city were entitled to 0.07 ha, in *aimag* centres 0.35 ha and in *soum* centres 0.5 ha. In rural areas, up to 100 ha of agricultural land may be given to a citizen and family who have worked in the agricultural sector, and up to 5 ha for vegetable growing (Article 29.3). *Aimags* can decide on the size of land to be given to corporations – up to 3000 ha for cereal and fodder crop production, up to 50 ha for vegetable production, and up to 1500 ha for commercial haymaking purposes.[33] We were informed that a good number of Mongolian corporations and legal entities had possession or use of large areas of agricultural land. This would raise the concern that there are inequalities in the land allocated between individuals and corporations. We were also concerned that the process of granting licenses for possession and use of land by companies and individuals may not have adequate transparency and accountability mechanisms that prevent favouritism and even corruption in the system.

Under the law, pastureland can still only be possessed collectively. Article 54 of the Law on Land defines responsibilities of local authorities in the preservation and use of pastureland. It requires that *soum* and *aimag* governors, in cooperation with relevant professional organizations and taking into consideration land use traditions, rational land use and conservation requirements, should carry out land management activities to ensure the preservation and rational use of national pastureland. During our mission, we welcomed the efforts made by Mongolia to strike a right balance between the competing policy needs of developing land and agricultural markets and the need to preserve public access to land, in particular pastureland, which is essential for the survival of herding communities and families. Being aware of mounting foreign pressure for further liberalization and privatization of land in Mongolia, we reminded the Government of its obligations under international human rights law to ensure access to food or to the means for its procurement. For farming and herding communities, which represent a large segment of Mongolian population, access to pastures and other land is crucial to their livelihoods.

11.3.3 Access to justice and human rights institutions

The Government has made important progress in establishing a National Human Rights Commission in 2000 and in drawing up the first national action plan on human rights, although progress on the plan of action was suspended during the election and a Committee of oversight had not been established at the time of our visit. However, we were very encouraged by the work of the National Human Rights Commission of Mongolia (NHRCM), which has been granted full political, economic and legal independence in line with the Paris Principles.

The mandate of the National Human Rights Commission is to promote and protect human rights and it must present annual reports on the human rights situation to the Parliament. It is responsible for monitoring compliance of domestic legislation with international standards. The NHRCM can receive individual complaints about constitutional rights or rights recognized in treaties ratified by Mongolia. Economic, social and cultural rights, including the right to adequate food, fall clearly within its mandate. The focus of the Commission has so far been on civil liberties and the administration of justice, but it has begun on poverty and economic, social and cultural rights. For example, its 2002 report addressed issues related to the right to health protection, education and social security, and labour rights, while the 2003 report addressed those rights in relation to the particular situation of groups such as children, disabled people and the extremely poor. The Commission has not yet worked on specific cases in relation to the right to food, although it did bring a case to court to challenge registration fees charged to new migrants in Ulaanbaatar on the basis of discrimination. This case was won, and there are no more official fees charged for registration, which significantly helps the poorest in gaining access to social services, although the process of registration still remains difficult.

In general, access to justice for the poor remains difficult, as although the judiciary is expected to be independent, judges are often inadequately trained on human rights issues, particularly for economic, social and cultural rights. The judicial system also suffers from large case backlogs and instances of corruption, and access to courts is hindered by long distances and high litigation costs.[34]

11.4 Policy framework for the right to food

11.4.1 Government policies and institutions

Mongolia has a number of policies and institutions in place to address issues related to food supply, food safety and nutrition, although there appears to be no comprehensive strategy fully addressing issues of food security in terms of access to food. Few policies take an explicitly rights-based approach, but the Government expressed a positive interest in building awareness of the issue of the right to food.

The National Plan of Action for Food Security, Safety and Nutrition adopted in October 2001 is the key government strategy relevant to the right to food and falls under the responsibility of the Ministry of Food and Agriculture. This plan addresses key questions of food supply, food safety and nutrition. It sets out important strategies for improving availability of food and promoting greater agricultural production, including of vegetables and milk, through programmes such as the Green Revolution and White Revolution programmes. During our mission and on our visits to a number of farms and factories we witnessed these important efforts to revive production of grain, processed meat and milk products. The Ministry plans to increase local food production, concerned that Mongolia imports over 70 per cent of its food.[35] In line with the 1995 Law on Food, the Action Plan also sets out important strategies to improve food safety, addressing public concerns that followed the liberalization of trade, when lower quality food imports flooded into the country. Finally, the Action Plan also sets out important strategies to improve nutrition, including encouraging greater consumption of vegetables through education and through promoting increased vegetable production and micronutrient fortification of certain basic staple foods. Although the plan addresses issues of poor nutrition, it fails to look at the link between the impacts of chronic under-consumption and extreme poverty. It defines food security largely as an issue of food availability (food supply through agricultural production), and does not address issues related to access to food. Nor does it contain statistics on or an analysis of the causes of undernourishment and food insecurity in Mongolia. Food accessibility is a key component of the right to food and it is essential to have a comprehensive strategy to address all aspects of food security, with responsibilities allocated between different ministries.

The Ministry of Health is responsible for a number of strategies in place to address nutritional deficiencies, with a priority focus on women and children. Programmes include a project for flour fortification to reduce iron-deficiency anaemia. A strategy on 'Prevention of Micronutrient Deficiency of Children under 5' is being drafted by the Ministry which will focus on the distribution of vitamins A and D and iron to children. The Government has also developed the project 'Goals for Children in Mongolia', which sets out goals to reduce rates of under-5 mortality and undernutrition, expand the coverage of vitamin D supplementation, increase rates of breastfeeding and ensure universal iodization of salt. The Ministry of Health is also promoting awareness of nutrition in order to promote healthy eating habits and, in collaboration with other Ministries, to promote food safety. All these are important policies to address nutritional deficiencies in the country. However, they remain focused on efforts to promote fortification or supplementation with micronutrients, without looking at the issue of under-consumption and resulting malnutrition in children and mothers. In our meeting with the Ministry of Health, we found that the senior officials did recognize the problem of undernourishment, but felt that this issue fell outside its competence.

The Ministry of Social Welfare and Labour has the overall responsibility for monitoring human development in Mongolia and implementing the Government's overall poverty reduction strategy. The Ministry is responsible for social safety nets, including the payment of pensions and unemployment benefits to those in the formal sector and direct assistance, including food support to the extremely poor through orphanages and feeding centres. It also sets the national minimum wage and is responsible for its enforcement. During our mission, we were concerned that the legal minimum wage was under US$ 30 (Tog 30,000) a month, considered insufficient by the National Commission on Human Rights to provide a decent standard of living for a worker and family.

The Government's overall poverty reduction strategy is outlined in the Economic Growth Support and Poverty Reduction Strategy Paper. The strategy paper briefly examines the question of undernourishment, recording that between 1990 and 2002, the national average caloric intake has fallen well below the national recommended levels.[36] It recognizes that a large number of families are suffering from a lack of food and that many of the poor cannot cover their food needs. However, it does not analyse the causes of food insecurity and it suggests that, compared to other countries with similar income levels, malnutrition is not a serious problem for Mongolia, except in rural areas and among poor people.[37] During our visit, we were also concerned that there were few concrete actions proposed to reduce food insecurity and undernourishment. The strategy rests on the belief that economic restructuring and rationalization of social safety nets will automatically generate economic growth, which will in turn automatically reduce poverty.[38] However, much of the restructuring already undertaken, including privatization and trade liberalization, has failed to automatically generate growth, and poverty alleviation will not occur in the context of rising inequality as the benefits will not trickle down to the poor. Privatization has often had the effect of increasing inequality, since the benefits of privatization have accrued to those elites closest to government officials. It is equally unlikely that a further rationalization of social safety nets will automatically generate economic growth; on the contrary, it may create even greater poverty, as so many people are dependent on pension incomes. We were encouraged that senior officials from the Ministry recognized these issues and informed us that there is now a shift towards 'livelihood support' that will prevent and slow down the rate of impoverishment of Mongolian families.

Mongolia's Disaster Management Agency has the responsibility for operating an early warning system for natural disasters – including *dzuds* – and coordinating responses to them. It also manages emergency fodder programmes, and food aid programmes. During our mission, we were concerned however that no overall responsibility for food aid appeared to have been allocated in Mongolia. Mongolia receives relatively high levels of food aid every year, including from the United States and France; most of this aid is not distributed as emergency food aid, but is locally monetized, with the funds then used to finance project budgets. But we were concerned that there seemed to be no responsibility for monitoring the impact of food aid on the Mongolian economy or for maintaining accountability on monetized aid. It would seem that there is therefore a need to allocate responsibility for the management of food aid to one particular institution.

In terms of responsibility for water management, Mongolia has no Ministry with overall responsibility for water. A National Water Committee has been established, which is responsible for the implementation of the National Water Action Plan and the coordination of responsibility among the different ministries; for example, the Ministry of Agriculture and Food is responsible for rural water supply, but the Ministry of Nature and the Environment is responsible for water conservation. We were concerned during our visit that both policies and the institutional framework for water management remain weak, which affects the regulatory capacity to prevent water pollution from mining, and other activities. We were encouraged that WHO is collaborating with the Government to improve the protection of natural water springs in urban areas, on which much of the urban population depends. However, we remain concerned that there appears to be no overall responsibility for ensuring adequate access to water for the poorest.

11.4.2 International agencies and donors

There are a large number of international agencies in Mongolia, including multilateral development banks (with a far greater involvement of the Asian Development Bank than the World Bank) and a number of the United Nations and specialized agencies, including FAO through its office in Beijing and its correspondents in Mongolia. The United Nations agencies in Mongolia have largely adopted a rights-based approach to development, although they have not focused attention on the right to food.

Mongolia receives one of the highest levels of international aid per capita. It is the fifth most aid-dependent country in the world,[39] with aid making up 20 per cent of the gross national product. During the period between 1991 and 2002, Mongolia received US$ 2.4 billion in bilateral and multilateral Official Development Assistance (ODA), about half of which in the form of grants and about half in concessional loans that will have to be repaid.[40] It receives an amount of of aid that is almost the amount of subsidies that it used to receive from the Soviet Union, yet the impact on poverty alleviation has been markedly different. Most of the aid has not been spent directly on poverty reduction. During the 1990s, most aid was allocated to physical infrastructure (37 per cent) and to 'economic management' (24 per cent), but only 1.2 per cent of total aid was spent on the National Poverty Alleviation Programme and 5 per cent on agricultural development in the rural sector, even though employment in this sector was growing.[41] This would suggest that the elimination of poverty and food insecurity has not been a priority for the major international donors, especially the Asian Development Bank and the World Bank. This appears to be changing, however, as the multilateral development banks begin to recognize the need to address poverty, rather than relying on benefits from economic growth eventually trickling down to the poor. Many of the United Nations agencies, such as UNDP and WHO, have worked hard to re-orient aid spending towards poverty reduction, although there is still little focus on issues of food insecurity and chronic undernourishment.

11.4.3 Non-governmental organizations

Important progress has been made in Mongolia with civil society organizations emerging since the transition. However, many of these organizations remain underdeveloped and weak in advocacy capacity, particularly in their advocacy for the poor. There are also a large number of international NGOs now working in Mongolia, many of which have focused on implementing a rights-based approach to their work, although few focus on the right to food. We met with local organizations, including the Centre for Human Rights and Development and the Mongolian Food Producers Association, as well as international NGOs, such as Action Contre la Faim and World Vision. All these organizations agreed that there was a problem of undernourishment in Mongolia, and were concerned that this was not a central issue for the main development donors. The representative of World Vision reported for example that a large number of people walk for up to an hour, even in the winter, to come to the two soup kitchens World Vision runs in Ulaanbaatar because this will be their only meal of the day.

11.5 Main findings and concerns

11.5.1 Progressive realization of the right to food

Under its commitment to the right to food, the Government of Mongolia is required to ensure the progressive realization of the right to food, using the maximum of available resources. This means that constant progress must be made in reducing levels of chronic food insecurity, hunger and poverty, by improving food availability, accessibility and adequacy, and by focusing on the most vulnerable.

During our visit, we were concerned that chronic undernourishment appears to have increased, rather than decreased in Mongolia, from 34 per cent to 38 per cent between 1990 and 2000, which amounts to a regression in the realization of the right to food. We were particularly concerned given that before 1990 malnutrition was rare, and, according to the UNDP, there was no recorded poverty or unemployment.[42] In 2005, 14 years after the economic transition, more than 35 per cent of Mongolians still lived under the poverty line and therefore with a systematic shortage of adequate food. Although the number of people living under the poverty line appears to have stabilized, inequality and the depth of poverty are reported to be increasing. This suggests that the poor are becoming poorer and will be increasingly unlikely to be able to meet their expenses for food in the future. While the Government has taken important steps to improve food availability and food safety, we were particularly concerned that the National Plan on Food Security does not address the question of undernourishment or access to food.

We were also concerned that Mongolia does not appear to be using the maximum available resources to address the situation of chronic undernourishment. Mongolia receives one of the highest levels of aid per capita in the world, yet it seems that most of these funds are not being used in ways that are alleviating food insecurity or poverty. Few concrete actions or institutions are in place to address the problem of access to food for the poorest. This may in part be the result of the lack of attention on food security by the donor community, particularly the multilateral development banks. It also appears to be partly due to reliance on 'trickle-down' economics, but this is not sufficient if it is failing to reach Mongolia's poor and hungry. We were also concerned by growing inequalities between rich and poor, between regions and between men and women.

In terms of the legal framework governing the right to food, we were encouraged by the establishment of the National Human Rights Commission which has the mandate to cover all human rights, including the right to food, and by the work that the Commission has already done on issues of poverty. We encouraged further work on the right to food as part of its work on poverty, as this would provide an important way of improving domestic monitoring of the right to food in Mongolia, as well as improving advocacy and accountability for the right to food.

11.5.2 Violations of the right to food

Under its commitment to the right to food, the Government undertakes obligations to respect, protect and fulfil the right to food, without discrimination. We were very encouraged to find comparatively few documented cases of violations of the right to food. We found little evidence of pervasive discrimination against ethnic or other groups that would amount to a violation of the right to food. We visited one prison to examine food conditions of detainees, but found that kitchen conditions were adequate and that the prison appeared to be providing food adequate in quantity and quality to its inmates.

However, we did find some documented cases of violations, including reports of cases of people starving to death, suffering from severe undernutrition, as well as cases of people excluded from social assistance. In its 2003 status report on human rights in Mongolia, the National Human Rights Commission reported that:

> During a survey in Ulaanbaatar, cases were reported on people who starved for days without any food, suffered from malnutrition and their mental health gradually degrading. In the social welfare centre at Songino-Khairkhan District, a 56-year-old citizen 'G' was suffering from a mental disorder caused by severe famine.[43]

Certain groups appear to be sometimes excluded from social assistance and services, such as unregistered migrants, single mothers, women-headed households, street children, the Tsaatan minority and people without identity documents. The National Human Rights Commission found that 41 per cent of poor people had no identity documents[44] and more than 50 per cent were not aware of their entitlements under the law. There are also concerns that some groups, especially women, migrants and rural and *ger* district populations, have been affected by inequities in the privatization process. In Ulaanbaatar for example, tenants were granted automatic free ownership of their apartments, but residents in the surrounding *ger* districts were not granted equivalent benefits or land titles.

11.5.3 Obstacles to the realization of the right to food

We believe that there are a number of key obstacles that affect the capacity of the Government to guarantee the progressive realization of the right to food.

The first obstacle to the full realization of the right to food in Mongolia has been the lack of attention paid to the problem of food insecurity and chronic undernourishment. The Government, apparently on the advice of the IMF and the multilateral development banks such as the Asian Development Bank and the World Bank, has tended to focus on the reorientation of the economy through 'shock therapy', rapid privatization and trade liberalization, without monitoring the impacts on the people's capacity to feed themselves. The focus of development efforts have been on privatization and economic growth, regardless of the cost in terms of social equality or environmental sustainability. Rapid de-industrialization has left Mongolia dependent on exports of primary products and it has shifted from being a net food-exporter to importing more than 70 per cent of its foodstuffs. Privatization and trade liberalization have not automatically generated broad, pro-poor economic growth, and much of new dynamism beginning to show in the economy appears to be coming from the profits of gold mining, but the benefits are unevenly spread and unsustainable.

Low incomes and wages and pervasive unemployment, exacerbated by the broader process of de-industrialization, continue to be the key obstacles to the realization of the right to food. The reliance on a trickle-down model of economic growth to fight poverty and hunger has not yet been successful. As Griffin noted, 'those who advocate a minimalist State, non-intervention and reliance on the market mechanism to reduce poverty have led the country to the brink of disaster'.[45] Government documents have noted that in the first years of transition, 'denial of State participation and coordination in the market economy and application of "shock therapy" in transition, created collapse and chaos in all sectors of the economy'.[46] The speed of liberalization did not allow Mongolia to build the efficiency of its existing industry that might have survived in an open world market. Privatization has also not automatically generated growth, as many privatized assets are in the same hands as they were before – previous managers or former government officials – yet there have been few efforts to build capacity or the skills of entrepreneurship or ensure adequate finance for development. Although some forms of allocation of land to herder families may enable them to invest in that land for the benefit of their families, the form of privatization implemented in the country has exacerbated inequalities and opened up new opportunities for corruption, particularly given the lack of transparency and accountability and the speed of the process. The economy remains unable to provide the employment necessary to lift more than one third of the population out of food insecurity and poverty.

The lack of public investment in herding livelihoods has also proved an obstacle to the realization of the right to food, particularly given that the 'pastoral safety net' provided necessary employment. Dismantling of the *negdels* left pastoralists without the public goods necessary for their survival, particularly in the harsh winters – water, shelter, and emergency fodder reserves. With no new collective institutions to provide these goods, herding has become increasingly unviable for small-scale herders. Yet pastoral livelihoods remain essential as part of the safety net for poor Mongolians, still providing employment to 45 per cent of the population and providing the best use of its key resource: land. The solidarity and rural–urban links between extended families also continue to provide urban families with essential meat and milk. It is essential to support pastoral livelihoods to stem the flow of urban migration, especially in a context where urban unemployment remains high and urban poverty is greater than rural poverty. It makes sense to invest in and support pastoral livelihoods, at least until sufficient employment is generated in the cities. Even subsistence level livelihoods are better than no livelihoods at all.

Mongolia's steppe ecosystem is fragile and vulnerable to overgrazing, degradation and deforestation, but the current land law has exacerbated the situation of overgrazing, heightening vulnerability to natural disasters. The 1994 Land Law codified an 'open access' regime to Mongolia's pastureland, which resulted in overgrazing in the most desirable areas because there are no limits on access to land. Some are now calling for the privatization of the pastureland to address overgrazing. However, privatization is not the best answer for herding livelihoods, which require mobility over large areas to manage climate-related risks. The choice does not need to be between open access and individual privatized ownership – the third possibility is common property, where a group is granted rights to land and can regulate the activities of its members and exclude non-group members from using that land.[47] A common property rights regime could give rights over seasonal pastures, including all the different types of pastureland needed during each of the four seasons, as well as water sources, providing security of tenure to the group and avoiding overgrazing, based on a leasing system whereby fees would be lower in less hospitable areas far from markets and with poor infrastructure, and higher in good grazing areas with easy market access and good infrastructure.[48] While nomadic pastoralism is well suited to the open steppes and is probably the best use of Mongolia's vast resource of land, this can remain sustainable only with an adequate pattern of mobility to avoid overgrazing and only with a focus on sustainability and the right to food for all, rather than purely on economic growth.

Mongolia also suffers from a large number of inherent obstacles that put it in a position of significant disadvantage in world trade that will make it difficult to generate economic growth in a context of fully liberalized trade. It is a huge, landlocked country that is geographically isolated with few road or rail communications and poor national and international market infrastructures. This 'tyranny of distance' and the lack of paved roads make competition for any product difficult because of transport costs. These obstacles make it very difficult for Mongolia to enter the world trading system on a level playing field, and this should be recognized and compensated for in trade liberalization. However, Mongolia has been persuaded to reduce all protection to its own economy and was encouraged to liberalize too rapidly, most of its industries collapsed without the time to build efficiency, leaving Mongolia little to compete with on international markets. It was assumed that liberalization would automatically generate growth, yet little could survive the onslaught of competition from goods from its huge neighbours in China and Russia, especially agriculture. Now having liberalized well beyond the requirements of the World Trade Organization, it will also be difficult for Mongolia to build up new industries. Left dependent primarily on cashmere, copper and gold, Mongolia has become vulnerable to volatile world commodity prices, even though it needs foreign exchange to purchase food imports.

After more than a decade of recession, the Mongolian economy is only just beginning to show dynamism, despite receiving one of the highest levels of aid in the world. While Mongolia needs international aid and support at present, there remains a danger that it will become too aid-dependent and that aid is not being spent on the poor. Mongolia's external debt stands at around US$ 1.3 billion, or 90 per cent of gross national income (GNI).[49] The debt burden will become an obstacle to the realization of the right to food in the future, by further limiting available resources to spend on fighting poverty and improving food security.

11.6 Conclusions and recommendations

In his report on the mission to Mongolia, presented to the Commission on Human Rights in March 2006, Jean Ziegler made the following conclusions and recommendations.

He was encouraged by the interest expressed by the Government in gaining a better understanding of the right to food. He was encouraged by the efforts of the Government to improve the availability and adequacy of food (supply and food quality). However, he believed that the problem of lack of access to food and the resulting chronic undernourishment deserves urgent attention, as do early warning mechanisms and preventative measures against natural disasters, such as the *dzuds*.

Jean Ziegler then recommended that:

(a) A comprehensive study on the situation of food insecurity and chronic undernourishment be carried out to determine the validity of existing statistics and the urgency of the problem. The linkages between poverty and the lack of access to sufficient food must be explored. Future studies on nutritional deficiencies should examine the extent to which nutritional deficiencies are due to chronic underconsumption;

(b) The legal framework to protect the right to food under domestic law be strengthened. Steps could be taken such as clarifying the relationship between international and domestic law and amending the 1995 Law on Food to include recognition that all Mongolians should be entitled to the right to adequate food. Mechanisms of accountability should also be established to ensure that Mongolians could seek access to justice if the right to food is not being met. The Government should also submit its overdue reports on its implementation of the human rights treaties to which it is a party;

(c) The excellent work of the National Human Rights Commission be supported and strengthened. The Commission has a crucial role to play in the realization of the right to food and should develop institutional capacities for research, monitoring and response to complaints on this issue. This should include monitoring of access to food and water of poor Mongolians and following up cases where people have been denied such access or where people have died of starvation, as well as monitoring the progressive realization of the right to adequate food in the context of the fight against chronic undernourishment;

(d) Government policies and programmes be developed to address food insecurity and the lack of access to food for Mongolia's population. Responsibilities should be fully established between Ministries. Addressing food insecurity should also be fully integrated into the national poverty reduction strategy. In collaboration with international donors, the Government should ensure that adequate resources are directed towards the most vulnerable and ensure equitable access to food and water as a priority, particularly international aid that should be used to alleviate poverty and food insecurity;

(e) Rural livelihoods be supported and greater investment undertaken to support the creation of pastoralist institutions to improve the provision of public goods and essential services, including well maintenance, emergency fodder stocks, winter shelters and veterinary services;

(f) Pastoral land not be privatized in the future, as this would not solve issues of overgrazing but rather exacerbate food insecurity and poverty. Institutions of common property and patterns of mobility should be considered to address overgrazing and improve sustainability;

(g) The institutional framework for the management of water resources be strengthened and responsibility allocated for ensuring access to water for all communities, including wells for rural populations and their animals, as well as water supplies for those living in urban centres which are not served, including the *ger* districts in Ulaanbaatar. There is also an urgent need to improve water quality;

(h) Overarching responsibility be established for the management of food aid. Mechanisms to monitor the impact of food aid on food security and the broader economy should be established, to ensure that food aid does not act as a disincentive to efforts to increase local production. Standard procedures should also be established for improved transparency and accountability for monetized food aid;

(i) Actions be taken to ensure that all groups have access to adequate social services and assistance, including not registered migrants and families without documents. The current restructuring of the social security system must include a review of the potential impacts on food security;

(j) Further reforms of the economy protect against the inequities that have characterized the liberalization and privatization process, particularly affecting women, and be monitored to ensure that they do not result in greater levels of undernourishment. Accountability and transparency should be improved to remove the potential for corruption and favouritism;

(k) Finally, the current model of economic development be revised to address problems of poverty and chronic undernourishment, otherwise it appears that Mongolia's poor and hungry will be increasingly left behind. Mongolia's inherent obstacles as a remote landlocked country must also be recognized at the international level and the rules of trade liberalization should permit development and the realization of the right to adequate food. Addressing food insecurity and poverty must be prioritized for the realization of the right to food.

12
Guatemala

12.1 Introduction

We (Jean Ziegler, Sally-Anne Way and Christophe Golay) visited Guatemala from 26 January to 4 February 2005.[1] During our visit, we had the honour to be received by Vice-President Eduardo Stein Barillas, Secretary for Food and Nutrition Security Andrés Botrán, and President of the Presidential Commission for the Coordination of Human Rights Policies (COPREDEH) Frank La Rue, as well as by the Minister and Deputy Minister for Foreign Affairs, the Minister of Agriculture and senior staff of the Ministries for Food Security, Health, Labour, Planning, Finance and Foreign Affairs. We welcomed the documentation provided to him by the Government with respect to the FAO Voluntary Guidelines on the Right to Food. We had the honour to be received by the wife of the President, Wendy W. de Berger and her Secretariat of Social Programmes and held meetings with senior members of the Secretariat of Social Welfare, the Women's Presidential Secretariat and the Defender of Indigenous Women. We appreciated meeting with Sergio Morales, the Ombudsman and the members of the Commission on the Strengthening of Justice. We were honoured to be received by Nobel Prize winner Rigoberta Menchu.

During our visit, we met with a wide range of civil society representatives. We appreciated participating in the 'National Forum on Right to Food as a Challenge to National Policy', an opportunity to catalyse greater action, and thank FAO, FIAN and the Platform of Human Rights for organizing the meetings. Álvaro Ramazzini, Bishop of San Marcos and the Pastoral de la Tierra organized a number of local forums to hear testimonies of different communities. We visited rural and urban areas, including Nebaj, Quiché, Chichicastenango, San Marcos, Chiquimula, Chor'ti and Zacapa and the Zone 18 and Zone 7 of Guatemala City.

Guatemala is a beautiful and wonderfully diverse country. Much of its terrain is mountainous and volcanic, with forested highlands in the west, fertile lowland coasts, and the tropical forest of the Petén. With a population of 12 million people, Guatemala is a multi-ethnic society, speaking 24 languages (Spanish, 21 Mayan languages, Xinca and Garifuna) amongst different ethno-linguistic groups of which the largest are the K'iché, the Kaqchiqel, the Man and the Q'eqchi. It has been a contested point, but it is now agreed that indigenous peoples make up more than half of Guatemala's population (63 per cent).[2] The majority of the population lives in rural areas (54 per cent), but Guatemala is becoming increasingly urbanized (46 per cent). Guatemala's economy is still largely based on exports of coffee and sugar, with agriculture providing work to at least 36 per cent of the population, although *maquila* (large factories producing finished goods for export) activities, extractive mining industries, energy, commerce, and services, including tourism, have become important economic sectors. Guatemala is not a poor country, but it is one of the countries with the most inequitable distributions of wealth in the world, and the majority of its population is poor and hungry, particularly indigenous peoples.

After a 36-year civil war in which more than 200,000 women, children and men were brutally killed or 'disappeared', Guatemala returned to peace with the Peace Accords of 1996 and a vision for a more inclusive future built on the respect of human rights and social justice. However, progress in implementation has been slow, and although the human rights situation has improved, violations of the right to food persist, particularly with persistent agrarian conflict. Poverty is widespread, and Guatemala has the highest level of malnutrition in Latin America, concentrated amongst the indigenous peoples. However, the election of a new Government dedicated to the respect of democratic principles in 2004 brought signs of hope, with public commitments to human rights and to make the fight against hunger a priority.

12.2 Hunger and food insecurity in Guatemala

12.2.1 Hunger and food insecurity

Chronic child malnutrition is more than twice as high in Guatemala than in most countries of Latin America and among the highest in the world (only higher in Yemen and Bangladesh).[3] Today, half of Guatemalan children under the age of five are stunted,[4] far more indigenous (70 per cent) than non-indigenous (36 per cent).[5] Acute malnutrition is concentrated in the poorest regions, particularly the northeast,[6] although in the wake of crises in the last decade, including the collapse in world coffee prices and localized droughts in 2001, acute malnutrition levels have increased in the east, south coast and the west, and there has even been the reappearance of kwashiorkor (a form of childhood malnutrition).[7] More than 15,000 Guatemalan children under the age of five die every year.

Widespread hunger and malnutrition in Guatemala is not simply a question of the availability of food, as Guatemala's land could theoretically feed the whole population. It is more related to inequities in the distribution of resources and people's access to food. The distribution of wealth in Guatemala is one of the most inequitable of all the countries in the world, and the concentration of wealth is extreme – 5.6 per cent of the richest households control 50 per cent of total income.[8] Economic growth has not reduced inequality, with the benefits of growth accruing mainly to the rich.[9] Land ownership is highly concentrated, with 2 per cent of the population owning up to 70–75 per cent of agricultural land. According to NGOs, 47 huge plantations take up over 3700 hectares, with vast tracts of land remaining uncultivated, while 90 per cent of small farmers survive on less than one hectare.[10] Such extreme inequality means that the majority of Guatemalans are excluded from development, with hunger and exclusion contributing to crime and social conflict. During our visit, a 15-year-old boy was killed on 24 January 2005 for stealing a fruit from Finca El Corozo, and four peasants were killed when they went looking for the child.[11]

Two thirds of Guatemala's people are too poor to feed themselves adequately – in more than 60 per cent of Guatemalan homes, spending on food does not meet minimum daily dietary requirements.[12] According to Government statistics, one third of Guatemalan families cannot afford even half a minimal food basket (2172 calories per person per day).[13] At the time of our visit, the statutory minimum wage was not set in relation to food costs and purchases only 56 per cent of the food basket. Food prices had increased faster than the minimum wage[14] and the price of tortillas, Guatemala's basic staple food, increased by 66 per cent over 2004.[15] More than half the population (56 per cent) lives in poverty,[16] mostly in rural areas in the north and northwest regions, the Department of San Marcos, and the southwest region.[17] Extreme poverty is highly concentrated among the indigenous peoples (70 per cent), particularly the Mam and the Q'echi, reflecting serious discrimination against indigenous populations.[18]

The hungry and malnourished are predominantly indigenous people and poor peasant farmers or agricultural workers living in rural areas.[19] Poor subsistence farmers lack access to sufficient, good quality land and survive on *microfincas* (smallholdings) of less than one hectare of unproductive land, while farmers told us they would need 25 hectares of fertile land to feed their families adequately. Hunger and malnutrition levels are closely linked to the quantity of land held – children of families possessing less than two *manzanas* of land (6987 m^2 = one *manzana*) are 3.2 times more likely to be malnourished than families possessing more than five *manzanas*.[20] On average, indigenous households hold 0.25 *manzanas* per person, whereas non-indigenous households have 1.5 *manzanas*, six times more land.[21] Many *campesinos* (peasant farmers) earn extra income as temporary agricultural workers during harvest on the coffee, sugar and fruit *fincas* (estate farms), but this still is insufficient to meet their nutrition needs.[22] Permanent workers on the *fincas*, often tied into a *colono* system (under which landowners provide subsistence plots in exchange for labour), also work for extremely low wages. The statutory minimum wage has risen in the last years, but many landowners have shifted to payment per task instead of per day to minimize the impact. Landowners often avoid paying legal entitlements by dismissing workers repeatedly to keep them on non-permanent contract status,[23] and often dismiss workers that negotiate for better conditions.[24] Persistent discrimination against indigenous peoples is reflected in an extremely high wage gap between indigenous and non-indigenous workers. Gender discrimination is also pervasive, and it is reported that many landowners do not even pay women or children for their work – they are considered husband's 'helpers'.[25] Women suffer multiple discrimination – as women, as poor, as rural residents and as indigenous,[26] – and rarely own land or other assets. Child labour also remains common in Guatemala, with around half a million children working in coffee and sugar plantations. Migrants are also particularly vulnerable to poverty and hunger.

After the collapse in world coffee prices, many landowners did not pay salaries to their workers, leaving many in extreme poverty. Agricultural workers on large *fincas* provided testimonies that they had not been paid for work already undertaken, and that the response to their claims was violent repression and forced eviction from the estates where they had lived all their lives. Church organizations, such as that led by Álvaro Ramazzini, Bishop of San Marcos, help families to survive by providing food donations and help workers to bring cases to local courts, although workers rarely win, and even when they do, legal orders are reportedly rarely enforced. Although the previous Government instituted a 'Policy Plan Concerning the Coffee Crisis and the Agrarian Conflict' (2002), and pledged US$ 100 million to coffee plantation owners, safety net programmes for the workers were not fully implemented.[27] Renting or leasing of land was encouraged, but farmers spoke of the semi-feudal nature of leasing agreements, requiring that half the harvest be given back to the landowner.

Land occupations increase as communities desperately search for ways of feeding themselves. Occupations occur mostly when landowners have violated labour rights, or where land ownership is disputed. There are often multiple claims to the same land, following a history of land expropriation by powerful landowners. We visited an Ixil indigenous community of 270 families in Antigua Xonka, occupying land they believe was expropriated from them. They issued legal proceedings in a local court but live under constant threat from the landowner who repeatedly sends private police squads to forcibly evict them and burn their crops, animals and makeshift shelters. They always return however, having nowhere else to go. They argue that none of the Ixil lands have been legally regularized or recognized, which allows *finceros* (estate owners) to keep taking more land from them. Although the Peace Accords set out a framework for regularization of indigenous lands and rights, lack of political will has left these issues unresolved.

The response of the Government to increasing land occupations has been forceful in the years preceding our visit. NGOs reported 40 forced evictions in the first six months of 2004, affecting 1500 families,[28] over half of which allegedly involved the use of extrajudicial executions, excessive force and the burning of crops and homes. The role of the authorities in protecting property should be recognized, but the use of disproportionate force that places property rights of large landowners above the right to food and the right to life is of serious concern. As Amnesty International noted:

> A particular characteristic of agrarian disputes in Guatemala is that the full weight of the law and judicial system is often levied in order to enforce evictions, but not to issues relating to labour rights of rural workers or land tenure of rural communities.[29]

In urban areas, hunger and malnutrition is closely linked to rural landlessness. Many of the urban hungry live in the *colonias* (legalized slums) or *asentamientos* (illegal slums) on the outskirts of Guatemala's cities. Unemployment levels are high and most people survive in the informal sector, mostly in petty trading. About 40 per cent of people are unemployed, underemployed or employed in non-paying jobs.[30] Human rights violations are common with poor working conditions, and wages insufficient to feed a family. Widespread violations of worker's rights are reported in the *maquila* factories that employ mainly young women at very low wages, although some *maquilas* are closing to move to even lower wage countries. In Guatemala City, we visited Bethania, a legalized slum where people were living in overcrowded shacks of tin and plastic, without sanitation, and where doctors in the local health centre estimated that at least 20 per cent of the children were suffering from malnourishment and more from diarrhoea, skin and fungal diseases. Many think that the high rates of criminality, violence and murder in Guatemala City are closely linked to extreme poverty and social exclusion. With few employment opportunities, young people join gangs involved in narcotics trafficking and terrorizing of the settlements, and even the bravest health workers can only work for a few hours a day in the morning when gangs are not present.

Access to water is problematic in urban areas, especially in illegal slums, but particularly in rural areas. Over 65 per cent of the rural population lack access to an improved source of fresh water, or sanitation. Municipalities are responsible for water, but at the time of our visit, only 4 per cent of the 331 municipalities treated the water they provide.[31] Access to water is also highly unequal – according to NGOs, if gold mining would be established in San Marcos, it would require 70,000 litres of water per hour for processing, which would reduce the river and springs on which many local residents depend. Risks of water contamination from open-pit cyanide leaching are also extremely high, particularly in the absence of a sound regulatory framework for water policy.

12.2.2 A history of social conflict

Guatemala's long history of economic inequality, exclusion of indigenous peoples and social conflict, largely explain the country's hunger and food insecurity today.

Inequities in the land regime

Guatemala has one of the most unequal land distributions in the world, given a long history of land expropriation from indigenous people.[32] Land expropriation started with the Spanish Conquest, but accelerated in the 1800s with the growth of coffee production. At that time, *ejidos* (communally-held indigenous lands) were nationalized or privatized into individual holdings, with the aim of consolidating the land into large *fincas* for commercialized coffee production. As the best coffee is cultivated at altitudes of between 800 m and 1500 m, many indigenous people were forced to relocate to steeper, less fertile ground for subsistence farming.[33] Lowlands were also expropriated for the growing of fruit – it is estimated that in the 1940s, one American-owned company owned 42 per cent of Guatemala's land. The pattern of land concentration was briefly interrupted in 1944 during the governments of Juan José Arévalo and Colonel Jacobo Arbenz Guzman, but a military coup in 1954 ended land redistribution and land was consolidated even further. Land concentration and growing landlessness contributed to Guatemala's ensuing 36-year civil war (see below), yet the war exacerbated the situation as the military and landowners forcibly controlled more land. Today, land remains highly concentrated, and many historical claims of indigenous communities and even claims of refugees and people displaced by the conflict are still not resolved.

Lack of labour rights

During the 1800s, forced labour of indigenous peoples supported the growth of the coffee plantations.[34] Land policies were deliberately designed to create cheap labour forces by reducing the land available for indigenous people's own subsistence activities.[35] Under the *Mandamiento* forced labour system for example, indigenous villages were forced to provide work crews of 60 people for 15–30 days to coffee plantations, and to provide free labour to build roads. Forced labour laws remained in place until the mid-twentieth century, with modern labour rights only established in the 1980s, although still not always enforced. The semi-feudal *colono* system persists in many regions today. Today, almost 70 per cent of employment is outside the formal sector and legal protection and workers faced limits on unionization.

The statutory legal minimum wage is set so low that it does not cover the cost of a minimum food basket.

Discrimination against indigenous peoples

Racial discrimination between the indigenous and *ladino* (of mostly mixed Maya-Spanish ancestry) populations persists in Guatemala. Although many of the legal institutions have been overturned, de facto discrimination persists, reinforcing discrimination in employment and ownership of resources, a key cause of concentration of hunger and malnutrition among indigenous peoples. The Peace Accords focused on fighting discrimination and recognizing the rights of indigenous peoples. However many organizations report that these are the least accomplished parts of the Accords.[36] We were shocked to see during our visit that even today many restaurants and bars will not serve people wearing indigenous dress. We were honoured to meet the well-known indigenous leader, Rigoberta Menchu who has remarkably brought, and won, Guatemala's first case on racial discrimination, which is a sign of progress.

Armed conflict

Guatemala's terrible 36-year conflict (1960–1996) erupted into a full-scale civil war in the 1980s, largely as a result of the social conflict generated by extreme inequality and social exclusion. Indigenous peoples and rural peasants became the targets of a repressive counterinsurgency effort by the military that 'reached genocidal proportions in the early 1980s, executing scorched earth warfare tactics, mandatory paramilitary civilian self-defence patrols, forced resettlement camps, and the militarization of the entire administrative apparatus of the country'.[37] During the conflict, more than 200,000 women, men and children were brutally killed or 'disappeared' and a million people were displaced from their homes and lands. Over 600 villages were completely destroyed and most of their residents massacred.[38]

12.2.3 The 1996 Peace Accords: framework for a more equitable future

With the Peace Accords that formally ended the war in 1996, a central aim was to reverse historical exclusion, discrimination and inequality. The 13 Accords provided a framework for deep political, economic, social and cultural change.[39] The 'Accord on Socio-economic Issues and the Agrarian Situation', laid out plans to increase social spending, improve access to education, health, public services, and land, to establish mechanisms to resolve agrarian conflicts and develop a rural development policy. These measures were to be financed by important tax reforms to raise government revenues from 8 to 12 per cent of GDP. The 'Accord on the Identity and Rights of Indigenous Peoples' proposed the recognition of Guatemala as a multi-ethnic, multicultural and multilingual nation, and identified specific measures for overcoming historical exclusion and exploitation, including measures on land rights, the regularization of land tenure of indigenous communities, the restitution of expropriated communal land and legal protection of the rights of indigenous peoples. However, the rejection of constitutional reforms in a referendum in 1999 slowed progress in turning these political commitments into reality, and the lack of political will has left many of the broader issues unresolved. According to the United Nations Mission in Guatemala (MINUGUA), progress on the fulfilment of the Peace Accords has been slow, partial and insufficient, and has faced much resistance from powerful groups.

12.3 Legal framework for the right to food in Guatemala

12.3.1 International obligations

Guatemala has an obligation to the right to food under the International Covenant on Economic, Social and Cultural Rights (Article 11). It is also party to other international instruments relevant to the right to adequate food, including the International Covenant on Civil and Political Rights (Article 6), the Convention on the Rights of the Child (Articles 24 and 27), the Convention on the Elimination of All Forms of Discrimination against Women (Articles 12 and 14), the International Convention on the Elimination of All Forms of Racial Discrimination (Article 5), and the Additional Protocol to the American Convention on Human Rights in the Area of Economic, Social and Cultural Rights ('Protocol of San Salvador') (Article 12). It means that Guatemala has the obligation to respect, protect and fulfil the right to food, without any discrimination.

Guatemala is also party to the ILO Indigenous and Tribal Peoples Convention, 1989 (No. 169). Under this Convention, the Government is required to respect indigenous peoples' rights to land and territories (Articles 13–17), including their collective aspects. These articles also require that indigenous peoples are not displaced from their lands, and that their rights to natural resources on their lands are specially safeguarded, including their right to participate in the use, management and conservation of these resources, and their right to be consulted and to assess any exploitation of resources on the land they own or possess.

12.3.2 Domestic constitutional and legislative framework

Guatemala also has a national constitutional obligation towards the right to food, specifically for vulnerable groups of children and elderly people. Guatemala's progressive 1985 Constitution (revised in 1993) includes the protection of economic, social and cultural rights without discrimination (Articles 50 and 51). The Constitution requires the Government to establish an effective national food system (Article 99), ensure social assistance for all (Article 94), and adopt a national framework law on water (Article 127). The Constitution also protects the rights of indigenous peoples, including access to land and the right to maintain traditional forms of land administration

(Articles 66–69). The right to property can be limited, if the State lawfully decides to expropriate private properties for public interest or social benefit (Article 40). The Constitution enshrines the right to work, freedom of association and the right to form and join trade unions, and equality between men and women (Articles 93–106). Under the Constitution, international human rights treaties take precedence over domestic law (Article 46). They must therefore be applied and taken into consideration by all organs of the Government – executive, legislative and the judiciary.

Guatemala's current legislative framework includes laws and government regulations that are important for the right to food. The Government has drafted an important new law on the national system for food and nutritional security, which entered into force on 2 May 2005. This recognizes the Government's international obligations towards the right to food and defines the right to food as:

> The right of every person to have physical, economic and social access at all times to food of adequate quantity and quality, in accordance with cultural preferences, preferably of national origin, and biologically adequate, in order to sustain a healthy and productive life. (Article 1)

This also recognizes the obligations of the Government to respect, protect and fulfil the right to food, and prohibits de jure and de facto discrimination in access to food and to the means to obtain food. Any such discrimination constitutes a violation of the law, which provides an excellent basis for the justiciability of the right to food. In the application of this law by the judiciary, violations should also include any violation of the obligations to respect, to protect and to fulfil the right to food.

A number of important laws have emerged out of the Peace Accords. The Law on Social Development (2001), the Urban and Rural Development Councils Act (2002), the Municipal Code (2002) and the General Law on Decentralization (2002) are important new laws that try to ensure more participation and effective decentralization. They give greater autonomy to Guatemala's 331 municipalities, allowing more participation of indigenous communities in departmental development councils and municipal administrative bodies. We saw a positive example of decentralization during our visit to the country, when we met with representatives of the *Mesa de desarrollo y seguridad alimentaria del area Ch'orti*, a coordinating body for the development and food security of four important municipalities – Jocotan, Camotan, Olopa and San Juan Ermita – in which 190,000 people are living. In ensuring participation and access to information, these municipalities have made considerable progress in the fight against hunger and malnutrition.

Despite important legislative progress, including substantial improvements of the Labour Code and the adoption of the Law on Land Registry, the national legal framework still remains inadequate on several important issues related to the right to food, including access to land and land tenure, water and mining. In a country with such a history of land conflicts and expropriations, the continued lack of an effective *cadastro* (land registry system), of an agrarian code, of the legal recognition of indigenous forms of land ownership and administration and of an agrarian jurisdiction to resolve land disputes is totally inadequate. All required under the Peace Accords, these elements are essential for the effective protection of the right to food in the country. The absence of any water law, despite being a constitutional commitment, is also of great concern. The Law on Mining is also of concern, as it does not provide adequate protection for the rights of indigenous communities over their natural resources, including their rights to be consulted in accordance with the ILO Convention No. 169. Finally, de jure discrimination against women remains institutionalized in Article 139 of the Labour Code, which describes rural women as 'helpers' of the male agricultural workers, rather than as workers entitled to receive their own salary, which has serious implications for women's right to food.

12.3.3 Access to justice and human rights institutions

Guatemala has a complex legal system, which includes customary law and community courts in indigenous peoples' areas, and State law and courts at the municipal, departmental and national levels (court of appeal and the Supreme Court). The Constitutional Court also has a special mandate to protect and enforce the Constitution. The Constitution guarantees free access to justice (Article 29) and victims of a violation of a fundamental right can use the procedure of *amparo* (right to due process) to claim their rights before the Supreme Court and the Constitutional Court. In practice, however, access to justice for victims of violations of the right to food is limited by several factors. These include the non-application of international human rights treaties and conventions by the judiciary, the lack of adequate protective national legislation, especially on land, water and mining, corruption and the lack of enforcement of existing legislation, administrative measures and judicial decisions, especially on labour. Indigenous peoples have particular difficulties in access to justice, given discrimination, the lack of legal interpreters, and the non-recognition of customary law and indigenous legal authorities. All these elements result in de facto impunity for violations of human rights.[40] Repeated threats against the judiciary and human rights defenders, including the Office of the Ombudsman, indigenous leaders, trade unionists, religious officials and journalists also persisted at the time of our visit, with more than 150 threats or attacks against human rights defenders reported from January 2004 to February 2005.[41]

Important progress has been made however in the strengthening of the Office of the Human Rights Ombudsman, headed by the courageous and outspoken Ombudsman, Sergio Fernando Morales Alvarado. His mandate includes the right to food, as it includes the promotion and protection of all human rights recognized in the Constitution and in international treaties ratified by Guatemala. In spite of serious budget limitations and threats and attacks against his staff and offices, the Human Rights Ombudsman is doing an impressive job in protecting vulnerable groups and individuals through mediation, conciliation, quasi-judicial decisions and legal assistance, as well as recording violations. A special section deals with economic, social and cultural rights and another thematic section is working on land and other issues related to the right to food. As the Law on the National System for Food and Nutritional Security (in Article 15. j) gives the Ombudsman an important mandate to monitor the Government's fulfilment of its obligations to respect, protect and fulfil the right to food, a special unit on the right to food was established within the Office to deal with this issue.

The Presidential Commission for the coordination of human rights policies COPREDEH, headed at the time of our visit by the well-respected Frank La Rue, also plays an important role in improving respect for human rights, as does the Congress's Human Rights Commission. These institutions were decisive in the recognition of the right to food in the elaboration of the new Law on the National System for Food and Nutritional Security, and have worked closely with the then Secretary for Food and Nutrition Security Andrés Botrán. Within COPREDEH, the Defender's Office for Indigenous Women provides mediation, conflict resolution and legal services for indigenous women. Another State institution, the Office of the Public Prosecutor, could have a more important role in the protection of the right to food, if the mandate of its Special Prosecutor for Crimes against Human Rights Defenders could include the right to food.

12.4 Policy framework for the right to food

12.4.1 Government policies and institutions

We were impressed during our visit by the awakening of public awareness of hunger and malnutrition in Guatemala. This was largely due to the new Government which, on election in 2004, declared the elimination of hunger to be one of its highest priorities. A potentially powerful legal and policy framework has being put in place for the realization of the right to food. The Secretary for Food and Nutrition Security was appointed to lead the *Frente Nacional Contra el Hambre* (National Front Against Hunger), and the President's wife, Wendy de Berger had also joined to bring the fight against hunger, focusing on the *Creciendo Bien* programme. Other programmes designed to address food insecurity includes the Programme for the Reduction of Chronic Malnutrition (*Programa de Reducción a la Desnutrición Crónica*), which aims to halve the level of child malnutrition over the next 10 years, as well as programmes such as *Guate Solidaria, Guate Crece* and *Guate Compite.*

A policy framework, the 2004 'National Policy on Food and Nutrition Security', explicitly recognizes Guatemala's obligation to realize the right to adequate food and nutrition. It sees food *availability* as problematic because of the increasing dependence on food imports and a fall in the production of basic staple foods. However, it recognizes that *access* to food is the key problem, given falling incomes, unemployment and low wages. Poor sanitation and lack of education, also affects food *utilization* especially amongst women. To improve food availability, the framework promotes greater local production of staple foods, and to improve access to food, it proposes income-generation opportunities, setting up food assistance programmes, and revising the statutory minimum wage.[42] It also requires improvements in budget allocations for food and nutrition security, although these are not specified. We were concerned that while the policy fully recognizes the right to food, it does not explicitly recognize the different obligations of the Government to respect, protect and fulfil the right to food (as laid out in the 2005 Law). We were also concerned that the policy does not address the structural causes of hunger and inequality, is not situated within the framework of the Peace Accords and does not address the complex issues of land, labour and fiscal reform.

The institutional framework has been strengthened with the creation of CONASAN (the National Council on Food and Nutrition Security), to promote programmes on food and nutrition security, and with the creation of SESAN (the Secretariat for Food and Nutrition Security) which is responsible for coordinating all the programmes and initiating concrete activities. The hunger early warning system SINASAN (National System for Food and Nutrition Security), monitors and evaluates the impact of food security programmes and provides an early warning to identify potential crisis situations. During our visit, we were encouraged that under the 2005 law, CONASAN would also have a responsibility to respond to the recommendations of the Human Rights Ombudsman in relation to the right to food.

Within the framework of the Peace Accords, some progress was made on the question of land with the establishment of CONTIERRA, an organization for mediating land disputes, but the lack of funding and institutional instability has meant that of the 909 cases that have come before the agency since 2005, very few have been resolved.[43] A land fund, FONTIERRA, was also created for market-based redistribution, providing credit for land purchases, and has redistributed 76,493 hectares to 15,996 families. However, this is far below demand of up to 300,000 rural families, and it continues to receive less than its mandated budgetary allocation. It is now generally agreed that FONTIERRA did not work effectively. Gender discrimination has also meant that only 11 per cent of the land credits have been granted to women.[44] The Government has established the legal framework for the *cadastro* (land registry), which will serve to clarify the disarray of existing land titles and multiple claims to the same land, as a result of historical expropriations. Many large landowners claim landholdings much greater than they have in official title, some having extended landholdings by force, and others having understated landholdings to avoid payment of land tax. However resistance from powerful landowners who do not want their boundaries formally delineated, as well as some resistance from indigenous communities (after a history of massacres) continues to slow the creation of the land registry. A crucial test for a future land registry will be how it mediates multiple claims to land, particularly avoiding formalizing ownership of land obtained via corruption or coercion. Some military and landowners continue to occupy land that was taken during the war, and there has been no adequate resolution of land claims of the many refugees and people displaced, nor has there been restitution of expropriated lands to indigenous people. As pointed out in the report of the Secretary-General on MINUGUA to the 59th session of the General Assembly, there has been little progress in 'creating an agrarian legal code, reviewing the status of idle lands and lands illegally acquired during the armed conflict: and establishing legal security for land held communally by indigenous groups'.[45]

The Ministry of Labour is responsible for the implementation of workers' rights, but often fails to enforce the *Código de Trabajo* and the minimum wage, given strong resistance from big business interests.[46] Workers are often afraid of reprisals if they claim their rights, given the lack of State protection against abuses by *patrones* (proprietors). Combating gender discrimination is the responsibility of the Foro de la Mujer, the Defensoria de la Mujer Indigena and the Secretaria Presidencial de la Mujer, established in response to the Peace Accords. However, women still face discrimination in relation to wages and land ownership, and often do not even have identity documents.[47]

Some progress on discrimination against indigenous peoples has been made with the establishment of the *Consejo Asesor sobre Pueblos Indigenas*, but its budget has remained very low. The Presidential Commission has stated that discrimination remains pervasive and aims at 'the maintenance of economic, political, sociocultural and spiritual control over the indigenous peoples'.[48] Little progress has been made on the recognition of indigenous law, of indigenous rights to land and their rights over the use and administration of natural resources on their territories,[49] with the justice system failing to resolve the claims of communities and individuals, but rather criminalizing social conflicts over land and the use of natural resources.[50]

In terms of responsibility for water policy, we were concerned that this did not seem to be a priority. There is no Ministry for Water, but responsibility is delegated to municipalities. Although a Commissioner on Water was appointed in 2004, there is still no national law on water, although such a law was envisaged in the 1985 Constitution, as the draft law was criticized by civil society and withdrawn from Congress. There is no national policy on drinking water and irrigation, despite the fact that 55 per cent of the rural population still has no access to drinking water.

12.4.2 United Nations specialized agencies

The mandate of MINUGUA, which oversaw the peace process under the astute guidance of Tom Koenigs, ended in 2004. Today, the United Nations system is represented through its specialized agencies, including the UNDP, FAO and the WFP. Issues of malnutrition, food security and agriculture were high on the agenda of the United Nations agencies when we undertook our visit. The United Nations 2004 Common Country Assessment for Guatemala and United Nations Development Assistance Framework process adopted a strong rights-based approach to the situation in Guatemala. It was particularly concerned about the lack of fulfilment of the Peace Accords, persistent impunity, lack of access to justice and the lack of real progress in economic, social and cultural rights, as well as women's rights and indigenous rights. OHCHR in Guatemala has taken up and very effectively promoted the issue of the right to food, and the United Nations country team, especially WFP, UNICEF and WHO have worked closely with the Government to promote the new legal and policy framework, as well as implementing programmes linked to food and nutrition security.

12.4.3 Non-governmental organizations and associations

Guatemala has a strong and vibrant civil society, comprising social movements and NGOs fighting for human rights, including the right to food. The key concern of most of the organizations with which we met, is the intensification of the rise in forced evictions and the criminalization of peasant protests. They have recorded 30 forced evictions with no due process since in 2005, with a disproportionate use of force that has resulted in at least 30 deaths. Many were particularly concerned about the general criminalization of the peasant movement and human rights defenders, seeing a rise in the arrest and detention of peasant leaders. Many organizations also called for better participation and for prior, informed consent on development policies and exploitation of indigenous lands for mining concessions. They denounce exclusionary development where local populations receive no benefit from the exploitation of Guatemala's natural resources. Bishop Alvaro Ramazzini, for example, has called for 50 per cent of the profits of gold mining to be returned to Guatemala, arguing that Guatemala's gold revenue should be spent on social services for the local indigenous populations. Many organizations were concerned that current Government programmes to fight hunger tended to be assistencialist and did not address the root of the problem. They see the model of export-orientated agriculture based on coffee and non-traditional exports as threatening traditional food security, and were concerned that the negative impacts of liberalization would be intensified with the passing of the Central American Free Trade Agreement (CAFTA).

12.5 Main findings and concerns

12.5.1 Progressive realization of the right to food

Under the right to adequate food, the Government of Guatemala is required to ensure the progressive realization of the right to food over time, to the maximum of its available resources.

During our mission, we welcomed the positive progress made in reducing poverty and malnutrition over the 1990s.[51] However, we were concerned that these gains appear to have been made mostly among the better off, with a widening gap between rich and poor.[52] We were also concerned by signs of regression since 1998, with both chronic malnutrition increasing (from 46.4 to 49.3 per cent between 1998 and 2002[53]) and the levels of extreme poverty rising (from 15.7 to 21.5 per cent between 2000 and 2002), particularly in rural areas.[54] FAO statistics suggested a serious increase in levels of undernourishment, from 16 to 24 per cent between 1990/1992 and 2000/2002.[55] Broader social indicators were also deteriorating, with Guatemala falling from rank 117 to 121 on the UNDP Human Development Index between 1999 and 2004. We concluded that this amounted to a regression in the realization of the right to food.

We were also concerned that Guatemala was not using the maximum available resources to fight hunger. Despite commitments in the Peace Accords to raise social spending to 12 per cent of the expenditure as a percentage of GDP, Guatemala still had one of the lowest levels of social spending in Latin America, with less than 5 per cent of the budget spent on social services, and only 1.5 per cent on health and nutrition.[56] As MINUGUA has reported 'One of the main limitations has been the chronic lack of Government funds, linked to the refusal by economic elites to pay higher taxes to finance an expansion in State services benefiting primarily the poor'.[57] The tax system was regressive, imposed largely through consumption taxes such as VAT which is charged even on basic food staples. The 'Fiscal Pact' signed in 2000 brought hope, but had not been realized.

12.5.2 Violations of the right to food

Under its commitment to the right to food, the Government undertakes obligations to respect, protect and fulfil the right to food, without discrimination, but we were concerned by reports of persistent violations of the right to food, some examples of which are outlined below.

Forced evictions by State agents

It was reported to us that more than 31 evictions occurred in the first six months of 2004, over half of which were violent.[58] In the case of the *Nueva Linda* farm (Champerico, Retalhuleu), it was alleged that on 31 August 2004, while some officials were negotiating a peaceful evacuation with the representatives of 22 communities who occupied the land three years ago, the

Civil National Police intervened violently, leaving 9 dead, over 40 injured and 13 detained, as well as the destruction of the communities' crops and houses.[59] In another case recorded at El Maguey farm (Fraijanes), it was alleged that a group of 86 peasant families had been forcibly evicted from their land by the police and the army on several occasions, with their crops and irrigations system destroyed, despite the recognition that they own the land in a Governmental Agreement dated 7 April 2003 and a Constitutional Court decision dated 4 May 2004.[60]

Expropriation of land of indigenous communities by third parties

The historical expropriation of land from indigenous communities was exacerbated during the conflict and continues today. Even with CONTIERRA supervision and local records of land ownership, the right to land of indigenous communities is consistently violated. In one case at *La Perla* farm (Quiché), it was alleged that the landowner extended his farm, under the repression of the army and paramilitary during the conflict, into the 2200 hectares that were recorded in the local property registry as belonging to two indigenous communities (Sotzil and Ilom). Despite being recognized by CONTIERRA, the situation of the indigenous families had not improved and their land tenure remained insecure.[61] Apart from living under constant threat of violent eviction, they lacked access to adequate food, water, health and education.

Impunity for violation of labour rights

Violations of labour rights in the Labour Code by powerful *patrones* were widespread. During our visit, we met with hundreds of agricultural workers on large estates, including *San Geronimo, La Doble Cota, Carolina, Alabama Grande* and *Las Delicias* farms, who were waiting for an administrative or judicial decision that will require employers to pay unpaid wages. The workers were living a precarious existence that threatened their right to food. In one case, at the *Nueva Florencia* farm (Colomba, Quetzaltenango), it was alleged that in 1997, immediately after having founded a union, 32 male and female workers were dismissed from the Nueva Florencia farm, without compensation. After seven years of legal proceedings, and despite two final decisions of the Constitutional Court in 2000 and 2003 ordering the reincorporation of the workers and the reimbursement of their unpaid salaries, the workers and their families were still without work.[62]

Exclusionary development and repression of peaceful protest

Demonstrations against exclusionary development were often met with violent repression that can amount to violations of the right to food. For example, in the long-standing, unresolved conflict over the construction of the Chixoy Dam, it was alleged that between 1980 and 1982, 440 persons of the Rio Negro community were brutally murdered and indigenous communities were forcibly evicted, their land, crops and housing destroyed for the dam construction. After persistent peaceful protests, an agreement was finally reached on 8 September 2004 between the Government, the Human Rights Ombudsman and the electricity company to negotiate compensation for indigenous communities and to provide the remaining community living near the dam with free running water and electricity. However, this agreement was suddenly voided when the electricity corporation presented a formal complaint against members of the dam-affected communities for participating in the protest, calling this an 'activity against national security'. In another example, indigenous communities alleged that the Government granted a mining licence to a corporation for the exploitation of a gold mine on their land without seeking their free and informed consent, and were concerned that their right to water and right to food will be violated by the open-pit cyanide leaching process of the gold mining that will poison drinking and irrigation water. During demonstrations against CAFTA in March 2004, it was reported that the army and the police employed tear gas, water cannons and rubber bullets, causing at least one death (Juan Lopez Velásquez on 14 March 2005[63]).

12.5.3 Obstacles to the realization of the right to food

In terms of per capita income, Guatemala is a comparatively rich country and the persistence and level of chronic hunger is absurd. There are a number of key obstacles to the realization of the right to food in Guatemala.

The first is Guatemala's model of exclusionary development that has concentrated wealth and power in the hands of a small elite. This persists today, given the continued resistance of powerful groups to structural change envisaged in the Peace Accords, particularly in relation to key structural issues of land, labour, non-discrimination and fiscal reform. The failure to resolve the land question, including 'land-grabbing' during the war and the historical inequities of land ownership, as well as the failure to resolve the issues of the cadastre, individual and collective land titles, restitution and redistribution of land will continue to be a serious obstacle to the right to food. Market-based land reform does not appear to be adequate to redress extreme inequality and the unjust, historical expropriation of the land. We were concerned during our visit by a perception among the elite that the indigenous people are 'stupid' for claiming their land. Discrimination against indigenous peoples and women, reflected for example in inadequate labour rights, also continues to be serious obstacles.

A second serious obstacle to the right to food is persistent impunity for violations of human rights, and the lack of equality before the law for Guatemala's people, evident in the unequal protection of land and labour rights of peasants, in discrimination against indigenous peoples and in the criminalization of social protest. For example, while the non-payment of salaries to workers is classed as a minor misdemeanour, social protest and land occupation is considered a crime and the full force of the law is brought down on peasants and indigenous populations. There remains a tendency to privilege the interests of the economic elite over those of the majority of people, as seen in the policy of forced evictions which put a higher priority on defending private property than on defending the right to life and the right to food.

The model of export-orientated agriculture has long been an obstacle to the realization of the right to adequate food. Guatemala provides a clear example of how agricultural modernization has created greater hunger and poverty, as peasants have been pushed off their land to make way for large-scale plantations. Today, liberalization is devastating the remaining peasants[64] and the production of basic staple foods has been hit by competition from cheap imports. Since 1990, the production of basic grains has declined nationally, while imports of staple commodities have increased by 170 per cent over the same period.[65] Only 20 per cent of food is now locally produced. While powerful interests in Guatemala may benefit from export-orientation and trade liberalization, the poor are finding it increasingly difficult to subsist, particularly in a context of lack of alternative employment. Free trade agreements, such as CAFTA, are likely to exacerbate the loss of livelihoods and increase food insecurity for indigenous and peasant communities. One study of the possible future impacts of CAFTA, suggests that while its impacts might be positive for urban areas, they will likely be negative for rural households.[66] While there is a transition period envisaged for rice and beans (15–18 years), there are concerns that yellow maize will displace the production of white maize.

While we were impressed by the efforts of the current Government to fight hunger, we were concerned by the lack of continuity between administrations, given the limited four-year term of each Government. While each new Government spends time and resources on new strategies and new laws, little time is left for concrete implementation. We therefore hope that all the policies and laws being put in place in relation to hunger and poverty will be maintained and implemented by the next administration. In 2005, the Government was establishing long-term programmes, and aimed to raise social awareness of hunger, so that the people will ensure the continuity of the programmes.

12.6 Conclusions and recommendations

In his report on the mission to Guatemala, presented to the Human Rights Council in March 2006, Jean Ziegler made the following conclusions and recommendations.

Jean Ziegler was very encouraged by the commitment of the current Government towards making the right to food a priority. However, he remained concerned that child malnutrition was so high and more than 60 per cent of

Guatemalans survived with an income that did not cover their basic food needs, preventing them from exercising their right to food. He therefore urged the full implementation of the new legal and policy framework to fully realize the right to food of all Guatemalans, including indigenous peoples. This should be implemented within the framework of the Peace Accords, promoting social justice, equity, participation and respect for human rights.

He then made the following specific recommendations:

(a) Given the situation of hunger and extreme poverty, the realization of the right to food must become an urgent priority in Guatemala. Any violation of the right to food should be considered to be fully justiciable under the new Law on the National System for Food and Nutrition Security. In the application of this law by the judiciary, violations should be understood to include both de jure and de facto discrimination in access to food and to the means to obtain food, as well as violations of the specific obligations to respect, to protect and to fulfil the right to food;
(b) The right to land of indigenous communities must be recognized, and communities should be protected from the forcible expropriation of their lands. Any evictions that take place should be conducted in accordance with human rights law. Impunity for violations of the right to food must be challenged, and all Guatemalans should be treated equally before the law. Legitimate peaceful protest should be permitted without repression. The detention and killing of peasant leaders and human rights defenders should be stopped. The Government should adopt a policy to decriminalize social and land conflicts and provide training and tools to the security forces, the Ombudsman and the judiciary to deal with those conflicts within a framework that respects the right to food. The right to property should not be placed above the right to life and the right to food;
(c) The commitments under the Peace Accords toward land rights, labour rights, and fiscal reform should be fully implemented to promote a more inclusive society based on human rights and social justice. Land rights, labour rights and non-discrimination must be fully respected;
(d) Racial discrimination against indigenous communities is not acceptable and must be urgently addressed through a broad national campaign. 'Land-grabbing' of indigenous lands, as in the *La Perla* case, must be stopped;
(e) Pervasive discrimination against women, particularly indigenous women, must be addressed, and the rights of women must be recognized, including in the access to and ownership of productive resources. The Labour Code should be amended to eliminate discrimination against rural women;

(f) The Law on Land Registry should be implemented without delay and an Agrarian Code to regulate the access, use and tenure of land should be elaborated, which recognizes indigenous forms of land ownership and respects the right to food. The establishment of an agrarian jurisdiction for the resolution of land conflicts should become the first priority of the Government, and must be given adequate funding and a mandate to enforce law against land-grabbing. The draft water legislation should contain provisions setting out institutional responsibility, establishing an institution for the resolution of conflicts and providing redress for victims of violations of the right to water. The Law on Mining should be amended to ensure protection of the rights of indigenous people over their natural resources, as provided by ILO Convention No. 169, and the mining policy should be reviewed to bring it into accordance with human rights law;

(g) A special unit, with adequate human and financial resources, should be established within the Office of the Human Rights Ombudsman to monitor the realization of the right to food and the obligations of the State to respect, protect and fulfil the right to food, as required by the new Law on the National System for Food and Nutritional Security. Better funding and protection should also be accorded to the human rights institutions, including the Office of the Defender of Indigenous Women of the Presidential Commission for the Coordination of Human Rights Policies (COPREDEH);

(h) Workers' rights should be respected, including the right of association, and the national minimum wage should be increased to cover the basic food basket;

(i) Participation of indigenous peoples should be included in the institutional and policy framework for the fight against hunger, as it is already in the Commission on Food Security;

(j) To overcome hunger and malnutrition, which are predominantly prevalent in rural areas, a comprehensive rural development strategy should be agreed with all social sectors and put in place. The model of exclusionary development and export-orientated agriculture that has created and is deepening extreme inequality in the ownership of resources must be reversed with a comprehensive strategy that directly improves food security and access to resources, through the implementation of agrarian reform and the promotion of investment in small-scale peasant agriculture;

(k) The 'National Policy on Food and Nutrition Security' should be revised to ensure that it reflects the obligations of the State to respect, protect, and fulfil the right to food. Due consideration should be given to CESCR General Comment No. 12 on the right to adequate food and the FAO Voluntary Guidelines on the Right to Food;

(l) It should be ensured that the obligations of the Central American Free Trade Agreement (CAFTA) are consistent with Guatemala's human rights obligations. A full study on the potential impacts of CAFTA should be carried out, and safety nets should be established prior to measures being implemented, to protect the national production of staple foods (including maize and beans) and the right to food of rural communities that are likely to be negatively affected, otherwise free trade will bring greater hunger;

(m) The progressive realization of the right to food should be monitored as part of the Government's national policy. Indicators should include not only statistics on malnutrition, but also statistics on undernourishment, poverty and inequality and should be linked to the Millennium Development Goals. Implementation of policies and programmes on food and nutrition should address the structural causes of hunger and poverty, and should take care not to create aid dependency or 'clientelistic' relations;

(n) Finally, we recognize that important progress is being made by the current Government in its fight against hunger and malnutrition, particularly the Government of Guatemala's efforts to catalyze action at the international and regional levels, including through the Latin America Conference on Chronic Hunger within the context of the Millennium Development Goals that was held on 11 and 12 September 2005 and which launched a new campaign for Hunger-free Latin America by 2020.

13
India

13.1 Introduction

We (Jean Ziegler, Sally-Anne Way and Christophe Golay) visited India on an official mission from 20 August to 2 September 2005.[1] We welcomed the invitation and the commitment of the Government of India to engage in open and frank discussions on the human right to food. During our visit, we were honoured to be received in Delhi by Sharad Pawar, Minister of Agriculture; R.N. Das, Secretary of the Department of Food; and Anita Chaudhary, Joint Secretary of the Department of Food. We very much appreciated their organization of a comprehensive programme that allowed us to speak to Union, state and district officials in Delhi, Madhya Pradesh and Orissa. We were particularly honoured to be received by Abhijit Sen and the Planning Commission, and by M.S. Swaminathan of the National Commission on Farmers and a number of other leading Indian academics. We also appreciated being able to benefit from the experience of the United Nations system in India and particularly appreciated advice from the United Nations Development Programme, WFP and FAO. We received valuable advice from Denis von der Weid, director of the non-governmental organization, Antenna.

We benefited from meeting with a wide range of representatives from civil society organizations working on right to food issues, including members of the Right to Food Campaign, Supreme Court lawyer, Colin Gonsalves and economist Jean Dreze. We participated in the national 'Judicial colloquium on the right to food', held on 27–28 August 2005 in Delhi, an initiative of the Right to Food Campaign to bring together 70 senior judges from across India to discuss the human right to food. We met civil society organizations in Delhi, Bhopal and Shivpuri in Madhya Pradesh and in Bhubaneswar, Orissa, and FIAN collaborated in the organization of meetings. We were honoured to be received by communities in a large number of villages in the rural areas of Madhya Pradesh and Orissa as well as in urban areas and slums in these states and in Delhi.

India is an incredibly diverse and fascinating country, the birthplace of some of the world's most ancient cultures, with a population of more than 1 billion people, predominantly Hindu but also Muslim, Christian and Sikh, speaking 15 national languages and a myriad of local languages. It is a nation that has become a world power. Huge advances have been made since India's independence barely 60 years ago when non-violent resistance led by Mohandas Gandhi and Jawaharlal Nehru brought the end of British rule. Today India has a solid democratic system, grounded in a complex federal State made up of 28 separate states and seven union territories. The states are very different, socially but also ecologically, with the climate varying from tropical monsoon in the southern states to more temperate climates in the northern areas. The central parts of India are affected by drought (including Madhya Pradesh, Andhra Pradesh, Gujarat and Rajasthan) and the Bay of Bengal is often affected by cyclones and flooding. Other natural disasters are common, including earthquakes such as the terrible quake that devastated India-administered Kashmir killing thousands of people in October 2005 and the tsunami of December 2004 that killed at least 11,000 people, injuring and displacing thousands more across the south-eastern coastal areas of the country.

The vast majority of Indian people (70 per cent) still lives in rural areas and depend on agriculture for their livelihoods (65 per cent). The Indian economy is still largely based on agriculture, but industry (especially textiles, chemicals, mining and computer software) and services are becoming increasingly important. Although today the threat of famine has been conquered, hunger and poverty remain a chronic and pervasive problem, exacerbated by widespread discrimination under the caste system and against women. In the recent years the issue of hunger has come back into the political spotlight, with debates about the paradox of mounting foodgrain stocks in the face of reported deaths from starvation and widespread undernourishment. This paradox of 'hunger amidst plenty' and the fact that the poor may not have benefited from the recent economic growth of 'India Shining', may have contributed to the victory in 2004 of the new Congress-led coalition, the United Progressive Alliance. This new Government, with the release of its Common Minimum Programme, brought new hope for more concrete progress towards the realization of the right to food.

13.2 Hunger and food insecurity in India

13.2.1 Hunger and food insecurity

India has made impressive progress in overcoming the threat of famine that plagued its history and overshadowed the early years of independence. The 1943 West Bengal famine, which killed more than three million people, was India's last and largest famine although India also faced serious food shortages in the first few decades of independence.[2] Since independence in 1947, however, concentrated investment in agricultural production and rural infrastructure has quadrupled the production of rice and wheat, and India has become self-sufficient in basic food production. With rapid transport of foodgrains to areas facing shortages under the Public Food Distribution System (PDS), India has conquered the threat of large-scale famines even though many regions are regularly affected by drought, flooding, cyclones and other natural disasters. Although the growth in foodgrain production has slowed in recent years it has remained above population growth rates, so at the national level India has enough food to feed its population of well over one billion people.[3]

Nonetheless, despite these impressive gains household-level food security has not been achieved, levels of malnutrition, undernourishment and poverty remain very high and there are signs that hunger and food insecurity have increased since the second half of the 1990s. Nearly two million Indian children die every year as a result of serious malnutrition and preventable diseases.[4] Nearly half suffer from moderate or severe malnutrition, with 47 per cent of children underweight and 46 per cent stunted in their growth. This is one of the highest levels of child malnutrition in the world, higher than most countries in Sub-Saharan Africa.[5] Malnutrition is most severe among children in rural areas but is also high in urban areas.[6] Nearly a third of children (30 per cent) are born underweight, which means that their mothers are themselves underweight and undernourished. Malnutrition also increases during early childhood, particularly for girl children, reflecting persistent social discrimination against girl children who appear to be fed less than boy children. Micronutrient deficiencies are endemic and have a disastrous effect on physical and mental development. More than 80 per cent of women, infants and adolescent girls suffer from anaemia and iron intake is estimated to be below 50 per cent of the recommended daily allowance. Vitamin A deficiencies, particularly blindness, as well as iodine disorders have been recorded among children in hundreds of districts. Although the Tenth Five Year Plan 2002–2007 included the prevention, detection and management of micronutrient programme, we were informed that the Indian Council of Medical Research's studies have shown that National Nutrition Goals have not been met.

The majority of the Indian population is still poor, with 25 per cent living below the national poverty line and 80 per cent living on less than US$ 2 per day,[7] which means that many people simply cannot afford adequate food to sustain a healthy and productive life. According to FAO, India is home to the largest share of the world's undernourished population, and more than 200 million Indian children, women and men eat less than the daily minimum calorie requirement.[8] Official Indian statistics suggest that this situation may be even worse, with more than half (53 per cent) of the population estimated to be undernourished in the Government's own report on progress towards achieving the MDGs.[9] It is estimated that the poorest 30 per cent of households eat less than 1700 kilocalories per day per person (well below the international minimum standard of 2100 kilocalories per day)[10] even if they spend 70 per cent of their income on food.[11] Average calorie consumption has been falling over recent decades – but while this is explained as a shift away from basic staple food among higher income families, it is also a sign of increasing food insecurity among the poorest. Over the last decade, in rural areas consumption of basic staple foods fell by 2.14 per cent but total calorie consumption fell by 1.53 per cent, which suggests that many people are eating less food rather than a more diversified diet,[12] especially with the price of basic foods increasing faster than real agricultural wages over the 1990s.

Although government statistics suggest that poverty fell across India from 36 to 26 per cent between 1993 and 2000, there is considerable debate about whether poverty has actually fallen or whether the drop in poverty is the result of changes in the data collected.[13] One explanation may be that the assumed cost of a minimum food basket no longer reflects the real cost of food in India.[14] Poverty remains concentrated in the states of Bihar, Uttar Pradesh, Orissa, Madhya Pradesh, Maharastra and Karnataka, especially in rural areas of eastern India (east Uttar Pradesh, North Bihar, North Bengal, coastal Orissa, Assam and Tripura) and central tribal India (Bundelkhand, Jharkhand, Vidarbha, Madhya Pradesh, Chattisgarh, Rajasthan, Western Orissa and Telangana).[15] There are concerns about evidence of rising inequality since the beginning of the 1990s as it seems that under recent economic growth, the better off western and southern states have been doing better than the poorer northern and eastern states.

The hungry and malnourished are primarily children, women and men living in rural areas and are dependent on agriculture, working as casual workers but also as sharecroppers and tenant or marginal farmers with less than one hectare of land. Agricultural wages are very low and increasingly precarious, minimum wages not always enforced and many people lack work during the agricultural lean season. In some states, feudalistic patterns of land ownership persist, despite legal abolition and the official Land Ceilings Act that aimed to limit land concentration. In Madhya Pradesh, for example, we found large landholdings still belong to the family of the former *Zamindari* king. Over the 1990s, the evidence suggests that concentration in land ownership increased, with many more households becoming landless and dependent on casual agricultural labour (45 per cent of households).[16] We were also concerned to receive reports of the increasing 'casualization' and insecurity of labour contracts, including serious concerns regarding workers on tea plantations across India.[17] Since the late 1990s, it has been reported that at least 60,000 workers have lost their jobs as the international price of tea has fallen, and millions of others face wage cuts, more insecure contracts and rising malnutrition that include cases of starvation. ActionAid reported that more than 240 workers died from starvation and suicide between March 2002 and February 2003 in just four tea gardens in West Bengal.

Scheduled castes and tribes suffer most from hunger and malnutrition, making up 25 per cent of the rural population but 42 per cent of the poor.[18] As a result of discrimination, many low-caste Dalits are expected to work as agricultural labourers without being paid, many held in debt bondage by their higher caste employers. Although debt bondage is illegal, it is estimated that there are between 20 to 60 million bonded labourers in India, 85 per cent of them belonging to scheduled castes and scheduled tribes. Widespread discrimination prevents Dalits from owning land, as they are seen as the 'worker class', and even if they receive land (as a result of redistribution and agrarian reform programmes in some states), such land is frequently taken by force by higher caste people in the area. Lower castes are also often restricted from using village wells, as we observed in Shivpuri District. Tribal peoples, particularly those living in forest and hill areas, are extremely marginalized, many having lost access to traditional forest livelihoods and food resources through the creation of Forest Reserves, and many remain without food ration cards or access to government services. Tribal peoples also suffer disproportionately from displacement because of development projects such as dams, power plants, coal mines and mineral industries.[19] There are no official statistics on the number of people displaced, but NGOs and academics estimate that dam projects alone have displaced up to 33 million people who have lost their lands and livelihoods.[20] Around 40–50 per cent of the displaced are tribal people even though they make up only 8 per cent of the population, reflecting the serious discrimination against tribal peoples.

Women and children, particularly girl children, tend to suffer disproportionately from hunger and malnutrition as a result of discrimination. Women are particularly vulnerable as a result of social customs that women should eat last and eat least. Women are paid less than men for the same work, with the average agricultural wage rate per day for women being about Rs16.4, while it is Rs23.4 for men.[21] Traditionally, women cannot inherit formal title to land (except in regions that practice matrilineal inheritance), which is increasingly problematic in the context of the feminization of agriculture. Child labour persists and we were particularly concerned to receive reports of child labour on farms contracted to transnational corporations, such as cottonseed production in Andhra Pradesh, where young girls have been employed instead of men to reduce the cost of labour.[22]

In urban areas the hungry and malnourished are predominantly people surviving in the informal sector as well as vulnerable groups that are excluded from access to public services and food ration cards such as migrants, refugees, the homeless, the displaced, informal slum dwellers and street children.[23] The sick and elderly, who have no family members to support them, are also extremely vulnerable. Increasing urbanization is closely linked to poverty and food insecurity in rural areas and shrinking rural wages is contributing to distress-induced migration to urban areas, seen in the rapid development of slum and squatter settlements in India's towns and cities.[24] More than 21 per cent of India's urban population now live in slums with inadequate sanitation, housing and access to safe drinking water, severely affecting food consumption and absorption.

13.2.2 Recent developments

Today it is widely recognized within India that, although the 1990s saw a period of sustained economic growth as India moved towards a more market-oriented economy, this growth did not benefit all Indians equally.[25] Middle and upper classes in urban areas have benefited under India Shining but the poorest have suffered a decline in living standards and rising food insecurity. With the liberalization of the agricultural sector and ongoing withdrawal of the State from agriculture there have been deep cuts in public investment in agriculture that have not been made up by private investment. The shift towards a more export-oriented economy has seen a shift from subsistence to cash crops, reducing the cultivation of grains, pulses and millet for household food consumption.[26] With cash crops requiring increasingly expensive inputs such as seeds and fertilizer, many farmers have been pushed heavily into debt, which seems to explain the crisis of farmer suicides (reported to have reached 10,000 cases by the end of 2004). It has also brought greater pressure to consolidate landholdings for more capital-intensive commercial farming, with landless households increasing dramatically over the 1990s to around 45 per cent of rural households. Along with falling agricultural wages and rising food prices, these trends seem to have contributed to growing food insecurity among the poorest, especially in rural areas.

Unlike many other countries that have been subjected to the shock therapy of structural adjustment programmes, India has taken a measured approach to withdrawing the State from the economy and has long maintained the world's largest food-based safety net, the Public Food Distribution System. The 1990s, however, saw a shift in the PDS away from a universal system to a targeted system in 1997, with the central aim of reducing the overall size and cost of the food distribution system. However, this did not work well, given that reduced sales of subsidized food under the Targeted PDS,[27] combined with increased procurement by the Government,[28] swelled national foodstocks, and led to huge increases in the costs of stocking food.[29] This 'created the appalling paradox of huge excess stocks of foodgrain held with the FCI, adding to costs and therefore to the losses, and therefore leading to a substantially higher food subsidy, even as problems of hunger and malnutrition among the poor became more acute'.[30]

In the year 2000 the press reported on people dying from starvation, especially in the drought-stricken regions of Rajasthan, while food rotted in the government storage facilities. Reports suggested that food was being thrown into the sea or exported internationally at highly subsidized prices to reduce storage costs rather than being distributed to the hungry and starving. With growing public outrage at the paradox of starvation amidst overflowing foodstocks, led to a ground-breaking public interest litigation being launched by People's Union for Civil Liberties (PUCL) against the Government before India's Supreme Court. PUCL petition argued that the right to food was part of the right to life of all Indian citizens and demanded that the country's food stocks be used without delay to prevent hunger and starvation. Interim orders of the Supreme Court ordered assistance be extended to those at risk of starvation. It ordered the full implementation of all the food-based schemes across India (see details below). This landmark case has brought the issue of the right to food as a human right back into public debate.

13.3 Legal framework for the right to food in India

13.3.1 International obligations

India is party to the International Covenant on Economic, Social and Cultural Rights, the main international instrument protecting the right to food. India has ratified all international treaties relevant to the right to food, including the International Covenant on Civil and Political Rights (Article 6), the Convention on the Rights of the Child (Articles 24 and 27) and the Convention on the Elimination of All Forms of Discrimination against Women (Articles 12 and 14). This means that, under its international commitments, the Government of India is obliged to respect, protect and fulfil the right to food of all Indians, without any discrimination.

13.3.2 Domestic constitutional and legislative framework

In 1950, three years after independence, India adopted a progressive Constitution aimed at securing all its citizens social, economic and political justice, equality and dignity. The Constitution prohibits discrimination and recognizes all human rights. Civil and political rights are recognized as directly justiciable fundamental rights, and economic, social and cultural rights are defined as directive principles of State policy. Article 47 of the Constitution states that: 'The State shall regard the raising of the level of nutrition and the standard of living of its people and the improvement of public health as among its primary duties.'

Although the right to food is not directly justiciable, its inclusion in the directive principles of State policy serves to guide interpretation of fundamental rights, including the right to life protected by Article 21.[31] For the Supreme Court, '(the) right to life guaranteed in any civilised society implies the right to food, water, decent environment, education, medical care and shelter'[32] and the right to life protected by Article 21 includes the right to water[33] and 'the right to live with human dignity and all that goes along with it, namely, the bare necessities of life such as adequate nutrition, clothing and shelter over the head (...)'.[34] The State has a constitutional obligation to take steps to ensure a dignified life to all individuals.

The Constitution provides special protection for women and children (Article 39 (f)) as well as for scheduled castes and scheduled tribes (Article 46), prohibits discrimination, including in the use of public sources of water (Article 15.2 (b)), and abolishes untouchability (Article 17). Many laws protect access to resources, including the Scheduled Castes and Scheduled Tribes (Prevention of Atrocities) Act, 1989, which prohibits wrongful occupation, cultivation or transfer of any land owned by or allotted to a member of a Scheduled Caste or a Scheduled Tribe (3.1.iv) and any wrongful dispossession of land or interference with the enjoyment of rights over any land, premises or water (3.1.v). The new amendments to the Hindu Succession Act, 1956, increase the protection of women's right to ownership and inheritance. Various State laws have also been adopted to abolish the feudal system and provide land for the most vulnerable (notably Land Ceiling Acts). However, de facto discrimination remains widespread in India.

In 2005, two important new laws regarding the right to food were adopted by the Indian Parliament. The Right to Information Bill guarantees the right to information to all citizens and recognizes many correlative obligations at all levels of government, which should improve transparency and accountability. The passing of the National Rural Employment Guarantee Act recognizes employment as a matter of right for the first time. It entitles anyone to be employed on public works within 15 days as unskilled manual labour at the statutory minimum wage, although this is restricted to rural areas and to a maximum of 100 days of work per household per year.

Under India's complex federal system, both the Union and state governments have responsibilities regarding the right to food. In general the Union Government is responsible for elaborating, monitoring and financing programmes to ensure access to food and water, while state governments are responsible for implementation. State governments also legislate on irrigation, agricultural land tenure, ceiling, transfer and on the minimum wage. In some areas, independent tribal authorities have important powers. In Scheduled Areas, tribal advisory councils must be consulted on any issue related to the Scheduled Tribes, and in Tribal Areas, tribal district councils have important autonomy in the allotment, occupation or use of the land, the management of forests (other than reserved forests) and the inheritance of property. At the local level, municipalities and *panchayats* (self-governments) are responsible for the supply of drinking water. *Panchayats*, in which seats are reserved for the Scheduled Castes, Scheduled Tribes and for women, have increasing power over land acquisition since the Panchayats (Scheduled Areas) Act, 1996, and in the management of the food-based schemes since directions were delivered by the Supreme Court.[35]

13.3.3 Access to justice and human rights institutions

All victims of violations of the right to food should have access to effective remedies, including access to justice to claim their right. India provides one of the best examples in the world in terms of the justiciability of economic, social and cultural rights, with the right to life interpreted extensively by the Supreme Court to include the right to food. Under the Constitution, public-interest litigation is permitted to protect the basic human rights of the most vulnerable, which explains why so many social movements have sought appropriate remedies before the Supreme Court. In 2001, the PUCL approached the Supreme Court on behalf of starving people. Their original petition addressed the situation in six states, but the Supreme Court broadened its scope to cover the entire country. For the Supreme Court, the Government has a direct responsibility to prevent starvation:

> The anxiety of the Court is to see that the poor and the destitute and the weaker sections of the society do not suffer from hunger and starvation. The prevention of the same is one of the prime responsibilities of the Government – whether Central or the State. Mere schemes without any implementation are of no use. What is important is that the food must reach the hungry.[36]

To ensure the fulfilment of the right to food, the Supreme Court directed that all destitute people be identified and included in existing food-based schemes and directed state governments to implement fully all these schemes, including the Targeted Public Distribution Scheme (TPDS), the Antyodaya Anna Yojana (AAY), the Integrated Child Development Scheme (ICDS) and the Mid-Day Meals Scheme (MDMS). The Supreme Court also directed the most vulnerable, including the primitive tribes, to be placed in the AAY lists to ensure their access to food at a highly subsidized price. To increase access to information, it directed that all its orders and the lists of beneficiaries be made publicly available. The Supreme Court also directed that Chief Secretaries/Administrations of the states/Union territories should be held responsible in case of starvation or malnutrition deaths or persistent default in compliance with the orders. These directions have significantly improved the implementation of many food security schemes in many states, particularly since the Court has also appointed two Commissioners to monitor the implementation of its orders.

The PUCL case represents a great advance in the justiciability of the right to food as a human right, as the orders of the Supreme Court in this case have transformed the policy choices of the Government into enforceable, justiciable rights of the people. Although this relates primarily to the obligation to fulfil the right to food, the Court has also made judgments that are related to the obligations to respect and to protect the right to food. It has, for example, protected the right to water of Dalits against discrimination by the upper castes,[37] the right to livelihood of traditional fisherpeople against the shrimp industry (*Aquaculture case*),[38] and the right to livelihood of scheduled tribes against the acquisition of land by a private company (*Samatha case*).[39] For the Supreme Court, 'any person who is deprived of his right to livelihood except according to just and fair procedure established by law, can challenge the deprivation as offending the right to life conferred by article 21'.[40] It is now essential that small farmers who are arbitrarily evicted from their land, or women or members of the Scheduled Castes or Scheduled Tribes who are deprived of their access to productive resources, should have the same access to justice before the Supreme Court.

Despite these advances in the justiciability of the right to food, there remain difficulties in enforcing existing legislation, in ensuring the implementation of court decisions and in ensuring access to justice for the poor. The decisions of the Supreme Court in the *Aquaculture case* and *Samatha case* have, for example, never been fully implemented. Article 39A of the Constitution requires the State to provide free legal aid to ensure that the most vulnerable will have access to justice. Lack of implementation, high costs, long delays in court proceedings and the lack of full independence of the judiciary at the local level have made the judicial system virtually inaccessible. One way of improving this situation would be for all states to set up the human rights courts and a special court as required under the Protection of Human Rights Act, 1993, and the Scheduled Castes and Scheduled Tribes Act, 1989.

The need to establish independent monitoring mechanisms is essential. In India, the National Human Rights Commission (NHRC) has been established under the Protection of Human Rights Act, 1993, in accordance with the Paris Principles[41] and 15 States have their own human rights commission. Their mandate includes the promotion and protection of all human rights, including the right to food. The National Commission for Minorities, the National Commission for Women and the Scheduled Castes and Scheduled Tribes Commission also address the specific needs of the most vulnerable. During our mission, we welcomed the work of the NHRC on the right to food, particularly in one specific case, in Orissa in 1996, when a Commission's inquiry concluded that 17 deaths were attributable to malnutrition and hunger. The Commission continues to monitor the situation today. We strongly encouraged the NHRC and the 15 state commissions to initiate other inquiries on complaints of alleged starvation or malnutrition deaths. We also recommended that a National Commission for Children be established to protect their specific needs.

13.4 Policy framework for the right to food

13.4.1 Government policies and institutions

A wide range of policies and programmes are in place to address food insecurity and malnutrition, mostly elaborated and financed by the central

Government and implemented by state governments, although these programmes have not been explicitly articulated around India's obligations towards the right to food.

Since independence, India's policies and programmes have focused on increasing both the national *availability* of food as well as the physical and economic *access* to food, although the *adequacy* of food has been a less central focus. The drive for national food self-sufficiency in rice and wheat production aimed to increase national food availability, eliminate the risks of famine and chronic food shortages and reduce dependency on food imports and food aid (particularly after India suffered when food aid was slow in coming in the 1970s as punishment for India's critical stance on the war in Vietnam).[42] Food self-sufficiency was achieved with public investment in agriculture and rural infrastructure and the introduction of Green Revolution technologies, quadrupling wheat and rice production from 50 million metric tonnes to well over 200 million tonnes in less than 50 years. Today, as India begins to liberalize the agricultural sector, there remains a strong preference for maintaining a certain level of food self-sufficiency, driven partly by the Government of India's awareness that national demand is so large that it could not be met by international markets along with the recognition that two thirds of the population still rely on agriculture for employment.[43] However, it is recognized that the drive for national food self-sufficiency has produced uneven progress, with production concentrated in irrigated, better quality lands of large farmers in the Punjab, Haryana and western Uttar Pradesh but bypassing small farmers in the rain-fed agricultural areas of central and eastern India.[44] Therefore, although food availability increased at the national level, this has not translated into household food security. There is therefore a need for greater investment in smallholder production in less developed areas to promote simultaneously food availability and access to food.[45]

Efforts to improve *access* to food at the household level have focused on generating economic growth and employment as well as on the provision of a food-based social safety net, including PDS, the largest food distribution programme in the world. In many respects, PDS is a colossal achievement: it has been successful in eliminating famine and in quadrupling foodgrain production. It involves the Food Corporation of India buying foodgrains in the surplus states (offering minimum support prices for rice and wheat), transporting it to 15,000 government *godowns* (storage facilities) in deficit states, and distributing the foodgrains through over half a million 'fair-price shops', where families are entitled to buy a fixed amount of rice and wheat at subsidized prices. Conceived as a universal scheme, the Government of India shifted to a Targeted Public Food Distribution System in 1997. Under the targeted system, the poorest families (below-poverty-line households) are entitled to buy a fixed amount of foodgrain at highly subsidized prices, whereas less poor (above-poverty-line households) can buy a specified amount at prices closer to the market price. State governments are responsible, with the participation of the local authorities, *Panchayati Raj*, for identifying the households that fall below the poverty line (rather than this being defined at the central level by the central Government). During our mission, we found problems in practice with below-poverty-line lists still not finalized and not always listing the poorest in the villages. The very poorest households are also entitled to the Antyodaya Anna Yojana Scheme (AAY), under which they have access to 35 kg of foodgrain per month (since 2002) at highly subsidized prices.

Although PDS has been successful in averting famine, it is beset by pervasive corruption. Union Government officials estimated for us that approximately 36 per cent of the foodgrains distributed were diverted onto the black market. PDS works best in the states of Kerala and Tamil Nadu, where it is accepted that the transparency and accountability of local government officials were much higher. Nonetheless, there are many problems across India and we found problems of overcharging, irregular opening hours of fair price shops, many of the poorest people not having ration cards, as well as people being so poor that they could not even afford the subsidized prices.[46] More broadly, however, even though the PDS has been successful in averting famine it has not managed to address chronic undernourishment, largely because it simply does not distribute enough food. PDS entitlements meet only 10–30 per cent of individual food needs and in 1997, with the shift to a targeted system, the entitlement changed to a *family* entitlement of 10 kg of rice or wheat per household per month, equivalent to only 18 per cent of recommended daily intake (assuming a five-member family). This entitlement was increased to 35 kg in 2002. It is also widely recognized that PDS has not always reached the poorest people in the poorest states and has tended to be biased towards the better-off living in urban areas. However, the shift away from a universal scheme towards a targeted scheme appears to have made PDS less effective. Its impact in addressing chronic hunger, undernourishment and malnutrition has not been helped by the continued focus on production rather than consumption, including monitoring 'off-take', rather than human in-take. Speaking to local officials, we found a tendency to deny that any starvation deaths occurred, with reported deaths generally blamed on unrelated diseases such as measles.

Large-scale food-for-work programmes managed by central and state governments such as the Sampoorna Grameen Rozgar Yojana (SGRY) programme, focus on ensuring guaranteed employment for a specified number of days during the lean agricultural season when work for agricultural labourers is scarce. The dual aim is to provide food security through employment (paid partly in foodgrains, partly in cash), and to build common assets such as roads. Although well designed, we found that there remain problems. The implementation of these programmes varies across states, as work is not always guaranteed for 100 days (studies show that most workers are only granted work for 7–21 days) and there have been reports of corruption and concerns that the schemes are not always well targeted towards people from scheduled castes and scheduled tribes.

The Integrated Child Development Services Programmes (ICDS) is one of the largest programmes in the world aiming to provide integrated nutrition, health and early child development services for children from 0–6 years, under the responsibility of the Department of Women and Child Development. We observed the operation of *Anganwadi* Centres in rural villages, where we saw how check-ups on children's nutritional status were carried out to monitor severe and acute malnourishment, with food and nutritional supplements given to mothers of children identified as malnourished. According to the State government officials with whom we spoke, the ICDS has contributed to enormous progress in improving child nutrition and reducing child mortality. However, we noted that there seemed to be a tendency to overstate progress in monitoring levels of malnutrition, as progress appeared to be extremely rapid but did not seem to accord with the national statistical surveys. Some other problems were drawn to our attention, including the lack of storage facilities for food, occasional diversion of supplies by staff and lack of availability of the right quantities of food at the centres at the appropriate time as well as the financial constraints of state governments that have limited the nutritional supplements available for the ICDS.[47] Predominantly distributing rice and wheat, even the ICDS does not sufficiently promote nutrition as well as food security.

The Mid-Day Meals Scheme aims to provide meals to schoolchildren under the responsibility of the Department of Education as well as the Ministry of Rural Development and the Ministry of Urban Affairs and Employment, and is implemented by the state governments. The dual aim is to ensure nourishment of children and encourage school attendance. Central government provides the foodgrains and state governments are expected to meet the costs of non-food expenses including cooking, transport and delivery of foodgrain to schools as well as arranging for cooking, serving and supplying micronutrients. Under an order from the Supreme Court, schools were required to serve cooked rice and *dal* (lentils) or vegetables to primary school children from January 2002, although this order has not been equally implemented across the different states. During our mission, we were also concerned by reports that, in the Mid-Day Meals Scheme, parents of upper-caste children have protested against women of scheduled castes or tribes being employed to cook or serve meals.

In terms of more broadly addressing the discrimination against tribal peoples and scheduled castes, a number of special programmes have been established by the Ministry of Social Justice and the Ministry of Empowerment and Tribal Affairs. These have included the Village Grain Bank Scheme, initiated in 1997, which aims to prevent starvation deaths of tribal people living in remote areas, especially those who are not reached by PDS. Affirmative action programmes have also aimed to increase access to education and employment for scheduled castes and scheduled tribes, although social discrimination persists. Although land reform schemes have been carried out in a number of states to distribute government lands to scheduled castes and tribal peoples, lack of political will has brought many of these initiatives to a halt, and in some states, such as Madhya Pradesh, the feudalistic *zamindari* system persists. Many people who have been granted lands have been forcibly evicted by higher castes with impunity. Loss of access to productive resources, such as forest tribal peoples being excluded from forests or shrimp-farmers displacing smallholder farmers, means that there is a lack of judicial and administrative protection for access to productive resources for the poorest.

In relation to addressing food security problems arising from the loss of livelihoods from development-induced displacement, a National Policy on Relief and Rehabilitation of Project Affected Families was instituted in 2004, with the Tenth Plan making a commitment to ensure resettlement and rehabilitation, including gender-sensitive programmes that ensure that women have legal rights to land and that women's livelihood and food security activities are recognized in the context of rehabilitation. However, this does not seem to have been fully implemented in practice.

13.4.2 Non-governmental organizations and associations

India has a vibrant and strong civil society and the role of civil society action in addressing hunger and poverty has been well recognized. Numerous projects initiated by civil society have had important impacts on the fight against hunger and malnutrition and the fight for the rights of the most vulnerable in different regions across India. Over the last decade, FIAN has been very involved in promoting the right to food and denouncing violations in different regions of India. Additionally, a wide range of national organizations are working on many issues related to food security and human rights. The NGO Antenna has worked to improve micronutrient deficiencies through low-cost investment in spirulina, which is used as a nutritional supplement. More recently the Right to Food Campaign, a coalition of different organizations, has started to work together after the success of the public-interest litigation brought by the PUCL, using legal strategies as well as broader social mobilization strategies to call for public action to fight starvation and chronic hunger. The Right to Food Campaign has held public hearings in Orissa, Madhya Pradesh, Jharkand, Maharashtra, Rajasthan as well as Delhi, bringing government officials to hear personal testimonies of people living in communities suffering from hunger, and has also served a monitoring role in trying to ensure the implementation of Supreme Court orders under the PUCL case. The Campaign also uses the 2005 Right to Information Act to challenge corruption, demanding that information on entitlements and ration cards be made publicly available. The Campaign also demands that employment and working conditions are seen as part of the right to food, and have had success with the passing of the national Employment Guarantee Act.

13.5 Main findings and concerns

13.5.1 Progressive realization of the right to food

Despite the progress made in the progressive realization of the right to food in India since independence, we were concerned that there are signs of regression, particularly amongst the poorest. In monitoring progress towards the Millennium Development Goals (MDGs), the Planning Commission has noted that India was not currently on track to achieve the goals set in relation to malnutrition and undernourishment. According to government statistics, levels of undernourishment fell from 62.2 to 53 per cent between 1990 and 2000, and the proportion of stunting in children fell from 54.8 cent to 47 per cent, but this was not fast enough to reach the Goals. The FAO has also recorded that much of the progress made in the early 1990s was lost in the late 1990s, with the number of victims of hunger increasing by 18 million people in the second half of the decade.[48] We were also concerned by the fall of foodgrain availability to 152 kg per capita, 23 kg less than in the early 1990s,[49] and by the decline in calorie consumption.[50] As pointed out by Utsa Patnaik, burgeoning foodstocks do not necessarily reflect 'over-production', but rather 'underconsumption'. With real agricultural wages declining, food prices and unemployment rising, there are signs of increasing food insecurity.

The Government is required to spend the maximum of available resources on ensuring the right to food but spending is falling, given pressures to reduce simultaneously public investment in agriculture and public spending on safety-nets. Investment in rural development has already fallen from 14.5 per cent of GDP before 1990 to less than 6 per cent of GDP, but investment in rural development and smallholder is essential to fight poverty and improve the right to food.[51] Spending on the Public Food Distribution System averaged 0.5 per cent of GDP before 1997,[52] increasing to 1.1 per cent of GDP,[53] but this was a result of storage costs after the shift to the targeted system, which suggests that the universal system was more cost-efficient.

13.5.2 Violations of the right to food

We were concerned that we received a large number of reports of alleged violations of the right to food during our visit. These include the following.

Starvation deaths

Reports of more than 250 starvation or malnutrition deaths in 2004 and 2005 in the States of Rajasthan, Jharkhand, Bihar, Madhya Pradesh and West Bengal were presented to us at the Judicial Colloquium on the

Right to Food.[54] In its fifth report to the Supreme Court, Commissioner Dr Saxena reported on hundreds of alleged hunger-related deaths in the same states and in Chattisgarh, Uttar Pradesh, Orissa, Karnataka, Andhra Pradesh, Assam, Kerala and Maharastra. We received many other reports on alleged starvation or malnutrition deaths, including by FIAN[55] and the Asian Human Rights Commission with the Manabadhikar Suraksha Mancha.[56] In Orissa, when we visited villages, we received testimonies by women who had lost their children to hunger and malnutrition. As Chief Justice of the Uttar Pradesh High Court, A.W. Ray, said in his conclusion of the Judicial Colloquium on the Right to Food, 'in a country where there is plenty of food, every child, woman and man dying from hunger is assassinated'.

Discrimination against the Scheduled Castes and the Scheduled Tribes

Most of the victims of starvation are women and children, members of the Scheduled Tribes and Scheduled Castes, with their deaths mainly due to discrimination in access to food or productive resources, evictions or the lack of implementation of the food-based schemes. Despite an extensive legal framework prohibiting discrimination and untouchability, discrimination persists, particularly in rural areas.[57] In Madhya Pradesh and Orissa, we observed that access to village water wells is still not allowed for Dalits and that even if members of the Scheduled Castes or Scheduled Tribes were granted lands, higher castes often take the land away. Reports were also received that in Uttar Pradesh and Uttaranchal, Dalit families were forcibly evicted from their land by upper castes, and sometimes forced to work for them.[58] In Harinagar, Kashipur, it was reported that 154 Dalit families had been forcibly evicted from their land and remained landless despite a decision by the Supreme Court in their favour in 1996.[59] As former Chief Justice R. Mishra said in a meeting with us, 'low-caste people receive the land, but the upper caste enjoys it'. These are crimes punishable by imprisonment and fine under the Scheduled Castes and Scheduled Tribes (Prevention of Atrocities) Act, 1989, but the law is not enforced.[60]

Obligation to respect: displacements or evictions by the State, without adequate resettlement and rehabilitation

We received numerous complaints about forced displacements of communities as a consequence of State development projects without adequate resettlement and rehabilitation. The case of the Narmada Dam is of particular concern, as despite clear directions by the Supreme Court in 2000,[61] thousands of affected people were still not adequately resettled and rehabilitated when we undertook the mission. It is alleged that in 2005 11,000 families in Madhya Pradesh, 1500 families in Maharashtra and 200 families in Gujarat were still to be rehabilitated, although their villages have already been submerged.[62] In Hazaribagh, Jharkhand, a state coal-mining project allegedly led to involuntary resettlements of thousands of people and the destruction of their sources of livelihood without adequate rehabilitation and compensation.[63] As provided by law, national and State policies and Supreme Court orders, every affected family should be adequately resettled and rehabilitated and the 'land for land' principle respected. We received many complaints from tribal communities who lost their means of livelihood when evicted from the forest as a consequence of the implementation of the Forest Act, 1980.

Obligation to protect: lack of protection against the activities of private companies

In Orissa, we received complaints about the alleged impact of mining activities on the right to food of tribal communities in Kashipur and Lanjigarh. It was reported that tribal communities had been forcibly evicted from their land to allow private mining activities, in violation of the Constitution and despite clear directions by the Supreme Court from 1997 that the lands in scheduled areas cannot be leased out to non-tribals or to companies.[64] In Bhopal, we met with the Government of Madhya Pradesh and representatives of the people affected by the gas disaster of 1984, in which 7, 00 people died in the first days and 15,000 people died in the following years.[65] In 2005, 20 years after the tragedy, water wells in the area were still contaminated and, despite clear directions by the Supreme Court in May 2004, the water requirements were still not met.[66] We also received complaints alleging that uncontrolled water extraction in the states of Kerala and Tamil Nadu was causing a severe shortage of water for the local population.[67] Impact assessment studies and prior consultation of the affected communities must always be conducted before any licence is granted to a private company, and in case of violations of the right to food, land or water, all victims must be adequately resettled, rehabilitated and compensated.

Obligation to fulfil: lack of implementation of the food-based schemes

In each of his reports, Commissioner Dr. Saxena points to the lack of implementation of the food-based schemes in most of the states. In May 2003 the Supreme Court concluded that the states of Bihar, Jharkhand and Uttar Pradesh had not even begun to implement its directions for supply of cooked Mid-Day Meals.[68] In 2005 in Arunachal Pradesh, Assam, Manipur, severely malnourished children were not covered by the programme. In this district, many of the most vulnerable persons had not been granted ration cards. The Supreme Court recognized these schemes as legal entitlements to all beneficiaries, including those living in tribal villages or illegal slums, which means that their non-implementation amounts to a violation of the right to food.

13.6 Conclusions and recommendations

In his report on the mission to India, presented to the Human Rights Commission in March 2006, Jean Ziegler made the following conclusions and recommendations.

He was encouraged by the commitment of the Government of India and by the vision of the Indian State in ensuring food security. He welcomed the work of the Supreme Court, which is an example to the world in advancing understanding of the justiciability of the human right to food. He also welcomed the adoption by the Government of the Rural Employment Guarantee Act and the entitlements enshrined in food-based programmes. However, he was concerned that India still has the largest number of permanently and chronically undernourished people and one of the highest rates of child malnutrition in the world, and that hunger and malnutrition have been increasing since the second half of the 1990s.

He then made the following specific recommendations:

(a) The right to food is a human right and an essential part of the right to life. Even as substantial progress is being achieved in ensuring food security, monitoring of the severity of chronic undernourishment and malnutrition and accountability for starvation or malnutrition deaths must be instituted, including by the national and state human rights commissions and the local *panchayat* bodies. As suggested by the Supreme Court, independent Public Service Commissions could contribute to this monitoring. All public administration officers should be trained with respect to human rights and the right to food;[69]

(b) A framework law with a national strategy for the implementation of the right to food should be instituted, in accordance with CESCR General Comment No. 12 on the right to food. This should establish benchmarks and indicators for the investment of the right to food;

(c) All Union and state governments must follow and implement all orders and judgments of the Supreme Court. Non-implementation of the food-based schemes enshrined as entitlements amounts to a violation of the right to food. In the case of Bhopal, the state authorities should ensure a regular supply of adequate safe water for all affected communities. Access to justice, including to the Supreme Court for victims of violations of the obligations to respect, protect and fulfil the right to food must be ensured;

(d) The human rights courts and the special courts required under the Protection of Human Rights Act, 1993, and the Scheduled Castes and Scheduled Tribes (Prevention of Atrocities) Act, 1989, should be established in all states with a mandate that protects their independence and includes the right to food;

(e) All Indians should be treated equally before the law. The Scheduled Castes and Scheduled Tribes (Prevention of Atrocities) Act, 1989, should be fully implemented, and atrocities committed should be prosecuted and brought to justice;
(f) Land and agrarian reform should be implemented to strengthen smallholder agricultural livelihoods. Existing agrarian reform legislation should not be undermined to serve the interests of large landholdings of landlords and agribusiness;
(g) The Land Acquisition Act should be amended, or new legislation adopted, to recognize a justiciable right to resettlement and rehabilitation for all displaced or evicted persons, including those without formal land titles and including women;[70]
(h) Minimum wage legislation and the Employment Guarantee Act should be fully enforced. Decisive action must be taken against widespread evasion, particularly for agricultural labour and the informal sector. The minimum wage should be indexed to the cost of a basic food basket, which must be sufficient to purchase the minimum daily calorie requirement;
(i) The Right to Information Act should be respected in relation to all programmes, including making publicly available all information on entitlements. This should include eligibility criteria under the Public Food Distribution System at the level of the fair price shops. Corruption must be challenged at all levels of the system and all public officials and shop licensees held accountable for any diversion of resources;
(j) Dams, mining and infrastructure projects must not be implemented if this entails displacement and irreversible destruction of people's livelihoods. Such projects should only be carried out with the consent of communities and on the condition that due legal process, proper resettlement, rehabilitation (under the 'land for land' principle) and compensation to all victims is guaranteed;
(k) A national early-warning system should be established that records starvation deaths to generate emergency response and improve accountability. Proper methods of documenting starvation and malnutrition-related deaths should be developed with the participation of the civil society;
(l) PDS must be strengthened to ensure that it reaches all those in need and that the prices do not make it impossible for the poor to buy the subsidized rations. Cash transfers could also be introduced to improve access to food. In the context of a more market-oriented economy, programmes and social transfers must remain in place to prevent starvation deaths and continue investment in the right to food. Such programmes must be implemented as a matter of right and not as benevolence and must be subject to review by the courts;
(m) Implementation of all food-based schemes must be improved by incorporating the human rights principles of non-discrimination, partici-

pation, transparency and accountability. Monitoring of all food-based programmes, including PDS, must include monitoring of impacts on malnutrition and undernourishment;

(n) Food security programmes should include elements to ensure nutritional security and to address micronutrient deficiencies. National initiatives for fortification of salt and flour should be complemented by low-cost local initiatives, including promoting small-scale horticulture production and supplementary food being distributed to children and women under ICDS and the Mid-Day Meals Scheme;

(o) Food security programmes must also place more emphasis on protecting and promoting sustainable livelihoods. Public investment in smallholder agriculture is essential, given that two thirds of the population still depends on agriculture, and employment is currently only being generated in the high-tech sector that will not be able to absorb all those left unemployed, if public investment in agriculture is abandoned;

(p) Finally, greater liberalization of trade in basic staple foods should not be pursued as long as subsidies in the developed countries keep international prices at artificially low levels, otherwise India will suffer from competition from dumped agricultural products that will undermine its own production, especially of rice and wheat.

14
Lebanon

14.1 Introduction

Jean Ziegler visited Lebanon from 11 to 16 September 2006 upon the invitation of the Government and in accordance with the Special Rapporteur's mandate established by Commission on Human Rights resolutions 2000/10 and as transferred by the General Assembly in resolution 60/251 to the Human Rights Council which extended the mandate by its decision 102.[1] This mission was undertaken independently from the Commission of Inquiry established on the basis of Council resolution S-2/1.

The visit to Lebanon was requested in relation to concerns raised by the international community regarding the impact on the right to food of the war between Israel and the armed forces of the Lebanese political party, Hezbollah. Initial concerns were raised regarding limits on humanitarian access to people trapped during the war, with certain areas in Lebanon cut off from access to humanitarian aid for prolonged periods of time during the 34 days of hostilities. In 21 July 2006, Jean Ziegler, in concert with a number of other United Nations human rights experts, issued a press release calling for the immediate cessation of hostilities and for unrestricted and secure passage of humanitarian assistance. The massive displacement of almost 1 million people also disrupted access to food across the country. With the loss of much of this year's harvest, the destruction of roads, agricultural and water infrastructure, fields littered with unexploded bombs and the disruption of agricultural and fishing livelihoods, serious concerns were also raised regarding the longer term impact of the war on the right to food and water.

Jean Ziegler also requested authorization to visit Israel to investigate the situation of the right to food of the affected Israeli population, but he received no response from the Government of Israel. In his report to the Human Rights Council, he therefore covered only the situation in Lebanon.

The objective of the mission was to investigate the situation of the right to food in Lebanon from the perspective of international human rights and humanitarian law.

During his visit, Jean Ziegler held constructive dialogues with the Lebanese authorities, including the Acting Minister for Foreign Affairs, the Ministers of Agriculture, Health, Social Affairs, Energy and Water, as well as with the Parliamentary Commission on Human Rights, the High Relief Council and members of Parliament. He also held meetings with a wide range of United Nations agencies, national and international NGOs, academics and individuals. He was able to visit the southern suburbs of Beirut and travelled to the south of the Litani River, where he was able to talk directly to local authorities and affected families, agricultural workers, farmers and fishermen.

14.2 General context

The mission followed the war that took place from 12 July to 14 August 2006 between Hezbollah and Israel, following Hezbollah's capture of soldiers in a raid across the border between Israel and Lebanon. It was reported that during the 34 days of the war the Israeli forces launched more than 7000 air attacks and 2500 attacks by sea as well as heavy artillery shelling. The war has had far-reaching effects on the Lebanese population. According to the Government of Lebanon, the war resulted in 1189 killed (mostly civilians), 4399 injured, 974,189 displaced and between 15,000 and 30,000 homes destroyed.[2]

On 11 August 2006, the Security Council adopted resolution 1701 (2006) in which the Council called for a full cessation of hostilities based upon, in particular, the immediate cessation by Hezbollah of all attacks and the immediate cessation by Israel of all offensive military operations. On the same day, the Human Rights Council, having convened a special session on the war, adopted resolution S-2/1, in which it called upon Israel to immediately stop military operations against the civilian population and civilian objects resulting in death and destruction and serious violations of human rights. It also decided to urgently establish and immediately dispatch a high-level commission of inquiry comprising eminent experts on human rights law and international humanitarian law, to assess and investigate, *inter alia*, the extent and impact of Israeli attacks on human life, property, critical infrastructure and the environment. The fighting continued after the adoption of the resolutions and even intensified up to the last moment, the cessation of hostilities taking effect on 14 August 2006.

14.3 Legal framework related to the right to food in Lebanon

As the International Court of Justice has reaffirmed,[3] both human rights law and, as lex specialis, international humanitarian law are applicable during armed conflicts and situations of occupation. These include the war in Lebanon, where all provisions of international human rights and humanitarian law protecting the right to food were applicable. It is important to note in that context that both Israel and Lebanon are parties to the International Covenant on Economic, Social and Cultural Rights and to the Convention on the Rights of the Child, the two main human rights instruments for the protection of the right to food, as well as to the Geneva Conventions of 12 August 1949. It is also important to note that while only Lebanon is a party to the Protocol Additional to the Geneva Conventions and relating to the Protection of Victims of International Armed Conflicts (First Additional Protocol, adopted in 1977), most of its provisions that are relevant to the right to food are considered part of customary international law and are therefore binding on all States and all parties to a conflict, regardless of status and ratification.[4]

The right to food is primarily the right to be able to feed oneself through physical and economic access to food, as defined in General Comment No. 12 of the CESCR. The right to food entails obligations of Governments towards their people, but also towards people living in other countries. This is particularly true for States parties to the International Covenant on Economic, Social and Cultural Rights, including Israel and Lebanon that have undertaken to cooperate, without any territorial or jurisdictional limitations, to realize the right to food. In time of an armed conflict, the most important human rights obligation of Governments is the obligation to respect the right to food, which means refraining from restricting, inhibiting or preventing people's access to food. As the right to food also includes access to clean, safe drinking water and irrigation water necessary for subsistence production, there is also a minimum obligation to refrain from restricting access to water or the destruction of water infrastructure. The right to food also obliged Governments to ensure that any individual or group affected by the war and without access to productive resources will have access to humanitarian assistance.

As outlined in our Chapter 5 on the right to food in armed conflict, there are a range of provisions contained in the Geneva Conventions of 1949 and in the Additional Protocols of 1977 that are particularly relevant to the protection of the right to food. International humanitarian law aims primarily to protect persons not taking or no longer taking part in hostilities, such as civilian populations, and one of its basic principles is that parties to an armed conflict must at all times distinguish between the civilian population and combatants and between civilian objects and military objectives, and direct attacks only against military objectives. One of its core rules is that indiscriminate attacks are strictly prohibited. Accordingly, one of its most important provisions is Article 54, paragraph 2, of the First Additional Protocol which establishes that:

> It is prohibited to attack, destroy, remove or render useless objects indispensable to the survival of the civilian population, such as foodstuffs,

agricultural areas for the production of foodstuffs, crops, livestock, drinking water installations and supplies and irrigation works...

Parties to a conflict are therefore prohibited from attacking not only civilians, but also the infrastructure for food, water and agricultural production that is necessary to their survival. Failing to respect this obligation would constitute a grave breach of international humanitarian law and a war crime.[5] The destruction of drinking water installations would be particularly problematic, but the systematic destruction of roads, bridges, ports and food factories, even if perceived on one side as military objectives, would also be prohibited and may also constitute a war crime if it causes excessive loss of life or injury to civilians or damage to civilian objects, or widespread, long-term and severe damage to the natural environment.[6]

International humanitarian law also limits the right of the parties to a conflict to choose methods or means of warfare, including by prohibiting parties to employ weapons, projectiles and material and methods of warfare of a nature to cause superfluous injury or unnecessary suffering. It follows that using cluster munitions in populated civilian areas, given the injuries and suffering that it will cause and given the effects that do not discriminate between military and civilian objectives, is likely to result in many violations of international humanitarian law. The dispersal of unexploded bomblets from cluster bombs also raises other serious concerns, not only as to their immediate affects on civilian life, but also in relation to the after-effects in terms of damage to agricultural fields, as well as life and civilian infrastructure.

International humanitarian law also contains many rules that protect the right to food for populations caught in armed conflict. These rules cover both the rights of affected civilians to receive aid and the rights of humanitarian agencies to deliver it. According to Articles 70 and 71 of the First Additional Protocol, the parties to an armed conflict shall allow and facilitate rapid and unimpeded passage of all relief consignments, equipment and personnel. They must encourage and facilitate effective international coordination of the relief actions and ensure the safety of medical and humanitarian personnel. States must facilitate and protect these operations, and must not divert or obstruct the passage of humanitarian assistance. The deliberate impeding of humanitarian operations and targeting of personnel, installations, material, units or vehicles involved in humanitarian assistance constitute war crimes.[7]

14.4 Main findings and concerns related to the right to food and water

14.4.1 During the war

During the war, a combination of destruction of road and transport infrastructure and denial of safe transit by the Israeli armed forces made it very difficult for humanitarian agencies to transport food and other relief, especially to the approximately 22,000 people left trapped in the area south of the Litani River, where there are 38 localities under the control of the United Nations Interim Force in Lebanon (UNIFIL). While the majority of the population fled their homes, those left behind were the elderly, the sick and the poor, including women and children. Amnesty International reported, for example, that more than 200 people trapped in the villages of Aitaroun and Bint Jbail, including women, children, and elderly and disabled people, were facing food shortages.[8] It also reported that the destruction of water infrastructure left thousands of people dependent on filthy water collected in ponds and ditches[9] and that for at least a week, no humanitarian organization was able to reach these villages.[10] According to the High Relief Council, in Markaba, a village of about 10,000 habitants, 128 people were left stranded between 6 and 13 August, without food and water.[11] UNIFIL also reported on several occasions that it was prevented from distributing food and undertaking other emergency work in its area of operations.

On 7 August 2006, the Government of Israel informed the United Nations agencies that any vehicle except those of UNIFIL travelling south of the Litani River within 5–30 km of the Israeli-Lebanese border could be attacked. As a consequence, the World Food Programme and other United Nations humanitarian agencies suspended all operations for the delivery of emergency assistance in the south. On the same day, an Israeli air strike destroyed the last remaining open crossing over the Litani River, effectively cutting off the southern port city of Tyre and the surrounding region, as the main Qasmiyeh road bridge had been destroyed by earlier air strikes. On 8 August 2006, it was reported that Israeli military dropped leaflets warning that it would attack any vehicle travelling south of the Litani River on suspicion of 'transporting rockets and arms for the terrorists'.[12] This prevented not only the movement of humanitarian assistance vehicles, but also of trucks transporting agricultural produce to markets and distribution points. According to Human Rights Watch, on 18 July Israeli air strikes hit a convoy of the United Arab Emirates Red Crescent Society, destroying a vehicle containing rice, sugar and other food, and killing the driver.[13] The destruction by the Israeli forces of hundreds of bridges and road networks impeded aid assistance convoys and made reconstruction a long-term project.

The refusal of safe passage by the Israeli armed forces not only disrupted the humanitarian food aid; it also had often dramatic consequences for the population fleeing their bombed villages and for families trapped in the ruins of their houses. It was for example reported that on 20 July 2006, 23 persons, mostly from the Al-Ghanam-family, fled in a truck from their village of Marwaheen to the north. On the way they were hit by a shell from an Israeli boat. Minutes later an Israeli helicopter appeared in the sky and fired a missile into the burning truck. Only one person survived: a four-year-old girl, with severe burns over most of her body.[14] Many of the families trapped under the ruins of their houses called for help, often over their cellular phones. Delegates of the International Committee of the Red Cross (ICRC) said that they could hear the voices, but it was impossible to send help, because the cranes, mechanical diggers and ambulances were immobilized.[15]

One quarter of Lebanon's population, about one million people, were forced to leave their homes and agricultural lands, which disrupted normal access to food and left tens of thousands dependent on food aid. Almost half of those displaced fled to central Beirut and the surrounding area, while others fled to the Syrian Arab Republic or other countries. Those who could not rely on friends and family were often crowded in squalid conditions in temperatures reaching 45°C in the parks, schools and public institutions in central Beirut, where humanitarian agencies did manage to deliver food rations and water supplies. Food aid was delivered by the High Relief Council of the Government, either directly or through local NGOs.[16] Food aid was also delivered by political parties, private donors, and local and international NGOs. As a result, while the diet of thousands of displaced people was disrupted, the nutritional status of the majority was not seriously threatened.[17]

In his discussions with the Ministry of Agriculture and the Ministry of Social and Family Affairs, Jean Ziegler was informed that apart from the material damage, the psychological damage and deep trauma of the war will have long-term effects on the civilian population that will affect the reconstruction of traditional economic and social life, particularly in rural areas. The loss of family members, as well as the loss of normal functions for those who are permanently injured, including amputates, contribute to psychological stress.

14.4.2 After the war

Food, agriculture and livelihoods

Most of the hundreds of thousands of Lebanese displaced by the war started to return to their villages and towns as soon as the cessation of hostilities was declared. Many of these towns and villages had been partially or totally destroyed. Food supplies were generally available immediately after the end of the war, despite the aerial and sea embargo. Many families returning to their villages took with them food aid that had been distributed to them in centres set up for displaced people. The blockade had, however, affected the variety of food commodities that could be found and thus the quality of people's diet. Food prices had also increased by between 10 and 15 per cent. For example, wheat flour, the main ingredient of the Lebanese staple food, bread, rose in price by 15 per cent as a result of the sea and land blockade that prevented imports during the war and in the weeks after. The impact of the loss of much of this wheat harvest and the harvests of vegetables and fruits will also have an impact.[18] Two months after the war, thousands of already poor families were still relying on food aid and assistance. Oxfam reported, for example, that in Zebqine, a small village of 300 families in South Lebanon, most of the population had returned to their homes and lands, but with the destruction of local shops and the devastation of agricultural fields, the food supply was precarious and it was almost wholly dependent on food aid.[19]

The longer term impact of the war on livelihoods was the key concern after the war. The right to food is not primarily about food aid, but about the right to be able to feed oneself through an adequate livelihood. Jean Ziegler found that the livelihoods of a large part of the population had been disrupted by the war, and the process of reconstructing livelihoods had been slow. The many testimonies he gathered during his visit, provided evidence that loss of livelihoods and sources of income was the main threat for the future well-being of many thousands of families, particularly in rural areas. Many people with whom he spoke informed him that they were very concerned about their livelihood prospects. The war took place at the peak of the fishing and fruit harvest season, affecting the people who earn their livelihoods from these sectors both directly in terms of damage but, more importantly, indirectly in terms of lost markets and revenues.[20] Much farmland had been affected by bombing and will continue to be affected by unexploded bombs that continue to make access to many fields impossible. The destruction by the Israeli forces of agricultural and water infrastructures will also have long-term impacts on livelihoods and access to food and water.

According to Oxfam, up to 85 per cent of Lebanon's farmers lost some or all of their harvest.[21] Most of these farmers have small farms of 1 ha or less and are generally poor. In the south of Lebanon, the majority of villages are dependent on agriculture as the sole source of income and livelihood for families. Across Lebanon, FAO estimates that agriculture provides direct employment for 9 per cent of the Lebanese population, but another 40 per cent of the population is involved in work that is indirectly related to agriculture.[22] The main agricultural regions are in the south, in the Nabatiyeh and Beqaa regions, all of which have suffered as a result of the war, particularly Baalbeck, Herml and West Baqaa in the Beqaa region, as well as in Akkar in the north and the coastal area of Damour.[23] The war resulted in the devastation of thousands of hectares of orchards, tobacco fields and olive groves by fire, the destruction of potato and banana plantations and the burning of hundreds of hectares of greenhouses. According to the Ministry of Agriculture of the Government of Lebanon, tens of thousands of head of livestock and poultry were killed and agricultural infrastructure, such as roads, machinery, buildings, farms and agro-processing factories, were destroyed.[24] The Ministry of Agriculture estimated that immediate and direct losses in agriculture amount to several hundreds of millions of United States dollars.

The war prevented farmers from harvesting and from irrigating their fruit and vegetable crops, and the land and sea blockade prevented any exports. The war took place at the peak time for the harvest (mainly stone fruits and potatoes) destined for export, but much of this year's harvest perished on the ground, as bombing forced farmers to abandon their lands and transport to market became impossible. With the loss of income from harvests, many farmers have become heavily indebted as they usually repay their debts during the harvest season (May–October) to secure credit for the following planetary season. The Ministry of Agriculture was concerned that this would lead to a downward spiral of debt and poverty for Lebanese farmers.

It was reported that agricultural fields have also been rendered useless until unexploded bombs littering the land can be removed or exploded. According to the United Nations Mine-Action Centre (UNMAC), hundreds of thousands of pieces of unexploded ordnance (UXO), mostly cluster bombs (anti-personnel weapons that spray bomblets indiscriminately over a wide area), will need to be cleared before agriculture can be re-established. It was reported that more than 1.2 million cluster bombs were dropped by the Israeli forces, and that about 90 per cent were dropped in the last 72 hours of the war when the Israeli forces were already aware that a ceasefire was imminent.[25] As of 19 September 2006, the United Nations had identified 516 individual cluster bomb strike locations.[26] UNMAC estimates that the failure rate of these cluster bomb sub-munitions is between 30 and 40 per cent. It can therefore be expected that many hundreds of thousands of unexploded cluster sub-munitions are scattered throughout the southern region.[27] Complete clearing of the south could take up to 10 years.[28] It was also estimated that from 14 August to 17 September, 83 civilians were injured and 15 died as a result of mines and cluster bombs.[29] It was also estimated that a large area of grassland used for animal grazing was also contaminated by cluster bombs.[30] Jean Ziegler was concerned that due to limited resources for clearing lands from bombs, mine clearance personnel were understandably giving priority to urban centres and roads, rather than agricultural fields. This means that many farmers were attempting to explode the bombs on their own, which is extremely dangerous. Clearing the fields had become urgent, as in the upcoming rainy season, cluster bombs and other munitions will sink into the mud and/or become camouflaged by the spring grasses, effectively becoming like landmines. Clearing the land of these unexploded bombs was essential to enable the reconstruction of livelihoods. The long-term damage of Israel's last flurry to flood the land with cluster bombs was difficult to estimate.[31]

The destruction of infrastructure in relation to agriculture, including the destruction of agricultural land and civilian infrastructure such as ports, roads, warehouses, food industries, bridges and markets, had made and will continue to make the production of food and its distribution throughout the country extremely difficult. It has been estimated that 145 bridges and overpasses and 600 km of roads were destroyed or damaged.[32] Jean Ziegler was also concerned at the destruction of agro-processing factories and plants, such as the Liban Lait dairy farm and processing plant in the Bekaa valley, the leading producer of milk and dairy products in Lebanon.[33]

The Ministry of Social and Family Affairs told Jean Ziegler that more than 70 per cent of the rural population was unemployed. With the destruction of farms and of 124 medium-sized and large factories, many of them agricultural processing factories, many people had been forced out of work. Many workers were already in a precarious situation before the war: rural farm workers earn only US$ 300 per month and there is normally work only eight months of the year; small farmers who own their own land earn about US$ 500 per month. Unemployed after the war, there is little to live on as Lebanon has no unemployment benefit or insurance for those forced out of work, although the Ministry has established emergency assistance programmes to provide families with financial and psycho-social support. Jean Ziegler was also concerned to find that one of the vulnerable groups of people particularly badly affected were Palestinian refugees living in unregistered camps, or 'gatherings', who do not benefit from the services of UNRWA and do not have the same rights as Lebanese, in terms of inheritance, ownership or work. There are nine 'gatherings' in the area of Tyre and nine in the Bekaa area, and the majority of the Palestinian families survive on casual agricultural work, and/or fishing, which have disappeared since the war, making it more difficult to feed their families. He visited two of these 'gatherings' in the south: Jall al-Bahr and Wasta. A serious concern that has been raised is that the poorest agricultural labourers, including Palestinians, will also be most at risk from UXO as they will be too desperate not to accept work to clear the fields.

Fisheries

Fishing activities and livelihoods have also been seriously affected by the war. An estimated 8000 families in the north and south of Lebanon rely on fishing for their livelihoods, including fisherfolk, fish cleaners, market sellers and boat repairers. It as been reported that people were unable to go out fishing due to destruction of boats, insecurity and the naval blockade imposed during the war. The ports of Tyre and Ouzai have been heavily damaged: more than 400 boats were reportedly destroyed, in addition to fishing nets, fish markets, warehouses and related facilities.[34] Jean Ziegler visited the port of Ouzai, which was reportedly hit by 23 attacks and which, at the time of the visit, had still not resumed working as fisherfolk no longer had boats nor the resources to repair them or buy new ones. The fisherfolk he met spoke about the precarious situation which they had to face. Jean Ziegler was shocked to see the port of Deliah where, at the time of his visit, the sea was covered by the thick carpet of the oil spill preventing fisherfolk from returning to work.

Jean Ziegler also visited Jiyyeh, where about 15,000 tons of oil spilled into the sea following the Israeli bombing of four fuel tanks on 14 July 2006. In addition, 55,000 tons of oil stored in the tanks exploded, causing a plume of polluting smoke 60 km high.[35] A preliminary assessment of the impact of the oil spill found that damage to the shoreline was extensive, with the oil slick measuring up to 50 cm thick in some places and beaches had been heavily contaminated.[36] Lebanon has a 220 km coastline, with two large bays, 12 peninsulas and a number of river deltas, about two thirds of which were affected by the pollution. It has been estimated that the massive oil spill should reach the Syrian coast by mid-September 2006. Jean Ziegler was able to speak with leaders of the fishing cooperatives and with NGOs regarding the short- and long-term damage of the bombardment of the Jiyyeh tanks. The United Nations Environment Programme, assisted by the French naval experts, estimated that the damage was as bad as the damage caused by the sinking of the tanker Erica on the north-west coast of France in 1999 and the Exxon Valdez disaster in Alaska in 1989. The long-term consequences remained to be seen; in the Exxon Valdez catastrophe, it took three years for the full effects to be felt on the ecosystem. Professor Richard Steiner, mandated by the Ministry of the Environment, the World Conservation Union and Green-Line, a Lebanese NGO, produced an assessment of how the food chain will be affected. As polluted algae are eaten by small fish, which are the prey of larger fish, it was expected that the pollution will move up the food chain. The French NGO Plan Action Mediterrannée also expressed concern that the fuel spilled contains class one carcinogenic substances like benzene that may have long-term impacts and increase the number of cancer cases. At a minimum, with the loss of fishing livelihoods, thousands of people needed basic support to survive until their livelihoods can be restored. The long-term effects of the oil spill on livelihoods must also include adverse impacts on the tourism industry, which provides employment for a large section of the Lebanese population.

Drinking water and agricultural irrigation

There have been shortages of potable water, especially in the south. A joint United Nations assessment team, including representatives of OCHA, UNICEF, UNHCR and WFP, that travelled from Tyre to Aitarou on 26 August 2006 found an urgent need for clean drinking and washing water in villages following extensive damage to the water network. In Tebnine, Aita Ech Chaab and Bint J'bail the need for water was a priority at the time of the mission of Jean Ziegler to Lebanon.[37] In some areas, only bottled water was available and the price of water was becoming unaffordable.[38] Concerns were raised about the threat of widespread outbreaks of waterborne disease; the first cases had been reported in the village of Yahoune. The authorities, the United Nations and many NGOs were working to provide the minimum standard of 15 litres of water per person per day.

Israeli bombing during the war destroyed wells, water mains, storage tanks, water pumping stations, distribution networks and water treatment works throughout southern Lebanon, and the irrigation canal attached to the Litani River was also hit.[39] The water service elsewhere in the country has also been disrupted, as water pipes running beneath roads had been extensively damaged when the roads above were bombed.[40] This has exacerbated water shortages, which were already a problem in Lebanon: prior to the war, most of the Lebanese territory was already facing a shortage of drinking water and the civil war had delayed water planning on the Litani River for more than 20 years.[41] According to the authorities, water infrastructure that had been extensively damaged included the pipelines from Ain El Zarka spring to the villages of eastern Saida and from Nabeh El Tasseh spring to the village of Aankoun, 31 water tanks in different areas and two artesian wells, Bfarwa well and a well in Fakher El Din.[42] UNICEF also reported that underground pipes and other water-related infrastructure had been seriously damaged or destroyed in many areas.[43]

The destruction of irrigation infrastructure also continued to hinder the re-establishment of agriculture after the war. The south of Lebanon is dry and arid, and the underground water level is very deep – about 600 m. Much of the agriculture in the region cannot be sustained by the rains alone. Without irrigation, it was expected that much of the next harvest, even if it can be planted, will be lost. Fadi Comair, Director-General of Hydraulic Resources of Lebanon, expressed concern that much of the complex system of the Litani canal, which provides irrigation water to southern Lebanon, had been destroyed. With many irrigation canals full of unexploded bombs, he estimated that it would take several years to clear the irrigation canals and repair the infrastructure. A shortage of fuel and electricity had also contributed to the water crisis, as water pumps require electricity or fuel-fed generators to run.[44] Electrical facilities, power plants and fuel stations had suffered extensive damage, and at least 20 fuel depots had been completely destroyed.[45]

14.5 Conclusions and recommendations

In his report on his mission to Lebanon, presented to the Human Rights Council in March 2007, Jean Ziegler made the following conclusions and recommendations.

The right to food and the right to water are protected under international human rights and humanitarian law. Given the essential nature of food and water to the survival of civilian populations, these rights entail central obligations in time of war, as well as in time of peace. In the light of the findings described above and the international obligations of the parties involved in the war, Jean Ziegler made the following recommendations:

(a) Violations of the right to food under international human rights and humanitarian law should be further investigated, including determining whether they constitute grave breaches of the Geneva Conventions and the First Additional Protocol and, possibly, war crimes under the Rome Statute of the International Criminal Court;

(b) The Commission of Inquiry established by the Human Rights Council should also investigate violations of the right to food and recommend measures for awarding reparation and determining accountability;

(c) The International Humanitarian Fact-Finding Commission established in accordance with the First Additional Protocol should be accepted by the Government of Israel and the Government of Lebanon to investigate violations of the right to food under international humanitarian law;

(d) Individuals should be held responsible for violations of the right to food and water. The United Nations High Commissioner for Human Rights in her statement to the Human Rights Council at its second special session noted that when legal obligations regulating the conduct of hostilities are violated, personal criminal responsibility may ensue, particularly for those in a position to command and control;

(e) International law regarding access for humanitarian agencies providing food and water to civilian populations must be respected at all times;

(f) According to international jurisprudence,[46] the Government of Israel should be held responsible under international law for any violation of the right to food of the Lebanese civilian population. Under international law, the Government of Israel has the obligation to ensure that all victims of violations of the right to food receive adequate reparation and compensation for the losses suffered during the war as well as for ongoing losses due to the disruption of livelihoods;

(g) The Government of Lebanon, in cooperation with United Nations agencies and international and national NGOs, should design programmes to support all those whose livelihoods have been devastated by the war, especially farmers, agricultural labourers and fisherfolk. The right to food and water must be a central part of the reconstruction effort;

(h) The Government of Lebanon, in cooperation with United Nations agencies and NGOs, must ensure that transitional measures are available to guarantee the access to food for all vulnerable groups and that the right to food is not compromised while long-term measures are put in place. This will require the provision of food assistance in the short term, but in the longer term it will require the re-establishment of livelihoods;

(i) The Government of Lebanon, with agencies and donors, must ensure that everyone has access to adequate quantities of clean drinking water. Reconstruction of water wells and water distributions networks must be a central priority;

(j) The Government of Lebanon should institute a moratorium on debt for small-scale farmers and fisherfolk to reverse the downward cycle of debt and impoverishment that will be caused by the loss of this year's harvest;

(k) The Government of Lebanon, with UNWRA, should ensure that unregistered 'gatherings' of Palestinians refugees are recognized as official camps and can be provided with all the basic services by the relevant authorities as well as by the Agency;
(l) The Government of Lebanon, in cooperation with donors, should also prioritize reconstruction of agricultural infrastructure, including irrigation networks;
(m) The Government of Lebanon, with bilateral and multilateral donors, should accelerate the clearing of cluster bombs from agricultural fields. The Government of Israel should provide the full details of its use of cluster munitions in order to facilitate the destruction of the UXO and the clearing of affected areas.

15
Bolivia

15.1 Introduction

We (Jean Ziegler, Sally-Anne Way and Christophe Golay) visited Bolivia from 29 April to 6 May 2007.[1] During our visit, we were honoured to be received by the President of the Republic, Evo Morales Ayma. We greatly benefited from meetings with the Minister for Rural Development and Agriculture, Dr Susana Rivero, the Minister of Health and Sport, Dr.Nila Heredia, and senior staff of the Ministry of Water, Ministry of Foreign Affairs and the Head of the National Insitute for Agrarian Reform. We also met with the Vice-President and other members of Bolivia's Constituent Assembly and appreciated the valuable insights from this meeting with Waldo Albarracin, the *Defensor del Pueblo*, Bolivia's human rights ombudsman.

We also appreciated meetings with a wide range of representatives from social movements, indigenous movements and NGOs. We visited rural communities and urban areas in the departments of La Paz and Oruro, and held meetings, *inter alia*, with communities in the urban areas of El Alto and miners and peasant communities in Oruro. The NGOs *Centro de Investigación y Promoción del Campesinado* (CIPCA) and Emmaus Bolivia, as well as FAO and WFP assisted in the organization of these visits.

Bolivia is the second poorest country in Latin America and has one of the highest levels of child malnutrition and under-nourishment in the continent. However, today Bolivia is in an historic moment of transition under the new Government of Evo Morales, who became Bolivia's first indigenous President in January 2006. Morales has promised to make the fight against malnutrition and extreme poverty the key focus of his administration.

Landlocked in the middle of South America, Bolivia ranges across the high altiplano and the Andes Mountains, to the tropical hills of the Yungas, the expansive forests of the Amazon and the lowland grassy plains of Santa Cruz. Nearly half of Bolivia's territory is covered by forest, and another third is semi-desert or arid. Its climate faces extreme variations of temperatures in the high altiplano as well as the hot humid temperatures of the Amazon lowlands, and it faces frequent natural disasters, especially droughts and floods. A country of 9.1 million people, the population is predominantly indigenous, with large populations of Quechua (30 per cent) and Aymara (25 per cent), and smaller ethnic groups, as well as mixed descent (30 per cent) and white populations (15 per cent), making Bolivia one of the most ethnically diverse countries in Latin America. Bolivia's economy has long been dependent on the export of minerals (especially silver and tin) and agricultural commodities (soya beans, sugar, wood) and more recently on natural gas and oil. However, despite the fact that Bolivia is a country rich in mineral resources, including natural gas and oil, and metals including silver, gold, iron, zinc and tin, the vast majority of its people have not benefited from this natural wealth and remain very poor. Millions still struggle to survive as subsistence farmers, agricultural labourers, informal miners and small traders or artisans in the informal sector, on incomes insufficient to meet basic food needs.

15.2 Malnutrition and food insecurity in Bolivia

15.2.1 The current situation of malnutrition and food insecurity in Bolivia

Chronic malnutrition affects more than one in four Bolivian children. The highest levels of malnutrition are among Bolivians living in rural areas, especially in the high plains of the altiplano regions of Potosi and Chuquisaca, but also in the valleys and tropical lowland departments of Beni and Pando.

Malnutrition levels are much higher among the poorest families.[2] Children in the poorest households have levels of malnutrition six times that of children born into the richest 20 per cent of households.[3] Families of indigenous Quechua, Aymara, Guaraní and other peoples are far more affected by chronic malnutrition (28 per cent) than non-indigenous children (16 per cent).[4] Many of Bolivia's minorities, such as the 38,600 *afrobolivianos* are also particularly affected by high levels of malnutrition. More than half of Bolivian children suffer from micronutrient deficiencies, particularly of iron, iodine and Vitamin A, and 80 per cent of children between six and 23 months suffer from anaemia. Child mortality levels remain high, but regional disparities are severe – a baby born in the richer department of Tarija is three times more likely to live to see its first birthday than a baby born in the poorer department of Oruro.[5]

Although Bolivia has vast natural wealth from mineral and energy resources, the majority of the population is still extremely poor. Nearly two thirds of Bolivians live below the national poverty line.[6] Around 35 per cent, mostly indigenous peoples, live in extreme poverty without access to a minimum *canasta basica*. This means that they cannot afford even the minimum amount of calories every day to sustain a healthy life.[7] Poor families spend a large proportion of their total income on food and have limited access to adequate, sufficiently nutritious food.

As a result of changing trade patterns, many have become dependent on cheap, low-quality imported noodles, rather than nutritionally rich Bolivian staples such as quinoa (a highly nutritious indigenous grain). Extreme poverty is concentrated among indigenous communities (49 per cent), rather than non-indigenous people (24 per cent) and poverty levels are much higher in rural areas. The poorest are mostly subsistence farmers who struggle to survive on small plots of land or as agricultural labourers on pitiful wages. However, there are also high levels of urban poverty, as rapidly increasing rural–urban migration over the last 30 years has pushed millions into the cities, especially to El Alto.

The poorest regions are the altiplano and the central and southern valleys, where indigenous populations and *campesinos* (peasant farmers) are dominant. The poorest departments are Potosi and Chuquisaca, followed by Beni, La Paz and Oruro. More than 60 per cent of the largely indigenous populations of Potosi and Chuquisaca are extremely poor and suffering from hunger, compared to fewer than 25 per cent of people living in Santa Cruz.[8] Santa Cruz and Cochabamba have the lowest levels of poverty, but rural and indigenous people in these areas remain very poor. Overall, the situation of the poor improved during the mid-1990s, but started to deteriorate again in 1999 and poverty levels are now back to those of 1990.[9] A sharp increase in inequality since the mid-1990s means that in Bolivia inequality is now among the greatest in the world, similar to levels seen in Brazil.[10] Nine out of ten Bolivians feel that such great inequality is socially unjust, and is the source of rising social conflict.[11]

In Bolivia's *Occidente* (or west), the poor and hungry are mostly indigenous people, living in rural areas and struggling to survive from small-scale and subsistence farming on the cold, windy plateau of the altiplano. The lands of the altiplano are difficult to cultivate given extremely high altitudes of 3500–4000 metres. Agriculture is dependent on uncertain rainfall and relies on crops that can survive the harsh climate. Most people have very small landholdings, barely large enough for subsistence. Landless families in rural areas are even poorer and work as sharecroppers or wage labourers, if they cannot afford to rent land. Most agricultural work is done by hand with little access to machinery even to plough the fields, and there has been little investment in irrigation and other infrastructure that would allow increased production. Highland families grow potatoes, oca (another edible tuber), fava beans and quinoa. Many keep animals such as sheep or llamas, but many of their products are sold rather than eaten, because of the need to generate income. This has resulted in very high levels of malnutrition, especially micronutrient malnutrition, among altiplano families because their diet is inadequate.

We found that the reason why many altiplano families are so poor is because the prices they receive for their crops are often below the cost of production. Unable to afford transport to markets, most are therefore dependent on intermediary traders who come to the villages with a truck to buy their milk or crops, but pay extremely low prices, while making large profits by selling the products in the cities.[12] The lack of transport for many remote families, widely dispersed across the altiplano is a serious obstacle to food security, as is the lack of inputs that would allow them to better utilize the land. Altiplano farming families are also vulnerable to a very uncertain climate. Whole crops can be wiped out by one heavy frost, hailstorm or summer drought. Climate change and the El Niño phenomenon appear to be causing an increase in extreme climatic events, with less rain and higher temperatures affecting productivity.[13] We spoke with Aymara families of Jintamarca near Guaqui, close to Lake Titicaca, who lost their entire potato crop after three days of heavy frost. As this is their staple food, they worried how they would survive and how they would be able to afford seeds to plant for the next harvest.

The harsh agricultural conditions, and past failures to invest in small-scale agriculture, account for the rapid urbanization of Bolivia, as millions have migrated to the cities, or abroad. Many also leave the land to toil in Bolivia's mineral mines – we saw at first hand the intolerable working conditions in the cooperative mines of Oruro, where both men and women miners work long shifts. Others leave in search of new lands in the tropical hills or lowlands of the Yungas and the valleys. These migrants or *colonizadores* clear small patches of forest for subsistence agriculture, growing crops adapted to the warmer climate, including yuca, rice, maize, bananas, cacao, coffee and coca. However, efforts to eradicate coca have also been accompanied by much violence and have angered many indigenous Bolivians, who see coca eradication not only as depriving them of livelihoods when the alternatives are bleak, but also as an attack on their cultural heritage.

The difficult conditions of subsistence agriculture stand in strong contrast to the modern agro-industrial plantations and cattle ranches that dominate Bolivia's eastern lowlands. While the vast majority of small farmers have low-quality landholdings of between less than half a hectare and five hectares, landholdings in the *Oriente* are characterized by huge extensions of over 5000 hectares, concentrated in the hands of a few powerful families. These extensions are highly developed, often highly mechanized and are focused on export-oriented agricultural production, including soya, sugar cane, sunflower oils and cattle. Mechanization means that these extensions provide much lower employment than small-scale farming and agricultural labourers are paid very low and insecure wages.[14] We were shocked to hear that many agricultural workers on large estates still work in feudal conditions of semi-slavery, or debt-bondage, particularly the Guaraní indigenous population of the Chaco. According to the *Defensor del Pueblo*, these workers are held in debt bondage or bound by duties to landholders and do not receive salaries for their work.

Although Bolivia does not suffer from a shortage of land,[15] inequalities in landholdings have been a key factor in deepening social conflict across the country. The vast majority of poor small-scale farmers together own only 1.4 per cent of the cultivated land, while the wealthiest 7 per cent of Bolivian landlords own 85 per cent of the cultivated land.[16] Although a 1953 agrarian reform programme broke up the traditional feudalistic *haciendas* in the highlands and the valleys, this system re-emerged in the eastern lowlands as huge tracts of land were granted to powerful political supporters of the regimes in power between the 1960s and the 1990s.[17] Inequalities of land ownership are particularly high in the southern state of Tarija, where 92 per cent of land is owned by 8 per cent of agricultural producers, while 80 per cent of the region's *campesinos* have no land title.[18] In the eastern lowlands, lands have been granted to indigenous peoples within the Tierra Comunitaria de Orígen (TCO) framework, but this has also been complicated and has not always provided secure tenure, given overlapping claims by settlers and large landowners which have generated further conflict.

Bolivia is also frequently faced with natural disaster. Many people we interviewed suggested that Bolivia is increasingly affected by unpredictable natural disasters as a result of climate change. In early 2007, Bolivia faced its worst floods in 25 years. While drought, hail and freezing temperatures devastated staple crops in the highlands, torrential rains and overflowing rivers caused serious floods in eight of Bolivia's nine departments, resulting in the deaths of 54 people and affecting the lives and livelihoods of over 450,000 people.[19] In the worst affected areas in Beni and Santa Cruz, at least 71,000 hectares of crops were destroyed and more than 11,000 cattle were lost in the rising water; at least 16,000 people were displaced from their homes in Santa Cruz. The Government declared a national emergency on 18 January 2007 and requested support from the international community on 7 February 2007. At the time of our visit, the floods had mostly receded, but thousands of people were left to rebuild their homes and livelihoods.

Millions of Bolivians continue to lack access to safe drinking water, as well as water for subsistence agriculture. The situation is particularly severe in rural areas, where up to 43 per cent of the population has no access to safe drinking water and 75 per cent have no sanitation,[20] the vast majority of whom are indigenous peoples.[21] The quality of existing drinking water is also problematic, given a continued lack of adequate water treatment. Water privatization under Bolivia's previous administrations aimed to improve the water quality and provision but gave rise to serious social conflict. In Cochabamba, water prices rose by 100–200 per cent after privatization.[22] For many families, this meant that up to half of their monthly income was spent on paying for water. Massive public protests broke out in February 2000, but the then President declared martial law and called for a state of emergency for 90 days. During this period, most civil rights were suspended, permitting the arrest and confinement of protesters without a warrant, restrictions on travel and political activity and a curfew, banning gatherings of more than four people and severely limiting freedom of the press. After persistent public protests, the Government was forced to back down and to break its contract with the private company. In a similar case of privatization in El Alto, a concession to a multinational company was halted in 2007, following widespread protests after communities were deprived of access to sufficient water as a result of increases in water prices and connection fees.

15.2.2 Social crisis and recent developments in Bolivia

The social crisis in Bolivia has its roots in a long history of extreme poverty and social exclusion of the majority of Bolivia's population. The history of colonial exploitation is still etched in the minds of Bolivia's poor, especially the indigenous population. Much of the Spanish empire's wealth was financed by Bolivia's rich deposits of silver and tin, mined by indigenous people forced to work as slaves. Thousands of indigenous peoples were also forced to work under nearly feudal conditions on large agricultural estates, denied the right to freely chosen work, the right to education and the right to vote. Even today, the vast majority of Bolivians are still extremely poor and struggling to feed their families and they question why they do not seem to benefit from Bolivia's wealth of natural and mineral resources. Protests have centred on opposition to privatization which is perceived as a new form of colonialism and the appropriation of Bolivia's wealth by foreign investors.

Bolivia's wealth of mineral resources includes silver, tin, zinc, tungsten, antimony, iron and gold, as well as oil and natural gas. Since the discovery of vast reserves in the 1990s, natural gas now dominates the country's exports (43 per cent of total exports in 2006). Natural gas and oil production have been increasing. Bolivia produces about 355 billion cubic feet of natural gas and has the second largest reserve of natural gas in South America, after Venezuela (with reserves estimated at between 24 and 53 trillion cubic feet).[23] More than 85 per cent of these natural gas reserves are located in the department of Tarija, with a further 10.6 per cent in Santa Cruz and 2.5 per cent in Cochabamba. Bolivia also has substantial oil reserves of at least 440 million barrels (proven reserves as of 2006) and produces about 64,000 barrels per day. Most of the oil is also located in south-western Bolivia, with 80 per cent in the department of Tarija. Rising international prices of natural gas and oil promise rising revenues, but the privatization of oil and gas reserves under the Sanchez de Lozada Government in the mid-1990s led to a decline in revenues accruing to the State. Following privatization, the Brazilian company, Petrobras, and Spanish Repsol-YPF became the dominant producers of both oil and natural gas in Bolivia, but the French company,

Total, Exxon of the United States of America, British Petroleum and British Gas, and other consortia are also involved in Bolivia.

However, growing public disillusionment with privatization led to protests against plans to export natural gas to the United States and Mexico via a Chilean pipeline and escalated into the 'gas war' of September and October 2003. During a month of social protests and blockades, social movements, representing indigenous peoples, peasant farmers and workers, fought street battles against the authorities. These protests were forcibly repressed and at least 59 people were killed in September and October 2003.[24] President Sanchez de Lozada was forced to resign from office and his Vice-President Carlos Mesa assumed the Presidency. Social movements drew up a list of demands called the October Agenda. They demanded the establishment of a Constituent Assembly to draw up a new constitution to re-establish participatory democracy as well as demanding the nationalization of Bolivia's national resources so that Bolivian wealth could finally benefit the Bolivian people.

Mesa acceded to these demands, including revising the constitution and holding a binding referendum on the export of natural gas. The Bolivian people voted overwhelmingly in the referendum for the development of oil and gas resources and for the imposition of a 50 per cent tax on extraction on all multinational companies. In May 2005, Congress passed the 2005 Hydrocarbons Law which introduced a direct tax on hydrocarbons of 32 per cent, adding to the 18 per cent royalty already paid and requiring a total tax contribution of 50 per cent. This led to huge increases in revenue to the Bolivian State, as the new tax was imposed across the industry. However, when more than 80,000 protestors surrounded the presidential palace to demand the full nationalization of the gas industry, Mesa was in turn forced to resign.

The elections of December 2005 marked a turning point as Bolivians elected Evo Morales Ayma with an absolute majority of almost 54 per cent, unprecedented in Bolivian elections. He was sworn in on 22 January 2006, the first indigenous President in a nation with a majority indigenous population. Morales promised fundamental change for the large majority of Bolivians, especially indigenous peoples, long excluded from such simple freedoms as the freedom from hunger and poverty. He promised that 500 years of colonialism were now over and that sovereignty would be re-established over resources for the benefit of the Bolivian people. On 1 May 2006 he announced the renationalization of the oil and natural gas industries. Under the terms of this 2006 nationalization decree (Decree 28701), foreign companies are not allowed to own the reserves (ownership is reserved for the State), but will be permitted to operate the fields for the Government. This affected mainly the production of Brazil's Petrobras in the largest gas fields of San Antonio and Sabalo, Spain's Repsol which operates the Margarity field, France's Total in Itau, and Britain's British Gas which operates in the La Vertiente, Escondido and Los Suris fields. Under new operational agreements signed in November 2006, the resources will formally lie in the hands of the Bolivian State gas company, Yacimientos Petrolíferos Fiscales Bolivianos (YPFB), but the foreign companies will operate as providers of services to YPFB and will be subject to new tax arrangements. Tax and royalties of 50 per cent of the income will be paid directly to the State, as well as a further tax, taking the total tax bill up to a maximum of 82 per cent, although when this is calculated after deduction of costs and investment, it is estimated that total tax bills will not exceed 60 per cent. All the foreign corporations have agreed to these demands and will continue to operate in Bolivia.

Under these new agreements successfully negotiated by the Government of President Evo Morales, there has been a massive increase in State revenues, which reached US$ 1.3 billion in 2006 and may reach US$ 1.5 billion in 2007, an enormous increase on revenues of only US$ 220 million in 2003.[25] This means that State revenues from oil and gas amounted to 9.7 per cent of GDP in 2006, compared to only 2.8 per cent in 2003.[26] The massive injection of revenue into State resources has already allowed the President to reverse a spiralling public deficit, reduce public debt and will allow increased investments in fighting hunger and poverty. Despite strong opposition from the traditional white and *mestizo* elites of the *Oriente*, Morales has publicly committed to make the fight against malnutrition, food insecurity, and poverty the key element of his agenda. Morales has announced that new expenditure will give priority to the Zero Malnutrition Programme. The 2007 National Development Plan also reflects commitments to sharply increase public expenditure, up to 14 per cent of GDP for the five-year period 2007–2012, compared to 10.5 per cent in 2006.[27]

Development expenditures at the local level will also increase as, under decentralization and the 2005 Hydrocarbons Law, two thirds of the proceeds of taxes and royalties from oil and gas will be transferred directly to Bolivia's regional departments (municipalities and *prefecturas*), which will see revenues rise to US$ 782 million in 2007 (compared to US$ 140 million in 2004).[28] The 2005 Law expressly establishes that resources from the hydrocarbon tax should be directed to health, education, roads and local development for employment generation. However, so far, there has been very little concrete investment at the local level and huge resources remain in bank accounts. There is a risk that under this decentralized revenue distribution, the central Government will not be able to ensure that municipalities prioritize expenditure on the Zero Malnutrition Programme or other programmes to meet the needs of the poorest. There is also a risk that the current distribution of these resources could contribute to increasing inequalities and conflicts between the regions. At present, the La Paz region receives only US$ 16 per capita compared to Pando which receives US$ 407 per head.[29] Allocating larger revenues to the producing regions may also generate conflict, as Tarija and Santa Cruz will receive larger revenues than any other region. Distribution of the hydrocarbon tax between regions is therefore a central and hotly debated issue which can only be resolved within the Constituent Assembly. Providing for transparency of expenditures and permitting participatory budgeting processes for expenditure decisions at the municipal and *prefectura* level will be essential.

These massive increases in government revenue will allow Bolivia, which has traditionally been dependent on international aid for its development, to finally take charge of its destiny and offer new hope to millions of poor and indigenous Bolivians that have remained excluded from Bolivia's wealth for so long.

15.3 Legal framework for the right to food in Bolivia

15.3.1 International obligations

Bolivia is party to the main international treaty that protects the right to food, the International Covenant on Economic, Social and Cultural Rights, and is therefore committed to realizing the right to food of its entire people. We noted that Bolivia has not reported recently on its realization of these rights to the CESCR and welcomed the Government's commitment to report soon to the Committee, with the support of international technical assistance. Bolivia has also ratified all the other key international human rights treaties relevant to the right to food, including the International Covenant on Civil and Political Rights (Article 6), the Convention on the Rights of the Child (Articles 24 and 27), the Convention on the Elimination of All Forms of Discrimination against Women (Articles 12 and 14) and the Additional Protocol to the American Convention on Human Rights in the Area of Economic, Social and Cultural Rights ('Protocol of San Salvador') (Article 12). This means that the Government of Bolivia is fully committed under international law to respect, protect and fulfil the right to food of all children, women and men in its territory.

Bolivia is also party to the ILO Convention No. 169 on Indigenous and Tribal Peoples (1989) which specifically protects the rights of indigenous peoples. Under this Convention, the Government is required to respect the rights of indigenous peoples to land and territories (Articles 13–17), including their collective aspects. These articles also require that indigenous peoples are not displaced from their lands, and that their rights to natural resources on their lands are safeguarded, including their right to participate in the use, management and conservation of these resources, and their right to be consulted and to assess any exploitation of resources on the land they own or possess. In Bolivia, Convention No. 169 has been adopted as part of domestic legislation (law 1257, 1991), like other international instruments. At the end of 2007, Bolivia was the first country to recognize as part of its domestic law the United Nations Declaration on the

Rights of Indigenous Peoples, adopted by the General Assembly in resolution 61/295.

15.3.2 Domestic constitutional and legislative framework

A Constituent Assembly was elected in July 2006, comprising 255 members, including 88 women, with the mandate to elaborate a new constitution. The new Constitution was adopted by the Constitutional Assembly on 14 December 2007 and by a popular referendum on 25 January 2009. The drafting of this new Constitution represented a unique opportunity for Bolivia to reaffirm the rights of those who have been historically excluded and oppressed. As the Vice-President Álvaro García Linera stated: 'this is the best moment to recreate and reinvent a new legal community in which all Bolivians will feel included'.[30] It also represented a unique opportunity for the right to food to be recognized as a fundamental human right of all Bolivians.

The new Constitution recognizes the right to food and the right to water as fundamental human rights of all Bolivians, with the correlative obligation of the State to guarantee food security, through safe, sufficient and adequate food for the whole population (Article 16). It also recognizes the direct applicability of all human rights, including the rights to health, housing, labour, basic services and social security, the specific rights of the most vulnerable, including children and the elderly, and the rights of the original indigenous and peasant people and nations, including their collective rights to land and territories. It also states that public expenses and national investments will be allocated, through participatory mechanisms, on a priority basis to social issues including food policies (Article 321); that genetically modified organisms are prohibited (Article 256); and that international human rights instruments proclaiming more favourable rights than the constitution shall take precedence (Article 257).[31]

Bolivia's legislative framework does not include a national law on the right to food or on food security, which would be important in determining the objectives and responsibilities of the relevant ministries and ensuring their coordinated activities. However, there are a large number of other laws, decrees and regulations that are of particular relevance for the realization of the right to food. This includes the *Ley de Reconducción Comunitaria de la Reforma Agraria* (2006) which outlines the system for regulating collective land titles for indigenous territories and indigenous communities, land for small farmers, and land for industrial farming (*empresa agropecuaria*). The law also established the National Institute for Agrarian Reform (INRA), charged with identifying and reclaiming unproductive or illegally obtained landholdings for redistribution to the landless. The *Ley del Medio Ambiente* (1992) protecting natural resources and the rights of indigenous people and farming communities against the negative activities of industrial and extractive companies and the *Ley de Fomento de la Lactancia Materna y Comercialización de sus Sucedáneos* (2006) promoting exclusive maternal breastfeeding for children under six months and prohibiting marketing of substitutes, in accordance with the International Code of Marketing of Breastmilk Substitutes, are also of particular relevance for the protection of right to food.

On the issue of water, the Government promulgated the *Ley de Promoción y Apoyo al Sector de Riego para la Producción Agropecuaria y Forestal* in October 2004, better known as the *Ley de Riego*. This law recognizes traditional water rights and uses and guarantees the right to water for irrigation for indigenous and farming communities. In February 2006, the new Government created a Ministry of Water to coordinate and oversee water issues through Law No. 3351. When we visited the country, the Ministry was in the process of drafting framework legislation on drinking water and sanitation systems which would expressly recognize access to water and water services for human consumption as basic human rights.

15.3.3 Access to justice and human rights institutions

Bolivia has a complex legal system, which includes State law and courts at the municipal, departmental and national levels, as well as customary law and traditional justice in areas of indigenous peoples. The Constitutional Tribunal has a special mandate to protect and enforce the constitution. The new Constitution, as well as the former Constitution, guarantees free access to justice for the poor and victims of a violation of a fundamental right can use the procedure of *amparo* (right to request a review of the constitutionality of a judgment or act) to claim their rights before the superior courts at the departmental level and the Constitutional Tribunal. In practice, however, access to justice for victims of violations of human rights, including the right to food, is limited.[32] Problems include the non-application of international human rights treaties and conventions by judges, corruption and the lack of independence of the judiciary. Indigenous peoples have particular difficulties in obtaining access to justice, given discrimination, the lack of legal interpreters, and the non-recognition of customary law and indigenous legal authorities. The compatibility and complementarity of modern and customary laws and systems of justice could be improved by the adoption of the draft law on the administration of justice of the original indigenous people and peasants community, in discussion at the national Congress, and by the adoption of the new constitution, which is very progressive in terms of access to justice in cases of violations of human rights.

In 1997, reforms to improve the efficiency and accountability of the judiciary and to broaden access to justice led to the establishment of three new institutions: the Constitutional Tribunal, the Judicial Council and the Office of the Ombudsman (*Defensor del Pueblo*). The Office of the Ombudsman is independent and is currently headed by the courageous and outspoken Ombudsman, Waldo Albarracín Sánchez. The Ombudsman has improved protection for vulnerable groups and individuals through mediation, conciliation, quasi-judicial decisions and legal assistance, as well as monitoring violations. His office has also put a special emphasis on many issues related to the right to food, including the right to land, labour rights, the right to a healthy environment, the rights of indigenous people, the rights of children and the rights of women. In view of the prospect of a new constitution that recognizes the right to food and the right to water as fundamental human rights, we hope that this focus will continue and that the office will be provided with adequate human and financial resources.

15.4 Policy framework for the right to food

15.4.1 Government policies and institutions

We were impressed by the personal commitment of President Evo Morales to the realization of the right to food. Fighting malnutrition has been made a key priority of his Government, through its Zero Malnutrition Programme, as well as other initiatives to promote food security and food sovereignty, land reform and the rights of indigenous peoples that should contribute to the realization of the right to food for all Bolivians.

The Zero Malnutrition Programme focuses on eradicating malnutrition among children under the age of five (with special emphasis on children up to the age of two, as well as pregnant women in poor areas), aiming to arrest the vicious cycle of malnutrition that limits their physical and intellectual development. The Ministry of Health is charged with implementing the programme, using a multisectoral approach which recognizes the multiple causes of malnutrition and food insecurity. This will address all the factors that limit physical and economic access to food – including lack of nutritional information, the high prevalence of diarrhoeal diseases given the lack of access to safe drinking water, discrimination and the lack of access to land and other productive resources. In April 2006, the institutional framework for fighting hunger was strengthened through the establishment of an intersectoral coordinating technical body of the National Council for Food and Nutrition (CONAN), which brings together all the relevant Ministries. CONAN's technical committee has made the promotion of the right to food one of its key priorities, elaborating new projects, such as the new draft *Ley del Desayuno Escolar*, to be implemented by departmental and municipal authorities.

During our mission, we welcomed the efforts of the Government to attempt to redistribute revenues in favour of the poorest groups of society, including children and the elderly. The Government's Supreme Decree No. 28899 of October 2006 set up a social programme called *Bono Juancito Pinto* which grants 200 bolivianos per school year to schoolchildren so that they can buy school materials. This programme aims to support poor families, allowing them to supplement their meagre budget to buy additional foodstuffs. It is reported that in 2007 this programme benefited more than 1 million children from over 13,000 schools. In addition, the Government recently approved the establishment of a social programme for the elderly, called *Renta Vitalicia Dignidad*, to be financed from the income tax from hydrocarbons. This programme aims to grant 200 bolivianos to each person over the age of 60 not currently receiving any type of pension. It is envisaged that the programme will reach approximately 800,000 persons.

We found that there was no comprehensive food security policy yet in place, but the Ministry of Agriculture has been charged with developing policies and regulatory legislation on food security and food sovereignty. The Minister of Agriculture informed us that there will be a new focus on food sovereignty. This will prioritize local production and will invest in small-scale family agriculture. The Minister believes that this will be the first time in Bolivia's history that the Government's efforts will focus primarily on small-scale agriculture, rather than on measures to support large-scale agro-industry. Given the importance of agricultural livelihoods to millions of Bolivia's poor, this new focus will have a positive impact on the realization of the right to food for Bolivia's small farmers.

In May 2006, the Government also launched a programme to revitalize land reform in Bolivia under the responsibility of INRA (*Instituto Nacional de Reforma Agraria* or National Agrarian Reform Institute). This will improve access to land for *campesinos*, communities and rural families. It will also give priority to eliminating the feudal practices of bonded labour (which still exist in the *Oriente*), as well as recognizing traditional forms of land tenure and restituting the lands of indigenous communities. The programme aims to speed up the process of land regularization to clarify existing land titles. In addition, INRA has been granted new powers to allocate existing public lands to landless *campesinos*, and to expropriate land for redistribution if this is unproductive and held for no productive economic or social use.

In June 2006, the Government also presented a new National Development Plan that is focused on reducing extreme poverty and inequality and redressing centuries of social exclusion and discrimination against indigenous peoples. The Plan sets concrete objectives, including reducing the percentage of the population living in poverty, from 58.9 per cent to 49.7 per cent and those living in extreme poverty from 34.5 per cent to 27.2 per cent by 2011, as well as reducing inequality. The minimum wage was also increased by 18.6 per cent to address extremely low salaries, although this is very difficult to enforce as 66 per cent of Bolivia's workers are engaged in the informal sector.

The institutional and policy framework for access to water has also been substantially strengthened with the creation of the new Ministry of Water. Given widespread social protests against privatization, the establishment of this Ministry is seen as key for elaborating a coherent national water strategy, even though municipalities will retain responsibilities in their regions. A new National Water Plan has been elaborated and the Government has announced concrete objectives to ensure access to drinking water for 1.9 million people and sanitation for 2 million people by 2010. The framework legislation governing access to drinking water and sanitation currently being developed will explicitly recognize access to water and water services for human consumption as a human right. The new law will also set out mechanisms to regulate the quality of water and sanctions for water pollution caused by industry or mining.

15.4.2 United Nations specialized agencies and bilateral assistance

The United Nations country team has also agreed in its development assistance framework (UNDAF) to support the Government's Zero Malnutrition Programme and other programmes that promote the right to food within the framework of its support to food sovereignty.[33] A joint programme on malnutrition brings together WFP, FAO, UNICEF, the Pan American Health Organization (PAHO), UNFPA and the United Nations Industrial Development Organization (UNIDO) and emphasizes nutritional education, supplementary feeding with fortified food and access to water, as well as promoting food security and food sovereignty. FAO is developing a specific programme to support the right to food. WFP is also providing emergency food assistance to victims of the recent floods and other emergencies and, in accordance with Government guidelines, 80 per cent of WFP's food aid is purchased locally. We visited one impressive WFP and FAO programme which works with the municipality of El Alto on nutritional security, constructing family vegetable greenhouses, and promoting appropriate technologies that allow plants to flourish at an altitude of 4000 metres, even in freezing winters.

Bolivia also receives important assistance from bilateral development agencies. Switzerland's bilateral assistance programme for example, through the Swiss Development Cooperation, has made working with Bolivia a key priority and has dedicated CHF 26 million to a variety of programmes, including projects on food security and malnutrition. Cuba assists Bolivia through financing the building of 26 hospitals in the poorest regions. Cuban doctors have also been sent to assist thousands of poor Bolivian families who have not previously had access to medical treatment.

15.4.3 Social movements and non-governmental organizations

Social movements, indigenous movements, women's movements, trade unions and civil society organizations are a powerful force in Bolivia and have been the driving force behind public protests for greater social justice and equal rights for all Bolivians. Civil society movements and organizations have pushed for more direct forms of participation in government where the people have a greater voice and role in policymaking. This has become possible with the election of President Evo Morales who has committed to opening up policy-making to participation and focusing on eradicating extreme poverty and malnutrition.

Human rights organizations have also had an important impact, with the *Capítulo Boliviano de Derechos Humanos, Democracia y Desarrollo* and the *Asamblea Permanente de Derechos Humanos de Bolivia* (APDHB) monitoring human rights in Bolivia. Until recently most human rights organizations have not traditionally worked on economic, social and cultural rights, but this is now changing as human rights and development organizations have come together in putting forward proposals to the Constituent Assembly. For example, a network of 125 organizations under the umbrella of the *Asociación de Instituciones de Promoción y Educación* (AIPE) has drawn up a proposal to include the right to adequate food in the new constitution, after conducting awareness-raising and consultations across the country.[34] Organizations working with *Agua Sustentable* have also advocated national laws on water issues and the inclusion of the right to water in the constitution.[35]

There are also many social and development NGOs contributing to the realization of the right to food in Bolivia. We had the opportunity to visit two schools in Oruro which provide 280 children aged between 5 and 12 from extremely poor families with access to daily food and basic education. The schools are directed by Julia and Fernando Sandalio who receive financial support from Emmaus France and Emmaus Switzerland. The French NGO *Voix Libre* finances daily food and basic education for more than 15,000 children from poor mining families so that they are not forced into child labour in the mines.

15.5 Main findings and concerns

15.5.1 Progressive realization of the right to food

Given its commitments under international and domestic law to the right to food, the Government of Bolivia has a legal obligation to ensure the progressive realization of the right to food over time, to the maximum of its available resources.

During our mission, we welcomed the positive progress made in reducing malnutrition and poverty, but were concerned that the situation of malnutrition and food insecurity in Bolivia remains grave. Chronic malnutrition of a large proportion of Bolivia's infant children is of most concern, as they may be permanently affected by stunted physical and intellectual development. Malnutrition levels fell from 28.3 per cent to 24.2 per cent between 1994 and 2003, but there have been recent signs of regression, particularly in the departments of Potosi, Beni and Pando.[36] Although infant mortality rates have fallen, Bolivia still has the second-highest infant mortality rate in Latin America.[37] High levels of extreme poverty affecting about 35 per cent of the population (and more than two thirds of people living in some regions) means that millions of Bolivians remain so poor that they cannot afford sufficient food to meet daily calorific requirements. Although there has been some progress over the last 10 years, it has been very slow. In some regions the situation is far worse, such as in Potosi and Chuquisaca, where the number of people living in extreme poverty remains well above 60 per cent.

We were also concerned to find that before 2006, the maximum of available resources had not been invested in guaranteeing the right to food for all Bolivians. Expenditure has not focused on effective nutritional programmes or improving the productivity of small-scale agriculture. Therefore we particularly welcomed the commitment of this Government to devoting greater resources to fighting malnutrition, food insecurity and poverty. We were very encouraged by the new tax arrangements under the Hydrocarbon Law in 2005 and the 2006 Presidential Decree, given the massive increases in revenue that have swelled the Government budget and the fact that the Zero Malnutrition programme, along with other similar programmes, will be a priority for expenditure. Given decentralization and the fact that local municipalities and *prefecturas* receive 60 per cent of this tax directly, we encouraged a coherent strategy across the different regions to encourage all municipalities to ensure that priority for expenditure is given to addressing malnutrition and food insecurity.

15.5.2 Violations of the right to food

Given its commitments to the right to food, Bolivia has the obligation to respect, protect and fulfil the right to food, without discrimination. During our mission, we were concerned to receive verbal reports from a number of organizations on violations of the right to food, particularly related to the displacement and eviction of families from their lands, the persistence of bonded labour and failure to pay minimum wages, and the pollution of water resources and contamination of fish stocks. However we were surprised that we received information on very few documented cases of specific violations during our visit. We believe that this may be due not so much to the lack of cases, but rather because most cases are not recorded as there are still very few organizations working from a right to food perspective in Bolivia. This suggests an urgent need for training to develop a better understanding of the right to food within the broader context of economic, social and cultural rights. We did receive details of a number of documented cases from the Office of the Ombudsman and civil society organizations relating to specific cases of violations, as detailed below.

Failure to prevent contamination of water sources and agricultural lands

In the departments of Potosi and Oruro, several communities are reported to have complained officially since 2002 of the water contamination affecting their land and livestock, as a result of the activities of the mining project Kori Kollo. Acid drainage and heavy metals deriving from mining operations have reportedly severely contaminated water resources. High levels of cyanide have been recorded in the soil, reportedly contributing to high levels of mortality and malformation in sheep and the contamination of soil, reducing the productivity of the land.[38] This has reportedly resulted in the loss of 50 per cent of livestock, affecting the livelihoods of farming communities dependent on selling milk and cheese products. Although local state authorities ordered an environmental impact assessment to be carried out, this order was still to be implemented when we visited Bolivia.[39] This may amount to a violation if the Government has failed in its duty to protect communities against the activities of third parties that have negatively affected the rights of these communities to adequate food.

Approximately 100 indigenous communities in the departments of Potosi, Chuquisaca and Tarija are also reportedly affected by the contamination of the basin of the Pilcomayo River by the extractive industry. Affected communities have reported that the impact of such water contamination over the years has caused 80 per cent loss of agricultural production, 60 per cent loss of livestock and 90 per cent loss of fish, greatly affecting people's access to sufficient and adequate food and means for its procurement.[40] We have been informed that the Office of the Ombudsman will conduct an inquiry into the contamination of the basin of the Pilcomayo River and recommend the appropriate remedial measures to be taken by the Government.

Failure to eliminate conditions of bonded labour

We received reports that forced labour, including situations of debt bondage, is still practised in some sectors in Bolivia, including the sugar cane industry, the Brazil nut industry and on private ranches (*haciendas*) in the region of the Chaco. The majority of labourers are held in some form of debt bondage. Estimates indicate that in 2003 there were approximately 21,000 forced labourers, including women and children, in the sugar cane industry in the Santa Cruz area and between 5000 and 6000 people became forced labourers on a permanent or semi-permanent basis in the Brazil nut industry in the Pando and Beni (province of Vaca Diez) regions.[41] Of particular concern is the situation of forced labour that the Guaraní people have to endure on some private ranches in the provinces of Santa Cruz, Chuquisaca and Tarija in the Chaco region. The ILO estimates that 7000 people from the Guaraní indigenous group are held in forced labour although the Government's figures in 1999 referred to 3179 people (578 families living on 106 ranches). They are held in debt bondage and in some cases threats and violence are common to prevent them from leaving the ranches. As they are paid extremely low wages which do not cover their basic living costs, they are forced to rely on credit from their employers. In addition, women and children are expected to work but are not paid at all. The Guaraní families on these ranches are rarely given any land to cultivate their own crops.

Failure to regulate advertising of milk formulas

While national law and policy promote breastfeeding to fight under-nutrition of babies and infants, this is reportedly being undermined by aggressive marketing by corporations promoting milk formulas that suggests that these formulas are more nutritious than breast milk. We received documented information of the persistence of aggressive marketing which contravened the national *Ley de Fomento a la Lactancia Materna y Comercialización de sus Sucedáneos* as well as the international standards encoded in the International Code of Marketing of Breast-milk Substitutes. We were informed that much of the obvious publicity by corporations would be banned after the adoption of the new regulation concretizing the national law.

Failure to provide adequate food and nutrition in prisons

We visited the prison of San Pedro in La Paz. We were alarmed by the nutritional status of many detainees in the prison, as the nutritional quality of the food does not meet international standards. The Government reached the same conclusion after a report was issued recognizing that many people in the prisons of San Pedro, Miraflores, Chonchocoro and Obrajes are underweight. Recently, the Government increased the daily payment for food per prisoner from 3.5 to 4.5 Bolivianos per day. This should improve the situation, but it is still essential to improve the nutritional value of the food distributed to prisoners.

15.5.3 Obstacles to the realization of the right to food

Clear obstacles to realizing the right to food of all Bolivians include discrimination, social exclusion and high levels of inequality, as well as the legacies of a colonial social structure. Previous administrations have prioritized an exclusionary economic model that has marginalized the poor and indigenous and failed to challenge the structures of clientelism and patronage of the traditional ruling elite. Bolivia has undertaken more economic reforms in line with the Washington Consensus than almost all developing countries.[42] However, the economic reforms and shock therapy policies imposed since 1985 have focused on generating export-led economic growth, rather than on poverty reduction. Liberalization, privatization and fiscal reform have been successful in controlling inflation, but have not delivered on the promises of trickle down to the majority of Bolivians. Most economic growth and foreign investment has occurred in export sectors such as oil, gas, mining and agro-industry, but these provide little employment in the economy and therefore have not contributed sufficiently to poverty reduction. Oil and gas now account for over 50 per cent of Bolivia's export earnings, but employ only 1 per cent of the population.[43] The approval of the hydrocarbons tax will therefore allow for greater equity in the distribution of Bolivia's natural wealth.

The promotion of investment in the export-oriented agro-industry has also failed to benefit the vast majority of small subsistence farmers. Despite the importance of small-scale agriculture in generating employment, there has been little investment in this kind of agriculture, particularly in the altiplano. Trade liberalization has also left small farmers facing unfair competition from the dumping of highly subsidized imports, including wheat, driving rapid urbanization over the last 30 years.[44] The lack of a human rights culture that recognizes the economic, social and cultural rights of all Bolivians appears to have been behind the demands of social movements for a new Constitution. The adoption of a new Constitution that protects the human right to adequate food and all human rights for all therefore marks a new start.

15.6 Conclusions and recommendations

In his report on the mission to Bolivia, presented to the Human Rights Council in March 2008, Jean Ziegler made the following conclusions and recommendations.

He found that Bolivia was in a dramatic moment of transition. Concrete change is essential to resolve serious social crisis and past failures to eradicate malnutrition and extreme poverty. He was impressed by the efforts of the current Government to focus attention on the tragedy of malnutrition and extreme poverty that affects such a large proportion of the population. He welcomed the President's success in increasing the budget of the Government to ensure that all Bolivians benefit from its oil and gas exports. Redistribution of some of the benefits of Bolivia's natural wealth should enable the Government to begin to redress expanding inequalities and help to realize the right to food for all Bolivians. The adoption of the new Constitution that recognizes the right to food of all Bolivians represents an important step towards this change.

He then offered the following recommendations:

(a) The new Constitution, recognizing the right to food and the right to water as fundamental rights, should be adopted. It would provide a useful framework for the right to food in Bolivia. The practical implications of its main principles, such as the recognition of the direct applicability of all human rights, including the rights to food and water, and of the international human rights treaties, should be explained through a national campaign.

(b) Framework laws on the right to food and the right to water should be adopted to fully entrench these rights, and allow for the identification of concrete goals, monitoring mechanisms and the allocation of responsibilities across all relevant ministries. Due consideration should be given to the CESCR General Comment No. 12 (1999) on the right to adequate food (Article 11) and the FAO Voluntary Guidelines on the Right to Food. All relevant actors should participate in this process, including the Government, the Office of the Ombudsman, civil society, including social movements, and all the United Nations agencies.

(c) Mechanisms of empowerment and accountability, and the possibility for victims to have access to effective remedies in case of violations of the right to food should be strengthened. The administration of justice should be more transparent and available for victims, including indigenous communities. The Office of the Ombudsman should create a special unit working on the right to food and the right to water, provided with adequate human and financial resources. The Government should take due account of all the recommendations of the Ombudsman.

(d) A comprehensive national development strategy for food security and food sovereignty, framed around the right to food, should be elaborated and implemented. The strategy should reflect the obligations of the State to respect, protect, and fulfil the right to food without discrimination. The strategy should focus on eradicating malnutrition and on reversing the extreme inequality that has resulted from export-orientated trade in agriculture, by investing in small-scale peasant agriculture, implementing effective agrarian reform and protecting the rights of peasants and indigenous peoples over their land, water and own seeds.

(e) The Government should accord the maximum of available resources to ensure that constant progress is made in combating the tragedy of malnutrition and extreme poverty. This must include directing new resources from the hydrocarbon tax directly to the Zero Malnutrition Programme and the programme *Renta Vitalicia Dignidad*, both at the national level and at the municipal level. As 60 per cent of the increased State revenues from the direct hydrocarbon tax is allocated directly to municipalities and *prefecturas*, these regional administrations must be encouraged to direct these funds towards these programme priorities. The progressive realization of the right to food should be monitored as part of the Government's national policy. Indicators should include not only statistics on malnutrition, but also statistics on under-nourishment, poverty and inequality.

(f) The eradication of slave-like conditions of bonded labour must be a priority and all labourers should be freed from their debt or other forms of bondage. The programme of agrarian reform should also be speeded up to regularize land titles, improve protection of the lands of indigenous communities and improve access to land for *campesinos*, communities and rural families.

16
Cuba

16.1 Introduction

We (Jean Ziegler, with Christophe Golay and Claire Mahon) visited Cuba from 28 October to 6 November 2007.[1] During our visit, we were honoured to be received by Carlos Lage Dávila, Vice-President of the State Council, Ricardo Alarcón de Quesada, President of the People's Power National Assembly, and Felipe Pérez Roque, Minister for Foreign Affairs. We benefited from constructive dialogue with other government ministers, including the Ministers of Agriculture, Economy and Planning, Education, Food Industry, Fisheries, Internal Trade, Labour and Social Security, and with senior staff of other ministries. In addition, we held useful meetings with representatives of United Nations agencies and the diplomatic community.

We also appreciated meetings with civil society organizations and academics. We travelled extensively in the east of the country, including in Holguín, Granma and Santa Clara, where we met the Presidents of the Provincial Assemblies and other senior provincial government officials. We also visited other locations such as Santa Cruz del Norte and Pinar del Río, where we met the President of the Provincial Assembly and other officials. In addition, we met with members of various types of agriculture production cooperatives and visited shops for subsidized food, health care centres for pregnant women, day care centres for the elderly, a hospital and two prisons.

The purpose of the mission was to examine the realization of the right to food in relation to Cuba's international and national commitments to respect, protect and fulfil this right. The mission took place at an important moment of transition in the relationship between Cuba and the Human Rights Council. In June 2007, the Council ended the mandate of the Personal Representative of the High Commissioner for Human Rights on the situation of human rights in Cuba. At the time, Cuba undertook commitments to collaborate with the Council. The invitation extended to the Special Rapporteur on the Right to Food was a clear illustration of these commitments. We welcomed the opportunity to visit Cuba and the commitments undertaken by the Government of Cuba on Human Rights Day (10 December) 2007, namely, that invitations will be extended to other special procedures and that Cuba will sign both of the key international human rights Covenants.

Cuba is a fascinating country and by far the largest of the Caribbean islands (110,860 km^2). It is covered by mountainous areas, such as the easterly Sierra Maestra, and Pico Turquino, the westerly Sierra de los Órganos, and the central Sierra de Trinidad. The rest is flat or rolling terrain. Forests cover 25 per cent of the land. The climate is semi-tropical. Cuba is subject to hurricanes, drought and floods. The population of 11.2 million people predominantly comprises Spanish and African descendants and a smaller group of Asian descendants. Cuba's economy has always been dependent on exported agricultural commodities (sugar and tobacco). Today, the most important export is nickel. A primary source of foreign income is tourism. The Cuban economy has suffered severely from the collapse of the Soviet bloc and the United States trade embargo. It has now emerged from a long 'special period'. With new opportunities for regional cooperation, including through the Bolivarian Alternative for the Americas (ALBA) with Venezuela, Bolivia and Nicaragua, Cuba has the potential to win 'the battle for life' that José Marti, the hero of the fight for independence, was calling for.

16.2 Malnutrition and food insecurity in Cuba

16.2.1 The current situation of malnutrition and food insecurity

Household food security has always been one of the highest priorities of the Government. In 1959, the Government decided that feeding its people was a matter of State responsibility. It established a subsidized national feeding programme designed to ensure that the entire population receives at least 50 per cent of the necessary nutritional requirements. Cuba does not produce enough food to feed its population and is reliant upon food imports. According to Vice-President Mr Carlos Lage Dávila, Cuba imports 54 per cent of the calories consumed and 64 per cent of the protein. It is difficult to grow all the food required in Cuba: tropical agriculture is difficult and cereals must be imported. This makes Cuba highly vulnerable to fluctuations in world food prices and changes in the policies of its major trading partners. For decades, Cuba has been significantly affected by the United States trade and financial embargo as well as the break-up of the Soviet Union. As a result, Cuba suffered a severe economic crisis in the 1990s, with significant food shortages affecting the whole population.

Despite these obstacles, there has been important progress in reducing malnutrition and hunger in Cuba since the early 1990s. Today, malnutrition is not considered a significant problem and the Government estimates that it affects less than 2 per cent of the population.[2] The WHO estimates that

2.3 per cent of children under the age of five suffer from grave or moderate undernourishment, one of the lowest figures in the developing world.[3] The corresponding figure was 3.9 per cent in 2000, and 0.4 per cent of these children were deemed severely underweight.[4] This is considered as a significant decrease since the 1990s. The number of people in the total population suffering from undernourishment has declined sharply, falling from 2 million in 1996 (18 per cent of the population), to 200,000 in 2002 (2.5 per cent).[5]

As the FAO has stated, this means that Cuba is one of the few countries in the developing world to achieve the objectives of the 1996 World Food Summit, that is, to halve the number of undernourished people by 2015.[6] Likewise, Cuba has probably already achieved Target 2 of Millennium Development Goal 1, namely, to reduce by half the proportion of people who suffer from hunger.

In 1995, the average Cuban's daily calorie intake was 1993 Kcal. This increased to 3279 Kcal in 2006 (the recommended average is 2400 Kcal).[7] Despite a high calorie count, the Cuban diet does not achieve the recommended nutritional intake for fats: in 2006 the fat content was 54.7 grams, as compared with the recommended rate of 75 g.[8] Protein intake is in line with recommended levels and has significantly increased since the 1990s, rising from 49.66 g in 1995 to 89.90 g in 2006. Data are not disaggregated to reflect the difference between vegetable and animal proteins, although in 2002 it was estimated that the average intake of animal proteins was below recommended levels.[9]

Inadequate diet is particularly a problem in the eastern provinces, where fat consumption levels are less than 50 per cent of the recommended daily intake. Carbohydrate consumption is relatively high and consumption of fruit and vegetables is low, creating mineral and vitamin deficiencies. In 1999, the Institute of Physical Planning and the WFP showed that five eastern provinces, Las Tunas, Holguín, Granma, Santiago de Cuba and Guantánamo, are the most vulnerable to food insecurity in the country. Recurrent droughts in these provinces create loss of harvests.

Throughout Cuba, the number of children with low birthweights has been decreasing, dropping from 9 per cent in 1993 to 5.9 per cent in 2004.[10] Infant mortality has fallen in Cuba, from 13.2 per thousand in 1990 to 5.3 in 2006. The mortality rate for children under five has declined (from 13 per thousand in 1990 to 7 in 2006), showing that Cuba is on track for attaining MDG 4.[11] However, it is estimated that 14–24 per cent of expectant mothers begin their pregnancy underweight, and weight increase during pregnancy is insufficient for 15.6 per cent of women.[12] These conditions affect children's low birthweight and subsequent nutritional status.

According to the WFP, approximately 40 per cent of children under the age of two and 30 per cent of expectant mothers suffer from iron-deficiency anaemia.[13] The situation is worse in the eastern provinces, where 29.1 per cent of children between 6 and 24 months and 42.6 per cent of children between 6 and 12 months suffer from anaemia.[14] Obesity has also become a risk factor of late: 13.5 per cent of children under five, 7.95 per cent of adult men and 15.4 per cent of women, suffer from obesity.[15] Finally, the number of deaths from diabetes has risen by 30 per cent since 2001.[16]

In Cuba, 95.6 per cent of the population has access to safe drinking water.[17] The National Institute of Hydraulic Resources (INRH) estimates that 75.3 per cent of Cubans have a water connection in their house, 15.1 per cent have easy access to water, and 5.2 per cent have access to a water public service. However, 4.4 per cent of the population, mainly isolated groups in mountainous regions, do not have regular access to water. The United Nations estimates that 98 per cent of urban dwellers and 95 per cent of rural residents have access to improved drinking water sources.[18]

Scant research is available on the level of poverty in Cuba. In 2006, the mean monthly wage in State-owned and mixed entities was 387 national pesos, a gradual but steady increase from 252 pesos in 2001.[19] However, the average in the eastern provinces of Santiago de Cuba, Guantánamo and Holguín is less.[20] The average also varies according to labour sectors, with the agricultural, forest, fisheries and hunting sector the third lowest. The purchasing power of the average salary is very limited and has been decreasing in recent years (although the nominal salary has increased). The NGO Welt Hunger Hilfe estimates that 80–90 per cent of family income is spent on food (as housing, health services and education are provided free of charge) and that a family of four people needs 1400 pesos per month to meet its basic needs. Approximately 60–70 per cent of Cubans rely on foreign currency remittances to buy food. Acting President Raúl Castro Ruz has confirmed that 'because of the extreme objective difficulties that we face, wages today are clearly insufficient to satisfy all needs'.[21]

Those particularly vulnerable to poverty and food insecurity in Cuba include people living in the eastern provinces, women, children and elderly. Female-headed households are particularly at risk of poverty and food insecurity. The share of households headed by women rose from 28.2 per cent in 1981 to 40.64 in 2002. The growing number of elderly people in Cuba also poses a threat to the stability of the food production system. With a robust life expectancy of 75 years for men and 78 years for women, Cuba faces the future challenge of providing food security with a declining agricultural workforce.

16.2.2 The dissolution of COMECON

Cuba joined the Council for Mutual Economic Support (COMECON) in 1972. The country relied on sugar and nickel to fund imports, particularly oil, from its Soviet trading partners. In 1989, Cuba imported 50 per cent of the population's calorie intake and 59 per cent of protein. From 1991, imports decreased by 75 per cent over four years, impacting significantly on food availability. A new economic strategy was needed to deal with what was officially named the 'Special Period'.

Gross Domestic Product (GDP) fell 33 per cent between 1989 and 1993, which made it difficult for the social system to function, reducing availability of goods, services and financial resources and affecting food security. Food availability in Cuba decreased substantially, as this affected food production and imports as well as the supply of food commodities distributed through the rationing system. Edible fat, animal protein and dairy products were the most affected among the staple food items.[22]

One of the key features of the Special Period was the damage to the agricultural and transportation sectors, which relied on oil from the former USSR. Production of meat and dairy products was severely affected due to the high dependency on fuel in the production process and farming methods. We visited the 'Unidad Básica de Produción Cooperativa' (UBPC) 'Francisco Suárez' in the Bayamo municipality, where 35 workers milk 826 cows daily by hand, involving long working days and low levels of milk production (5.2 litres per day per cow). Before the Special Period, this dairy farm, like many in Cuba, was mechanized and production levels were much higher.

Fertilizers and pesticides also became scarce during the Special Period, reducing agricultural productivity. In 2003, Cuba purchased 11 times less fertilizer than in 1989, 3.12 times less diesel and 11.1 times less chemicals.[23] The transport sector was left in disarray with no fuel and no spare parts.

The Government responded to these events by taking measures to promote agricultural recovery. In 1993, State farms were dismantled and turned into farming cooperatives (UBPCs). Supply-and-demand markets were created to enable people to purchase food outside government stores. Remittances from abroad and holdings of foreign currency were legalized. Self-employment was also authorized. We were impressed by the examples of creativity applied in dealing with the problems of the special period. For example, organic permaculture farming (*organopónico*) was developed in order to produce fruits and vegetables in private or communal gardens within the city areas without the need for fuel-based inputs. Produce from these *organopónicos* is sold directly to the consumers and in the free vegetable markets.

Another among the many examples of structural change is the drastic reduction of sugar cane production. Under COMECON, Cuba produced 7–8 million tons of sugar per year. Today, the production is around 1.2 million tons, mainly destined for internal consumption. More than 95 sugar mills have been closed and 1.3 million hectares have been converted to alternative production. The conversion process affected over 100,000 workers who have been assigned to other functions. We visited Empresa Agropecuaria 'Camilo Cienfuegos' in Santa Cruz del Norte, where we were received by Mr Ulises Rosales del Toro, Minister of Sugar Industries. This used to be one of the biggest sugar mills in Cuba, the former Hershey mill, and sugar cane used to cover around 12,000 hectares. Today, this land, where 2600 people live at present, is entirely devoted to the production of vegetables, fruit and cattle. The large sugar mill buildings have been converted into a ceramic factory and a pasta factory. We were told that in this case none of the more than 4000 workers (or their families) from the original sugar mill were displaced or lost their jobs.

16.2.3 The reinforcement of the United States embargo

The United States embargo, imposed in 1962, was extended in 1963 to prohibit travel, financial and commercial transactions with Cuba. Through the Torricelli Act (1992) and the Helms-Burton Act (1996), it has been further intensified to apply extraterritorially, making it difficult for companies to do business with both Cuba and the United States. According to the Cuban government, the embargo has cost the Cuban economy over US$ 89 billion since its introduction and resulted in US$ 258 million of losses in the food sector during May 2006 to April 2007.[24] The United States embargo has been repeatedly condemned by the General Assembly as a violation of international law, most recently in October 2007.[25]

The hardship imposed by the embargo has significantly impacted upon the realization of the right to food in Cuba. Food importation is a difficult and expensive process. While one-way trade with the United States has been permitted for a limited number of products, US ships must return in ballast. Foreign ships carrying food to Cuba are prohibited from entering the United States for a period of six months. Food must be imported from distant countries via circuitous routes, increasing the cost of delivery. The embargo impacts the quality of the food imported because of the long transport times and the need to stockpile supplies for longer than would otherwise be required. FAO has stated the following:

> The import of food products for human consumption, particularly those destined for social programmes, is affected by the embargo, as restrictions limit their quantity and quality, thus having a direct effect on the food security of the vulnerable segments of the population.[26]

For example, over 80 per cent of dairy imports to Cuba consist of milk powder for use in the social programme, imported from New Zealand and the European Union. Rice is shipped from China and Vietnam, taking 45 days to reach Cuba. By way of comparison, it would cost one third of the price to ship from the United States and would only take two days.

Increased transaction costs also affect the import of food. US products must be paid for in advance in cash or through letters of credit drawn on third country banks. The Government estimates that incremental (transaction) costs for food and agricultural imports incurred in 2006 due to the embargo amounted to US$ 62.8 million.[27] Since restrictive new payment regulations were introduced in 2005, agricultural imports from the United States fell from US$ 392 million to US$ 340 million during the period 2004–2006.[28] US rice imports, for example, were down by 11 per cent in 2006.[29]

The embargo also affects the cost and availability of inputs needed for the agricultural, fisheries and livestock production processes. Fuel, fertilizers, insecticides, agricultural implements, veterinary pharmaceuticals and other equipment are affected by the ban on purchasing products from the United States.[30] This restriction particularly affects the meat production industry due to the lack of animal feeds, minerals, vitamin supplements, genetic materials and incubation equipment.[31] We saw the impact of this first-hand at a number of farming cooperatives, when we visited the 'Leopoldo Reyes' cooperative in Pinar del Río province. Of the cooperative's 27 tractors, all over 30 years old, only 3 were in operation, using a combination of spare parts from the others. The cooperative now relies primarily on animal traction. This method is widespread in Cuba, where some 250,000 bulls are at work as substitutes for broken-down tractors.

16.2.4 Increases in world food prices

Low levels of domestic production and reliance on food imports make the country susceptible to external crises. In recent years, prices of fuel and food products on the world market have exploded. In 2007, a ton of wheat in the world market traded at US$352, whereas the average price during 2004–2005 was US$154. Cuba now needs additional funds to sustain the existing level of food supply. For example, the Government spent US$146 million on importing milk in 2006; this year it estimates US$204 million for the same amount and US$340 million in 2008 – significantly more than the US$105 million it spent in 2004.

16.3 Legal framework for the right to food in Cuba

16.3.1 International obligations

During our mission, we welcomed the declaration of the Government of Cuba on Human Rights Day (10 December) 2007 that it will sign the International Covenant on Economic, Social and Cultural Rights and the International Covenant on Civil and Political Rights. Cuba has already ratified other key international human rights treaties relevant to the right to food, including the Convention on the Rights of the Child (Articles 24 and 27) and the Convention on the Elimination of All Forms of Discrimination against Women (Articles 12 and 14). It has also accepted two important instruments for the protection of the right to food, namely, the Universal Declaration of Human Rights (Article 25) and the Right to Food Guidelines. Cuba has always been very active in the promotion of the right to food in the Human Rights Council, the former Commission on Human Rights and the General Assembly. The Minister for Foreign Affairs confirmed to us that

Cuba considers the right to food to be a fundamental human right. This means that the Government of Cuba is fully committed under international law to respecting, protecting and fulfilling the right to food of all children, women and men in its territory.

16.3.2 Domestic constitutional and legislative framework

The Constitution of the Republic of Cuba was adopted in 1976 and subsequently amended in 1992 and 2002. Its Preamble introduces the fact that the entire Constitution was inspired by a wish of José Marti: 'I want the fundamental law of our republic to be the tribute of Cubans to the full dignity of man'.

The first aim of the Constitution is to ensure the enjoyment of political freedom, social justice, individual and collective well-being and human solidarity (Article 1). It prohibits any form of discrimination and guarantees equality between men and women, as well as among all human beings (Articles 36, 41-42, 44). The Constitution recognizes in particular economic, social and cultural rights, including the right to food, health, education, work, social security and social assistance (Articles 43-52). It also recognizes that the rights of the most vulnerable groups, including children, young people, pregnant women and elderly, must be particularly safeguarded (Articles 36, 37, 40 and 44). The State has a constitutional obligation to guarantee that every man or woman who is able to work, has the opportunity to have a job with which to contribute to the good of society and to the satisfaction of individual needs; that no disabled person is left without adequate mean of subsistence; and that no child is left without schooling, food and clothing (Article 9). The Constitution also states that parents have a duty to provide nourishment for their children (Article 38), a principle that is described in detail in the Family Code.

Cuba's legislative framework does not include a national law on the right to food or on food security, which would be important to determine the objectives and responsibilities of the relevant ministries and ensure their coordinated activities. However, there are a large number of other laws, decrees and regulations that are of particular relevance for the realization of the right to food. These include two laws on agrarian reform, adopted in 1959 and 1963, that limit land ownership to 65 hectares, distribute the land to those who work on it, and set up the National Institute of Agrarian Reform. The Constitution adopted in 1976 guarantees that small farmers should have access to land and to means of food production, which is an essential component of the right to food. It recognizes that small farmers have the right to legal ownership of their lands and other real estate and personal property necessary to work their land, as well as the right to group together, including through the establishment of cooperatives. It also provides that the State must back small farmers' individual production and give all possible support to the cooperative form of agricultural production (Articles 19 and 20). The

National Association of Small Farmers (ANAP), founded in 1961 and currently comprising 350,000 peasants, is entitled to participate in agricultural and food security policy-making at the highest level of Government.[32]

Other laws of particular importance for the right to food include the Labour Code (1984), which acknowledges the equal rights of women and men in the workplace and their right to a sufficient salary, and the Law on Social Security (1979), which protects people without income, including unemployed people and single pregnant women, and recognizes the right of peasants to social security. A Decree on Water Resources regulates the supply and rational use of water resources and acknowledges the priority accorded to drinking water and sanitation, while the Environmental Law entrusts the National Institute for Hydraulic Resources (INRH) with the functions of monitoring and developing the management of water resources, protecting natural resources and promoting sustainable agriculture. In March 2007, the Council of Minister approved a decree to institutionalize the National Council on Water, created in 1997 to coordinate and oversee water issues. We had been informed that a draft Food Law has been discussed by the National Assembly but has never been adopted.

The Cuban legal framework has been commended for its impact towards the elimination of racial discrimination and the realization of the economic, social and cultural rights of women and children, including by the Committee for the Elimination of Racial Discrimination, the Committee on the Rights of the Child and the Special Rapporteur on violence against women, who visited Cuba in 1999.[33] By addressing the structural causes of hunger and by prioritizing the rights of the most vulnerable groups, including children, the legal framework in Cuba has greatly contributed to the realization of the right to food, the reduction of child mortality and the achievement of the objectives of the World Food Summit. Today, Cuba ranks 51st out of 177 States listed by UNDP in its Human Development Report, an impressive achievement for a developing country.

16.3.3 Access to justice and human rights institutions

The CESCR underlined a fundamental principle of human rights law in paragraph 33 of its General Comment No. 12 (1999) on the right to adequate food:

> Any person or group who is a victim of a violation of the right to food should have access to effective judicial or other appropriate remedies at both national and international levels. All victims of such violations are entitled to adequate reparation, which may take the form of restitution, compensation, satisfaction or guarantees of non-repetition.

In Cuba, the court system consists of a Supreme Court, provincial courts, municipal courts and military courts. Although these instances enjoy functional independence, they are subordinate to the National Assembly of People's Power and the Council of State. There is no Constitutional Court, but the Constitution recognizes that anybody who suffers damages or injuries unjustly caused by a State official or employee in connection with the performance of his or her public functions has the right to claim and obtain appropriate compensation or indenisation (Article 26). Such complaints can be addressed to the Office of the Attorney General of the Republic, which is responsible for ensuring that State agencies, economic and social entities and citizens comply fully with the Constitution, the law and other legal regulations (Article 127). The Office of Attorney-General of the Republic was established in 1997 as the main defender of the rights of citizens, through the State Procurator's Act. The Attorney-General is also subordinate to the National Assembly and the Council of State and receives instructions directly from the Council of State. The Constitution further recognizes that every citizen has the right to address complaints and petitions to the authorities and to be given attention or a reply within a reasonable length of time (Article 63). This means that everybody is entitled to administrative remedies in case of violations of his/her right to food.

We discussed with the Ministry of Justice and the Ministry of Internal Trade about the possibilities for people to complain in case of violations of their right to food, for example if their entitlements under the *libreta* (food rationing) system were not met. The Minister of Internal Trade explained that 840 consumer protection offices were available to receive this kind of complaint; he was unable to provide figures on how many complaints are filed every year but stated that no complaint had ever been received by the Ministry. There is a lack of information provided on this kind of remedies and a lack of trust from the population as to their effectiveness. In many places we visited, we saw that information was available on many human rights issues, including on the rights of children to food, education, health in hospitals and the rights of consumers in marketplaces. However, we are concerned that many people with whom we discussed were not aware of the availability of remedies in cases of violations or did not believe in their effectiveness. The promotion and protection of the right to food could be improved by the establishment of an independent institution in charge of receiving and dealing with complaints of violation of human rights, including the right to food, and providing adequate remedies. This has also been recognized as a key component of the right to food in the Right to Food Guidelines, adopted by all FAO Member States in 2004:

> States that do not have national human rights institutions or ombudspersons are encouraged to establish them. Human rights institutions should be independent and autonomous from the government, in accordance with the Paris Principles. States should encourage civil society organizations and individuals to contribute to monitoring activities undertaken

by national human rights institutions with respect to the progressive realization of the right to adequate food.[34]

16.4 Policy framework for the right to food

16.4.1 Government policies and institutions

Food and nutrition programmes

We observed how the Government aims to ensure that its whole population is provided with 50 per cent of their nutritional requirements, at a heavily subsidized price, through the national food rationing system (*libreta*). The *libreta* allows each family to purchase rationed items for the 'basic food basket' (*canasta básica*), namely cereals, fish, rice, pasta, meat, oil, eggs, bread, sugar and coffee. In addition to this, Cubans can buy non-quota products at the 18,160 government-run stores and outlets, although the range of products available is limited. The remainder of peoples' food supplies are purchased at agricultural markets (*mercados agropecuarios*), some of which are government-owned and operated (559), while others operate on a supply-and-demand basis rather than applying fixed prices (208). Some products are only available for purchase in foreign currency (Cuban convertible pesos, or CUCs), which makes it difficult for residents earning only local currency to purchase them. Given the prices in these markets and the low salaries of Cuban workers, many people are forced to purchase basic food on the black market. Thus, the daily task of completing a balanced diet for the family is sometimes a complicated process in Cuba.

The cost of food under the *libreta* is very cheap. One litre of milk, despite costing the State 2.4 local pesos, costs the consumer 25 cents in local currency (one cent CUC). Eighty grams of bread costs five cents in local currency. However, the food rationing supply depends on product availability, which in turn depends on agricultural production, foreign imports and adequate transportation. Food rations are sometimes delivered late. During our visit, we observed that some government-run stores were better stocked than others. For example, one such store we visited in Camagüey was apparently regularly without stocks of eggs, and was only able to store meat products for a very limited period of time as the refrigeration system was in a state of disrepair.[35]

Many Cubans also rely on a social consumption scheme, which provides subsidized lunches in workplaces and schools or food in hospitals, maternity residences, centres for the elderly or other social centres. We visited a number of such sites. According to government figures, over 350,500 people benefit from this scheme. In addition, individuals belonging to particularly vulnerable groups, such as children, pregnant women, the sick or the elderly, may be entitled to additional food and nutritional supplements. For example, children up to seven years receive one litre of milk a day. In the east of the country, children up to 14 years and adults above 64 years receive an additional supplement to their diet: this programme benefits 1,347,000 people.[36] An array of other food and nutrition programmes exists, for example, the National Health System's Food and Nutrition Monitoring System, the Nutrition Education Programme, and the National Plan for the prevention and control of iron deficiency and anaemia in the Cuban population.

Cuba's extensive system of State-organized social workers provides a mechanism for monitoring the realization of the right to food. There are 42,128 social workers in Cuba, who ensure that families receive appropriate social support by *inter alia* identifying nutritional deficiencies and the need for food supplements. A social workers' study of 2,143,995 children in Cuba found that 109,001 suffered from nutritional problems.[37] Now 71,794 children receive free food supplements, in addition to regular monitoring. A further 7356 adults suffering from chronic diseases receive a special diet. Social workers can identify families who suffer because of food unavailability or unaffordability, although the options for remedying such problems are limited.

Cuba has a free, universal and compulsory education programme for children up to 14 years of age (9th grade). Boarding and half-boarding schools have been established for children of working mothers and those located in isolated areas. Half-board schools provide children with a small snack and lunch. Full boarding schools provide children with all meals. Despite efforts made by the Government to meet the minimum daily nutritional requirements, the results of a 1999–2000 study indicate that children in day care centres received 76 per cent of the recommended levels of meat products, whereas children in half-boarding schools received 60 per cent and those in boarding schools only 65 per cent.[38] Similarly, results showed that vegetable and fat intakes were below recommended levels.

Various government agencies are involved in protecting and promoting the right to food in Cuba. The Ministry of Economy and Planning administers the Plan of Action for Nutrition, a framework for ensuring food security that focuses on increasing domestic agricultural production and equitable distribution, particularly for vulnerable groups. A National Council for Food Distribution consists of representatives of the Ministry of Economy and Planning, the Ministry of Transport and social workers. Various national food security and nutrition programmes apply a multisectoral approach, involving the Ministries of Food Industries, Agriculture, Fisheries, Health, Education, Transport and others. The importation of food products, 94 per cent of which are used in the *canasta básica*, is coordinated by *Alimport*.

Agricultural production policies and agrarian reform

In Cuba, half of the 6629.6 million hectares of agricultural land is cultivated (3124.3 Mha). There are five main types of land holdings: State farms (150); some private farms (approximately 150,000 farm their own small landholdings with family labour[39]); Basic Units of Agricultural Production (UBPCs, 1762); Agricultural Production Cooperatives (CPAs, 739); and Credit and Service Cooperatives (CCSs, 2201).[40] UBPC members cooperatively farm State land under a usufruct arrangement. CPAs are forms of collective land ownership: former private farmers join together in government-organized cooperatives, in exchange for inputs from the State. CCSs emerge when small farmers who privately own their land cooperate to collectively share access to credit and some inputs and services, such as irrigation, seed, fertilizer and chemical products.

Producers' income is based on productivity. UBPC members are entitled to retain any surplus income after sale of their production, whereas CPA members distribute profits as per their cooperative agreements. Once the State quota is filled, farmers are entitled to keep a small percentage of their produce for personal consumption and to sell surpluses through the free supply-and-demand markets. Intermediation of agricultural products is illegal.

Most agricultural producers are required to sell the majority of their production directly to the State collection agency, ACOPIO, at fixed prices. In return, the State sells the farmers inputs. ACOPIO has been criticized for setting some selling prices below production costs, long delays in paying producers, and a failure to provide critical production inputs.

Since 1993, the proportion of agricultural land directly managed by the State has decreased from 70 per cent to 30 per cent. Even so, production outputs are determined by the production quotas set by the Ministries of Agriculture and Sugar, on the basis of the quantities needed to maintain food supplies, particularly for the libreta system.

From 1959 to 1990, the Cuban agricultural sector began to diversify its output, focusing on livestock production, rice, citrus, coffee, poultry, pork and reforestation. Since 1990, the Ministry of Agriculture has developed programmes for egg production, pork production, urban agriculture, production of root vegetables, protected crops, as well as a mechanism for rice silage and warehousing. Currently, the principal agricultural products are root vegetables, other vegetables, rice, citrus and other fruits, eggs, pork and honey. Cuba has been focusing on increasing pork production in order to satisfy demand for protein. In 2007, pork production reached 150,000 tons. Yet this progress is hindered by the cost of production inputs, the price of which has risen because of the embargo.

Since 1959, the Cuban agricultural sector has been plagued by inefficiencies and obstacles. Equipment failures and lack of inputs delay or reduce harvests. Investment in modernizing equipment and technologies is limited. Two million hectares of previously productive land were left uncultivated and have now been taken over by *marabú*, a thorny bush with a strong root system, inedible for livestock. In some provinces, it covers 49 per cent of the land.[41]

In 2007, the National Commission for the Updating of Agricultural Policy was created to address the need to enhance domestic food production by achieving greater self-sufficiency through diversification and increased output. In March 2007, it initiated two reforms: eliminating debts to producers and changing the payment system for non-State producers; and increasing the price paid to milk and meat producers. Both measures are designed to stimulate production and have already had a positive impact. For example, the UBPC 'Francisco Suárez', which we visited, increased its productivity by 15 per cent when the State dairy increased the price it paid for the UBPC's milk from two pesos per litre to 2.5 pesos. Such measures will need to be expanded.

Another problem is storage. FAO calculates that worldwide, approximately 25 per cent of food crops are lost to rodents, pests and climatic destruction. Figures are lacking for Cuba, but in our conversations with farmers and provincial officials, we learnt that part of each harvest is lost due to lack of silos, particularly in the east. Working together with the Swiss Agency for Cooperation and Development, the Government has launched a programme of thousands of household silos in three eastern provinces. ANAP produces these silos in a sustainable manner. These silos, which are metallic and are three metres high and two metres wide, have a simple aeration system and preserve provisions from destruction. Rice can be kept for over four months, and the silos can withstand hurricanes.

Major challenges to the reform of the agricultural sector remain, as identified by the national authorities in late 2006, including inefficiencies in management, work productivity and average number of hours of worked, and distribution of production. We welcome the steps taken, in particular as highlighted in the speech by Raúl Castro Ruz on 26 July 2007, to encourage a national debate on these problems and the future of agricultural reform in Cuba. Cuba has taken a great step forward in acknowledging previous errors, inefficiencies and other internal obstacles, which have hampered fulfilment of the right to food.[42] This unprecedented explicit recognition that significant structural and conceptual changes are needed in order to address shortages in food production is an opportunity to be welcomed by Cubans.

Water and sanitation

Water services are subsidized by the Government, with beneficiaries charged an average of one peso per person per month for water use. Levels of water supply are adequate and water is generally safe for drinking. Water supply, however, is not always regular and the hydraulic distribution network is not very well maintained, with a high percentage of water loss. Although sanitation coverage is high, in some suburban areas of big cities sanitation services are inadequate and sewerage systems are deficient.

The National Institute for Hydraulic Resources (INRH), established in 1962, is in charge of water supply and sanitation. INRH proposes water and sanitation policies to the Cabinet in coordination with relevant ministries such as the Ministries of Economy and Planning, Health, Financing and Prices and Construction. Local authorities are also involved in service provision.

The National Institute for Hydraulic Resources has implemented a number of programmes under the *Voluntad Hidráulica* policy. One such programme aims to modernize the water infrastructure and introduce new technology, another to rehabilitate pumping stations and increase the efficient use of energy, and yet another to renovate the drinking water network. We visited the factory Hidroplast, built under the third programme, which produces new pipes for the water network. INRH also works on enhancing the quality of the water supplied. Through these efforts, Cuba has achieved the MDG targets related to population coverage of safe drinking water and sanitation.

Civil defence

In Cuba, there is a comprehensive National Civil Defence System to prevent and respond to natural disasters. This has greatly strengthened local actors' capacity to reduce the risks of natural disaster. The *Grupo de Alimentos*, a coordinating body comprising five ministries, guarantees the supply of food in case of natural disasters.

While better prepared than almost all of the neighbouring countries, Cuba is often badly affected by natural disasters. During our mission, tropical storm Noel attacked the east of the country. The storm destroyed buildings, bridges, roads and harvests. Although over 74,000 people became homeless, no one was killed. The storm came from the Dominican Republic, where more than 120 lives were lost.

16.4.2 United Nations specialized agencies

The United Nations Country Team recently developed the United Nations Development Assistance Framework (UNDAF) for the period 2008–2012. This framework document establishes fives areas of concentration, one of which is food security. The United Nations agencies working on the ground in Cuba include UNDP, FAO, WHO, WFP, the United Nations Educational, Scientific and Cultural Organization (UNESCO), UNICEF, UNFPA, UNEP, UNIDO and HABITAT. United Nations activities in Cuba involve improving national agricultural production levels and reducing reliance on food imports, supplementing micronutritional deficiencies, particularly anaemia in children under five, as well as education about nutrition and diet.

WFP focuses on the east of the country, where it works to supply nutritional supplements to 375,000 children over the age of five. FAO provides technical assistance through projects supporting the intensification and diversification of agricultural production and increasing food quality and economic accessibility of food. WHO works in the eastern region to increase the availability and consumption of animal protein. UNDP allocates a maximum of 2 million dollars per year for projects linked to production and agricultural activities, food and the feeding of HIV patients. UNICEF also works on strengthening children's nutrition.

The Government of Cuba conducts successful bilateral cooperation, including with Canada, Spain and Switzerland.

The work of United Nations agencies is hampered by the United States embargo, which has a negative impact on the effectiveness of development resources, increases administrative costs, and prevents the importation of project materials.[43]

The work of other international organizations is also impeded by the United States embargo. Staffs of the World Bank and the IMF are prohibited from travelling to Cuba. Furthermore Cuba is not a member of the Inter-American Development Bank and, although remaining a member of the Organization of American States, the current Government has been excluded from participation in this regional organization since 1962.[44] This affects the country's ability to access external multilateral financing for development programmes, potentially useful for rehabilitating and modernizing its agricultural infrastructure and equipment.[45]

16.4.3 Civil society

During our visit, we met with a variety of different social movements. We were grateful to Monsignor de Cespedes, who explained the work that the Catholic Church is doing with Caritas at the local level, supported by Caritas International, which is conducted in a free and open manner. Other sources indicate that the Cuban Government is reluctant to enter into cooperation with foreign organizations, particularly in times of natural disaster.

We had an opportunity to visit various institutions of civil society. For example, under the guidance of Eusebio Leal, we visited the Covent of Bethlehem in Old Havana, where we saw the community work being carried out in the day care centre for senior citizens.

We met with representatives from international NGOs to discuss their food security projects. These NGOs included primarily Welt Hunger Hilfe, CARE International, Grupo de Voluntariado Civil Italia, Entrepueblos, and ACSUR-Las Segovias. CARE International undertakes water and sanitation, and agro-breeding projects. ACSUR-Las Segovias addresses food sovereignty in the eastern region, promoting sustainable rural habitats and strengthening of local actors. Entrepueblos works in UBPCs with the Cuban Council of Churches. Welt Hunger Hilfe has a range of projects that assist with the decentralization of food production and support urban agriculture in Havana and the eastern provinces.

We also met with representatives from the Federation of Cuban Women, who are working with WFP to reduce the prevalence of anaemia in pregnant women.

16.5 Main findings and concerns

16.5.1 Progressive realization of the right to food

Cuba has made impressive progress towards the realization of the right to food. Cuba has already met the targets of the 1996 World Food Summit and MDG1, for example, halving the proportion of people suffering from hunger by 2015.[46] Cuba has also already achieved the Millennium Development Goals 2 (universal primary education), 3 (gender equality) and 4 (reduction of child mortality), and expects to fully achieve Goals 1, 5 and 6 by 2015.[47] We noted throughout our visit that, despite difficult times and adverse external circumstances, the Government has taken seriously its obligation to realize the right to food and not to regress on the progress made thus far.

We believe that important challenges to the progressive realization of the right to food in Cuba remain. For example, further steps need to be taken to reduce the prevalence of anaemia, particularly for children and pregnant women, and in the eastern region. In addition, the Government needs to step up its efforts to promote a balanced diet, which includes the required intake of fats and animal proteins, fruits and vegetable; moreover measures are needed to address the increased risk of obesity in the population, which is the result of an unbalanced diet.

Despite the intended inclusiveness of the *libreta* system, Cubans continue to face difficulties in accessing affordable food in light of their insufficient income, particularly those who do not belong to any of the groups at particular risk and have to obtain 50 per cent of their minimum food requirements from non-subsidized mechanisms such as agricultural markets. This situation has worsened in recent years. In addition, the limited number of products available in national currency has impeded the Government's ability to ensure economic access to sufficient and adequate food to the whole population. While measures are being initiated to improve this, further progress is required.

16.5.2 Main concerns

Rural exodus

Rural exodus is constant and massive in Cuba. Paradoxically, this is a result of the impressive social achievements of the Cuban revolution. In 1959, 43 per cent of Cuban men and 51 per cent of women were illiterate. In 2007, the corresponding figure was 0.3 per cent (men and women aggregated). Today, Cuba has over 700,000 university students, three times the per-capitanumber of Switzerland. By 2007 Cuba had one medical doctor for every 168 inhabitants, whereas in 1959 there were only 6000 doctors in all of Cuba, 3000 of whom left for the United States within the year.

Rural exodus is common in almost all developing countries. In most countries, it is caused by the lack of schools, hospitals and social mobility in the countryside. This is not the case in Cuba. In Cuba, rural exodus is motivated by the high professional quality of its inhabitants. A son or a daughter of a peasant family who holds a university degree does not want to plough the field at temperatures of 30°C, under tropical conditions which make work in agricultural production very hard. But without a productive peasantry, Cuba will not reduce its food imports and massively increase its own food production. One solution is to invest in fertilizers and mechanization and to increase prices paid to producers.

The right to food of unrecognized internal migrants

We were informed that the right to food of unrecognized internal migrants may be at risk. These migrants are people who move from one place to another without properly fulfilling the necessary administrative procedures. According to the right to food and the constitutional right of all citizens to live in any sector, zone or area (Article 43 of the Constitution), all Cubans should receive the subsidized food basket through the *libreta* system, wherever they live. However, we received information that many internal migrants might not be benefiting from the *libreta* in their new place of residence because of the difficulties for the Government to know whether they have moved to another place other than their official place of residence, as a result of which their subsidized basket continues to be allocated in their former place of residence. It is difficult to evaluate the extent of this problem, but there is a trend suggesting that internal migration has been on the rise, with thousands of internal migrants seeking to improve their living conditions by moving to the capital city every year.

The lack of food in government-run stores

We visited a number of government-run stores in which all food products were available. However, we also visited stores where the food products that should be accessible to the population through the *libreta* system were not all available. Under the *libreta* system, people have the right to receive the full list of food products to meet their nutritional needs. We are aware of the current limitations on agricultural production, transportation and distribution in the country. However, a maximum of available resources must be used to guarantee that all government-run stores are able to ensure availability at all times of all the food products that are listed as entitlements under the *libreta* system.

Access to adequate food for all prisoners

We visited one female and one male prison at the *Combinado del Este*, near the city of Havana. Officials of the prison administration explained that the United Nations Standard Minimum Rules for the Treatment of

Prisoners states that all prisoners have the right to drinking water and to adequate food (article 20). They explained that in 2007 they guaranteed a minimum of 2,600 Kcal per day to inmates, and that inmates are entitled to receive food from their families, who can visit every 21 days or every 30 days without limit. According to the officials, 84 per cent of inmates benefit from this possibility. We were informed that 24 inmates of the male prison tend a vegetable garden of four hectares, which allows them to complement their diet with a variety of vegetables. The remaining facilities visited seemed adequate and well managed and the inmates with whom we spoke seemed to be satisfied with the food and diet provided by the prison administration. However, we also received allegations that some prisoners suffer from nutritional disorders and gastrointestinal problems caused by inadequate diet and that some of them have not received proper medical attention.

16.5.3 Obstacles to the realization of the right to food

One of the key external obstacles to the realization of the right to food in Cuba is the United States embargo, which increases food prices through transport and transaction costs and limits importation of food production inputs. Coupled with the rising price of food commodities, Cuba faces considerable hurdles in enhancing self-sufficiency and domestic food production. Other countries commonly deal with such obstacles by complementing domestic efforts with international cooperation and assistance and access to credit. However, accessing the resources of the World Bank, IMF and the Inter-American Development Bank is not currently an option for Cuba. Cuba is also affected by extreme weather conditions, which impact on the economic and social situation, particularly in the east. In Cuba's tropical climate, food production, especially wheat and other grains, is difficult, and complete self-sufficiency is not possible.

There are further internal obstacles. Agricultural decapitalization, deindustrialization, and lack of labour, have reduced production. Poor land management creates further obstacles: much of the fertile land is covered by *marabú* and requires rehabilitation. Inefficiencies often stem from overcentralization. Low wages prevent access to affordable food. In addition, lack of agro-production incentives, prohibition of intermediates and curbs on farmers' market freedom all limit efficiency. One solution could be to liberalize food production, distribution and sales. However, this could well contradict the revolution's objective of equality. Dependency on food imports cannot be easily overcome by liberalization, as this would inevitably lead to inequalities and difficulties for the State in fulfilling its social promise, for example, due to the impossibility of buying milk at an affordable price to distribute through the *libreta*. Reforms, clearly needed in the agricultural sector to increase productivity and reduce dependency on food imports, will have objective limits.

16.6 Conclusions and recommendations

In his report on our country mission to Cuba, presented to the Human Rights Council in March 2008, Jean Ziegler presented the following conclusions and recommendations.

He welcomed the declaration which Acting President Raúl Castro Ruz made on 26 July 2007, namely, that the Government will give priority to reform in the agricultural sector, specifically through increasing support to small farmers to increase both livelihoods and production. He remained concerned that external problems, in particular the United States embargo and world food prices, as well as internal contradictions will create major difficulties for the complete realization of the right to food.

He was very encouraged by Cuba's commitments to increase its cooperation with the Human Rights Council. He welcomed the declaration made by Felipe Pérez Roque, Minister for Foreign Affairs on 10 December 2007 to the effect that Cuba will sign both the International Covenant on Economic, Social and Cultural Rights and the International Covenant on Civil and Political Rights in early 2008 and extend invitations to other special procedures of the Council.

He then made the following specific recommendations:

(a) The Government of Cuba should continue to strengthen its cooperation with the Council and the United Nations. It should promptly ratify the International Covenant on Economic, Social and Cultural Rights and the International Covenant on Civil and Political Rights. It should also extend standing invitations to all special procedures of the Human Rights Council in 2008.
(b) A framework law on the right to food should be adopted, allowing for the identification of concrete goals such as the eradication of malnutrition, the improvement of monitoring mechanisms and the allocation and coordination of responsibilities across all relevant ministries. The drafting of this framework law would represent an excellent opportunity to discuss the possibilities for reforms in the agricultural sector and increase both livelihood and production, while at the same time ensuring access to food for everyone. All relevant actors should participate in this process, including representatives of small farmers, civil society, social movements and United Nations agencies. Due consideration should be given to Right to Food Guidelines of FAO and General Comment No. 12 (1999) of the CESCR on the right to adequate food.
(c) Access to justice in relation to the right to food should be improved. The courts should be mandated to deal with human rights violations, including the right to food. An independent institution charged with receiving and processing complaints and providing remedies for violations, should be established, in accordance with the 2004 Right to Food

Guidelines adopted by all FAO Member States, as existing consumer offices fail to address this need.

(d) The constitutional right of every citizen to live in any sector, zone or area should be fully implemented, in conjunction with the right to food of every Cuban. Measures should be taken to facilitate the allocation of the subsidized basket to internal migrants who have moved without properly fulfilling the necessary administrative procedures. All Cubans should receive the subsidized food basket through the *libreta* system, wherever they live.

(e) The Government should prioritize intensification of recent policies to increase agricultural production and efficiency, particularly diversification of food production, use of non-State farming cooperatives, the *organopónico* movement and free supply-and-demand vegetable markets. The Government should enact further steps to ensure that farmers achieve profitable returns, through reductions in the quota system and legalization of secondary markets. Measures should be taken to stimulate capitalization and investment in the agricultural industry and to guarantee the independent operation of cooperatives.

(f) Only around three million hectares are cultivated, out of a possible six million hectares of fertile land. The *marabú* weed is invading millions of hectares of good land. The Government should implement a national programme to eradicate *marabú* in order to reclaim lost agricultural land and to establish incentives to promote the cultivation and use of this land.

(g) Special attention should be given to the urgent problem of food transport. Food is lost when adequate transport is not available due to lack of fuel or spare parts. At present, not all the more than 18,000 government-run stores receive the food to which they are entitled each month. Reform of the transport system is therefore urgent. Steps should be taken to improve or avoid unreliability and inefficiencies in the transport and food distribution system, and to reduce product loss, for example through decentralization of food production and by moving production closer to consumption points.

(h) In order to combat loss of harvest, the Government should extend the current programme of construction of family silos, currently implemented in only three eastern provinces, to the entire country.

(i) The Government should take further steps to enable individuals to access food that is available, accessible, acceptable, adaptable, and of good quality. Reforms are needed to expand the range and quality of food products available; to ensure food affordability; to ensure an adequate level of animal protein in diets; and to guarantee greater consumer sovereignty. More varied and nutritional food should be included in the basic food basket.

(j) Social security programmes should be strengthened in order to ensure coverage for all, including those that may be neglected under the current system. The Government, United Nations agencies and NGOs must work together to improve the progressive realization of the right to food for vulnerable groups, by intensifying measures to further reduce the prevalence of anaemia, by developing strategies for promoting a healthy diet, and by combating obesity. Data should be collected on a disaggregated basis to facilitate the monitoring of progress.

(k) To the United States, the Special Rapporteur recommends in the strongest way the removal of the illegal embargo against Cuba. Cuba should be granted open access to export markets, and the unnecessary cost and inconvenience that the embargo places on the system of food importation in Cuba should be eliminated. Cuba should be entitled to access the credit facilities of the World Bank, IMF and the Inter-American Development Bank. The travel ban on staff of the World Bank and other international organizations should be lifted, and the inconveniences created for United Nations staff, scientists, civil society members and others working to develop Cuba's capacity to realize the right to food should be eased.

17
Conclusion

It is clear that there is still much work to be done to make the right to food a reality, both in times of peace and in times of war. We are fighting for a world in which, as Martin Luther King hoped, the word 'hunger', like other words of oppression such as slavery, racism and discrimination, will disappear and can be taken out of the dictionary forever.

Hunger and malnutrition still sentence millions of people to underdevelopment and death. It is an outrage that over one billion people still suffer from hunger and chronic malnourishment and that more than five million children die from hunger or hunger-related illnesses each year. This silent massacre occurs in a world which is richer than ever before and already produces more than enough food to feed the global population.

There is no secret as to how to eradicate hunger. There is rather a need for political commitment to challenge existing policies, inequities and corruption across the world that are making the poor, poorer and the rich, richer. We need political solutions, rather than complicated technical solutions to hunger. There is rather a need to challenge the growing inequities between rich and poor around the world. Widening inequalities will simply result in even greater poverty, as the profits of economic growth will go to the rich. But we should all be concerned about reducing the poverty and marginalization of poor countries and poor peoples which will stabilize the world. As Josué de Castro, the world-renowned Brazilian economist and former President of the FAO Council wrote metaphorically 50 years ago: 'In Brazil, no one sleeps because of hunger. Half because they are hungry and the other half because they are afraid of the hungry.'[1]

Eradicating hunger and poverty is not only a question of finding resources. It is also a question of challenging structural injustices and inequities of power that allow human rights abuses to take place. It is also a question of challenging economic inequalities and adopting a principled and fair approach to global economic trade.

The eradication of hunger and violations of the human right to food is the most urgent priority facing Governments today. Hunger and people's lack of access to sufficient productive resources to be able to feed themselves will continue to create conflicts and force children out of school into forced labour, including recruitment into armed forces. Hunger will also continue to force people to flee their own countries. The answer is not a criminalization of those who suffer from hunger. The answer is to take immediate action to respect, protect and fulfil the right to food of every human being.

We would like to conclude this book by highlighting where the structural problems and the new threats are, and where hope is.

17.1 Where are the structural problems?

17.1.1 Schizophrenia in the UN system and in States' policies
The non-acceptance of the right to food
We firmly believe that a key obstacle to the realization of the right to food is the profound internal contradictions operating in the United Nations system. On one hand, United Nations agencies such as FAO, WFP, UNDP and UNICEF emphasize social justice and human rights and do excellent work in promoting the right to food, for example evidenced by the FAO Right to Food Guidelines. On the other hand, the Bretton Woods institutions, along with the Government of the United States of America and the WTO, refuse to recognize the mere existence of a human right to food and impose on the most vulnerable States the Washington Consensus emphasizing liberalization, deregulation, privatization and the compression of State domestic budgets, a model which in many cases produces greater inequalities. In particular, three aspects of this general process of privatization and liberalization create catastrophic consequences for the right to food: the privatization of institutions and public utilities, the liberalization of agricultural trade and the market-assisted model of land reform.

Our two missions to Niger showed clearly how the market-based paradigm of development, largely imposed by IMF and the World Bank, has been harmful to food security for the most vulnerable.[2] Cost-recovery policies in health centres, for instance, mean that many poor children are not being treated for malnutrition. The privatization of Government support services, including the logistics and distribution system OPVN and the National Veterinary Office, has exacerbating food insecurity among small-scale farmers and pastoralists. Niger has wealth of 20 million head of cattle, sheep and camels, which are historically much sought after and exported widely. The animals constitute essential revenue for millions of nomads and peasants. But the privatization of the national veterinary office has produced a disaster: many pastoralists can no longer afford the prices of vaccinations, medicines and vitamins charged by the commercial traders.

The schizophrenia of the United Nations system is also particularly evident in relation to land issues.[3] Despite the importance placed on agrarian reform models that promote transformative, redistributive reform by the international community, the contradictions continue. In the 1996 Declaration of the World Food Summit, land reform constituted a key part of stated commitments. In the Final Declaration of the 'International Conference on Agrarian Reform and Rural Development' organized by the FAO and the Government of Brazil in March 2006, 95 States recognized that one important way to ensure the fulfilment of the right to food is to establish appropriate land reform to secure access to land for marginalized and vulnerable groups, and to adopt adequate legal frameworks and policies to promote traditional and family agriculture.[4] However, at the same time, agencies such as the World Bank are in contrast promoting new models of agrarian reform which emphasise the market and are compatible with the 'Washington Consensus', a paradigm which is 'inherently opposed to policy interventions aimed at achieving social equity'.[5]

The World Bank's 'market-assisted' or 'negotiated' models of land reform seek to overcome elite resistance to land reform by offering credit to landless or land poor farmers to buy land at market rates from large landholders with the State playing a part only in mediation and the provision of credit. But these models shift the logic of agrarian reform away from a concept of a right to land and redistribution, towards a view that access to land is only possible through purchase of the land at market prices, despite a context of historically produced inequities. Despite the criticism drawn in the past by many NGOs and social movements who claim that it is undermining more transformative programmes of agrarian reform,[6] the practice continues.

We saw the limits of the 'market-assisted' model during our mission to Guatemala.[7] Despite the fact that the government is making impressive efforts to change the situation, Guatemala remains one of the most inequitable countries in the world. Land ownership is highly concentrated, with 2 per cent of the population own up to 70–75 per cent of agricultural land, while 90 per cent of small farmers survive on less than one hectare. This situation is the result of a long history of land expropriation from indigenous people, exacerbated by a 36-year civil war (1960–1996) during which military and landowners forcibly controlled more land. In this particular context, the promotion by the World Bank of a market-based redistribution of land, concretized by the creation of a land fund, FONTIERRA, to provide credit for land purchases, is particularly ineffective. It precludes the adoption of more important measures required under the Peace Accords of 1996, including the creation of an effective *cadastro* (land registry system), the elaboration of an agrarian code recognizing indigenous forms of land ownership and the establishment of an agrarian jurisdiction to resolve land disputes.

The lack of coherence of States' policies

The second aspect of this 'schizophrenia' is that many States are not at all coherent in their own practices. Far too often one part of a government makes commitments to protect and promote the right to food, while another part of the government takes decisions or implements policies that directly undermine this right.

The great majority of States have recognized the right to food in the World Food Summit Declarations and the Right to Food Guidelines. 160 States are parties to the ICESCR, and 190 to the Convention on the Rights of the Child. They have to respect, protect and fulfill the right to food in all their policies and decisions. Unfortunately today, there is also an increasing lack of coherence in government policies which can mean for example, that while they remain committed to a rights-based approach to development, at the same time, they might engage for example in trade policies that could have negative effects on human rights in other countries.

Wide disparities in economic power between the States means that powerful States negotiate trade rules that are neither free nor fair. These trade rules severely affect small farmers and threaten food security,[8] especially in developing countries that have been required to liberalize agriculture to a much greater extent than developed countries.[9] The heavy production and export subsidies that OECD countries grant their farmers – more than US$349 billion in 2006 (almost US$1 billion per day) – means that subsidized European fruit and vegetables can be found in a market stall in Dakar, Senegal, at lower prices than local produce. Although developed countries, including the European Union, made promises at the WTO Hong Kong conference in December 2005 to eliminate export subsidies that result in dumping, there has been little concrete progress so far. In Mexico, it is estimated that up to 15 million Mexican farmers and their families (many from indigenous communities) may be displaced from their livelihoods as a result of the North American Free Trade Agreement and competition with subsidized United States maize.[10]

Coherence would be possible by putting human rights at the centre of all government policy and to refrain from policies and programmes that may negatively affect the right to food of people in other countries. This primacy of human rights is recognized in the Declaration and Plan of Action of the World Conference on Human Rights in Vienna (1993), where all States recognized that human rights are 'the first responsibility of Governments' (paragraph 1).

17.1.2 Exclusion and discrimination

Exclusion and discrimination are particularly evident in the case of women and indigenous and tribal people, who are also among the most vulnerable to hunger and malnutrition.[11] Women play vital roles in the production and preparation of food, in agriculture and in earning incomes to feed their families, and as mediators of nutrition education within the family, if they themselves are educated. It is now widely agreed that women produce the 60–80 per cent of food crops in developing countries and play a crucial role in food security of households. And it is increasingly recognized that the health of women is crucial to the health of whole societies, because malnourished women are more likely to give birth to malnourished and underdeveloped babies. New scientific evidence in nutrition calls for a 'life-cycle' approach to nutrition which recognizes the intergenerational links in nutritional status.[12] Underweight and malnourished mothers are more likely to give birth to underweight babies, whose mental and physical capacities may be severely stunted. Regis Debray has called these children 'crucified at birth'. These children may never recover and in turn have malnourished babies, passing hunger on through the generations.

Despite their key role in ensuring food security, 70 per cent of the world's hungry are women or girls. Women often face discrimination in gaining secure access to and control over other productive resources, such as land, water and credit, as they are often not recognized as producers or juridical equals. According to the FAO, while the proportion of women heads of rural households continues to grow, reaching more than 30 per cent in some developing countries, less than 2 percent of all land is owned by women.[13] Despite legal and often constitutional rights in many countries, women still face severe obstacles to inheritance, purchase and control of land. In many countries, despite formal protection against discrimination, women are lacking any real access to land and this problem is further exacerbated by a lack of inheritance rights. For Meaza Ashenafi, Executive Director of the Ethiopian Women Lawyers Association (EWLA), 'almost in all regions, women do not have any access to land whatsoever. They don't have the right to inherit, and the only option is to get married and have a husband. But when the husband dies, they are also kicked off their land'.[14]

Indigenous and tribal peoples also face exclusion and discrimination impacting upon their right to food. Indigenous and tribal peoples encompass approximately 5000 distinct peoples and around 350 million people, with the vast majority living in developing countries. It has long been understood that, due to long historical processes of colonization, exploitation and political and economic exclusion, indigenous peoples are among the most vulnerable to poverty, hunger and malnutrition. Various studies have, over an extended period of time, established that the living standards for indigenous peoples 'were at the bottom of the socio-economic scale' and 'indigenous peoples the world over are usually among the most marginalized and dispossessed sectors of society'. This problem continues to be of alarm, as a result of continued discrimination in access to productive resources. In Guatemala for instance, where the Government has made important efforts to change this situation, it is still clear that indigenous peoples face much higher levels of poverty and malnutrition than the rest of the population. While half of all Guatemala children under the age of five are stunted, malnutrition is much higher among indigenous children, with 70 per cent stunted in their growth compared to 36 per cent of non-indigenous children.[15]

Refugees from hunger are among the most excluded and discriminated people.[16] They are also among those who suffer most from the lack of coherence in States' policies. To be coherent, States must extend legal protection to protect people fleeing from hunger and other severe violations of their right to food. We also call for the creation of a new legal instrument to recognize them as 'refugees from hunger' and grant them, at the very minimum, the right of non-refoulement with temporary protection, so that they would not be sent back to a country where hunger and famine threaten their lives.

17.1.3 Powerful non-state actors: transnational corporations

A phenomenon that affects the right to food is the increasing control of vast sectors of the world economy by transnational corporations.[17] Today, the top 200 corporations control around a quarter of the world's total productive assets. Many transnational corporations have revenues far exceeding the revenues of the Governments of the countries in which they are operating. Concentration has produced huge transnational corporations that monopolize the food chain, from the production, trade, processing, to the marketing and retailing of food, narrowing choices for farmers and consumers. As we noted earlier, just ten corporations, including Aventis, Monsanto, Pioneer and Syngenta, control one third of the US$23 billion commercial seed market and 80 per cent of the US$28 billion global pesticide market.[18] Another ten corporations, including Cargill, control 57 per cent of the total sales of the world's leading 30 retailers and account for 37 per cent of the revenues earned by the world's top 100 food and beverage companies.[19]

The participation of private sector corporations in food and agriculture sectors may improve efficiency, but such concentration of monopoly power also brings a danger that neither small producers, nor consumers will benefit. The design of genetically modified seeds for example, has largely been about creating vertical integration between seed, pesticides and production to increase corporate profits. The FAO revealed that 85 per cent of all plantings of transgenic crops are soybean, maize and cotton, modified to reduce input and labour costs for large-scale production systems, but not designed 'to feed the world or increase food quality'.[20] No serious investments have been made in any of the five most important crops of the poorest countries – sorghum, millet, pigeon pea, chickpea and groundnut. Only 1 per cent of research and development budgets of multinational corporations are spent on crops that might be useful for the developing world in arid regions.[21]

There is also the growing power of transnational corporations over the supply of water, as this is increasingly liberalized across the world. In many cases, private sector participation in water services has been made a precondition for the provision of loans and grants to developing countries by the IMF and the World Bank. Just two companies, Veolia Environnement, formerly Vivendi Environnement, and Suez Lyonnaise des Eaux, control a majority of private concessions worldwide.

Evidence on water privatization suggests that, while in some cases it can bring increased efficiency; it often means higher prices, which the poorest cannot afford. The case of Cochabamba, Bolivia, is now famous. A study on the privatization of water services in Manila[22] shows some positive effects, with 1 million more people being connected to the network between 1997 and 2003, but the price also rose by 425 per cent, making it too expensive for the poor. The study suggests that the poorest are doubly discriminated against because the price is at its highest in poorest communities and water quality has deteriorated rapidly in the poorest parts of the city. The study concluded that there was no independent mechanism for accountability and affected populations were not able to participate in the process. The same conclusions have been presented by WaterAid and Tearfund, in a study funded by the Government of the United Kingdom, on the effects of water privatization in ten developing countries.[23]

Despite the fact the transnational corporations increasingly control our food and water system, there are still relatively few mechanisms in place to ensure that they respect standards and do not violate human rights. As former Secretary-General Boutros Boutros-Ghali stated in 1996, 'the global reach of TNCs is not matched by a coherent global system of accountability'.

In many cases, transnational corporations have voluntarily chosen to abide by human rights standards, adopting internal policies and Codes of Conduct. Nestlé is one of them. But several NGOs raised concerns that Nestlé dominates the market for breastmilk substitutes in many countries and that some of its marketing practices violate the internationally agreed International Code of Marketing of Breastmilk Substitutes.[24] United Nations agencies, including UNICEF, have expressed similar concerns.[25]

Important intergovernmental instruments applying to private transnational corporations' activities include the OECD Guidelines, under which all adhering Governments (the OECD States, Argentina, Brazil and Chile) are bound to establish national contact points to handle complaints of violations by a transnational corporation, and the ILO Tripartite Declaration of Principles Concerning Multinational Enterprises and Social Policy. However, their supervision mechanisms are very weak. An excellent set of instruments has been proposed to fill this gap: the Norms on the Responsibilities of Transnational Corporations and Other Business Enterprises with Regard to Human Rights.[26] Unfortunately, they have not yet received the necessary attention by the Human Rights Council.

17.2 What are the new threats?

17.2.1 Desertification[27]

Many of the ongoing food crises are the result of the impact of serious drought, desertification and land degradation and rising conflict over deteriorating resources. In arid regions around the world, as the land becomes as hard as concrete and the wells dry up, thousands of families are forced to leave their villages. But where can they go? To the slums which encircle the ever-growing cities of Africa, Asia and Latin America. Deprived of their lands and their subsistence, families suffer from permanent unemployment, hunger and desperation.

The destruction of ecosystems and the degradation of vast agricultural zones across the world, especially in Africa, have created tragedies for small farmers and pastoralists who have depended on their land to secure their right to food. It is now estimated that there are around 25 million 'ecological refugees' or 'environmental migrants',[28] people who have been forced to flee from their lands as a result of natural disasters, including floods, drought and desertification, and end up struggling to survive in the slums of the world's megacities. Land degradation causes migration and intensifies conflict over resources, particularly between pastoral and farming communities, as witnessed in the Niger and in Ethiopia.[29] Many conflicts in Africa, including the conflict in the Darfur region of the Sudan, are linked with progressively worsening droughts and desertification that have contributed to conflict over resources.[30]

Eradicating hunger and fully realizing the right to food will therefore also depend on addressing the global problems of desertification and land degradation. Effective implementation of the United Nations Convention to Combat Desertification in Countries Experiencing Serious Drought and/or Desertification, particularly in Africa, is required.[31]

Globally, desertification and land degradation now affect over one billion people in over 100 countries,[32] including millions of people in both North and South, in both developing and developed countries. Dryland regions, where the land is arid or semi-arid and particularly vulnerable to the risk of degradation, comprise over 44 per cent of the world's cultivated land and support one third of the world's population (two billion people).[33] The vast majority of people living in drylands, about 1.4 billion, live in Asia (including China and Mongolia) and another 270 million people live in Africa, but 140 million people in Europe and 177 million in the Americas are also affected.[34] However, the impacts of land degradation are most severe in developing countries, particularly in Africa, where millions of people are wholly dependent on land for their livelihoods as farmers or pastoralists, and where there are few alternative livelihoods. The African drylands are home to 325 million people, 46 per cent of the population of the continent.[35] Countries with the greatest dryland populations are Nigeria, South Africa, Morocco, Algeria, the Sudan and Ethiopia.[36] Today, in Africa, approximately 500 million hectares of land are affected by degradation, including two thirds of the region's productive agricultural land.[37] The last four decades of repeated drought in the Sudano-Sahelian region have left people and their land increasingly vulnerable to degradation and desertification, and the resulting destitution. In the last year, droughts and food crises have spread across the drylands of the Sahel and the Horn of Africa threatening millions of people with hunger and starvation, as reported above.

Hunger is highly concentrated in arid countries where rainfall is low and uncertain, but where people nevertheless remain dependent on agricultural economies, especially in Africa. In Niger, for example, close to 95 per cent of productive land is dryland and the population is predominantly rural, chronically poor and subject to repeated food crises.[38] In Zimbabwe, the overwhelming majority of the poor live in rural areas and poverty is deepest in the low-rainfall areas of Matabeleland South, Masvingo and Matabeleland North provinces.[39] In Chad, which has an agricultural economy reliant on volatile rains, four fifths of the population is rural and an even higher proportion is poor.[40] Levels of undernourishment are particularly high across sub-Saharan Africa, with 34 per cent of its population, or 186 million people, chronically undernourished.[41] Sub-Saharan Africa is also the only region in the world where food production per capita is not expected to be able to keep up with population growth[42] and where food insecurity is increasing.[43]

It is estimated that 50 per cent of the world's 1 billion hungry people live on marginal, dry and degraded lands, according to the Millennium Project Task Force on Hunger.[44] Half of the world's hungry people therefore depend for their survival on land which is inherently poor, and may be becoming less fertile and less productive as a result of the impacts of repeated droughts, climate change and unsustainable use of the land. This means that eradicating hunger will require addressing desertification and land degradation as a key element of realizing the right to food. The Millennium Project report suggests that

> [a]bout half of food-insecure people in developing countries are farm households in higher-risk lands with low or highly unreliable rainfall, inherently poor or degraded soils, unfavourable topography and remoteness from markets and public services. These are mainly located in sub-humid and semiarid regions – generally referred to as drylands, and in hillsides and mountains in the humid tropics, in comparison with irrigated areas or fertile valley bottoms.[45]

The poor are often blamed for land degradation and desertification. It is assumed that, faced with the imperative of short-term survival, they may have no other choice than to act against their long-term interests by degrading their land, as they strive to meet their short-term basic needs for food, shelter and a livelihood.[46] Overgrazing, deforestation, extensification and intensification of agriculture and unsustainable population growth are causes of land degradation and desertification.[47] However, it is important to recognize that these immediate causes are usually linked to much broader causes.[48] Many factors affect land degradation, including people's lack of access to water, agricultural inputs, credit and agricultural infrastructure that would allow sustainable agriculture. The poor often have little choice but to live on land that is inherently poor and risk prone, with limited access to water and other infrastructure services, sometimes because they have been pushed off more fertile lands by wealthier landowners. The broader impacts of global climate change, economic globalization, and political and economic marginalization can all affect livelihoods in dryland areas.[49] A whole range of different factors at local, national and global levels in each country have an impact on land degradation and desertification, including inappropriate government policies.[50]

Although the poor are often blamed for land degradation, inappropriate national and international policies for the drylands have sometimes been more to blame. In the past, policies have been based on misunderstandings of the ecological dynamics of dryland regions and of traditional land use practices, particularly pastoralism.[51] Although pastoralists were long blamed for overgrazing, it is now recognized that pastoralist strategies are very well adapted to the special risks that characterize drylands, as long as pastoralists are able to follow the rains with their animals. Unfortunately, there has been a tendency to impose modern models of land management which have encouraged fencing and privatization of the land to create ranching systems that restrict the movement of animals and people, have been ill-adapted to the drylands and have resulted in overgrazing and land degradation. More recently, however, many experts have come to recognize that the traditional way of life of nomadic pastoralists is very well adapted to managing the risks and making the best use of marginal drylands.[52]

While overpopulation is often a factor that causes land degradation, it does not inevitably lead to land degradation and desertification. In Kenya, for example, the previously highly degraded lands of the Machakos district are in a much better state today that they were in the 1930s, despite the population having increased by more than five times. The introduction of terracing, small-scale water-harvesting and the planting and protection of trees, and substantial investment in infrastructure, including markets and development, have facilitated a rehabilitation of degraded land.[53] In Ethiopia, in regions where there has been significant investment in the land and infrastructure, particularly in small-scale water-harvesting, the land has been rehabilitated to become substantially more productive.[54] In fact, investment in small-scale water-harvesting can be one of the key elements in improving the realization of the right to food in arid regions.

Unfortunately, however, despite evidence that investment in drylands, including public investment in sustainable water management, is essential to rehabilitate land and to reduce the impact of land degradation on hunger, few resources are directed towards rural drylands. Hunger and food insecurity persist not only because of the low productivity and the threat of drought, but because of the lack of adequate investment in these areas and the lack of recognition of the rights of the people who live in them. International efforts to combat hunger – including poverty reduction strategies – still pay little attention to the problems of land degradation and desertification. Investment in rural development in terms of government and donor expenditure continues to fall, and drylands are accorded a very low level of priority, disproportionate to their size, population and need. Donors do respond to severe droughts by offering food aid, but offer little in the way of longer term development aid that would break the cycle of repeated drought, degradation and destitution. And while food aid saves lives, it does not save livelihoods – it is not a long-term solution, as found in Ethiopia and Niger.[55]

It is essential to invest in long-term development that reduces vulnerability to drought and desertification. This is possible. For example, Niger's water resources are quite vast. Beneath Niger's desert lies one of the largest fresh water aquifers in the world, and there is significant potential for better management of the Niger River and rainwater run-off.[56] Investing in small-scale water harvesting and digging wells where appropriate have reduced the vulnerability to drought of people dependent on rain-fed agriculture and has allowed some people in Niger to grow three crops per year. Although the cost of a well depends on its depth and is difficult when the water line can be as far down as 80 m, in many regions water is accessible at a relatively shallow 6 m. In Niger one quarter of the children die before they reach the age of five; this tragedy could be prevented. The main problem has been the lack of finance available to invest in small-scale water management to improve food security.

It is encouraging to see that, in the drive to implement the Millennium Development Goals, there is growing international awareness of the need to invest in drylands to fight hunger. The Millennium Project Task Force on Hunger placed special emphasis on marginal rural areas, including drylands, and argued that reaching the Millennium Development Goals on hunger will require investment in these lands. The report of the Task Force argues that '[t]o ignore marginal lands would consign millions to poverty and abandon vast areas of genuine potential'.[57]

With repeated droughts and repeated famines, especially in Africa, it is clear that there is an urgent need to invest and to build resilience to drought, which comes repeatedly and regularly, if not predictably, to dryland regions. It is unacceptable that drylands are still accorded such a low level of priority, disproportionate to their size, population and need. It is vital States focus on the full implementation of the Convention to Combat Desertification, and of the International Covenant on Economic, Social and Cultural Rights, to ensure the full realization of the right to food in the drylands.

For all the States parties to the International Covenant on Economic, Social and Cultural Rights, realizing the right to food is not merely a policy choice, but a legal obligation. There is a legal obligation on Governments to respect, protect and fulfil the right to food of all those under their jurisdiction, including people living in marginalized drylands. This means respecting and protecting appropriate livelihood strategies, but also where necessary supporting livelihoods to fight hunger and realize the right to food. All Governments also have extraterritorial obligations towards the realization of the right to food.[58] This means that all Governments must support the realization of the right to food in other countries, including for people living in marginalized drylands.

17.2.2 Biofuels[59]

An emerging issue has the potential to threaten the realization of the right to food: global plans to increase rapidly the production of 'biofuels' or what is termed by many environmental and social organizations in developing countries, 'agrofuels'.[60] Rushing to turn food crops – maize, wheat, sugar, palm oil – into fuel for cars, without first examining the impact on global hunger is a recipe for disaster. It is estimated that to fill one car tank with biofuel (about 50 litres) would require about 200 kg of maize – enough to feed one person for one year.[61]

Already, the new Executive Director of WFP, Josette Sheeran, has cited new obstacles for the organization, including climate change, soaring commodity prices, caused partly by the rapid growth of major countries like China and India, commodity costs and rising demand for biofuels, which in turn is pushing up global grain prices.[62]

The former President of the State Council of the Republic of Cuba, Fidel Castro Ruiz, has warned that it is a 'sinister idea to transform food into fuel'.[63] Lester Brown from the Earth Policy Institute, briefing the United States Senate in June 2006 suggested that, 'the stage is now set for direct competition for grain between the 800 million people who own automobiles, and the world's two billion poorest people'.[64] Increasingly unconvinced of the positive net impact of the production of agrofuels on carbon dioxide emissions, NGOs have called for a global moratorium on the expansion of agrofuels until the potential social, environmental and human rights impacts can be fully examined and appropriate regulatory structures put in place to prevent or mitigate any negative impacts.[65]

The sudden explosion of interest in agrofuels is evident in massive increases in investment and the setting of ambitious renewable-fuel targets across the Western countries. The European Union requires that agrofuels provide 5.75 per cent of member States' transport power by 2010 and 10 per cent by 2020.[66] The United States has set targets to increase usage of agrofuel for energy to 35 billion gallons per year. The former President of the United States, George W. Bush, and the President of Brazil, Luiz Inácio Lula da Silva, signed an agreement in March 2007 committing those two countries to increase their ethanol production. But why are agrofuels so suddenly being promoted? One answer is that Governments are finally waking up to the need to do something about global warming and climate change. Another answer is that Governments see the need to reduce dependence on oil for strategic reasons in the current war on terror. In his 2007 State of the Union message, President Bush was explicit about this goal:

> It's in our vital interest to diversify America's energy supply ... Let us build on the work we've done and reduce gasoline usage in the United States by 20 per cent in the next 10 years. When we do that we will have cut our total imports by the equivalent of three quarters of all the oil we now import from the Middle East.[67]

Garten Rothkopf, author of a new report commissioned by the Inter-American Development Bank, Blueprint for Green Energy in the Americas, has argued that Latin America will be the new Middle East: 'Latin America will be the Persian Gulf of biofuels, except that of course Latin America is much more stable as a source of energy.'[68] Another reason is pressure from the agro-industrial interests that will benefit from a rapid expansion in the production of agrofuels. As oil prices rise, it becomes more viable to invest in alternative energies, the 'green gold' of biofuels.

We use the term 'agrofuels' interchangeably with the more commonly used expression of 'biofuels'. Using the term 'agrofuels' highlights how the interests of the agro-industrial monopolies will dominate over the interests of the world's poor and hungry, especially in the developing world. As E. Holt-Giménez of Food First has argued, the myths of the green and pure image of 'biofuel' are being used to 'obscure the political-economic relationships between land, people's resources and food, and fail to help us to understand the profound consequences of the industrial transformation of our food and fuel systems'.[69]

If there are not conscious efforts to ensure that producing biofuels does not bring greater hunger in its wake, then the poor and hungry will be the victims of these new fuels.

Agrofuel

The two main types of agrofuel are bioethanol and biodiesel. Both are produced from a variety of food crops. Bioethanol is produced from sweet and starchy crops, which can be fermented to produce alcohol – mostly sugar cane and maize, but also sugar beet, potatoes, wheat or even manioc (the staple food of many African nations). Biodiesel is produced from vegetable oils by reaction of the oil with methanol.[70] The oils used are mostly from soya, palm or rapeseed, but also from peanuts, coconuts and many other oil-rich plants. P. Garde in his study on biofuels in Senegal points out that most of the plants used for agrofuels are food products and form the basic staple foods of millions of people in the poorest regions of the world, including in Africa, where food security is already seriously in peril.[71]

These food crops can be directly converted into energy and can be used to fuel cars and other transport. Up to 10 per cent of bioethanol can be mixed into normal petrol and can run in any car. Cars with specialized engines can also run on 100 per cent bioethanol, although so far Brazil is the only country to have made substantive progress with these cars. Biodiesel can also be blended directly into standard diesel and can be used by standard diesel engine cars. Adding between 5 and 10 per cent of biofuel to petrol and diesel can simply replace additives that oil companies normally add to improve combustion. Current forecasts therefore suggest that biofuels will account for less than 5 per cent of total transport fuel use in 2010. 'Because most liquid biofuels will be consumed as blends with gasoline or petroleum diesel, biofuels will for some time to come be complements to petroleum-based transport fuels, not major competitors with them', the Director of Research of the Global Subsidies Initiative, Ronald Steenblik, has observed.[72] This means that, so far, oil companies do not feel threatened by the shift towards agrofuels. On the contrary, the global corporate monopolies of oil, grain, cars and biotechnology are rushing to consolidate partnerships: Archer Daniels Midland Company (ADM) with Monsanto, Chevron with Volkswagen, BP and DuPont with Toyota.[73]

Global production of agrofuels is currently dominated by one continent (the Americas) and one type of fuel (bioethanol). This bioethanol is produced mostly from maize (in the United States) or sugar cane (in Brazil). The United States has doubled its production of bioethanol over the past five years and has now overtaken Brazil as the dominant producer. Brazil, which produced over 12 million tons of ethanol in 2006, much of it for the domestic market, plans to become a dominant producer for the global market by 2025.[74] By contrast, Europe's production of ethanol, at 3.5 million tons, is still relatively low. However, Europe dominates the production of biodiesel, using rapeseed oil and palm oil predominantly imported from India and Malaysia, although biodiesel production remains one tenth of total ethanol production.[75] Other than Brazil, few developing countries produce significant amounts, but China, Colombia, India and Thailand have started production. So far, production is focused on food crops in the 'first generation' of agrofuels and there has been little production and investment in what are known as 'second-generation' cellulose-based fuels which could convert non-food crops and agricultural wastes (e.g. the fibrous stalks of wheat) for production.

Global consumption of agrofuels is low, but will rise rapidly under targets set in the European Union, the United States and Latin America. The European Union has set targets requiring that agrofuels provide up to 10 per cent of transport fuels by 2020.[76] The United States has also set targets to increase the use of agrofuel. But the target objectives cannot be met by agricultural production in the industrialized countries. It has been estimated that Europe would have to devote 70 per cent of its arable lands to agrofuel production to meet these objectives and the United States would have to convert its entire production of maize and soya into ethanol and biodiesel.

Therefore, the industrialized countries of the North are very interested in the production of the countries of the southern hemisphere to meet these needs.[77] According to FIAN International, the United States and the European Union are heavily dependent on imports from Latin America of soya, sugar cane and palm oil, some African countries, such as Nigeria, Cameroon, Ivory Coast and Ghana, for palm oil and Asian countries, including India, Indonesia and Malaysia, which are the main palm oil producers. Such production is also much cheaper in developing countries. For example, it is much cheaper to produce a litre of ethanol in Brazil (15 Euro cents) than in the United States (30 Euro cents) or Europe (50 Euro cents).[78]

The impact of biofuels on the right to food

Increasing the production of biofuels could bring positive benefits for climate change and for farmers in developing countries, including by improving food security, if the benefits trickle down. However, it is also important to examine the potential of biofuels to threaten the realization of the right to food. It is unacceptable that increasing production of biofuels should lead to greater hunger. The greatest risk is that dependence on the agro-industrial model of production will fail to benefit poor peasant farmers and will generate violations of the right to food. As the Brazilian Landless Workers' Movement argues, 'the current model of production for bio-energy is sustained by the same elements that have always been the cause of the oppression of our peoples' – the appropriation of land, concentration of ownership and the exploitation of the labour force.[79]

There are a number of key concerns to highlight. These include increasing of food prices, increasing competition over land and forests, and forced evictions, the degradation of employment and conditions of work, and increasing prices and scarcity of water.

According to many studies, the production of biofuels was one of the main causes of the food crisis of 2007 and 2008.[80] According to a study by the World Bank, the increase in production of agrofuels is responsible for 70–75 per cent of the increase in food prices between 2002 and 2008, mainly because it resulted in a decrease in the supply of food commodities and the substitution of food crops by crops for the production of agrofuels, in particular maize.[81] Mexico, for example, faced food riots in February 2007 after the price of maize tortillas rose by over 400 per cent in January 2007, severely affecting the poorest for whom the basic staple tortilla makes up 45 per cent of family expenses.[82] Although Mexico was traditionally a net exporter of maize, it has become a net importer because of so-called 'free-trade' agreements, which have opened up Mexican markets to unfair competition with the dumping of subsidized maize exports from the United States and have displaced Mexican production. With the production of biofuels in the United States, the price went up and the Mexican consumers were not able to afford it any more.

The prices of basic staple foods are likely to continue to increase, threatening economic access to sufficient food, particularly for the poorest who already spend a high proportion of their incomes on food. The well-regarded think tank, International Food Policy Research Institute (IFPRI), has estimated that prices will continue to rise in the near future if the production of biofuels is increased. It is estimated that there could be a rise of 41 per cent in the international price of maize between now and 2020. The prices of vegetable oil crops, especially soya and sunflower seeds could increase by 76 per cent by 2020, and wheat prices could increase by 30 per cent. In the poorest regions of sub-Saharan Africa, Asia and Latin America, the price of manioc could rise by 135 per cent by 2020.[83] IFPRI believes that this will set up a battle of 'food versus fuel', unless there are urgent investments in moving to the second generation of biofuels that will not depend so much on food products. The consequences of such a continued increase in food prices would be grave. IFPRI projects that the number of people suffering from undernourishment would increase by 16 million people for each percentage point increase in the real price of staple food. This could mean that 1.2 billion people would be suffering from hunger by 2025.

Although increasing food prices should theoretically benefit millions of people working as peasant farmers in developing countries, this is not always the case. Many farming families are net buyers of staple foods, as they do not have enough land to be self-sufficient, and will therefore be affected by rising consumer prices. In addition, prices received by farmers at the farm gate are often exploitatively low, particularly for remote farmers with little choice of whom to sell their crops to, and often do not reflect global prices because of the greed of intermediaries. If increased agricultural production is to benefit poor peasant farmers, it will be essential to build mechanisms, such as cooperatives and non-exploitative out-grower schemes, that would ensure a trickle-down to the poorest.

A structural increase in the prices of food crops will intensify competition over land and other natural resources, including forest reserves. This will pit peasant farmers and indigenous communities of forest dwellers against massive agribusiness corporations and large investors who are already buying up large swathes of land or forcing peasants off their land. The Belgian human rights organization Human Rights Everywhere (HREV) has documented forced evictions, the appropriation of land and other violations of human rights in the palm oil plantations in Colombia, documenting responsibilities of all the actors along the production chain.[84] Forced evictions constitute clear violations of the obligations to respect and protect people's existing access to food, and all corporations involved in the production of biofuels should avoid complicity in these violations.

Lessons must be learned from the more recent expansion of soya production across Latin America, which has contributed to the deforestation of vast swathes of the Amazonian basin and has resulted in the forcible eviction of many peasants and indigenous peoples from their lands. Cases have been documented in Brazil, Colombia, Argentina, Paraguay and Indonesia. In some cases, agribusiness companies urge peasants to sell their land, in others the companies occupy land without informing the communities who have been living there for decades. In Paraguay, where the area planted with soya has more than doubled since the 1990s (mainly in the regions of Itapúa, Alto Paraná and Canindeyú), many indigenous communities do not possess land titles and have been reportedly forcibly evicted. In Argentina, peasants and indigenous families have reportedly been evicted from their land in the provinces of Córdoba, Santiago del Estero, Salta, Mendoza, Misiones and Jujuy. In the Colombian region of Chocó, communities of indigenous people and people of African descent have reportedly been evicted from their land after oil palm growing companies occupied the land. Similar cases have been recorded in Indonesia and Cameroon.

Although the increase in agrofuel production could offer better employment, MST in Brazil has already protested the 'slavery' conditions faced by workers on the country's sugar-cane plantations. Alexandre Conceicao, a member of the MST national leadership in the northern state of Pernambuco, has warned that 'the social cost of this policy is the overexploitation of labour with an army of seasonal workers who cut one ton of sugar cane for 2.50 reals (1.28 dollars) in precarious conditions which have already caused the deaths of hundreds of workers', and Camila Moreno, an expert in agrarian development at the Rural University of Rio de Janeiro, has warned that the growth of the ethanol industry is breathing life into 'a modern-day version of the sugar plantation slave-labour past'.[85]

Although promises are being made that the production of biofuels will provide more jobs,[86] there are risks that, given competition over land with peasant farmers, biofuel production may result in greater unemployment. In Brazil, it is estimated that 100 hectares dedicated to family farming generate at least 35 jobs, while 100 hectares dedicated to industrial farming of sugar cane and oil palm plantations provide only 10 jobs, and of soybeans half a job.[87] If industrial farming takes over land formerly dedicated to family farming, the net effect will be fewer jobs. The possibilities for agrarian reform to increase access to land for landless families may also be halted. Biofuels can, however, be produced by non-industrial family farming that provides more employment: in Brazil, 30 per cent of sugar cane production is in the hands of 60,000 small producers.

Finally, the production of biofuels requires substantial amounts of water, diverting water away from the production of food crops. So far, few substantive studies have been undertaken to examine the impact of biofuel production on water resources and reflect the true environmental and social costs, although this was a central concern of the World Water Week international meeting held in Stockholm in August 2006. Rising prices of water would limit access to water for the poorest communities, in ways that would negatively affect the right to food.

Protecting the right to food through a moratorium on biofuel production

Rather than persuading us to use less energy, the false promise of agrofuels suggests that we can help the climate by simply changing fuels. Yet many studies have shown that agrofuels may not even be 'carbon-neutral' or make much contribution to setting off carbon dioxide emissions, once account is taken of the fossil fuels that are still needed to plant, harvest and process food crops for biofuels under highly mechanized industrial models of production. Agrofuel production is unacceptable if it brings greater hunger and water scarcity to the poor in developing countries.

The recommended response is a five-year moratorium on biofuel production using current methods, to allow time for technologies to be devised and regulatory structures to be put in place to protect against negative environmental, social and human rights impacts. Many measures can be put in place during such a moratorium to ensure that biofuel production can have positive impacts and respect the right to adequate food. Such measures include promoting the need to reduce overall energy consumption and maintaining focus on all other methods of improving energy efficiency, and moving immediately to 'second generation' technologies for producing biofuels, which would reduce the competition between food and fuel. Agricultural wastes and crop residues could be used. As IFPRI has pointed out: 'the efficient exploitation of agricultural wastes presents significant potential for developing bio-energy without unduly disrupting existing agricultural practices and food production or requiring new land to come into production'.[88] Common crop residues that can be used include maize cobs, sugar cane bagasse, rice husks and banana leaves. In this way, biofuel production could be complementary to existing agriculture, rather than competing with it, and would not require massive diversion of food, land and water resources away from food production. Food prices would therefore remain stable, but farmers would have profitable ways of disposing of agricultural waste products, benefiting both consumers and producers.

Finally, it should be ensured that biofuel production is based on family agriculture, rather than industrial models of agriculture, in order to ensure more employment and rural development that provides opportunities, rather than competition, to poor peasant farmers. Organizing cooperatives of small farmers to grow crops for larger processing firms would provide much more employment than the concentration of land into heavily mechanized expanses and plantations. As ActionAid has pointed out 'Biofuel could even be an important tool to fight hunger and poverty if it comes together with a set of appropriate policies involving smallholder farmers.'[89]

17.3 Where is hope?

17.3.1 The Right to Food Guidelines

The Right to Food Guidelines, which were adopted in November 2004 by the FAO Council, mark an important step in the definition and implementation of the right to food.[90] The adoption of these guidelines gives us hope for the future in terms of government-level commitments to improving enjoyment of the right to food.

The Right to Food Guidelines are ground-breaking in the sense that they provide an internationally accepted definition of the right to food. The definition adopted by governments (see paragraphs 16 and 17) closely follows the definition adopted by the CESCR. It also follows the interpretation offered by the Committee that States are obliged to *respect, protect* and *fulfil* the right to adequate food. This has important implications for the acceptance of this framework across all economic, social and cultural rights.

The Right to Food Guidelines are also ground-breaking in recognizing the international dimension related to the right to food, and addressing questions of, for example, international trade, food aid and embargoes. This is important because it extends understanding of the right to food beyond the traditional relation between a State and its citizens towards a greater recognition of 'extraterritorial' obligations. This set of guidelines also addresses questions of non-State actors, encouraging direct responsibility for respecting the right to food and improved regulation of markets to ensure food security.

The Guidelines also show how the right to food can be incorporated into government strategies and institutions.[91] They show how the key human rights principles – non-discrimination, participation, transparency, accountability and access to justice – can be incorporated into a rights-based approach to food security. They also call on States to promote 'broad-based economic development that is supportive of their food security policies' (guideline 2.1), to 'pursue inclusive, non-discriminatory and sound economic, agriculture, fisheries, forestry, land use, and, as appropriate, land reform policies' (guideline 2.5) and to incorporate the right to food into poverty reduction strategies. They also urge States to 'take account of shortcomings of market mechanisms in protecting the environment and public goods' (guideline 4.10) and that, particularly for women (guideline 8.3) and vulnerable groups (guideline 8.1). The Right to Food Guidelines call on States to set up mechanisms to inform people of their rights and improve access to justice for the right to food (guideline 7).

Since 2004, several Governments implemented the Right to Food Guidelines at the national level.[92] Brazil provides one of the best examples. In January 2002, the Brazilian government adopted a national policy of food and nutrition security, introducing structural measures and a national programme of food security – the zero hunger programme – based on social assistance.[93] A National Council of Food and Nutrition Security was set up to develop and guarantee the implementation of these measures in September 2006. It was created as a forum for discussion between government and civil society, reporting directly to the President, with the aim of coordinating the policies of various governmental institutions and the efforts of civil society and representatives of the most vulnerable groups.[94] Finally, the Brazilian Congress passed a law creating the national system of food and nutrition security, which sanctioned the system put in place by the government and recognized the right to food and related obligations of the State.[95]

This example of Brazil demonstrates the value governments and others ascribe to the legal entrenchment of rights. A corollary to this is the ability of victims to enforce such rights. This ability of victims to legally enforce the right to food and other economic, social and cultural rights has been problematic without an international complaints mechanism, such as provided for in the Optional Protocol to the International Covenant on Economic, Social and Cultural Rights.

17.3.2 The adoption of the Optional Protocol to the ICESCR and progress in the justiciability of the right to food

The Optional Protocol to the International Covenant on Economic, Social and Cultural Rights was adopted by consensus by the Human Rights Council in June 2008 and by the General Assembly on 10 December 2008, 60 years after the adoption of the Universal Declaration of Human Rights.

The adoption of the Optional Protocol marks significant progress at the international level in the development of the practical framework for the understanding and implementation of economic, social and cultural rights, including the right to food. During our missions to countries such as Brazil, Ethiopia, Bangladesh, Guatemala, India, Mongolia and others, we found that it is sometimes very difficult for poor people, especially peasant farmers, to have access to justice before local and national tribunals. The entry into force of the Optional Protocol will greatly improve access to justice for victims of violations of the right to food, by allowing individuals or groups to bring a complaint directly to the CESCR.

The Optional Protocol to the International Covenant on Economic, Social and Cultural Rights is an instrument that gives the CESCR the mandate to consider individual communications (complaints) from victims of violations of all economic, social and cultural rights contained in the Covenant. It also establishes an inquiry mechanism for investigating grave or systematic violations of economic, social and cultural rights.

In its future role as quasi-judicial mechanism, the CESCR will certainly build upon the recent developments in case law at national and regional levels, which prove that the right to food is inherently justiciable.[96]

India provides one of the best examples in the world in terms of the justiciability of the right to food.[97] The Constitution of India prohibits discrimination and recognizes all human rights. The right to life is recognized as a directly justiciable fundamental right (Article 21), while the right to food is defined as a directive principle of State policy (Article 47). Through interpreting these provisions, the Supreme Court of India has found that the Government has a *constitutional obligation* to take steps to fight hunger and extreme poverty and to ensure a dignified life to all individuals. In a decision in 2001, the Supreme Court concluded that the Government has a direct responsibility to prevent starvation.[98] To ensure the fulfilment of the right to food, the Supreme Court directed that all destitute people be identified and included in existing food-based schemes and directed state governments to implement fully all these schemes, including the Targeted Public Distribution Scheme (TPDS), the Antyodaya Anna Yojana (AAY), the Integrated Child Development Scheme (ICDS), the Mid-Day Meals Scheme (MDMS). The Supreme Court also directed the most vulnerable, including the primitive tribes, to be placed in the AAY lists to ensure their access to food at a highly subsidized price. In the past, the Court has also made judgments that protected the right to water of Dalits against discrimination by the upper castes,[99] the right to livelihood of traditional fisherpeople against the shrimp industry (*Aquaculture case*),[100] and the right to livelihood of scheduled tribes against the acquisition of land by a private company (*Samatha case*).[101]

In South Africa, all economic and social rights have been declared justiciable under South African law. The South African Bill of Rights, incorporated into the 1996 Constitution, explicitly provides (section 27, paragraph 1 (b)) that every person has the right to have access to sufficient food and water, subject to progressive realization. This legal recognition of the right to food enabled, for example, artisanal fishers in South Africa to initiate and win a case before the High Court of Cape Town in 2007. The fisherfolk brought the case to the High Court of Cape of Good Hope to challenge their effective exclusion from access to fishing resources.[102] The Court examined the case and the Government and the fishermen reached a friendly agreement, which took a number of months. It allowed 1000 fishermen to have immediate access to the sea. In a judgement in 2007, the Court took responsibility for ensuring the implementation of the agreement and it obliged the Government to review the law while respecting the right to food in this context.[103]

17.3.3 The strategy of food sovereignty

A third area of hope is the focus on food security. For some time now, civil society organizations have been calling for a new focus on 'food sovereignty' that challenges the current model of agricultural trade, which they see as cultivating an export-oriented, industrial agriculture that is displacing peasant and family agriculture. The concept of food sovereignty is not the same as the concept of the right to food, but there are some close links between them.

So what does food sovereignty mean? So far, there are few academic studies or systematic papers on the concept of food sovereignty. Rather, it is a concept still in the process of being conceptualized and iteratively debated among civil society organizations, after first being proposed by the global social movement of peasant and family farmers, Via Campesina. For Via Campesina:

> Food sovereignty is the right of peoples to define their own food and agriculture; to protect and regulate domestic agricultural production and trade in order to achieve sustainable development objectives; to determine the extent to which they want to be self-reliant; [and] to restrict the dumping of products in their markets.[104]

Via Campesina had originally developed and introduced the concept in 1996, introducing it into the discussions at a parallel meeting held by NGOs and civil society organizations (CSOs) during the 1996 World Food Summit. Since 1996, the concept has gained support from other farmers and civil society organizations, both in the South and in the North. During the World Food Summit: five years later in 2002, a NGO/CSO 'Forum on food sovereignty', attended by representatives of over 400 civil society and farmer organizations, defined the concept of food sovereignty as:

> Food sovereignty is the right of peoples, communities, and countries to define their own agricultural, labor, fishing, food and land policies which are ecologically, socially, economically and culturally appropriate to their unique circumstances. It includes the true right to food and to produce food, which means that all people have the right to safe, nutritious and culturally appropriate food and to food-producing resources and the ability to sustain themselves and their societies.
>
> Food sovereignty means the primacy of people's and community's rights to food and food production, over trade concerns. This entails the support and promotion of local markets and producers over production for export and food imports.
>
> ... Food sovereignty requires:
>
> – **Placing priority** on food production for domestic and local markets, based on peasant and family farmer diversified and agro-ecologically based production systems;
>
> – **Ensuring fair prices** for farmers, which means the power to protect internal markets from low-priced, dumped imports;
>
> – **Access to land, water, forests, fishing areas and other productive resources** through genuine redistribution;

– **Recognition and promotion of women's role** in food production and equitable access and control over productive resources;
– **Community control over productive resources**, as opposed to corporate ownership of land, water, and genetic and other resources;
– **Protecting seeds**, the basis of food and life itself, for the free exchange and use of farmers, which means no patents on life and a moratorium on the genetically modified crops; and
– **Public investment** in support for the productive activities of families, and communities, geared toward empowerment, local control and production of food for people and local markets.[105]

The first key element in the concept of food sovereignty is the reclamation of national and individual sovereignty over food security policy. CSOs charge that, under WTO Agreements, countries are losing control of their ability to decide their own food and agricultural policies. Countries have found themselves in a position where they are deprived of certain policy options (such as tariffs on food imports). Under WTO rules, it is also very difficult to reverse liberalization already undertaken. In this demand for reclaiming policy space, food sovereignty runs close to the concept of 'multifunctionality'. The Norwegian proposal referred to in section 4.1, for example, suggests that 'every country should be granted flexibility in national policy design to foster domestic agricultural production necessary to address domestic non-trade concerns'.[106]

Food sovereignty holds that each country should have the right to determine the extent to which it wants to be self-reliant in domestic production for basic food needs. A stable trading system can contribute to improving overall food availability, but food security cannot always be assured through food imports. Poor countries may not have sufficient foreign exchange. Poor people may not be able to afford to buy food imports, especially when this displaces local farming and therefore devastates rural incomes. The concept of food sovereignty is not anti-trade, but rather is against the priority given to exports and against the dumping of imported, subsidized food in local markets which destroys local farmers' livelihoods. It seeks to guarantee food security first, by favouring local production for local markets. The central idea is that small-scale, peasant agriculture should be protected for its role in ensuring food security, employment and environmental objectives – as long as that protection does not threaten the livelihoods of other farmers in other countries.

Food sovereignty does not rule out subsidized protection, but explicitly establishes a corollary right of importing countries to impose protective tariffs to protect themselves against dumping of any subsidized exports. As has been noted 'one of the goals is to stop the race to the bottom in terms of price and the resulting disintegration of rural communities'[107] in both the North and the South. Subsidies are therefore permitted, but only to support small farmers producing for domestic markets and not for export. Under the logic of food sovereignty, subsidies should never be permitted to large-scale farming or the export sector.

Food sovereignty emphasizes locally oriented small-scale peasant agriculture producing for consumption inside the country, as opposed to the current model of export-oriented, industrialized agriculture. CSOs believe that the export-oriented model is forcing the industrialization of the food chain, precipitating the decline of small farms and peasant farming, in the North as well as in the South, to the benefit of the large agribusiness corporations. Millions of farmers are losing their livelihoods in the developing countries, but small farmers in the northern countries are also suffering. In the United Kingdom of Great Britain and Northern Ireland, for example, 20,000 farm workers left agriculture in the year 1999, allowing ever-greater concentration of the land.[108] The same is happening around the rest of Europe and in the United States. Food sovereignty suggests that small-scale farmers have much in common, both in the North and the South. Food sovereignty is an attempt to find common ground and resolve the opposition that has been created through the issue of subsidies, by recognizing that subsidies have primarily benefited larger farmers and agribusiness corporations.

Food sovereignty also embodies a call for greater access to resources by the poor, especially women, challenging what is perceived as a growing concentration of ownership of resources. Food insecurity, like poverty, is usually the result of a lack of access to productive resources, rather than the overall availability of food. Food sovereignty calls for equitable access to land, seeds, water, credit and other productive resources so that people can feed themselves. This implies challenging existing relations of power and distribution, through for example, engaging in agrarian reform. It also implies challenging the increasing concentration of ownership of agricultural trade, processing and marketing by transnational agribusiness corporations through, for example, improving competition law (anti-trust law) at a transnational level and through the prohibition of the appropriation of knowledge through intellectual property-rights regimes. It calls for recognition of communities' rights to their local, traditional resources, including plant genetic resources, and for protection of farmers' rights to exchange and reproduce seeds.[109]

Finally, the concept of food sovereignty also recognizes the right of countries to refuse technologies considered inappropriate, on the basis of the precautionary principle. It also recognizes the right of consumers to be able to decide what they consume, and how and by whom it is produced. This means that consumers should be able to choose food produced in their own countries, without this being seen as a restraint on trade. It also means that consumers should be able to choose whether they want to eat genetically modified organisms (GMOs) products; labelling for genetically modified ingredients may be seen as an indirect trade barrier. Food sovereignty demands the protection of consumer interests, including regulation for food safety that embodies the precautionary principle and the accurate labelling of food and animal feed products for information about content and origins. It also demands the participation of consumers, as well as producers, in standard-setting, whether at national level or international level. For instance, the FAO/World Health Organization Codex Alimentarius Commission, which sets international standards for food safety recognized by WTO, is criticized by CSOs for failing to include the participation of small producers and consumers, and being rather heavily influenced by the lobbying and participation of the large agribusiness, food and chemical corporations. Food sovereignty seeks to redress this balance.

How then is food sovereignty linked to the concept of the right to food? The right to food means that governments are legally bound as States parties to the International Covenant on Economic, Social and Cultural Rights to ensure food security for their citizens, in any political or economic system. Governments are legally bound to respect, protect and fulfil the right to food, when they have ratified the International Covenant. They are duty-bound to finding the best way of ensuring food security for all their people, as the right to adequate food is only realized 'when every man, woman and child, alone or in community with others, has physical and economic access at all times to adequate food or means for its procurement'.[110] In the face of mounting evidence that the current world trading system is hurting the food security of the poorest and most marginalized, and generating ever-greater inequalities, it is now time to look at alternative means that could better ensure the right to food. Food sovereignty offers an alternative vision that puts food security first and treats trade as a means to an end, rather than as an end in itself.

These three areas – the government commitment demonstrated through the voluntary guidelines, the developments in justiciability mechanisms such as the Optional Protocol to the International Covenant on Economic, Social and Cultural Rights and the visions encompassed in the concept of food security – all offer substantial reason to hope that in the future the normative framework for the right to food will continue to improve and expand.

Annexures

1. The work of the Special Rapporteur on the right to food and his team

The mandate of the UN Special Rapporteur on the Right to Food

At its fifty-sixth session, the Commission on Human Rights adopted resolution 2000/10, in which it decided to appoint a Special Rapporteur on the Right to Food for a period of three years. On 4 September 2000, the Chairperson of the Commission appointed Mr. Jean Ziegler, from Switzerland, as Special Rapporteur.

The role of the Special Rapporteur on the Right to Food is to ensure that governments are meeting their obligations to respect, protect and fulfil the right to food of all people. The Commission on Human Rights created the role of Special Rapporteur on the Right to Food 'in order to respond fully to the necessity for an integrated and coordinated approach in the promotion and protection of the right to food'. Resolution 2000/10 outlined the mandate of the Special Rapporteur, requesting the Special Rapporteur to accomplish the following main activities:

(a) To seek, receive and respond to information on all aspects of the realization of the right to food, including the urgent necessity of eradicating hunger;
(b) To establish cooperation with Governments, intergovernmental organizations, in particular the Food and Agriculture Organization of the United Nations, and non-governmental organizations, on the promotion and effective implementation of the right to food, and to make appropriate recommendations on the realization thereof, taking into consideration the work already done in this field throughout the United Nations system;
(c) To identify emerging issues related to the right to food worldwide.

Thematic reports

Jean Ziegler submitted his first report to the Commission in April 2001 at its 57th session. In his report, he recommended that the Commission make it clear that the term 'food' covers not only solid foods but also the nutritional aspects of drinking water. He also expressed the view that the right to food is of such theoretical and practical importance for the economic, social and cultural development of peoples and individuals that it should be the subject of a debate at the General Assembly of the United

Nations. At that session, the Commission adopted resolution 2001/25 on the right to food by a roll-call vote of 52 votes to one (the United States voted against). In this resolution, the Commission commended the Special Rapporteur for his valuable work in the promotion of the right to food (paragraph 7). It reconfirmed his mandate as spelt out in resolution 2000/10 and further requested him to pay attention to the issue of drinking water, taking into account the interdependence of this issue and the right to food (paragraph 9).

The Special Rapporteur presented a report each year to the Commission on Human Rights and to the General Assembly between 2001 and 2006. When the Commission on Human Rights was dismantled, the mandates of the Special Rapporteur on the Right to Food and the other experts of the Commission on Human Rights were transferred by the General Assembly in resolution 60/251 to the Human Rights Council which extended the mandate by its decision 2006/102. The Special Rapporteur's first report to the Human Rights Council was submitted in January 2007. He then presented a last report to the General Assembly in October 2007 and a final report to the Human Rights Council in March 2008. Jean Ziegler's mandate finished at the end of April 2008 after the appointment of Professor Olivier de Schutter as the new Special Rapporteur on the Right to Food.

Country missions

The Special Rapporteur and his team also undertook country missions to look at the situations of the right to food in different countries in the various regions of the world. On country missions, the focus was to examine the progress in realizing the right to food over time, monitor the situation of vulnerable groups especially those that suffer from discrimination, as well as to monitor compliance with the obligations to respect, protect and fulfil the right to food.

During the course of his mandate, the Special Rapporteur conducted 11 official country missions to 10 countries:

- Niger (27 August to 3 September 2001, and again in 2005)
- Brazil (1–18 March 2002)
- Bangladesh (23 October to 4 November 2002)
- The Occupied Palestinian Territories (3–12 July 2003)
- Ethiopia (16–27 February 2004)
- Mongolia (14–24 August 2004)
- Guatemala (26 January to 4 February 2005)
- India (20 August to 2 September 2005)
- Lebanon (11–16 September 2006)
- Bolivia (29 April to 6 May 2007)
- Cuba (28 October to 6 November 2007)

Two unofficial preparatory missions were also undertaken, to Venezuela (10–15 July 2001) and Brazil (1–7 August 2001), to explore the situation of the right to food in these countries and prepare for future official missions. In Venezuela, the Special Rapporteur examined the first results of the Government's 'Plan Bolivar' and the fight against malnutrition, and also gave a speech at the special session of the Latin American Parliament in Caracas. In Brazil, the Special Rapporteur addressed a meeting organized by the MST (Landless Workers Movement) Central Committee and the Lawyers Association of Sao Paolo, and visited MST *asentamientos* and *acampamentos*.

Urgent appeals

The terms of the mandate entrusted to the Special Rapporteur also requested him to 'seek, receive and respond to information on all aspects of the realization of the right to food, including the urgent necessity of eradicating hunger'. In the context of this part of his mandate, the Special Rapporteur received a large number of communications alleging violations of the right to food and related rights worldwide. Such communications were received from national, regional and international NGOs, as well as intergovernmental organizations and other United Nations procedures concerned with the protection of human rights. This process is an important means of cooperation with Member States, as it opens a constructive dialogue about specific cases that can be remedied.

Each year efforts were made to better publicize the right to food mandate and raise awareness among civil society. As a result, each year there was a marked increase in the cases reported to the Special Rapporteur and on which he called governments attention. However, the communications presented in no way reflect the full extent of the serious obstacles that still remain in the realization of the right to food of all around the world.

During 2006 for example, the Special Rapporteur sent a total of 46 communications concerning the right to food to 22 Member States as well as seven communications to other actors including international and regional financial institutions (the World Bank and the Asian Development Bank), national development agencies (the *Agence française de développement*) and transnational corporations. Many of these communications were sent jointly with other relevant thematic or country-based special procedures, and were addressed to, *inter alia*, the Governments of Australia, Brazil, Chile, Colombia, the Democratic Republic of the Congo, the Democratic People's Republic of Korea, Ecuador, India, Indonesia, Israel, the Lao People's Democratic Republic, Mexico, Myanmar, the Philippines, the Republic of Moldova, the Sudan and the United States of America. Communications were also sent to the European Union. Approximately half related to allegations of violations of the obligation to respect the right to food on the part of State agents, for example, forced evictions from land that inhibited peoples' access to food. The remaining communications related to allegations that relevant authorities failed to protect or fulfil the right to food.

Out of the 46 communications sent, 16 replies from 12 Governments were received along with one reply from a multinational company. The Special Rapporteur welcomed these replies which he considered a useful way to engage in constructive dialogues in relation to specific cases, issues or situations. Almost half of the Governments failed to respond at all.

In 2007, the Special Rapporteur sent a total of 61 communications concerning the right to food to 31 Member States as well as eight communications to other actors including international and regional financial institutions (the World Bank and the Asian Development Bank), regional organizations (European Commission) national development agencies (*Agence Française de Developpement*), transnational corporations and private foundations (Bill and Melinda Gates Foundation). Where appropriate, the Special Rapporteur sent joint urgent appeals or letters with one or more special procedures of the Human Rights Council where the allegations raised relate to the right to food as well as to rights addressed under other mandates. Out of the 61 communications sent to Member States, 33 replies were received and out of the 8 communications sent to other actors, 8 replies were received.

The Research Unit on the Right to Food

The Research Unit on the Right to Food was created in 2001 to provide research support to the UN Special Rapporteur on the Right to Food, in collaboration with the United Nations Office of the High Commissioner for Human Rights. The Research Unit on the Right to Food was located at the Graduate Institute of Development Studies in Geneva from 2001 to 2007 and at the newly created Graduate Institute of International and Development Studies in 2008. It was financially supported by the Swiss Agency for Development and Cooperation. In July 2008, at the end of the mandate of Jean Ziegler as UN Special Rapporteur, the Research Unit on the Right to Food completed its work and two of its members, Christophe Golay and Claire Mahon, joined a new Project on Economic, Social and Cultural Rights, based at the Geneva Academy of International Humanitarian Law and Human Rights.

The Research Unit helped to prepare the Special Rapporteur's reports to the UN Commission on Human Rights and to the UN General Assembly, and assisted in country missions to examine the right to food around the world. The Research Unit also worked to disseminate information about the right to food, included through the website www.righttofood.org, and to develop networks of organizations working on the right to food and reporting violations of the right to food.

The staff of the Research Unit on the Right to Food were: Sally-Anne Way (2001–2007), Christophe Golay (2001–2008) and Claire Mahon (2007–2008).

2. The right to food: Commission on Human Rights Resolution 2000/10

The Commission on Human Rights,

Recalling the Universal Declaration of Human Rights, which provides that everyone has the right to a standard of living adequate for her/his health and well-being, including food,

Recalling also the provisions of the International Covenant on Economic, Social and Cultural Rights in which the fundamental right of every person to be free from hunger is recognized,

Recalling further the Universal Declaration on the Eradication of Hunger and Malnutrition,

Bearing in mind the Rome Declaration on World Food Security and the Plan of Action of the World Food Summit, held in Rome from 13 to 17 November 1996,

Recalling all its previous resolutions in this regard, in particular resolution 1999/24 of 26 April 1999,

Recognizing that the problem of hunger and food insecurity have global dimensions and that they are likely to persist and even to increase dramatically in some regions, unless urgent, determined and concerted action is taken, given the anticipated increase in the world's population and the stress on natural resources,

Reaffirming that a peaceful, stable and enabling political, social and economic environment, both at a national and an international level, is the essential foundation which will enable States to give adequate priority to food security and poverty eradication,

Reiterating, as did the Rome Declaration, that food should not be used as an instrument of political or economic pressure, and reaffirming in this regard the importance of international cooperation and solidarity, as well as the necessity of refraining from unilateral measures not in accordance with international law and the Charter of the United Nations which endanger food security,

Convinced that each State must adopt a strategy consistent with its resources and capacities to achieve its individual goals in implementing the recommendations contained in the Rome Declaration and Plan of Action of the World Summit and, at the same time, cooperate regionally and internationally in order to organize collective solutions to global issues of food security in a world of increasingly interlinked institutions, societies and economies, where coordinated efforts and shared responsibilities are essential,

Stressing the importance of reversing the continuing decline of official development assistance devoted to agriculture, both in real terms and as a share of total official development assistance,

1. *Reaffirms* that hunger constitutes an outrage and a violation of human dignity and, therefore, requires the adoption of urgent measures at the national, regional and international levels for its elimination;
2. *Also reaffirms* the right of everyone to have access to safe and nutritious food, consistent with the right to adequate food and the fundamental right of everyone to be free from hunger so as to be able fully to develop and maintain their physical and mental capacities;
3. *Considers* intolerable that 825 million people, most of them women and children, throughout the world and particularly in developing countries, do not have enough food to meet their basic nutritional needs, which infringes their fundamental human rights and at the same time can generate additional pressures upon the environment in ecologically fragile areas;
4. *Stresses* the need to make efforts to mobilize and optimize the allocation and utilization of technical and financial resources from all sources, including external debt relief for developing countries, to reinforce national actions to implement sustainable food security policies;
5. *Encourages* all States to take steps with a view to achieving progressively the full realization of the right to food, including steps to promote the conditions for everyone to be free from hunger and as soon as possible enjoy fully the right to food;
6. *Takes note with interest* of the updated study on the right to adequate food and to be free from hunger submitted by Mr Asbjørn Eide to the Sub-Commission on the Promotion and Protection of Human Rights, in accordance with Sub-Commission decision 1998/106 (E/CN.4/Sub.2/1999/12);
7. *Also takes note with interest* of the report submitted by the United Nations High Commissioner for Human Rights on the right to food, in accordance with Commission resolution 1999/24 (E/CN.4/2000/48 and Add.1);
8. *Welcomes* the work already done by the CESCR in promoting the right to adequate food, in particular its General Comment No. 12 (1999) on the right to adequate food (art. 11 of the International Covenant on Economic, Social and Cultural Rights), in which the Committee affirmed, *inter alia*, that the right to adequate food is indivisibly linked to the inherent dignity of the human person and is indispensable for the fulfilment of other human rights enshrined in the International Bill of Human Rights and is also inseparable from social justice, requiring the adoption of appropriate economic, environmental and social policies, at both the national and international levels, oriented to the eradication of poverty and the fulfilment of all human rights for all;

9. *Recommends* that the High Commissioner organize a third expert consultation on the right to food, following those held in 1997 and 1998, this time with a focus on implementation mechanisms at country level, inviting experts from all regions to share their experience;
10. *Decides*, in order to respond fully to the necessity for an integrated and coordinated approach in the promotion and protection of the right to food, to appoint, for a period of three years, a special rapporteur, whose mandate will focus on the right to food;
11. *Requests* the Special Rapporteur on the right to food, in the fulfilment of her/his mandate, to accomplish the following main activities:
    (a) To seek, receive and respond to information on all aspects of the realization of the right to food, including the urgent necessity of eradicating hunger;
    (b) To establish cooperation with Governments, intergovernmental organizations, in particular the Food and Agriculture Organization of the United Nations, and non-governmental organizations, on the promotion and effective implementation of the right to food, and to make appropriate recommendations on the realization thereof, taking into consideration the work already done in this field throughout the United Nations system;
    (c) To identify emerging issues related to the right to food worldwide;
12. *Requests* the High Commissioner to provide all necessary human and financial resources for the effective fulfilment of the mandate of the Special Rapporteur;
13. *Requests* the Special Rapporteur to submit a report on the implementation of the present resolution to the Commission at its 57th session;
14. *Requests* Governments, relevant United Nations agencies, funds and programmes, treaty bodies, as well as non-governmental organizations, to cooperate fully with the Special Rapporteur in the fulfilment of her/his mandate, *inter alia* through the submission of comments and suggestions on ways and means of realizing the right to food.

52nd meeting
17 April 2000
[Adopted by a roll-call vote of 49 votes to 1, with 2 abstentions.]

3. The right to food: Commission on Human Rights Resolution 2001/25

The Commission on Human Rights,

Recalling the Universal Declaration of Human Rights, which provides that everyone has the right to a standard of living adequate for her/his health and well-being, including food,

Recalling also the provisions of the International Covenant on Economic, Social and Cultural Rights in which the fundamental right of every person to be free from hunger is recognized,

Recalling further the Universal Declaration on the Eradication of Hunger and Malnutrition,

Bearing in mind the Rome Declaration on World Food Security and the Plan of Action of the World Food Summit, held in Rome from 13 to 17 November 1996,

Recalling all its previous resolutions in this regard, in particular resolution 2000/10 of 17 April 2000,

Reaffirming that all human rights are universal, indivisible, interdependent and interrelated,

Recognizing that the problem of hunger and food insecurity has global dimensions and that they are likely to persist and even to increase dramatically in some regions, unless urgent, determined and concerted action is taken, given the anticipated increase in the world's population and the stress on natural resources,

Reaffirming that a peaceful, stable and enabling political, social and economic environment, both at a national and an international level, is the essential foundation which will enable States to give adequate priority to food security and poverty eradication,

Reiterating, as did the Rome Declaration, that food should not be used as an instrument of political or economic pressure, and reaffirming in this regard the importance of international cooperation and solidarity, as well as the necessity of refraining from unilateral measures not in accordance with international law and the Charter of the United Nations which endanger food security,

Convinced that each State must adopt a strategy consistent with its resources and capacities to achieve its individual goals in implementing the recommendations contained in the Rome Declaration and Plan of Action of the World Food Summit and, at the same time, cooperate regionally and internationally in order to organize collective solutions to global issues of food security in a world of increasingly interlinked institutions, societies and economies, where coordinated efforts and shared responsibilities are essential,

Stressing the importance of reversing the continuing decline of official development assistance devoted to agriculture, both in real terms and as a share of total official development assistance,

1. *Reaffirms* that hunger constitutes an outrage and a violation of human dignity and, therefore, requires the adoption of urgent measures at the national, regional and international levels for its elimination;
2. *Also reaffirms* the right of everyone to have access to safe and nutritious food, consistent with the right to adequate food and the fundamental right of everyone to be free from hunger so as to be able fully to develop and maintain their physical and mental capacities;
3. *Considers* it intolerable that 826 million people, most of them women and children, throughout the world and particularly in developing countries, do not have enough food to meet their basic nutritional needs, which infringes their fundamental human rights and at the same time can generate additional pressures upon the environment in ecologically fragile areas;
4. *Stresses* the need to make efforts to mobilize and optimize the allocation and utilization of technical and financial resources from all sources, including external debt relief for developing countries, to reinforce national actions to implement sustainable food security policies;
5. *Encourages* all States to take steps with a view to achieving progressively the full realization of the right to food, including steps to promote the conditions for everyone to be free from hunger and as soon as possible enjoy fully the right to food, as well as to elaborate and adopt national plans to combat hunger;
6. *Takes note* of *The State of the World's Children 2001* report on early childhood of the United Nations Children's Fund and, in this context, recalls that the nurturing of young children merits the highest priority;
7. *Takes note with appreciation* of the report of the Special Rapporteur on the right to food, submitted in accordance with Commission resolution 2000/10 (E/CN.4/2001/53), and commends the Special Rapporteur for his valuable work in the promotion of the right to food;
8. *Requests* the Special Rapporteur, in the fulfilment of his mandate, to continue to carry out the following main activities:
   (a) To seek, receive and respond to information on all aspects of the realization of the right to food, including the urgent necessity of eradicating hunger;
   (b) To establish cooperation with Governments, intergovernmental organizations, in particular the Food and Agriculture Organization of the United Nations, and non-governmental organizations on the promotion and effective implementation of the right to food and to make appropriate recommendations on the realization thereof, taking into consideration the work already done in this field throughout the United Nations system;
   (c) To identify emerging issues related to the right to food worldwide;

9. *Also requests* the Special Rapporteur, in discharging his mandate, to pay attention to the issue of drinking water, taking into account the interdependence of this issue and the right to food;
10. *Further requests* the Special Rapporteur to contribute effectively to the medium-term review of the implementation of the Rome Declaration on World Food Security and the Plan of Action of the World Food Summit by submitting to the United Nations High Commissioner for Human Rights his recommendations on all aspects of the right to food;
11. *Encourages* the Special Rapporteur to mainstream a gender perspective in the activities relating to his mandate;
12. *Requests* the High Commissioner to provide all the necessary human and financial resources for the effective fulfilment of the mandate of the Special Rapporteur;
13. *Welcomes* the work already done by the CESCR in promoting the right to adequate food, in particular its General Comment No. 12 (1999) on the right to adequate food (art. 11 of the International Covenant on Economic, Social and Cultural Rights), in which the Committee affirmed, *inter alia*, that the right to adequate food is indivisibly linked to the inherent dignity of the human person and is indispensable for the fulfilment of other human rights enshrined in the International Bill of Human Rights and is also inseparable from social justice, requiring the adoption of appropriate economic, environmental and social policies, at both the national and international levels, oriented to the eradication of poverty and the fulfilment of all human rights for all;
14. *Also welcomes* the convening by the High Commissioner in Bonn, from 12 to 14 March 2001, of the Third Expert Consultation on the Right to Food, with a focus on implementation mechanisms at country level, hosted by the Government of Germany, and takes note with interest of the report of the Third Expert Consultation (E/CN.4/2001/148);
15. *Recommends* that the High Commissioner organize a fourth expert consultation on the right to food, with a focus on the realization of this right as part of strategies and policies for the eradication of poverty, inviting experts from all regions;
16. *Requests* the Special Rapporteur to submit a preliminary report to the General Assembly at its 56th session and a final report on the implementation of the present resolution to the Commission at its 58th session;
17. *Invites* Governments, relevant United Nations agencies, funds and programmes, treaty bodies and non-governmental organizations, to cooperate fully with the Special Rapporteur in the fulfilment of his mandate, *inter alia* through the submission of comments and suggestions on ways and means of realizing the right to food.

70th meeting
20 April 2001
[Adopted by a roll-call vote of 52 votes to 1]

4. The right to food: Human Rights Council Resolution 7/14

The Human Rights Council,

Recalling all previous resolutions on the issue of the right to food, in particular General Assembly resolution 62/164 of 18 December 2007 and Council resolution 6/2 of 27 September 2007, as well as all resolutions of the Commission on Human Rights in this regard,

Recalling also the Universal Declaration of Human Rights, which provides that everyone has the right to a standard of living adequate for her or his health and well-being, including food, the Universal Declaration on the Eradication of Hunger and Malnutrition and the United Nations Millennium Declaration,

Recalling further the provisions of the International Covenant on Economic, Social and Cultural Rights, in which the fundamental right of every person to be free from hunger is recognized,

Bearing in mind the Rome Declaration on World Food Security and the World Food Summit Plan of Action and the Declaration of the World Food Summit: five years later, adopted in Rome on 13 June 2002,

Reaffirming the concrete recommendations contained in the Voluntary Guidelines to Support the Progressive Realization of the Right to Adequate Food in the Context of National Food Security, adopted by the Council of the Food and Agriculture Organization of the United Nations in November 2004,

Bearing in mind paragraph 6 of its resolution 60/251 of 15 March 2006,

Reaffirming that all human rights are universal, indivisible, interdependent and interrelated, and that they must be treated globally, in a fair and equal manner, on the same footing and with the same emphasis,

Reaffirming also that a peaceful, stable and enabling political, social and economic environment, at both the national and the international levels, is the essential foundation that will enable States to give adequate priority to food security and poverty eradication,

Reiterating, as in the Rome Declaration on World Food Security and the Declaration of the World Food Summit: five years later, that food should not be used as an instrument of political or economic pressure, and reaffirming in this regard the importance of international cooperation and solidarity, as well as the necessity of refraining from unilateral measures that are not in accordance with international law and the Charter of the United Nations and that endanger food security,

Convinced that each State must adopt a strategy consistent with its resources and capacities to achieve its individual goals in implementing the recommendations contained in the Rome Declaration on World Food Security and the World Food Summit Plan of Action and, at the same time, cooperate regionally and internationally in order to organize collective solutions to global issues of food security in a world of increasingly interlinked institutions, societies and economies where coordinated efforts and shared responsibilities are essential,

Recognizing that the problems of hunger and food insecurity have global dimensions and that there has been virtually no progress made on reducing hunger and that it could increase dramatically in some regions unless urgent, determined and concerted action is taken, given the anticipated increase in the world's population and the stress on natural resources,

Noting that environmental degradation, desertification and global climate change are exacerbating destitution and desperation, causing a negative impact on the realization of the right to food, in particular in developing countries,

Expressing its deep concern at the number and scale of natural disasters, diseases and pests and their increasing impact in recent years, which have resulted in massive loss of life and livelihood and threatened agricultural production and food security, in particular in developing countries,

Stressing the importance of reversing the continuing decline of official development assistance devoted to agriculture, both in real terms and as a share of total official development assistance,

Welcoming the theme 'The right to food', chosen by the Food and Agriculture Organization of the United Nations to mark World Food Day on 16 October 2007,

Taking note of the Final Declaration adopted at the International Conference on Agrarian Reform and Rural Development of the Food and Agriculture Organization of the United Nations in Porto Alegre, Brazil, on 10 March 2006,

1. *Reaffirms* that hunger constitutes an outrage and a violation of human dignity and therefore requires the adoption of urgent measures at the national, regional and international levels for its elimination;
2. *Also reaffirms* the right of everyone to have access to safe and nutritious food, consistent with the right to adequate food and the fundamental right of everyone to be free from hunger, so as to be able to fully develop and maintain his or her physical and mental capacities;
3. *Considers it intolerable* that more than 6 million children still die every year from hunger-related illness before their fifth birthday and that there are about 854 million undernourished people in the world and that, while the prevalence of hunger has diminished, the absolute number of undernourished people has been increasing in recent years when, according to the Food and Agriculture Organization of the United Nations, the planet could produce enough food to feed 12 billion people, twice the world's present population;

4. *Expresses its concern* that women and girls are disproportionately affected by hunger, food insecurity and poverty, in part as a result of gender inequality and discrimination, that in many countries, girls are twice as likely as boys to die from malnutrition and preventable childhood diseases, and that it is estimated that almost twice as many women as men suffer from malnutrition;

5. *Encourages* all States to take action to address gender inequality and discrimination against women, in particular where it contributes to the malnutrition of women and girls, including measures to ensure the full and equal realization of the right to food and ensuring that women have equal access to resources, including income, land and water, to enable them to feed themselves and their families;

6. *Encourages* the Special Rapporteur on the right to food to continue mainstreaming a gender perspective in the fulfilment of his mandate, and encourages the Food and Agriculture Organization of the United Nations and all other United Nations bodies and mechanisms addressing the right to food and food insecurity to integrate a gender perspective into their relevant policies, programmes and activities;

7. *Reaffirms* the need to ensure that programmes delivering safe and nutritious food are inclusive and accessible to persons with disabilities;

8. *Encourages* all States to take steps with a view to achieving progressively the full realization of the right to food, including steps to promote the conditions for everyone to be free from hunger and, as soon as possible, to enjoy fully the right to food, and to create and adopt national plans to combat hunger, and recognizes in this regard the great efforts and positive developments with respect to the right to food in some developing countries and regions, including those highlighted in the report of the Special Rapporteur;

9. *Stresses* that improving access to productive resources and public investment in rural development is essential for eradicating hunger and poverty, in particular in developing countries, including through the promotion of investments in appropriate, small-scale irrigation and water management technologies in order to reduce vulnerability to droughts;

10. *Recognizes* that 80 per cent of hungry people live in rural areas, and 50 per cent are small-scale farm-holders, and that these people are especially vulnerable to food insecurity, given the increasing cost of inputs, and the fall in farm incomes; that access to land, water, seeds and other natural resources is an increasing challenge for poor producers; and that support by States for small farmers, fishing communities and local enterprises is an element key to food security and provision of the right to food;

11. *Stresses* the importance of fighting hunger in rural areas, including through national efforts supported by international partnerships to stop

desertification and land degradation and through investments and public policies that are specifically appropriate to the risk of drylands, and, in this regard, calls for the full implementation of the United Nations Convention to Combat Desertification in Those Countries Experiencing Serious Drought and/or Desertification, particularly in Africa;

12. *Also stresses* its commitments to promote and protect, without discrimination, the economic, social and cultural rights of indigenous peoples, in accordance with international human rights obligations and taking into account, as appropriate, the United Nations Declaration on the Rights of Indigenous Peoples, and acknowledges that many indigenous organizations and representatives of indigenous communities have expressed in different forums their deep concerns over the obstacles and challenges they face for the full enjoyment of the right to food, and calls upon States to take special actions to combat the root causes of the disproportionately high level of hunger and malnutrition among indigenous peoples and the continuous discrimination against them;

13. *Requests* all States and private actors, as well as international organizations within their respective mandates, to take fully into account the need to promote the effective realization of the right to food for all, including in the ongoing negotiations in different fields;

14. *Recognizes* the need to strengthen national commitment as well as international assistance, upon request and in cooperation with affected countries, towards a better realization and protection of the right to food, and in particular to develop national protection mechanisms for people forced to leave their homes and land because of hunger or natural or man-made disasters affecting the enjoyment of the right to food;

15. *Stresses* the need to make efforts to mobilize and optimize the allocation and utilization of technical and financial resources from all sources, including external debt relief for developing countries, and to reinforce national actions to implement sustainable food security policies;

16. *Recognizes* the need for a successful conclusion of the Doha Development Round negotiations of the World Trade Organization as a contribution to creating international conditions that permit the realization of the right to food;

17. *Stresses* that all States should make every effort to ensure that their international policies of a political and economic nature, including international trade agreements, do not have a negative impact on the right to food in other countries;

18. *Recalls* the importance of the New York Declaration on Action against Hunger and Poverty, and recommends the continuation of efforts aimed at identifying additional sources of financing for the fight against hunger and poverty;

19. *Recognizes* that the promises made at the World Food Summit in 1996 to halve the number of persons who are undernourished are not being

fulfilled, and invites once again all international financial and development institutions, as well as the relevant United Nations agencies and funds, to give priority to and provide the necessary funding to realize the aim of halving by 2015 the proportion of people who suffer from hunger, as well as the right to food as set out in the Rome Declaration on World Food Security and the United Nations Millennium Declaration;

20. *Reaffirms* that integrating food and nutritional support, with the goal that all people at all times will have access to sufficient, safe and nutritious food to meet their dietary needs and food preferences for an active and healthy life, is part of a comprehensive response to the spread of HIV/AIDS, tuberculosis, malaria and other communicable diseases;

21. *Urges* States to give adequate priority in their development strategies and expenditures to the realization of the right to food;

22. *Stresses* the importance of international development cooperation and assistance, in particular in activities related to disaster risk reduction and in emergency situations such as natural and man-made disasters, diseases and pests, for the realization of the right to food and the achievement of sustainable food security, while recognizing that each country has the primary responsibility for ensuring the implementation of national programmes and strategies in this regard;

23. *Calls upon* Member States, the United Nations system and other relevant stakeholders to support national efforts aimed at responding rapidly to the food crises currently occurring across Africa and expresses its deep concern that funding shortfalls are forcing the World Food Programme to cut operations across different regions, including Southern Africa;

24. *Invites* all relevant international organizations, including the World Bank and the International Monetary Fund, to promote policies and projects that have a positive impact on the right to food, to ensure that partners respect the right to food in the implementation of common projects, to support strategies of Member States aimed at the fulfilment of the right to food and to avoid any actions that could have a negative impact on the realization of the right to food;

25. *Encourages* the Special Rapporteur on the right to food and the Special Representative of the Secretary-General on the issue of human rights and transnational corporations and other business enterprises to cooperate on the subject of the contribution of the private sector to the realization of the right to food, including the importance of ensuring sustainable water resources for human consumption and agriculture;

26. *Recognizes* the negative impact of massive rises in prices of food on the realization of the right to food, particularly on people in developing countries with a high level of dependence on food imports for the fulfilment of nutritional national requirements;

27. *Takes note* of the report of the Special Rapporteur on the right to food, and of his valuable work in the promotion of the right to food in all

parts of the world and expresses its appreciation for the work and commitment of the first mandate-holder to achieving the realization of the right to food;
28. *Encourages* the new mandate-holder on the right to food to discharge his/her activities taking into account the important achievements in the fulfilment of the mandate in recent years;
29. *Supports* the realization of the mandate of the Special Rapporteur as extended for a period of three years by the Council in its resolution 6/2 of 27 September 2007;
30. *Requests* the Secretary-General and the United Nations High Commissioner for Human Rights to provide all the necessary human and financial resources for the effective fulfilment of the mandate of the Special Rapporteur;
31. *Welcomes* the work already done by the CESCR in promoting the right to adequate food, in particular its General Comment No. 12 (1999) on the right to adequate food (Article 11 of the International Covenant on Economic, Social and Cultural Rights), in which the Committee affirmed, *inter alia*, that the right to adequate food is indivisibly linked to the inherent dignity of the human person and is indispensable for the fulfilment of other human rights enshrined in the International Bill of Human Rights, and is also inseparable from social justice, requiring the adoption of appropriate economic, environmental and social policies, at both the national and the international levels, oriented to the eradication of poverty and the fulfilment of all human rights for all;
32. *Recalls* General Comment No. 15 (2002) of the Committee on the right to water (Articles 11 and 12 of the Covenant), in which the Committee noted, *inter alia*, the importance of ensuring sustainable water resources for human consumption and agriculture in the realization of the right to adequate food;
33. *Reaffirms* that the Voluntary Guidelines to Support the Progressive Realization of the Right to Adequate Food in the Context of National Food Security, adopted by the Council of the Food and Agriculture Organization of the United Nations in November 2004, represent a practical tool to promote the realization of the right to food for all, contribute to the achievement of food security and thus provide an additional instrument in the attainment of internationally agreed development goals, including those contained in the Millennium Declaration;
34. *Requests* the Advisory Committee to consider potential recommendations for approval by the Council on possible further measures to enhance the realization of the right to food, bearing in mind the priority importance of promoting the implementation of existing standards;

35. *Welcomes* the continued cooperation of the High Commissioner, the Committee and the Special Rapporteur, and encourages them to continue their cooperation in this regard;
36. *Calls upon* all Governments to cooperate with and assist the Special Rapporteur in his/her task, to supply all necessary information requested by him/her and to give serious consideration to responding favourably to the requests of the Special Rapporteur to visit their countries to enable him/her to fulfil his/her mandate more effectively;
37. *Decides* to convene a panel discussion on the realization of the right to food in the period of its main session of 2009;
38. *Recalls* the requests made by the General Assembly, in its resolution 62/164, that the Special Rapporteur submit to it an interim report at its 63rd session on the implementation of that resolution and to continue his work, including by examining the emerging issues with regard to the realization of the right to food within his existing mandate, and by the Council that the Special Rapporteur submit to it a comprehensive report on the fulfilment of his/her mandate in 2009, in accordance with its annual programme of work;
39. *Invites* Governments, relevant United Nations agencies, funds and programmes, treaty bodies and civil society actors, including non-governmental organizations, as well as the private sector, to cooperate fully with the Special Rapporteur in the fulfilment of his/her mandate, *inter alia*, through the submission of comments and suggestions on ways and means of realizing the right to food;
40. *Decides* to continue the consideration of this matter under the same agenda item in 2009 in accordance with its annual programme of work.

40th meeting
27 March 2008
[Adopted without a vote]

5. List of the Special Rapporteur's reports to the United Nations

Annual reports to the Commission on Human Rights

E/CN.4/2001/53 (2001)
E/CN.4/2002/58 (2002)
E/CN.4/2003/54 (2003)
E/CN.4/2004/10 (2004)
E/CN.4/2005/47 (2005)
E/CN.4/2006/44 (2006)

Annual reports to the Human Rights Council

A/HRC/4/30 (2007)
A/HRC/7/5 (2008)

Annual reports to the General Assembly

A/56/210 (2001)
A/57/356 (2002)
A/58/330 (2003)
A/59/385 (2004)
A/60/350 (2005)
A/61/306 (2006)
A/62/289 (2007)

Country mission reports

E/CN.4/2002/58/Add.1 (Niger)
E/CN.4/2003/54/Add.1 (Brazil)
E/CN.4/2004/10/Add.1 (Bangladesh)
E/CN.4/2004/10/Add.2 (Occupied Palestinian Territories)
E/CN.4/2005/47/Add.1 (Ethiopia)
E/CN.4/2005/47/Add.2 (Mongolia)
A/60/350 (Niger)
E/CN.4/2006/44 (Niger)
E/CN.4/2006/44/Add.1 (Guatemala)
E/CN.4/2006/44/Add.2 (India)
A/HRC/2/8 (with A/HRC/2/8/Corr.1) (Lebanon)
A/HRC/7/5/Add.2 (and A/HRC/4/30/Add.2) (Bolivia)
A/HRC/7/5/Add.3 (Cuba)

6. Main recommendations of the Special Rapporteur on the right to food to the Members States of the United Nations and international organizations

This annexure summarizes the recommendations which were submitted throughout the seven year mandate in various reports presented by the Special Rapporteur to the General Assembly, Commission on Human Rights, and Human Rights Council.

General recommendations on realizing the right to food and its legal framework

Hunger is not inevitable. The lack of progress in meeting the objectives of the World Food Summit and Millennium Goal No. 1 to halve the number of hunger victims by 2015 is unacceptable. All States should take immediate action to realize the human right to food of all their people.

Concrete steps should be taken immediately to reduce hunger and malnutrition. Immediate measures to reduce hunger and malnutrition, even in States which have limited resources, should include the following:

1. *Nutritional education*. This must emphasize the importance of micronutrients as well as calories, focusing especially on the importance of vitamins, minerals and iodine;
2. *Universal school lunches*. Programmes of food distribution in schools and in crèches are one of the most efficient forms of fighting child malnutrition in both rural and urban areas. Daily school meals should be extended to all needy children and meal vouchers introduced in compulsory schools;
   - *Maternal breastfeeding*. It is vital that maternal breastfeeding be encouraged by authorities as the best form of combating malnutrition in babies. This means that the 1981 WHO International Code of Marketing of Breast-milk Substitutes must be enforced;
   - *Family gardens*. Almost everywhere in the world a majority of families in extreme rural poverty could be granted access to a few square metres of land. This would help to develop a food local security strategy to improve nutrition at the household level. The State should provide the poorest families with local seed and land for family vegetable gardens;
   - *Basic foods subsidies*. Basic foods should be State-subsidized and food tickets to be issued to the most deprived.

Questions of inequality of access to food and water must also be immediately addressed to ensure that there is no discrimination on the grounds of ethnicity, gender, religion or otherwise in access to food and water. Monitoring structures should also be put in place to monitor the progressive realization of improvements in access to food and water for people who are suffering from chronic malnourishment.

Governments should enshrine the right to food in a national law to meet their international obligations, develop a national strategy to realize the right to food, and take all necessary actions, including ensuring good governance and macroeconomic stability, to help combat hunger and malnutrition on their national territory.

Concrete steps must be taken to ensure that national legislation provides a framework that recognizes the State's obligations to respect, protect and fulfil the right to food of its people, in peace and in war. Governments should adopt an adequate legal framework to ensure the right to food for all, including and in particular for the most vulnerable. This should include a clear definition of the right to food and the obligations of the Government to respect, protect and fulfil the right to food, without discrimination, as well as provisions for strong, independent and adequately financed monitoring mechanisms.

Every Government should develop a national framework law conforming to the need to respect, protect and fulfil the right to food, recognizing obligations under international human rights and humanitarian law, in particular paragraph 29 of General Comment No. 12 of the CESCR. As recommended by the Third Expert Consultation on the Right to Food, held in Bonn, Germany, from 12 to 14 March 2001, the strategy should make an inventory or checklist of issue areas that require national regulation, such as guaranteeing access to productive resources for the food-insecure and the vulnerable, including land tenure and access to water. In addition, a review of existing legislation should be made to assess whether it contradicts the obligations under the right to adequate food or lacks adequate implementation.

Governments should appoint focal points on the right to food in national administrations that should coordinate the work of relevant ministries (agriculture, finance, social welfare, health and land). As provided for in paragraph 29 of General Comment No. 12, Governments should develop indicators and set benchmarks to allow verification of the progress of establishing the right to food at the country level. Setting benchmarks for food security and for water quality and quantity is vital to measure and monitor the progressive implementation of the right to food over time.

All Governments have the obligation to respect, protect and fulfil the right to food of their people. Governments should not implement any policies or programmes that run counter to their legal obligations to realize the right to food. The progressive realization of the right to food means that levels of food security should consistently improve over time. All arbitrary and discriminatory actions by Governments that restrict or exclude poor people from access to food, water and other productive resources constitute a violation of the right to food and the right to water.

Effective administrative and judicial remedies and recourse procedures should be implemented for everyone whose right to food is violated or neglected.

The right to food, along with other economic, social and cultural rights, must be treated as equal in status and implementation to civil and political rights.

Recommendations on the right to water and the right to food

Water is essential to human life. More than 400 million children do not have regular access to clean drinking water, leaving them vulnerable to disease and early death. Water must therefore be maintained as a common good and the right to water considered as a human right. All Governments must respect the human right of every person to have regular, healthy and unobstructed access to an amount of water adequate in quality and quantity to sustain life.

The nutritional aspects of water must be a component of the right to food, as millions suffer from diseases carried in water that are easily eradicable. As water is also essential for life, everyone must have access to drinking water on equal terms and irrigation water should also be accessible for poor peasants who depend on their land to feed themselves. This should include several elements, including reducing inequality of access to water at the national and international levels, taking into account the particular problems of countries suffering from severe water shortages.

Water should be treated as a public good and be protected through appropriate public services. Raising public awareness at the national and international levels to promote the conservation of water, to limit overconsumption and to reduce losses, leakage, pollution and wastage of water is also fundamental. Ensuring better purification and storage and setting benchmarks for water quality would reduce the risk of disease and contribute immeasurably to the nutritional aspects of water as a component of the right to food.

Governments should ensure fair distribution of and access to adequate quantity and quality of water, free from many easily eradicable diseases.

General Comment No. 15 on the right to water should be widely disseminated and debated to improve understanding of the right to water and the obligations that this entails to respect, protect and fulfil (facilitate and provide) the right to water. The close links between the right to food and the right to water should also be recognized, given that violations of the right to food are very often linked to problems in relation to the lack of access to water, or control over water supplies.

Recommendations on women and the right to food

The rights of women to access to land and to water must be recognized and guaranteed, given their key role in food security in households and in the production of food crops. It is essential to strengthen the rights of women to ensure the full realization of the right to food.

All Governments must take immediate action to address discrimination against women, particularly where this contributes to the malnutrition of women and girls. Social traditions that proscribe that women should eat last should be understood as a form of violence against women, particularly as this contributes to high rates of female mortality in certain regions of the world.

All Governments should improve the enforcement and implementation of existing legislation developed to protect women. This must include respecting women's right to food and ensuring that women have equal access to resources, including income, land and water, to enable them to feed themselves.

Governments should also take concrete action to improve the conditions of women to ensure that legal equality is transformed into substantive equality, taking note of the different starting points of men and women.

The international financial institutions should review programmes of economic restructuring to examine their gender-differentiated effects, recognizing the important role that the State must play in reducing inequality.

Recommendations on children and the right to food

All Governments should take immediate steps to eliminate child hunger. This should include programmes to address food security and adequate livelihoods, as well as nutritional security, especially in vitamin A, iron and iodine deficiencies and the promotion of breastfeeding. School meal programmes should be universalized and should ensure adequate nutrition for all children. Special programmes must be conceived for the 140 million children under 12 who still have no access to school.

All governmental and non-governmental armed forces must stop recruiting children as combatants or with other functions and release those who remain at their service, and measures must be taken to avoid the enlistment of child combatants who are forced into recruitment by hunger.

Recommendations on farmers and peasants and the right to food

Urgent attention be given to ensuring the livelihoods of poor peasant farmers who make up 75 per cent of the world's 1.2 billion poorest people, so that they would be able to feed themselves in dignity in accordance with the right to food. Models of export-oriented agriculture that threaten the livelihoods of millions of peasant farmers should be reviewed, particularly if economic restructuring does not result in new employment in other sectors.

Hunger is still primarily a rural problem, and the majority of those suffering from hunger depends on small-scale agriculture and pastoralism but do not have sufficient access to productive resources such as land, water, infrastructure and extension services. Improving access to productive resources and public investment in rural development is essential for eradicating hunger and poverty.

Access to land must be recognized as a fundamental element of the right to food. Agrarian reform should be taken seriously as a policy instrument to reduce hunger and poverty. It should promote truly transformative and redistributive change involving not just land, but also the necessary elements to make reform viable, including access to water, credit, transport, extension services and other infrastructure. In many countries, agrarian reform and the right to land are already provided for in national law, which needs to be effectively applied and enforced. 'Market-based' land reforms that undermine local legislation and constitutional commitments or undermine the possibility of a truly transformative and redistributive agrarian reform must be avoided.

Recommendations on fisherpeople and the right to food

In the case of communities dependent on fish and fishing resources, Governments must comply with obligations to respect, protect and fulfil the right to adequate food. This means that it must ensure that artisanal and subsistence fishers are not arbitrarily excluded from their access to fishing resources. Governments must also provide protection to small-scale fisheries against negative impacts of actions undertaken by corporations or other private actors. Priority must be given in the first instance to protecting livelihoods. Adequate compensation for any loss of existing access to resources must be instituted for those whose livelihoods and food security are not respected or protected. Where policies of restructuring the fishing industry are put in place, Governments must ensure that the needs of poor and marginalized communities are respected. Impact analysis of policy shifts must analyse potential impacts on all groups and ensure that all needs are met in a way that avoids potential for regression in the realization of the right to adequate food.

Recommendations on indigenous peoples and the right to food

International protection of indigenous peoples remains inadequate, and the right to food of indigenous peoples is frequently denied or violated, given systematic discrimination and the widespread lack of recognition of indigenous land and water rights. The United Nations Declaration on the Rights of Indigenous Peoples should be supported as a first step in the elaboration and adoption of a new binding instrument, such as an international convention on the rights of indigenous peoples.

All Governments should recognize that indigenous peoples suffer from disproportionately high levels of hunger and malnutrition and take special action to combat the causes, particularly the pervasive discrimination against indigenous peoples.

All Governments should respect, protect and fulfil the right to food of their indigenous populations, including by recognizing their right to land, resources and traditional subsistence activities, their intellectual property rights over their genetic and knowledge resources and their right to appropriate development that does not result in further marginalization, exploitation, poverty or hunger. Governments should recognize that the right to food is not only a positive right, but also a negative right that requires Governments to refrain from taking actions that negatively affect indigenous people's existing access to food, such as the displacement, dispossession or the destruction of traditional access to subsistence resources.

Recommendations on refugees from hunger

All Governments and international agencies should address the root causes of migration and armed conflict, including realizing the right to food in those countries where people have little option but to flee their own countries or where children are forced to enlist in armed groups in order to procure food for themselves and their families.

States should refrain from deporting people who have fled from their own countries as a result of hunger and violations of the right to food.

States should strengthen international and national protection mechanisms for people forced to leave their homes and land because of hunger or other severe violations of their right to food. In this regard, States should elaborate a new international legal instrument that will provide protections for all people fleeing from hunger who are not currently protected under international human rights, humanitarian or refugee law.

At a minimum, States should extend the principle of non-refoulement to people fleeing hunger and starvation owing to a state of necessity, and refrain from deporting them. Governments should not expel, return or extradite a person to another country when there are substantial grounds for believing that he/she would be in danger of suffering from hunger, chronic undernourishment or other severe violations of the right to food. Governments should duly recognize the state of urgency that compels these people to flee and that they are entitled to receive temporary protection on the basis of the principle of non-refoulement.

Recommendations on protecting food security and the right to food in international trade

All States should ensure that their international political and economic policies, including international trade agreements, do not have negative impacts on the right to food in other countries. In this context, European Union

Governments must ensure that EPA agreements with Asian, Caribbean and Pacific countries do not negatively affect the progressive realization of the right to food in those countries and include safeguard mechanisms to allow appropriate responses to any resulting food insecurity and hunger. All international trade agreements should include the participation of all stakeholders, including civil society. The implementation of the concept of food sovereignty should be discussed.

International trade obligations must also be reviewed to ensure that they do not conflict with the right to food. The unfairness of the current regime must be revised and developing countries allowed special protection, as it is in those countries that food security remains a daily struggle. WTO negotiations must take into account the suggestions of the developing countries and must consider the need to protect the right to food. Economic policy changes must not endanger life through malnutrition, but guarantee at least a basic minimum that respects at the very least the right to food and the right to life.

As far as structural adjustment programmes can increase social disparities and exclude many of the poorest of the poor households from access to minimum food requirements, the right to food should be a guiding principle in the process of the review of such programmes. Similarly, the right to food should be a guiding principle in poverty-related policies in the preparation of poverty reduction strategy papers.

In order to eliminate hunger and malnutrition, more emphasis needs to be put on small-scale farming, local food security and nutritional programmes. Whatever the weakness of the situation in a State, there are measures for local food security that can be taken immediately at very low cost, including programmes for nutritional education, universal school lunches, encouraging maternal breastfeeding and the provision of family gardens or small parcels of land and other elements that relate to securing land titles, micro-credit, local cooperatives and access to water.

Food sovereignty be considered as an alternative model for agriculture and agricultural trade, in order to meet State obligations to respect, protect and fulfil the right to food.

Action for local food security should also clarify the question of the organization of the provision of food and water in case of natural disasters, ensuring ethnic, gender and religious non-discrimination. Monitoring structures should also be put in place at the local level to monitor the consumption of food in sufficient quantity and high enough quality to ensure adequate growth of babies and children, as well as for women, the elderly and other vulnerable groups.

Stronger involvement of local authorities in delivering services and reaching food-insecure population groups should be encouraged. Decentralization means allocation of responsibility and budgets to local authorities, in accordance with the principle of subsidiarity.

Recommendations on the extraterritorial obligations of States and the right to food

All Governments must respect extraterritorial obligations by refraining from implementing any policies or programmes that negatively affect the right to food of people living outside their territories. Specifically, all Governments must refrain from dumping agricultural products in other countries and creating food insecurity. Inequities in WTO rules that disadvantage developing countries must be changed.

Recommendations on the responsibilities of international organizations

International organizations, such as the World Bank, IMF and WTO should recognize that they do have binding responsibilities towards human rights, including the right to food. International organizations should recognize their minimum obligation to refrain from promoting policies or projects that negatively impact or violate the right to food, particularly where no social safety nets are implemented. They should also recognize positive obligations to protect, by ensuring that partners do not violate the right to food in the implementation of common projects, and to support Governments in the fulfilment of the right to food.

All United Nations agencies, including the Bretton Woods institutions, must adopt a rights-based approach to their work to ensure that international human rights law is always respected.

Recommendations on the accountability of transnational corporations

All powerful private actors, particularly the 500 biggest transnational corporations that control 52 per cent of the world's gross global product, have an obligation to respect the right to food and the right to water, and to avoid complicity in violations of these rights carried out by others. Transnational corporations must respect regulatory frameworks set by Governments, as well as respect their direct obligations towards the right to food (including water) under international human rights law, national legislation, intergovernmental instruments and voluntary codes of conduct. Corporations must accept independent monitoring.

States also have an obligation to protect their citizens against negative impacts of transnational corporations on the right to food, including water. States must monitor and regulate the activities of their transnational corporations to ensure that they do not violate the right to food.

States should improve the international supervisory mechanisms for transnational corporations, especially those which control our food and water system, to ensure that they respect the right to food. This should include discussing and adopting the Norms on the Responsibilities of Transnational

Corporations and Other Business Enterprises with Regard to Human Rights.

Recommendations on biofuels and the right to food

States should establish a five-year moratorium on all initiatives to develop biofuels through converting food into fuel. This should provide time for an assessment of the potential impact on the right to food, as well as on other social, environmental and human rights, and should ensure that biofuels do not produce hunger.

States should ensure that biofuels are produced from non-food plants, agricultural wastes and crop residues, rather than food crops, in order to avert massive rises in the prices of food, water and land and the diversion of these resources away from food production. This will require immediate massive investment in 'second generation' technologies for producing biofuels.

States should adopt appropriate measures to ensure that biofuel production is based on family agriculture, rather than agro-industrial methods, in order to avert creating hunger and instead create employment and rural development that does not bypass the poor.

Recommendations on drought and desertification and the right to food

States should give priority to investments in long-term development projects that reduce vulnerability to drought and desertification, including through investing in small-scale water harvesting and management to improve food security.

Approximately 50 per cent of those suffering from hunger live on marginal and degraded lands, including drylands facing desertification. Fighting hunger in rural areas must therefore include fighting desertification and land degradation, through investments and public policies that are specifically appropriate to the risks of the drylands. Full implementation of the United Nations Convention to Combat Desertification is a global responsibility.

Preventing famine requires reducing vulnerability to drought, particularly in Africa. Investment in appropriate, small-scale irrigation and water management technologies must be a central part of strategies for reducing vulnerability to drought.

Recommendations on the right to food and armed conflict

International human rights law must be complemented by international humanitarian law that protects the right to food in situations of armed conflict. This must include the prohibition of starvation of civilians as a method of warfare and forced displacement, as well as respect for the rules on relief and humanitarian assistance, so that relief is not blocked, diverted or delayed.

All States should respect international humanitarian law to protect the right to food in situations of armed conflict. International humanitarian law must be respected by all parties to the conflict to ensure that civilian populations are not made the victims of war to which they are not party. The principles and rules which govern humanitarian assistance, particularly food assistance, must be respected in order to prevent the starvation of innocent people.

Recommendations on the right to food and humanitarian assistance

Governments and international agencies must guarantee safe passage in accordance with international humanitarian law and must ensure that relief assistance meets the specific food and nutrition needs of families and their children during emergency situations such as conflicts and natural disasters.

All Governments must respond to the food crises affecting African countries. Food security cannot be left to the vagaries of the market system. Emergency food aid must be provided; it should not be governed by market principles and food should be distributed free of charge. All Governments should support the Global Emergency Fund.

All Governments must respond to calls for emergency assistance to refugees, especially in the refugee camps of Eastern and Southern Africa where shortages are greatest. It is shocking that WFP is being forced to hand out rations that do not meet international standards for minimum daily calorie requirements per person. This is a violation of the right to food.

Recommendations on the Voluntary Guidelines on the Right to Food

The Voluntary Guidelines on the right to adequate food, accepted at the international level by Governments, should now be practically implemented and incorporated into government development programmes for food security and poverty reduction. Training for government officials and non-governmental organizations should be organized to raise awareness of the Guidelines and to improve realization of the right to food.

Recommendations on access to justice for violations of the right to food

Access to justice for victims of violations of the right to food is central to the protection of this right. Protection of the right to food at national, regional and international levels must be ensured by strengthening judiciaries and by ensuring the justiciability of the right to food. Governments should support the Optional Protocol to the International Covenant on Economic, Social and Cultural Rights.

Notes

1 Introduction: Hunger and the Right to Food

1. Of 815 million, 777 million were from developing countries, 27 million from transition countries and 11 million from industrialized countries. See Food and Agriculture Organization of the United Nations (FAO), The State of Food Insecurity in the World 2001, Rome, FAO, 2001, p. 2.
2. FAO, The State of Food Insecurity in the World 2005, Rome, FAO, 2005, p. 20.
3. FAO, The State of Food Insecurity in the World 2008, Rome, FAO, 2008, pp. 6–12.
4. Ibid.
5. Iron and zinc are vital for the development of mental abilities. Micronutrients contain other substances too (such as enzymes).
6. United Nations Children's Fund (UNICEF), *The State of World's Children 1998. Focus on Nutrition*, New York, Oxford University Press, 1998, p. 19.
7. Antenna, 'Malnutrition: un massacre silencieux', unpublished paper, Geneva, 2000.
8. See for example, Administrative Committee Coordination/Subcommittee on Nutrition (ACC/SCN), *Ending Malnutrition by 2020: An Agenda for Change in the Millennium*, final report to the ACC/SCN by the Commission on the Nutrition Challenges of the 21st Century, 2000; and ACC/SCN, *Fourth Report on the World Nutrition Situation: Nutrition throughout the Life Cycle*, Geneva, 2000, p. 53 (regarding HIV/AIDS).
9. See updated study on the right to food, submitted by Mr Asbjörn Eide in accordance with Sub-Commission decision 1998/106, E/CN.4/Sub.2/1999/12.
10. R. Debray and J. Ziegler, *Il s'agit de ne pas se rendre*, Paris, Editions Arléa, 1994.
11. G. McGovern, *The Third Freedom: Ending Hunger in Our Time*, New York, Simon and Schuster, 2001.
12. United Nations Millennium Project, Task Force on Hunger, *Halving Hunger, It Can Be Done*, New York, United Nations Development Programme (UNDP), 2005. Also International Fund for Agricultural Development, *Rural Poverty Report 2001: The Challenge of Ending Rural Poverty*, New York, Oxford University Press, 2001.
13. M.W. Rosegrant, S.A. Cline, W. Li, T.B. Sulser and R.A. Valmonte-Santos, *Long-Term Prospects for Africa's Agricultural Development and Food Security*, Washington, International Food Policy Research Institute (IFPRI), Discussion paper 41, August 2005.
14. FAO, The State of Food Insecurity in the World 2008, pp. 6–12.
15. M.W. Rosegrant, S.A. Cline, W. Li, T.B. Sulser, R.A. Valmonte-Santos, M.W. Rosegrant, S.A. Cline, W. Li, T.B. Sulser and R.A. Valmonte-Santos, *Long-Term Prospects for Africa's Agricultural Development and Food Security*.
16. G. Abi-Saab, 'Les sources du droit international: essai de déconstruction', In M. Rama-Montaldo, *Liber Amicorum en hommage au Professeur Eduardo Jimenez de Aréchaga*, Montevideo, Fundación de Cultura Universitaria, 1994, pp. 29–49.

386 Notes

17. J. Ritter and K. Gründer (eds), *Historisches Wörterbuch der Philosophie*, Basel, Verlag Schwabe, 1976, vol. 4, pp. 667–9.
18. Prior to this, the first World Food Conference was held in Rome in November 1974. On 16 November, it adopted a declaration, in which it solemnly declared that:
    1. Every man, woman and child has the inalienable right to be free from hunger and malnutrition in order to develop fully and maintain their physical and mental faculties. Society today already possesses sufficient resources, organizational ability and technology and hence the competence to achieve this objective. Accordingly, the eradication of hunger is a common objective of all the countries of the international community, especially of the developed countries and others in a position to help.
    FAO, *Report of the World Food Conference*,
    FAO document E/CONF.65/20, 1975, Part 1, chapter I.
    The Declaration goes on to say that it is a fundamental responsibility of Governments 'to work together for higher food production and a more equitable and efficient distribution of food between countries and within countries' (paragraph 2). Moreover, priority should be given to attacking 'chronic malnutrition and deficiency diseases among the vulnerable and lower income groups' (paragraph 2). In sum: 'As it is the common responsibility of the entire international community to ensure the availability at all times of adequate world supplies of basic food-stuffs by way of appropriate reserves, including emergency reserves, all countries should cooperate in the establishment of an effective system of world food security ...' (paragraph 12).
19. FAO, The State of Food Insecurity in the World 2001.
20. Ibid.
21. FAO Committee on World Food Security, Twenty-Seventh Session, *Fostering the Political Will to Fight Hunger*, Rome, FAO, 2001.
22. The Voluntary Guidelines on the Right to Food are available online, with publications on the right to food, at www.fao.org/righttofood.
23. See FAO Newsroom Focus, 'FAO Council adopts Right to Food Guidelines seen as landmark commitment to human rights', Rome, FAO, 24 November 2004.
24. Committee on Economic, Social and Cultural Rights (CESCR), *General Comment No. 12*, E/C.12/1999/5.
25. Ibid.
26. The International Bill of Human Rights comprises of the Universal Declaration of Human Rights (UDHR), the International Covenant on Economic, Social and Cultural Rights (ICESCR) and the International Covenant on Civil and Political Rights (ICCPR).
27. E/CN.4/Sub.2/1999/12.
28. In 2000 a report was submitted to the Commission on Human Rights by the United Nations High Commissioner for Human Rights on the right to food, in accordance with Commission resolution 1999/24, E/CN.4/2000/48 and Add.1.
29. The new Special Rapporteur created a website describing his activities at www.srfood.org.
30. Commission on Human Rights resolution 2001/25 of 20 April 2001, as approved by the Economic and Social Council at its substantive session of 2001.
31. In 2007, the Graduate Institute of Development Studies merged with the Graduate Institute of International Studies, to create the new Graduate Institute of International and Development Studies in Geneva.

2 The Definition of the Right to Food in International Law

1. See also E/CN.4/2001/53 and A/56/210.
2. See E/CN.4/2003/54, paragraph 36–51, as well as E/CN.4/2001/53 and resolution 2001/25 of the Commission on Human Rights.
3. See 'The Four Freedoms' speech by Franklin Delano Roosevelt, made on 6 January 1941 to the United States Congress.
4. For example, the right to food is also very closely linked to the right to life, which is protected under Article 6 of the ICCPR. The right to food of children is also specifically protected under Article 24 of the Convention on the Rights of the Child (CRC). Article 24, paragraph 2 (c), calls for appropriate measures to combat disease and malnutrition, including through the provision of nutritious foods and drinking water.
5. CESCR, *General Comment No. 12*, E/C.12/1999/5, paragraph 1.
6. See also the study of A. Eide, E/CN.4/Sub.2/1999/12, paragraph 52.
7. CESCR, *General Comment No. 12*, E/C.12/1999/5, paragraph 6.
8. Ibid, paragraph 7.
9. Ibid, paragraph 9.
10. Ibid, paragraph 11.
11. Ibid, paragraph 13.
12. 'Calorie' is a term used in physics; it is the unit used to measure the amount of energy consumed by the body. For details on the measurement method, see J-P. Girard (1991), *L'Alimentation*, Geneva, Georg.
13. On the justiciability of the right to food, see C. Golay (2009), *The Right to Food and Access to Justice: Examples at the National, Regional and International Levels*, Rome, FAO. See also C. Courtis, 'The Right to Food as a Justiciable Right: Challenges and Strategies', in *Max Planck Yearbook of United Nations Law*, Vol. 11, 2007, pp. 317–37; M. Borghi and L. Postiglione Blommestein (eds) (2006), *The Right to Adequate Food and Access to Justice*, Bruylant, Schulthess.
14. See also E/CN.4/2006/44.
15. A. Eide (1989), *Right to Adequate Food as a Human Right*, Human Rights Study Series No. 1, United Nations publication, New York, United Nations. An initial report by Eide in 1984 (E/CN.4/Sub.2/1984/22 and Add.1 and 2) was followed by the final report submitted in 1987. An interim report updating this study was submitted to the Sub-Commission at its 50th session (E/CN.4/Sub.2/1998/9). In 1999, Eide updated his study with document E/CN.4/Sub.2/1999/12, which, as he points out, should be read in conjunction with the 1998 update.
16. CESCR, *General Comment No.12*, E/C.12/1999/5, paragraph 15.
17. FAO, *Implementing the Right to Adequate Food: The Outcome of Six Case Studies*, FAO document IGWG RTFG/INF4, June 2004, p. 13.
18. CESCR, *General Comment No.3*, E/1991/23.
19. CESCR, *General Comment No.12*, E/C.12/1999/5, paragraph 6.
20. Ibid.
21. Ibid, paragraph 10.

3 The Right to Food of the Most Vulnerable People

1. See also A/58/330.

388 Notes

2. United Nations Administrative Committee on Coordination, Subcommittee on Nutrition (ACC/SCN) *4th Report on the World Nutrition Situation: Nutrition throughout the Life Cycle*, Geneva, 2000.
3. See FAO, *Women and the Right to Food. International Law and State Practice*, FAO, Rome, 2008.
4. See for example Chapters 6, 8 and 10 on the situation in Niger, Bangladesh and Ethiopia.
5. A. Sen, 'More than 100 Million Women are Missing', *New York Review of Books*, Vol. 37, No. 20, 20 December 1990.
6. See Chapter 8.
7. See Chapter 7.
8. R. Henriques, *Desigualdade Racial no Brasil: Evoluçao das Condições de Vida na Decada de 90*, Brasilia, Institute for Applied Economic Research (IPEA), 2001.
9. See FAO, Women and the Right to Food: International Law and State Practice.
10. See Chapter 6.
11. M. Molyneaux and S. Razavi (eds), *Gender Justice, Development and Rights*, Oxford, United Nations Research Institute for Social Development, Oxford University Press, 2003.
12. L. Cotula, *Gender and Law – Women's Rights in Agriculture*, FAO Legislative Study 76, Rome, FAO, 2002.
13. See Chapter 5.
14. See, for example, Convention No. 111 concerning Discrimination in Respect of Employment and Occupation, 1958, and Convention No. 100 concerning Equal Remuneration for Men and Women Workers for Work of Equal Value, 1951.
15. General Recommendation No. 19 of the Committee on the Elimination of Discrimination against Women, adopted at the 11th session, 1992, paragraph 9.
16. See also A/HRC/4/30.
17. UNICEF, *The State of the World's Children 2005 – Childhood Under Threat*, New York, UNICEF, 2005.
18. Child Rights Information Network, 26 September 2006.
19. UNICEF, *Progress for Children: A Report Card on Nutrition*, New York, UNICEF, 2006.
20. Ibid.
21. Ibid.
22. UNICEF, *Progress for Children: A Report Card on Water and Sanitation*.
23. Articles 23, 50, 89 of the Fourth Geneva Convention, 1949, and Article 70 of the First Optional Protocol, 1977. See Chapter 5.
24. UNICEF, *Progress for Children: A Report Card on Water and Sanitation*, New York, UNICEF, 2006.
25. Ibid.
26. J. Lee and S. Thorat, 'Dalits and the Right to Food: Discrimination and Exclusion in Food related Government Programmes', *Indian Institute of Dalit Studies Working Paper Series*, Vol. 1, No. 3, 2006.
27. See A/51/306.
28. *International Herald Tribune*, 24 August 2006.
29. R. Brett and I. Specht, *Young Soldiers: Why they Choose to Fight*, Bolder, Lynne Rienner, 2004.
30. See A/51/306 and Add.1.
31. See A/61/275.
32. Ibid.
33. R. Brett and I. Specht, Young Soldiers: Why they Choose to Fight.

34. Ibid.
35. Redress, *Victims, Perpetrator or Heroes? Child Soldiers before the International Criminal Court*, London, The Redress Trust, 2006.
36. R. Brett and I. Specht, *Young Soldiers: Why they Choose to Fight*.
37. C. Lata Hogg, *Child Recruitment in South Asian Conflicts: A Comparative Analysis of Sri Lanka, Nepal and Bangladesh*, London, The Royal Institute of International Affairs, 2006.
38. Redress, *Victims, Perpetrator or Heroes? Child Soldiers before the International Criminal Court*.
39. Ibid.
40. See Security Council Resolution 1612 (2005).
41. See A/61/275.
42. See also A/57/356.
43. United Nations Millennium Project, Task Force on Hunger, *Halving Hunger, It Can Be Done*, New York, UNDP, 2005.
44. International Fund for Agricultural Development (IFAD), *Rural Poverty Report 2001: The Challenge of Ending Rural Poverty*, New York, Oxford University Press, 2001.
45. Ibid.
46. See Chapter 7.
47. See Chapter 12.
48. R. Prosterman and T. Hanstad, 'Land Reform: Neglected, Yet Essential', *Rural Development Institute Reports on Foreign Aid and Development*, No. 87, Washington, 1995.
49. Ibid.
50. IFAD, *Rural Poverty Report 2001: The Challenge of Ending Rural Poverty*.
51. FAO, Contemporary Thinking on Land Reforms, Rome, FAO, 1998.
52. See D. Lehman, 'The Death of Land Reform: A Polemic', cited in FAO, Contemporary Thinking on Land Reforms.
53. FAO, *Report of the World Food Summit, 13–17 November 1996*, FAO document WFS 96/REP, Part 1, Appendix.
54. See FAO document C/2006/REP, Appendix G.
55. FAO, Contemporary Thinking on Land Reforms.
56. P. Rosset, 'Tides Shift on Agrarian Reform: New Movements Show the Way', *Food First Backgrounder*, Vol. 7:1, 2001.
57. Ibid.
58. FAO, Contemporary Thinking on Land Reforms.
59. IFAD, *Rural Poverty Report 2001: The Challenge of Ending Rural Poverty*.
60. K. Hoff, A. Braverman and J. E. Stiglitz (eds), *The Economics of Rural Organization*, New York, Oxford University Press for the World Bank, 1993, p. 236.
61. World Bank, *World Development Report 2000/2001: Attacking Poverty*, New York, Oxford University Press, 2001, p. 55.
62. R. Prosterman and T. Hanstad, 'Land Reform: Neglected, Yet Essential'.
63. P. Rosset, 'Tides Shift on Agrarian Reform: New Movements Show the Way'.
64. Ibid.
65. IFAD, *Rural Poverty Report 2001: The Challenge of Ending Rural Poverty*; FAO, *Contemporary Thinking on Land Reform*; P. Rosset, 'Tides Shift on Agrarian Reform: New Movements Show the Way'.
66. IFAD, *Rural Poverty Report 2001: The Challenge of Ending Rural Poverty*.
67. P. Rosset, 'Tides Shift on Agrarian Reform: New Movements Show the Way'.

68. FAO, *Contemporary Thinking on Land Reforms*.
69. IFAD, *Rural Poverty Report 2001: The Challenge of Ending Rural Poverty*.
70. S. Monsalve Suárez, 'Marcos legales y conflictos de tierras: análisis desde una perspectiva de derechos humanos', *Grupo Semillas, Revista no. 30–31*, 2007.
71. See Chapter 7.
72. S. Monsalve Suárez, 'Marcos legales y conflictos de tierras: análisis desde una perspectiva de derechos humanos'.
73. J. Ziegler, 'Schizophrénie des Nations Unies', *Le Monde diplomatique*, Paris, Novembre 2001.
74. Ibid.
75. P. Rosset, 'Tides Shift on Agrarian Reform: New Movements Show the Way'.
76. See, for example, 'Land for those who work it, not just for those who can buy it', Final declaration of the international seminar on the negative impacts of World Bank market-based land reform policy, April 2002, http://www.foodfirst.org/node/248.
77. See Chapter 12.
78. S. Monsalve Suárez, 'Marcos legales y conflictos de tierras: análisis desde una perspectiva de derechos humanos'.
79. See Chapter 6.
80. For example the declaration 'Land for those who work it, not just for those who can buy it'.
81. See also A/59/385.
82. See FAO Newsroom Focus, 'Aquaculture: Not Just an Export Industry', Rome, August 2003.
83. G. Kent, 'Fish Trade, Food Security and the Human Right to Adequate Food', Rome, FAO, 2003.
84. FAO, *The State of World Fisheries and Aquaculture 2002*, Rome, FAO, 2002.
85. Ibid.
86. Ibid. According to FAO statistics, about 47 per cent of the major marine fish stocks or species groups are fully exploited and offer no reasonable expectations for further expansion, another 18 per cent of stocks or species groups are over-exploited and 10 per cent have become significantly depleted or are recovering from depletion, leaving only 25 per cent of the main stocks or species groups underexploited or moderately exploited.
87. The Agreement for the Conservation and Management of Straddling Fish Stocks and Highly Migratory Fish Stocks, Articles 5(i) and 24, 1995.
88. World Wildlife Fund (WWF), *Turning the Tide on Fishing Subsidies: Can the World Trade Organization play a Positive Role?*, Washington, WWF, 2002.
89. G. Porter, *Fisheries and the Environment: Fisheries Subsidies and Overfishing: Towards a Structured Discussion*, United Nations Environment Programme (UNEP), Prepared and presented for the UNEP Fisheries Workshop, Geneva, 12 February 2001.
90. UNEP, *Fisheries and the Environment: Fisheries Subsidies and Marine Resources Management: Lessons Learned from Studies in Argentina and Senegal*, Geneva, UNEP, 2002.
91. Ibid.
92. FAO Newsroom Focus, 'Countries Debate Strategies for Managing Fleet Capacities and Combating Illegal Fishing', Rome, 1 July 2004.
93. International Collective in Support of Fishworkers, *Workshop on Gender and Coastal Fishing Communities in Latin America. 10 to 15 June 2000. Prainha do Canto*

Verde, Ceara, Brazil, Chenai, 2000, http://www.icsf.net/icsf2006/uploads/publications/reports/pdf/english/issue_2/chapter04.pdf.
94. G. Kent, 'Fish Trade, Food Security and the Human Right to Adequate Food.'
95. Ibid.
96. Ibid.
97. Foodfirst Information and Action Network (FIAN), the Russian Association of Indigenous Peoples of the North (RAIPON), the Institute for Ecology and Action Anthropology (INFOE), *The right to adequate food (art.11) and violations of this right in the Russian Federation. Parallel information to the fourth periodic report of the Russian Federation, submitted by the Russian Government to the CESCR (E/C.12/4/Add.10),* 2003.
98. FIAN, RAIPON, INFOE, The right to adequate food (Article 11) and violations of this right in the Russian Federation. Parallel information to the fourth periodic report of the Russian Federation, submitted by the Russian Government to the CESCR (E/C.12/4/Add.10).
99. High Court of South Africa (Cape of Good Hope Provincial Division), *Kenneth George and Others v. Minister of Environmental Affairs & Tourism*, Case No. EC 1/2005, Founding Affidavit. See also High Court of South Africa (Cape of Good Hope Provincial Division), *Kenneth George and Others v. Minister of Environmental Affairs & Tourism*, Case No. EC 1/2005, Affidavit by N. Jaffer; High Court of South Africa (Cape of Good Hope Provincial Division), *Kenneth George and Others v. Minister of Environmental Affairs & Tourism*, Case No. EC 1/2005, Supporting Affidavit by Jean Ziegler.
100. High Court of South Africa (Cape of Good Hope Provincial Division), *Kenneth George and Others v. Minister of Environmental Affairs & Tourism*, Case No. EC 1/2005, Judgment of 2 May 2007.
101. FAO, the State of World Fisheries and Aquaculture 2002.
102. J. Kurien, *The Blessing of the Commons: Small-Scale Fisheries, Community Property Rights, and Coastal Natural Assets*, Political Economy Research Institute, University of Massachusetts Amherst, Conference Paper Series No. 2, 2002.
103. H. Josupeit and N. Franz, Aquaculture – Trade, Trends, Standards and Outlooks, Rome, FAO, 2004.
104. R.L. Naylor, R.J. Goldburg, J.H. Primavera, N. Kautsky, M.C.M. Beveridge, J. Clay, et al. 'Effect of Aquaculture on World Fish Supplies', *Nature*, Vol. 405, 2000, pp. 1017–24.
105. Supreme Court of India, *S. Jagannath v. Union of India and Ors*, 1996.
106. S.C. Stonich and I. De La Torre, 'Farming Shrimp, Harvesting Hunger: The Costs and Benefits of the Blue Revolution', *Backgrounder*, Vol. 8, No. 1, 2002.
107. Supreme Court of India, *S. Jagannath v. Union of India and Ors*, 1996.
108. D.L. Lahiri (ed.), Pink Revolution: Right to Livelihood of the Coastal Poor. A Case Study on Shrimp Monoculture, Kolkata, India.
109. See also A/60/350.
110. The United Nations Declaration on the Rights of Indigenous Peoples has been adopted by the General Assembly in its resolution 61/295 of 13 September 2007. See S. Errico, 'The UN Declaration on the Rights of Indigenous Peoples is Adopted: An Overview', *Human Rights Law Review*, Vol. 7, 2007, pp. 756–9.
111. See A/60/350.
112. E/C.19/2005/2, section II, paragraph 7.

113. International Labour Office (ILO), *Indigenous Peoples Living and Working Conditions of Aboriginal Populations in Independent Countries*, Geneva, ILO, 1953, p. 89.
114. Commission on Human Rights, Study of the problem of discrimination against indigenous populations, E/CN.4/Sub.4/1986/7/Add.4.
115. See A/59/258, paragraph 10.
116. See E/C.19/2005/2, section II, paragraph 13.
117. World Bank, *Indigenous People and Poverty in Latin America: an Empirical Analysis*, Washington, World Bank, 1994, pp. 206–7.
118. World Bank, *Indigenous Peoples, Poverty and Human Development in Latin America: 1994–2004*, Washington, World Bank, 2005.
119. See E/C.19/2003/4.
120. Government of Guatemala, *Politica Nacional de Seguridad Alimentaria y Nutricional*, Guatemala City, 2004, p. 8. See also Chapter 12, this volume.
121. S. Thériault, G.Otis, G. Duhaime and C. Furgal, 'The Legal Protection of Subsistence: Prerequisite of Food Security for the Inuit of Alaska', *Alaska Law Review*, Vol. 22, No. 1, June 2005, p. 35.
122. See E/CN.4/2005/88/Add.2.
123. World Bank, *Guatemala: Livelihoods, Labor Markets, and Rural Poverty*, Washington, World Bank, Guatemala Poverty Assessment (Guapa) Program, Technical Paper No. 1, 2003, p. 25.
124. See E/CN.4/2002/97, paragraph 57.
125. Inter-American Court of Human Rights, *The Mayagna (Sumo) Indigenous Community of Awas Tingni v. The Republic of Nicaragua*, Judgement Summary and Order issued 31 August 2001.
126. See, on this subject, 'Learning the Lessons of Traditional Knowledge: Broadening the Base of Intellectual Property', *WIPO Magazine*, No. 1, January to February 2004, pp. 14–17, http://www.wipo.int/wipo_magazine/en/pdf/2004/wipo_pub_121_2004_01-02.pdf.
127. See Rural Advancement Foundation International (RAFI), Press release, 'Quinoa Patent Dropped', 16 May 1998, http://www.ukabc.org/quinoa.htm. RAFI became the ETC Group in 2001, see more information at http://www.etcgroup.org.
128. E/CN.4/Sub.2/2001/21, paragraph 67.
129. Malaysian Court of Appeal, *Adong bin Kuwau v. State of Johor*, Judgment of 21 November 1996.
130. Plataforma Interamericana de Derechos Humanos, Democracia y Desarollo (PIDhDD), FIAN Brasil, *El Derecho Humano a la Alimentación en America Latina*, PIDhDD, FIAN, 2004. FIAN, *The Human Right to Food in Guatemala*, Heidelberg, FIAN, October 2004.
131. See E/CN.4/2005/88/Add.2.
132. See resolution 2006/2.
133. See also A/HRC/4/30 and A/62/289.
134. Internally displaced persons are defined as persons who have been forced or obliged to flee or leave their homes or places of habitual residence, in particular as a result of or in order to avoid the effects of armed conflict, situations of generalized violence, violations of human rights or natural or human-made disasters, and who have not crossed an internationally recognized border. Internally displaced persons are protected under human rights instruments and the Guiding Principles on Internal Displacement (E/CN.4/1998/53/Add.2, annex). Principle 18 reaffirms the right of internally displaced persons to an

adequate standard of living and states that, at minimum, regardless of the circumstances, and without discrimination, competent authorities shall provide internally displaced persons with and ensure safe access to, inter alia, essential food and potable water.
135. See *Tribune de Genève*, 14 December 2006.
136. BBC News, 30 November 2006, http://news.bbc.co.uk/go/pr/fr/-/2/hi/europe/6160633.stm.
137. *Le Courrier*, Geneva, 10 December 2006.
138. Ibid.
139. Amnesty International, *Spain/Morocco: Hundreds of Migrants from sub-Saharan Africa*, 3 October 2005, Amnesty International Index EUR 41/012/2005.
140. Human Rights Watch, 13 October 2005, http://hrw.org/english/docs/2005/10/13/spain11866.htm.
141. Ibid.
142. BBC News, 10 September 2006, http://news.bbc.co.uk/go/pr/fr/-/2/hi/europe/5331896.stm.
143. See Amnesty International, 4 May 2000, http://web.amnesty.org/library/Index/ENGASA170212000?open&of=ENG-PRK.
144. BBC News, 27 October 2006, http://news.bbc.co.uk/go/pr/fr/-/2/hi/americas/6090060.stm.
145. Human Rights Watch, 11 August 2006, http://hrw.org/english/docs/2006/08/11/austra13964.htm.
146. International Organization for Migration (IOM), *World Migration Report 2005*, Geneva, IOM, 2005.
147. United Nations High Commissioner for Refugees (UNHCR), *State of the World's Refugees 2006*, New York, Oxford University Press, 2006.
148. Ibid.
149. UNHCR, Handbook on Procedures and Criteria for Determining Refugee Status under the 1951 Convention and the 1967 Protocol relating to the Status of Refugees, Geneva, UNHCR, 1992 (first edition 1979).
150. J.B. Davies, S. Sandström, A. Shorrocks and E.N. Wolff, *The World Distribution of Household Wealth*, Tokyo, United Nations University World Institute for Development Economics Research (UNU-WIDER), 2008.
151. Ibid.
152. S. Castles and M.J. Miller, *The Age of Migration. International Population Movements in the Modern World*, Fourth Edition, Basingstoke, Palgrave Macmillan, 2009.
153. FAO, The State of Food Insecurity in the World 2008, Rome, FAO, 2008, pp. 6–12.
154. J. Macrae and A.B. Zwi, 'Food as an Instrument of War in Contemporary African Famines: a Review of the Evidence', *Disasters*, Vol. 16, No. 4, 1992, pp. 299–321.
155. See A/61/306.
156. N. Myers, 'Environmental Refugees: an Emergent Security Issue', OSCE, 13th Economic Forum, Prague, 23–27 May 2005, http://www.osce.org/documents/eea/2005/05/14488_en.pdf.
157. Ibid.
158. M. Conisbee and A. Simms, *Environmental Refugees: The Case for Recognition*, London, New Economics Foundation Pocket Book, 2003.
159. Oxfam, 'Rigged Rules and Double Standards: Trade, Globalisation, and the Fight Against Poverty', 2002, http://www.ecolomics-international.org/n_san_oxfam_make_trade_fair_report_summary.pdf, date accessed 31 May 2010.

160. J. Pottier, 'Migration as a Hunger-Coping Strategy: Paying Attention to Gender and Historical Change', in H.S. Marcussen (ed.), *Institutional Issues in Natural Resources Management*, Roskilde, Roskilde University, 1993.
161. See UNHCR, *The State of the World's Refugees 2006*, Oxford, Oxford University Press, 2006.
162. See section 4.2.
163. United Nations Office of the High Commissioner for Human Rights (OHCHR), *Human Rights and Refugees*, Fact Sheet 20, Geneva, OHCHR, 1997.
164. A/60/316, paragraph 52.
165. Legal developments in Africa and Latin America have broadened the concept to protect those escaping generalized violence, foreign aggression, internal conflicts, massive violation of human rights or other circumstances seriously disturbing public order. Furthermore, some countries in other regions have established complementary protection regimes for persons who do not qualify as refugees under the 1951 Convention. In addition, the mandate of the UNHCR has been extended by the General Assembly to cover not only those persons who are refugees within the meaning of the 1951 Convention, but also persons outside their country of origin or habitual residence who are unable to return there owing to serious and indiscriminate threats to life, physical integrity or freedom resulting from generalized violence or events seriously disturbing public order and who, as a result, require international protection.
166. Cour d'Amiens, *Dame Ménard*, 22 April 1898.
167. Supreme Court of Canada (1984), 2 S.C.R. 232.

4 The Right to Food in an Era of Globalization

1. See E/CN.4/2006/44.
2. See also E/CN.4/2004/10, E/CN.4/2004/10.
3. See the report of Olivier de Schutter on his mission to the World Trade Organization (WTO) in June 2008, A/HRC/10/5/Add.2.
4. Interview of Peter Brabeck, *Weltwoche*, Zurich 19 January 2006.
5. See 'France Signals Real Change in Agriculture Policy', *The Guardian*, 12 June 2003.
6. President G.W. Bush address to the Future Farmers of America, Washington, 27 July 2001.
7. Cited in C. Raghavan, 'U.S. Farm Bill Gives One More Blow to New Round', www.twnside.org.sg/title/twe280c.htm, date accessed 31 May 2010.
8. A. Mittal, 'Giving Away the Farm: The 2002 Farm Bill', *Food First Backgrounder*, Summer 2002, Vol. 8, No. 3.
9. X. Diao, E. Diaz-Bonilla and S. Robinson, *How Much Does It Hurt? The Impact of Agricultural Trade Policies on, Developing Countries*, Washington, IFPRI, August 2003.
10. International Monetary Fund (IMF), *External evaluation of the ESAF (Enhanced Structural Adjustment Facility): Report by a group of independent experts*, Washington, IMF, June 1998.
11. Often government monopolies are simply replaced by monopolistic private companies or traders, who offer lower prices to farmers and charge higher prices to consumers. See S.A. Way and J. Chileshe, 'Trade Liberalisation and the Impact on Poverty: Zambia Case Study', in Oxfam/Institute of Development Studies, University of Sussex, *Liberalisation and Poverty*, Oxford, Oxfam, 1999.

12. K. Watkins, *Mexico: Globalization and Liberalization: Implications for Poverty, Distribution and Inequality*, New York, UNDP, Occasional Paper 32, 1997.
13. Friends of the Earth International, *Sale of the Century?: Peoples' Food Sovereignty, Part 1 – The Implications Of Current Trade Negotiations*, Amsterdam, Friends of the Earth International, 2001.
14. S. Murphy and S. Suppan, 'Introduction to the Development Box: Finding Space for Development Concerns in the WTO's Agriculture Negotiations', Manitoba, International Institute for Sustainable Development, 2003.
15. J. Morisset, 'Unfair Trade?: Empirical Evidence in World Commodity Markets Over the Past 25 Years', Policy Research Working Papers of the World Bank, No. 1815, Washington, World Bank, 1997.
16. Statement by the FAO at the WTO Ministerial Conference, fifth session, Cancún, Mexico, 10–14 September 2003, WTO document WT/MIN(03)/ST/61.
17. See the report of O. de Schutter, the current UN Special Rapporteur on the Right to Food, on his mission to WTO, A/HRC/10/5/Add.2.
18. World Bank, *World Development Report 2000/2001: Attacking Poverty*, New York, Oxford University Press, Published for the World Bank, 2001, p. 3.
19. *Action contre la faim*, Paris, Information Document, 31 October 1997.
20. A French version of the article appeared in *Courrier International*, No. 315, Paris, 14–20 November 1996.
21. J. Madeley, 'Trade and Hunger: An Overview of Case Studies on the Impact of Trade Liberalization on Food Security', *Globala Studier*, No. 4, Stockholm, Church of Sweden, Diakonia, Forum Syd, the Swedish Society for Nature Conservation and the Programme of Global Studies, 2000.
22. Of course the problems are different for net food importing countries that cannot grow sufficient food. For this reason, the Decision on Measures concerning the Possible Negative Effects of the Reform Programme on Least Developed and Net Food Importing Countries (Marrakesh Decision) was taken, but it has had little concrete effect so far. See WTO document TD/B/COM.1/EM.11/2 and Corr.1.
23. Often government monopolies are simply replaced by monopolistic private companies or traders, who offer poorer prices to farmers and charge higher prices to consumers. See S.A. Way and J. Chileshe, 'Trade Liberalisation and the Impact on Poverty: Zambia Case Study'.
24. IMF, *External evaluation of the Enhanced Structural Adjustment Facility (ESAF): Report by a group of independent experts*.
25. Ibid.
26. P.M. Rosset, 'The Multiple Functions and Benefits of Small Farm Agriculture in the Context of Global Trade Negotiations', *Foodfirst Backgrounder*, Winter 1999, Vol. 6, No. 4.
27. Ibid.
28. See WTO document TD/B/COM.1/EM.11/2 and Corr.1.
29. In the case of Zambia, for example, import tariffs were reduced under structural adjustment to well below their boundary levels under WTO.
30. It is also important to point out, however, that a cut in domestic support and export subsidies on food envisaged under agricultural trade reform may have a negative impact on developing countries that are net food importers (although food aid will generally be exempted). This is because there will be upward pressure on world agricultural prices of basic foodstuffs at the same time as price concessions are taken away. See WTO document TD/B/COM.1/EM.11/2 and Corr.1.

31. See, for example, C. Dommen, 'Raising Human Rights Concerns in the World Trade Organization: Actors, Processes and Possible Strategies', *Human Rights Quarterly*, Vol. 24, No. 1, 2002. Another difficult issue concerns strong developing country resistance to United States proposals to include trade and labour rights as part of the WTO agreements, but this matter is not treated here as this section focuses only on the impact of the Agreement on Agriculture on liberalization on food security (although this has often involved deregulation and removal of existing social protections, such as labour rights, under structural adjustment provisions).
32. Ibid.
33. WTO, 'The WTO Is Not After Your Water', in WTO, *GATS: Fact and Fiction*, WTO, Geneva, 2001.
34. WTO document G/AG/NG/W/101, paragraph 29.
35. Ibid., paragraphs 33 and 36.
36. See WTO document G/AG/NG/W/13.
37. D. Green and S. Priyadarshi, 'Proposal for a "Development Box" in the WTO Agreement on Agriculture', CAFOD Policy Paper, London, Catholic aid agency for England and Wales (CAFOD), 2001.
38. Ibid.
39. D. Rodrik, 'The Global Governance of Trade as if Development Really Mattered', New York, UNDP, 2001.
40. The World Bank argues that pre-existing inequality in a country affects the way in which the benefits of growth are distributed. When inequality in a country is very high, then growth will benefit the rich and not the poor, as growth in itself does nothing to reduce inequality. Reducing inequality requires the State to engage in active measures of redistribution, such as land reform – a classic form of redistribution that can be effective. See World Bank, *World Development Report 2000/2001: Attacking Poverty*, p. 55.
41. See also E/CN.4/2005/47.
42. S. Skogly, 'The Obligation of International Assistance and Co-Operation in the International Covenant on Economic, Social and Cultural Rights', in M. Bergsmo, *Human Rights and Criminal Justice for the Downtrodden: Essays in Honour of Asbjørn Eide*, Dordrecht, Kluwer Law International, 2003, pp. 403–20.
43. See E/CN.4/2004/10.
44. The European Court of Human Rights, *Loizidou* judgement of 23 March 1995, Series A. No. 310, p. 24, paragraph 62.
45. International Council on Human Rights Policy (ICHRP), *Duties sans frontières. Human rights and global social justice*, Versoix, ICHRP, 2003.
46. FIAN, Brot für die Welt and the Evangelischer Entwicklungsdienst, *Extraterritorial State Obligations*, Heidelberg, FIAN, 2004. These organizations also presented a parallel report to the CESCR on compliance of Germany with its international obligations, available at http://www.fian.org/resources/documents/others/extraterritorial-state-obligations/pdf, date accessed 31 May 2010.
47. 3D-Trade-Human Rights – Equitable Economy and Realizing Rights: The Ethical Globalization Initiative, US and EU Cotton Production and Export Policies and Their Impact on West and Central Africa: Coming to Grips with International Human Rights Obligations, 2004, http://www.3dthree.org/pdf_3D/1404-EGI-CottonBrief_FINAL.pdf, date accessed 31 May 2010.
48. S. Skogly, 'The Obligation of International Assistance and Co-Operation in the International Covenant on Economic, Social and Cultural Rights'.

49. F. Coomans and M.T. Kamminga (eds), *Extraterritorial Application of Human Rights Treaties*, Antwerp, Intersentia, 2004.
50. See CESCR, *General Comment No. 3*, /1991/23; *General Comment No. 12*, E/C.12/1999/5; *General Comment No. 15*, E/C.12/2002/11.
51. See E/CN.4/Sub.2/1999/12.
52. As stated by the European Court on Human Rights, human rights obligations do not stop when States are acting as members of international organizations. European Court on Human Rights, *Waite and Kennedy v. Germany*, 1999, paragraph 67. See also E. Petersmann, 'Time for integrating human rights into the law of worldwide organizations: Lessons from European Integration Law for Global Integration Law', Jean Monnet Working Paper 7/01, Jean Monnet Programme Publication, 2001, p. 14.
53. CESCR, *General Comment No. 3*, E/1991/23, paragraph 14.
54. Ibid, paragraphs 13-14.
55. Committee on the Rights on the Child, *General Comment No. 3*, CRC/GC/2003/3 paragraph 7.
56. States that have signed the Covenant, but not ratified it, have a minimum obligation to refrain from acts which would defeat its object and purpose. See Vienna Convention on the Law of Treaties, Article 18.
57. CESCR, *General Comment No. 12*, E/C.12/1999/5, paragraph 36.
58. United Nations Millennium Declaration, paragraphs 2 and 19.
59. CESCR, *General Comment No. 12*, E/C.12/1999/5, paragraph 36, and E/CN.4/Sub.2/1999/12, paragraph 131. S. Skogly, 'The Obligation of International Assistance and Co-Operation in the International Covenant on Economic, Social and Cultural Rights', pp. 419-20.
60. FIAN, Brot für die Welt and the Evangelischer Entwicklungsdienst, *Extraterritorial State Obligations: International Covenant on Economic, Social and Cultural Rights. Documentation in the form of a written report for the United Nations on the effect of German policies on social human rights in the South*, available at http://www.fian.org/resources/documents/others/extraterritorial-state-obligations/pdf, date accessed 31 May 2010.
61. CESCR, *General Comment No. 12*, E/C.12/1999/5, paragraph 37; *General Comment No. 15*, E/C.12/2002/11, paragraph 32.
62. Friends of the Earth International, Sale of the century? Peoples' Food Sovereignty, Part 1 – The Implications of Current Trade Negotiations.
63. See Chapter 6.
64. See section 4.4.
65. F. Coomans and M.T. Kamminga (eds) *Extraterritorial Application of Human Rights Treaties*.
66. See E/CN.4/2004/10, paragraphs 35-52.
67. CESCR, *General Comment No. 15*, E/C.12/2002/11, paragraph 33.
68. It applies to customary international law norms, such as the prohibition of slavery, genocide, torture, crimes against humanity and war crimes. See the cases of *Wiwa v. Royal Dutch Petroleum (Shell)* and *Bowoto v. ChevronTexaco, Doe v. Unocal* before US jurisdictions.
69. European Parliament, Resolution on EU standards for European enterprises operating in developing countries: towards a European Code of Conduct, adopted in 1999; The Parliament of Australia, Corporate Code of Conduct Bill, adopted in 2000.
70. CESCR, *General Comment No. 12*, E/C.12/1999/5, paragraph 17.

71. A 20:20 initiative was discussed during the World Summit for Social Development, in which donor countries would commit themselves to use 20 per cent of the aid for social priority areas, while developing countries would have to spend 20 per cent of their budget for social priority areas.
72. Only a few countries have achieved the goal of 0.7 per cent, notably the Netherlands, Sweden, Denmark, Norway and Luxembourg. As M. Craven rightly stated, 'it would be a clear signal...that a State was not committed to its obligation to assist other States if the amount of aid it provided to other States declined over a number of years'. M. Craven, *The International Covenant on Economic, Social and Cultural Rights. A Perspective on its Development*, Oxford, Clarendon Press, 1995, p. 150.
73. See E/1990/6/Add.21, paragraph 10.
74. See E/CN.4/2002/58.
75. CESCR, *General Comment No. 12*, E/C.12/1999/5, paragraph 38.
76. CESCR, *General Comment No. 12*, E/C.12/1999/5, paragraph 39.
77. See also A/60/350.
78. Some instances of violations are described in D.D. Bradlow and C. Grossman, 'Adjusting the Bretton Woods Institutions to Contemporary Realities', in G. Bernhard. and J.M. Griesgraber (ed.), *Development, New Paradigms and Principles for the 21st Century*, London, Pluto Press, pp. 27–59; see also B. Ghazi, 'The IMF, World Bank Group and the Question of Human Rights', PhD dissertation, Geneva, Graduate Institute of International Studies, May 2004.
79. World Bank Inspection Panel, Investigation Report on India: Coal Sector Environmental and Social Mitigation Project (Credit No. 2862-In), Washington, World Bank, November 2002.
80. B. Ghazi, 'The IMF, World Bank Group and the Question of Human Rights', PhD dissertation, Geneva, Graduate Institute of International Studies, May 2004, p. 44.
81. IMF, External evaluation of theEnhanced Structural Adjustment Facility (ESAF): report by a group of independent experts.
82. See section 4.1.
83. Oxfam, 'Rigged Rules and Double Standards: Trade, Globalisation, and the Fight Against Poverty', 2002, http://www.ecolomics-international.org/n_san_oxfam_make_trade_fair_report_summary.pdf, date accessed 31 May 2010.
84. International Federation for Human Rights (IFHR), *Les politiques de la Banque Mondiale à l'épreuve des droits humains*, Paris, IFHR, 2003; IFHR, *Understanding Global Trade and Human Rights*, Paris, IFHR, 2005.
85. 3D-Trade-Human Rights – Equitable Economy and FORUM-ASIA, *Practical Guide to the WTO for Human Rights Advocates*, 2004, http://www.3dthree.org/en/complement.php?IDpage=53&IDcomplement=55&IDcat=22.
86. FIAN, 'Questionable Advice, The Worldbank's Influence on Mining Laws in Africa – Human Rights Comments', Herne, FIAN Germany, 2004.
87. S. Skogly, *The Human Rights Obligations of the World Bank and the IMF*, London, Cavendish Publishing, 2001.
88. A. Clapham, *Human Rights Obligations of Non-State Actors*, New York, Oxford University Press, 2005.
89. M. Darrow, *Between Light and Shadow: The World Bank, the International Monetary Fund and International Human Rights Law*, Oxford, Hart Publishing, 2003.
90. B. Ghazi, 'The IMF, World Bank Group and the Question of Human Rights', PhD dissertation, Geneva, Graduate Institute of International Studies, May 2004.

91. See CESCR, *General Comment No. 3*, E/CN.12/1991/23; *General Comment No. 12*, E/C.12/1999/5; *General Comment No. 15*, E/C.12/2002/11.
92. E/CN.4/Sub.2/2000/13, E/CN.4/Sub.2/2001/10, E/CN.4/Sub.2/2003/14.
93. See B. Simma and P.Alston, 'The Sources of Human Rights Law: Custom, Jus Cogens, and General Principles', *Australian Year Book of International Law*, Vol. 12, 1992, pp. 82–108; H.G. Schermers and N.M. Blokker, *International Institutional Law: Unity within Diversity*, The Hague, Martinus Nijhoff Publishers, third revised edition, 1995, pp. 824 and 998; and S.I. Skogly, *The Human Rights Obligations of the World Bank and the IMF*, Chapter 4.
94. International governmental organizations that are not specialized agencies of the United Nations in accordance with Article 63 are still under obligation to respect their member States' obligations under the Charter as recognized in Article 103.
95. International Court of Justice (ICJ), *Interpretation of the Agreement of 25 March 1951 between the WHO and Egypt*, Advisory Opinion, ICJ Reports 1980, pp. 89–90, paragraph 37.
96. ICJ, Interpretation of the Agreement of 25 March 1951 between the WHO and Egypt, Advisory Opinion, ICJ Reports 1980, pp. 89–90, paragraph 37.
97. See A/RES/60/165.
98. WTO, *Understanding the WTO*, Geneva, WTO, 27 June 2005.
99. H.G. Schermers and N.M. Blokker, *International Institutional Law. Unity within Diversity*, fourth edition, Leiden, Martinus Nijhoff Publishers, 2003, pp. 992–3.
100. M. Darrow, *Between Light and Shadow: The World Bank, the International Monetary Fund and International Human Rights Law*, Oxford, Hart Publishing, 2003, p. 192 and chapter IV.
101. See for instance F. Gianviti, 'Economic, Social and Cultural Rights and the International Monetary Fund', Paper presented at a consultation convened by the CESCR and the High Council of International Cooperation of France, Geneva 7 May 2001 (unpublished paper); I.F.I Shihata (ed.), *The World Bank Inspection Panel. In Practice*, second edition, New York, Oxford University Press, 2000, p. 241.
102. Declaration of the World Food Summit 1996 and 'An International Alliance Against Hunger': Declaration of the World Food Summit: five years later, 2002. In both cases the United States of America formulated reservations to the recognition of the right to food as a legal right, but this only can make that country a persistent objector and does not preclude the formation of the right to food as a customary norm.
103. P. Sands and P. Klein (eds), *Bowett's Law of International Institutions*, fifth edition, Londond, Sweet and Maxwell, 2001, pp. 458–9; A. Clapham, *Human Rights Obligations of Non-State Actors*, chapter V; E.U. Petersmann, *Time for Integrating Human Rights into the Law of Worldwide Organizations. Lessons from European Integration Law for Global Integration Law*, p. 5.
104. E/CN.4/Sub.2/2003/14, paragraph 39.
105. For example B. Ghazi, 'The IMF, World Bank Group and the Question of Human Rights', PhD dissertation, Geneva, Graduate Institute of International Studies, May 2004, pp. 108–9 and 206–13.
106. CESCR, Statement on Globalization and Economic, Social and Cultural Rights, 18th session, 27 April to 15 May 1998, Geneva.
107. S. Skogly, The Human Rights Obligations of the World Bank and the IMF, p. 151.

108. See also E/CN.4/2004/10 and A/58/330.
109. See E/CN.4/Sub.2/1996/12, paragraph 72.
110. UNDP, *Human Development Report 2002*, New York, Oxford University Press, 2002, p. 10.
111. United Nations Conference on Trade and Development (UNCTAD) press release TAD/INF/PR/47, 12 August 2002.
112. Erosion, Technology and Concentration Action Group (ETC Group), 'Oligopoly, Inc. Concentration in Corporate Power: 2003', Communiqué, November/December 2003, Issue 82. See also M. Saam, B. Bordogna Petriccione and A. November, 'Les impacts des plantes transgéniques dans les pays en voie de développement et les pays en transition', *Les Cahiers du RIBios*, No. 5, 2004.
113. C. James, 'Global Status of Commercialized Transgenic Crops: 2002', *International Service for the Acquisition of Agri-Biotech Applications Briefs*, No. 27, 2002.
114. ETC Group, 'Oligopoly, Inc. Concentration in Corporate Power: 2003'.
115. ActionAid, *GM Crops – Going Against the Grain*, May 2003, http://www.actionaid.org/docs/gm_against_grain.pdf, date accessed 31 May 2010.
116. See A/58/330, paragraph 36.
117. N. Roseman, 'The Human Right to Water Under the Conditions of Trade Liberalisation and Privatization – A Study on the Privatization of Water Supply and Wastewater Disposal in Manila', Occasional Papers: International Development Cooperation, Bonn, Friedrich Ebert Foundation, 2003.
118. N. Laurie and C. Crespo, *Pro-Poor Water by Concession, Dream or Reality? Lessons From Bolivia*, Newcastle, University of Newcastle, 2003.
119. E. Gutierrez, B. Calaguas, J. Green and V. Roaf, *New Rules, New Roles: Does Private Sector Participation Benefit The Poor?*, WaterAid and TearFund, 2003.
120. L.O. Fresco, 'Which Road Do We Take? Harnessing Genetic Resources and Making Use of life Sciences, a New Contract for Sustainable Agriculture', European Discussion Forum 'Towards Sustainable Agriculture for Developing Countries: Options from Life Sciences and Biotechnologies', Brussels, 30–31 January 2003, www.fao.org/ag/magazine/fao-gr.pdf.
121. P.L. Pingali and G. Traxler, 'Changing Focus of Agricultural Research: Will the Poor Benefit from Biotechnology and Privatization Trends?', *Food Policy*, No. 27, 2002.
122. ActionAid, *GM Crops – Going Against the Grain*.
123. L.O. Fresco, 'Genetically modified organisms in food and agriculture: Where are we? Where are we going?', Keynote address at the Conference on 'Crop and Forest Biotechnology for the Future', Royal Swedish Academy of Agriculture and Forestry, September 2001.
124. The case of Canadian farmer Percy Schmeiser raises serious concerns. See Percy Schmeiser, 'Who Owns the Seeds?', *San Francisco Chronicle*, Opinion Editorial, 20 June 2003.
125. Ibid.
126. Europe-Third World Centre, *Transnational Corporations and Human Rights*, Geneva, CETIM, 2000.
127. See S. Lewis, 'Malnutrition as a Human Rights Violation', ACC/SCN, *SCN News*, No. 18, July 1999.
128. See A. Clapham, *Human Rights Obligations of Non-State Actors*. See also the report of J. Ruggie, Special Representative of the Secretary-General on the issue of human rights and transnational corporations and other business enterprises, on the protect, respect and remedy principles, A/HRC/8/5.

Notes 401

129. See E/C.12/2000/13.
130. See E/CN.4/2003/54, paragraphs 36–51.
131. Inter-American Court of Human Rights, *Velasquez Rodriguez v. Honduras*, 1989; European Court of Human Rights, *Guerra v. Italy*, 1998; Human Rights Committee, *Kitok v. Sweden*, 1985.
132. Center for Economic and Social Rights, 'Rights violations in the Ecuadorian Amazon: the human consequences of oil development', *Health and Human Rights: An International Journal*, Vol. 1, No. 1, 1994.
133. Inter-American Commission on Human Rights, *Report on the Situation of Human Rights in Ecuador*, OEA/Ser.L/V/II.96, doc. 10 rev.1, 24 April 1997.
134. Supreme Court of India, *Consumer Education and Research Centre v. Union of India*, 1995.
135. See E/C.12/1/Add.66, paragraph 30.
136. European Court on Human Rights, *Costello-Roberts v. United Kingdom*, 1993.
137. See also the report of Olivier de Schutter on Agribusiness and the right to food, A/HRC/13/33.
138. Organization for Economic Co-operation and Development (OECD), Working Party of the Trade Committee, *Codes of Corporate Conduct: An Inventory*, OECD document TD/TC/WP(98)74/Final, 29 May 1999.
139. See E/CN.4/Sub.2/2003/12/Rev.2.
140. United States Council for International Business (USCIB), 'UNHCHR Norms of Responsibilities of Transnational Corporations and Other Business Enterprises with Regard to Human Rights', January 2003, http://www.ioe-emp.org/fileadmin/user_upload/documents_pdf/memberpublications/english/csr_usa02_unhchrnorms.pdf.
141. See Commission on Human Rights' resolution 2003/16.
142. Sir G. Chandler, 'Commentary on the United States Council for International Business "Talking Points"', 20 November 2003.
143. See for example the litigation against Broken Hill Proprietary by people living near Ok Tedi River in Papua New Guinea.
144. For example, Cour supérieure du Québec, Canada, *Recherche Internationales Quebec v. Cambior Inc*, 1998, Arrêts du Québec No. 2554.
145. For example, Court of Appeal, *Sithole v. Thor Chemicals Holdings Ltd.*, decision of 3rd February 1999.
146. It applies to customary international law norms, such as the prohibition of slavery, genocide, torture, crimes against humanity and war crimes. See the cases of *Wiwa v. Royal Dutch Petroleum (Shell)* and *Bowoto v. ChevronTexaco, Doe v. Unocal* before US jurisdictions.
147. Supreme Court of India, *Consumer Education and Research Centre v. Union of India*, 1995.
148. P.T. Muchlinski, 'Human Rights and Multinationals: Is There a Problem?', *International Affairs*, Vol. 77, No. 1, 2001, pp. 31–48.

5 The Right to Food in Situations of Armed Conflict

1. See also A/56/210 and E/CN.4/2002/58.
2. Statement made by the International Committee of the Red Cross (ICRC) to the Commission on Human Rights at its 57th session on agenda item 10.
3. J. PEJIC, 'The Right to Food in Situations of Armed Conflict: The Legal Framework', *Revue internationale de la Croix-Rouge*, Vol. 83, 2001, pp. 1097–109.

4. See Chapters 9 and 14, on our visits to the Occupied Palestinian Territories and Lebanon.
5. See United Nations document CD/1478.
6. A/CONF.183/9.
7. First Additional Protocol to the Geneva Convention, Article 54, paragraph 1, and Second Additional Protocol, Article 14.
8. First Additional Protocol, Article 54, paragraph 2, and Second Additional Protocol, Article 14.
9. While there is no equivalent categorization of starvation of civilians as a war crime in non-international armed conflict under the Rome Statute, it may be said that such an act constitutes a serious violation of international humanitarian law when committed in internal armed conflict as well.
10. See 'Serb Charged Over Role in Sarajevo Siege', *The Independent*, London, 2 March 1996.
11. Second Additional Protocol, Article 17.
12. For international armed conflict, see Article 8, paragraphs 2(a)(vii) and (b)(viii) of the Statute; for non-international armed conflict, see Article 8, paragraph 2(e)(viii).
13. According to Articles 20 and 46 of the Third Geneva Convention.
14. According to Article 26 of the Third Geneva Convention.
15. According to Articles 89 and 127 of the Fourth Geneva Convention.
16. Resolution 46/182. Resolution 45/100 'stresses the important contribution made in providing humanitarian assistance by intergovernmental and non-governmental organizations working with *strictly humanitarian motives*' (emphasis added).
17. See International Court of Justice (ICJ), *Military and Paramilitary Activities in and against Nicaragua, Nicaragua v. United States of America*, Merits, Judgment, ICJ Reports 1986, paragraphs 242–3.
18. According to General Assembly resolution 46/182, the role of the United Nations has to be conducted under the leadership of the Secretary-General who 'should be supported by a secretariat based on a strengthened Office of the United Nations Disaster Relief Coordinator' and 'should work closely with organizations and entities of the United Nations system, as well as the International Committee of the Red Cross, the League of Red Cross and Red Crescent Societies, the International Organization for Migration and relevant non-governmental organizations' (paragraph 33).
19. Resolution 4(g)(2) of the 26th International Conference of the Red Cross and Red Crescent.
20. Intervention by P. Kung, from the ICRC, before the UN Security Council on 21 May 1997. See UN Security Council, Press Release SC/6371, 3778th meeting, 'Difficulty of providing military support for humanitarian operations while ensuring impartiality focus of Security Council debate', 21 May 1997.
21. Presentation by J-D. Tauxe, Director of Operations of the ICRC, Geneva, 45th Rose-Ross Seminar, Montreux, Switzerland, 2 March 2000.
22. This was reiterated by the ICRC in relation to Afghanistan. See ICRC, 'Afghanistan: ICRC call on all parties to conflict to respect international humanitarian law', communication to the press 01/47, 24 October 2001.
23. Article 23 of the Fourth Geneva Convention.
24. Article 8, paragraph 2(b)(xxv) of the Rome Statute.
25. First Additional Protocol, Article 70, paragraph 2.

26. Ibid, Article 70, paragraph 5. States could provide financial and/or material support for organizations involved in humanitarian assistance and, particularly those in the region concerned, could make available their logistical (airports, ports, telecommunication networks) and medical (hospitals, personnel) infrastructures. See U. Palwankar, 'Measures Available to States for Fulfilling their Obligation to Ensure Respect for International Humanitarian Law', *International Review of the Red Cross*, No. 298, January–February 1994, p. 23.
27. Ibid, Article 70, paragraph 3(c).
28. Ibid, Article 70, paragraph 4.
29. See Article 55 of the Fourth Geneva Convention, in the light of Articles 69 and 70 of the First Additional Protocol.
30. Additional Protocol I, Article 70, paragraph 1.
31. Ibid.
32. Fourth Geneva Convention, Article 23.
33. The articles that describe the legal regime which applies in this situation are Article 3 common to the Geneva Conventions and Article 18 of the Second Additional Protocol.
34. Article 18, paragraph 1, of the Second Additional Protocol reaffirms this right to offer services.
35. See L. Boisson de Chazournes and L. Condorelli, 'Common Article 1 of the Geneva Conventions Revisited: Protecting Collective Interests', *International Review of the Red Cross*, Vol. 82, No 837, March 2000, pp. 67–87.
36. According to Article 89 of the First Additional Protocol.
37. See General Assembly resolution 43/8.
38. See Article 39 of the Charter of the United Nations.
39. See Security Council resolution 794, 1992.
40. See Security Council resolution 764, 1992.
41. The Security Council expressed its willingness to respond '... including through the consideration of appropriate measures at the Council's disposal in accordance with the Charter of the United Nations'. See Security Council resolution 1265, 1999.

6 Niger

1. See E/CN.4/2002/58/Add.1.
2. UNDP, *Human Development Report 2001*, New York, Oxford University Press, 2001; Food and Agriculture Organization of the United Nations (FAO), *State of Food Insecurity in the World 2001*, Rome, FAO, 2001; FAO Niger, *Preparation of the National Programme for Global Food Security*, Niamey, FAO, 2001.
3. World Bank, 'Socio-Economic Differences in Health, Nutrition and Population in Niger', Paper prepared by R. G. Davidson, S. Rustein, K. Johnson, R. Pande and A. Wagstaff for the Health, Nutrition, Population (HNP)/Poverty Thematic Group of the World Bank, May 2000.
4. Statistics provided by Helen Keller International in Niger.
5. There are also distinct regional variations in malnutrition. For example, for severe and moderate child malnutrition, the departments of Maradi (21.1 per cent severe, 42.9 per cent moderate) and Zinder/Diffa (20.7 per cent, 37.9 per cent) are much more affected than Tillaberi (9.9 per cent, 24.8 per cent), Dosso (10 per cent, 24 per cent) and Niamey (4.8 per cent, 19.2 per cent). At the

time of our mission, the most recent data recorded that 25 per cent of people suffered from protein-energy malnutrition, but these data dated back to 1985. See UNDP, *Rapport National sur le Développment Humain. Niger 1998*, Niamey, UNDP, 1998.
6. See E/CN.4/2002/58/Add.1, Annex.
7. FAO, Elaboration du document de bilan commun de pays, *Sécurité alimentaire et nutrition*, rapport provisoire par Idrissa Soumana, consultant national, 2001.
8. République du Niger, Cabinet du premier ministre, Comité national du système d'alerte précoce et de gestion des catastrophes, *Stratégie opérationnelle de sécurité alimentaire pour le Niger*, Niamey, 2000, p. 17.
9. République du Niger, Ministère des ressources en eau, Liste des projets dont le financement est à rechercher et des fiches de synthèses, Niamey, 2000.
10. République du Niger, Cabinet du premier ministre, Conseil national de l'environnement pour un développement durable, *Programme d'action national de lutte contre la désertification et de gestion de ressources naturelles*, Niamey, 2000.
11. Article 2, paragraph 2, ICECSR.
12. Commission nationale des droits de l'homme et des libertés fondamentales, *Rapport annuel d'activités 2000*, Niamey, 2000.
13. See the document produced for CARE International for the 'Conférence sur l'opportunité de la relance du débat sur l'élaboration d'un code de la famille' by S. Fatoumata and E. Allagbada, Niamey, May 2000. This explains the content of the Family Code, compares the differences between the legal systems and analyses the factors for the blockage of the adoption of the Code.
14. On the development of this case, see Fédération internationale des Ligues des droits de l'homme (FIDH), Droit à l'eau potable au Niger. Enfants de *Tibiri* : quand l'eau se transforme en poison Privatisation de la distribution de l'eau : un processus à surveiller, Paris, FIDH, 2002.
15. See Jean Ziegler, 'Schizophrénie des Nations Unies', *Le Monde Diplomatique*, Paris, November 2001.
16. See A/60/350.

7 Brazil

1. See E/CN.4/2004/10/Add.1.
2. See in particular the report of the follow-up mission of Olivier de Schutter in Brazil in 2009, A/HRC/13/33/Add.6; Food and Agriculture Organization of the United Nations (FAO), *Right to Food. Lessons learned in Brazil*, Rome, FAO, 2007; FAO, *Right to Food Case Study: Brazil*, 2004, FAO document IGWG RTFG /INF 4/APP.1; F.L. Schieck Valente, 'The International Voluntary Guidelines and the Justiciability of the Human Right to Adequate Food in Brazil', In M. Borghi and L. Postiglione Blommestein (eds), *The Right to Adequate Food and Access to Justice*, Bruylant, Schulthess, 2006, pp. 303–5; A. Beurlen, *Directo Humano à Alimentação Adecuada no Brasil*, Curitiba, Juruá Editora, 2008.
3. The National Council on Food and Nutrition Security comprises 17 Brazilian governments representatives – notably the Ministers of social development and the fight against hunger, agriculture, fishing and provision, agricultural development, education, environment, planning, health and work and specialized secretariats – notably of farmers' organizations, agricultural workers, minorities, churches, universities, human rights organizations and the food industry – and 16 observers – notably the representatives of municipalities,

United Nations agencies, the World Bank, as well as the National Rapporteur on Human Rights related to food, water and agriculture.
4. Law 11.346 adopted on 15 September 2006.
5. Constitutional Amendment Project PEC 47/2003, adopted by the Brazilian Congress on 3 February 2010.
6. From 15.7 per cent to 10.5 per cent between 1989 and 1996. IPEA, the Secretary of State for Human Rights (SEDH) and the Ministry of Foreign Affairs (MRE), *A Seguranca Alimentar e Nutricional e o Direito Humano a Alimentacao no Brasil: Documento elaborado para a visita ao Brasil do Relator Especial da Comissao de Direitos Humanos da Organizacao das Nacoes Unidas sobre Direito a Alimentacao*, Brazilia, IPEA, SEDH, MRE, 2002.
7. In 2000, 33 out of every 1000 children die before age five compared to 48 in 1990.
8. UNDP, *Human Development Report 2002*, New York, Oxford University Press, 2002.
9. The definition of the extreme poverty line ('indigence' line) means that people living below this line are people whose income cannot guarantee the most basic need: food. At the time of our mission, of a total population of around 170 million people, 54 million Brazilians were living below the poverty line, and 22 million women, children and men suffered from extreme poverty. IPEA, SEDH, MRE, *A Seguranca Alimentar e Nutricional e o Direito Humano a Alimentacao no Brasil: Documento elaborado para a visita ao Brasil do Relator Especial da Comissao de Direitos Humanos da Organizacao das Nacoes Unidas sobre Direito a Alimentacao.*
10. Projeto Fome Zero, Instituto Cidadania, Fundaçao Djalma Guimaraes, *Uma Proposta de Politica de Combate a Fome no Brasil*, Brasilia, 2001.
11. Personal communication with the Special Rapporteur.
12. Government of Brazil, Ministry of Health, *Politica Nacional de Alimentacao e Nutricao*, Brasilia, 2002.
13. The FAO estimated availability of 2960 kilocalories per person per day in Brazil in 2002, significantly above the recommended minimum of 1900 kcal per person per day. IPEA, SEDH, MRE, *A Seguranca Alimentar e Nutricional e o Direito Humano a Alimentacao no Brasil: Documento elaborado para a visita ao Brasil do Relator Especial da Comissao de Direitos Humanos da Organizacao das Nacoes Unidas sobre Direito a Alimentacao.*
14. Global Justice Center, Pastoral Land Commission, and the Landless Workers Movement, 'Agrarian Reform and Rural Violence', In Global Justice, *Human Rights in Brazil 2000*, Sao Paulo, 2000.
15. 1996 Census of Agriculture in Brazil.
16. IPEA, SEDH, MRE, A Seguranca Alimentar e Nutricional e o Direito Humano a Alimentacao no Brasil: Documento elaborado para a visita ao Brasil do Relator Especial da Comissao de Direitos Humanos da Organizacao das Nacoes Unidas sobre Direito a Alimentacao.
17. World Bank, *Attacking Brazil's Poverty*, Volume I, World Bank, Washington, 2001.
18. IPEA, SEDH, MRE, *A Seguranca Alimentar e Nutricional e o Direito Humano a Alimentacao no Brasil: Documento elaborado para a visita ao Brasil do Relator Especial da Comissao de Direitos Humanos da Organizacao das Nacoes Unidas sobre Direito a Alimentacao.*
19. R. Henriques, Desigualdade Racial no Brasil: Evolucao das Condicoes de Vida na Decada de 90, Rio de Janeiro, IPEA, 2001; IPEA, SEDH, MRE, A Seguranca

Alimentar e Nutricional e o Direito Humano a Alimentacao no Brasil: Documento elaborado para a visita ao Brasil do Relator Especial da Comissao de Direitos Humanos da Organizacao das Nacoes Unidas sobre Direito a Alimentacao.
20. See Report of UN Special Rapporteur on racial discrimination, E/CN.4/1996/72/Add.1.
21. R. Levine *The History of Brazil*, Westport, Greenwood Press, 1999.
22. UNDP, *Human Development Report 2002*. Between 1977 and 1999, the Gini coefficient measure of inequality has remained at a constant level of 0.60 with few exceptions, one of the highest in the world. IPEA, SEDH, MRE, *A Seguranca Alimentar e Nutricional e o Direito Humano a Alimentacao no Brasil: Documento elaborado para a visita ao Brasil do Relator Especial da Comissao de Direitos Humanos da Organizacao das Nacoes Unidas sobre Direito a Alimentacao*, p. 19.
23. Ibid.
24. World Bank, Attacking Brazil's Poverty.
25. Personal communication with Senator Bernardo Cabral, President of the Justice Commission. FAO, The Right to Food in Practice. Implementation at the National Level, FAO, Rome, 2006, p. 14. On 3 February 2010, the Article 6 of the Brazilian Constitution was finally amended to include the right to food among the social rights recognized in the Constitution.
26. Article 208-VII.
27. Article 68, Ato das Disposições Constitucionais Transitórias, Law 7688.
28. Presidential Decree 591 of 6 July 1992 proclaimed that the ICESCR will be implemented and fulfilled entirely. Law 8.069 of 13 July 1990 relates to the CRC.
29. See Constitutional Court of South Africa, *The Government of the Republic of South Africa and Others v. Irene Grootboom and Others*, 2000 (11) BCLR 1169 (CC), Decision of 4 October 2000.
30. Letter to the Special Rapporteur from the Permanent Mission of Brazil in Geneva, 4 June 2002.
31. IPEA, SEDH, MRE, *A Seguranca Alimentar e Nutricional e o Direito Humano a Alimentacao no Brasil: Documento elaborado para a visita ao Brasil do Relator Especial da Comissao de Direitos Humanos da Organizacao das Nacoes Unidas sobre Direito a Alimentacao*.
32. Ibid.
33. Clientelism is the term used to describe how persons or groups of higher status (patrons) take advantage of their authority and resources to protect and benefit those with inferior status (clients) in exchange for loyalty and/or votes.
34. A. de Melo, 'A Execucao Orcamentaria da Uniao de 2001', Nota Tecnica de Instituto de Estudos Socioeconomicos (INESC), Brasilia, INESC, 2002.
35. Ibid.
36. Law 8.913.
37. Provisional Measure 2.027.
38. Following R. Bastide, *Images du Nordeste Mystique en Noir et Blanc*, Paris, Pandora/Actes Sud, 1978.
39. Article 2, paragraph 1, ICESCR.
40. IPEA, SEDH, MRE, *A Seguranca Alimentar e Nutricional e o Direito Humano a Alimentacao no Brasil: Documento elaborado para a visita ao Brasil do Relator Especial da Comissao de Direitos Humanos da Organizacao das Nacoes Unidas sobre Direito a Alimentacao*.
41. World Bank, *Attacking Brazil's Poverty*.
42. Ibid.

43. Ibid.
44. Letter dated 28 March 2002 from the Assessor Executivo da Comissão dos Direitos Humanos da Ordem dos Advogados.
45. Letter to Brazilian authorities dated 29 April 2002.
46. By FIAN, Comissão Pastoral da Terra (CPT) and other organizations.
47. Global Justice Center, Pastoral Land Commission, and the Landless Workers Movement, 'Agrarian Reform and Rural Violence'.
48. CPT, *Conflitos no Campo. Brazil 2000,* Sao Paulo, CPT, 2001, p. 13.
49. FIAN, *Brazil: Landless rural workers arrested in Pará and in Sao Paulo,* Urgent actions, 15 March 2002.
50. The Federal Government has the constitutional capacity to intervene under Article 34 of the Constitution.
51. CPT, Conflictos no Campo. Brazil 2000, pp. 69–77.
52. Statement by Ambassador Luiz Felipe de Seixas Corrêa, before the Working Group on Contemporary Forms of Slavery, Geneva, 30 May 2002.
53. J. Benvenuto Lima. and L. Zetterstrom (eds), *Extreme Poverty in Brazil: The Situation of the Right to Food and Adequate Housing,* Plataforma Interamericana de Direitos Humanos, Democracia e Desenvolvimento, Secao Brasiliera, 2002.
54. FIAN, *Brazil: Threats in Irapé, Minas Gerais,* Urgent actions, 25 January 2002.
55. Joao Pedro Stedile in *Caros Amigo,* Revista Sao Paulo, No. 39.
56. M. Moore and E.S. Lieberman, 'Tax rates in Brazil and South Africa', *Governance and Development Review IDS,* Institute of Development Studies, University of Sussex, 2002.
57. See Political Statement of the NGO/CSO Forum, Rome, 14 June 2002, http://www.foodfirst.org/progs/global/food/finaldeclaration.html. See also section 17.3.

8 Bangladesh

1. See E/CN.4/2004/10/Add.1.
2. UNDP, *Human Development Report 2002,* New York, Oxford University Press, 2002.
3. United Nations, *Common Country Assessment. Bangladesh,* Dhaka, United Nations, 2000.
4. United Nations, Common Country Assessment. Bangladesh.
5. IFPRI, *Food for Schooling in Bangladesh,* Washington, IFPRI, 2001.
6. IMF, *Bangladesh: Interim Poverty Reduction Strategy Paper,* IMF Country Report No. 03/177, June 2003.
7. Ibid, p. 6.
8. World Bank, *Bangladesh: Progress in Poverty Reduction,* Background Paper, Paris, Bangladesh Development Forum, March 2002.
9. IMF, *Bangladesh: Interim Poverty Reduction Strategy Paper,* p. 14.
10. Articles 44 and 102 of the Constitution.
11. Constitution, Article 8, paragraph 2. Article 32 of the Constitution states that 'No person shall be deprived of life or personal liberty save in accordance with law'.
12. Orders in the Supreme Court of Bangladesh High Court Division, Strict Direction on Radioactive Milk, 48 DLR 1996 438.
13. Orders in the Supreme Court of Bangladesh High Court Division, Writ Petition No. 3034 (1999).

14. This is the same in India. See Supreme Court of India, *People's Union for Civil Liberties v. Union of India & Ors*, 2001, and information about the case at www.righttofoodindia.org.
15. UNDP, 'Human Security in Bangladesh: In Search of Justice and Dignity', UNDP, Dhaka, 2002, p. 106.
16. United Nations, *Common Country Assessment: Bangladesh*, p. 51.
17. UNDP, 'Human Security in Bangladesh: In Search of Justice and Dignity', p. 43.
18. Supreme Court of Bangladesh, *Mohiuddin Farooque v. Bangladesh*, 49 (1997) DLR AD 1.
19. UNDP, *Human Security in Bangladesh: In Search of Justice and Dignity*, pp. 44–6.
20. IMF, Bangladesh: Interim Poverty Reduction Strategy Paper, p. 7.
21. Only 43 per cent had access to sanitation (61 per cent in urban areas and 41 per cent in rural areas). UNICEF Bangladesh, *Arsenic Mitigation in Bangladesh*, Dhaka, UNICEF, 2001.
22. B.K. Caldwell, J.C. Caldwell, S.N. Mitra and W. Smith, *Tubewells and Arsenic in Bangladesh: Challenging a Public Health Success Story*, National Centre for Epidemiology and Population Health, Australian National University, Canberra, June 2002.
23. Ibid.
24. IMF, *Bangladesh: Interim Poverty Reduction Strategy Paper*.
25. Ibid, p. 3.
26. World Bank, *Bangladesh: Progress in Poverty Reduction*.
27. IMF, *Bangladesh*: Interim Poverty Reduction Strategy Paper.
28. United Nations, *Common Country Assessment: Bangladesh*, p. 56.
29. Ibid.

9 The Occupied Palestinian Territories

1. See E/CN.4/2004/10/Add.2.
2. As of 15 August 2003. Sources: Palestinian Independent Commission for Citizens Rights, information at www.piccr.org, and Israeli Defence Forces, information at www.idf.il.
3. Z. Abdeen, G. Greenough, M. Shahin, M. Tayback, *Nutritional Assessment of the West Bank and Gaza Strip*, United States Agency for International Development (USAID), Johns Hopkins University, Al-Quds University, CARE International, September 2002.
4. C. Bertini, Personal Humanitarian Envoy of the Secretary-General, *Mission Report*, 11–19 August 2002, paragraphs 53–54.
5. Ibid.
6. Ibid.
7. World Bank, *Twenty-Seven Months – Intifada, Closures and the Palestinian Economic Crisis: An Assessment*, Jerusalem, World Bank, May 2003, p. 36; R. Bocco, M. Brunner, I. Daneels, J. Husseini, F. Lapeyre and J. Rabah, *Palestinian Public Perceptions on Their Living Conditions*, Geneva, Institut Universitaire d'Etudes du Développement, 2003, p. 51.
8. Z. Abdeen, G. Greenough, M. Shahin and M. Tayback, *Nutritional Assessment of the West Bank and Gaza Strip*.

9. World Bank, *Twenty-Seven Months – Intifada, Closures and the Palestinian Economic Crisis: An Assessment*.
10. Ibid.
11. Ibid.
12. Z. Abdeen, G. Greenough, M. Shahin and M. Tayback, *Nutritional Assessment of the West Bank and Gaza Strip*, p. 59.
13. Ibid.
14. World Bank, *Twenty-Seven Months – Intifada, Closures and the Palestinian Economic Crisis: An Assessment*, p. xii.
15. See G. Levy, 'There's a wall in the way', *Ha'aretz*, Jerusalem, 8 September 2003; A. Burg, 'The End of Zionism? A Failed Israeli Society is Collapsing', *International Herald Tribune*, 6 September 2003.
16. World Bank, *Twenty-Seven Months – Intifada, Closures and the Palestinian Economic Crisis: An Assessment*, pp. 2–3 and 26.
17. Ibid, p.3.
18. Amnesty International, 'Surviving under siege: The impact of movement restrictions on the right to work', Amnesty International document MDE 15/001/2003, September 2003.
19. Ibid.
20. C. Bertini, Personal Humanitarian Envoy of the Secretary-General, *Mission Report*, 11–19 August 2002.
21. World Bank, *Twenty-Seven Months – Intifada, Closures and the Palestinian Economic Crisis: An Assessment*, p. 47.
22. C. Bertini, Personal Humanitarian Envoy of the Secretary-General, *Mission Report*, 11–19 August 2002.
23. BBC News, *Activist who died for conviction*, 17 March 2003, http://news.bbc.co.uk/2/hi/middle_east/2856433.stm.
24. G. Levy, 'There's a wall in the way'.
25. T. Honig-Parnass, 'All's Clear for Full-Scale War against the Palestinians', *Between the Lines*, June 2003, p. 6.
26. Ibid.
27. United Nations Office for the Coordination of Humanitarian Affairs (OCHA), *Humanitarian Monitoring Report on the 'Bertini Commitments'*, OCHA, Jerusalem, June 2003.
28. See the ruling of the Israeli High Court of Justice in the *Beit-El* case, High Court of Justice 606, 610/78, *Suleiman Tawfiq Ayyub et al. v. Minister of Defence et al.*
29. ICJ, *the Legality of the Threat or Use of Nuclear Weapons*, Advisory Opinion of 8 July 1996.
30. Ibid.
31. For example in its resolution 56/204 of 21 December 2001.
32. ICESCR and ICCPR, common Article 1.
33. E/C.12/1/Add 90, paragraph 31.
34. See E/CN.4/1992/26 and CCPR/CO/78/ISR.
35. As defined in the 1995 Interim Agreement, Article XI.
36. Ibid, Article XIX; Declaration of Independence of 15 November 1988.
37. See, for example, M. Abdel Hamid, 'Why Fatah Doesn't Participate in the Morass of Reform', *Between the Lines*, August 2002.
38. World Bank, *Twenty-Seven Months – Intifada, Closures and the Palestinian Economic Crisis: An Assessment*, p. 46.
39. Ibid, p. 42.

40. 1995 Interim Agreement, Annex III, Appendix I, Article 40.
41. B'Tselem, *Thirsty for a solution: The Water Crisis in the Occupied Territories and its Resolution in the Final-Status Agreement*, Jerusalem, B'Tselem, July 2000.
42. See information at http://www.idf.il.
43. United Nations, *Humanitarian Plan of Action 2003: Occupied Palestinian Territory*, New York and Geneva, United Nations, November 2002, p. 22.
44. Z. Abdeen, G. Greenough, M. Shahin and M. Tayback, *Nutritional Assessment of the West Bank and Gaza Strip*, p. 51.
45. Ibid, p. 60.
46. B'Tselem, *Not even a drop: the water crisis in Palestinian villages without a water network*, Jerusalem, B'Tselem, 2001.
47. C. Bertini, Personal Humanitarian Envoy of the Secretary-General, *Mission Report: 11–19 August 2002*, paragraph 46.
48. Ibid, paragraph 45.
49. World Bank, *Twenty-Seven Months – Intifada, Closures and the Palestinian Economic Crisis: An Assessment*, p. 46.
50. Palestinian National Information Center (PNIC), *Palestinian Economic Losses due the Israeli Siege, Closures and Aggressions* (Sept. 29, 2000 to May 31, 2003), Gaza, PNIC, 2003.
51. OCHA, *Humanitarian Monitoring Report on the 'Bertini Commitments'*.
52. World Bank, *Twenty-Seven Months – Intifada, Closures and the Palestinian Economic Crisis: An Assessment*, p.19.
53. B'Tselem, *Thirsty for a solution. The Water Crisis in the Occupied Territories and its Resolution in the Final-Status Agreement*.
54. See E/CN.4/2004/6. Also ICJ, *Legal Consequences of the Construction of a Wall in the Occupied Palestinian Territory*, Advisory Opinion of 9 July 2004, pargraphs 133–134.
55. B'Tselem, *Behind the Barrier: Human Rights Violations As a Result of Israel's Separation Barrier*, Jerusalem, B'Tselem, 2003.
56. Humanitarian and Emergency Policy Group and the Local Aid Coordination Committee, *The Impact Of Israel's Separation Barrier On Affected West Bank Communities*, Update No. 2, 30 September 2003.
57. Ibid.
58. Document prepared by the Ministry of Defence and given to the Special Rapporteur at his meeting with the Chief Engineer.
59. 'The Eastern Wall: the last remaining steps for completing Plan Bantustan', *Between the Lines*, June 2003, p. 9.
60. See the review *News from Within*, June 2003, p. 8.
61. Amnesty International, 'Surviving under siege: The impact of movement restrictions on the right to work'.
62. OCHA, Humanitarian Monitoring Report on the 'Bertini Commitments'.
63. See *Le Monde*, 6 December 2002.
64. OCHA, Occupied Palestinian Territory Humanitarian Update: 4–21 April 2003, Jerusalem, OCHA, 2003.
65. OCHA, Humanitarian Monitoring Report on the 'Bertini Commitments'.
66. Amnesty International, 'Surviving under siege: The impact of movement restrictions on the right to work'.
67. E. Bronner, 'Israel's Barrier Stokes Conflict', *International Herald Tribune*, 9 August 2003.
68. A. Burg, 'The End of Zionism? A Failed Israeli Society is Collapsing'.
69. I. Pappe, 'The Language of Hypocrisy', *News from Within*, June 2003.

10 Ethiopia

1. See E/CN.4/2005/47/Add.1.
2. S. Lautze, Y. Aklilu, A. Raven-Roberts, H. Young, G. Kebede and J. Leaning, *Risk and Vulnerability in Ethiopia: Learning from the Past, Responding to the Present, Preparing for the Future*, Addis Ababa, United States Agency for International Development, 2003.
3. OCHA, *2004 Humanitarian Appeal for Ethiopia. A Joint Government and Humanitarian Partners' Appeal*, Addis Ababa, 10 December 2003.
4. Ibid.
5. S. Lautze, Y. Aklilu, A. Raven-Roberts, H. Young, G. Kebede and J. Leaning, Risk and Vulnerability in Ethiopia: Learning from the Past, Responding to the Present, Preparing for the Future, p. 10.
6. This refers to liberalization carried out under World Bank programmes – Ethiopia is not yet a member of the WTO.
7. World Bank, *Country Assistance Strategy for Ethiopia*, Washington, World Bank, 2003.
8. FAO/WFP, *Crops and Food Supply Assessment: Mission to Ethiopia*, Rome, FAO/WFP, 12 January 2004.
9. IFPRI, *Ending the Cycle of Famine in Ethiopia*, Washington, IFPRI, 2003.
10. Ibid.
11. Discussions with the representatives of WFP in Ethiopia.
12. T. S. Jayne and D. Molla, 'Toward a Research Agenda to Promote Household Access to Food in Ethiopia', Addis Ababa, Ministry of Economic Development and Cooperation, Food Security Research Project, Working Paper 2, 1995.
13. UNDP, *Human Development Report 2003*, New York, Oxford University Press, 2003.
14. United Nations, *Common Country Assessment for Ethiopia*, Addis Ababa, United Nations, 1999.
15. FAO/WFP, Crops and Food Supply Assessment: Mission to Ethiopia.
16. UNDP, Human Development Report 2003.
17. S. Lautze, Y. Aklilu, A. Raven-Roberts, H. Young, G. Kebede and J. Leaning, Risk and Vulnerability in Ethiopia: Learning from the Past, Responding to the Present, Preparing for the Future.
18. UNDP, *Human Development Report 2004*, New York, Oxford University Press, 2004.
19. D. Rahmeto and A. Kidanu, Consultations with the Poor: A Study to Inform the World Development Report (2000/01) on Poverty and Development. Ethiopia Report, Washington, World Bank, 1999.
20. C. Robinson, Nothing to Fall Back on: Why Ethiopians are Still Short of Food and Cash, Dublin, Christian Aid, 2003.
21. A. Solomon, A. Workalemahu, M.A. Jabbar, M.M. Ahmed and B. Hurissa, 'Livestock Marketing in Ethiopia: A Review of Structure, Performance and Development Initiatives', Nairobi, International Livestock Research Institute, Socio-economics and Policy Research Working Paper 52, 2003.
22. United Nations Children's Fund (UNICEF) and the Federal Democratic Republic of Ethiopia, *The Situation of Ethiopian Children and Women: A Rights-Based Analysis*, Addis Ababa, UNICEF, 2002.
23. The Government had said that this report was being prepared with the civil society.
24. F. Nahum, Constitution for a Nation of Nations: The Ethiopian Prospect, Addis Ababa, Red Sea Press, 1997.

25. See Federal Appeals Court of Argentina, *Viceconte v. Ministry of Health and Social Welfare*, decision of 2 June 1998.
26. See Supreme Court of India, *People's Union for Civil Liberties v. Union of India & Ors*, 2001.
27. Meeting with M. Ashenafi during our mission in Ethiopia.
28. Proclamations No. 210/2000 and No. 211/2000.
29. Human Rights Watch, *World Report 2003*, New York, Washington, Human Rights Watch, 2003.
30. Ethiopian Human Rights Council (EHRC), *The Human Rights Situation in Ethiopia: 19th Regular Report*, Addis Ababa, EHRC, 2003. See also Human Rights Watch, *World Report 2003*; United States Department of State, *Ethiopia: Country Report on Human Rights Practices 2003*, Washington, Bureau of Democracy, Human Rights, and Labor, 25 February 2004.
31. UNDP and United Nations Capital Development Fund, Lessons from Experience in Decentralizing Infrastructure and Service Delivery in Rural Areas: Country Case Study: Ethiopia, Addis Ababa, UNDP, 2003.
32. United Nations Economic Commission for Africa (ECA), *Fiscal Decentralization in Africa: A Review of Ethiopia's Experience*, Addis Ababa, United Nations ECA, 2003.
33. Ministry of Finance of Ethiopia, 2003 Annual Progress Report on Ethiopia: Sustainable Development and Poverty Reduction Programme, Addis Ababa, Ministry of Finance, 2003.
34. OCHA, Ponds filled with challenges: Water harvesting – experiences in Amhara and Tigray. Assessment Mission 30 September to 13 October 2003, Addis Ababa, OCHA, 2003.
35. Ibid.
36. Irin News, 15 March 2004.
37. Ministry of Finance of Ethiopia, 2003 Annual Progress Report on Ethiopia: Sustainable Development and Poverty Reduction Programme.
38. S. Devereux and K. Sharp, 'Is Poverty Really Falling in Rural Ethiopia?', Institute for Development Studies, University of Sussex, Paper presented at the conference 'Staying Poor: Chronic Poverty and Development Policy' at the University of Manchester, 7 to 9 April 2003.
39. EHRC, The Human Rights Situation in Ethiopia, 19th Regular Report.
40. United States Department of State, Ethiopia: Country Report on Human Rights Practices 2003.
41. Ibid.
42. Ibid.
43. United States Department of State, *Ethiopia: Country Report on Human Rights Practices 2002*, Washington, Bureau of Democracy, Human Rights, and Labor, 31 March 2003.
44. World Organization Against Torture, 'Ethiopia: Concerns About A Commission of Investigation Attempting to Cover up State Involvement in Acts of Genocide', press release, Geneva, 27 April 2004.
45. J. Stiglitz, 'FMI, la preuve par l'Ethiopie', *Le Monde Diplomatique*, avril 2002.
46. Ministry of Finance of Ethiopia, 2003 Annual Progress Report on Ethiopia: Sustainable Development and Poverty Reduction Programme.
47. Ibid.
48. T. Tafesse, The Nile Question: Hydropolitics, Legal Wrangling, Modus Vivendi and Perspectives, Münster, LIT Verlag, 2001.

11 Mongolia

1. See E/CN.4/2005/47/Add.2.
2. See O. Bruun, P. Ronnast and L. Narangoa, *Mongolia, Transition from the Second to the Third World*, Stockholm, Swedish International Development Cooperation Agency (SIDA), 2000.
3. Department of Economic and Social Affairs to Mongolia, *Economic Vulnerabilities and Human Security in Mongolia*, Ulaanbaatar, Government of Mongolia, June 2004, p. 15.
4. Government of Mongolia, Economic Growth Support and Poverty Reduction Strategy, Ulaanbaatar, 2003, p. 2.
5. Nutrition Research Centre of the Ministry of Health, WHO, UNICEF and the United States Centers for Disease Control and Prevention, *Preliminary report of a survey assessing the nutritional consequences of the* dzud *in Mongolia*, 2001.
6. Nutrition Research Centre of the Ministry of Health, WHO, UNICEF and the United States Centers for Disease Control and Prevention, *Final report of a survey assessing the nutritional consequences of the* dzud *in Mongolia*, Ulaanbaatar, 2001.
7. K. Griffin, 'Urban-Rural Migration and Involution in the Livestock Sector', In K. Griffin (ed.) *Poverty Reduction in Mongolia*, Canberra, Asia Pacific Press, 2003, p. 57.
8. K. Griffin, 'The Macroeconomics of Poverty', in Ibid, p. 15.
9. FAO, *The State of Food Insecurity in the World 2003*, Rome, FAO, 2003, Table 1.
10. Recommended measure of food intake of population, 1997.
11. Government of Mongolia, National Report on the Implementation of the Millennium Development Goals in Mongolia, Ulaanbaatar, 2004, pp. 14–15.
12. Government of Mongolia, *III National Nutrition Survey*, Ulaanbaatar, 2004.
13. Government of Mongolia, *National Nutrition Survey*, Ulaanbaatar, 1999.
14. Government of Mongolia, *III National Nutrition Survey*, Ulaanbaatar, 2004.
15. UNDP, *Human Development Report Mongolia 2003*, Ulaanbaatar, UNDP, 2003, p. 28.
16. Government of Mongolia, Economic Growth Support and Poverty Reduction Strategy, p. 14.
17. Ibid, p. 16.
18. Ministry of Health and UNICEF, *Family Violence and its Health Consequences*, Ulaanbaatar, Government of Mongolia, 2004.
19. Government of Mongolia, Economic Growth Support and Poverty Reduction Strategy, p. 10.
20. World Bank, Mongolia: Participatory Living Standards Assessment 2000, Washington, World Bank, 2001.
21. UNICEF, Save the Children UK and the National Board for Children, *The living conditions of the children in peri-urban areas of Ulaanbaatar*, Ulaanbaatar, 2003, p. 14.
22. Ibid, p. 11.
23. World Bank, *Mongolia: Participatory Living Standards Assessment 2000*.
24. This has been pointed out by S. Devine of the Department of Anthropology and Health and Behavioural Sciences of the University of Colorado: 'The cost in lives and productivity to Mongolia from malnutrition, especially micronutrient defi-

ciencies, can be measured, but only if agencies collect specific information and share it among researchers'.
25. Methodologies used for determining the national poverty line in Mongolia are discussed in K. Griffin, 'The Macroeconomics of Poverty', in *Poverty Reduction in Mongolia*, pp. 30–5.
26. UNDP, *Human Development Report Mongolia 2003*, p. 13, and information provided in discussions with the Ministry for Social Welfare.
27. World Bank, Mongolia: Participatory Living Standards Assessment 2000.
28. Ministry of Labour and Social Welfare of Mongolia, UNDP and the Population Teaching and Research Center, *Urban Poverty and In-Migration*, Ulaanbaatar, 2004, pp. 66, 71 and 88.
29. WHO, Ministry of Health and the Directorate of Medical Services, *Survey Report on the internal migration and its public health consequences*, Ulaanbaatar, 2003, p. 26.
30. UNDP, *Human Development Report Mongolia 2003*, p. 31.
31. See CCPR/C/79/Add.120, paragraph 7.
32. National Human Rights Commission of Mongolia, *Report on Human Rights and Freedoms in Mongolia*, Ulaanbaatar, 2003, pp. 30–1.
33. Ministry of Food and Agriculture, *Legal and administrative guidelines for investors in food and agriculture sector*, Ulaanbaatar, Government of Mongolia, March 2004.
34. United Nations, *United Nations Development Assistance Framework for Mongolia 2002–2006*, Ulaanbaatar, United Nations, June 2001, p. 12.
35. World Vision, *The Status of Food Insecurity in Mongolia*, Ulaanbaatar, World Vision, 2004, p. 7.
36. Government of Mongolia, *Economic Growth Support and Poverty Reduction Strategy*, p. 10.
37. Ibid, p. 135.
38. Ibid, p. i.
39. T. McKinley, 'The National Development Strategy and Aid Coordination', in K. Griffin, *Poverty Reduction in Mongolia*, p. 136.
40. Department of Economic and Social Affairs to Mongolia, *Economic Vulnerabilities and Human Security in Mongolia*, p. 33.
41. T. McKinley, 'The National Development Strategy and Aid Coordination', p. 138.
42. UNDP, *Human Development Report Mongolia*, 2003, p. 36.
43. National Human Rights Commission of Mongolia, *Report on Human Rights and Freedoms in Mongolia*, p. 33.
44. Ibid, p. 34.
45. K. Griffin, *Poverty Reduction in Mongolia*, p. xvii.
46. Department of Economic and Social Affairs to Mongolia, *Economic Vulnerabilities and Human Security in Mongolia*, p. 36, quoting the Mongolia Consultative Group of the Ministry of Finance and Economy.
47. A. Ickowitz, 'Poverty and the Environment', in K. Griffin, *Poverty Reduction in Mongolia*, pp. 97–9.
48. K. Griffin, 'Urban to Rural Migration', in *Poverty Reduction in Mongolia*, p. 69.
49. Department of Economic and Social Affairs to Mongolia, *Economic Vulnerabilities and Human Security in Mongolia*, pp. 30 and 33.

12 Guatemala

1. See E/CN.4/2006/44/Add.1. See also the report of the follow-up mission of Olivier de Schutter in Guatemala in 2009, A/HRC/13/33/Add.4.
2. Comision para Esclarecimiento Historico, *Guatemala: Memoria de Silencio*, Washington, American Association for the Advancement of Science, 1999.
3. World Bank, *Guatemala: Poverty in Guatemala*, Report of the Poverty Reduction and Economic Management Unit, Washington, World Bank, February 2003, p. 83.
4. United Nations, *Situacion de la Seguridad Alimentaria y Nutricional de Guatemala*, Guatemala City, United Nations Group for Food and Nutrition Security, September 2003, p. iii.
5. Government of Guatemala, *Política Nacional de Seguridad Alimentaria y Nutricional*, Guatemala City, 2004, p. 8.
6. Sistema Mesoamericano de Alerta Temprana para la Seguridad Alimentaria (MFEWS), *Special Report: MFEWS Food Security Overview*, Guatemala City, MFEWS, December 2004, p. 13.
7. United Nations, Situacion de la Seguridad Alimentaria y Nutricional de Guatemala, p. iii.
8. Ibid, p. 14.
9. Ibid, p. 13.
10. FIAN, *The Human Right to Food in Guatemala*, Heidelberg, FIAN International, October 2004.
11. See the newspaper article 'Campesinos realizan masiva protesta fúnebre', *El Periodico*, 27 January 2005.
12. United Nations, *Common Country Assessment. Guatemala*, Guatemala City, United Nations, 2004, p. 17.
13. MFEWS, *Special Report: MFEWS Food Security Overview*.
14. Ibid.
15. Between November 2003 and December 2004. Ibid, p. 17.
16. World Bank, *Guatemala: Poverty in Guatemala*, p. 8.
17. United Nations, *Situacion de la Seguridad Alimentaria y Nutricional de Guatemala*, p. 16.
18. Guatemala's poverty lines are defined in relation to food consumption – extreme poverty line is based on the annual cost of a 'food basket' (minimum caloric requirement of 2172 kilocalories per person per day) and the poverty line is defined as the food basket, plus an allowance for non-food items.
19. World Bank, *Guatemala: Poverty in Guatemala*, p. 49.
20. United Nations, *Common Country Assessment: Guatemala*, p. 16.
21. Ibid, p. 14.
22. Ibid, p. 16.
23. World Bank, *Guatemala: Poverty in Guatemala*, p. 52.
24. FIAN, *The Human Right to Food in Guatemala*, p. 6.
25. Ibid, p. 9.
26. See E/CN.4/2005/72/Add.3.
27. R. Vakis, 'Guatemala: Livelihoods, Labour Markets, and Rural Poverty', Washington, World Bank, Guatemala Poverty Assessment Programme, Technical Paper No. 1, 2003.

28. Colectivo de Organizaciones Sociales, *Otra Guatemala es Posible: Acuerdos de Paz, Unidad y lucha de las organizaciones sociales*, Guatemala City, 2004.
29. Amnesty International, *Memorandum to the Government of Guatemala: Amnesty International's concern regarding the current human rights situation*, London, Amnesty document AMR 34/014/2005.
30. United Nations, *Common Country Assessment: Guatemala*, p. 15.
31. Government of Guatemala, *Política Nacional de Seguridad Alimentaria y Nutricional*, p. 11.
32. World Bank, *Guatemala: Poverty in Guatemala*, p. 30.
33. R. Vakis, 'Guatemala: Livelihoods, Labour Markets, and Rural Poverty'.
34. World Bank, *Guatemala: Poverty in Guatemala*, p. 33.
35. Ibid.
36. FIAN, *The Human Right to Food in Guatemala*, p. 7.
37. World Bank, *Guatemala: Poverty in Guatemala*, p. 36.
38. Ibid.
39. FIAN, *The Human Right to Food in Guatemala*.
40. See E/CN.4/2003/104/Add.2, paragraph 63 of the report of the Special Representative of the Secretary-General on the situation of human rights defenders.
41. Amnesty International, *Memorandum to the Government of Guatemala: Amnesty International's concerns regarding the current human rights situation*.
42. Government of Guatemala, *Política Nacional de Seguridad Alimentaria y Nutricional*, p. 23.
43. FIAN, *The Human Right to Food in Guatemala*, p. 5.
44. Ibid, p. 8.
45. See A/59/307, paragraph 54.
46. United Nations, *Common Country Assessment: Guatemala*, p. 14.
47. Ibid, pp. 9–10, p. 24.
48. Ibid, p. 21.
49. Ibid, p. 10.
50. Ibid, p. 13.
51. United Nations System in Guatemala, *Millennium Development Goals: Report on Progress Made in Guatemala*, Guatemala City, United Nations, 2003.
52. United Nations, *Situacion de la Seguridad Alimentaria y Nutricional de Guatemala*, p. iii.
53. Encuesta Nacional de Salud Materno Infantil del 2002, cited in Government of Guatemala, *Política Nacional de Seguridad Alimentaria y Nutricional*, op.cit.
54. United Nations, Situacion de la Seguridad Alimentaria y Nutricional de Guatemala, pp. 13–14.
55. Food and Agriculture Organization of the United Nations (FAO), *State of World Food Insecurity 2004*, Rome, FAO, 2004.
56. United Nations, Situacion de la Seguridad Alimentaria y Nutricional de Guatemala, p. 16.
57. See A/59/307, p. 13.
58. Amnesty International, *Memorandum to the Government of Guatemala: Amnesty International's concern regarding the current human rights situation*.
59. FIAN, *The Human Right to Food in Guatemala*; Colectivo de Organizaciones Sociales, Acuerdos de Paz: Unidad y lucha de las organizaciones sociales.
60. Plataforma Interamericana de Derechos Humanos, Democracia y Desarollo (PIDhDD), FIAN Brazil, *El Derecho Humano a la Alimentación en América Latina*, PIDhDD, FIAN Brazil, 2004 ; FIAN, *The Human Right to Food in Guatemala*.

61. PIDhDD, FIAN Brazil, El Derecho Humano a la Alimentación en América Latina; FIAN, *The Human Right to Food in Guatemala*.
62. Pastoral de la tierra interdiocesana, Pastoral de la tierra de Quetzaltenango, Seis Días que se Convierten en Seis Años, 2004 ; FIAN, *The Human Right to Food in Guatemala*; PIDhDD, FIAN Brazil, El Derecho Humano a la Alimentación en América Latina.
63. FIAN, 'Guatemala: Repression against peasant women and men', urgent actions 2005, http://www.fian.org/cases/letter-campaigns/guatemala-repression-against-peasant-women-and-men, date accessed 31 May 2010.
64. United Nations, Situacion de la Seguridad Alimentaria y Nutricional de Guatemala, p. 24.
65. MFEWS, Special Report: MFEWS Food Security Overview, p. 8.
66. M. Cabrer and J. A. Fuentes Knigt, *El CAFTA y el desarollo humano en Centroamerica*, Guatemala City, UNDP, 2004, p. 28.

13 India

1. See E/CN.4/2006/44/Add.2.
2. World Food Programme (WFP), *Enabling Development: Food Assistance in South Asia*, New Delhi, Oxford University Press, 2001, p. 61.
3. G.J. Gill, J. Farrington, E. Anderson, C. Luttrell, T. Conway, N.C. Saxena and R. Slater, *Food Security and the Millenium Development Goal on Hunger in Asia*, London, Overseas Development Institute, Working Paper 231, 2003.
4. A. Sharma, 'Realisation of Rights of the Indian Child: Measures for Implementation of the CRC', *PRAYAS Journal*, Vol. II, No. 1, 2000.
5. UNDP, *Human Development Report 2005*, New York, Oxford University Press, 2005.
6. FAO, *State of World Food Insecurity 2004*, Rome, FAO, 2004, p. 22.
7. World Bank, *World Development Indicators*, Washington, World Bank, 2005.
8. FAO, State of World Food Insecurity 2004.
9. Government of India, Planning Commission, *Progress Towards Achieving the MDGs in India*, New Delhi, 2005, p. 146.
10. FAO, State of World Food Insecurity 2004.
11. S. Jha and D.U. Deininger, *Public Expenditures on Food and Nutrition Security Programs in India: Are They Meeting the Challenge?*, Washington, World Bank, South Asia Rural Development Unit, Working Paper, 2003, p. 2.
12. FAO, *State of World Food Insecurity 2004*, p. 12; Government of India, Planning Commission, Progress towards achieving the MDGs in India, p. 194.
13. A. Deaton and J. Drèze, 'Poverty and Inequality in India: A Re-examination', *Economic and Political Weekly*, 7 September 2002, p. 3745.
14. Poverty in India is officially measured in terms of monthly per capita expenditure of Rs 49 in rural areas and Rs 57 in urban areas at 1973 all-India prices, which could then buy an energy consumption of 2400 calories/day in rural areas and 2100 calories/day in urban areas.
15. G.J. Gill, J. Farrington, E. Anderson, C. Luttrell, T. Conway, N.C. Saxena and R. Slater, *Food Security and the Millenium Development Goal on Hunger in Asia*.
16. National Sample Survey data cited in J. Gosh, *Trade Liberalization in Agriculture: An Examination of Impact and Policy Strategies with Special Reference to India*, New York, UNDP, Human Development Report Office, Occasional Paper 2005/12, 2005, p. 14.

17. ActionAid, *Tea Break: A Crisis Brewing in India*, London, ActionAid, May 2005.
18. G.J. Gill, J. Farrington, E. Anderson, C. Luttrell, T. Conway, N.C. Saxena and R. Slater, *Food Security and the Millenium Development Goal on Hunger in Asia*.
19. Government of India, Planning Commission, *Mid-Term Appraisal of 10th Five-year Plan*, New Delhi, 2005.
20. R. Hemadri, H. Mander and V. Nagaraj, *Dams, Displacement, Policy and Law in India*, Contributing Paper to the World Commission on Dams, Cape Town, World Commission on Dams, July 1999.
21. M.S. Swaminathan Research Foundation (MSSRF) and WFP, *Atlas of the Sustainability of Food Security*, Chennai, MSSRF, 2004, p. 130.
22. D. Venkateswarlu, Child Labour and Transitional Seed Companies in Hybrid Cottonseed Production in Andhra Pradesh, The Netherlands, India Committee of the Netherlands, 2003.
23. G.J. Gill, J. Farrington, E. Anderson, C. Luttrell, T. Conway, N.C. Saxena and R. Slater, *Food Security and the Millenium Development Goal on Hunger in Asia*.
24. S. Chakravarty and S. Dand, *Food Insecurity in India: Causes and Dimensions*, Vastrapur, Indian Institute of Management Ahmedabad, 2005, p. 3.
25. M.S. Swaminathan, P. Medrano, D. J. Gustafson and P. Sharma (eds), *National Food Security Summit 2004. Selected Papers*, New Delhi, WFP, 2004, p. 15.
26. Ibid.
27. Declining from over 19 million tonnes in 1996/97 to 12 million tonnes in 2000/01.
28. Increasing from 21 million tonnes to 58 million tonnes by the end of 2001.
29. P. Sharma, 'Agricultural Policy Reform for Poverty Alleviation: Some Current Issues', in M.S. Swaminathan, P. Medrano, D.J. Gustafson and P. Sharma (eds), *National Food Security Summit 2004. Selected Papers*, p. 276.
30. J. Gosh, Trade Liberalization in Agriculture: An Examination of Impact and Policy Strategies with Special Reference to India, p. 10.
31. 'No person shall be deprived of his life or personal liberty except according to procedure established by law.'
32. Supreme Court of India, *Chameli Singh & Others v. State of Uttar Pradesh*, 1996.
33. Supreme Court of India, *Narmada Bachao Andolan v. Union of India*, 2000.
34. Supreme Court of India, *Francis Coralie Mullin v. Union Territory of Delhi and Others*, 1981.
35. Supreme Court of India, *People's Union for Civil Liberties v. Union of India & Ors*, 2001.
36. Ibid.
37. Supreme Court of India, *State of Karnataka v. Appa Balu Ingale*, 1993.
38. Supreme Court of India, *S. Jagannath v. Union of India*, 1996.
39. Supreme Court of India, *Samatha v. State of Andhra Pradesh*, 1997.
40. Supreme Court of India, *Olga Tellis v. Bombay Municipal Corporation*, 1985.
41. United Nations General Assembly Resolution 48/134.
42. P. Sharma, 'Agricultural Policy Reform for Poverty Alleviation: Some Current Issues', p. 274.
43. WFP, Enabling Development: Food assistance in South Asia, p. 65.
44. Ibid, p. 63.
45. D. Gustafson, 'Building a Hunger-Free India From the Ground up: The Importance of Smallholder Agriculture for Poverty Reduction and Food Security', in M.S. Swaminathan, P. Medrano, D.J. Gustafson and P. Sharma (eds), *National Food Security Summit 2004. Selected Papers*.

46. N.C. Saxena, 'Reorganizing Policies and Delivery for Alleviating Hunger and Malnutrition', in M.S. Swaminathan, P. Medrano, D.J. Gustafson and P. Sharma (eds), *National Food Security Summit 2004. Selected Papers*, pp. 413–14.
47. Government of India, Planning Commission, *Progress towards achieving the MDGs in India*.
48. FAO, *State of World Food Insecurity* 2004, p. 6.
49. MSSRF and WFP, *Atlas of the Sustainability of Food Security*, p. 170.
50. Government of India, Planning Commission, *Mid-Term Appraisal of 10th Five-year Plan*, p. 194.
51. U. Patnaik, 'The Republic of Hunger', in C. Gonsalves, P.R. Kumar and A. K. Srivastava (eds), *Right to Food*, Second Edition, New Delhi, Human Rights Law Network, 2005, p. 483.
52. Government of India, Planning Commission, *Mid-Term Appraisal of 10th Five-year Plan*.
53. S. Jha and D.U. Deininger, *Public Expenditures on Food and Nutrition Security Programs in India: Are They Meeting the Challenge?*.
54. Human Rights Law Network, *Food Security and Judicial Activism in India*, New Delhi, Human Rights Law Network, 2007.
55. FIAN Andhra Pradesh, *List of Hunger and Starvation Deaths for 'Public Hearing on Hunger'*, FIAN Andhra Pradesh, 2005.
56. Asian Human Rights Commission and the Manabadhikar Suraksha Mancha, *People's tribunal on starvation in Jalangi, West Bengal*, Hong Kong, Asian Human Rights Commission, 2005.
57. G. Agrawal and C. Gonsalves (eds), *Dalits and the Law*, New Delhi, Human Rights Law Network, 2005.
58. FIAN Uttar Pradesh, *Report on cases of violations of the right to food in Uttar Pradesh*, FIAN Uttar Pradesh, 2005.
59. Ibid.
60. National Human Rights Commission (NHRC), *Report on Prevention of Atrocities Against Scheduled Castes*, New Delhi, NHRC, 2004.
61. Supreme Court of India, *Narmada Bachao Andolan v. Union of India*, 2000.
62. *Report of the Indian People's Tribunal on Environment and Human Rights on the Narmada Dam*, 2005, http://www.narmada.org/IPT_Report.pdf, date accessed 31 May 2010.
63. FIAN, *Update on the Enjoyment of the Right to Food and Water in India*, Heidelberg, FIAN International document d39e, December 2004.
64. Supreme Court of India, *Samatha v. State of Andhra Pradesh*, 1997.
65. Amnesty International, *Clouds of Injustice. Bhopal Disaster 20 years On*, London, Amnesty International, 2004.
66. Ibid.
67. FIAN, *Update on the Enjoyment of the Right to Food and Water in India*.
68. Supreme Court of India, *People's Union for Civil Liberties v. Union of India & Ors*, 2001.
69. Ibid.
70. NHRC, *Annual Report 2002–2003*, New Delhi, NHRC, 2003.

14 Lebanon

1. See A/HRC/2/8 and A/HRC/2/8/Corr.1.

2. See information of the High Relief Council at www.lebanonundersiege.gov.lb. See also Human Rights Watch, *World Report 2007: Events of 2006*, New York, Human Rights Watch, 2007, p. 489.
3. See ICJ, *Legal Consequences of the Construction of a Wall in the Occupied Palestinian Territory*, Advisory Opinion of 9 July 2004, paragraph 106.
4. See J-M. Henckaerts and L. Doswald-Beck, *Customary International Humanitarian Law*, Geneva, ICRC, 2005.
5. First Additional Protocol, Article 85, paragraph 3; Rome Statute of the International Criminal Court, Article 8, paragraph 2(b).
6. Ibid.
7. Rome Statute of the International Criminal Court, Article 8, paragraph 2(b).
8. Amnesty International, *Israel/Lebanon -Deliberate destruction or 'collateral damage'? Israeli attacks on civilian infrastructure*, London, Amnesty International document MDE 18/007/2006, 22 August 2006.
9. Ibid.
10. Amnesty International, 'Imprisoned for Refusing to Attack', Web Action, London, Amnesty International document MDE 02/011/2006, 9 August 2006.
11. High Relief Council, 12 September 2006.
12. See Agence France Presse (AFP), 'Israel Says it Will Bomb all Moving Vehicles South of Litani River', 8 August 2006.
13. Human Rights Watch, *Lebanon. Fatal strikes. Israel's Indiscriminate Attacks Against Civilians in Lebanon*, New York, Human Rights Watch, Vol. 18, No. 3(E), August 2006.
14. See *International Herald Tribune*, 22/23 of July 2006.
15. R. Huguenin, ICRC spokesperson in Tyre, quoted in *Le Matin* (Switzerland), 13 August 2006.
16. The High Relief Council told Jean Ziegler that it had distributed, for a family of four, 26 kg packages of food including rice, sugar, tea, jam, lentils, salt, milk, every two weeks. They also distributed hygiene kits and packets of food and items for babies.
17. See WFP, *Lebanon Crisis: WFP Rapid Food Security Assessment 27 August to 10 September 2006*, WFP, 13 September 2006.
18. See WFP, *Lebanon Crisis: WFP Rapid Food Security Assessment 27 August to 10 September 2006*.
19. Oxfam, *Real Time Evaluation Report – Lebanon Crisis: Response: October 2006*, Oxford, Oxfam, 2006.
20. Ibid.
21. Oxfam International, 'Lebanese farmers in crisis after month of war', press release of 31 August 2006, http://www.oxfam.org/en/news/pressreleases2006/pr_060931_lebanon.
22. FAO, *First Assessment Report. Lebanon*, Rome, FAO, September 2006.
23. Government of Lebanon, Ministry of Agriculture, *Preliminary Report: War Damage Assessment in the Agricultural Sector*, September 2006.
24. Ibid.
25. See M. Rapoport, 'What Lies Beneath', *Haaretz*, 8 September 2006; AFP, 'Over 1.2 million cluster bombs dropped on Lebanon', 13 September 2006.
26. See United Nations Joint Logistics Centre, *Consolidated Situation Report. Lebanon Crisis*, United Nations, 16 September 2006.
27. See OCHA, *Lebanon: Cluster Bomb Fact Sheet*, OCHA, 19 September 2006.
28. See Associated Press, 'L'ONU demande à Israël de préciser les emplacements visés au Liban par des bombes à sous-munitions', 19 September 2006.

29. See UNDP, *Information on Mine and UXO Victims*, UNDP, 2006.
30. See United Nations Joint Logistics Centre, *Consolidated Situation Report. Lebanon Crisis*.
31. FAO, *First Assessment Report: Lebanon*.
32. United Nations press release, 26 August 2006.
33. Discussion with Nabil de Freige, Member of Parliament, President of the Economic and Industry Commission, 15 September 2006.
34. FAO, *First Assessment Report: Lebanon*.
35. World Conservation Union (IUCN) and Green Line, *Lebanon oil spill rapid assessment/response mission. Final report*, 11 September 2006, http://www.greenline.org.lb/new/pdf_files/document_2_lebanon_oil_spill_rapid_assessment_and_response_mission.pdf, date accessed 31 May 2010.
36. Ibid.
37. OCHA, *Situation Report No. 35: Lebanon Response: 30 August 2006*, OCHA, 2006.
38. Action Contre la Faim, 'Au Sud Liban: des milliers de personnes survivent sans un accès minimum à l'eau potable', 28 August 2006.
39. See South Lebanon Water Establishment, *Needs Assessment Report*, 10 September 2006.
40. Amnesty International, *Israel/Lebanon: Deliberate destruction or 'collateral damage'? Israeli attacks on civilian infrastructure*.
41. See H.A. Amery, 'Assessing Lebanon's Water Balance', in D. B. Brooks and O. Mehmet (eds), *Water Balances in the Eastern Mediterranean*, Ottawa, International Development Research Centre, 2000.
42. Action Contre la Faim, 'Au Sud Liban: des milliers de personnes survivent sans un accès minimum à l'eau potable', 28 August 2006.
43. UN press release, 22 August 2006.
44. Ibid.
45. Ibid.
46. See ICJ, *Legal Consequences of the Construction of a Wall in the Occupied Palestinian Territory*, Advisory Opinion of 9 July 2004, paragraphs 152, 153 and 163.

15 Bolivia

1. See A/HRC/7/5 and A/HRC/4/30/Add.2.
2. See United Nations, Ministry of Health and National Council for Food and Nutrition (CONAN), *Support to the implementation of the national Zero Malnutrition Programme*, La Paz, 2007.
3. UNDP, *Objetivos de Desarollo del Milenio: La Paz*, La Paz, UNDP, 2007.
4. Unidad de Análisis de Políticas Sociales y Económicas (UDAPE), Naciones Unidas, Organización Internacional del Trabajo, *Pueblos Indígenas Orginarios y Objetivos de Desarrollo del Milenio*, La Paz, 2006.
5. World Bank, *Bolivia: Towards a New Social Contract, A Country Social Analysis*, Volume II, Washington, World Bank, 2006.
6. UDAPE, Naciones Unidas, Organización Internacional del Trabajo, *Pueblos Indígenas Orginarios y Objectivos de Desarrollo del Milenio*.
7. The poverty line for extreme poverty is calculated according to ability to access the *canasta basica* or basic food basket of the minimum daily requirement of calories.
8. R. Viscarra and J. Rushton, *Productive Strategies for Poor Rural Households to Participate Successfully in Global Economic Processes: Country Report for Bolivia*,

422 Notes

London, Overseas Development Institute, International Development Research Center, May 2006.
9. World Bank, *Bolivia: Towards a New Social Contract: Options for the Constituent Assembly*, Washington, World Bank, 2006.
10. The World Bank estimates the Gini coefficient for income at 0.58, although inequality in land distribution is even higher.
11. World Bank, *Bolivia: Towards a New Social Contract: Options for the Constituent Assembly*.
12. J. Prudencio and G. Ton, *Integración regional y producción campesina: La urgencia de políticas de soberanía alimentaria*, Cochabamba, Fundación Agrecol Andes, 2005.
13. S. Klasen, M. Gross, R. Thiele, J. Lay, J. Spatz and M. Wiebelt, *Operationalising Pro-Poor Growth, A Country Case Study on Bolivia*, October 2004, p. 24, http://siteresources.worldbank.org/INTPGI/Resources/342674-1115051237044/oppg-bolivia.pdf.
14. UNDP, *La economia más allá del gas, informe tematico sobre el desarollo humano*, La Paz, UNDP, 2006.
15. Out of 8 million hectares classified as productive for agriculture, only 2.5 million hectares are currently exploited.
16. Food and Agriculture Organization of the United Nations (FAO), *Perfiles nutricionales por paises: Bolivia*, Rome, FAO, 2001. The overall Gini coefficient for land inequality stood at 0.768 in 1989. See S. Klasen, M. Gross, R. Thiele, J. Lay, J. Spatz and M. Wiebelt, *Operationalising Pro-Poor Growth, A Country Case Study on Bolivia*.
17. World Bank, *Bolivia: Towards a New Social Contract: Options for the Constituent Assembly*.
18. FAO, *Perfiles nutricionales por paises: Bolivia*.
19. United States Agency for International Development (USAID), *Bolivia - Floods*, Washington, USAID, 23 March 2007.
20. UDAPE, Naciones Unidas, Organización Internacional del Trabajo, *Pueblos Indígenas Orginarios y Objectivos de Desarrollo del Milenio*.
21. Ibid.
22. Public Citizen, *Water Privatization Fiascos: Broken Promises and Social Turmoil*, Washington, Public Citizen, 2003.
23. See United States Energy Information Administration (EIA), *Country Analysis Briefs: Bolivia*, Washington, EIA, October 2006.
24. Human Rights Watch, *Bolivia: Strengthen Investigation into Protest Deaths*, 21 December 2003, http://www.hrw.org/english/docs/2003/12/22/bolivi6847.htm.
25. Data given during our visit by the Ministerio de Hidrocarburos y Energia.
26. IMF, *IMF Executive Board Concludes 2007 Article IV Consultation with Bolivia*, Public Information Notice No. 07/80, 17 July 2007, http://www.imf.org/external/np/sec/pn/2007/pn0780.htm.
27. Ibid.
28. World Bank, *Bolivia: Towards a New Social Contract: Options for the Constituent Assembly*, pp. 87–91.
29. Ibid.
30. Álvaro García Linera, 'La Ley de Convocatoria a la Asamblea Constituyente en la Coyuntura Nacional' in Defensor del Pueblo, *Ley de Convocatoria a la Asamblea Constituyente, Derechos Humanos y Defensor del Pueblo*, La Paz, Defensor del Pueblo, 2005.
31. Bolivia's former Constitution also sets out very important principles that have been reaffirmed in the new Constitution. It recognized the diversity of

the population of Bolivia, its multi-ethnicity and multiculturalism (Article 1). It prohibited any form of discrimination and guarantees equality between men and women (Article 6). It also recognized that the rights to life, health and security, the right to a fair remuneration, sufficient to ensure a dignified existence for the worker and his/her family, and the right to a healthy environment are fundamental human rights (Article 7). It also provided that the State must recognize, respect and protect the economic, social and cultural rights of indigenous people living in Bolivia, in particular their rights to lands of origin (under the Tierra Comunitaria de Orígen framework), to the sustainable use of natural resources, to identity, values, customs and institutions (Article 171).

32. Defensor del Pueblo, *Informe IX del Defensor del Pueblo al Congreso Nacional*, La Paz, Defensor del Pueblo, 2006. See also Inter-American Commission on Human Rights, *Access to Justice and Social Inclusion: the Road towards Strengthening Democracy in Bolivia*, Washington, Organization of American States, Inter-American Commission on Human Rights, 2007.
33. United Nations, *Marco de Asistencia de las Naciones Unidas para el Desarrollo 2008–2012*, La Paz, United Nations, February 2007.
34. AIPE, *Constitucionalización del derecho humano a una alimentación adecuada*, La Paz, AIPE, 2007. Other documents of AIPE are available at www.aipe.org.bo.
35. Agua Sustentable, *Propuestas constitucionales del agua*, La Paz, Agua Sustentable, 2007, www.aguasustentable.org, date accessed 31 May 2010.
36. Stunting measured by height for age. See UDAPE, Naciones Unidas, Organización Internacional del Trabajo, *Pueblos Indígenas Originarios y Objetivos de Desarrollo del Milenio*, p. 21.
37. Some progress is due to demographic changes and urbanization. See P. Espinoza, E. Yañez and G. Gray Molina, *¿Demografía o políticas públicas?: La paradoja del avance en necesidades básicas insatisfechas en Bolivia*, Working Paper 01/05, La Paz, UNDP, 2005.
38. Inter-American Commission on Human Rights, *Informe de derechos humanos de los pueblos indígenas afectados por las industrias de la minería, gas y petróleo, y el caso de las familias cautivas en el Chaco boliviano*, Washington, Organization of American States, Inter-American Commission on Human Rights, 2005.
39. Ibid. Also Defensor del Pueblo, *Informe IX del Defensor del Pueblo al Congreso Nacional*.
40. Inter-American Commission on Human Rights, *Informe de derechos humanos de los pueblos indígenas afectados por las industrias de la minería, gas y petróleo, y el caso de las familias cautivas en el Chaco boliviano*.
41. B. Sharma, *Contemporary Forms of Slavery in Bolivia*, London, Anti-Slavery International, 2006.
42. S. Klasen, M. Gross, R. Thiele, J. Lay, J. Spatz and M. Wiebelt, *Operationalising Pro-Poor Growth, A Country Case Study on Bolivia*, p. 4.
43. Ibid, p. 15.
44. Ibid.

16 Cuba

1. See A/HRC/7/5/Add.3.
2. Institute for Nutrition and Food Hygiene (INFH), presentation made during our visit in Havana on 5 November 2007.

3. See Millennium Development Goal Indicators, The official United Nations site for MDG Indicators, available at http://mdgs.un.org/unsd/mdg/.
4. Ibid.
5. Ibid.
6. FAO, *The State of Food Insecurity in the World 2006*, Rome, FAO, 2006.
7. INFH, presentation made during our visit in Havana on 5 November 2007.
8. Ibid.
9. Ibid.
10. United Nations Development Programme (UNDP), *Millennium Development Goals Cuba. Second Report*, New York, UNDP, 2005.
11. See Millennium Development Goal Indicators, The official United Nations site for MDG Indicators, available at http://mdgs.un.org/unsd/mdg/.
12. National Bureau of Statistics, *2006 Statistical Yearbook for Cuba*, Havana, National Bureau of Statistics, Demographic Publications, 2007.
13. See World Food Programme (WFP), *Development Project – Cuba*, document WFP WFP/EB.1/2001/9-A, pp. 5–6.
14. INFH, presentation made during our visit in Havana on 5 November 2007.
15. Ibid.
16. See WFP, Development Project – Cuba, pp. 5–6.
17. Ibid.
18. See Millennium Development Goal Indicators, The official United Nations site for MDG Indicators, available at http://mdgs.un.org/unsd/mdg/.
19. See WFP, Development Project – Cuba, pp. 5–6.
20. Respectively 360, 359 and 374. See Ibid.
21. Speech by First Vice-President Raúl Castro Ruz delivered on 26 July 2007, http://www.cubaminrex.cu/english/Speeches/RCR/RCR_260707.htm.
22. See WFP, Development Project – Cuba, pp. 5–6.
23. Government of Cuba, Ministry of Agriculture, presentation made during our visit in Havana on 29 October 2007.
24. See report A/62/92, paragraph 25.
25. See resolution 62/3.
26. See A/62/92, paragraph 84.
27. Government of Cuba, Ministry of Internal Trade, presentation made during our visit in Havana on 2 November 2007.
28. See A/62/92, paragraph 83.
29. See A/62/92, paragraph 84.
30. See A/62/92, paragraph 81.
31. See A/62/92, paragarph 27.
32. The National Association of Small Farmers (ANAP) membership comprises 150,000 farmers farming their own individual farms and 200,000 farmers farming their own land through Credit and Service Cooperatives.
33. CERD/C/304/Add.60, CRC/C/15/Add.72, E/CN.4/2000/68/Add.2.
34. Voluntary Guideline 18.1.
35. In the village of Crucero de Piedrecita.
36. Government of Cuba, Ministry of Interior Commerce, presentation made during our visit in Havana on 2 November 2007.
37. National Social Workers Programme, presentation made during our visit in Havana on 29 October 2007.
38. See WFP, Development Project – Cuba, pp. 5–6.
39. CERD/C/304/Add.60, CRC/C/15/Add.72, E/CN.4/2000/68/Add.2.

40. Government of Cuba, Ministry of Agriculture, presentation made during our visit in Havana on 29 October 2007.
41. Meeting with Alexander Rodríguez Rosada, President of the Provincial Assembly, Villa Clara, 31 October 2007.
42. Government of Cuba, Ministry of Agriculture, presentation made during our visit in Havana on 29 October 2007.
43. See A/62/92, paragraph 81.
44. Resolution of the 8th Organization of American States Meeting of Consultation of Ministers of Foreign Affairs, 1962.
45. See A/62/92, paragraph 81.
46. FAO, *The State of Food Insecurity in the World 2006*, Rome, FAO, 2006.
47. United Nations, *United Nations Development Assistance Framework 2008–2012*, Havana, United Nations, 2007.

17 Conclusion

1. Josué de Castro, *The Geography of Hunger*, New York, Little, Brown, 1952.
2. See Chapter 6.
3. See section 3.3.
4. See FAO Document/C/2006/REP.
5. FAO, *Contemporary Thinking on Land Reforms*, Rome, FAO, 1998.
6. For example, 'Land for those who work it, not just for those who can buy it', Final declaration of the international seminar on the negative impacts of World Bank market-based land reform policy, April 2002, http://www.foodfirst.org/node/248.
7. See Chapter 12.
8. Oxfam, 'Rigged Rules and Double Standards: Trade, Globalisation, and the Fight Against Poverty', 2002.
9. S. Way and J. Chileshe, 'Trade Liberalisation and the Impact on Poverty: Zambia Case Study', In Oxfam/Institute of Development Studies, University of Sussex, *Liberalisation and Poverty*, Oxford, Oxfam, 1999.
10. Friends of the Earth International, *Sale of the Century?: Peoples' Food Sovereignty, Part 1 – the Implications of Current Trade Negotiations*, 2003, www.foe.co.uk/resource/reports/qatar_food_sovereignty_1.pdf, date accessed 31 May 2010.
11. See sections 3.1 and 3.5.
12. Administrative Committee Coordination/Subcommittee on Nutrition (ACC/SCN), *Fourth Report on the World Nutrition Situation: Nutrition throughout the Life Cycle*, Geneva, 2000.
13. FAO, Women's Right to Land: A Human Right, Rome, FAO, 2002.
14. See Chapter 10.
15. See Chapter 12.
16. See section 3.5.
17. See section 4.4.
18. Erosion, Technology and Concentration Action Group (ETC), Communiqué, November/December 2003, Issue 82.
19. Ibid.
20. L.O. Fresco, 'Which Road Do We Take? Harnessing Genetic Resources and Making Use of life Sciences, a New Contract for Sustainable Agriculture', European Discussion Forum 'Towards Sustainable Agriculture for Developing Countries:

Options from Life Sciences and Biotechnologies', Brussels, 30–31 January 2003, www.fao.org/ag/magazine/fao-gr.pdf.
21. P.L. Pingali and G. Traxler, 'Changing Focus of Agricultural Research: Will the Poor Benefit from Biotechnology and Privatization Trends?', *Food Policy*, No. 27, 2002.
22. N. Roseman, 'The Human Right to Water Under the Conditions of Trade Liberalisation and Privatisation – a Study on the Privatisation of Water Supply and Wastewater Disposal in Manila', Occasional Papers: International Development Cooperation, Bonn, Friedrich Ebert Foundation, 2003.
23. E. Gutierrez, B. Calaguas, J. Green and V. Roaf, *New Rules, New Roles: Does Private Sector Participation Benefit the Poor?*, WaterAid and TearFund, 2003.
24. Europe-Third World Centre, *Transnational Corporations and Human Rights*, Geneva, CETIM, 2000. For more information, see at www.ibfan.org.
25. See S. Lewis, 'Malnutrition as a Human Rights Violation', ACC/SCN, *SCN News*, No. 18, July 1999.
26. See E/CN.4/Sub.2/2003/12/Rev.2.
27. See A/61/306.
28. International Federation of Red Cross and Red Crescent Societies (IFRC), *World Disasters Report*, Geneva, IFRC, 2003.
29. See chapters 6 and 10 above.
30. M. Leighton, 'Desertification and Migration', in P. M. Johnson, K. Mayrand and M. Paquin, *Governing Global Desertification: Linking Environmental Degradation, Poverty and Participation*, Aldershot, United Kingdom, Ashgate, 2006.
31. See the text of the Convention at www.unccd.int/convention/text/convention.php?annexNo=0.
32. International Year of Deserts and Desertification, http://www.iydd.org/, date accessed 31 May 2010. Desertification is defined as 'land degradation in arid, semi-arid and dry sub-humid areas resulting from various factors, including climatic variations and human activities' in Article 1 of the United Nations Convention to Combat Desertification.
33. Millennium Ecosystems Assessment, *Ecosystems and Human Wellbeing: Desertification Synthesis*, Washington, World Resources Institute, 2005, p. 1.
34. R.P. White and J. Nackoney, 'Drylands, People, and Ecosystems Goods and Services: A Web-Based Geospatial Analysis', Washington, World Resources Institute, 2003.
35. This includes the entire continent, not only sub-Saharan Africa.
36. Poverty and Environment Initiative, *Attacking Poverty, While Improving The Environment: Towards Win-Win Policy Options*, Paper published under the auspices of the UNDP and the European Commission, 1999, http://www.unpei.org/PDF/Attacking-Poverty-win-win-Eng.pdf, date accessed 31 May 2010.
37. P.M. Johnson, K. Mayrand and M. Paquin, 'The United Nations Convention to Combat Desertification in Global Sustainable Development Governance', In P. M. Johnson, K. Mayrand, and M. Paquin, *Governing Global Desertification: Linking Environmental Degradation, Poverty and Participation*.
38. See E/CN.4/2006/44.
39. IFAD, *Rural Poverty Report 2001: The Challenge of Ending Rural Poverty*, New York, Oxford University Press, 2001.
40. Ibid.
41. FAO, *The State of Food Insecurity in the World 2000*, Rome, FAO, 2000.

42. FAO, 'Assessment of the World Food Security Situation', Paper prepared for the 26th session of the Committee on World Food Security, 18–21 September 2000, Rome, FAO, 2000.
43. FAO, *The State of Food Insecurity in the World 2000*.
44. United Nations Millennium Project, Task Force on Hunger, *Halving Hunger, It Can Be Done*, New York, UNDP, 2005.
45. Ibid.
46. S. Devereux, 'Food Insecurity in Ethiopia', Discussion Paper for the United Kingdom Department for International Development, Institute of Development Studies Sussex, October 2000.
47. See A. McCulloch, S. Babu and P. Hazell (eds), *Strategies for Poverty Alleviation and Sustainable Natural Resource Management in the Fragile Lands of Sub-Saharan Africa*, Feldafing, Germany, Deutsche Stiftung fur Internationale Entwicklung (DSE), 2000.
48. S.A. Way, 'Examining the Links between Poverty and Land Degradation: From Blaming the Poor towards Recognising the Rights of the Poor', in P. M. Johnson, K. Maynard, and M. Paquin, *Governing Global Desertification: Linking Environmental Degradation, Poverty And Participation*.
49. Y. D. Evers, *The Social Dimensions of Desertification: Annotated Bibliography and Literature Review*, London, International Institute for Environment and Development (IIED) and United Nations Research Institute for Social Development (UNRISD), 1996.
50. M. Leach and R. Mearns (eds) *The Lie of the Land: Challenging Received Wisdom on the African Environment*, Oxford, James Currey, 1996; T. Forsyth and M. Leach with I. Scoones, 'Poverty and Environment: Priorities for Research and Policy: An Overview Study', Paper prepared for the UNDP and European Commission, Institute of Development Studies Sussex, September 1998.
51. I. Scoones (ed.) *Living with Uncertainty: New Directions in Pastoral Development in Africa*, London, Intermediate Technology Publications, 1994.
52. R. Øygard, T. Vedeld and J. Aune, 'Good Practices in Drylands Management', Paper prepared by Noragric Agricultural University of Norway for the World Bank, Washington, 1999.
53. M.F. Tiffen and M.J. Mortimore, *More People. Less Erosion: Environmental Recovery in Kenya*, Chichester, J. Wiley, 1994.
54. See Chapter 10.
55. See Chapters 6 and 10.
56. This includes 2 million m^3 of renewable water and 2000 million m^3 of non-renewable water in subterranean aquifers, as well as the Niger River with 30 million m^3 per year, of which only 1 per cent is exploited. See République du Niger, Ministère des ressources en eau, *Liste des projets dont le financement est à rechercher et des fiches de synthèses*, Niamey, 2000.
57. United Nations Millennium Project, Task Force on Hunger, *Halving Hunger, It Can Be Done*, New York, UNDP, 2005.
58. E/CN.4/2006/44.
59. See also A/62/289.
60. See E. Holt-Giménez, 'The biofuel myths', *International Herald Tribune*, 10 July 2007.
61. G. Gendron, Radio Canada, 12 August 2007.
62. See 'Let us make hunger a part of history', *UN Special*, July 2007, Invité du mois, Josette Sheeran.

63. Fidel Castro Ruiz, *Granma*, 27 March 2007.
64. Cited in D. Howden, 'The fight for the world's food', *The Independent*, 23 June 2007.
65. See E. Holt-Giménez, 'The biofuel myths'.
66. Directive 2003/30/EC on the promotion of the use of biofuels or other renewable fuels for transport.
67. Address to the United States Congress on 23 January 2007.
68. Cited in Marcela Sanchez, 'Latin America – the 'Persian Gulf' of biofuels?', *Washington Post*, 23 February 2007.
69. E. Holt-Giménez, 'The biofuel myths'.
70. See L. Peskett, R. Slater, C. Stevens and A. Dufey, *Biofuels, Agriculture And Poverty Reduction*, London, Overseas Development Institute, Natural Resource Perspectives Series, June 2007.
71. P. Garde, *Les biocarburants au Sénégal comme outil de développement: oasis ou mirage*, Genève, Mémoire présenté à l'Institut de Hautes Etudes Internationales et du Développement, 2007.
72. See Global Subsidies Initiative, Biofuels at What Cost ? Government support for ethanol and biodiesel in the United States, Geneva, October 2006.
73. E. Holt-Giménez, 'The biofuel myths'.
74. G. Dupuy, 'La nouvelle bataille des champs', *L'Express*, 19 April 2007.
75. UNCTAD, 'Challenges and opportunities for developing countries in producing biofuels', UNCTAD document UNCTAD/DITC/COM/2006/15, 27 November 2006.
76. Directive 2003/30/EC on the promotion of the use of biofuels or other renewable fuels for transport.
77. See 'Biocarburants: l'arnaque', *Courrier International*, No. 864.
78. Ibid, p. 13.
79. Movimento dos Trabaladores Rurais Sim Terra (MST), Full tanks at the cost of empty stomachs: the expansion of the sugarcane industry in Latin America, Sao Paulo, MST, 28 February 2007.
80. See C. Golay, 'The Food Crisis and Food Security: Towards a New World Food Order?', *International Development Policy Series*, Volume 1, pp. 215–32.
81. D. Mitchell, 'A Note on Rising Food Prices', Washington, World Bank Policy Research Working Paper, July 2008.
82. See BBC News, 'Mexicans Stage Tortilla Protest', 1 February 2007.
83. See P. Hazell and R. K. Pachauri (eds), *Bioenergy and Agriculture: Promises and Challenges*, Washington, International Food Policy Research Institute, 2006.
84. F. Mingorance, 'The Flow of Palm Oil: Colombia-Belgium/Europe. A Study from a Human Rights Perspective', Bruxelles, Human Rights Everywhere, 2007.
85. See F. Frayssinet, 'Guest brings Biofuel Argument Summit', Inter Press Service, 5 June 2007.
86. A. J. Ferriera Simões, 'Biofuels will help fight hunger', *International Herald Tribune*, 6 August 2007.
87. E. Holt-Giménez, 'The biofuel myths'.
88. D. Howden, 'The Fight For The World's Food', *The Independent*, 23 June 2007.
89. See ActionAid press release, Fortaleza, Brazil, 5 July 2007, www.actionaid.org/pages.aspx?PageID=34&ItemID=287.
90. The Voluntary Guidelines on the Right to Food are available online, with publications on the right to food, at www.fao.org/righttofood.

91. FAO, Right to Food in Action. Examples of How FAO Member Countries Make it Happen, Rome, FAO, 2007.
92. Ibid.
93. F.L. Schieck Valente, 'Understanding Human Rights Approaches to Food and Nutritional Security in Brazil. Learned Revisited', in M. Borghi, L. Postiglione Blommestein (eds), *For an Effective Right to Adequate Food*, Fribourg, Éditions universitaires, 2002, pp. 261-97.
94. The National Council on Food and Nutrition Security comprises 17 Brazilian governments – notably Ministers of social development and the fight against hunger, agriculture, fishing and provision, agricultural development, education, environment, planning, health and work, and specialised secretariats – notably of farmers' organizations, agricultural workers, minorities, churches, universities, human rights organizations and the food industry – and 16 observers – notably representatives of municipalities, of the United Nations agencies, the World Bank, as well as the National Rapporteur on Human Rights related to food, water and agriculture.
95. Law 11.346 adopted on 15 September 2006.
96. On the justiciability of the right to food at the national, regional and international levels, see C. Golay, *The Right to Food and Access to Justice: Examples at the National, Regional and International Levels*, Rome, FAO, 2009. See also C. Courtis, 'The Right to Food as a Justiciable Right: Challenges and Strategies', *Max Planck Yearbook of United Nations Law*, Vol. 11, 2007, pp. 317-337 ; M. Borghi and L. Postiglione Blommestein (eds), *The Right to Adequate Food and Access to Justice*, Bruylant, Schulthess, 2006.
97. See Chapter 13.
98. Ibid.
99. Supreme Court of India, *State of Karnataka v. Appa Balu Ingale*, 1993.
100. Supreme Court of India, *S. Jagannath v. Union of India*, 1996.
101. Supreme Court of India, *Samatha v. State of Andhra Pradesh*, 1997.
102. High Court of South Africa (Cape of Good Hope Provincial Division), *Kenneth George and Others v. Minister of Environmental Affairs & Tourism*, Case No. EC 1/2005, Founding Affidavit. See also High Court of South Africa (Cape of Good Hope Provincial Division), *Kenneth George and Others v. Minister of Environmental Affairs & Tourism*, Case No. EC 1/2005, Affidavit by N. Jaffer ; High Court of South Africa (Cape of Good Hope Provincial Division), *Kenneth George and Others v. Minister of Environmental Affairs & Tourism*, Case No. EC 1/2005, Supporting Affidavit by Jean Ziegler.
103. High Court of South Africa (Cape of Good Hope Provincial Division), *Kenneth George and Others v. Minister of Environmental Affairs & Tourism*, Case No. EC 1/2005, Judgment of 2 May 2007.
104. La Via Campesina, 'Priority to people's food sovereignty', Declaration of 1 November 2001.
105. See 'Food Sovereignty: A Right For All', Political Statement of the NGO/CSO Forum for Food Sovereignty, 14 June 2002, www.foodfirst.org/progs/global/food/finaldeclaration.html.
106. Government of Norway, Ministry of Agriculture, 'Multifunctional Agriculture: the case of Norway', Publication Number M-0722E, http://www.regjeringen.no/lmd/html/multifunc/multifunc1.html, date accessed 31 May 2010.
107. D. E. Ray and the Agricultural Policy Analysis Center, 'Food Sovereignty', *MidAmerica Farmer Grower*, Vol. 21, No. 34, 22 August 2003.

108. Friends of the Earth International, Sale of the Century?: Peoples' Food Sovereignty, Part 1 – the implications of current trade negotiations, Amsterdam, Friends of the Earth International, 2001.
109. Via Campesina, 'Priority to people's food sovereignty', Declaration of 1 November 2001.
110. CESCR, *General Comment No. 12*, E/C.12/1999/5.

Index

access to credit *see* credit
access to justice *see* justice
access to land *see* land
Action contre la Faim 3, 176, 228
ActionAid 92, 206, 260, 349
Afghanistan 1, 6, 32
African Charter on Human and Peoples' Rights 116
African Commission on Human and Peoples' Rights 96
Agence française de développement 359, 360
agrarian conflict 239, 240
agrarian reform 20, 27, 35–41, 139, 141, 142, 153, 223, 255, 270, 275, 294, 299, 301, 302, 309, 317, 328, 329, 334, 350, 355, 378
agricultural policy 70, 72, 150, 262, 267
agrofuels *see* biofuels
aid *see* humanitarian aid
Alaska 53
Algeria 134, 339
Alien Tort Claims Act 83, 100
amparo 300
anaemia *see* iron deficiency
Angola 32
Argentina 92, 98, 338, 348
armed conflict
   and child combatants 31–3, 378
   and children 30, 31–3, 101, 105, 106
   and right to food 19, 101–8, 242, 279, 379, 383
   and women 101, 103, 105, 106
arsenic 158–9, 166–7, 169–72, 173
Asian Development Bank 227, 228, 230, 359, 360
Australia 62, 82, 100, 359
Aventis 91, 337

Bangladesh 1, 7, 11, 24, 35, 44, 48, 92, 155–74, 351
Belgium 10, 134
Benin 115
biofuels 343–9, 382
bioprospecting 54

biotechnology *see also* genetically modified organisms
   and impact on access to food xiii, 93
blockade *see* embargo
Bolivia 11, 54, 92, 290–309, 311, 338
bondage *see* forced labour
Bosnia and Herzogovina 107, 108
Brazil 11, 25, 31, 34, 35, 36, 38, 39, 50, 77, 98, 135–54, 296, 334, 338, 343, 345, 348, 350, 351, 359
breastfeeding 31, 93, 106, 144, 225, 300, 307, 375, 378, 381
Breast-milk Substitutes, International Code of Marketing 31, 93, 98, 99, 307, 338
Burma *see* Myanmar
Burundi 32, 62

Cambodia 217
Cameroon 346, 348
Canada 44, 45, 82, 100, 325
Cape Verde 44, 60
Cargill 91, 337
Center for Economic and Social Rights 96
Central American Free Trade Agreement 249, 252, 253, 256
Chad 340
child combatants 31–3, 378
child labour 31–3, 261
child soldiers *see* child combatants
children
   in armed conflict 30, 31–3, 101, 105, 106
   girl 25, 28
   protection under international law 29–30
   vulnerability to hunger and malnutrition 1–4, 28, 29, 31–2, 113, 133, 156, 167, 216, 217, 225, 237, 260, 291, 312, 313, 318, 378, 381
Chile 46, 50, 98, 338, 359
China 6, 37, 47, 61, 214, 215, 232, 339, 343, 345

431

432 *Index*

civil society organizations *see* non-governmental organizations
climate change 58, 63, 293, 294, 340, 341, 343, 344, 346, 368
Colombia 32, 36, 55, 92, 136, 345, 347, 348, 359
colonization 51, 53, 194, 295, 296, 307, 336
Commission on Human Rights 10–11, 89, 95, 97, 99, 131, 141, 181, 316, 357–8
Committee on Economic, Social and Cultural Rights 8, 10, 13, 16, 19, 30, 37, 38, 56, 57, 78, 79, 80, 83, 84, 86, 89, 94, 95, 97, 98, 116, 141, 183, 199, 255, 274, 279, 298, 309, 318, 329, 350, 351, 375
commodity prices 71, 72, 232, 343
communications (to the Special Rapporteur) 359
companies *see* corporations
compensation 46, 90, 273
Congo, Democratic Republic of 7, 32, 33, 62, 369
constitutional
 norms in Ethiopia 199–200, 209
 obligations 243
 protection of property rights 38
 protection of the right to food 39, 89
 reform in Bolivia 296, 299–300, 304, 308
 reform in Guatemala 243, 245
 right to agrarian reform 41
 rights in Bangladesh 160, 161
 rights in Brazil 38–9, 139–40, 151, 152
 rights in Cuba 317, 319, 327, 330
 rights in India 263–4, 266, 352
 rights in Mongolia 221–2
 rights in Niger 117
 rights in South Africa 97, 352
contamination
 arsenic 158–9, 166–7, 169–72, 173
 of water 96, 306
Convention on the Elimination of All Forms of Discrimination Against Women 25, 27, 38, 116, 129, 139, 159, 173, 199, 221, 243, 263, 298, 316
Convention on the Elimination of Racial Discrimination 243
Convention on the Rights of the Child xiv, 29, 33, 79, 88, 116, 139, 159, 199, 221, 243, 263, 279, 298, 316, 335
Convention relating to the Status of Refugees 61, 63, 64, 65, 66
corporations
 accountability of 68, 82, 94–100, 337–8, 382
 communications to 359–60
 impact of 54, 91–3, 261, 307, 337–8, 355
 responsibilities of xv, 68, 77, 90, 91–100, 337–8, 350, 382
 States obligations vis-à-vis 30–1, 46, 49, 57, 81, 275, 299, 382
 violations by 46, 50, 93–4, 209, 273, 295, 337–8, 352
corruption xiii, 19, 35, 91, 168, 170, 234, 269
Côte d'Ivoire 32, 92, 115, 130, 346
credit, access to xiii, 25, 27, 35, 93, 127, 199, 208, 284, 288, 322, 341, 342, 355, 378
Cuba 7, 11, 31, 37, 75, 134, 303, 310–31, 343

debt servicing xiii, 132, 210, 297
decentralization 45, 195, 202, 220, 244, 297, 305, 325, 328, 330, 381
Declaration on the Rights of Indigenous Peoples 50–1, 56
deficiencies *see* nutrition, deficiencies in
Democratic People's Republic of Korea *see* Korea, Democratic People's Republic of
Democratic Republic of Congo *see* Congo, Democratic Republic of
Denmark 134
desertification 63, 115, 127, 132, 338–41, 382, 383
disaster *see* natural disasters
disaster relief *see* humanitarian aid
discrimination *see also* non-discrimination
 in food distribution policies 65
 and indigenous people 50–1, 58, 238, 239, 252–3, 295, 298, 335, 379
 and migrants 224, 230, 239
 racial 138, 242, 261, 266, 269, 272, 318
 and refugees 65, 261

discrimination – *continued*
  in social assistance 230
  and women 9, 23–8, 138, 144, 169, 173, 209, 210, 230, 254, 258, 269, 272, 335–6
displacement 19, 30, 49, 57, 84, 90, 102, 103, 112, 149, 168, 187, 204, 208–9, 242, 243, 261, 272–3, 275, 277, 283, 335, 379
Dominican Republic 75
drought
  in Bangladesh 156
  in Bolivia 291
  in Ethiopia 195–7, 203, 209
  in Niger 114, 121, 126, 134
  and right to food 4, 34, 339, 341, 342, 382, 383
dumping xiv, 77, 353, 354, 381

Ecuador 54, 96, 359
Egypt 40, 59, 211
El Salvador 75
embargo 105, 311, 315–16, 325, 328, 331
employment 20, 36, 37, 41, 42, 43, 48, 49, 50, 58, 73, 76, 90, 114, 137–8, 141, 142, 144, 147, 164, 166, 171, 191, 198, 203, 205, 210, 218, 226, 229, 231, 239, 240, 248, 251, 252, 255, 260, 261, 268, 269, 270, 274, 275, 276, 283, 285, 293, 295, 302, 305, 307, 309
Ethiopia 11, 20, 194–213, 339, 341, 351
European Commission 360
European Court of Human Rights 78, 97
European Union 44, 59, 60, 69, 86, 89, 134, 315, 335, 343, 345, 346, 359, 380
evictions *see* displacement; forced evictions
expropriation 40, 179, 188, 191, 192, 200, 239, 244, 245, 248, 251, 302
extraterritorial obligations 9, 64, 78–83, 95, 134, 315, 343, 350, 381

famine
  and armed conflict 107
  in Bangladesh 158, 163, 169
  in Ethiopia 195–8, 202, 205, 206, 210
  generally 3, 36, 39, 114, 383
  in India 258, 267
  in Mongolia 216
  in Niger 112, 114, 120, 134
  and refugees 58–9, 60
  in Somalia 107–8
farmers
  and agricultural investment 196
  associations 213
  and food security xiv, 34, 203, 204, 329, 348, 378
  and land reform 36, 40, 212, 223, 270, 317, 334, 378
  small scale 36, 73, 76, 77, 141, 211, 216, 267, 270, 285, 293, 294, 317, 353
  subsistence 114, 197, 220, 291
  and trade liberalization 70–2, 85–6, 335, 347
FIAN 36, 46, 78, 80, 86, 135, 146, 149, 236, 257, 272, 346
Finland 60
fisheries 42–9, 168, 285–6, 316, 320, 350
fisherpeople 41–9, 285, 288, 352, 378
fish-farming 42–9
fishing 34, 41–9, 52–3, 277, 283, 286, 306, 353, 378
floods
  in Bangladesh 156, 157, 158, 163, 164, 171, 174
  in Bolivia 291, 294, 303
  in Ethiopia 209, 225
  in India 258, 259
  in Niger 114, 115, 126
food aid *see* humanitarian aid
Food and Agriculture Organization xiii, 1, 3, 6, 20, 23, 25, 27, 35, 36, 39, 43, 44, 66, 73, 83, 92, 93, 98, 111, 121, 131, 144, 164, 176, 206, 217, 219, 227, 236, 249, 255, 259, 271, 283, 303, 309, 312, 315, 319, 323, 324, 329, 330, 332, 333, 334, 336, 337, 350, 356
food basket 260, 291, 321, 327, 330
food crisis 1, 3, 125–6, 163, 178, 196, 202, 207, 339, 346, 347
food insecurity
  in Bangladesh 163–6, 169
  in Bolivia 291–7, 305
  in Brazil 141–4
  in Cuba 311–15
  in Ethiopia 195–8

food insecurity – *continued*
  generally 4, 15–22, 341
  in Guatemala 237–40
  in India 258–62, 266–7, 271
  in Mongolia 215–20, 226, 228, 233, 234, 235
  in Niger xiv, 112–13, 119, 134
  in the Occupied Palestinian Territories 177
  in the world xiii, 73, 340
food security
  in Bolivia 299, 301, 302, 309
  concept of 7, 18, 75
  in Cuba 311, 317
  in Ethiopia 206, 207, 211–12
  generally 9, 46, 76, 77, 84, 90, 210, 346, 350, 376, 377, 378, 380, 381, 383, 384
  in Guatemala 244, 247, 249, 255
  in India 265, 267
  in Mongolia 225, 229, 233, 234
  trade and 68–72, 85, 249, 380
  and women 23–8
food sovereignty 41, 301, 302, 309, 352–3, 355–6, 380, 381
forced displacement *see* displacement
forced evictions 19, 38, 84, 90, 102, 103, 149, 187, 200, 240, 249, 250, 251, 253, 254, 270, 272–3, 347, 359
forced labour 61, 149, 241, 261, 293–4, 306, 309, 332, 333, 348
fortification *see* nutrition, improvement of
France 7, 134, 296

Gambia 44
gender *see also* women
  dimensions of the right to food 24–7, 169–70, 239, 248, 261, 377
  disparity 167, 169
General Assembly 87, 89, 97, 98, 104, 107, 181, 182, 299, 316, 351
General Comment
  No. 3 on States Parties obligations 21
  No. 12 on right to food 10, 13, 16, 19, 20, 21, 27, 37, 38, 56, 94, 98, 141, 185, 255, 274, 279, 309, 318, 329, 375, 376
  No. 15 on right to water 95
genetically modified organisms 19, 92–3, 337, 355

Geneva Conventions 101, 102, 103, 106, 107, 181, 182, 184, 191, 192, 199, 279, 287
Germany 7, 134, 376
Ghana 346
Guatemala 11, 35, 40, 51, 52, 53, 55, 236–56, 334, 336, 351
Guinea 32, 44
Guinea-Bissau 44

Haiti 1, 75
HIV 2, 4, 77, 197, 203, 325
Honduras 75
Human Rights Council xiv, 11, 56, 278, 288, 310, 316, 329, 338
humanitarian
  aid 20, 83, 164, 172, 178, 180, 195, 196–7, 206, 207, 208, 209, 212, 213, 216, 227, 233, 234, 256, 267, 277, 282, 283
  assistance 104–8, 134, 191, 281, 294, 303, 342, 383
  catastrophe and crisis 175, 177, 185, 190, 192, 196, 202, 207
  law 28, 101–4, 181, 182, 191, 192, 199, 278, 279–80, 288, 375, 383
Hungary 92
hunger
  and biofuels 346–9
  in Bolivia 292, 296
  in Brazil 136–8, 147, 150, 152, 153
  and children 29, 31–2
  cost 2–4
  in Cuba 311, 318
  definition 2
  in Ethiopia 195–9
  extreme 1, 2, 58
  global figures xiii, 1, 6–7, 332
  in Guatemala 237–40, 252, 253
  in India 258–62, 263, 268, 271, 272, 274
  and indigenous people 51, 379
  and land reform 36, 41
  in Mongolia 215–20, 231, 235, 237–40
  and refugees 58–63
  and the right to food 15–22, 28, 375, 378, 380, 383
  and trade 72
  and undernourishment 1–4

importation, food 218, 230, 232, 253, 267, 308, 311, 313, 314, 315, 320, 324, 327, 328, 331
India 7, 11, 30, 31, 35, 37, 44, 47, 48, 49, 85, 100, 168, 171, 197, 257-76, 343, 345, 346, 351, 352, 359
indigenous people
 in Bangladesh 161
 in Bolivia 291, 292, 294, 295, 296, 298, 299, 300, 301, 302, 303, 306, 309
 in Brazil 140
 in Ecuador 96
 in Guatemala 237, 240, 241, 242, 243, 245, 246, 248, 251, 252-3, 254, 255
 and intellectual property rights 53-4, 379
 in Mexico xv, 81
 and right to food 35, 45, 50-7, 77-8, 81, 84-5, 90, 334, 335-6, 379
 and right to land 38, 40, 348
Indonesia 35, 36, 47, 85, 92, 346, 348, 359
inheritance rights *see* women
intellectual property rights 53-4, 74, 379
Inter-American Commission on Human Rights 96
Inter-American Court of Human Rights 53
internally displaced persons 59, 64
International Committee of the Red Cross 101, 104, 106, 180, 181, 182, 282
International Covenant on Civil and Political Rights 57, 116, 139, 159, 199, 200, 221, 263, 298, 316, 329
International Covenant on Economic, Social and Cultural Rights 10, 16, 18, 20, 27, 28, 29, 37, 41, 56, 64, 86, 88, 116, 139, 159, 182, 183, 199, 200, 220, 243, 263, 279, 298, 316, 329, 335, 342, 351, 356
International Criminal Court 33, 103, 105, 107
International Food Policy Research Institute 3-4, 7, 70, 347, 349
International Fund for Agricultural Development 36, 39
international humanitarian law *see* humanitarian law
International Labour Organization 28, 33, 51-2, 55, 56, 98, 243, 245, 255, 298, 306, 338
International Labour Organization Convention No. 169 on Indigenous People 38, 55, 243, 245, 255, 298
International Monetary Fund xiv, 26, 68, 69, 70, 73, 79, 81, 84-90, 92, 129, 143, 147, 150, 153, 206, 230, 325, 328, 331, 337, 381
International organizations 84-90, 381
iodine deficiency 29, 156, 197, 217, 259, 291, 378
Iran 7
iron deficiency 29, 197, 217, 225, 259, 291, 312-13, 324, 331, 378
Israel 175-93, 277, 279, 280, 281, 284, 286, 288, 359
Italy 59, 60

Japan 37, 44, 62, 69, 82
justice, access to 9, 55, 119, 140, 148, 152, 161, 171, 174, 199, 200, 223, 233, 245, 300, 329, 350, 384
justiciability 160, 161, 244, 266, 351, 384

Kazakhstan 214
Kenya 7, 35, 60, 75, 217, 341
Korea, Democratic People's Republic of 1, 6, 61, 359
Korea, Republic of 37
Kosovo 32

labourers *see* employment
land
 access to xiii, 24, 25, 27, 34-7, 38, 41, 58, 93, 169, 210, 245, 317, 355, 377, 378
 reform *see* agrarian reform
 tenure *see* tenure
Landless Workers Movement 135, 145-6, 346
landlessness 34, 36, 39, 137
Lao People's Democratic Republic 359
Lebanon 11, 277-89

liberalization *see* agrarian reform; agricultural policy; trade
Liberia 32, 62
Libyan Arab Jamahiriya 59, 134

Madagascar 92, 217
Malawi 35
Malaysia 345, 346
Maldives 44
Mali 60, 63
malnutrition
  in Bangladesh 156, 172
  in Bolivia 290–7, 303, 304, 305, 308, 309
  in Brazil 136, 137, 152, 153
  and children 28, 29, 31–2, 113, 133, 136, 156, 216, 217, 225–6, 240, 259, 312, 377
  in Cuba 311–13
  definition 1, 2
  effects 2–4, 29, 137
  in Ethiopia 195–9, 206
  in Guatemala 237, 250
  in India 259, 260, 266–7, 269, 271
  and indigenous people 51–2, 379
  in Mongolia 216, 217, 219, 220, 225, 226, 229
  in Niger 114, 133
  in the Occupied Palestinian Territories 175, 177–9, 185, 192
  and the right to food xiii, 1, 15–22, 28, 375
  and women 23–8, 167, 173, 259, 269, 301, 312, 336, 377
Malta 59
Mauritania 44, 59, 60, 63
Mexico xiv–xv, 36, 61, 70, 81, 92, 136, 335, 346, 359
migration 34, 36, 58–63, 112, 126, 224, 231, 234, 239, 261, 293, 326–7, 330, 339, 379
Millennium Development Goals 4, 21, 29, 34, 51, 79, 165, 217, 219, 256, 259, 271, 312, 324, 326, 342, 374
Moldova, Republic of 359
Mongolia 1, 11, 214–35, 339, 351
Monsanto 91, 337, 345
Morocco 59, 60, 82, 134, 339
multinational corporations *see* corporations

Myanmar 32, 359

national human rights institutions
  in Bangladesh 168, 174
  in Bolivia 300
  in Brazil 140
  in Cuba 318, 319–20
  in Ethiopia 195, 201, 207–8, 212
  generally 100
  in Guatemala 245, 255
  in India 265, 266, 274
  in Mongolia 224, 226, 229, 230, 233
  in Niger 118, 132
natural disasters 34, 156, 157, 163, 169, 171, 202–3, 215, 216, 232, 233, 294, 324, 325, 339, 381, 383
Nepal 32, 92, 97
Nestlé 93, 98, 338
New Zealand 315
Nicaragua 53, 75, 311
Niger xiv, 11, 25, 29, 40, 81, 111–34, 333, 339, 340, 342
Nigeria 92, 96, 115, 339, 346
nomadic people 114, 129, 198, 214, 215, 218, 232, 341
non-discrimination
  and food security xiii, 9
  obligation of 21–2, 27–8, 84, 160, 335–6, 376
non-governmental organizations
  in Bangladesh 155, 161, 162, 165, 166, 168, 170
  and biofuels 343
  in Bolivia 290, 303–4, 305, 309
  in Brazil 135, 141, 142, 153, 351
  and child combatants 33
  in Cuba 310, 325, 331
  in Ethiopia 194, 202, 204, 206, 209, 213
  and fishing rights 44–5, 46, 49
  and food security 76
  in Guatemala 236, 237, 240, 249
  in India 257, 261, 270–1, 275
  in Lebanon 278, 282, 286, 288
  in Mongolia 228
  in Niger 111, 112, 117, 118, 119, 124, 130, 133
  in the Occupied Palestinian Territories 176, 180, 183, 185, 191
  and the right to food 36, 39, 40, 41, 78, 80, 84, 86, 93, 97, 98, 99, 104, 334, 338, 343, 353–4, 355, 356

non-governmental organizations – *continued*
  and trade liberalisation 72, 74, 85
  and the work of the Special Rapporteur 359
non-refoulement 380
non-retrogression 21
non-state actors *see* corporations; international organizations
Norms on the Responsibilities of Transnational Corporations and Other business Enterprises 99–100
Norway 7, 33, 74, 75, 134, 354
nutrition
  deficiencies in 23, 29, 156, 114, 197, 217, 219, 233, 259, 269, 276, 291, 378, 312
  improvement of 164, 225–6, 244, 247, 254, 269, 276, 303, 304, 321, 336

obesity 313, 331
Occupied Palestinian Territories 11, 175–93, 359
OECD Guidelines for Multinational Enterprises 82, 95, 98, 338
Office of the High Commissioner for Human Rights 4, 10–11, 64, 249, 360
ombudsman 97, 162, 168, 195, 201, 208, 212, 245, 246, 247, 252, 254, 255, 300, 306, 309, 319
Optional Protocol to the International Covenant on Economic, Social and Cultural Rights 351–2, 356, 384

Pakistan 35, 75, 92
Palestine *see* Occupied Palestinian Territories
Paraguay 348
pastoralists 114, 115, 128, 132, 195, 198, 199, 216, 223, 231, 234, 342
peasants 34–5, 39, 71, 77, 129, 200, 242, 252–3, 292, 299, 300, 309, 327, 346, 347, 348, 353, 355, 377, 378
Philippines 35, 36, 47, 92, 338, 359
pollution 30
Portugal 60
poverty
  in Bangladesh 172
  in Bolivia 290, 291, 295, 296, 302, 304, 308, 309
  in Brazil 136–8, 147
  in Cuba 313
  in Ethiopia 195–9, 206, 207
  in Guatemala 237–40, 253
  in India 258–62, 267–8
  and indigenous people 51–2
  in Mongolia 218, 222, 228, 229, 231, 235
  in the Occupied Palestinian Territories 185, 192
  reduction strategies 41, 85, 165, 234, 342, 380, 384
  rural 34–5, 113, 137, 157, 196–8, 378
  urban 216, 261–2, 293
prisoners 148, 152, 184, 190, 230, 307, 327
privatization
  in Bolivia 294, 295–6, 302, 307
  in Ethiopia 203, 210
  in Mongolia 223, 226, 230–2, 234
  in Niger 130, 132, 134
  and the right to food xiii–xv, 26, 81, 333
  of water 91–2, 97, 294, 295–6, 302, 337–8, 377
progressive realization (of the right to food)
  in Bolivia 304–5
  in Brazil 166–7
  communications about 359–60
  concept of 20–1
  in Cuba 326
  in Ethiopia 207–8
  in Guatemala 250, 256
  in India 271
  in Mongolia 228
  monitoring 375, 376
  in Niger 123, 131
property rights 38, 39, 254
protests 39, 57, 249, 251–2, 254, 294, 295, 296, 302, 303
Protocol of San Salvador 243, 298

rationing, of food 314, 319, 320
refugees from hunger 58–67, 337, 379–80

remedies 19, 49, 56, 95, 96, 125, 131, 151, 152, 173, 210, 213, 265, 309, 318, 319, 329, 351–2, 376
retrogression *see* non-retrogression
right to food, definition of 4, 15–18
Russian Federation 44, 46, 50, 214, 232

safety, food 141, 161, 197, 222, 224, 225, 229, 356
Saudi Arabia 134
school lunch programmes 31, 142, 143, 276, 321, 375, 381
Security Council 33, 107, 181, 184, 278
seeds 77, 93, 293, 309, 322, 354, 355
Senegal 44, 59, 60, 63, 70, 86, 92, 343
Sierra Leone 32, 62, 113
slavery *see* forced labour
Social and Economic Rights Action Center 96
Somalia 32, 107
South Africa 31, 35, 36, 46, 50, 77, 97, 100, 197, 339, 352
Soviet Union 311, 313, 314
Spain 59, 63, 296, 325
Special Rapporteur on the Right to Food
country missions 358–9
mandate 10–11, 357
role 10–11
team 11, 360
thematic reports 357–8
urgent appeals 359–60
Sri Lanka 44, 75, 92
starvation
of civilians in armed conflict 20, 100, 102, 107, 108, 383
in Ethiopia 202
fleeing from 64, 65, 380
in India 260, 262, 263, 265, 271–2, 274
in Niger 112, 133
prevention of 58
in Somalia 108
structural adjustment 26, 40, 73, 85, 90, 129, 130, 171, 231, 262, 380
subsidies xiv, 74, 76, 77, 262, 267, 276, 308, 311, 320, 335, 354–5, 375
Sudan 211, 339, 359
Sweden 33, 134
Swiss Development Cooperation Agency xv, 130, 323, 360
Switzerland 7, 134, 325

Syngenta 91, 337
Syrian Arab Republic 282

Taiwan 37
Tanzania 7
tenure, land, security of 3, 25, 34, 35, 36, 38, 40, 132, 203, 204, 210, 212, 223, 239, 240, 242, 245, 248, 251, 264, 275, 294, 381
Texaco 96
Thailand 48, 345
trade
impact on right to food xiii–xiv, 68–77, 78, 82, 85–6, 90, 249, 256, 380, 311, 332, 335, 352–3, 356
liberalization xiii–xv, 40, 70, 72–4, 76, 85–6, 130, 152, 196, 230–1, 232, 234, 235, 249, 253, 262, 267, 276, 307, 308, 333, 335, 354
negotiations 72–3, 153, 335, 346, 354, 380
transnational corporations *see* corporations
Tunisia 59, 92

Uganda 7, 32, 33, 73, 75
undernourishment *see* hunger
unemployment *see* employment
UNICEF 93, 131, 133, 165, 176, 206, 218, 219, 249, 286, 287, 303, 324, 325, 333
United Kingdom of Great Britain and Northern Ireland 82, 92, 100, 296, 338, 355
United Nations Development Programme 91, 131, 133, 176, 206, 217, 221, 228, 229, 249, 257, 318, 324, 325, 333
United Nations High Commissioner for Refugees 61, 62, 64, 83, 286
United Nations Sub-Commission for the Promotion and Protection of Human Rights 10, 79, 86, 89, 99
United States of America xiii, xv, 44, 61, 69, 71, 81, 82, 100, 131, 134, 167, 311, 315, 325, 326, 328, 331, 333, 343, 345, 346, 355, 359
Universal Declaration of Human Rights 5, 15, 29, 56, 79, 82, 97, 98, 162, 200, 298–9, 316, 351, 379

urbanization 34, 37, 41, 137, 215, 237, 261, 293, 308

Venezuela 7, 37, 134, 136, 311, 359
Via Campesina 145, 353
violations (of the right to food)
  in armed conflict 103, 242, 383
  in Bolivia 209, 301, 305–6
  in Brazil 140, 152
  communications regarding 359
  by corporations 46, 50, 93–4, 209, 273, 295
  in Cuba 319, 329
  in Ethiopia 208–9
  generally 19, 38, 50, 51, 56, 84, 347, 351, 377, 380
  in Guatemala 237, 250–2
  in India 271–3, 274
  in Lebanon 287, 288
  in Mongolia 229, 230
  in Niger 124–5, 131
  in the Occupied Palestinian Territories 185–9
  and refugees from hunger 64, 65
vitamin A deficiencies 156, 197, 225, 259, 291, 378
Vivendi 125
Voluntary Guidelines on the Right to Food xiii–xiv, 6–9, 13, 19, 83, 98, 255, 309, 315, 329, 330, 333, 335, 350, 356, 384

war *see also* armed conflict
  civil, in Guatemala 40, 237, 241, 242
  civil, in Liberia 32
  in Ethiopia 195
  generally xiii, 383
  in Lebanon 278, 280–7
  in Somalia 107–8
water, right to
  access to 25, 35, 74, 93, 97, 202, 211, 220–1, 277, 279, 280, 286, 287, 288, 294, 300, 303, 318, 341, 355, 376, 377, 378, 381, 383
  in Bangladesh 156, 158, 160, 165, 167, 171, 173
  and biofuels 348–9
  in Bolivia 294, 299, 300, 302, 303, 304, 305, 306, 308
  and children 28, 29–30, 33, 221

  contamination 96, 306
  in Cuba 313, 323–4, 328
  in Ethiopia 197, 198, 200, 202, 203, 204, 207, 211, 212, 213
  generally 80, 99, 376
  in Guatemala 240–1, 243, 245, 248
  in India 262, 274
  in Lebanon 280–9
  in Mongolia 217, 227, 234
  in Niger 113, 121, 125, 128, 131
  in the Occupied Palestinian Territories 179, 185, 186–8, 191, 192
  privatisation 91–2, 97, 294, 295–6, 337–8, 377
women *see also* gender
  in armed conflict 101, 103, 105, 106
  in Bangladesh 156, 159, 162, 170, 173
  in Bolivia 301
  in Cuba 313, 317, 318, 325, 326
  discrimination and food 9, 23–8, 138, 144, 209, 210, 213, 230, 239, 248, 261, 270, 335–6, 377, 381
  in Ethiopia 197, 198–9, 200, 209, 210, 213
  in Guatemala 239, 248, 254
  in India 261, 269, 270, 272
  inheritance rights 38, 169, 198–9, 217, 248, 261
  in Niger 115, 124, 128, 129, 132
  protection under international law 27–8, 350
  right to land 27–8, 38
workers *see* employment
World Bank xiv, 26, 36, 39, 40, 52, 68, 69, 71, 72, 77, 80, 81, 84–90, 92, 133, 142, 147, 178, 183, 186, 187, 206, 218, 228, 230, 325, 328, 331, 334, 337, 346, 359, 360, 381
World Food Programme xiii, 28, 66, 84, 111, 131, 133, 164, 176, 180, 190, 194, 206, 249, 281, 286, 303, 312, 324, 325, 333, 343, 383
World Food Summit
  1996 Summit xiv, 4–7, 88, 165, 312, 318, 326, 353, 374
  2002: five years later 6–7, 88
  Declaration on Food Security 5–6, 35, 39, 334, 335

World Food Summit – *continued*
    Plan of Action 5–6, 18, 35
World Health Organization 133, 172, 227, 228, 249, 311, 324
World Trade Organization xiii, xiv, 26, 54, 68, 69, 70, 73, 74, 76, 77, 79, 81, 84–90, 130, 131, 153, 333, 335, 354, 356, 380, 381

Zambia 31, 70, 73, 85
Zimbabwe 35, 39, 75

CPSIA information can be obtained at www.ICGtesting.com
Printed in the USA
LVOW102122161012

303178LV00006B/1/P